MIGRATION AND SETTLEMENT

A Multiregional Comparative Study

Migration and Settlement

A Multiregional Comparative Study

Edited by

Andrei Rogers
University of Colorado, Boulder, U.S.A.

and

Frans J. Willekens
Netherlands Interuniversity Demographic Institute,
The Netherlands

D. Reidel Publishing Company

A MEMBER OF THE KLUWER ACADEMIC PUBLISHERS GROUP

Dordrecht / Boston / Lancaster / Tokyo

Library of Congress Cataloging in Publication Data

Main entry under title:

Migration and settlement.

 (GeoJournal library)
 Bibliography: p.
 Includes indexes.
  1. Migration, Internal—Cross-cultural studies. 2. Migration,
Internal—Case studies. 3. Demography—Cross-cultural studies. I.
Rogers, Andrei. II. Willekens, Frans. III. Series.
HB1952.M539 1986   304.8   85-25626
ISBN 90-277-2119-X

Published by D. Reidel Publishing Company
P.O. Box 17, 3300 AA Dordrecht, Holland

Sold and distributed in the U.S.A. and Canada
by Kluwer Academic Publishers,
190 Old Derby Street, Hingham, MA 02043, U.S.A.

In all other countries, sold and distributed
by Kluwer Academic Publishers Group,
P.O. Box 322, 3300 AH Dordrecht, Holland

Printed in The Netherlands

To Our Marias

FOREWORD

The life table technique, by which the observed number of persons exposed to risk and the number dying can be converted into probabilities of dying and expectation of life, has been central to the study of mortality. That technique, now 300 years old, represents transitions (one way only!) between life and death.

The results of elementary demography may be generalized to more than one decrement, as well as to increments, and to transitions in all directions and among many states rather than just two. This has been done in one form or another by a number of writers, including Schoen (1975), Hoem (1977), and most extensively and persistently by Andrei Rogers (1975 and subsequently). They had in mind applications to matters far different from mortality, including marriage and divorce, labor force, and especially migration. Rogers discovered the power of matrix theory to express complex relations in simple form, and in that way brought the methodology within reach of every student of population. Expressions for probabilities, expectations, stationary populations, and other columns of the life table carry over to multiple decrement—increment virtually unchanged, except that the elements are matrices rather than the scalars of the ordinary life table. With standard computer software it is not even necessary for the analyst to calculate the inverse of a matrix.

To see the economy of the methods used here think of calculating probabilities in a marriage table without matrices, say to find the probability that a person now 20 years of age will have been married and divorced by 40. The calculation would include such terms as the chance of being married by age 21, then divorced by age 22 and remaining in the divorced state; of being married by age 21 and divorced at age 22, then remarried by age 30 and divorced again by age 37, etc. With 60 single years of age, from 15 to 75, say, even if only two states are recognized, the number of terms involved in calculating the probability without the convenience of matrices would be something like 2^{60} or about 10^{18}. The formula would require 10^{16} or so pages to write out, or more books than in all the world's libraries. The number of terms is so great because every combination of circumstances would need to be taken into account. The matrix formula avoids explicit consideration of this detail and handles all combinations without any detailed specification by the user.

This ready accessibility of multistate calculations has been extensively exploited for the presentation of migration data, as several chapters of this book show. Andrei Rogers had teams of workers in the 17 countries where IIASA had National Member Organizations, applying the theory to the statistics of those countries. The operation involved scientists from East and West, developing a common attack on matters of interest to all − the process of migration in particular, as well as birth and death and population projection. Estimates are needed of future population for regions within a country as well as for the country as a whole, and the multiregional formulas at least provide a consistent set by region, sex, and age. A permanent residue of the IIASA work has been left in the form of methods now incorporated in routine national calculations.

This book is primarily methodological. What are the real issues to which the methods here exhibited can be applied? These are innumerable, and a few examples will have to suffice. All countries have internal migration, with flows persistent enough to be usefully projected into the future. The South of Italy and the North of the US continue to be the source of immigrants for the North and the South of those countries, respectively. Such migration creates a wide range of problems: of employment, of housing, of water supply. Insofar as the self-selection of migrants is toward more vigorous and generally more capable people, those left behind are less able to look after themselves and their community and to pay the taxes. Migration is in general beneficial to the nation, as it is to the individuals moving, but some way of mitigating the difficulties that it generates is badly needed. Techniques of analysis such as are presented in this book arrange the data on movement so that they can be effectively used by the policy analyst.

Once the labor force is categorized into employed and unemployed, even down to occupation groups, then it is possible to show transitions among these so that probabilities of unemployment, for instance, and expected length of time in unemployment can be readily obtained. Similarly with marriage and divorce. Both unemployment and divorce are obstinate features of advanced societies, and more knowledge of their characteristics is badly needed. Especially valuable is sensitivity analysis, answering the question "What difference does it make to the outcome if such and such an input parameter is altered?". We have some useful theory showing how to do this, again in convenient matrix formulas, from Frans Willekens (1977).

Not only do the methods await application, but they await also some extensions. Chief of these is recognition of heterogeneity. Like the life table, the methods represented in this book implicitly suppose that every individual of given age in the population has exactly the same probability of dying, giving birth, moving, becoming unemployed, etc., as every other individual. That is a very strong (i.e., unrealistic) assumption. We know that some people are more robust than others, that some are more likely to move than others, that some are accident-prone and others not. This variation in probabilities holds at a given age, and within all identifiable groups. Differences between identifiable groups can always be handled by separate tables, but not so differences that are unobservable. For the simple life table it turns out that unobserved differences in what Vaupel and Yashin (1983) call "frailty" always have the effect of making the expectation of life as published in the usual life table too large to apply to an average individual. My own experimenting suggests that the amount of overstatement of the standard life table because of concealed heterogeneity is about one year.

Much work remains to be done, but the material of this book as it stands is a generous source of methods that one hopes will have the welcome it deserves. The book merges from nearly ten years of research at the International Institute for Applied Systems Analysis in Laxenburg, and summarizes one of IIASA's most successful projects.

Nathan Keyfitz
IIASA

References

Hoem, J. (1977) A Markov Chain Model of Working Life Tables. *Scandinavian Actuarial Journal*, 1–20.

Rogers, A. (1975) *Introduction to Multiregional Mathematical Demography*. New York: John Wiley.

Schoen, R. (1975) Constructing Increment–Decrement Life Tables. *Demography* 12(2): 313–324.

Vaupel, J. and Yashin, A. (1983) *The Deviant Dynamics of Death in Heterogeneous Populations*. Research Report RR-83-1. Laxenburg, Austria: International Institute for Applied Systems Analysis.

Willekens, R. (1977) Sensitivity Analysis in Multiregional Demographic Models. *Environment and Planning A* 9: 653–674.

PREFACE

Shortly after the publication of the book *Introduction to Multiregional Mathematical Demography* (Wiley, 1975), the two of us moved with our families to join the International Institute for Applied Systems Analysis (IIASA) in Laxenburg, Austria, for what we thought would be a stay of not more than a year or two. At that time the techniques of multiregional mathematical demography were not widespread, and a number of demographers voiced skepticism about the usefulness of the multiregional perspective. It seemed appropriate, therefore, to establish an applied research project that would both help to expand and disseminate the new methodology, and demonstrate its utility by means of national case studies. In doing this the project would, it was hoped, exemplify IIASA's mission as an international institution dedicated to high-quality, applied, interdisciplinary collaborative research.

To launch this research project a small group of scholars from about a dozen countries met at Schloss Laxenburg in December 1975 and allowed themselves to be persuaded to participate in a comparative study of the multiregional population dynamics in IIASA nations. Little did they know how much work was to be involved, nor indeed did we — their persuaders. Our plans for a two-year study escalated, and the research effort ultimately lasted eight long years. Over the course of this period, a team of some forty IIASA scientists and national collaborators contributed to the theory, methods, and applications involved in what came to be called the Migration and Settlement Study. Ten of this group have contributed as authors to this volume. Without the active support and interaction of this network of enthusiasts for multiregional population analysis, the book could not have been written. We therefore offer our sincere thanks to them all, and particularly wish to acknowledge the contributions of IIASA scientists Luis Castro, Peer Just, Young Kim, Jacques Ledent, Kao-Lee Liaw, Dimiter Philipov, and Richard Raquillet, and of the following national collaborators: *Austria* — Michael Sauberer; *Bulgaria* — Dimiter Philipov; *Canada* — Marc Termote; *Czechoslovakia* — Karel Kühnl; *Federal Republic of Germany* — Reinhold Koch and Hans-Peter Gatzweiler;

Finland — Kalevi Rikkinen; *France* — Jacques Ledent and Daniel Courgeau; *German Democratic Republic* — Gerhard Mohs; *Hungary* — Klara Bies and Kalman Tekse; *Italy* — Domenico Campisi, Agostino La Bella, and Giovanni Rabino; *Japan* — Zenji Nanjo, Tatsuhiko Kawashima, and Toshio Kuroda; *Netherlands* — Paul Drewe; *Poland* — Kazimierz Dziewonski and Piotr Korcelli; *Soviet Union* — Svetlana Soboleva; *Sweden* — Åke Andersson and Ingvar Holmberg; *United Kingdom* — Philip Rees; and *United States* — Larry Long and William Frey.

A major activity of the Migration and Settlement Study was the development of computer software and the assembly of an international data bank on regional population stocks, and interregional patterns of fertility, mortality, and migration. We are grateful to Peer Just, Walter Kogler, Dimiter Philipov, and Friedrich Planck for their devoted work in handling data for 139 regions in 17 countries and in writing and running the large number of programs involved in managing this special data base.

In supplying the necessary demographic data several individuals in national statistical agencies were particularly helpful: Arne Arvidsson of the Swedish Central Bureau of Statistics was instrumental in supplying Swedish migration data of unique detail and quality. Karel Kühnl, the Czechoslovakian national collaborator, obtained a unique body of data on migration by cause. Larry Long of the US Bureau of the Census contributed special US tabulations, and Svetlana Soboleva, the national collaborator from the USSR, managed to obtain a unique unpublished data set on internal migration in the Soviet Union. Finally, a number of anonymous workers at national statistical agencies in several IIASA nations contributed to the assembly of the demographic data used in this comparative study.

Over the eight years of its life, the Migration and Settlement Study produced innumerable working papers, research reports, and journal articles. In doing so it was immeasurably aided by the team behind the printed word at IIASA, a group we wish to acknowledge and thank. Without Maria Rogers' unstinting devotion to the conversion of the manuscripts and typescripts crafted in a myriad of dialects of written English and mathematics into a clear, simple, and communicative language, the products of the Migration and Settlement Study would have been much poorer. But for Susanne Stock's amazing abilities on an IBM typewriter, the chapters in this book would never have met their deadlines. She bore with great charity a million corrections and changes.

At the final and frantic editing stage several authors were of great assistance. Kao-Lee Liaw plunged his way through the whole book and left no sloppy concepts unchallenged. Marc Termote likewise found in the most innocuous sentences sleeping illogicalities in chapter after chapter. Philip Rees assisted with British grit in getting tardy chapters up to the deadline on time. Steve Flitton very ably edited the final manuscript, and Bob Duis saw to its publication.

Finally, we wish to express our gratitude to IIASA, a unique institution, and to Roger Levien, its Director for seven of this study's eight years, for giving us the opportunity and support to carry out this research endeavor.

To all these people and to all their families who lost a little of them to the Migration and Settlement Study, we extend our sincere thanks.

Andrei Rogers
Frans Willekens

CONTENTS

PART ONE

Introduction

CHAPTER ONE

Introduction

Andrei Rogers and Frans Willekens

The "population problem" in most parts of the world has two distinct dimensions: growth (positive or negative) and spatial distribution. Concern about population growth has focused attention on fertility patterns and has fostered family planning and family allowance programs in scores of countries. The issue of population distribution, on the other hand, has only recently received serious analytical attention, as programs to encourage the development of economically declining regions, to stem the growth of large urban centers in less developed countries, and to revitalize the central cores of metropolitan areas have become parts of national agendas all over the globe.

The unanticipated postwar baby boom had a salutary influence on demographic research. Extrapolations of past trends appropriately adjusted for expected changes in the age, sex, and marital compositions of the population were very much wide of the mark. So long as trends were stable, demographic projections prospered; but when a "turning point" occurred, the projections floundered. The net result was increased pressure to consider the complex relationships between fertility patterns and socioeconomic development.

But the poor predictive performance also had another important effect — it stimulated research in improved methods for *measuring* fertility and for understanding the *dynamics* by which it, together with mortality, determines the age composition of a population. Inasmuch as attention was principally directed at national population growth, measurement of internal migration and of the *spatial* dynamics through which geographical mobility affects a national settlement pattern was neglected. This neglect led Dudley Kirk (1960) to conclude, in his 1960 Presidential address to the Population Association of America, that the study of migration was the stepchild of demography. Sixteen years later, Sidney Goldstein (1976) echoed the same theme in his Presidential address to the same body, and in 1983, Kirk asserted that his conclusion of 23 years ago was still valid (Kirk 1983).

The pressing need for improved methods of measuring migration and understanding its important role in spatial population dynamics led the

3

International Institute for Applied Systems Analysis (IIASA) in 1976 to organize a multinational study of internal migration and population distribution patterns in the countries of its National Member Organizations (NMOs). Recently
developed techniques of multiregional demographic analysis (Rogers 1975a, b)
provided the unifying methodological framework for this study, which was
undertaken by scholars from the 17 countries of the Institute's NMOs: Austria,
Bulgaria, Canada, Czechoslovakia, Finland, France, the German Democratic
Republic, the Federal Republic of Germany, Hungary, Italy, Japan, the Netherlands, Poland, the Soviet Union, Sweden, the United Kingdom (UK), and the
United States (US). A list of the scholars and their national reports appears in
the Appendix to this chapter.

1.1 The Migration and Settlement Study at IIASA

Representatives from 12 countries met in London in October 1972 to
found the International Institute for Applied Systems Analysis, situated in
Laxenburg on the outskirts of Vienna, Austria. The founders put forward three
goals for the Institute: (1) to strengthen international cooperation; (2) to
advance the science and art of systems analysis; and (3) to apply systems
analysis to a wide range of societal problems.

During the past decade, institutions from five additional countries have
joined this unique nongovernmental East—West research institute, and scholars
from more than two dozen nations have contributed to its activities.

One of the principal research areas at IIASA during the past seven years
has been its Program on Human Settlements and Services. An important component of this program has been the Migration and Settlement Study, a study
that was organized primarily to expand and disseminate a new methodology —
multiregional demography — to scholars and professionals dealing with population issues in the IIASA nations and elsewhere.

Multiregional demography focuses on the evolution of spatially interdependent regional populations. It considers their sizes, age compositions, and
geographical distributions, as well as the changes of these characteristics
over time. The principal argument of the multiregional perspective is that it is
not enough simply to examine a single regional population when studying its
evolution. One must simultaneously also consider the several regional populations that are interacting with it. The ability afforded by such a perspective
to trace out the demographic impacts of interregional migration flows and of
regionally differentiated regimes of mortality, and fertility makes multiregional demography an especially useful tool for projecting subnational populations.

IIASA's study of migration and settlement began with two basic components: a set of computer programs for multiregional demographic analysis
and a network of collaborating investigators in the Institute's NMO countries.

The principal goal was a case study of each country to be carried out by a scholar from that country. Each study was to use a common methodology and to follow a common outline of substantive topics. Much of the data analysis was to be carried out at IIASA using a standard package of computer programs (Willekens and Rogers 1978), and most of the scholars involved had to be trained in the methodology by those at IIASA familiar with the mathematical theory. The success of this training led the Institute to offer short courses on multiregional demography in Austria, Mexico, and Bulgaria.

The Migration and Settlement Study was concluded in 1982, seven years after its initiation. An important outcome of the study was the set of 17 national reports written by 27 scholars. Each report presents a national overview of recent regional patterns of fertility, mortality, and internal migration, illustrates the application of multiregional demographic techniques and the additional insights into population redistribution that can be gained from it, and concludes with a very brief review of population distribution issues and policies.

Common to the preparation of each national case study were the following steps. First, the national investigator assembled available data on population stocks, births, deaths, and origin–destination-specific migration flows for the set of regions to be studied, using official published or unpublished sources. The regions were delineated by the national investigator and generally consisted of contiguous, administratively defined units of territory that completely divided up the country and for which migration data were available. The number of regions in each country ranged from a minimum of four to a maximum of 13, giving rise to a total of 139 regions for the 17 countries.[1]

Following the assembly of the available data, the national investigator and the IIASA project staff proceeded to infer missing data and to estimate the input variables needed for the study's package of computer programs. The programs were then executed at IIASA and the outputs were transmitted to the national investigator for examination and possible modification. After several iterations a final set of outputs was obtained, and this set was then analyzed and described in the national report.

The activities of the international network of collaborating scholars, who were producing the national reports, were complemented by the theoretical research of the IIASA core staff. The need to infer missing migration data, for example, led to the development of a unified strategy for estimating missing elements in a flow matrix in ways that preserve, in some sense, the structure of the whole data set (Willekens *et al.* 1981). The regularities in age patterns of migration observed in the data collected during the study suggested a formal mathematical description of the age profiles of migration rates and methods for inferring such profiles from inadequate or inaccurate data

---

[1]A 20-region analysis was carried out for Italy, but the national report focused primarily on the results of the five-region disaggregation.

(Rogers and Castro 1981a). Differences in the sources of migration data used in the study motivated an intensive investigation of alternative estimators of migration propensities (Ledent 1980c, 1981).

Questions regarding population prospects in the IIASA countries formed an integral part of the case study reports. They motivated IIASA scientists to examine the possible redistributive consequences of fertility reduction to bare replacement levels and the resulting spatial stabilization of a national population (Rogers and Willekens 1978). A concern with the need to reduce the dimensionality and associated computational requirements of large-scale population projection models was the stimulus for production of methods for "shrinking" such models to a more manageable size (Rogers 1976b). The search for an improved understanding of the long-term consequences of current trends led to fundamental extensions of the theory of stable spatial population dynamics (Liaw 1980a). And a desire to improve the accuracy of simple population projections was reflected in the development of models for generating multiregional population projections disaggregated by region of birth (Philipov and Rogers 1981).

The theoretical work of the Migration and Settlement Study has received wide dissemination. It served as the focus of two sessions on mathematical demography at the annual meetings of the Population Association of America (in 1979 and 1981). Two special issues of the journal *Environment and Planning A* were devoted to an exposition of its principal findings (the May 1978 and May 1980 issues); and a substantial part of a National Science Foundation-sponsored conference on multidimensional mathematical demography focused on its theoretical advances (Land and Rogers 1982). The study's principal contributions to the theory of multiregional mathematical demography are contained in six research reports, which, together with the 17 national case studies, have been issued as a three-volume boxed set, available from the Publications Department of IIASA (see Appendix). The theory, applications, and data reported therein form the basis of this book.

1.2 The Organization and Contents of this Book

This book is the product of a concerted effort by a team of 10 scholars to provide an integrated overview of the principal empirical findings produced by a study carried out by a much larger number of researchers. The empirical foundation of the book is the large data base provided by the national case studies. The underlying methodological perspective of the authors is multiregional demography. And the intended outcome is an improved understanding of regional demographic patterns and multiregional population dynamics in the 17 developed countries that support IIASA's National Member Organizations.

1.2.1 *Part One*

Part One of this book introduces the Migration and Settlement Study, previews the book's contents, and considers a number of details related to the study's data base.

Empirical studies in multiregional demography often begin with data, set out in tabular form, that describe changes in stocks that have occurred over two or more points in time. These changes arise as a consequence of increments and decrements associated with events, such as births and deaths, and with the migration of individuals between different regions. When all of the appropriate elements in such tables have been filled in with numbers, they generally are referred to as *accounts*. And when, as is often the case, some data are unavailable, ingenuity and statistical estimation techniques are used to supply the missing entries.

In Chapter 2, Philip Rees and Frans Willekens consider some of the problems of data collection, account construction, and estimation of missing data brought forth by the national reports. They contrast the two accounting frameworks that were implicitly adopted in the 17 case studies: movement accounts, which focus on *migrations* as recurrent events, and transition accounts, which focus on *migrants* and their places of residence at two different times. The different time and age frameworks used in the IIASA study also come under close scrutiny, and the particular problems of incomparability that they give rise to are identified. The regions used in the Migration and Settlement Study are listed and identified on maps, and methods that were used for dealing with the estimation of missing migration flows are set out.

1.2.2 *Part Two*

The data collected as inputs to the multiregional life table and population projection programs executed at IIASA were assembled primarily to demonstrate the application of a new demographic methodology and not to carry out a comparative study. Consequently, virtually no attention was given to problems of comparability. Nevertheless, the availability of age-specific mortality, fertility, and migration data for 139 regions in 17 countries proved to be seductive and led to an attempt to "compare the incomparable". Part Two reports on this attempt. Its three chapters assess the degree of regional variation in mortality, fertility, and migration patterns that prevailed among IIASA's NMO countries in the 1970s.

Marc Termote examines the record for mortality in the IIASA nations in Chapter 3 and finds that regional disparities continue to exist in these countries today, with such disparities being primarily a result of the considerable regional differences in infant and young-adult mortality. After an illuminating critical assessment of the quality of mortality data in IIASA nations, an analysis that also carries over to the fertility and migration chapters, Termote describes the mortality regimes in the 139 regions, focusing on regional differences in such indicators as life expectancies, gross death rates, and age-specific death rates. For each of these indicators and for each country he presents low and high regional values, the national average, and the mean absolute deviation (the latter also expressed as a percentage of the national figure). He concludes that a moderate amount of regional variation still exists in the number of years one may expect to live and that regional disparities for males are higher than those for females, with both becoming more pronounced as spatial disaggregation is increased.

In the latter half of his chapter, Termote introduces the economist's *shift—share* method of accounting for regional differences. Using global indices of regional disparities, the author finds a somewhat more diverse regional pattern of variation for mortality than before. For example, whereas previously the Soviet Union showed the largest regional variations in mortality levels, the scaling of each regional observation by population size reduces its exhibited variation dramatically and elevates that of the UK to first place. This leads Termote to underline the importance of introducing a weighting process in constructing measures of regional disparity, since large regional differences are less important if the regional populations are small.

Young Kim analyzes the fertility regimes in the IIASA countries in Chapter 4, finding that the Federal Republic of Germany and the German Democratic Republic exhibited the lowest levels in the 1970s. Comparing differentials across regions, she discovers that the Soviet Union, Italy, and Canada showed the greatest regional differentials. In place of Termote's mean absolute deviation as an index of variation, Kim adopts Tukey's (1977) methods of exploratory data analysis — a form of analysis that focuses on medians, on lower and upper quartiles, and on interquartile ranges. Box-plot diagrams set out visually the differences among the 17 countries.

Again turning to Tukey's methods, Kim borrows the technique of "median polish" to examine the age patterns of fertility rates. The Soviet Union, Italy, and Canada show the highest regional variations once again. The lowest differentials and the most uniform age patterns are shown by Sweden and the German Democratic Republic. Kim concludes that high-fertility countries tend also to show large regional fertility differentials in levels and age patterns. Such a pattern was not observed for mortality according to Termote.

Comparative studies of national migration patterns are especially hampered by the unresolved problem of how to standardize areal units to reflect the influence that their particular areal delineations have on various measures of mobility. In the Migration and Settlement Study not only do data describe flows of individuals between regions of different sizes and shapes, but also they do so for different calendar years, variable intervals of time, and incompatible data collection systems. This makes them almost totally unsuited for comparative analysis. Nevertheless, in Chapter 5 Andrei Rogers and Luis Castro describe and compare across several nations an apparently universal regularity in migration data — the profile of age-specific migration rates.

Upon examining more than 600 age profiles, the authors find striking similarities in the age patterns of migration rates in the IIASA nations. Besides demonstrating that persistent regularities are exhibited by these profiles, they also show that such regularities may be expressed by a mathematical curve that has at most 11 parameters and in many instances only seven. Calling this curve a model migration schedule, they argue that much of the national and regional variation exhibited by the schedules in IIASA's study arises from changes in the values of four variables: the position parameter of the curve's labor force component, its degree of symmetry, the schedule's level of child dependency, and the degree to which the migration rates of infants and adolescents mirror those of their parents. These four parameters may be used to define several families of migration schedules, into which the schedules examined in the Migration and Settlement Study can be classified.

1.2.3 *Part Three*

Although the IIASA countries show considerable variation in national rates of fertility, they nevertheless are all tending toward rates of reproduction that are below replacement levels. By the end of the 1970s, not enough children were being born to replace their parents in 13 of the 17 countries; in the remaining four countries (Bulgaria, Czechoslovakia, Poland, and the Soviet Union) the number of children born was only slightly above replacement level. Consequently, in most IIASA nations the share of the elderly (that is, those 65 years of age and over) in the total population increased during that decade. Population aging and spatial redistribution in IIASA nations are the two principal processes illuminated by the Migration and Settlement Study. The three chapters in Part Three of this book address different aspects of these two processes.

The most recent national projections published by the United Nations (1981) project a total population of 1.1 billion for the 17 IIASA nations in the year 2000. In Chapter 6, Andrei Rogers compares these UN projections with those contained in the individual national reports of the Migration and Settlement Study. A reasonably close agreement is found for most countries with the notable exception of Canada, for which the UN projects a surprisingly high total of 34.8 million.

Although an overall aging or "graying" of IIASA's national populations is in prospect, at the subnational level a few regions, mainly those centered on large cities, may expect a decline in the number and proportion of elderly people. The largest decline will probably occur in West Berlin: between 1974 and 2000, the number of people 65 years of age and over is expected to decrease by 55% and the proportion of elderly is projected to drop from 22% to 14%. While West Berlin's elderly population could halve, Vienna's may drop by as much as 35%. In 1971, one out of every five persons in Vienna was older than 65; by the year 2000, it is expected to be one out of every seven.

Projections to the year 2000 also show the following regions gaining substantially in their share of total national population: British Columbia in
Canada, the Vorarlberg province of Austria, Berlin in the German Democratic
Republic, the Kanto region in Japan, the Western states of the US, and the
Central Asian Republics of the Soviet Union. Those with declining shares of
national populations include Vienna in Austria, Quebec in Canada, the West
region in the Netherlands, the North region in France, and the Kyushu region
in Japan.

Chapter 7 is a sample of the national reports produced for the Migration
and Settlement Study. It contains three revised and abridged case studies: the
report on the United Kingdom by Philip Rees, the report on the Soviet Union
by Svetlana Soboleva, and the report on Canada by Marc Termote. These three
studies were particularly selected for inclusion in the chapter because they
illuminate important facets of multiregional demography.

Philip Rees identifies five fundamental choices regarding data and estimation methods, concluding that the length of the period over which migration
is measured most influences the spatial allocation of regional life expectancies
in the UK. The use of multiregional demographic techniques to study sectorally
rather than spatially defined populations is illustrated in Svetlana Soboleva's
report on urbanization in the Soviet Union. And temporal variations in a multiregional growth regime are examined by Marc Termote, who uses Canadian
data collected over two consecutive quinquennial time intervals to do so.

Large urban agglomerations in many highly urbanized countries are
either experiencing absolute population decline or growing at rates lower than
those exhibited by smaller settlements. These trends apparently are related
to declining rates of national population growth, patterns of economic inter-
sectoral change, and interregional shifts in the migration of people and jobs.
In Chapter 8, Piotr Korcelli examines several hypotheses regarding population
dynamics in large urban regions, using data drawn from the Migration and Settlement Study.

Korcelli analyzes observed relationships between population growth,
urbanization, and city size, considers the relative contributions of migration
and natural increase to urban population growth and decline over time, examines the overall spatial mobility of populations in urban regions, questions the
concept of hierarchical migration, and identifies characteristic age profiles of
interurban migration.

1.2.4 *Part Four*

Part Four of this book is devoted to a brief exposition of multiregional
mathematical demography and to methodological advances generated by the
Migration and Settlement Study in methods of life table construction and in
stable population theory. Rates, probabilities, and projections are the

principal foci of three chapters whose contents are considerably more mathematical than those of the earlier eight chapters.

A short course on multiregional mathematical demography is offered by Andrei Rogers and Frans Willekens in Chapter 9. Starting with a brief consideration of age patterns in the fundamental components of demographic change and an overview of prospective and retrospective observation plans, the authors go on to review the mathematical theory of transition probability estimation, life table construction, and population projection.

The life table is a central concept in classical mathematical demography. Its use to express the facts of mortality in terms of survival probabilities and their combined impact on the lives of a cohort of individuals born at the same moment has been so successful that demographers have been accused of being incapable of thinking about population change and mortality from any other starting point (Keyfitz 1968, p.3). It can be argued, therefore, that the natural starting point for thinking of multiregional population change is the multiregional life table: its theoretical derivation and its empirical calculation.

Jacques Ledent and Philip Rees focus in Chapter 10 on the crux of the life table construction problem: the estimation of age-specific survival probability transition matrices using data either on interregional *moves* or on interregional *transitions*. Since the data on interregional migration flows can come in the form of *move* counts or *people* counts, the estimation methods used must be specific to each kind of data. Irrespective of the form of the data, however, no statements about probabilities can be made without a conversion, at some point in the analysis, of information on moves to information on individuals who have moved. Ledent and Rees show how this conversion can be carried out.

Presenting an assessment of the various choices faced by the prospective builder of a multiregional life table, they conclude that, for a given data set, methodological choices regarding the transformation of the data into appropriate transition probabilities have relatively little effect on the functions of a multiregional life table. The nature of the migration data, however, is an element of prime importance. Ledent and Rees contend that transition data are to be preferred to movement data. Moreover, in the case of transition data, they argue that use of a five-year age interval and a five-year time period is a reasonable compromise between the desire to reduce the errors introduced by age aggregation and the desire to decrease the dependence of the life table model on the so-called Markovian assumption (which holds that the future evolution of a population is independent of its past history and is a function only of current conditions).

The survivorship proportions found in a multiregional life table have an important and fundamental application to population projection. Multiregional projection models are of two kinds: continuous age–time Lotka renewal equation models and discrete age–time Leslie cohort-survival models. Both may be used to generate expected future population figures evolving from assumed or predicted changes in model parameter values. They also give the demographer a tool for examining the asymptotic properties of a projection carried out with fixed coefficients.

Kao-Lee Liaw sets out, in Chapter 11, the analytical solution of a multiregional population projection that is generated by a discrete age–time model with a constant multiregional growth regime. He shows that a stable distribution across ages and regions is implicit in every multiregional population projection matrix. Deviations from these age compositions and regional shares, in the starting age-by-region distribution, ultimately disappear, but in the short to medium term they create fluctuations and disturbances in age profiles and in regional allocations.

Liaw applies the analytical solution to data on multiregional population change in Sweden. Focusing on an 18-age-group, eight-region, female population in 1974, he illustrates how population waves and spatial redistribution are transmitted by the various components of the analytical solution. He finds that for the Swedish data regional stability in age composition is achieved much sooner than stability in the spatial allocation of the national population.

Chapter 12 concludes the book. Focusing on the accomplishments of the Migration and Settlement Study, it discusses the three principal themes to which the study's methodological research contributed: spatial population dynamics, measurement and analysis of migration patterns, and formal demographic methods for modeling transitions between states other than regions.

1.3 Expositional Details

In assembling, compiling, and reporting the results described in this volume, a number of editorial decisions had to be made, some for reasons of expediency, others for reasons of style. A uniform notation had to be imposed, and the same ordering of countries, regions, and related details had to be enforced. To clarify the reasons for some of the choices made, a few of the more important of such expositional details are identified in this section.

1.3.1 *Reference Years*

The years for which data were assembled in the Migration and Settlement Study varied from nation to nation, spanning a period from 1970 to 1978. Furthermore, those studies that relied on migration data obtained from national censuses, rather than registers, of necessity used transition data referring to a time interval longer than a single year, being five years in the case of Canada and seven years in the case of France, for example. And in several national case studies the fertility and mortality data that were used represented an average taken across several years, in order to remove the irregular influences of episodic events.

To simplify the exposition, a single reference year was associated with each national study. In all cases, except for Canada, this was the year for which the data on population stocks were collected. For Canada, however, this population stock was taken to be the average of the enumerated populations in 1966 and 1971. Nevertheless, for consistency we assign it the reference year of 1971.

1.3.2 *National and Regional Identification*

The order in which the 17 national reports were produced is not the order in which they are listed in the various tables of this book. All countries are identified by the name adopted by the author for the title of the national report (e.g., the Soviet Union instead of the USSR), and the list of the 17 countries is in alphabetical order. For ease of reference, however, the Federal Republic of Germany and the German Democratic Republic are listed in the tables and figures as FRG and GDR, respectively.

The names of regions have in almost all cases been translated into their English equivalents, but their listing retains the order used by the author in the national report's computer outputs. Maps delineating the 139 regions examined in the study and the names of these regions are given in Chapter 2.

1.3.3 *Mathematical Notation*

A transparently simple yet powerful notational system is an important ingredient of effective strategies to understand and deal with complex problems of a mathematical nature. In extending the principal theory of uniregional population mathematics to multiregional population systems, we generalize conventional demographic notation as set out, for example, in Keyfitz (1968). Although we did not distinguish notationally between continuous and discrete functions in our earlier efforts (Rogers 1975a, b, Willekens and Rogers 1978), we have elected to do so in this book.

In the notation used in this book, the regional dimension is expressed by means of superscripts that refer to regions of residence at successive ages and successive points in time. The age and time indices are subscripts positioned directly below the corresponding superscripts. The exact age is denoted by a small x (or y); the age interval is represented by a capital X (or Y). The age group X may also be written as $(x, x+h)$, with h being the width of the age interval. The index h is generally omitted when that interval is taken to be one or five years. The exact time is denoted by t and the time interval by T. The length of the time interval is u, hence $T = (t, t+u)$.

It is frequently necessary in multiregional demographic analysis to consider two or more reference ages and reference points in time. A multiregional life table, for instance, yields an estimate of the number of persons who will be living in region j at exact age y, among those currently x years old and living in region i and who have lived at some prior age z in region k. The prior age z is the age at which an initial event occurred and it therefore defines a cohort. If $z = 0$, the migration experience of a birth cohort is being considered.

To distinguish the cohort-defining age from the current and higher ages, we position the first at the left of the variable and the latter at the right side. Thus

$$_z^k l_{xy}^{ij}$$

denotes the number of persons in the life table population of region i at exact age x who were residents of region k at exact age z and will be living in region j at exact age y. If $y = x + h$, the subscript y is deleted. Hence $_z^k l_x^{ij}$ is the number of people who will be in j at exact age $x + h$.

A dot in place of a superscript (subscript) is an indication that the variable has been summed over all regions (ages) included in the range of that superscript (subscript). For instance, the k-born life table population of region j at exact age $x + h$ may be denoted by

$$\sum_{i=1}^{N} {}_0^k l_x^{ij} = {}_0^k l_x^{\cdot j} \;,$$

where N indicates the number of regions. The dot is omitted when the context makes clear the meaning of the variable without it. Hence $_0^k l_x^{\cdot j}$ is also written as $_0^k l_{x+h}^{j}$.

In multiregional life table and projection models, a number of variables are defined, the values of which are independent of the initial event. The indication of the initial event is therefore omitted. For instance, the life table model assumes that the probability that a person of age x in region i will be in region j after h years is independent of the migration history of the person, including his or her place of birth. The probability is therefore denoted by p_x^{ij}, where

$$p_x^{ij} = {}_0^{\cdot} l_x^{ij} / {}_0^{\cdot} l_x^{i} = l_x^{ij} / l_x^{i} \;.$$

Analogously, in the projection model, it is assumed that the proportion of x- to $(x + h)$-year-old persons living in region i at time t who will be residing in region j at time $t + u$ (with $u = h$) is independent of the migration histories of the persons. It is denoted by s_x^{ij}.

Appendix 1: Selected IIASA Publications of the Migration and Settlement Study (three-volume boxed set)

Volume 1   MODELS, METHODS, AND COMPUTER PROGRAMS

RR-78-6   Migration and Settlement: Selected Essays
            A. Rogers (ed.) (1978), 10(5) reprinted from special issue of *Environment and Planning A*

> Model migration schedules and their applications
> *A. Rogers, R. Raquillet, and L. Castro*
> The spatial reproductive value and the spatial momentum of zero population growth
> *A. Rogers and F. Willekens*
> Job-search perspectives on migration behaviour
> *J. Miron*
> Regional multiplier analysis: a demometric approach
> *J. Ledent*
> A dynamic linear-programming approach to the planning of national settlement systems
> *A. Propoi and F. Willekens*
> Optimization of rural—urban development and migration
> *R. Kulikowski*
> Migration and settlement in Bulgaria
> *D. Philipov*

RR-78-13   Migration and Settlement: Measurement and Analysis
            A. Rogers and F. Willekens

> Spatial population dynamics
> *A. Rogers and F. Willekens*
> Sensitivity analysis in multiregional demographic models
> *F. Willekens*
> Shrinking large-scale population-projection models by aggregation and decomposition
> *A. Rogers*
> Demometrics of migration and settlement
> *A. Rogers*

RR-78-18   Spatial Population Analysis: Methods and Computer Programs
            F. Willekens and A. Rogers

RR-80-10   Essays in Multistate Mathematical Demography
            A. Rogers (ed.) (1980),12(5) reprinted from special issue of*Environment and Planning A*

> Introduction to multistate mathematical demography
> *A. Rogers*
> Multistate demographic accounts: measurement and estimation procedures
> *P. Rees*
> Multistate life tables: movement versus transition perspectives

CHAPTER TWO

Data and Accounts

Philip Rees and Frans Willekens

The Migration and Settlement Study at IIASA was based on the demographic data of 17 countries, disaggregated into 139 regions. This chapter describes in general terms the countries studied, the data bank developed, the estimation techniques employed, and the consequences of data problems encountered in carrying out the study.

We begin by considering some of the characteristics of the countries included in the study. Table 2.1 provides a set of basic indicators for all countries, extracted from the individual national reports and from the *World Development Report* (World Bank 1980). The set of countries includes three of the most extensive in the world (the Soviet Union, Canada, and the US) together with 13 moderately and small-sized European countries and Japan. In population size the countries range from Finland (under 5 million in 1978) to the Soviet Union (261 million in 1978). According to the World Bank, the total population of the IIASA countries in 1978 comprised 969 million people, about 23% of the world total. In terms of level of development the IIASA nations in 1978 were 17 of 30 countries with per capita incomes over US$3000 per annum and 17 out of 39 countries where the life expectancy at birth was 70 years or over. The Migration and Settlement Study thus investigated the regional population dynamics in a set of relatively rich, developed countries, a majority of which fall in the World Bank's "industrialized countries" category, and a minority of which fall in its "centrally planned economies" class.

For methodological and for practical reasons, the analysis of these countries was limited in scope in order to make the execution of the task feasible. To carry out a 17-nation study it was necessary that the methodology adopted be specified and fixed prior to the start of the study. To change the methods used midway through the study would have been foolish, for it is on such grounds that many projects fail.

Table 2.1 Basic demographic and economic indicators for IIASA nations in 1978.

Country	Area (thousands of square kilometers)	Population (millions)	Average annual crude rate of population growth, 1970–1978 (per thousand)	Crude birth rate (per thousand)	Crude death rate (per thousand)
Austria	84	7.5	2	11	12
Bulgaria	111	8.8	5	16	11
Canada	9976	23.5	12	16	8
Czechoslovakia	128	15.1	7	18	11
FRG	249	61.3	1	9	12
Finland	337	4.8	4	14	9
France	547	53.3	6	14	10
GDR	108	16.7	−2	13	13
Hungary	93	10.7	4	16	12
Italy	301	56.7	7	13	9
Japan	372	114.9	12	15	6
Netherlands	41	13.9	8	13	8
Poland	313	35.0	9	19	9
Soviet Union	22402	261.0	9	18	10
Sweden	450	8.3	4	12	11
United Kingdom	244	55.8	1	12	12
United States	9363	221.9	8	15	9

Country	Life expectancy at birth (years)	Total fertility rate (per woman)	Gross national product per capita (US $)	Percentage of population of working age	World Bank classification[a]
Austria	72	1.7	7030	63	IC
Bulgaria	72	2.3	3230	66	CPE
Canada	74	1.9	9180	66	IC
Czechoslovakia	70	2.4	4720	64	CPE
FRG	72	1.4	9580	65	IC
Finland	72	1.7	6820	68	IC
France	73	1.9	8260	63	IC
GDR	72	1.8	5710	63	CPE
Hungary	70	2.2	3450	66	CPE
Italy	73	1.9	3850	64	IC
Japan	76	1.8	7280	68	IC
Netherlands	74	1.6	8410	65	IC
Poland	71	2.3	3670	66	CPE
Soviet Union	70	2.4	3700	65	CPE
Sweden	75	1.7	10210	64	IC
United Kingdom	73	1.7	5030	64	IC
United States	73	1.8	9590	65	IC

[a]IC, industrialized country; CPE, centrally planned economy.
Source: World Bank (1980, pp.110–111).

The project had the following important and recognized limitations:

- The age classification was by five-year groups.
- The regions were limited in number.
- The temporal frame of reference was limited to one period in the recent past. (The end dates vary from 1970 to 1978.)
- The system studied was limited to the country concerned and inter-actions with the rest of the world were not generally included in the multiregional analyses. The studies concentrated on the internal redistri-bution of national populations.
- Further classifications of population – by birthplace or by ethnic or socioeconomic group – were not attempted.

Detailed comments are made on each of these limitations in the course of this chapter. In future studies many of them can and will be eliminated, but in the first such effort of comparing the population dynamics of regions within a set of 17 countries, the limitations, we believe, were justified.

This chapter sets out a systematic presentation of the accounting frame-works within which the multiregional population analyses of the Migration and Settlement Study were embedded. The concepts are described in general terms in Section 2.1. Time and age frameworks are developed in Section 2.2. Section 2.3 deals with the spatial frameworks adopted in the individual national studies, and Section 2.4 describes the estimation problems and pro-cedures associated with the stocks, events, and flow data used as input to the multiregional analysis. An overview of some of the principal problems encoun-tered in comparing the results and the lessons to be learned for future work is presented in the last section.

2.1 Accounting Frameworks

Multiregional demographic analysis aims at a better understanding of the dynamics shaping the growth and spatial distribution of population. To accom-plish this goal, it describes the process of change in the population size (stock) and composition in terms of flows of people moving between various states of the "demographic system". The flow perspective requires flow data. These data may conveniently be arranged in an accounting framework. Accounts are not only convenient data representation schemes, but they also provide a useful framework for evaluating the completeness and accuracy of the available data and for estimating the missing data.

Population accounts are two- or multidimensional tables of population flows. All flows are accounted for by including all possible states of origin as row classes for the account matrices and all possible states of destination as column classes. Flows may be given for the total population (aggregate accounts) or for each of several population categories (disaggregate accounts). In multiregional analysis, age-disaggregated accounts are used, that is, all flows must be given for each of the (five-year) age groups considered in the study. A complete exposition of population accounts is beyond the scope of this chapter; the reader is referred to other works for details (Stone 1971, Illingworth 1976, Rees and Wilson 1977, Rees 1980, 1981). We limit ourselves to the presentation of the two types of accounts that are fundamental in spatial population analysis, since they relate to different ways of measuring migration flows: movement accounts and transition accounts. This distinction has important implications for the analysis and interpretation of the results, as we show below.

2.1.1 *Movements and Transitions*

Quite distinctive instruments are used to measure migration flows. Registration systems are generally used in Europe, where each change of address (and hence each move) must be registered with the local authorities. Other countries, like Canada, the UK, and the US, derive migration statistics from a retrospective question in the national census. The data generated by registration and census differ in at least two respects:

•   Registration data are "prospective" data, whereas census data are "retrospective". This distinction is important for the estimation of the population that is at risk of experiencing demographic events, as will be illustrated in Chapter 10.
•   Registration systems generally record each move: a passage from one state to another. The statistical data that represent the number of passages are said to be *movement data*. In the census, respondents are asked to state what their address (place of residence) was some fixed number of years ago. Individual moves are not recorded; only the transition that a person made between the start and end of the given time interval is recorded. These data representing migration are therefore referred to as *transition data*.

The distinction between movements and transitions is illustrated in Figure 2.1. The figure shows the mobility experience of eight individuals during the interval from t to $t + u$. Each line represents the "lifeline" of an individual. Every time a person (and his or her lifeline) crosses the boundary between region i and region j, a migration occurs. A person can make several migrations within the interval. Migrants (3) and (8) make two migrations, for example. Although a migrant can make several migrations within an interval, only one transition can be recorded. Person (3), for instance, will not be represented in the transition count, despite having moved to region j for a short period in the time interval. Some transitions – for example, a person

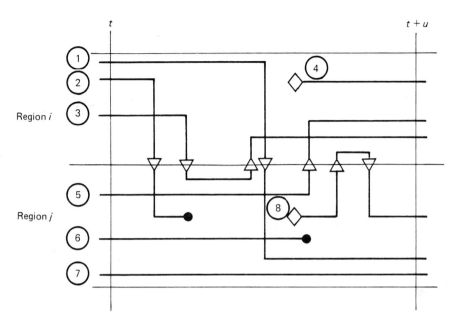

Figure 2.1 Transitions from the initial state to the final state and movements of individuals represented by lifelines (−). ∇, a move from region i to region j; Δ, a move from region j to region i; ◇, a birth; •, a death.

alive in region i at time t and dead in region j later in the period − carry information on the additional move that must have taken place. The distinction between movements and transitions is numerically important only for migration; for birth and death totals the movement and transition counts are identical.

In the Migration and Settlement Study, both registration-based movement data and census-based transition data were employed. Movement data were used in 11 of the 17 national studies and transition data were employed in the remaining six. The argument against the collection of both types of statistics by national statistical offices has been that duplication is thereby avoided and costs saved. However, the measures of migration are sufficiently different in numerical magnitude to suggest that this argument is unfounded. Views are now beginning to shift and some countries (e.g., the UK) that have in the past relied on census measures have now developed a registration and survey-based system of data collection.

The distinction between movements and transitions is crucial in spatial population analysis. Researchers on migration (Courgeau 1973a, Rees 1977a) have long been aware of this distinction but its implications for population models, such as the multiregional life table model, have only recently been realized (Ledent 1980a; Chapter 10 of this book). A major implication is that

the life table probabilities, which are transition probabilities, should be calculated differently for movement and transition data. We elaborate on this
implication in the next section. First, however, we show how different types
of data lead to different accounts.

2.1.2 Movement Accounts and Transition Accounts

Accounts provide a useful framework for distinguishing between movements and transitions. The structure of a movement account is shown in Table
2.2; the analogous transition account is presented in Table 2.3. Each account
involves a set of regions internal to the country, there being 1,2,...,N internal
regions, and an external region, o, called here "the outside world". To these
"existing" states we must add the entry point of birth or immigration and the
exit point of death or emigration. In both accounts initial population stocks
are linked to final population stocks via accounting equations. For the moment,
age and sex are not included.

In the movement case, for typical region i and for a time interval T,
which is from t to $t + u$, the accounting equation is

$$K_{t+u}^i = K_t^i - O_T^{id} - \sum_{j \in I} O_T^{ij} - O_T^{io} + O_T^{bi} + \sum_{k \in I} O_T^{ki} + O_T^{oi} , \qquad (2.1)$$

that is,

stock at end of period = stock at start of period − outflows + inflows.

The interpretation of the variables included in the movement accounting equation is given in Table 2.2 and in the Glossary.

The corresponding equation for the transition accounts that links initial
and final populations is

$$K^{\cdot\cdot, si} = \left[K^{ei, \cdot\cdot} - \sum_{\substack{j \in I \\ j \neq i}} K^{ei, sj} - K^{ei, so} - K^{ei, di} - \sum_{\substack{j \in I \\ j \neq i}} K^{ei, dj} - K^{ei, do} \right]$$

$$+ \sum_{\substack{j \in I \\ j \neq i}} K^{ej, si} + K^{eo, si} + K^{bi, si} + \sum_{\substack{j \in I \\ j \neq i}} K^{bj, si} + K^{bo, si} , \qquad (2.2)$$

where the terms in brackets define the diagonal entry in the accounts,
$K^{ei, si}$, which refers to persons who survive and stay in regions over the
period. This has substantive meaning, in contrast to $\bar{O}^t$, which has none.
Notice that $K^{bi, \cdot\cdot} = O^{bi}$, $K^{\cdot\cdot, dj} = O^{dj}$, $K^{ei, \cdot\cdot} = K_t^i$, and $K^{\cdot\cdot, sj} = K_{t+u}^j$.

Table 2.2 Movement account for a multiregional system within a single country in a single period T.

State prior to move in period		State after move in period						
		Destination region					Death	Total
		Internal regions				Outside world		
		1	2	$\cdots$	N	o		
Origin regions								
Internal regions 1		$\bar{O}^1$	O_T^{12}	$\cdot\cdot$	O_T^{1N}	O_T^{1o}	O_T^{1d}	K_t^1
	2	O_T^{21}	$\bar{O}^2$	$\cdots$	O_T^{2N}	O_T^{2o}	O_T^{2d}	K_t^2
	$\vdots$	$\vdots$	$\vdots$	$\vdots$	$\vdots$	$\vdots$	$\vdots$	$\vdots$
	N	O_T^{N1}	O_T^{N2}	$\cdots$	$\bar{O}^N$	O_T^{No}	O_T^{Nd}	K_t^N
Outside world		O_T^{o1}	O_T^{o2}	$\cdots$	O_T^{oN}	ϕ	ϕ	$O_T^{o\cdot}$
Birth		O_T^{b1}	O_T^{b2}	$\cdots$	O_T^{bN}	ϕ	ϕ	$O_T^{b\cdot}$
Total		K_{t+u}^1	K_{t+u}^2	$\cdots$	K_{t+u}^N	$O_T^{\cdot o}$	$O_T^{\cdot d}$	

Definitions of variables

$\bar{O}^i$ residual accounts balancing term for region i (no substantive meaning). This term is to be distinguished from the term that often appears in the diagonal of movements tables: the total number of movements within the region, which might be expressed as O_T^{ii}.

O_T^{ij} migrations (moves) from region i to region j.

O_T^{io} emigrations (moves) from region i to the outside world.

O_T^{id} deaths in region i.

K_t^i population at the start of the period in region i.

O_T^{oj} immigrations (moves) from the outside world to region j.

σ item ignored or set to zero.

$O_T^{\cdot o}$ the total number of immigrations to internal regions from the outside world. The $\cdot$ refers to summation over all possible future states in the period.

O_T^{bi} births in region i.

K_{t+u}^j population at the end of the period in region j.

$O_T^{\cdot o}$ the total number of emigrations from the internal regions to the outside world. The $\cdot$ refers to summation over all possible past states in the period.

$O_T^{\cdot d}$ the total number of deaths in the internal regions.

2.1.3 *The Migration and Settlement Study from an Accounting Perspective*

We can now place the multiregional analysis of the Migration and Settlement Study within these two accounting perspectives. Two aspects are of principal importance: the method of survival probability estimation and the degree of closure of the system.

(1) *Methods of Calculating the Life Table Survival Probabilities.* Methods of calculating survival probabilities from different types of data are discussed in detail in Chapter 10. Two main approaches to probability estimation may be distinguished: the movement and the transition approaches.

In the movement approach, movement data are used and the survival probabilities are estimated from

$$\mathbf{p}_x = [\mathbf{I} + (h/2)\mathbf{m}_X]^{-1}[\mathbf{I} - (h/2)\mathbf{m}_X] \, , \tag{2.3}$$

where $\mathbf{p}_x$ is a matrix of multiregional survival probabilities for age transition x to $x + h$, $\mathbf{m}_X$ is a special matrix of *annual* migration and mortality rates (see Chapter 9 for details), $\mathbf{I}$ is the identity matrix, and h is the age interval. In the transition approach, two subapproaches can be used, depending on whether "stayer" numbers are available. If no such numbers are available (subapproach A), equation (2.3) or a slightly improved version of it (Chapter 10) can be used with annual-equivalent migrant rates. But if stayer numbers are available (subapproach B), conditional survivorship proportions $\bar{\mathbf{s}}_X$ can be calculated. Conditional survival probabilities are computed from interpolation between successive $\bar{\mathbf{s}}_X$ matrices using

$$\bar{\mathbf{p}}_X = \frac{1}{2}(\bar{\mathbf{s}}_{X-H} + \bar{\mathbf{s}}_X) \tag{2.4}$$

or some more sophisticated interpolation technique, and then the survival probabilities obtained by post-multiplying by an adequate matrix accounting for mortality.

All national studies except that for France employed equation (2.3) to estimate survival probabilities: for 11 countries movement data were available, and transition data were obtained for five (Table 2.4). In the French study, a method involving transition approach B (Ledent with Courgeau 1982) was applied in which seven-year migration and stayer proportions conditional on survival were adjusted to correspond to a five-year time interval (by raising the matrix of rates to the power 5/7) and then used to compute survival probabilities using conventional mortality rates and an interpolation technique.

Transition approach B was applied by Ledent and Rees (1980) to the UK data subsequent to the national study. A comparison was made between the results of the two transition subapproaches for a common three-region system (East Anglia, the South East, and the Rest of Britain). In life table analysis, these results differed significantly: the percentage of life predicted to be

Table 2.3 Transition account for a multiregional system within a single country in a single period T. [a]

Initial state in period	Final state in period										
	Survival s at time t					Death d in period $t, t+u$					Total
	Internal regions			Outside world, o	N	Internal regions			Outside world, o	N	
	1	2	...			1	2	...			
Existence e at time t											
Internal regions 1	$K^{e1,s1}$	$K^{e1,s2}$	...	$K^{e1,so}$	$K^{e1,sN}$	$K^{e1,d1}$	$K^{e1,d2}$	...	$K^{e1,do}$	$K^{e1,dN}$	$K^{e1,\cdot\cdot}$
Internal regions 2	$K^{e2,s1}$	$K^{e2,s2}$	...	$K^{e2,so}$	$K^{e2,sN}$	$K^{e2,d1}$	$K^{e2,d2}$	...	$K^{e2,do}$	$K^{e2,dN}$	$K^{e2,\cdot\cdot}$
...	...	...		...	...	...	...		...	...	...
N	$K^{eN,s1}$	$K^{eN,s2}$	...	$K^{eN,so}$	$K^{eN,sN}$	$K^{eN,d1}$	$K^{eN,d2}$	...	$K^{eN,do}$	$K^{eN,dN}$	$K^{eN,\cdot\cdot}$
Outside world o	$K^{eo,s1}$	$K^{eo,s2}$	...	ϕ	$K^{eo,sN}$	$K^{eo,d1}$	$K^{eo,d2}$	...	ϕ	$K^{eo,dN}$	$K^{eo,\cdot\cdot}$
Birth in $t, t+u$											
Internal regions 1	$K^{b1,s1}$	$K^{b1,s2}$	...	$K^{b1,so}$	$K^{b1,sN}$	$K^{b1,d1}$	$K^{b1,d2}$	...	$K^{b1,do}$	$K^{b1,dN}$	$K^{b1,\cdot\cdot}$
Internal regions 2	$K^{b2,s1}$	$K^{b2,s2}$	...	$K^{b2,so}$	$K^{b2,sN}$	$K^{b2,d1}$	$K^{b2,d2}$	...	$K^{b2,do}$	$K^{b2,dN}$	$K^{b2,\cdot\cdot}$
...	...	...		...	...	...	...		...	...	...
N	$K^{bN,s1}$	$K^{bN,s2}$	...	$K^{bN,so}$	$K^{bN,sN}$	$K^{bN,d1}$	$K^{bM,d2}$	...	$K^{bN,do}$	$K^{bN,dN}$	$K^{bN,\cdot\cdot}$
Outside world o	$K^{bo,s1}$	$K^{bo,s2}$	...	ϕ	$K^{bo,sN}$	$K^{bo,d1}$	$K^{bo,d2}$	...	ϕ	$K^{bo,dN}$	$K^{bo,\cdot\cdot}$
Total	$K^{\cdot\cdot,s1}$	$K^{\cdot\cdot,s2}$	...	$K^{\cdot\cdot,so}$	$K^{\cdot\cdot,sN}$	$K^{\cdot\cdot,d1}$	$K^{\cdot\cdot,d2}$	...	$K^{\cdot\cdot,do}$	$K^{\cdot\cdot,dN}$	$K^{\cdot\cdot,\cdot\cdot}$

[a]Time subscripts are deleted for convenience.

Definitions of variables

T period from time t to $t+u$.

u length of period T.

t time at start of period.

K transitions or persons making a transition.

$K^{ei,sj}$ persons in existence in region i at time t who survive in region j at time $t+u$.

$K^{ei,dj}$ persons in existence in region i at time t who die in region j before time $t+u$.

$K^{bi,sj}$ persons born in region i in period T to $T+u$ who survive in region j at time $t+u$.

$K^{bi,dj}$ persons born in region i in period T to $T+u$ who die in region j before time $t+u$.

$K^{ei,\cdot\cdot}$ population of region i at time t.

$K^{bi,\cdot\cdot}$ births in region i in period T.

$K^{\cdot\cdot,dj}$ deaths in region j in period T.

$K^{\cdot\cdot,sj}$ population of region j in period T.

$K^{eo,\cdot\cdot}$ immigrants from the outside world to internal regions in period T.

$K^{bo,\cdot\cdot}$ infant immigrants from the outside world to internal regions in period T.

$K^{\cdot\cdot,so}$ surviving emigrants from internal regions to the outside world in period T.

$K^{\cdot\cdot,do}$ nonsurviving emigrants from internal regions to the outside world in period T.

Table 2.4 The Migration and Settlement national studies classified
by approach to multiregional life table construction.

Movement approach (movement data employed)	Transition approach (transition data employed)
Occurrence/exposure rates used to derive survival probabilities	A. Migrant rates used to derive survival probabilities
Bulgaria	Austria
Czechoslovakia	Canada
FRG	Japan
Finland	United Kingdom
GDR	United States
Hungary	
Italy	
Netherlands	B. Survivorship rates used to derive
Poland	survival probabilities
Soviet Union	
Sweden	France

spent in the region of birth differed by 4.5% in the case of the smallest region,
East Anglia. The difference can ultimately be attributed to the way the diagonal terms were handled in these particular applications.

(2) *Degree of Closure of the Multiregional Systems.* The importance of
migration streams external to the country's multiregional system was usually
discussed in each national report if it was considered relevant, but external
migration flows were not incorporated in the multiregional analysis. This is a
common practice in life table analysis, where life histories are drawn of persons born in the country considered and where a life expectancy, which is
comparable to the conventional concept, can only be calculated by assuming
that people do not leave the multiregional system. Excluding external migration is an appropriate practice for analysis of a stable population, where the
asymptotic behavior of a population with fixed demographic rates is investi-
gated. The practice is, however, not suited for population forecasting, since
external migration affects both population size and population distribution. At
the time the Migration and Settlement Study was carried out, the necessary
computer programs for incorporating external flows in projections were still
under development and there were great difficulties in assembling comparable
international migration statistics for regions within countries. It was therefore decided not to include external migration. It is, however, useful to assess
the importance of external migration as a component of population change.

How important are external migration flows? The percentage contribution
of external migration to the combined total of internal interregional migration
and external migration was estimated by Rees and Willekens (1981) for the

countries for which the relevant figures are available. For three countries — the UK, Canada, and the Federal Republic of Germany — more than half of the migration flows are external; for three countries — Sweden, the Netherlands, and France — between a quarter and a half of the migration flows are external. For the Soviet Union, external migration makes up only 2% of total migration flows. Of the remaining countries we guess that for Finland, Austria, US, and Italy, external migration contributes between 5 and 25% of total flows, whereas for Japan, German Democratic Republic, Hungary, Poland, Bulgaria, and Czechoslovakia, external flows are probably less than 5% of the total.

What kinds of effects are introduced by ignoring external migration flows in instances where they are important? Three effects may be distinguished.

The effect on the computation of overall life expectancies (either uni-regional or multiregional) will be fairly unimportant. More important in this respect may be the method of estimating mortality probabilities from mortality rates for the first age interval.

The effect on the computation of projected populations will be of some importance, especially if emigration and immigration are very differently distributed within the country concerned. This is certainly the case in the UK, France, and the Netherlands, in which immigration flows are concentrated in the capital regions (the South East, the Paris Region, and North and South Holland, respectively) and in which emigration flows are more evenly distributed. In the case of Sweden, the Stockholm region received about 40% of the total immigration in 1978–1979. Without the net gain in the foreign migration flow, the Stockholm region would have experienced a population decline (Holmberg, private communication).

The major effect, however, will be on those products of multiregional population analysis that involve "matrix" results — for example, the matrix of life expectancies by place of birth and place of residence. A significant proportion of the lives of people living in a country with a high emigration rate is likely to be spent outside that country. This aspect is not within the demographic system covered in the Migration and Settlement Study.

2.2 The Time and Age Frameworks

Demographic processes take place continuously over time, age, and space. To measure the processes, discrete time and age intervals and discrete spatial units are generally introduced. In this section, we focus on time and age intervals used in the Migration and Settlement Study. In the next section, we review the spatial units. First, however, some remarks are made on the sex specificity of the analysis.

Sex-specific population, fertility, mortality, and migration data were not available for all countries. Where these data were available, they were aggregated to correspond to persons (i.e., including both sexes) prior to the

analysis in most studies, though occasionally separate analyses were carried
out for each sex. The aggregation was made simply to limit the amount of output that national investigators had to digest and describe.

Single-sex models were employed for the demographic analyses instead of
the more customary female-dominant models. It was assumed that the births
were distributed according to the age group of the mother at the time of con-
finement. Although the distribution by average age of both parents will differ
slightly from the distribution by age of the female parent only, this difference
is usually negligible and has been ignored.

2.2.1 *Time Frameworks: Selection of Base Period and Approxi-*
mation of Population at Risk and Person-Years Lived

The population stock data needed for multiregional population analysis
should fulfill two functions in an ideal framework. They should serve as constraints on population change over the period and to estimate the population
"at risk" for events during the period. Thus if we were to build population
accounts prior to our multiregional analysis, we would need data for
beginning-of-period and end-of-period populations, and an estimate of the
populations at risk for births, deaths, and movements, which might be either
the average of beginning- and end-of-period populations, the midperiod population estimate, or a multiregional population at risk computed from associated
transition accounts (Rees and Wilson 1975). The populations at risk for transition data would be the beginning-of-period populations since, here, survivorship proportions (probabilities) and not rates are calculated from the data.
The total length of time for which the population at risk can experience an
event is denoted by the person-years lived. It is equal to the population at
risk times the average length of the observation interval.

However, the actual frameworks used in the Migration and Settlement
Study are, in several cases, far from ideal, even if one ignores the absence of
underpinning population accounts. In general, the studies that employ movement data derived from registration data were able to match the periods used
for births, deaths, and migration flow data precisely and to use the midperiod
or average population stocks as populations at risk in their rate calculations
(Finland, Sweden, the Federal Republic of Germany, Bulgaria, Czechoslovakia,
and Italy). Because of lack of adequate data, other movement-based studies
employed beginning- or end-of-period populations (German Democratic Republic, Netherlands, Hungary, Soviet Union, and Poland), thereby introducing
errors into their subsequent rate calculations. The errors are likely to be
small, however, since the time interval of the period of study is one year.

Transition-based studies faced the problem that the periods of measurement of transition data, being keyed to the census data, were not the same as
those for the birth and death data. The solution in the case of the Canadian
study, for example, was to compute the requisite vital statistics from detailed

(monthly) time series. If available at all, only birth, death, and migrant totals are normally available for separate months. Age-specific monthly figures must therefore be estimated. In other cases some of the discrepancies in time reference were left unresolved or only partially adjusted for.

The errors that result from the misspecification of the time reference of the input components are probably not great for the one-year-period transition data. The degree of error depends on the degree of instability in fertility and mortality rates during the period. The procedure adopted in the Canadian study, compiling birth and death statistics for all the years in the period of transition, is recommended.

Conversely, the discrepancies highlight the inadequacy of periodic censuses for monitoring migration behavior unless these censuses are quinquennial and linked (as in the Canadian practice). In the UK, the pressure from population practitioners has persuaded the Office of Population Censuses and Surveys to exploit partial register data (from the National Health Service Central Register) to generate movement data for quarterly and annual periods (Ogilvy 1980a, b).

2.2.2 Age–Time Frameworks

All of the national studies adopted five-year age groupings as the level of disaggregation for which it was feasible to gather or estimate the necessary input data. Movement data on births, deaths, or migrations are generally classified either by age of the person at the time of the event or by year of birth of the person, or, equivalently, by age at the beginning or end of the interval. At the time of the study, the distinction was not made clear in the data that were submitted for the analysis. It was assumed that all data were classified by age at the time of the event. The data are said to be period data (see Chapter 9). Events over one year could therefore be counted in space abcd on the Lexis diagram in Figure 2.2(a) (period observation) and extrapolated (by multiplying by five) to fill space aefd [see also Figure 2.3(a)].

The number of moves recorded during the observation interval divided by the person-years lived gives the annual period migration rate. If the population at risk is approximated by the average midperiod population, the migration rate for movement data is as follows:

$$m_X^{ij} = \frac{O_{XT}^{ij}}{u K_{X,t+u/2}^{i}}, \tag{2.5}$$

where O_{XT}^{ij} represents the number of moves from i to j during the time interval T by persons who were x to $x+h$ years old at the time of moving, and $K_{X,t+u/2}^{i}$ denotes the number of people aged x to $x+h$ in region i at time $t+u/2$ (midperiod).

In transition approach B, transitions (of migrants) are counted when cohorts move from being aged $x-h$ to x at time t to being aged x to $x+h$ at

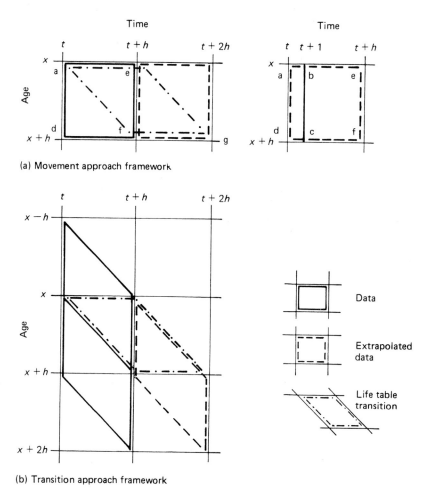

(a) Movement approach framework

(b) Transition approach framework

Figure 2.2 Lexis diagrams showing the age—time frameworks of the movement and transition approaches.

time $t + h$, as in Figure 2.2(b) (with $h = u$). The age is measured at the end of the period and the observation plan is a period—cohort observation plan (see Chapter 9). It is easy to see how the all-age transition accounts of Table 2.3 can be converted into age-specific accounts. All that is needed is the addition of a subscript, say x, to indicate the parallelogram of interest [with points (x, t), $(x + h, t)$, $(x + h, t + h)$, and $(x + 2h, t + h)$ in Figure 2.2(b)]. The accounts are reduced in size because the births portion in the aggregate representation simply becomes the first, infant cohort.

In transition approach A, when census data are available, the migrant rates that are used (period rates, Figure 2.3) cannot be derived directly. The

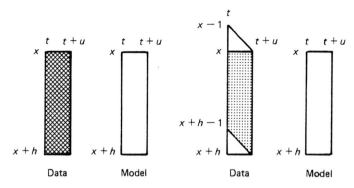

(a) Movement approach: one-year data
    $(h-5, T-1)$

(b) Transition approach A: one-year data
    $(h-5, T-1)$

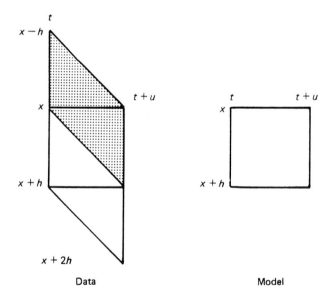

(c) Transition approach A: five-year data $(h-5, T-5)$

Movements as events in
age–time space

Transitions as events in
age–time space

Figure 2.3 The problem of matching data and model.
Source: Ledent and Rees (1980, figure 4).

annual period rates should be estimated from data in adjacent age groups:

$$m_X^{ij} = \frac{(1 - u/2h)K_X^{ij} + (u/2h)K_{\cdot,X+H}^{ij}}{uK_{X,t+u/2}^{i}} , \tag{2.6}$$

where K_X^{ij} is the number of persons in region j and in age group $(x, x + h)$ at time $t + u$ who were in region i at time t. The age interval for this group at time t is between exact ages $x - u$ and $x - u + h$. Figures 2.3(b) and (c) show how equation (2.6) applies to one-year and to five-year census migrant data, respectively.

In the UK, this equation was used to convert the data to the model age—time space [Figure 2.3(b)]. In the Austrian and Canadian studies, where five-year census migrant data were used, slightly different equations were used to derive the mobility rates. However, Ledent and Rees (1980, table 25) show that the error introduced does not have serious effects on multiregional statistics produced by summing over the age subscript.

2.2.3 Period Length of Migration Measurement

The period for which all movement data were gathered was one year. Figure 2.2(a) shows that these data are extrapolated to an imaginary five-year period in the multiregional population analysis [because of the h terms on the right-hand side of equation (2.3)]. If, instead, we had measured movements over five years, and the underlying migration pattern had not changed, we would have recorded the same number of moves. Moves, like births and deaths, are additive over time.

In the studies where transition data were used, the periods were one year (Japan, the UK, and the US), five years (Austria and Canada), and seven years (France). The seven-year French migration matrix was raised to the power 5/7 in order to make the lengths of the time interval u and the age interval h equivalent. The other data matched requirements as to h and u and so were not adjusted. A comparison in Table 2.5, of the UK national case study and the later analysis based on five-year migration data reveals a profound difference between the outcomes in terms of distribution of life among regions of residence for the one-year- and five-year-based analyses. The principal reason appears to be that the transition probabilities are not homogeneous across subgroups of the population. Some subgroups have much higher transition probabilities than others. This was demonstrated in a general sense by Kitsul and Philipov (1981).

What implications do these findings have for comparing the results of the 17 national studies? Clearly, they mean that we are unable to compare results with precision unless the studies concerned use the same type of migration data and period length. The differences that can be generated are displayed in Figure 2.4. The figure presents retention percentages, that is, the observed population-weighted average percentages of life expected to be lived in the

Table 2.5 Life expectancies and percentage distributions of residency for three regions of the United Kingdom.[a]

Region of birth	Percentage of life spent resident in:			Life expec- tancy (years)
	East Anglia	South East	Rest of Britain	
(a) *One-year migration and deaths data*				
East Anglia	41	26	33	72.4
South East	4	65	31	72.5
Rest of Britain	2	16	81	71.5
(b) *Five-year migration and deaths data*				
East Anglia	56	20	24	72.8
South East	4	74	23	72.5
Rest of Britain	2	12	87	71.7

[a]Not all the percentages sum to 100 because of rounding errors.
Source: Ledent and Rees (1980, Appendix A.3.1, runs 7–15).

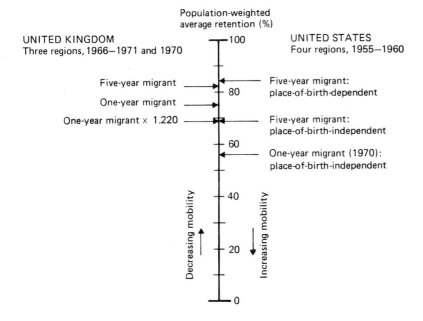

Figure 2.4 The effect of different migration data types on life table regional retention percentages.
Sources: United Kingdom: computed from data in Table 2.5 and population figures given in Ledent and Rees (1980, appendix A2.1). United States: computed from Ledent (1981, p.44, table 5) using population figures in Rogers (1976b, p.523) for 1958.

region of birth for a three-region UK system (East Anglia, the South East, and the Rest of Britain) and a four-region US system (averages are calculated over the regions).

The figure indicates that on the basis of five-year migration data a person in the UK may, on the average, expect to spend 82% of his or her lifetime in the region of birth. The retention percentage is 75 if one-year migrant data are employed. The statistic labeled "one-year migrant × 1.220" needs some explanation. The one-year complements of the retention figures (100 minus the retention percentage, that is, the percentage of life expected to be spent outside the region of birth) were multiplied by the average number of migrations per transition for interregional migration plans reported by Ogilvy (1980a). Thus 69% is a guess as to the result that might have been obtained if movement data had been used.

The equivalent US figure using five-year migrant data is 69%. The difference of 13% between this figure and its UK counterpart means that persons born in the US are expected to spend 13% more of their lives outside their birth region than are persons born in the UK, for the particular set of regions being studied. Similarly, we can compare directly the one-year migrant figures for the UK and US. The average retention level in the US regions is only 56%, compared with 75% for the UK regions, a wider difference of 19%. Ledent (1981), however, was able to use migration data tabulated by place of birth of the migrant and to compute a life expectancy matrix dependent on place of birth (the four region-of-birth matrices weighted by their share of national births in the period), in which 84% of life is likely to be spent in the region of birth.

A comparison of the UK figures demonstrates the importance of having the same type of migration data and period length if results are to be comparable. Differences in retention percentages are made up of differences due to the use of:

- a movement rather than transition concept, 75 − 69 = 6 points
- a one-year rather than five-year period, 82 − 75 = 7 points.

The difference of 13 percentage points between the US and the UK five-year migration propensity would have been masked if the UK one-year migrant data or the movement data had been used.

Is there anything that could have been done in the national studies to avoid the disturbing incomparabilities resulting from differences in the type of migration data and in period lengths? The answer must be "probably not", on two counts. First, interregional migration statistics are expensive demographic data to collect and are usually assembled and tabulated in only a few ways. The only countries in which there appears to have been any choice are the UK (one-year and five-year migration tables, 1971 census) and the Soviet Union (two-year migration tables, 1970 census: registration-based movement tables for single years). For Hungary, movement data were used, although the 1970 census collected five-year transition data; these data have, however, not been tabulated. For Japan, 1970 one-year transition data were used; movement data were generated by a registration system, but these data were not tabulated for age categories (Nanjo 1981). In member countries of the European Communities, transition data (one- and sometimes two-year periods) are nowadays collected as part of labor force surveys; the migration data are generally not tabulated. The second argument is that the nature of the differences and their effects has only become clear because the Migration and Settlement Study has been carried out.

We turn next to an examination in detail of the spatial frameworks adopted in the national studies, an important aspect of data comparability that we have so far neglected.

2.3 The Spatial Frameworks: Regions Used

The concept of a "region" has been much argued about in the social sciences, particularly in geography (Grigg 1967, Haggett *et al.* 1977). Two views have been in conflict. The first sees countries as being divided up into functional, "real" regions that organize a human activity (commuting, trade, traffic, information flows, and control). The second view identifies regions by using classificatory principles of uniform grouping with a contiguity constraint addressed to the purpose at hand. The regions used for administrative or planning purposes may have the characteristics of either functional or formal regions or a mixture of both or of neither, being *ad hoc* products of historical evolution, usually associated with a collective regional consciousness.

Geographers have put forward strong arguments that the evolution of the population distribution within a country should be studied using functional urban regions, as in Berry and Gillard (1977) and Hall and Hay (1980). Researchers build up their regions by adding to significant employment centers those areal units (operational taxonomic units) that have strong connections in terms of journey-to-work flows. The changes in population and employment in the system of functional urban regions are then studied, and in some instances (Kennett 1980) the components of population change (natural increase, net migration, gross migration flows) are also examined.

There are, however, problems associated with the adoption of such regional units: some practical, some methodological. First, in most countries functional urban regions are not adopted as the areal units for publication of the necessary population stock, vital, and migration statistics disaggregated by age and sex. To estimate the missing data items would be a major research task in itself. Second, there tend to be many functional urban regions within a country (70 in Sweden, about 130 in Great Britain, over 200 in the US). As a result, the migration flow matrices would be extremely sparse and any analysis

Table 2.6 The regions used in the Migration and Settlement Study.

Country	Scale of regions		
	Coarse	Medium	Fine
1 Austria	4 *Länder* aggregations[a]	9 *Länder*[bd] (states)	95 *Gemeinden* (communities)
2 Bulgaria	–	7 regions[bd]	28 districts
3 Canada	–	10 provinces[bd]	
4 Czecho-slovakia	2 republics	10 regions[bd]	12 administrative regional units
5 FRG	–	10 *Länder*[bd] and West Berlin	58 functional urban regions
6 Finland	–	12 *läani* (provinces)[bd]	16 economic regions
7 France	8 ZEATs (planning zones)[bd]	22 regions[c]	95 departments
8 GDR	5 regions[bd]	10 and 15 regions (districts)[cd]	219 *Kreise* (counties)
9 Hungary	–	6 economic planning regions[bd]	25 counties and towns[c]
10 Italy	5 regions[bd]	–	20 administrative units[acd]
11 Japan	–	8 regions[bd]	47 prefectures
12 Nether-lands	5 geographic regions[bd]	11 provinces[cd]	40 COROP regions 129 economic geographic areas
13 Poland	–	13 regions[bd]	22 *voivodships* (until 1975), 49 *voivodships* (since 1975)[c]
14 Soviet Union	urban and rural areas[ad]	8 units: 7 urban regions and 1 rural remainder[bd]	15 republics
15 Sweden	–	8 regions[bd]	24 counties[c] 70 A-Regions
16 United Kingdom	2 standard regions and remainder of country[a]	10 standard regions[bd]	20 metropolitan countries and region remainder 61 counties and Scottish regions
17 United States	4 regions[bd]	9 census divisions[a]	50 states

[a]Secondary multiregional analysis carried out at this scale.
[b]Principal multiregional analysis carried out at this scale.
[c]Additional single-region analysis carried out at this scale.
[d]Data provided in Research Report at this scale for multiregional analysis.

Notes for Table 2.6

Austria:	The four macroregions are groupings of the nine *Länder*.
Bulgaria	The seven regions are groupings of 28 administrative districts.
Canada:	The Canadian study omits the Yukon and Northwest Territories from the multiregional analysis. The provinces are administrative units.
Czechoslovakia:	Seven of the regional units fall in the Czech Socialist Republic and three in the Slovak Socialist Republic.
FRG:	The *Länder* are administrative regions.
Finland:	The provinces are administrative units.
France:	The ZEATs are the *zones d'étude et d'aménagement du territoire*, originally defined for the regionalization of the Sixth National Plan. They are groupings of the 22 programming regions.
GDR:	The multiregional analysis of the German Democratic Republic was carried out principally using five macroregions, though some analysis was done with 10 and 15 regions. The 15 regions are the administrative districts of the German Democratic Republic (*Bezirke*). The macroregions are aggregations of the administrative districts.
Hungary:	The six regions are groupings of the 25 administrative districts.
Italy:	The five regions are amalgamations of the 20 administrative units.
Japan:	The eight regions are aggregations of the 47 administrative prefectures.
Netherlands:	The five regions are groups of the 11 administrative provinces and the Ijsselmeer polders. The COROP regions are functional urban regions.
Poland:	The 13 regions are groupings of the 49 (post-1975) administrative *voivodships*. Before 1975 there were 22 *voivodships*.
Soviet Union:	The urban regions are not contiguous.
Sweden:	The regional units are amalgamations of counties (administrative units).
United Kingdom:	The United Kingdom regional analysis covers 11 regions: the eight standard regions of England, plus Wales, Scotland, and Northern Ireland. In the multiregional analysis Northern Ireland was omitted. Three regions (coarse regionalization) are used in the United Kingdom analysis in Chapter 7 and in the Ledent and Rees (1980) study. The standard regions are aggregations, for statistical purposes, of the administrative counties.
United States:	The four regions are aggregations of the nine census divisions, which are amalgamations of the 50 administrative states.

Source: Rees and Willekens (1981, pp.44–45), with corrections by authors.

based on them would be rather unreliable. There would also be the problem of coping with the large number of regions to be handled in computer data-processing operations.

Of course, demographic analysis of functional urban regions is perfectly possible on the basis of a single region or an aggregated system (e.g., n systems of three regions consisting of the functional urban region, the rest of the country, and the rest of the world), as Long and Frey (1982) have shown in their study of the US. In general, such an analysis on a comparative basis would pose substantial data problems.

As a result of these problems a decision was taken early in the Migration and Settlement Study to leave the delineation of regions to the national investigators. They were asked to decide upon a policy-relevant set of regions into which their country could be divided and for which most population data could be obtained without too much difficulty. The number of regions to be identified was constrained to be less than or equal to 12, which was felt to be a maximum for the purposes of the project (largely a learning exercise for the participants) and to which the version of the computer program used was constrained. (For Poland, 13 regions were used and the program was executed on a larger computer in Warsaw; a 20-region output for Italy was produced also by a larger computer in Turin.)

What kinds of regions were chosen by the authors of the national studies and what problems of comparability do they pose?

Table 2.6 sets out the names and numbers of regions that exist and are used in each country. The regional sets are classified into coarse (less than six regions in the set), medium (6–15 regions), and fine (more than 15 regions). Multiregional analyses were carried out at either the coarse or the medium scale or both; in some studies additional single-region analyses were carried out at the fine scale (e.g., Koch and Gatzweiler 1980, Campisi *et al.* 1982). The coarse scale consists of sets of regions that are aggregations of medium-scale regions, for which all the necessary data were available.

A majority of the regional sets used consisted of aggregations of administrative (governmental or planning) areas. In some cases (e.g., Sweden and Japan) this aggregation was made by the authors; in others (e.g., the UK and France) the aggregations were widely used for statistical reporting purposes by government agencies. In other studies the regions analyzed were used for planning or policy purposes. The *lääni* of Finland, the provinces of Canada, the economic planning regions of Hungary, the geographic regions of the Netherlands, the *Länder* of the Federal Republic of Germany, and the *Länder* of Austria all fall into this category.

The boundaries of the regions used in the principal multiregional analyses of the country studies are shown in Figures 2.5(a) and (b), and the names are spelled out in full in Table 2.7. A few comments are in order about the nature and scale of some particular regions.

A couple of regionalizations fail to be exhaustive of the national territory. Northern Ireland is omitted from the UK multiregional analysis because
of the lack of published data on migration to Northern Ireland from the
regions of Great Britain. The second instance is the omission of the Yukon and
Northwest Territories from the Canadian study on the grounds of their small
population and unreliable data.

The varying scale of regions (both in area and in population) gives rise to
problems of comparability both within countries and between them. Courgeau
(1973b) has studied the relationship between the level of migration (migration
rate) and the number of units into which the national territory is divided [Fig-
ure 2.6(a)]. He proposes a power function to express this relationship. A
parallel proposition is given in Figure 2.6(b), where the migration level is an
inverse power function of the average areal size. The migration rates of country A are consistently higher than those of country B when equivalent
numbers of regions are taken into account. It might be quite feasible to
observe a higher interregional migration level for country B, however, if the
number of units involved were sufficiently greater, as is the case when studies
1 and 2 are compared in Figure 2.6(a).

A similar effect can occur when two regions are compared within a country. The smaller the region, other things being equal, the higher the observed
outmigration rates. But the propensity of migrants to move over given distances may be exactly the same. Thus the *Länder* of Bremen and Hamburg are
much smaller than the other *Länder* of the Federal Republic of Germany, and
the migration levels observed are much higher.

Of course, the Bremen and Hamburg *Länder* are under-bounded definitions of their respective functional urban regions (Koch and Gatzweiler 1980,
figure 5), and thus a major part of their higher than average migration levels is
probably a result of the suburbanization processes overlapping *Länder* boundaries.

The biggest contrast between and within sets of regions, however, is the
contrast between the regions of the Soviet Union and the other countries.
The Soviet Union regions are collections of urban islands in a rural sea; only
the rural remainder preserves the property of contiguity. Seven of the eight
"regions" are small in collective area extent, and the eighth is vast. Since the
Soviet Union is currently in the process of rapid urbanization (Soboleva 1980),
this particular regionalization is especially pertinent but difficult to compare
with other regionalizations.

It is clear from the discussion that there are considerable problems in
comparing the regional patterns of mortality, fertility, and migration in the 17
IIASA countries. It is also clear that no uniform criteria or regionalization
rules are yet available to deal with the problem of the dependence of migration levels on regional disaggregation. Regional population dynamics must be
viewed on a variety of scales and Table 2.6 tells us that this is what many of
the study's authors did intuitively: they studied population and migration

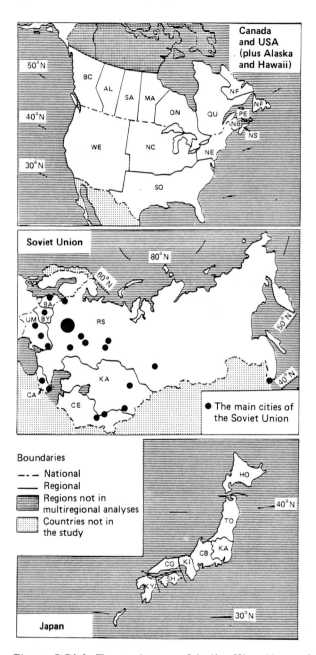

Figure 2.5(a) The regions used in the Migration and Settlement Study: North America, the Soviet Union, and Japan.

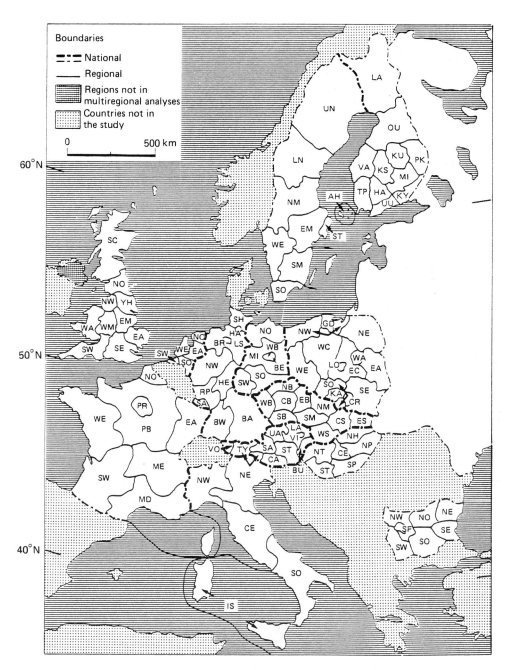

Figure 2.5(b) The regions used in the Migration and Settlement Study: Europe.

Table 2.7 Names of the regions and reference years used in the multiregional population analyses.

1. *Austria* (1971)
BU Burgenland
CA Carinthia
LA Lower Austria
UA Upper Austria
SA Salzburg
ST Styria
TY Tyrol
VO Vorarlberg
VI Vienna

2. *Bulgaria* (1975)
NW North West
NO North
NE North East
SW South West
SO South
SE South East
SF Sofia

3. *Canada* (1971)
NF Newfoundland
PE Prince Edward Island
NS Nova Scotia
NB New Brunswick
QU Quebec
ON Ontario
MA Manitoba
SA Saskatchewan
AL Alberta
BC British Columbia

4. *Czechoslovakia* (1975)
CB Central Bohemia
SB Southern Bohemia
WB Western Bohemia
NB Northern Bohemia
EB Eastern Bohemia
SM Southern Moravia
NM Northern Moravia
WS Western Slovakia
CS Central Slovakia
ES Eastern Slovakia

5. *Federal Republic of Germany* (1974)
SH Schleswig–Holstein
HA Hamburg
LS Lower Saxony
BR Bremen
NW North Rhine–Westphalia
HE Hessen
RP Rhineland–Palatinate
BW Baden–Württemberg
BA Bavaria
SA Saarland
WB West Berlin

6. *Finland* (1974)
UU Uusimaa
TP Turku and Pori
AH Ahvenanmaa
HA Häme
KY Kymi
MI Mikkeli
PK Pohjois–Karjala
KU Kuopio
KS Keski–Suomi
VA Vaasa
OU Oulu
LA Lappi

7. *France* (1975)
PR Paris Region
PB Paris Basin
NO North
EA East
WE West
SW South West
ME Middle East
MD Mediterranean

8. *German Democratic Republic* (1975)
NO North
BE Berlin
SW South West
SO South
MI Middle

9. *Hungary* (1974)
CE Central
NH North Hungary
NP North Plain
SP South Plain
NT North Trans-Danubia
ST South Trans-Danubia

10. *Italy* (1978)
NW North West
NE North East
CE Center
SO South
IS Islands

11. *Japan* (1970)
HO Hokkaido
TO Tohoku
KA Kanto
CB Chubu
KI Kinki
CG Chugoku
SH Shikoku
KY Kyushu

12. *Netherlands* (1974)
NO North
EA East
WE West
SW South West
SO South

13. *Poland* (1977)
WA Warsaw
LO Łódź
GD Gdańsk
KA Katowice
CR Krakow
EC East Central
NE Northeast
NW Northwest
SO South
SE Southeast
EA East
WC West Central
WE West

14. *Soviet Union* (1974)
RS Urban areas of the RSFSR
UM Urban areas of the Ukrainian and Moldavian SSRs
BY Urban areas of the Byelorussian SSR
CE Urban areas of the Central Asian Republics (Uzbek, Kirgiz, Tadzhik, and Turkmen SSRs),
KA Urban areas of the Kazakh SSR
CA Urban areas of the Caucasian Republics (Georgian, Azer-baijan, and Armenian SSRs)
BA Urban areas of the Baltic Republics (Estonian, Latvian, and Lithuanian SSRs)
RU Rural areas of the USSR

15. *Sweden* (1974)
ST Stockholm
EM East Middle
SM South Middle
SO South
WE West
NM North Middle
LN Lower North
UN Upper North

16. *United Kingdom* (1970)
NO North
YH Yorkshire and Humberside
NW North West
EM East Midlands
WM West Midlands
EA East Anglia
SE South East
SW South West
WA Wales
SC Scotland

17. *United States* (1970)
NE Northeast
NC North Central
SO South
WE West

Source: Rees and Willekens (1981, pp.48–49), amended.

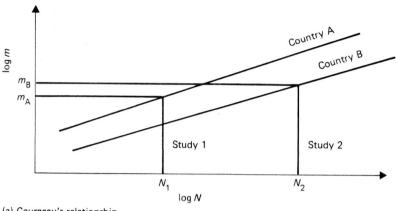

(a) Courgeau's relationship

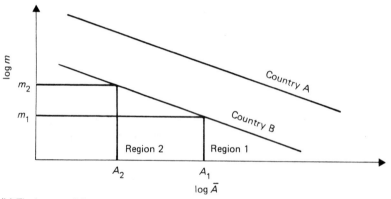

(b) The inverse of Courgeau's relationship

Figure 2.6 Migration rate as a function of (a) the number and (b) the average areal size of measurement units, along logarithmically scaled coordinate axes (N is the number of regions into which the country has been divided, and $\bar{A}$ the average area of a region).

patterns using coarse, medium, and fine levels of resolution. As we show in the next section, however, the difficulties in preparing the data for multiregional population research generally restrict analysis to the medium scale.

2.4 The Estimation of Model Inputs

The first step in each of the 17 studies was the estimation of the necessary input data on population stocks, births, deaths, and migration flows for the regions chosen. For one reason or another none of the data gathered and published by national statistical offices were quite in the correct form for analysis. Official data must often be adjusted or disaggregated to yield variables for input to population models. Sometimes this work of estimation is needed because the data are missing; more often, estimations are carried out because retabulation of the original census or register files is prohibitively costly in money or time.

We believe that five principles should govern the estimation process:

(1) The data should correspond to the variables input to the population model.
(2) The data should be corrected for known under- or overenumeration.
(3) The time points or periods of data collection should match those of the model.
(4) The data should apply to regions used in the model.
(5) The age disaggregation of the input data should match that demanded in the model.

Application of these principles leads to estimation involving concept adjustment, correction for under- or overenumeration, temporal adjustment, regional adjustment, and age disaggregation.

2.4.1 *Population Stocks*

Population stocks can be measured in several ways. The population can be enumerated in a census, counted by a register, or estimated using accounting principles from previous counts, from demographic event and flow counts, and from other correlated data series such as electoral registers and housing statistics (Office of Population Censuses and Surveys 1980b).

Concept adjustment is occasionally necessary for population stocks. Census populations are tabulated in one of two ways: as either the enumerated (*de facto*) population actually present in a household on census night or the "usually resident" (*de jure*) population counted by place of usual residence, census night visitors being transferred back to households of usual residence. In the UK censuses of 1966 and 1971, for example, the main region-by-age-by-sex population stock tables are for *de facto* populations, and the detailed group numbers must be adjusted to a "usually resident" total. In countries with a registration system, the population stock refers to the *de jure* population.

Correction for under- or overenumeration may be applied to census- or register-based population stocks data if a measure of likely error is available in the form of a post-census survey for census-derived populations or in the form of a census for register-derived populations. [Andersson and Holmberg (1980) include a discussion of errors associated with register counts.]

Regional adjustment is rarely necessary for study periods of only one year and in statistical systems in which the building blocks (*départements* in

France, states and counties in the US, *Länder* in Austria and the Federal
Republic of Germany) remain fixed over long periods of time. Where radical
changes have taken place in the local government system of units and boundaries (as in Poland or the UK) the reconstruction of spatially compatible time
series of demographic data is involved and prone to error. Every time a spatial
revision takes place, the time series must be adjusted.

The need for further age disaggregation of population stock data is rare.
In order that reasonable life expectancy estimates can be made, the population age breakdown (by five-year age groups) should extend to at least 85
years. Where the age breakdown of regional populations was insufficient,
deconsolidation proportions were applied to disaggregate an age group such as
60+ into quinquennial age groups 60–64, 65–69, . . . , 80–84, 85+. The deconsolidation proportions were derived either from national population data (as in
the Bulgarian study), from equivalent regions within the country, or from other
countries (as in the Soviet Union study, where deconsolidation proportions
from Poland were used).

A particularly unusual age grouping is used by the German Democratic
Republic. For planning purposes, age groups 0–1, 1–3, 3–6, 6–10, 10–15,
15–18, 18–21, 21–25, followed by the five-year age groups 25–30, 30–35, and
so on, are considered in statistical publications. For the Migration and Settlement Study, this age grouping was rearranged into five-year age groups on the
basis of the age composition at the national level, which was recorded in single
years of age. Unfortunately, however, the disaggregation was extended only to
the 75+ age group. (The same insufficient age disaggregation was also carried
out in Finland.)

2.4.2 *Deaths and Births*

Concept adjustment is not normally required for death data since death
registrations are tabulated, as a matter of course, by area of usual residence.
Underenumeration in developed countries is not regarded as serious and the
existence of combined birth and death registration systems ensures accuracy
of the reported information.

Adjustment of the death data to the relevant period is occasionally
needed if an intercensal period is used to match the time span of the migration
data. Annual counts of deaths for regions can be adjusted by applying temporal fractions based on quarterly or monthly national data. Termote (1980)
describes such procedures in the Canadian report.

Occasionally, the age disaggregation of death data was insufficiently
detailed for model input, as in the Bulgarian and UK studies. Since a detailed
age composition of deaths was available at the national level, broad age classes
were disaggregated using national data. In the case of Bulgaria, the data were
disaggregated in proportion with the national age structure of deaths within
the broad age classes. For the UK, deaths in broad age classes were

disaggregated using national death *rates* for the age groups that compose the age classes. The procedure is described by Rees (1980). It implies that the *shape* of the national mortality curve within an age class is imposed on to the region, whereas the *level* of the curve is determined by the number of deaths in the age class in the region.

In one case, age-classified data had to be aggregated: both UK and Bulgarian regional death tables distinguish between deaths under one year of age and deaths at ages one to four. This disaggregation has long been recognized as necessary in "abridged" single-region life tables, although in most developed countries it has relatively little effect on average life expectancies. [Rees (1979a, p.51) suggests that adopting the finer disaggregation lowers the calculated life expectancies for British regions by about three weeks.]

Little needs to be added to this discussion when birth data are considered. The only estimation problem concerned the meaning of the age classification in relation to the population model, and this we have already discussed.

2.4.3 *Migration Flows: Minor Problems*

We concentrate in this section on the problems of estimating migration flows sufficiently classified by age for input to the multiregional population models, after first referring to the problems of concept adjustment, underenumeration, and regional adjustment.

The various migration concepts used in the IIASA countries have been discussed in some detail in preceding sections. The conceptual differences between movement and transition data and between transition data over short and long time intervals have been noted. Choices between concepts were occasionally available to the national investigators (e.g., for the UK) but, in general, insufficient information was available to transform one type of migration data into another, even if a model of the process could be proposed (Kitsul and Philipov 1981).

These major conceptual differences were not the only problems faced in the national case studies. In the Hungarian case study, the authors were faced with two sets of migration statistics, those described as temporary and those described as permanent. Each person can have a temporary place of residence in addition to his or her permanent residence. Although a migration is normally defined as a change of permanent residence, in countries or regions where restrictions are placed on changes in permanent residence — usually because some attempt is being made to limit the growth of the largest metropolis in a country — temporary migrations (visits) may take on a rather permanent character. This has happened to a major degree in Hungary, and Bies and Tekse (1980) therefore added temporary and permanent migration together before using them as inputs to their multiregional population analysis. This raises regional migration levels in Hungary above those observed in other East European countries in the Migration and Settlement Study.

Underenumeration and misreporting are always a potential problem in the collection of migration statistics. In censuses the most mobile of the population are the most likely to be missed. Retrospective census questions upon which the migration statistics rely depend on accurate recall by the respondent and accurate classification by census clerical staff. The usual assumption that researchers make is that the errors will tend to cancel out. Registration systems avoid most of these difficulties, but not entirely, as Andersson and Holmberg's (1980) discussion of the Swedish system reveals. An additional problem associated with many censuses is that the migration question is only asked or tabulated for a sample (e.g., 10, 25, or 50%) of the population.

2.4.4 *Migration Flows: The Problem of Age*

Estimation of missing migration flows using five-year age groups proved to be the greatest problem in preparing the national data sets for input to the multiregional computer programs. This involved substantial research into the application and further development of techniques, developed in regional science and transportation science, to infer spatial interaction flows from incomplete data (Willekens 1977b, Willekens *et al.* 1981). Recently, the estimation methods have been simplified and extended to allow for the combination of various sources of prior information in order to produce the best estimates possible (Willekens 1982). The review presented in this section draws on this research; however, the numerical results shown are identical to those obtained by the entropy-maximization technique proposed by Willekens *et al.* (1981).

A major feature of the estimation method is its focus on the structure of the whole data set to predict values of missing elements. The structural representation of migration data is provided by accounts. The strategy to predict (or estimate) missing cell values in migration tables consists of five stages:

(1) Set up the accounting frames. (The account is a multidimensional contingency table.)
(2) Develop a model of the data in the accounts. (Although various models of data structures are available, the parametric log-linear model has been found most appropriate for our purposes since its parameters denote particular effects of interaction between the cross-classified variables.)
(3) Enter the available data into the account. (Fill the account as far as possible and list other prior information separately.)
(4) Determine the parameter values of the parametric model on the basis of the different types of prior information, supplemented by hypotheses about certain structural relationships in the data to be estimated.
(5) Apply the model to infer the values of the missing elements.

Step 4 may be skipped, that is, the missing elements may be predicted directly from the available data without explicitly estimating the model parameters. This shortcut will be followed in this section. The steps will now be discussed in greater detail.

Model the Data in the Account. Multiregional population analysis requires migration flows by age and by region of origin and of destination. The required data may be arranged to constitute a three-dimensional account of region of origin, region of destination, and age. (Only the first quadrants of the movement and transition accounts are of interest since they contain all the required data on internal migration.)

The investigation of large data sets may be made by fitting models to the data. During the past decade, analytical techniques have been developed for structural analysis of multidimensional contingency tables (e.g., Bishop *et al.* 1975). These techniques, which were originally designed to identify patterns of association among several cross-classified categorical variables, may be fruitfully applied for estimating missing cell values in the contingency table or account. In fact, the problem of estimating cell values in a multidimensional account is equivalent to the problem of quantifying appropriate interaction effects (Willekens 1982). This can easily be seen by appropriately modeling the data. The model is represented by the first equation in Table 2.8. It is a multiplicative or log-linear model. It has eight terms, the number of terms depending on the dimension of the account or on the number of cross-classified variables (in this case three: region of origin i, region of destination j, and age group X). Each term represents a particular structural effect on the cell values. The cells contain either the number of migrations O_X^{ij} or the number of transitions K_X^{ij}. In the table, we use O_X^{ij}.

According to the model, the expected cell count of a complete contingency table, a table without structural zeros, is the product of various effects. The overall effect w is a size effect; it is the geometric mean of all expected cell counts (Table 2.8). The main effects denote the impacts on O_X^{ij} of relative size differences between the various univariate marginals. For instance, w_X is the effect of the average age composition of the migrants on O_X^{ij}. When all else is equal, large age groups result in large migration flows. The age effect is the ratio between the geometric mean of the Xth layer and the overall geometric mean. The term w_X^i represents the interaction effect between age and origin. The pattern of interaction denoted by this term is the average interaction over all origin–age tables (i.e., for all possible destinations j). The pattern may differ for each destination, which results in values of w_X^{ij} different from unity.

By introducing this multiplicative model, we have transformed the problem of predicting the O_X^{ij} values into a problem of estimating the parameters

Table 2.8 Multiplicative formulation of a linear model.

Model	$O_X^{ij} = w w^i w^j w_X w^{ij} w_X^i w_X^j w_X^{ij}$
Overall mean effect	$w = \left[\prod_{i,j,X} O_X^{ij} \right]^{1/rcl}$
Main effects	$w^i = \dfrac{1}{w} \left[\prod_{j,X} O_X^{ij} \right]^{1/cl}$

w^i and w_X: analogous

First-order interaction effects (two-way or pairwise interaction):

$$w^{ij} = \frac{1}{z} \left[\prod_X O_X^{ij} \right]^{1/l}$$

with $z = w\, w^i w^j w_X$

w_X^i and w_X^j: analogous

Second-order interaction effects (three-way interaction):

$$w_X^{ij} = \frac{1}{z'} O_X^{ij}$$

with $z' = w\, w^i w^j w_X w^{ij} w_X^i w_X^j$

Constraints $\displaystyle\prod_i w^i = \prod_j w^j = \prod_X w_X = 1$

$\displaystyle\prod_i w^{ij} = \prod_j w^{ij} = \prod_i w_X^i = \prod_X w_X^i = \prod_j w_X^j = \prod_X w_X^j = 1$

$\displaystyle\prod_i w_X^{ij} = \prod_j w_X^{ij} = \prod_X w_X^{ij} = 1$

r: number of rows; c: number of columns; l: number of layers.

w_X^{ij}, i.e., of quantifying the interaction effects. The parameters may be derived, and the migration flows may be determined from the available data.

Enter the Available Data into the Account. In countries where migration information is not abundantly available, existing data are generally limited to aggregate information about flows. We might, for example, know the total migration flows between origins and destinations (aggregated over age), the total outmigration flows from origins by age group (aggregated over destinations), or the total inmigration flows to destinations by age group (aggregated over origins). Each of the known items is a two-dimensional array or matrix, which is a marginal (bivariate) total of the three-dimensional account, and may be entered at the appropriate place (O^{ij}, $O_X^{i\cdot}$, $O_X^{\cdot j}$). The estimation problem, for which three bivariate marginal totals are given, is referred to by Willekens *et al.* (1981) as the "three-face (3F)" problem, since the available data can be imagined as constituting the three faces of a cube (Figure 2.7).

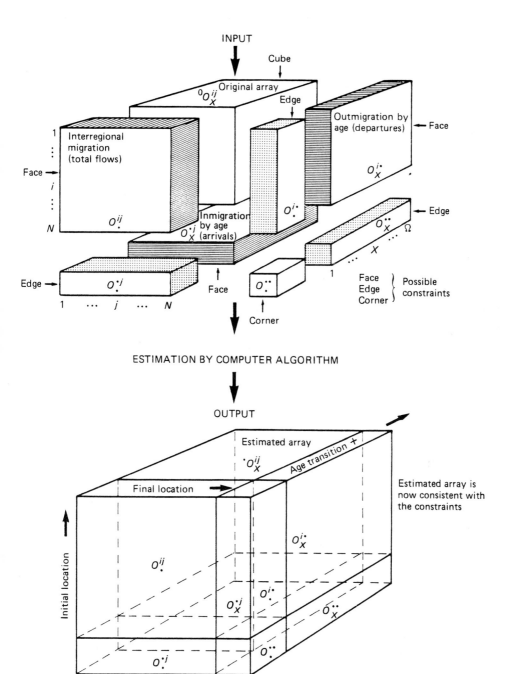

Figure 2.7 A diagrammatic representation of the migration estimation problem.

Although the 3F problem is common in the Migration and Settlement Study, migration flows may be predicted from less data. In a two-face (2F) problem, only two of the three faces (bivariate marginal totals) are given. There are three varieties of the 2F problem. In a one-face and one-edge (1FE) problem, we would only know the contents of some face together with an edge. The edges represent univariate marginal totals ($O_X^{..}$, $O_.^{i.}$, $O_.^{.j}$); hence there are three variations of the 1FE problem. The data limitation is most severe when only the three edges are known: in the 3E problem, the available data are limited to a single age composition of the migrants, a vector of departures by region, and a vector of arrivals by region.

The 3F, 2F, 1FE, and 3E problems represent various situations of data availability. Data limitations experienced in a few countries participating in the IIASA study can be related to the four types of problem. In the studies of Finland, Sweden, the Federal Republic of Germany, and Poland the necessary migration flow data disaggregated by five-year age groups were available and no further estimation was required.

In the studies of Canada, Austria, and France migration flows were classified by five-year age groups, but conversion of the classification to the appropriate age—time framework had to be carried out. In the case of Canada special tabulations for infant migrants, aged 0—4 at the end of the period, were obtained by cross-classifying place of current residence at the time of the census against place of birth. For the Netherlands and Bulgaria full 3F problems had to be solved. Between these two extremes were situations in which the age breakdown was by 10- or 15-year age groups for interregional migration flows (UK 1 and 2). In other cases the age-classified data available were not for quinquennial ages (the German Democratic Republic) or were not sufficiently disaggregated at the older ages (Japan, Canada, the UK, the Soviet Union, and Bulgaria). In these cases model migration schedules or other interpolative—extrapolative techniques had to be used.

Approximate the Missing Migration Flows. Migration flows may be approximated directly from marginal totals without first estimating the model parameters. The estimation procedure starts with a set of preliminary estimates (guesses) of the unknown migration flows. To design a set of appropriate preliminary estimates, prior information on migration, other than marginal totals, may be used. For instance, we may disregard intraregional migration and thereby force the diagonal elements of the age-specific migration matrices to be zero. Information on locational preferences may be introduced in the set of off-diagonal preliminary estimates. In the Migration and Settlement Study we did not have additional information on migration that would warrant special attention to be given to the design of a set of preliminary estimates. Therefore, the estimation procedure was started from a uniform distribution:

$$^{0}O_X^{ij} = 1 \quad \text{for all } i, j, X,$$

where $^0O_X^{ij}$ denotes the preliminary estimate of the O_X^{ij} element. In most cases, we could deduct the intraregional migration flows from the given marginal totals and hence limit the estimation problem to interregional migration. (Diagonal elements were forced to be zero: $O_X^{ii} = 0$ for all i, X.)

The estimation technique that was applied is an extension of the entropy method, widely used in transportation science and geography to infer spatial interaction flows from aggregate data. The algorithm is an iterative procedure. However, it can be shown that in three of the four problem types, the iteration takes only one step, that is, the estimation problem has a closed-form solution.

Table 2.9 Maximum-likelihood estimates in three-dimensional accounts.[a]

Case	Available data	Log-linear model	Closed-form cell estimates
3E	$\{O^{i\cdot}_{\cdot}, O^{\cdot j}_{\cdot}, O_{X}^{\cdot\cdot}\}$	$O_X^{ij} = w\, w^i w^j w_X$	$\hat{O}_X^{ij} = (1/N^2)O^{i\cdot}_{\cdot}O^{\cdot j}_{\cdot}O_X^{\cdot\cdot}$
1FE	$\{O^{ij}, O_X^{\cdot\cdot}\}$	$O_X^{ij} = w\, w^i w^j w_X w^{ij}$	$\hat{O}_X^{ij} = (1/N)O^{ij}O_X^{\cdot\cdot}$
2F	$\{O^{ij}, O_X^{\cdot j}\}$	$O_X^{ij} = w\, w^i w^j w_X w^{ij} w_X^j$	$\hat{O}_X^{ij} = O^{ij}O_X^{\cdot j}/O^{\cdot j}_{\cdot}$
3F	$\{O^{ij}, O_X^{i\cdot}, O_X^{\cdot j}\}$	$O_X^{ij} = w\, w^i w^j w_X w^{ij} w_X^j w_X^i$	No closed-form solution
CI[b]	$\{O_X^{ij}\}$	$O_X^{ij} = w\, w^i w^j w_X w_X^i w_X^j w_X^{ij} w^{ij}$	O_X^{ij} given

[a]In this table, N is the overall total $O^{\cdot\cdot}_{\cdot}$.
[b]CI: complete information.

Table 2.9 shows the solutions to the various types of estimation problem in three-dimensional accounts. Also given is the associated log-linear model. The list of parameters shows which effects are present in the estimates. The parameters not shown are unity, because the array of preliminary estimates consists of equal cell values. Since such a set of preliminary estimates represents a uniform distribution, all interaction effects are absent and the only interaction effects contained in the final estimates of migration flows are those exhibited by the given marginal totals. For instance, in the 1FE problem, only one bivariate marginal total is given and hence only one set of first-order interaction effects is different from unity. If a set of preliminary estimates is used that deviates from the uniform distribution, then the higher-order interaction effects of the final estimates are those exhibited by the preliminary estimates.

In the 3F problem, no closed-form solution exists, and the estimates must be determined by an iterative procedure. Willekens *et al.* (1981) propose an iterative multiproportional adjustment algorithm, which gives a solution of the desired characteristics and which is equivalent to iterative proportional fitting algorithms (Bishop *et al.* 1975, pp. 83–97).

2.5 Conclusion

An important objective of the Migration and Settlement Study was a quantitative assessment of recent migration patterns and spatial population dynamics in all of IIASA's 17 countries. By involving scholars of each country and by using a methodology that was considered the best then available and that was being developed at IIASA, substantial research capabilities were built up in the different countries. The application of a common methodology to different data sets provided a first step toward producing comparative results. Comparability is, however, severely handicapped by the considerable degree of incomparability of the input data, in particular the migration data. We have already noted the deviations that exist between movement and transition data and the limitations on the time period for which transition data are available. A consequence is that we can perhaps compare Finland, Sweden, the German Democratic Republic, the Netherlands, Hungary, the Soviet Union, the Federal Republic of Germany, Poland, and Bulgaria in one set (movement data over one year), Canada, France, and Austria in another (transition data over five or seven years), and the UK and US in a final set (transition data over one year).

Within the first set, the high levels of interregional migration propensity stand out in Finland, Hungary, and the Soviet Union. In the case of Hungary these may be associated with the inclusion of temporary migrations in the migration flow input data; in the Soviet Union the high levels are undoubtedly associated with the urban—rural region definitions adopted. In Finland, however, migration levels between provinces appear to be genuinely high.

Poland, the Germany Democratic Republic, and Bulgaria show the lowest migration propensities in the first set of countries. In Poland's case there has been a strongly secular decline in postwar migration rates. The Netherlands, Sweden, and the Federal Republic of Germany fall in the middle of the range of observations.

In the second set, Canada shows substantial regional contrasts in retention level, with the regions of net outmigration (Saskatchewan, Manitoba, and the four Atlantic provinces) retaining the least fraction of their birth cohorts. Mobility levels in France and Austria appear to be lower and more even over the regions (although the French levels are influenced by the longer period of measurement of the original data — seven years).

The comparability of the results of the Migration and Settlement Study is further handicapped by the wide range in sizes of the regions considered. To these problems may be added differences in base period. The reason for this lack of a uniform base year is that not all participating countries had the necessary data available for the same year. In countries with registration systems, migration data become available annually and hence a recent year could be selected as the base for the study. Countries that do not have a registration system must rely on a census for their migration data. Since all basic data on the components of demographic change should relate to the same period, fertility and mortality data generally were collected for the period (or mid-period) to which the migration data refer. [An alternative strategy could have been to assemble as much data as possible for a given year (1975, say) and to assemble other data for the nearest available period.]

We wish to issue a final warning against comparing the incomparable. A uniform methodology was used throughout in the hope of obtaining truly comparable results for all participating countries. Severe data limitations, however, as well as the focus on individual national reports and the building up of research capabilities in the 17 countries, prevented the generation of fully comparable input data within the time and budget constraints imposed on the study. Thus the findings of the national studies must be assessed very carefully in relation to the nature of the inputs used.

The principal purpose of this chapter has been to provide the reader with a framework within which the 17 studies can be set and to provide the user of multiregional demographic programs with a guide for preparation of input data sets in new situations.

In this review of accounting frameworks and data inputs we have often been critical of what has been done. Only in that way can future analyses be improved and our understanding of spatial population behavior be increased. Yet despite the severe problems attending comparison of separate national studies, we feel such an approach was justified. Only by confronting the theory of multiregional population analysis with the problems of implementation in a wide variety of contexts could its content and applicability be improved. We therefore conclude this chapter by discussing in what ways we would recommend the research specification be improved, should anyone wish to repeat and update the exercise in the future.

- External (international) migration should be included in the population projection exercises.
- To avoid the effect of age groupings, single-year-of-age data should be used; and to reduce the huge data set to manageable proportions, model schedules of age-specific migration rates should be used.
- If migration and settlement studies ought to generate directly comparable results, attention should be given to the harmonization of the available migration statistics: this should be a priority for future comparative analyses.
- Given a choice between different migration data types and period lengths, we would recommend a comparative analysis using transition data for a time interval equal to the age interval (Ledent and Rees 1980), preferably classified by region of birth as well (Ledent 1981, Philipov and Rogers 1981) and with movement data. Such a comparative analysis is carried out by Ledent and Rees in Chapter 10.

- The problem of adopting sets of regions more attuned to the detailed settlement structure of developed countries (a system of many city regions) might be solved by dropping the requirement that they be studied as a single multiregional system (Long and Frey 1982). Instead, they could be studied as a set of smaller (three-region) systems: the city region, the rest of the country, and the rest of the world. Most of the important statistical outputs of multiregional population analysis would be generated for such systems and for many other and more meaningful regions. The migration data estimation problems would be fairly straightforward, although there might be problems of consistency between the aggregate and regional projections to be solved.
- Careful attention should be paid to some of the detailed problems of data estimation analysis, such as age classification of migration, proper time specification of populations at risk, and comparable treatment of intraregional migration: these can all have a nonnegligible effect on results.

PART TWO

Components of Change

CHAPTER THREE

Mortality

Marc Termote

In the beginning of what was later to be known as demography, mortality was the most popular subject. One may even state that demography was born thanks to mortality. An interesting feature of the early works on mortality is their focus on regional differentials.

3.1 Revival of Mortality Analysis

Demography began with such scholars as Graunt, who compared the demographic situation in London with that in an English rural parish in the 1600s; Halley, who proposed the first life table based on the mortality regime of Wroclaw; and Short, who continued the study of regional mortality differentials in the eighteenth century. It was not until the last quarter of the nineteenth century that fertility and – to a much lesser extent – migration started to receive more than incidental and sporadic interest. Finally, after World War I, when mortality became increasingly "under control", at least in most industrialized countries, fertility took over as the dominant topic in population analysis.

In the last decade or so, mortality has again grown in popularity among students of demography. This is a consequence of the rapid aging of populations due to the considerable drop in fertility levels. The revival of mortality studies is also a result of some important changes in mortality itself. Even though it has been accepted for some time that the life span of human beings could not be extended significantly, it was taken for granted that the average duration of life could still be increased. In recent years, however, many of the most industrialized countries of the world have experienced a total halt, sometimes even a reversal, in the secular trend of increasing life expectancies.[1] At

---

[1] A recent study on mortality trends in the 21 member countries of the Council of Europe shows, however, that the worsening of mortality conditions observed at the beginning of the 1970s could be transitory. Indeed, new gains in life expectancy seem to have been made, particularly for the older age groups (Caselli and Egidi 1981).

present, the worsening of mortality conditions is concentrated in certain age groups (young adults of both sexes, males 45 and over, and — in some countries — infants). Moreover, this deterioration does not seem to be limited to the most industrialized nations. One possible explanation for the recent slowing of population growth in some developing countries is the increase in mortality because of malnutrition and starvation. For most developing countries, however, there has been no deterioration of mortality conditions, but rather a deceleration of mortality decline (United Nations 1982).

Regional mortality differentials have always existed, even in countries with overall high levels of life expectancy. While some differences may be attributed to "exogenous" factors (e.g., climatic and biological), most have socioeconomic causes, which implies that some groups still have less access to a country's economic, social, and medical benefits than do others. Although not much can be done to lengthen a life span, there is still room to extend the average duration of life, by giving equal access to the highest existing standard of life expectancy to all human beings.

Life expectancy may be considered as an indicator not only of a population's average level of well-being but also of the degree of social justice achieved in the population. The most tangible sign of progress in our human society has been the increase in the number of years each individual is expected to live. One should thus ask the question: Who is benefiting from this increase in the average life expectancy? Moreover, among all demographic phenomena, mortality is (with immigration) the variable most liable to intervention and control through policy measures.

Because mortality varies with place of residence, much could be done by national policymakers to equalize conditions. On the one hand, even within highly advanced countries like France and Switzerland, expectation of life for males at birth may differ by as much as five years (between French *départements* or Swiss *cantons*). This mortality differential increases to 11 years (for females as well) if we consider the nearly 260 administrative regions that constitute the 10 Common Market countries, the four Scandinavian countries, the Iberian peninsula, Austria, and Switzerland (van Poppel 1980). On the other hand, under mortality conditions prevailing today in most of Europe, the elimination of death caused by malignant tumors would increase life expectancy by only three years (Preston *et al.* 1972). It is clear that policy measures aimed at giving to all regions the mortality regime "enjoyed" by the most advanced would be highly rewarding.

Demography, more than any other social science, is highly dependent on statistical data and analytical tools. Thanks to IIASA's international study of migration and settlement, a rich stock of regional data was collected and new concepts and measures were developed. A considerable impetus has thus been given to the demographic analysis of regional differentials. The purpose of this chapter is to summarize mortality differentials in the 17 countries of the IIASA study.

This summary will be made in two ways: first, by comparing the various regional mortality patterns (Section 3.3); and second, by measuring the overall level of regional mortality differentials for each country (Section 3.4). In both cases, attention is devoted to interregional rather than international comparisons, because the various case studies emphasize the interregional redistribution of their populations and because comparability of mortality data between countries poses definite problems. Therefore, we begin with a critical analysis of the mortality data used in the different countries.

3.2 Critical Analysis of the Data

To interpret correctly the outputs of our analysis of regional mortality differentials in the various countries, we need to know as precisely as possible the quality of the inputs.

One of the main merits of IIASA's Migration and Settlement Study has been to use the same methodology for all national case studies. This eliminates one obstacle of comparability, but there still remains the problem of data comparability. It would be dangerous to infer an international pattern from the results; only a few broad generalizations can be made. Even in a field like mortality, where there is a long tradition of data collection, an international standardization of definitions, collecting procedures, and tabulation categories is still lacking. There is even a lack of standardization within some countries; data problems still exist for particular regions. Moreover, the author of each case study was solely responsible for the choice of such factors as the period of analysis, the regional disaggregation, and the procedure for estimating missing data. This obviously introduces a second complication. Because of these international comparability problems, in this chapter we emphasize interregional mortality differentials within a country, giving only marginal attention to differentials across countries.

The most important mortality data problems encountered in this study are: the time dimension, the spatial dimension, and the population coverage of these data.

3.2.1 The Time Dimension

A multiregional demographic analysis requires regional data on fertility, migration, and mortality, preferably for the same period. Because data on migration usually are available only for some specific periods (a census period, for instance), mortality could be analyzed only for the same period or for a particular year of this period. Unfortunately, this period is rarely the same for the various countries. (For example, censuses were held at different times, or if they were held at the same time, the migration question did not refer to the same year of previous residence.) When data for several periods were available (as in the case of countries where migration data were obtained from a population register with yearly tabulation), the choice of the period was left to the author of each case study, and usually the most recent year was chosen.

As a result, the periods of analyses are widely dispersed. In five cases, mortality data going back to 1971 or before were used: Canada (1966–1971), Austria (1969–1973), the UK (1970), Japan (1970, except for one region where the data of one of the prefectures refer to 1973), and the US (1970, with 1958 as an additional reference year for which unpublished data were used). Twelve national case studies refer to data for 1974 or later: for the Federal Republic of Germany, Finland, Hungary, the Netherlands, the Soviet Union, and Sweden, 1974 data were used; while for Bulgaria, Czechoslovakia, France, and the German Democratic Republic, 1975 data were taken; the Polish analysis was based on 1977 data (but computations were also made on unpublished 1973 data with another regional disaggregation) and the Italian study used 1978 data. Finally, a second Canadian study (Termote 1983) provides the results that are included here for an additional reference year, and deals with the 1971–1976 mortality conditions. It is obvious that an international comparison of mortality conditions observed at periods so far apart is highly questionable.

Even though, on the whole, developed countries have not experienced a marked increase in life expectancy at birth over the last decade, some countries in the Migration and Settlement Study showed a rather significant gain. For instance, the Japanese figure increased from 71.7 to 74.8 years (total population) between 1968 and 1976, and the US figure increased from 70.3 to 72.6 between 1968 and 1975. In such a situation, a comparison of the US 1970 data with, for example, the Polish 1977 data would be difficult to justify, because the bias imposed by using a different reference year would be larger than the international disparity actually observed for a same given year. (In 1975, the difference in life expectancy at birth between Poland and the US was about two years.)

In most cases, the mortality data used in the IIASA study refer to one-year periods. This is a serious drawback, not only for international comparisons, but also for national mortality analyses. Observations limited to one year may introduce episodic impacts, such as a flu epidemic or a change in the collecting or tabulating procedure. In a study where the main focus is limited to regional mortality differentials within a country, however, this problem is not as important. We may assume that these disparities are not significantly affected by such phenomena, and that they are relatively stable over time.

The way deaths are registered and tabulated may also introduce some bias. For most countries, death statistics refer to the data of occurrence of the event. However, in some cases (e.g., the UK) data on deaths are tabulated by date of registration rather than occurrence; it is difficult to estimate the temporal and regional bias (spatial variations in this time lag) introduced by this procedure.

3.2.2 *The Spatial Dimension*

Clearly the number and size of the regions affect considerably the results of any analysis of regional disparities. One may expect that the larger the number of spatial units used for a given country, the larger the spatial discrepancies observed. Moreover, these regional units usually correspond to administrative units,[2] which vary in population size and area, thus leading one to weight mortality indicators of a large region the same as those of a small region (where the "law of large numbers" may not apply, particularly with respect to age categories). Therefore, not only is it difficult to interpret the results of an analysis of regional discrepancies within a given country, but also it is perilous to use such results for an international comparison. We will simply emphasize that this regional disaggregation is quite different from one case study to another, ranging from four macroregions for the US to 20 regions for Italy, and that each of the US macroregions is larger (in population size and area) than most of the other countries considered.

For the analysis at the national level a more specific example of the impact of regional delineation may be given. According to the results of the second Canadian study (see Chapter 7), based on 1971–1976 data, male life expectancy at birth varied from 68.6 years (in Quebec) to 78.0 years in Saskatchewan), if we use the ten provinces as regional units. Suppose we now divide Quebec into six regions, five of them referring to the Montreal region (which contains half of Quebec's population), and four of these five being larger than the smallest Canadian province (Prince Edward Island). The range of male life expectancy at birth now extends from 58.7 to 74.1 years (Wilkins 1980), a 15.4-year difference for the 15 regional units instead of the 2.4-year difference for the ten regional units. This is, of course, an extreme case, but considering that all regional aggregations are in some way "particular", it serves to illustrate how sensitive the results of an analysis of regional differentials may be.

3.2.3 *Population Coverage*

Who is covered by these mortality statistics, and to what extent are these deaths registered? More specifically, do the mortality data of a country include deaths among all nations or only those of people who have resided in the country? For example, do they include deaths among immigrants, among nationals residing temporarily outside the country, among persons having no fixed place of residence? Do these data include stillbirths; what is the rate of underregistration or incomplete registration; when registration is incomplete, for instance with regard to age, how has this problem of incomplete

---

[2]The Soviet study represents a partial exception, inasmuch as seven "urban" regions and one "rural" macroregion comprising all rural areas were used.

registration been solved? Since it would be rather fastidious to discuss these questions for each of the 17 countries, only a global view will be presented.

As a general rule, the data refer to deaths of those individuals who had their main residence in the country and who were either citizens or immigrants to the country. This implies that deaths of residents temporarily outside the country are included. (The problem here is one of underregistration and time lag in registration.) Thus deaths occurring among military and diplomatic personnel stationed outside the country, among students attending school in a foreign country, or among tourists are registered in the "official" place of residence. The same is valid for the regional level: deaths occurring in region A of a particular country among people whose main place of residence was in region B will be included in the death statistics of region B. There is at least one exception to this general rule: Japan. Mortality data for this country refer to Japanese nationals who, at the moment of their death, were in Japan.

A particular problem arises with persons having no fixed place of residence. Their deaths may be ascribed to the region of occurrence of the event, to the region of birth of the deceased, to their last known official place of residence (if any), or to a fictitious place of residence. The most appropriate system seems to be the one used in the Netherlands, where persons having no fixed place of residence are entered separately in the central register of the population, so that they are all assumed to reside and die in a special, nonexistent region, which serves as an accounting device.

Stillbirths are usually excluded from mortality data; only deaths among infants born alive are supposed to be entered in the death statistics. There are, however, some exceptions to this rule. For instance, mortality data for the Soviet Union exclude infants born alive — after less than 28 weeks' gestation, whose weight is less than 1000 grams, and whose length is less than 35 cm — if they die within seven days of birth. French mortality data exclude deaths of infants who die before the registration of their birth. And in some countries, statistics on stillbirths are suspect, because hospitals either do not want to recognize that a "viable" baby died under their responsibility or prefer to inflate the number of births in their institution to obtain increased financial funding.[3] Underregistration and incomplete registration or tabulation may be important problems, because their impact is usually highly localized, being concentrated in some particular region or age group.

It is rather difficult to estimate the rate of underregistration of deaths; usually this rate has an insignificant impact. There is, however, one case where a marked bias is observed. In Canada, the total number of deaths in the

---

[3]At least among West European countries, however, international differences in the definitions and the collecting of data do not seem to have a significant impact on the measures of infant mortality (Höhn 1981).

province of Quebec had to be corrected for 228 "not reported" deaths in 1975 and 166 in 1976; these unreported deaths were attributed to the 0–1 age group, and represent about 18% of the total number of reported deaths for this age group in this region, a quite remarkable bias.

Even if all deaths were registered, there remains the problem of incomplete registration, particularly with respect to age. Information available for the Quebec region indicates that those deaths with "age unknown" represent about 0.5% of all reported deaths. Of course, one may always disaggregate these deaths among the different age groups according to the known distribution, but this may introduce a new bias, because most of such deaths are probably concentrated in the older age groups.

In some cases, deaths may be correctly reported, but the tabulation of these statistics may be incomplete, particularly in the last, open-ended, age group. In the Soviet Union and Bulgaria, for instance, the last age group for which the death rate is available is 70 and over. Because the age structures and mortality patterns in the older age groups of the Soviet Union and Poland are believed to be similar, the 70+ death data were disaggregated into four age groups (70–74, 75–79, 80–84, and 85+) for the Soviet study by using Polish age-specific mortality rates. Most of the national case studies used a disaggregation into 18 age groups; there are, however, two cases where only 16 age groups were used: Finland and the German Democratic Republic.

According to standard practice, age classification is based on the number of completed years of life. (In France, however, classification for ages 5 and over is based on the difference between year of birth and year of death.) In the Migration and Settlement Study, where five-year age groups are used, an infant who lived only one hour and one who lived 4 years + 360 days are both entered into the 0–4 age group, just as an individual who lived 85 years + one day and one who lived 110 years are both entered into the 85+ age group. This introduces imprecision in the computation of age-specific death rates and therefore in the significance of many mortality indicators.

Finally, the important distinction between *de facto* and *de jure* populations should be taken into account, because it may explain some considerable biases in the computation of regional death rates. When these rates are obtained by dividing the number of deaths among a *de facto* population by the number of inhabitants in the *de jure* population, one may obtain a significant underestimation of the mortality level in regions of heavy outmigration and emigration.

3.3 Regional Analysis of Some Mortality Indicators

We begin our analysis with a description of the mortality regime observed in each of the 17 countries of the IIASA study. Rather than analyze in detail the age-specific death rates in each region of each country, we summarize the mortality regime by selecting some global mortality indicators – indicators chosen in such a way as to allow for a meaningful interregional analysis.

Five mortality indicators are used in this comparative analysis. An initial way to measure the mortality level of a region is to add all age-specific death rates and then multiply by the age interval (five, in our case). This is called the *gross death rate* (GDR) or "equivalent average death rate". (Appendix 3A gives the GDRs for each region in the Migration and Settlement Study.) Such a measure gives the same weight to each age-specific death rate. But, from the individual's point of view as well as from a macrodemographic perspective, dying at age 1 and dying at age 80 are quite different. We therefore also consider a more traditional indicator: the total number of years expected to be lived by a newborn baby (if he/she remains in the region of birth during his/her entire lifetime). This is called the *expectation of life at birth* (e_0). An interregional comparison of the gross death rate and of the expectation of life at birth, however, does not provide any idea of regional differentials in age-specific death rates. To obtain some indication of this, we consider the mortality conditions for three age groups: 0–4 (because infant mortality is an important indicator of medical and social progress), 15–29 (because the recent increase in the death rate at these low-mortality ages is probably a result of specific socioeconomic factors), and 65 and over (because most deaths in a region – and most of its GDR – are from this age group).

Often-used indicators, such as the crude death rate and the mean age at death, are not considered here. These measures are too dependent on the age composition of the population. We could have presented the mean age of the mortality schedule, but empirical results show that by eliminating the effects of the age structure in this way, not much regional disparity is left. In other words, the sometimes considerable regional differences in the observed mean age of death are almost totally a result of the differences in age compositions of the populations.

Probabilities of surviving in the region at some given ages (for instance, at exact ages 20 and 65) show a remarkable regional uniformity, and are therefore not analyzed here. When migration is taken into account, considerable regional differences do appear, but since these differences primarily reflect migration behavior and not mortality, we do not analyze them in this chapter.

Clearly, we cannot produce here all values obtained for each of the five indicators in the 139 regions of our IIASA sample. It is sufficient to present a few figures that allow us to estimate the importance of these differentials, without having to describe in detail the mortality conditions observed in each region.

For each of the five mortality indicators, we present, for each country, the lowest and highest observed regional figure as well as the national average value. The highest absolute deviation is a rough measure of regional disparity. This is why we will also show the *mean absolute deviation* (MAD), defined as the sum of the differences between the regional values and the national figure,

divided by the number of regions. This mean absolute deviation is then
expressed as a percentage of the national average value of the indicators
(MAD/N).

Table 3.1 Regional differentials in life expectancy at birth (e_0) [a]: both sexes combined.

Country (reference year: number of regions)	National (N)	Lowest	Highest	MAD	MAD/N(%)
Austria (1971:9)	70.5	69.6	71.7	0.6	0.8
Bulgaria (1975:7)	70.9	69.9	71.8	0.5	0.7
Canada (1971:10)	72.5	71.5	73.8	0.6	0.8
Czechoslovakia (1975:10)	70.3	68.7	71.5	0.6	0.8
FRG (1974:11)	71.9	70.4	72.8	0.5	0.7
Finland (1974:12)	71.7	69.9	72.8	1.1	1.5
France (1975:8)	73.5	70.2	74.7	1.1	1.5
GDR (1975:5)	71.7	70.8	72.2	0.5	0.6
Hungary (1974:6)	69.0	68.4	69.8	0.3	0.5
Italy (1978:5)	74.1	73.5	75.3	0.5	0.7
Japan (1970:8)	72.2	71.2	72.6	0.5	0.7
Netherlands (1974:5)	74.7	74.0	75.7	0.5	0.6
Poland (1977:13)	70.6	69.4	71.8	0.6	0.9
Soviet Union (1974:8)	69.3	68.2	73.5	1.7	2.5
Sweden (1974:8)	75.2	74.4	75.9	0.4	0.6
United Kingdom (1970:10)	71.9	70.3	73.5	0.9	1.3
United States (1970:4)	70.8	69.9	71.8	0.7	0.9
Additional aggregation					
GDR (1975:10)	71.7	70.8	72.9	0.4	0.5
Italy (1978:20)	74.1	72.1	75.6	0.9	1.3
Netherlands (1974:11)	74.7	73.6	75.7	0.5	0.6
Additional reference year					
Canada (1976:10)	73.2	72.2	74.3	0.5	0.7
Poland (1973:9)	70.9	70.1	72.5	0.5	0.8
United States (1958:4)	69.4	68.5	70.4	0.6	0.9

[a]The life expectancies at birth for each region of the Migration and Settlement
Study are given in Appendix 3A.

Table 3.1 presents these various figures for the (single-region) expectation of life at birth. The table shows that still in the 1970s, and even in the most advanced countries of the world, there are considerable regional disparities in the number of years one may be expected to live. In some countries, both small (Hungary and Sweden) and large (Japan, Canada, and the US), the highest absolute deviation is relatively small (1.3–2.1 years). But in others (the UK, France, and the Soviet Union), this range is twice as large. As previously stated, the particular regional disaggregation significantly affects the values presented here and thus precludes any serious international comparison. Nevertheless, one observes in some cases marked regional disparities in the expectation of life. Moreover, we show later that for those countries where another, more refined, regional disaggregation is available, this conclusion is even more pronounced.

With the regional delineation considered here, the range of regional life expectancies at birth extends from 68.2 to 75.9 years (a difference of 7.7), and the lowest regional life expectancies vary from 68.2 to 74.4 (a difference of 6.2), while the highest vary from 69.8 to 75.9 (a difference of 6.1). We also note that in only two countries (France and the Netherlands) does the highest regional value exceed the lowest Swedish regional value (as observed at comparable years).

By looking only at the extreme values, we tend to magnify the importance of these regional differentials. Once one considers the mean absolute deviation instead of the highest absolute deviation, the regional variation is much less marked. Most countries show a MAD in the 0.3—0.7 year range; in only three countries (Finland, France, and the Soviet Union) is this mean deviation of life expectancy at birth more than one year, and only in one of these three does it represent more than 2% of the national life expectancy.

On the whole, regional disparities in life expectancy at birth seem, therefore, to be relatively small. This conclusion should, however, be qualified. There are at least two important reasons for such a result. First, by taking the total population of both sexes combined we may dilute some marked regional differences, which are observed only for subgroups of the population. Second, the regional disaggregations used in the Migration and Settlement Study are particularly rough. By considering only a small number of regions (e.g., the four regions of the US), one minimizes the probability of the appearance of regional disparities.

Let us first deal with the male—female disaggregation. In only seven of the countries of the IIASA study has a disaggregation by sex been made. Table 3.2 presents, for each of these countries, the extreme values and mean absolute deviations of life expectancy at birth for the male and female populations separately. These values clearly show that regional disparities are higher for males than for females. The mean absolute deviation of male life expectancy, considered by itself or related to the national value, is always higher than the corresponding value for the female population. [The same conclusion may be inferred from the results obtained by van Poppel (1980) in his study on regional disparities in European countries.] These regional differences, however, remain relatively small. For the seven countries, the mean deviation of male life expectancy varies from one half to one year, which represents only between 0.7 and 1.4% of the national life expectancy.

With the data available, the impact of regional disaggregation on the importance of regional disparity in life expectancy may be tested in only a few cases. Table 3.3 presents the extreme values of life expectancy at birth for seven countries at two significantly different levels of regional disaggregation. More refined regional disaggregations for France, Italy, Sweden, and the UK

Table 3.2 Regional differentials in life expectancy at birth: males and females.

Country (reference year: number of regions)	National (N)	Lowest	Highest	MAD	MAD/N(%)
(a) *Males*					
Canada (1971:10)	69.3	68.4	70.8	0.7	1.0
FRG (1974:11)	68.5	66.5	69.4	0.7	1.0
Finland (1974:12)	67.2	64.9	68.4	1.0	1.4
France (1975:8)	69.6	66.1	71.0	0.8	1.2
Japan (1970:8)	69.5	68.2	70.1	0.7	0.9
Sweden (1974:8)	72.5	71.7	73.2	0.5	0.7
United Kingdom (1970:10)	68.7	67.1	70.5	1.0	1.4
(b) *Females*					
Canada (1971:10)	76.1	75.0	77.5	0.7	0.9
FRG (1974:11)	74.9	73.4	75.7	0.4	0.5
Finland (1974:12)	76.2	74.0	78.3	0.9	1.2
France (1975:8)	77.5	74.7	78.4	0.8	1.1
Japan (1970:8)	74.8	74.1	75.4	0.3	0.4
Sweden (1974:8)	78.2	77.4	78.8	0.4	0.5
United Kingdom (1970:10)	75.0	73.3	76.5	0.9	1.2
Additional reference year					
(a) *Males*					
Canada (1976:10)	69.7	68.6	71.0	0.6	0.9
(b) *Females*					
Canada (1976:10)	77.1	76.1	78.3	0.6	0.8

(from 5–10 regions to 20–24 regions) lead to marked increases in the differences between these extreme values, at least for the male population. As noted above, regional disparities are much less significant for female populations.

Thus regional disparities in life expectancy at birth are mostly (1) relatively low, (2) larger for males than for females, and (3) increasing markedly, at least for males, when a more refined regional disaggregation than the one used in most national case studies is adopted. Is this conclusion also valid when other mortality indicators are used? Instead of considering life expectancy at birth, where the mortality regime experienced at each age is weighted by age itself, one may look at the gross death rate, which sums the various age-specific death rates and thus better reflects the overall level of the mortality curve. (It is actually the integral of the function describing the mortality curve.) By including the open-ended age interval, one assumes that the age-specific death rate for the 85+ group is that of the 85–89 group for all countries. Moreover, since the death rate increases rapidly in this group, the measure is heavily weighted by these ages, making the gross death rate more unreliable as higher (and more unreliable) rates for old ages are included.

The extreme regional values of these gross death rates for the total population are presented in Table 3.4. As previously mentioned, Finland and the German Democratic Republic have age-specific death rates for only 16 age

Table 3.3 Regional differentials in life expectancy at birth for different levels of regional disaggregation: males and females or both sexes combined.

Country (reference year: number of regions)	Lowest	Highest	Difference
France			
Males			
(1975:8)	66.1	71.0	3.9
(1974–1976:21)[a]	65.7	70.7	5.0
Females			
(1975:8)	74.7	78.4	3.7
(1974–1976:21)[a]	74.1	77.7	3.6
GDR			
Total			
(1975:5)	70.8	72.2	1.4
(1975:10)	70.8	72.9	2.1
Italy			
Total			
(1978:5)	73.5	75.3	1.8
(1978:20)	72.1	75.6	3.5
Netherlands			
Total			
(1974:5)	74.0	75.7	1.7
(1974:11)	73.6	75.7	2.1
Poland			
Total			
(1973:9)	70.1	72.5	2.4
(1977:13)	69.4	71.8	2.4
Sweden			
Males			
(1974:8)	71.7	73.2	1.5
(1974–1977:24)[a]	71.0	73.6	2.6
Females			
(1974:8)	77.4	78.8	1.4
(1974–1977:24)[a]	77.3	79.2	1.9
United Kingdom			
Males			
(1970:10)	67.1	70.5	3.4
(1974–1977:24)[a]	65.0	71.3	6.3
Females			
(1970:10)	73.3	76.5	3.2
(1974–1977:24)[a]	73.4	76.9	3.5

[a]Data taken from van Poppel (1980).

groups; since they are not comparable, the absolute values for these two countries have not been presented.

As Table 3.4 shows, the range of regional gross death rates is much wider than that of regional life expectancies. In most of the countries considered, the highest gross rate is more than 10% above the lowest rate; in three cases

Table 3.4 Regional differentials in the gross death rates for the total population: both sexes combined.

Country (reference year: number of regions)	National (N)	Lowest	Highest	MAD	MAD/N(%)
Austria (1971:9)	2.9	2.8	3.1	0.1	3
Bulgaria (1975:7)	3.0	2.5	3.9	0.3	11
Canada (1971:10)	2.3	2.1	2.6	0.1	6
Czechoslovakia (1975:10)	3.1	2.9	3.4	0.2	6
FRG (1974:11)	2.7	2.6	3.0	0.1	3
Finland (1974:12)[a]	—	—	—	—	5
France (1975:8)	2.2	2.0	2.6	0.2	7
GDR (1975:5)[a]	—	—	—	—	3
Hungary (1974:6)	3.0	3.0	3.2	0.1	2
Italy (1978:5)	2.4	2.3	2.5	0.1	3
Japan (1970:8)	2.8	2.7	3.0	0.1	2
Netherlands (1974:5)	2.3	2.1	2.5	0.1	4
Poland (1977:13)	2.6	2.4	2.8	0.1	4
Soviet Union (1974:8)	2.3	2.0	2.3	0.1	4
Sweden (1974:8)	2.4	2.3	2.5	0.1	4
United Kingdom (1970:10)	2.7	2.4	3.0	0.2	6
United States (1970:4)	2.4	2.2	2.4	0.1	3
Additional aggregation					
GDR (1975:10)[a]	—	—	—	—	3
Italy (1978:20)	2.4	2.2	2.7	0.1	5
Netherlands (1974:11)	2.3	2.1	2.5	0.1	4
Additional reference year					
Canada (1976:10)	2.2	2.1	2.4	0.1	5
Poland (1973:9)	2.6	2.2	2.8	0.1	5
United States (1958:4)	2.7	2.6	2.9	0.1	4

[a]Age-specific death rates were available for 16 rather than 18 age groups and are therefore not included in this comparison.

it is even more than 25% higher; and in one case the highest rate is more than 50% larger than the lowest rate. Whereas the mean absolute deviation of the regional values for life expectancy at birth seldom represented more than 1% of the national value, the MAD for the gross death rate represents 5% or more of the national rate in eight of the 15 countries, reaching 11% in one country. Thus the level of regional mortality curves, as measured by the gross death rate, varies much more than the level of the regional life expectancies at birth.

Until now we have considered the mortality level as a whole, that is, by taking all age-specific death rates simultaneously (these rates being either weighted, as in the life expectancy, or unweighted, as in the gross death rate). Next, we turn to the regional disparities in the age-specific death rates themselves for three representative age groups: 0–4, 15–29, and 65 years and over.

Table 3.5 Regional differentials in death rates (per thousand) for the infant (0−4) age group: both sexes combined.

Country (reference year: number of regions)	National (N)	Lowest	Highest	MAD	MAD/N (%)
Austria (1971:9)	5.4	4.7	6.2	0.3	5
Bulgaria (1975:7)	5.8	5.3	6.5	0.4	6
Canada (1971:10)	4.5	4.0	5.8	0.4	9
Czechoslovakia (1975:10)	5.3	4.2	7.3	0.7	13
FRG (1974:11)	4.4	3.8	5.1	0.3	7
Finland (1974:12)	2.8	2.0	3.5	0.3	10
France (1975:8)	3.7	3.4	5.0	0.4	10
GDR (1975:5)	3.6	3.4	4.0	0.1	3
Hungary (1974:6)	9.3	7.4	11.4	1.0	11
Italy (1978:5)	3.4	2.6	4.2	0.3	8
Japan (1970:8)	3.8	3.4	4.2	0.2	6
Netherlands (1974:5)	2.5	2.4	2.6	0.1	3
Poland (1977:13)	6.0	4.8	7.0	0.4	7
Soviet Union (1974:8)	9.0	4.6	14.1	2.4	26
Sweden (1974:8)	2.1	1.8	2.8	0.3	12
United Kingdom (1970:10)	4.2	3.7	4.8	0.3	8
United States (1970:4)	5.0	4.6	5.8	0.4	9
Additional aggregation					
GDR (1975:10)	3.6	2.8	4.2	0.3	9
Italy (1978:20)	3.4	1.6	4.8	0.7	21
Netherlands (1974:11)	2.5	2.1	3.0	0.2	7
Additional reference year					
Canada (1976:10)	3.7	3.3	4.5	0.3	9
Poland (1973:9)	6.4	5.7	7.0	0.3	5
United States (1958:4)	6.8	6.1	8.1	0.7	10

Table 3.5 shows, for the 17 countries, the extreme values of the regional *infant mortality* rates as well as the mean absolute deviation of these rates around the national average. Clearly, regional disparities are much larger for infant mortality than for total mortality (measured by life expectancy at birth and gross death rate). In almost half of the IIASA study countries (seven of the 17), there is more than a 50% difference between the highest and lowest regional mortality rates, and in all 17 countries this percentage is above 20. Moreover, in each case the mean absolute deviation represents at least 5% of the national average, and in eight countries it represents 10% or more.

Abstracting from problems of international comparability, one may also observe that the range between the lowest and the highest infant death rates is particularly large. The highest observed rate is almost nine times larger than the lowest rate. If one considers only minimum or maximum rates, the range is of course much smaller, but still considerable. The highest minimum rate is four times larger than the lowest minimum rate, and the highest maximum rate is five times larger than the lowest maximum rate. The data also

show that the maximum rate observed in the Netherlands (2.6 per thousand in
the North region) is lower than the minimum rate observed in most countries.
Only three other countries (Finland, Italy in the 20-region analysis, and
Sweden) have minimum rates that are below the highest rate observed in the
Netherlands.

Thus even in the 1970s, within a group of the most advanced countries of
the world, large disparities in infant mortality still exist. With such differences, one may reasonably conclude that there is room for considerable progress in the probability of survival of infants. As the additional observation
periods for Canada and the US show (Table 3.5), a reduction of infant mortality
is possible over a relatively short period. Unfortunately, from the scarce evidence available, it does not seem that this decrease would easily lead to a
reduction in regional disparity.

The second age group considered in this analysis of regional differentials
is the group of *young adults*, aged 15–29. To summarize the mortality level,
we computed the gross death rate over these ages. We did this by summing the
death rates observed for the three five-year age groups contained in the
15–29 category and multiplied by five.

Table 3.6 presents the extreme regional values and mean absolute deviation obtained for each of the 17 countries. Just as in the case of infant mortality, regional mortality differentials for young adults (15–29) are much larger
than those for total (all ages) populations. In seven of the 17 countries, the
highest regional mortality rate for young adults is more than 50% above the
lowest rate, and in all but one country it is more than 30%. Moreover, the mean
absolute deviation represents at least 5% of the national average in all countries but one, and in 10 countries it represents more than 10%.

As expected, the range is even wider when we compare regions of different countries. One may notice that the highest observed gross rate (0.038)
is almost five times larger than the lowest (0.008). The data in Table 3.6 also
show that the maximum rate observed in the UK (0.011) is lower than (or equal
to) the minimum rate observed in most countries. Only four countries (Finland,
Italy, the Netherlands, and Sweden) have minimum rates that are below the
maximum rate of the UK. If one considers only the minimum rates observed in
each country, the range is relatively narrow: 0.008–0.017, a twofold figure,
which should be compared with the fourfold variation observed between the
minimum infant mortality rates. The range is considerably wider, however, for
the maximum rates. The highest maximum rate (0.038) is almost four times
larger than the lowest maximum rate (0.011), but this variation is still much
smaller than that observed for infant mortality.

For three countries, additional reference periods allow us to analyze the
evolution of the regional mortality regime for young adults. The data for
Canada and the US show that the mortality rate for the 15–29 age group is
increasing not only at the national level but also in each of their regions. In
Poland, however, only the regions containing the main urban areas have

Table 3.6 Regional differentials in gross death rates for the 15–29 age group: both sexes combined.

Country (reference year: number of regions)	National (N)	Lowest	Highest	MAD	MAD/N(%)
Austria (1971:9)	0.018	0.014	0.023	0.002	12
Bulgaria (1975:7)	0.013	0.011	0.016	0.002	12
Canada (1971:10)	0.016	0.013	0.019	0.002	12
Czechoslovakia (1975:10)	0.014	0.011	0.016	0.001	9
FRG (1974:11)	0.015	0.013	0.017	0.001	8
Finland (1974:12)	0.015	0.008	0.023	0.003	18
France (1975:8)	0.015	0.013	0.017	0.001	5
GDR (1975:5)	0.014	0.012	0.015	0.001	7
Hungary (1974:6)	0.014	0.012	0.017	0.001	9
Italy (1978:5)	0.010	0.009	0.012	0.001	12
Japan (1970:8)	0.014	0.013	0.019	0.002	11
Netherlands (1974:5)	0.010	0.009	0.012	0.001	14
Poland (1977:13)	0.019	0.011	0.020	0.003	15
Soviet Union (1974:8)	0.027	0.015	0.038	0.007	27
Sweden (1974:8)	0.010	0.008	0.013	0.001	12
United Kingdom (1970:10)	0.010	0.010	0.011	0.000	3
United States (1970:4)	0.020	0.017	0.022	0.002	8
Additional aggregation					
GDR (1975:10)	0.014	0.012	0.016	0.001	7
Italy (1978:20)	0.010	0.008	0.016	0.002	17
Netherlands (1974:11)	0.010	0.008	0.015	0.001	14
Additional reference year					
Canada (1976:10)	0.019	0.013	0.022	0.002	10
Poland (1973:9)	0.015	0.001	0.017	0.002	10
United States (1958:4)	0.018	0.014	0.021	0.003	14

experienced such an increase. All three countries show increases in their lowest and highest regional rates. In Canada and the US the deterioration of mortality conditions among young adults seems to be accompanied by a reduction in regional mortality differentials. Insofar as young-adult mortality is related to traffic accidents, one may assume that this reduction is partially a result of increased diffusion of car ownership.

The last age group we consider is the *old age group* (65 years and over). Here, too, we use the gross death rate as a summary measure of the mortality level. It is not surprising that the GDR for the 65-and-over age group represents about 90% of the total rate and, therefore, that regional differentials in the GDRs for these ages are highly similar to those observed for the GDR over all age groups. A comparison between Table 3.7, which gives regional differentials in the gross death rates for the 65 and over population, and Table 3.4 clearly shows this.

To obtain a more precise idea of the regional mortality differences of older age groups, we should consider the death rates of each age group

Table 3.7 Regional differentials in gross death rates for the 65 and over age group: both sexes combined.

Country (reference year: number of regions)	National (N)	Lowest	Highest	MAD	MAD/N(%)
Austria (1971:9)	2.7	2.5	2.8	0.1	4
Bulgaria (1975:7)	2.7	2.2	3.6	0.3	12
Canada (1971:10)	2.1	1.9	2.3	0.1	6
Czechoslovakia (1975:10)	2.8	2.6	3.1	0.1	5
FRG (1974:11)	2.5	2.4	2.6	0.1	2
Finland (1974:12)[a]	—	—	—	—	5
France (1975:8)	2.0	1.8	2.3	0.1	7
GDR (1975:5)[a]	—	—	—	—	3
Hungary (1974:6)	2.7	2.7	2.9	0.0	1
Japan (1970:8)	2.5	2.4	2.7	0.1	2
Netherlands (1974:5)	2.1	1.9	2.2	0.1	4
Poland (1977:13)	2.3	2.1	2.5	0.1	5
Soviet Union (1974:8)	2.0	1.7	2.0	0.1	6
Sweden (1974:8)	2.2	2.1	2.3	0.1	3
United Kingdom (1970:10)	2.4	2.2	2.7	0.2	7
United States (1970:4)	2.0	1.9	2.1	0.1	4
Additional aggregation					
GDR (1975:10)[a]	—	—	—	—	3
Italy (1978:20)	2.2	2.0	2.4	0.1	4
Netherlands (1974:11)	2.1	1.9	2.3	0.1	4
Additional reference year					
Canada (1976:10)	2.0	1.8	2.1	0.1	5
Poland (1973:9)	2.3	2.0	2.5	0.1	5
United States (1958:4)	2.3	2.2	2.5	0.1	4

[a]Age-specific death rates were available for 16 rather than 18 age groups and are therefore not included in this comparison.

separately. The oldest five-year age group for which data are available for every one of the 17 countries is the 70–74 group, because for Finland and the German Democratic Republic the last age group is 75 and over. Because regional differences in age distribution within an age group having a large interval would make any comparison highly disputable, we have chosen to limit our analysis to the 70–74 age group.

Table 3.8 presents the minimum and maximum regional death rate values for this age group as well as the mean absolute deviation from each national average. The range between the extreme regional values is much smaller for old-age (i.e., 70–74) mortality than for infant (Table 3.5) or young-adult (Table 3.6) mortality. In 13 of the 17 countries, the ratio between the maximum and minimum regional values is smaller for the 70–74 age group than for the two other age groups considered, and only in Bulgaria is the highest regional mortality rate more than 50% above the lowest. Moreover, in only one country does the mean absolute deviation represent more than 10% of the national average,

Table 3.8 Regional differentials in death rates (%) for the 70–74 age group: both sexes combined.

Country (reference year: number of regions)	National (N)	Lowest	Highest	MAD	MAD/N (%)
Austria (1971:9)	5.1	4.6	5.4	0.2	4
Bulgaria (1975:7)	5.2	4.2	7.2	0.7	13
Canada (1971:10)	4.0	3.3	4.4	0.3	8
Czechoslovakia (1975:10)	5.4	4.6	6.3	0.4	8
FRG (1974:11)	4.8	4.4	5.1	0.2	3
Finland (1974:12)	4.8	4.5	5.6	0.3	7
France (1975:8)	3.7	3.3	4.7	0.3	8
GDR (1975:5)	5.2	5.0	5.8	0.2	4
Hungary (1974:6)	5.2	4.9	5.4	0.1	3
Italy (1978:5)	3.9	3.6	4.1	0.2	4
Japan (1970:8)	4.8	4.4	5.2	0.2	4
Netherlands (1974:5)	3.8	3.3	4.2	0.2	5
Poland (1977:13)	4.7	4.1	5.1	0.3	6
Soviet Union (1974:8)	3.8	3.3	3.9	0.2	5
Sweden (1974:8)	3.6	3.4	3.9	0.2	5
United Kingdom (1970:10)	4.9	4.4	5.4	0.3	7
United States (1970:4)	4.4	4.0	4.7	0.2	4
Additional aggregation					
GDR (1975:10)	5.2	4.7	5.8	0.3	5
Italy (1978:20)	3.9	3.4	4.6	0.3	7
Netherlands (1974:11)	3.8	3.3	4.5	0.2	5
Additional reference year					
Canada (1976:10)	3.9	3.3	4.3	0.3	7
Poland (1973:9)	4.6	3.9	5.1	0.3	6
United States (1958:4)	4.9	4.6	5.4	0.3	5

while for infant and young-adult mortality this is the case in eight and ten countries, respectively. When we compare countries, we observe that the highest regional death rate (7.2%) is only two times larger than the smallest rate (3.3%), whereas in the case of infant and young-adult mortality the ratio between the smallest and the largest rate is from 1 to 9 and from 1 to 5, respectively.

The data in Table 3.8 also show that the maximum rates observed in the Soviet Union and Sweden (3.9%) are smaller than the lowest rates observed in most of the other countries. When we consider only the observed minimum or maximum rates in each country, the range is relatively narrow: the minimum rate varies from 3.3 to 5.0 and the maximum rate from 3.9 to 7.2. Again, this variation is much smaller than those observed for infant and young-adult mortality.

For seven countries we are able to disaggregate these old-age mortality rates by sex (Table 3.9). It is no surprise that males have an old-age mortality rate that is almost twice that of females. (In the case of France, the national

Table 3.9 Regional differentials in death rates (%) for the 70—74 age groups: males and females

Country (reference year: number of regions)	National (N)	Lowest	Highest	MAD	MAD/N(%)
(a) *Males*					
Canada (1971:10)	5.2	4.2	5.6	0.5	9
FRG (1974:11)	6.5	5.9	7.6	0.3	5
Finland (1974:12)	6.9	5.5	7.8	0.5	7
France (1975:8)	5.2	4.6	6.9	0.5	10
Japan (1970:8)	6.0	5.7	6.7	0.2	3
Sweden (1974:8)	4.8	4.5	5.4	0.3	6
United Kingdom (1970:10)	6.9	6.0	7.7	0.5	7
(b) *Females*					
Canada (1971:10)	3.0	2.5	3.3	0.2	8
FRG (1974:11)	3.6	3.4	3.8	0.1	3
Finland (1974:12)	3.5	3.2	4.2	0.3	8
France (1975:8)	2.6	2.3	3.3	0.2	9
Japan (1970:8)	3.7	3.4	4.1	0.2	4
Sweden (1974:8)	2.7	2.6	2.9	0.1	3
United Kingdom (1970:10)	3.6	3.3	4.1	0.3	8
Additional reference year					
(a) *Males*					
Canada (1976:10)	5.2	4.3	5.7	0.4	8
(b) *Females*					
Canada (1976:10)	2.8	2.3	3.2	0.3	9

rate for males is double that for females). Regional disparities, however, are the same for males and females, except in Sweden, where they are twice as large for males. There are two countries (Canada and France) where, for both males and females separately, the value of MAD/N is larger than for the two sexes combined. This indicates that the disparities, while being of the same magnitude for each sex, have a different regional pattern. More data, over a larger number of countries and over a larger number of regions, are needed to explore this question.

The global picture that emerges is one of continued regional disparities in life expectancy — particularly for males — in these 17 developed countries, with the disparities being primarily a result of the considerable differences in infant and young-adult mortality.

3.4 A Global Measure of Regional Mortality Differentials

There are two main ways to analyze regional differences in a mortality regime. The first is based on age-specific death rates (or probabilities). These may be summarized through the use of traditional mortality indicators (crude and gross death rates, life expectancy, mean age, etc.), as was done in the previous section, or they may be parameterized by fitting a mathematical function to them. The second is based on the regional differences in these rates. These differences are used directly as inputs in the analysis of regional discrepancies.

The parameterizing approach as developed by Brass (1971, 1977) and extended by Zaba (1979) and others was found to be unsuitable for analyzing regional mortality differentials. Because interregional differences appear mainly in the youngest age groups, smoothing the various regional mortality curves makes them more or less similar, and by regressing on the basis of 18 observations (age groups), the same weight is given to the observations for which there are no regional differentials as to those for which there are. As a result, the two or three age groups for which significant regional differences may exist are lost among a large number of "undifferentiated" observations. Instead of emphasizing these differences, the model dampens them. As a tool for estimating missing data and for projection, the Brass model is undoubtedly useful, but it is not appropriate for analyses of interregional differences (at least with the kind of data available for this study).

Instead of creating smooth curves approximating the survival probabilities (expressed in the form of logits) as in the Brass approach, one may directly use the curve representing the age-specific death rates and find a mathematical function for this curve, as proposed by Heligman and Pollard (1980), for example. To be meaningful, however, such an application requires single-year death rates, whereas the regional data available for the Migration and Settlement Study refer to five-year age groups.

With the regional mortality data available, we concluded that parameterization is not the correct approach for studying regional differentials. We thus turned to a second approach, which consists of analyzing directly the regional differences in age-specific death rates. How do we measure the degree of above- or below-average mortality in a region compared with a given (national) standard? How do we describe the age profile of these mortality differentials, that is, what age groups account for the divergence?

To measure the overall level of a region's mortality differential, we applied a method widely used in regional economic analysis: the so-called shift—share method. This method decomposes a region's growth (in our case, the negative growth of mortality) into two main components: the growth resulting from the population composition (the structural effect) and the growth resulting from regional dynamics (the competitive effect). The first expresses the calculated number of deaths in the region if one applies the national (standard) age-specific death rates to the given population age structure of the region. It represents the number of deaths expected in the region if there are no regional mortality differentials. The second component reflects the number of deaths that did or did not occur in the region, corresponding to the region's age-specific rates being above or below the national average. If

K_X^i = the number of inhabitants of age X in region i

$m_X^{i\,d}$ = the death rate at age X in region i

m_X^{d} = the national death rate at age X

$K_{\cdot}^{i\,d}$ = the total (all ages) number of deaths in region i,

then

$$K_{\cdot}^{i\,d} = \sum_X K_X^i m_X^{d} + \sum_X K_X^i (m_X^{i\,d} - m_X^{d}) \ . \qquad (3.1)$$

The regional mortality differential component presents three interesting features. First, it is the sum of age-specific differentials, weighted by the importance of the corresponding age group. This offers an important advantage. When the absolute number of deaths is small (either because of a small region or an age group with a high rate of survival), it often happens that the value for the death rate is not very meaningful (particularly when mortality data refer to a one-year period). In such a case, expressing the differentials in relative terms may be misleading: if the death rate is 1/10000 in one region, the slightest difference compared with the national level will represent a large percentage. But this large relative difference is not meaningful. From the individual's point of view, it is the absolute level, and therefore the absolute difference, that matters, rather than the relative difference. Also, large relative differences are often based on small numbers, reflecting possibly random phenomena. Therefore, it is important to express differentials in absolute terms and to weight them by the number of individuals exposed to this higher or lower mortality risk. By doing so, one introduces a built-in correction, where large absolute differences, when they are due to small numbers, have only a minor impact on the computed level of overall mortality, either because the age-specific death rate (and thus the number of deaths) is low anyway, or because the population figure is small.

This weighting process largely eliminates the impact of the level of regional disaggregation. With most indicators of regional disparity, the finer the disaggregation, the larger the national measure of disparity. This is because, explicitly (as when the mean absolute deviation is used) or implicitly (as when comparing, for instance, the results of regional parameterization), one gives the same weight to each regional observation. Here, however, because each of the m regional observations is actually the weighted sum of a finite number n of subregional observations, the national measure of regional disparity, being itself regionally weighted, will (under some condition to be explained later) be the same with m or with mn, thus eliminating one of the main obstacles to international comparisons.

The second feature of the regional component is related to the first. Combining age structure and mortality differentials may lead to a possible drawback, because the results obtained reflect not only the level of above- or below-average mortality but also the difference in age structure between the region and the national standard. To take this into account, we will further decompose the regional component (R) into two parts, so that

$$R^i = \sum_X K_X^i (m_X^{id} - m_X^{\cdot d}) \tag{3.2}$$

$$= \sum_X \left[\frac{K_X^{\cdot}}{K_{\cdot}^{\cdot}} K^i_{\cdot} \right] (m_X^{id} - m_X^{\cdot d}) + \sum_X \left[K_X^i \frac{K_X^{\cdot}}{K_{\cdot}^{\cdot}} K^i_{\cdot} \right] (m_X^{id} - m_X^{\cdot d}) , \tag{3.3}$$

where the first term on the right-hand side of (3.3) expresses the number of deaths corresponding to regional mortality differentials, while the second term reflects the effect of the interaction between differences in age structure and differences in mortality conditions. The first term of (3.3), which represents a standardized measure of regional mortality differentials, has the same sign as the nonstandardized measure of (3.2). Differences in age structure may reduce or increase the level of above- or below-average mortality of a region but not change above- or below-average mortality into below- or above-average mortality.

The equations presented above lead only to absolute numbers. To obtain from them a measure of above- or below-average mortality, one has to relate the all-age total number of unexpected (excess) deaths or unexpected survivals (missing deaths) of a region to the number of expected deaths. In other words, the number of deaths in the region relating to the differences in the death rates [obtained from (3.2) or (3.3)] is divided by the number of deaths expected when no such differences exist [obtained from the first term on the right-hand side of (3.1)]. We thus define our observed, nonstandardized *index of mortality differential* (IMD) *for a given region* i *as*

$$\text{IMD}^i = \frac{\sum_X K_X^i (m_X^{id} - m_X^{\cdot d})}{\sum_X K_X^i m_X^{\cdot d}} \tag{3.4}$$

and our standardized index (i.e., standardized for differences in age structure) as

$$*\text{IMD}^i = \frac{\sum_X [(K_X^{\cdot}/K_{\cdot}^{\cdot}) K^i_{\cdot}] (m_X^{id} - m_X^{\cdot d})}{\sum_X K_X^i m_X^{\cdot d}} \tag{3.5}$$

If positive, the index shows that the region has an overall above-average mortality level. A negative index would denote a below-average level. The value of the index (multiplied by 100) represents the percentages of excess (or missing) deaths that correspond to the difference between the region's death rates (and age profile) and the national rates. The index of mortality differential is thus equivalent to the standardized mortality ratio -1, as may be seen by dividing equation (3.1) by $\sum_X K_X^i m_X^{\cdot d}$.

Until now, we have only obtained a measure of the level of the above- or below-average mortality of a particular region. We also want to derive a national measure that will express the degree of regional disparity within the whole system. The third feature, then, or the regional mortality differential component can be expressed by a mathematical property of the regional component. Let us consider this regional differential component for a given age group X in a given region i. We have, as in equation (3.2),

$$R^i = \sum_X K_X^i(m_X^{id} - m_X^{\cdot d})$$

$$= K_X^i m_X^{id} - K_X^i m_X^{\cdot d} .$$

(3.2)

When summed over all regions of a particular system (country), one obtains

$$\sum_i R_X^i = \sum_i K_X^i m_X^{id} - \sum_i K_X^i m_X^{\cdot d} = 0 .$$

(3.6)

In other words, for a given age group the total number of expected deaths necessarily equals the total number of observed deaths, so that the sum over all regions of the regional differential component necessary equals zero. This zero-sum game property leads to two national measures of regional disparity particularly useful in our analysis.

If, for a given age group X, the sum of the regional differential components necessarily equals zero, it implies that the number of excess deaths in the regions of above-average mortality equals the number of missing deaths in the below-average regions. If we add these total numbers of excess deaths and missing deaths [i.e., if we take the sum over all regions of the absolute value of each $K_X^i(m_X^{id} - m_X^{\cdot d})$], we have the total number of deaths that should be "transferred" between regions to obtain uniform regional mortality conditions over the whole system. By relating this new total to the total number of deaths observed at age X in the country, we then obtain an *index of regional mortality disparity for age group* X *in country* j:

$$^j\text{IMD}_X = \frac{\sum_i |K_X(m_X^{id} - m_X^{\cdot d})|}{^j K_X^{\cdot d}}$$

or

$$^j\text{IMD}_X = \frac{2\sum_i [K_X(m_X^{id} - m_X^{\cdot d})]}{^j K_X^{\cdot d}} \quad \text{for } (m_X^{id} - m_X^{\cdot d}) > 0 .$$

(3.7)

It is now easy to derive an overall (all ages) national measure of regional mortality disparity. Because the total number of excess deaths equals the total number of missing deaths for each X in j when we sum over all age groups in country j, we necessarily obtain the same equality, and therefore

$$\sum_X \sum_i R_X^i = \sum_X \left[\sum_i K_X^i (m_x^{i\,d} - m_X^{\cdot d}) \right] = 0 \ .$$

Correlatively, if we consider all age groups and sum the various regional components R^i over all regions, we also necessarily obtain zero. That is, the total number of excess deaths in all regions of above-average mortality equals the total number of missing deaths in all regions of below-average mortality. Thus

$$\sum_X \sum_i R_X^i = \sum_i \left[\sum_X K_X^i (m_x^{i\,d} - m_X^{\cdot d}) \right] = 0 \ .$$

If we add these total numbers of excess deaths and missing deaths [i.e., if we take the sum over all regions of the absolute value of each $\sum_X K_X^i (m_X^{i\,d} - m_X^{\cdot d})$],

we have the total number of deaths that, irrespective of age, should be transferred between regions in order to obtain uniform regional mortality conditions over the whole system. By relating this new sum to the total number of deaths observed in all ages of the population, we finally obtain a *global national index of regional mortality disparity in country* j:

$$^j\mathrm{IMD} = \frac{\sum_i | \sum_X K_X^i (m_X^{i\,d} - m_X^{\cdot d}) |}{^j K^{\cdot d}} \tag{3.8}$$

or

$$^j\mathrm{IMD} = \frac{2\sum_i \left[\sum_X K_X^i (m_X^{i\,d} - m_X^{\cdot d}) \right]}{^j K^{\cdot d}} \tag{3.8'}$$

$$\text{for } (m_X^{i\,d} - m_X^{\cdot d}) > 0 \ .$$

From the latter equation, one may easily see that this index will not be affected by the level of regional disaggregation, as long as the aggregation has homogeneous above- or below-average mortality, that is, as long as macroregions are constructed with subregions for which $m_X^{i\,d} - m_X^{\cdot d}$ has the same sign. And, of course, if a region is only slightly above (or below) the average [if its $|\sum_X K_X^i (m_X^{i\,d} - m_X^{\cdot d})|$ is relatively small] then aggregating with regions of below- or above-average mortality does not make much difference. For each particular age group, as well as for all ages together, the total nonstandardized number and the total standardized number of excess (or missing) deaths are not necessarily the same. Therefore, if we want a measure of regional mortality disparity that is not biased by regional differences in age structure, we will have to substitute the first term on the right-hand side of equation (3.3) for equation (3.2) in the numerator of equation (3.8), so that the *standardized global index* will be

$$j_{\text{IMD}*} = \frac{\sum\limits_i \left| \sum\limits_X [(K_X^{\cdot} / K_{\cdot}^{\cdot}) K_{\cdot}^i] (m_X^{i\,d} - m_X^{\cdot d}) \right|}{j K_{\cdot}^{\cdot d}}, \tag{3.9}$$

the equality between equations (3.8) and (3.8') being invalid in this case.

Equations (3.4), (3.5), (3.7), (3.8), and (3.9) provide us with the needed tools for analyzing regional mortality differentials in each country of the IIASA study sample. The results obtained from equations (3.4) and (3.5) are given in Appendix 3B. Some particularly interesting cases are described in our global analysis. Two principal questions remain: What is the degree of regional disparity in the mortality conditions of each country, and to what extent does this regional disparity vary with age groups?

Table 3.10 Index of regional mortality disparity in the IIASA countries.

Country (reference year: number of regions)	Observed	Standardized
Austria (1971:9)	2.6	2.8
Bulgaria (1975:7)	6.4	6.8
Canada (1971:10)	4.4	4.6
Czechoslovakia (1975:10)	4.6	4.8
FRG (1974:11)	2.9	2.9
Finland (1974:12)	6.3	6.3
France (1975:8)	6.3	6.6
GDR (1975:5)	3.0	2.9
Hungary (1974:6)	1.3	1.4
Italy (1978:5)	4.0	3.8
Japan (1970:8)	2.8	2.8
Netherlands (1974:5)	3.2	3.4
Poland (1977:13)	3.1	3.1
Soviet Union (1974:8)	2.9	3.3
Sweden (1974:8)	3.5	3.4
United Kingdom (1970:10)	7.8	7.8
United States (1970:4)	2.9	2.9
Additional aggregation		
GDR (1975:10)	3.3	3.2
Italy (1978:20)	6.5	6.6
Netherlands (1974:11)	3.4	3.5
Additional reference year		
Canada (1976:10)	4.5	4.7
Poland (1973:9)	3.5	3.4
United States (1958:4)	4.2	4.0

Table 3.10 provides us with some answers to the first of these questions. From the data shown, some important conclusions on the level of regional mortality disparity in the IIASA study countries may be derived.

(1) The overall level of observed regional mortality disparity, as measured through the index of equation (3.8), varies considerably between countries. The index actually ranges from 1.3 in Hungary to 7.8 in the UK, a sixfold variability. This means that in Hungary only 1.3% of the total number of deaths should be redistributed across regions in order to obtain identical mortality conditions (i.e., regions of above-average mortality have 0.65% excess deaths, and regions of below-average mortality have 0.65% missing deaths); in the UK, this percentage is six times larger.

(2) As mentioned before, because of the weighting process implied in the construction of our index, this international comparison is not affected by the number of regions as such, but rather by the way regions are aggregated. More precisely, the index of regional mortality disparity in a given country will not be affected by the number of regions as long as they have a homogeneous average mortality — as long as all macroregions of above- or below-average mortality comprise only subregions of above- or below-average mortality.

To illustrate this point, let us consider the results for the German Democratic Republic, Italy, and the Netherlands. For these countries, five macroregions were obtained by grouping, respectively, 10, 10, and 11 regions. As may be seen from Table 3.10, reducing the number of regions by half (as in the case of the German Democratic Republic and the Netherlands) only slightly reduced the index of regional mortality disparity. This implies that in these cases, the homogeneity condition was almost totally fulfilled during the aggregation process. In Italy, however, reducing the number of regions from 20 to five significantly reduced the index (from 6.5 to 4.0), because only two of the five macroregions (the Central region and the Islands) have homogeneous average mortality levels (see Appendix 3B). The difference between the indices of regional disparity obtained at two different levels of aggregation does not reflect so much the degree of disaggregation as the degree of intraregional heterogeneity in the higher-level regions.

(3) With these considerations in mind, we group the 17 countries of our sample according to their level of regional mortality disparity, ignoring problems of differences in definitions and periods of observations. Three main groups may be considered: nine countries where regional differentials are low (Hungary, 1.3; Austria, 2.6; Japan, 2.8; Federal Republic of Germany, 2.9; Soviet Union, 2.9; US, 2.9; German Democratic Republic, 3.0; Poland, 3.1; and Netherlands, 3.2), four countries where these disparities are in the middle range (Sweden, 3.5; Italy, 4.0; Canada, 4.4; and Czechoslovakia, 4.6), and four countries where regional mortality differentials are relatively high (Finland, 6.3; France, 6.3; Bulgaria, 6.4; and UK, 7.8).

(4) We see that there is no clear relation between the level of mortality and that of regional mortality disparity. The often assumed direct relation of countries with low mortality having lower regional differentials than countries with high mortality was not observed in our sample. Let us compare the results of Table 3.10 with the data on national life expectancy at birth presented in Table 3.1. In the group of countries where regional disparities are low, there are countries with relatively low life expectancy (Hungary and the Soviet Union) as well as countries with a relatively high life expectancy (the Netherlands, the Federal Republic of Germany, and Japan). Similarly, in the group of countries where regional disparities are high, there are countries with relatively low life expectancies (Bulgaria) as well as countries with relatively high life expectancies (France). When interpreting this absence of relation between levels of mortality and regional disparity, one should consider that all countries of our IIASA sample actually are low-mortality countries. It may be assumed that once a country has a level of life expectancy of 69–75 years, any possible impact of the overall mortality conditions on regional death rates will be minimal; the regional mortality regime in these cases is mainly determined by regional (economic, climatic, etc.) conditions.

(5) For three countries we have information on the evolution of regional disparity over time. In two of these countries, there were similar decreases in the regional mortality disparity indices: a decline of 10% over a four-year period in Poland and 30% over a 12-year period in the US. In Poland, this reduction was achieved at a time when life expectancy at birth was slightly declining, whereas in the US it was concomitant with a marked increase in the expectation of life at birth. In Canada, there were also marked increases in life expectancies, but they were not accompanied by significant changes in regional mortality disparity levels. In interpreting these results, one should remember that Canadian mortality data refer to five-year periods and thus may be considered as better expressing a temporal evolution, whereas mortality data for all other countries of our sample (except Austria) refer to a one-year period. Comparing mortality conditions between two years may be disputable, because too many "accidental" or episodic phenomena may effect the basic trend. (This is certainly the case with Poland, as will be shown below.)

(6) As already stressed, one advantage of the measure of regional disparity adopted in this study is that it allows for a standardization, which eliminates differences in age structures and thus estimates only regional differentials in mortality. It is clear from a comparison between the observed and the standardized indices (Table 3.10) that regional differences in the age structure are not marked enough to affect significantly our measure of regional disparity. Only in the Soviet Union and Bulgaria are there considerable differences between the two types of indices. The Soviet situation is probably related to the particular type of regional disaggregation used (seven groups of urban areas and one rural area).

A comparison of the observed and standardized regional indices given in Appendix 3B shows that for most regions the differences between the regional and national age structures are not important enough to have a significant impact on their level of above- or below-average mortality. The most striking exceptions are the Sofia region of Bulgaria, for which the level of above-average mortality (when compared with the national level) increases from 8% (when differences in the mortality regime are combined with those of the age structure) to 22% (when differences in the age structure are eliminated), and the urban areas of the Central Asian Republics of the Soviet Union, for which an above-average mortality of 5% totally disappears in the standardized results. Other cases where the elimination of differences in age structure significantly changes the results are in Austria (the Vorarlberg region), Bulgaria (the North West region), France (the North region), Italy (the regions of Campania and Toscana), and the Netherlands (the regions of Zeeland, Noord Brabant, and Limburg). In Canada, Czechoslovakia, Finland, the German Democratic Republic, Hungary, Japan, Poland, Sweden, the UK, and the US, each region has a level of above- or below-average mortality that is not significantly affected by differences in age structure.

Let us now turn to the levels of regional above- or below-average mortality as such. Since differences between observed and standardized indices are negligible for most regions, we shall limit our discussion to the standardized measure of above- or below-average mortality. Among the 139 regions of our sample, there are 16 regions for which the standardized indices are equal to or greater than 10% (in absolute value), that is, for which the number of excess or missing deaths represents at least 10% of the number of deaths that would have been observed if the national mortality regime had been applied; 11 of these are regions of above-average mortality.

The two regions with the highest above-average mortality are the North region in France (27%) and the Sofia region in Bulgaria (22%). Other regions of high above-average mortality are North Bohemia (16%) in Czechoslovakia; Scotland (14%) and the North West (11%) in the UK; Saarland (12%) in the Federal Republic of Germany; the East region (12%) in France; Pohjois–Karjala (12%), Mikkeli (11%), and Oulu (10%) in Finland; and Quebec (10%) in Canada. There are no regions of high above-average mortality in Austria, the German Democratic Republic, Hungary, Japan, Poland, the Soviet Union, Sweden, and the US in the regional disaggregation adopted for the Migration and Settlement Study.

Five regions have a marked below-average mortality level: the urban areas of the Byelorussian Republic (−23%) and Caucasian Republics (−13%) in the Soviet Union, East Anglia (−11%) in the UK, Vorarlberg (−10%) in Austria, and the Paris region (−10%) in France.

Another way to look at spatial discrepancies is to consider the relative number of spatial units that are close to the national average, avoiding international comparisons because of the dependence on the regional disaggregation used. If all regions of a given country have an index of mortality differential close to zero, however, we may assume that this country shows a rather uniform regional pattern. Let us consider that, as long as the standardized index of mortality differential for a region is between −4 and +4%, its level of below- or above-average mortality is small enough to be ignored. There are 78 regions that fall into this category out of the total of 139 regions.

But in some countries, all regions (in Hungary) or almost all regions (in the Federal Republic of Germany, the German Democratic Republic, Japan, and the US) show mortality conditions [summarized by equation (3.5)] close to the national average, while in other countries (Bulgaria, Finland, Italy, the Soviet Union, and the UK), only a small minority are close to the national standard. All countries of the latter group (except the Soviet Union) have a high index of regional mortality disparity (Table 3.10). In Bulgaria, Finland, Italy, and the UK, therefore, not only are there relatively many regions where the mortality regime is significantly different from the national standard, but also these regions of above- or below-average mortality represent an important share of the national total, making the national level of regional disparity relatively high. In the Soviet Union, however, even though five of the eight regions have mortality conditions with as much as a 23% departure from the national standard, they account for only a small percentage of the total number of deaths in the country. Thus the overall level of regional mortality discrepancy is moderate.

This shows clearly the importance of introducing a weighting process in constructing a measure of regional disparity. Large regional differentials are less important if the regions are small. For instance, the high level of below-average mortality in Vorarlberg (−10%) and of above-average mortality in Saarland (12%) do not prevent Austria and the Federal Republic of Germany from being countries with a low overall level of regional mortality disparity, while the same high level in Quebec (10%) takes Canada into the middle-range group. This is mainly because Quebec represents almost 30% of Canada's population, whereas each of the two other regions represents only about 2% of their respective national population. Similarly, small regional differentials become important in populous regions. This explains why Sweden, with small differentials, has an overall middle-range index of regional disparity, while Japan and the US, with more or less the same set of regional indices, are in the group of countries with low regional mortality disparity.

The same holds true for age weighting. Large (absolute) regional differences in the death rate for a given age group are not important if the death rate is low or if the population represents only a small part of the total population. This is obviously not the case for age groups with high death rates and large shares of the total population. This was accounted for in the equations on which the previous results are based. Our regional indices of mortality differential and our national indices of regional mortality disparity are age-weighted indices.

To what degree does this regional mortality disparity vary between age groups? To discuss this question, we applied equation (3.7) to each of the 18 age groups in each of the 17 countries of the IIASA study. The results are presented in Table 3.11. The main conclusion is that regional disparities in death rates are much lower for old age groups (65 years and over) than for other age groups. Our measure of regional disparity is based on absolute differences in death rates [$m_X^{id} - m_X^{\cdot d}$ in equation (3.7)]. Had we used relative differences ($m_X^{id} / m_X^{\cdot d}$), as is often done with other measures of regional disparity, we would have had even higher disparities for the young and adult age groups, and lower disparities for old age groups because a given absolute difference obviously produces a larger relative difference when the death rate is low than when it is high.

To analyze the age profile of regional mortality disparities in each country, we will use the national figure (last column of Table 3.11) as a reference point. This total is different and necessarily higher than that obtained previously from equation (3.4) (Table 3.10), because adding over age groups in the latter analysis neutralizes the above- and below-average mortality that exists in the particular ages of a given region. This neutralization is appropriate when one wants to estimate the overall level of mortality differential for each region; however, when one wants to analyze the age profile of regional disparities, one must emphasize the age groups. The national value, therefore, should represent the sum of all differentials (positive or negative) observed in each age group in each region but should not be interpreted as a measure of overall regional disparity in the country.

To substantiate our conclusions regarding the relatively lower regional disparities for old-age mortality, let us look more closely at the values in Table 3.11. For the three oldest age groups (75−79, 80−84, and 85+), the index of regional disparity is below the national figure in almost all countries. The main exception is Bulgaria, but, as we discuss later, there is a serious data problem in this case. For the earlier three age groups (60−64, 65−69, and 70−74), this index is also below the national total in a majority of countries, and in those countries where the index is above the national value the difference is in most cases rather small.

The opposite is true of infant mortality (0−4), child mortality (5−9 and 10−14), and young-adult mortality (15−19, 20−24, and 25−29). In almost all countries the index of regional disparity is significantly higher, often two or three times that of the national total. There are only two countries where the index for infant (0−4) mortality is below the all-age index: Bulgaria and Poland. For child mortality, there is no exception and for young-adult mortality, only one exception (the UK).

For the six remaining five-year age groups (between 30 and 59), the majority of the countries have an index of regional disparity significantly above the all-age figure. For the 35−39 and 40−44 age groups, there are only two countries (Bulgaria and Canada) with below-average values, whereas for the other age groups (30–34 and 45–59) there are four exceptions (Bulgaria always being one of them). However, if, on the whole, regional disparities are above average for all age groups between 30 and 59, they are usually much lower than the ones observed for the younger (0–29) age groups.

In summary, the global picture of regional mortality disparity by age shows an age composition of three main groups (0–29, 30–59, and 60 and over) and a declining trend of regional mortality differentials with age. The first two groups almost always show above-average levels of regional disparity; the old age group shows relatively small regional differentials.

There are four countries for which the general age pattern just described is not valid according to Table 3.11. In France and Japan, the highest regional disparities are found in the second main age group rather than the first (between 20 and 39 years of age in Japan, and 35 and 54 years in France). The age profile of regional discrepancies looks rather irregular for the UK. Above-average levels of regional disparity in the infant and child age groups (0–14) are followed by low levels for young adults (15–29). The highest indices of regional disparity are observed for the middle-age groups (35–54), as in France, resulting in relatively high old-age regional disparities even though they are almost all below average. From the information available, it is difficult to see whether this particular pattern reflects some real phenomena specific to the UK, or whether it also is the result of some data problems.

Bulgaria is a fourth exception to the general pattern of regional disparity by age. Here it seems obvious that a large part of the irregular profile is because of data problems, as can be quickly seen from the Bulgarian figures in Table 3.11. For instance, the value of the index at ages 30–34, 40–44, 50–54, and 60–64 is negligible. This is probably because of the way regional mortality data have been estimated for these groups. In Bulgaria, these data are available only for 10-year age groups after age 24, before which the index seems indeed to behave normally. Another feature of the Bulgarian pattern lies in the old age groups. Because the last group for which regional mortality data are available in Bulgaria is age 70 and over, data for each of the four groups thereafter had to be estimated from the 70+ total. It seems this estimation was performed by assuming identical levels of regional disparity for all four age groups, and has led to levels of regional disparity that are very large indeed. As a result, the Bulgarian pattern is quite different from those of all other countries in the study and probably does not reflect reality accurately.

Let us now consider the various national levels of regional disparity for each age group separately (the columns of Table 3.11). This is brief, however, because problems of international comparability remain, even though the index of disparity eliminates some problems of regional disaggregation.

The most important infant mortality regional disparities are observed in Italy (with the index close to 20%), but Czechoslovakia, Hungary, the Soviet Union, and Sweden also have an index above 10%. Austria and Poland have particularly low indices. Finland shows the highest levels of regional disparity for

Table 3.11 Index of regional mortality disparity, by age group and by country.

Country (reference year: number of regions)	Age group									
	0–4	5–9	10–14	15–19	20–24	25–29	30–34	35–39	40–44	45–49
Austria (1971:9)	4.7	10.1	8.4	11.1	14.2	13.4	9.6	12.0	6.2	4.6
Bulgaria (1975:7)	6.2	11.5	17.8	10.0	11.8	10.4	0.2	8.9	0.1	8.2
Canada (1971:10)	6.8	15.8	11.4	8.9	12.6	9.8	10.1	5.4	4.5	4.1
Czechoslovakia (1975:10)	13.1	19.3	14.8	11.8	8.0	7.6	10.9	9.0	8.5	8.0
FRG (1974:11)	6.3	4.2	7.6	14.2	6.5	8.7	6.9	5.6	18.3	9.8
Finland (1974:12)	7.4	23.6	25.8	12.3	13.7	17.1	16.2	12.8	14.1	9.3
France (1975:8)	8.7	8.5	7.6	8.8	9.0	5.2	8.3	13.1	14.9	12.1
GDR (1975:5)	6.3	9.9	9.2	7.6	3.8	7.7	7.7	7.0	4.0	4.8
Hungary (1974:6)	12.8	17.4	8.1	13.5	12.3	10.0	8.9	9.1	6.8	2.6
Italy (1978:5)	18.1	18.6	7.1	14.8	15.6	8.1	6.8	6.6	10.3	12.9
Japan (1970:8)	6.0	4.3	5.6	7.2	12.7	9.6	10.3	7.9	6.3	6.8
Netherlands (1974:5)	4.4	7.2	16.6	14.8	13.4	3.7	5.0	3.1	6.0	3.6
Poland (1977:13)	5.0	9.5	13.4	73.0	10.4	14.7	10.9	7.0	6.4	7.3
Soviet Union (1974:8)	12.6	11.9	11.0	26.0	31.4	17.0	17.9	13.4	13.6	8.9
Sweden (1974:8)	0.3	11.8	19.7	19.5	11.8	10.2	12.2	8.4	11.0	9.8
United Kingdom (1970:10)	8.8	10.6	8.6	2.7	3.9	4.6	6.7	12.4	10.6	12.2
United States (1970:4)	9.3	6.4	12.3	9.5	7.1	10.0	11.6	11.69	9.8	10.1
Additional aggregation										
GDR (1975:10)	7.9	10.8	14.1	8.0	5.9	7.9	7.7	7.0	4.0	7.4
Italy (1978:20)	19.1	12.3	13.1	14.8	15.6	10.2	8.8	8.9	15.2	14.0
Netherlands (1974:11)	7.5	15.16	16.9	15.3	15.3	6.6	8.6	5.5	6.5	4.6
Additional reference year										
Canada (1976:10)	6.8	15.5	12.5	11.7	13.5	11.7	9.3	5.5	5.3	4.0
Poland (1973:9)	3.8	12.8	9.8	9.7	10.4	7.8	5.1	6.2	6.5	6.5
United States (1958:4)	11.4	9.2	7.7	12.8	14.9	16.2	15.3	12.8	11.0	8.0

Table 3.11 (*continued*)

Country (reference year: number of regions)	Age group								
	50–54	55–59	60–64	65–69	70–74	75–79	80–84	85+	Total
Austria (1971:9)	4.1	3.4	3.1	2.9	2.2	2.5	3.6	2.5	3.4
Bulgaria (1975:7)	0.1	5.5	0.0	11.6	12.6	12.6	12.6	12.6	9.7
Canada (1971:10)	5.5	7.9	7.7	6.8	6.5	5.1	4.3	4.2	6.0
Czechoslovakia (1975:10)	3.7	5.8	6.1	7.0	6.7	5.5	3.9	3.4	5.8
FRG (1974:11)	6.1	6.5	7.4	4.9	3.3	3.7	2.8	3.2	4.6
Finland (1974:12)	9.5	10.2	7.5	5.9	6.5	←—	5.4	—→	7.3
France (1975:8)	10.3	8.7	7.6	6.9	6.9	6.1	5.8	4.3	6.8
GDR (1975:5)	4.5	4.5	3.9	3.1	3.7	←—	2.6	—→	3.3
Hungary (1974:6)	2.1	5.6	3.7	1.6	2.5	2.3	2.5	2.5	3.6
Italy (1978:5)	11.9	9.6	6.4	5.5	4.2	3.5	4.1	2.9	5.6
Japan (1970:8)	5.0	4.2	3.4	3.1	3.0	3.5	2.9	1.5	4.0
Netherlands (1974:5)	6.6	4.3	3.2	4.4	3.1	3.8	3.6	1.6	3.7
Poland (1977:13)	7.3	7.8	5.7	3.8	4.0	4.4	4.5	6.0	6.2
Soviet Union (1974:8)	7.0	4.4	6.4	9.3	1.5	1.5	1.5	1.5	6.7
Sweden (1974:8)	6.8	7.3	5.2	4.9	4.0	5.3	4.5	2.5	5.0
United Kingdom (1970:10)	12.0	9.7	9.3	7.8	7.8	7.1	6.6	6.4	7.9
United States (1970:4)	6.9	5.7	3.7	3.7	2.8	3.6	3.1	3.9	4.9
Additional aggregation									
GDR (1975:10)	6.6	4.7	5.1	4.3	4.4	←—	2.8	—→	3.9
Italy (1978:20)	13.8	12.4	9.6	8.5	16.6	5.9	5.6	4.1	7.8
Netherlands (1974:11)	6.9	5.5	4.2	5.1	3.6	4.6	4.2	2.5	4.6
Additional reference year									
Canada (1976:10)	4.7	6.2	7.4	67.6	6.2	5.7	4.7	2.6	5.7
Poland (1973:9)	6.3	5.5	4.4	4.4	6.0	4.4	6.2	6.0	5.4
United States (1958:4)	6.6	6.9	6.5	5.6	4.9	4.7	5.1	4.5	6.6

child (5–9 and 10–14) mortality (with indices around 25%), followed by Czechoslovakia. Also, the Netherlands has high levels of regional disparity (around 15%) for the three age groups between 10 and 24, while Sweden has high indices (close to 20%) for the 10–19 age group and the Soviet Union has indices around 30% for the 15–24 age group.

A record level of regional disparity was reached by Poland in 1977; this country shows a 73% index of mortality disparity in the 15–19 age group. But, once again, data problems may be responsible for this extreme situation. This disparity is mainly caused by the Polish East region, which shows an abnormal death rate of 7 per thousand at ages 15–19, while all other regions have a rate in the range of 0.5–0.8 per thousand. Moreover, as Table 3.11 shows, in 1973 the Polish level of disparity at age 15–19 was only 10%. Even if the Polish value is disregarded, the overall 15–19 age group shows a rather wide range of regional disparity, as does the 20–24 age group.

Starting with the 25–29 age group, the range of the index becomes less important, with maximum values reaching 18 in the Soviet Union for ages 30–34 and in the Federal Republic of Germany for ages 40–44, 12 in France, the UK, and Italy at ages 45–54, and less than 8 after ages 65–69 (ignoring the Bulgarian figures), whereas the minimum values decline from 3 for ages 25–39 to less than 2 in the older age groups. Thus not only is there less regional disparity within countries when age increases, but also there is less international variability in these disparities.

The figures for additional reference years in Table 3.11 provide sketchy information on the temporal evolution of regional mortality disparities by age. Between 1958 and 1970 the US showed a marked reduction in regional disparities for most age groups. Actually, there is an increase only among older children (10–14) and adults in the 45–54 age group. Its northern neighbor, Canada, shows quite a different evolution; between the periods 1966–1971 and 1971–1976 the index increased or remained about the same in most age groups, the only exceptions being 30–34, 50–59, and 85 and over. The Canadian pattern seems to be valid for Poland as well (between 1973 and 1977), where the level of regional mortality disparity also increased for most age groups (the main exceptions being in the older age groups).

One could conclude that since these disparities are lowest for the older age groups (65 and over), where also most deaths occur, the whole problem of regional inequality with respect to death is somewhat deflated. After all, if only a small minority of a country's population is affected by really important regional mortality differentials, we can more easily disregard them. Thus it is worthwhile considering the part that each of the main age groups (0–29, 30–59, and 60 and over) represents in the overall level of above- or below-average mortality for the 139 regions of the study and in the overall national level of regional disparity. For the sake of brevity, only the national results will be analyzed here. Table 3.12 provides the percentage of national mortality

Table 3.12 Percentage of mortality disparity in the 0–29 and 60+ age groups.

Country (reference year: number of regions)	0–29	60+
Austria (1971:9)	14	67
Bulgaria (1975:7)	6	88
Canada (1971:10)	16	64
Czechoslovakia (1975:10)	9	75
FRG (1974:11)	7	70
Finland (1974:12)	10	77
France (1975:8)	6	71
GDR (1975:5)	6	79
Hungary (1974:6)	27	53
Italy (1978:5)	12	60
Japan (1970:8)	18	52
Netherlands (1974:5)	12	70
Poland (1977:13)	25	51
Soviet Union (1974:8)	33	33
Sweden (1974:8)	8	72
United Kingdom (1970:10)	4	75
United States (1970:4)	16	50
Additional aggregation		
GDR (1975:10)	7	86
Italy (1978:20)	10	65
Netherlands (1974:11)	12	70
Additional reference year		
Canada (1976:10)	16	65
Poland (1973:9)	12	68
United States (1958:4)	20	52

disparities (measured in terms of excess and missing deaths) accounted for by the age groups of high (0–29) and low (60 and over) mortality disparities.

The values in this table identify the relative contributions of age-specific regional mortality differentials to the overall national differentials. In seven of the 17 countries, about two-thirds (between 64 and 72%) of the impact of regional mortality differentials is concentrated among old age groups. In other words, the main part of regional mortality disparities is accounted for by age groups for which these disparities are relatively low anyway. These seven countries have low overall disparity levels (Austria and the Federal Republic of Germany), as well as middle-range or high levels (France). In five other countries, three quarters or more of the regional disparity is accounted for by old age groups: Bulgaria (88%), the German Democratic Republic (79%), Finland (77%), and Czechoslovakia and the UK (75%). Bulgaria, Finland, and the UK are countries with high regional disparities, having only a marginal part of their mortality differentials occurring in infants, children, and young adults (0–29). In other words, a significant decrease in overall regional mortality disparity in these countries will not be obtained by policy measures for young ages, even though in some cases mortality differentials are particularly high at these ages (e.g., in Finland).

Finally, there are five countries where a considerable part of overall regional mortality disparity is a result of younger-age (0–29) differentials, with only about half of the overall disparity being accounted for by the elderly (60+). The Soviet Union represents an extreme case, with one third of the overall disparity being in the 0–29 age group and only one third in the older age groups (but rather important data problems have been encountered here). Hungary, Poland, Japan, and the US (with, respectively, 27, 25, 18, and 16%) are the four other countries where a significant reduction in disparities could be obtained by policy measures promoting more uniform and lower death rates for the 0–29 age group. In these countries (except for Poland, for which data errors may exist), a considerable part of the overall regional disparity is actually due to infant mortality differentials; thus any intervention in infant mortality could be rewarding in terms of regional equality.

3.5 Conclusion

Depending on the definition of regional mortality disparity used, conclusions on the level of mortality inequalities will be highly divergent.

If we consider life expectancy at birth and analyze only the maximum differences between the highest and lowest regional values, we could conclude that even in the most socioeconomically advanced countries regional mortality disparities are still significant. If these disparities are measured by using the mean absolute deviation between regional and national life expectancies, however, we would conclude that the differences are rather marginal.

By using the gross death rate instead of life expectancy at birth, one obtains still larger regional disparities (measured by dividing the mean absolute deviation by the national figure), and, as expected, once one considers age- (and sex-) specific death rates, these differentials may become quite striking. From the data available it is clear that, on the whole, these regional mortality deviations are high for infant and young-adult mortality but low for old-age mortality.

Instead of summarizing the mortality regime through traditional indicators or comparing regional age-specific rates, we measured regional mortality disparity in terms of the percentage of deaths in a country that represent these regional (age-specific) differences. We began with the overall level of above- or below-average mortality observed in each region. From this we obtained a global (national) measure of regional disparity, by relating the total number of deaths observed in the country. In this analysis, regional differences in the age structure of the population were taken into account, but the results showed that in most cases they had no significant impact on the level of regional disparity.

The main conclusion of this second type of analysis is that, within countries, there are still striking regional differences in mortality, with 16 (of the 139) regions showing a level of above- or below-average mortality representing more than 10% or more (in three regions, more than 20%) of the number of deaths that would have been expected if the national mortality regime had been applied. We also observed marked differences among countries in the national level of regional disparity. This international comparison was made possible because our national measure of regional disparity takes into account some of the problems resulting from differences in regional disaggregation. Finally, an analysis by age group shows that, on the whole, most of the above- or below-average mortality for a region is concentrated in the older age groups, which are also those for which regional disparities are usually the lowest. A policy implication of this is that, in most of the countries of our IIASA sample, policy measures that favor a decrease in infant and young-adult mortality rates and a decline in regional disparity of these rates would have only a marginal impact on the overall regional mortality disparities. Even though differentials are lower for old-age groups, policy interventions favoring these groups would be more rewarding for the overall regional disparity.

But our analysis is merely descriptive. We did no more than estimate, using various indicators and measures, the degree of regional disparity in the mortality regime of the various countries of the IIASA study. No attempt has been made to explain these disparities, although some indications are given. For instance, some countries have an inverse relation between infant and old-age mortality, which could be a result of natural selectivity — where only the fittest survive and survive longer — as well as socioeconomic and environmental factors. (Factors that lead to high infant mortality may also represent favorable conditions for old-age survival.) This brings us to an analysis of urban–rural mortality differentials. From the data available, however, we could not derive any clear relation between urbanization and mortality levels. Some regions of our sample are highly urbanized (some actually being city regions). Their level of mortality is in some cases above the national average, in others below. In some countries, where the overall level of urbanization is high, small regional mortality disparities exist, whereas others with the same level or urbanization have relatively large differences.

Perhaps the final conclusion that should be derived from this analysis is that no conclusion should be made. Indeed, even the merely descriptive results obtained are disputable. We have mentioned serious data problems. Even for such a "vital" phenomenon as mortality, in the statistically most advanced countries of the world there are still considerable problems of data quality. Among all the social disciplines, demography is probably the field where respect for the critical analysis of data has been strongest. One of the first tasks of multiregional demographers is to push toward a higher quality in the data they use, now that many methodological problems have been resolved.

Another reason for not drawing conclusions from our results is that they are based on highly contingent observations. It should be remembered that, except for two countries, all our data are for single years. To derive any conclusion on a one-year observation is obviously disputable. To obtain more meaningful results we should use, for example, yearly averages of five-year data; there are too many incidental, sporadic phenomena that otherwise may intervene. Extending the period of observation is, however, not enough. We are still left with all the problems arising from the static nature of this type of analysis. To progress toward a more explanatory analysis and to obtain some policy-oriented results, we need to analyze the temporal evolution of regional mortality disparities. Since reliable data are available in some countries, such a temporal regional analysis is not merely a utopian dream.

Clearly our analysis is limited. But because regional mortality differentials are still observed in many of the so-called advanced countries of the world and because these inequalities have social implications that are of interest to policymakers, we hope that this first step will be followed by many more advances.

APPENDIX 3A: The Gross Death Rate and the Expectation of Life at Birth for each Region in the Migration and Settlement Study

Country (reference year) and region	Population (1)	GDR (2)	Expectation of life e0 (3)	GDR(0-4) (4)	GDR(15-29) (5)	GDR(65+) (6)	GDR(70-74) (7)
Austria (1971)							
Burgenland	272119.	3.13	69.57	0.026	0.022	2.811	0.263
Carinthia	525728.	2.89	70.27	0.031	0.020	2.601	0.255
Lower Austria	1414161.	2.98	70.27	0.026	0.022	2.681	0.256
Upper Austria	1223444.	3.04	70.52	0.027	0.018	2.761	0.268
Salzburg	401766.	2.87	71.17	0.025	0.017	2.594	0.251
Styria	1192100.	3.03	70.06	0.029	0.020	2.728	0.263
Tyrol	540771.	2.77	71.68	0.024	0.017	2.509	0.237
Vorarlberg	271473.	2.78	71.57	0.026	0.014	2.516	0.231
Vienna	1614841.	2.88	70.85	0.027	0.014	2.591	0.254
Austria	7456403.	2.94	70.54	0.027	0.018	2.653	0.256
Bulgaria (1975)							
North West	1042803.	2.46	71.79	0.026	0.016	2.192	0.208
North	1400117.	2.72	71.37	0.028	0.012	2.460	0.235
North East	1486719.	3.15	69.94	0.033	0.015	2.868	0.277
South West	696466.	3.05	71.02	0.029	0.015	2.788	0.274
South	2164076.	3.23	70.61	0.028	0.013	2.962	0.288
South East	866834.	3.08	70.56	0.031	0.014	2.811	0.272
Sofia	1069975.	3.87	70.40	0.027	0.011	3.610	0.359
Bulgaria	8726990.	2.96	70.90	0.029	0.013	2.687	0.260
Canada (1971)							
Newfoundland	507750.	2.42	72.21	0.029	0.013	2.150	0.198
Prince Edward Island	110085.	2.20	72.51	0.026	0.015	1.916	0.177
Nova Scotia	772500.	2.39	71.92	0.023	0.018	2.099	0.204
New Brunswick	625674.	2.36	72.23	0.024	0.018	2.078	0.193
Quebec	5904307.	2.56	71.52	0.023	0.016	2.270	0.218
Ontario	7331987.	2.36	72.71	0.020	0.014	2.088	0.206
Manitoba	975655.	2.22	73.26	0.023	0.016	1.971	0.186
Saskatchewan	940790.	2.09	73.79	0.026	0.019	1.851	0.167
Alberta	1545537.	2.17	73.62	0.022	0.018	1.923	0.178
British Columbia	2029147.	2.21	72.93	0.022	0.018	1.940	0.182
Canada	20743436.	2.35	72.51	0.022	0.016	2.073	0.200
Czechoslovakia (1975)							
Central Bohemia	2300705.	3.17	70.10	0.027	0.013	2.870	0.282
Southern Bohemia	667998.	3.00	70.85	0.024	0.012	2.713	0.253
Western Bohemia	872296.	3.34	69.77	0.022	0.013	3.022	0.310
Northern Bohemia	1138800.	3.39	68.74	0.030	0.016	3.050	0.317
Eastern Bohemia	1224599.	2.96	71.22	0.021	0.013	2.684	0.265
Southern Moravia	1985174.	2.95	71.46	0.024	0.011	2.679	0.259
Northern Moravia	1875294.	3.15	70.28	0.024	0.014	2.842	0.272
Western Slovakia	1966889.	2.92	70.36	0.027	0.013	2.612	0.254
Central Slovakia	1455491.	2.92	70.42	0.027	0.016	2.611	0.239
Eastern Slovakia	1316921.	2.98	69.90	0.036	0.015	2.671	0.230
Czechoslovakia	14801667.	3.07	70.31	0.026	0.014	2.762	0.268

Mortality

Country (reference year) and region	Population (1)	GDR (2)	Expectation of life e0 (3)	GDR(0-4) (4)	GDR(15-29) (5)	GDR(65+) (6)	GDR(70-74) (7)
Fed.Rep.of Germany (1974)							
Schleswig-Holstein	2584343	2.72	72.11	0.019	0.015	2.465	0.242
Hamburg	1733802	2.70	71.85	0.021	0.013	2.430	0.230
Lower Saxony	7265539	2.65	71.68	0.023	0.017	2.381	0.240
Bremen	723990	2.72	71.79	0.021	0.013	2.440	0.231
N.Rhine-Westphalia	17218626	2.75	71.48	0.024	0.013	2.478	0.249
Hessen	5576082	2.74	72.37	0.022	0.014	2.495	0.233
Rhineland-Palatinate	3687561	2.76	71.68	0.023	0.015	2.490	0.239
Baden-Wuerttemberg	9226239	2.61	72.76	0.019	0.014	2.375	0.222
Bavaria	10849123	2.71	72.03	0.022	0.016	2.458	0.234
Saarland	1103325	2.90	70.60	0.026	0.016	2.603	0.254
West Berlin	2034366	2.96	70.37	0.022	0.023	2.646	0.252
Fed.Rep. of Germany	62002996	2.72	71.86	0.022	0.015	2.460	0.239
Finland (1974)							
Uusimaa	1073485	1.18	72.41	0.013	0.015	0.890	0.223
Turku and Pori	691672	1.18	72.82	0.013	0.015	0.912	0.223
Ahvenanmaa	22009	1.18	72.82	0.010	0.008	0.894	0.225
Hame	657049	1.34	72.25	0.014	0.014	0.926	0.229
Kymi	345985	1.42	70.51	0.016	0.019	1.018	0.247
Mikkeli	212200	1.42	70.32	0.017	0.016	1.094	0.280
Pohjois-Karjala	177870	1.38	69.90	0.012	0.018	1.042	0.254
Kuopio	251320	1.34	70.47	0.014	0.019	0.999	0.263
Keski-Suomi	238814	1.34	71.03	0.014	0.013	1.028	0.268
Vaasa	423043	1.22	72.32	0.016	0.016	0.953	0.234
Oulu	400853	1.34	70.56	0.014	0.023	0.999	0.252
Lappi	196232	1.29	70.44	0.012	0.023	0.934	0.255
Finland	4690532	1.25	71.66	0.014	0.015	0.952	0.238
France (1975)							
Paris Region	9876665	2.04	74.64	0.017	0.013	1.801	0.169
Paris Basin	9647540	2.26	73.26	0.018	0.016	1.994	0.187
North	3913250	2.64	70.24	0.025	0.015	2.298	0.237
East	4905810	2.48	72.25	0.020	0.015	2.198	0.209
West	6889705	2.32	73.03	0.017	0.017	2.054	0.186
Southwest	5553655	2.20	74.37	0.017	0.016	1.973	0.175
Middle East	6129105	2.30	73.63	0.017	0.015	2.054	0.191
Mediterranean	5464635	2.07	74.72	0.018	0.016	1.845	0.164
France	52380364	2.24	73.48	0.018	0.015	1.989	0.185
German Dem.Rep.(1975)							
North	2085383	1.34	71.25	0.020	0.015	1.075	0.270
Berlin	1098174	1.43	70.81	0.018	0.013	1.148	0.288
Southwest	2529805	1.32	71.74	0.020	0.012	1.073	0.268
South	7134846	1.27	72.21	0.017	0.013	1.020	0.252
Middle	3972041	1.34	71.36	0.019	0.014	1.071	0.270
German Dem.Rep.	16820250	1.31	71.74	0.018	0.014	1.053	0.262

Mortality

Country (reference year) and region	Population (1)	GDR (2)	Expectation of life e0 (3)	GDR(0-4) (4)	GDR(15-29) (5)	GDR(65+) (6)	GDR(70-74) (7)
Hungary (1974)							
Central	2968109.	2.99	68.36	0.057	0.012	2.652	0.265
North Hungary	1357973.	3.07	68.92	0.045	0.014	2.744	0.261
North Plain	1543604.	2.97	69.28	0.044	0.016	2.657	0.245
South Plain	1451260.	3.06	68.97	0.042	0.017	2.728	0.254
North Trans-Danubia	1823844.	3.02	69.81	0.037	0.013	2.711	0.268
South Trans-Danubia	1303694.	3.16	68.78	0.049	0.014	2.850	0.267
Hungary	10448484.	3.03	68.99	0.046	0.014	2.710	0.261
Italy (1978)							
North West	15424582.	2.52	73.46	0.015	0.011	2.282	0.207
North East	10394756.	2.39	73.87	0.013	0.012	2.146	0.198
Center	10790837.	2.25	75.27	0.014	0.009	2.053	0.182
South	13471822.	2.45	73.99	0.021	0.009	2.229	0.193
Islands	6518288.	2.37	74.55	0.018	0.009	2.166	0.184
Italy	56600292.	2.41	74.07	0.017	0.010	2.185	0.195
Japan (1970)							
Hokkaido	5184287.	2.80	71.65	0.019	0.015	2.537	0.249
Tohoku	11392179.	2.96	71.20	0.021	0.016	2.693	0.262
Kanto	30257930.	2.78	72.43	0.018	0.013	2.534	0.240
Chubu	17401128.	2.80	72.42	0.019	0.014	2.565	0.238
Kinki	16511391.	2.76	72.56	0.017	0.013	2.521	0.234
Chgoku	6996961.	2.68	72.45	0.019	0.016	2.437	0.222
Shikoku	3904014.	2.78	71.52	0.021	0.019	2.510	0.232
Kyushu	13017290.	2.72	71.59	0.021	0.017	2.450	0.233
Japan	104465176.	2.78	72.16	0.019	0.014	2.532	0.239
Netherlands (1974)							
North	1473611.	2.24	74.74	0.013	0.012	2.026	0.188
East	2592786.	2.38	74.40	0.013	0.011	2.165	0.192
West	6150477.	2.31	75.06	0.012	0.009	2.104	0.190
South-West	332891.	2.11	75.69	0.012	0.012	1.914	0.164
South	2948600.	2.46	73.97	0.013	0.011	2.236	0.210
Netherlands	13488365.	2.33	74.71	0.012	0.010	2.119	0.192
Poland (1977)							
Warsaw	2207161.	2.37	71.39	0.027	0.013	2.061	0.213
Lodz	1099132.	2.64	69.96	0.035	0.014	2.311	0.231
Gdansk	1287689.	2.41	71.49	0.027	0.015	2.116	0.220
Katowice	3557261.	2.79	69.79	0.030	0.014	2.454	0.253
Cracow	1143864.	2.40	71.82	0.024	0.011	2.116	0.231
East-Central	2930837.	2.69	70.19	0.032	0.020	2.382	0.233
Northeast	2398497.	2.43	71.33	0.029	0.019	2.137	0.206
Northwest	2106814.	2.49	69.93	0.033	0.017	2.148	0.249
South	2505722.	2.61	70.84	0.028	0.016	2.312	0.239
Southeast	4208485.	2.60	70.88	0.030	0.017	2.306	0.243
East	2479828.	2.64	69.40	0.028	0.051	2.329	0.229
West-Central	4712562.	2.61	70.86	0.030	0.015	2.313	0.235
West	4059724.	2.47	70.37	0.031	0.017	2.146	0.240
Poland	34697580.	2.58	70.56	0.030	0.018	2.267	0.234

Mortality

Country (reference year) and region	Population (1)	GDR (2)	Expectation of life e0 (3)	GDR(0-4) (4)	GDR(15-29) (5)	GDR(65+) (6)	GDR(70-74) (7)
Soviet Union (1974)							
Urban areas of the:							
RSFSR	88230272.	2.34	69.44	0.043	0.025	1.999	0.195
Ukrainian+Mold.SSRs	29527222.	2.30	71.50	0.028	0.017	2.004	0.196
Byelorussian SSR	4549020.	2.01	73.49	0.024	0.015	1.747	0.172
Central Asian Rep.s	8681624.	2.10	68.27	0.071	0.024	1.723	0.167
Kazakh SSR	7348350.	2.27	68.55	0.049	0.028	1.887	0.184
Caucasian Republics	6918171.	2.12	71.51	0.044	0.015	1.823	0.178
Baltic Republics	4334008.	2.30	71.70	0.023	0.020	1.997	0.196
Rural areas of USSR	101280288.	2.32	68.23	0.048	0.038	1.942	0.192
Soviet Union	250868944.	2.31	69.32	0.045	0.027	1.958	0.192
Sweden (1974)							
Stockholm	1486821.	2.32	75.03	0.009	0.009	2.106	0.187
East Middle	1397129.	2.43	75.13	0.010	0.010	2.244	0.185
South Middle	763793.	2.33	75.42	0.014	0.012	2.150	0.177
South	1157556.	2.26	75.92	0.009	0.011	2.082	0.171
West	1603323.	2.33	75.57	0.011	0.009	2.149	0.175
North Middle	853655.	2.53	74.52	0.011	0.012	2.332	0.193
Lower North	400292.	2.47	74.37	0.013	0.012	2.265	0.188
Upper North	494569.	2.47	74.87	0.010	0.012	2.284	0.197
Sweden	8157138.	2.37	75.21	0.011	0.010	2.182	0.182
United Kingdom (1970)							
North	3359700.	2.92	71.14	0.021	0.010	2.627	0.259
Yorkshire + Humbers.	4811900.	2.84	71.23	0.024	0.011	2.554	0.260
North West	6788700.	2.95	70.61	0.024	0.010	2.635	0.270
East Midlands	3362800.	2.70	72.06	0.020	0.010	2.430	0.246
West Midlands	5178000.	2.77	71.68	0.022	0.010	2.487	0.252
East Anglia	1673500.	2.41	73.51	0.019	0.010	2.182	0.219
South East	17315502.	2.47	73.19	0.019	0.010	2.227	0.221
South West	3763700.	2.59	72.89	0.019	0.010	2.345	0.227
Wales	2733900.	2.89	71.16	0.021	0.011	2.593	0.259
Scotland	5199100.	2.98	70.26	0.023	0.011	2.653	0.269
United Kingdom	54186800.	2.69	71.94	0.021	0.010	2.416	0.244
United States (1970)							
Northeast	49040708.	2.44	70.99	0.023	0.017	2.113	0.233
North Central	56571668.	2.38	71.26	0.024	0.019	2.064	0.221
South	62795372.	2.34	69.90	0.029	0.022	1.972	0.220
West	34804200.	2.22	71.82	0.023	0.021	1.910	0.202
United States	203211920.	2.36	70.84	0.025	0.020	2.026	0.221

APPENDIX 3B: Observed and Standardized Index of Mortality Differentials for Each Region in the Migration and Settlement Study

Country, reference year, and region		IMD	
		Observed	Standardized
Austria	Burgenland	7	7
(1971)	Carinthia	−1	−1
	Lower Austria	2	2
	Upper Austria	2	3
	Salzburg	−4	−5
	Styria	3	3
	Tyrol	−8	−9
	Vorarlberg	−7	−10
	Vienna	−2	−1
Bulgaria	North West	−12	−7
(1975)	North	−5	−4
	North East	7	8
	South West	−1	−0
	South	5	6
	South East	3	3
	Sofia	8	22
Canada	Newfoundland	2	2
(1971)	Prince Edward Island	−4	−2
	Nova Scotia	3	3
	New Brunswick	1	1
	Quebec	8	10
	Ontario	−0	−0
	Manitoba	−6	−5
	Saskatchewan	−11	−9
	Alberta	−8	−9
	British Columbia	−5	−4
Czechoslovakia	Central Bohemia	4	3
(1975)	Southern Bohemia	−3	−3
	Western Bohemia	9	9
	Northern Bohemia	14	16
	Eastern Bohemia	−4	−4
	Southern Moravia	−6	−5
	Northern Moravia	2	2
	Western Slovakia	−3	−3
	Central Slovakia	−4	−5
	Eastern Slovakia	−2	−4

Country, reference year, and region		IMD	
		Observed	Standardized
FRG	Schleswig–Holstein	−2	−2
(1974)	Hamburg	−1	−1
	Lower Saxony	−1	−1
	Bremen	−0	−0
	North Rhine–Westphalia	3	3
	Hessen	−3	−3
	Rhineland–Palatinate	1	1
	Baden–Wuerttemberg	−6	−6
	Bavaria	−1	−1
	Saarland	11	12
	West Berlin	8	6
Finland	Uusimaa	−5	−5
(1974)	Turku and Pori	−7	−6
	Ahvenanmaa	−7	−5
	Häme	−4	−4
	Kymi	7	7
	Mikkeli	13	11
	Pohjois–Karjala	11	12
	Kuopio	8	8
	Keski–Suomi	6	6
	Vaasa	−4	−4
	Oulu	8	10
	Lappi	8	8
France	Paris Region	−9	−10
(1975)	Paris Basin	1	1
	North	24	27
	East	11	12
	West	3	3
	South West	−4	−4
	Middle East	1	1
	Mediterranean	−9	−8
GDR	North	3	3
(1975)	Berlin	9	9
	South West	1	1
	South	−3	−3
	Middle	2	2
Hungary	Central	1	1
(1974)	North Hungary	1	1
	North Plain	−3	−3
	South Plain	−0	−0
	North Trans-Danubia	−2	−1
	South Trans-Danubia	3	3

Country, reference year, and region		IMD	
		Observed	Standardized
Italy	North West	6	6
(1978)	North East	1	1
	Central	−7	−7
	South	0	0
	Islands	−3	−4
Japan	Hokkaido	4	4
(1970)	Tohoku	8	8
	Kanto	−2	−2
	Chubu	−2	−2
	Kinki	−3	−3
	Chugoku	−4	−3
	Shikoku	2	2
	Kyushu	2	2
Netherlands	North	−2	−2
(1974)	East	2	2
	West	−2	−2
	South West	−10	−7
	South	7	9
Poland	Warsaw	−6	−5
(1977)	Łódź	3	3
	Gdańsk	−6	−6
	Katowice	8	8
	Krakow	−5	−5
	East Central	2	2
	North East	−7	−7
	North West	4	4
	South	−1	−1
	South East	−1	−1
	East	3	3
	West Central	−1	−1
	West	1	0
Soviet Union	Urban areas of the:	1	1
(1974)	RSFSR		
	Ukrainian and Moldavian		
	Republics	−7	−6
	Byelorussian Republic	−21	−23
	Central Asian Republics	5	0
	Kazakh Republic	4	5
	Caucasian Republics	−12	−13
	Baltic Republics	−7	−7
	Rural areas of the USSR	2	3

Country, reference year, and region		IMD	
		Observed	Standardized
Sweden			
(1974)	East Middle	2	2
	South Middle	−3	−3
	South	−5	−5
	West	−3	−3
	North Middle	6	6
	Lower North	1	1
	Upper North	5	6
United Kingdom	North	8	8
(1970)	Yorkshire and Humberside	6	6
	North West	11	11
	East Midlands	−0	−0
	West Midlands	2	3
	East Anglia	−11	−11
	South East	−9	−9
	South West	−5	−5
	Wales	7	7
	Scotland	13	14
United States	North East	2	1
(1970)	North Central	−1	−1
	South	3	3
	West	−7	−7
Additional aggregation			
GDR	Rostock	3	3
(1975)	Neubrandenburg and Schwerin	3	3
	Berlin	9	9
	Erfurt, Gera, and Suhl	1	1
	Leipzig and Halle	0	0
	Karl-Marx-Stadt	−4	−4
	Dresden	−8	−7
	Cottbus	−2	−2
	Frankfurt	3	3
	Postdam and Magdeburg	3	3

Country, reference year, and region		IMD	
		Observed	Standardized
Additional aggregation			
Italy	Piemonte	4	4
(1978)	Valle d'Aosta	14	14
	Lombardia	10	11
	Liguria	−3	−2
	Trentino−Alto Adige	6	6
	Veneto	5	5
	Friuli−Venezia Giulia	6	5
	Emilia−Romagna	−5	−4
	Toscana	−10	−8
	Umbria	−9	−8
	Marche	−9	−8
	Lazio	−6	−7
	Abruzzi	−8	−8
	Molise	−7	−6
	Campania	10	13
	Puglia	−4	−5
	Basilicata	−4	−4
	Calabria	−7	−8
	Sicilia	−2	−3
	Sardegna	−7	−7
Additional aggregation			
Netherlands	Groningen	−5	−4
(1974)	Friesland	−1	−1
	Drenthe	−1	−1
	Overÿssel	4	4
	Gelderland	1	1
	Utrecht	−1	−1
	Noord Holland	0	0
	Zuid Holland	−4	−4
	Zeeland	−10	−7
	Noord Brabant	5	7
	Limburg	10	13
Additional reference year			
Canada	Newfoundland	3	4
(1976)	Prince Edward Island	−4	−2
	Nova Scotia	3	3
	New Brunswick	1	2
	Quebec	8	10
	Ontario	−1	−1
	Manitoba	−5	−4
	Saskatchewan	−10	−8
	Alberta	−6	−7
	British Columbia	−5	−4

Country, reference year, and region		IMD	
		Observed	Standardized
Additional reference year			
Poland	Warsaw	−11	−9
(1973)	Krakow	−1	−1
	Łódź	3	3
	Poznań	−1	−1
	Wrocław	2	2
	Białystok	−6	−5
	Gdańsk	−0	−1
	Katowice	8	8
	Lublin	−2	−2
Additional reference year			
United States	North East	5	4
(1958)	North Central	−5	−4
	South	3	3
	West	−5	−5

Note: The "observed" index is obtained from equation (3.4), the "standardized" index from equation (3.5).

CHAPTER FOUR

Fertility

Young J. Kim

Before reliable data on births for large population aggregates became available, the study of fertility lacked quantitative analyses. By the end of the eighteenth century, Malthus had stimulated interest in the quality of population data, but because he considered fertility levels to be essentially constant, studies of mortality were stressed throughout the nineteenth century. Only when it became obvious, at the turn of the twentieth century, that these levels were not constant but were actually falling in many West European countries, did serious interest in fertility analysis arise and develop into a science that has come to receive enormous attention from demographers in recent years.

Differences in both the levels and age patterns of fertility in the 17 IIASA countries and in the 139 regions forming these countries are the primary concern of this chapter. Our aim is to summarize and describe observed fertility differentials but not to search for explanatory factors associated with them. Before examining these differentials, we briefly review the basic measures of fertility analysis and discuss the limitations of available data, as well as define the measures that are used in the subsequent sections. In Section 4.3 we make comparisons of the levels of fertility between countries and between regions within countries, without regard to differing age patterns of fertility. We then examine the levels and age patterns simultaneously by fitting a linear model that includes both location and age effects to the age-specific fertility rates of regional populations. This is done first for the national age-specific rates, for which the location and age effects are estimated. The same analysis is next carried out using the regional age-specific rates within each country. In Section 4.5, the relational two-parameter Gompertz fertility model is fitted to the age pattern of fertility. The goodness-of-fit is examined visually by comparing a fitted curve and the observed age pattern, but a statistical test is not used to assess the quality of the fit. A summary concludes the chapter.

4.1 Basic Fertility Measures

We begin this chapter with a discussion of several commonly used measures of fertility, the most basic of which is the *crude birth rate* (CBR): the ratio of the number of births in a year to the average population in thousands (or more exactly, in thousand person-years of exposure) during that year. Using this measure for a comparison of fertility levels within a country over time or of various countries at a given time, however, would confound the effects of the age and sex compositions of the respective populations with differences in their fertility. In an effort to refine the denominator (the average population) more closely so that it represents the population at risk of giving birth, the *general fertility rate* (GFR) — the ratio of the number of births in a year to the number of thousand person-years of females in the childbearing ages, usually 15–44 — is often used instead. And since the risk of childbearing varies greatly with age even within the childbearing years, this idea may be further extended to define the *age-specific fertility rate* (ASFR): the ratio of the number of births to a mother in a given age group (usually a five-year age interval) to the number of thousand person-years of females in that age group. Although these female rates are widely accepted because of their convenience, they are rather arbitrary in the sense that each birth requires two parents, who are not generally of the same age.

Reducing the six or seven values of age-specific rates into a single fertility index involves the assignment of proper weights to each age group. The *total fertility rate* (TFR) is obtained by assigning equal weights of unity to each age group. This measure represents a mean parity of a cohort of women at the end of its childbearing age, assuming that the childbearing years are unaffected by mortality and that the cohort experiences given age-specific fertility rates at each age. A modification of this rate to include only female births produces the *gross reproduction rate* (GRR), a measure of replacement for a female population under the assumption of no mortality.

Similarity in the pattern of age-specific fertility rates in various populations has led researchers to look for a simple model that describes patterns using only a small number of parameters. There have been essentially two approaches presented in this endeavor. The first fits probability density functions, such as gamma, beta, and Hadwiger functions, to a curve (for example, see Hoem *et al.* 1981). The second fits curves that are generated from observed empirical fertility patterns with a small number of parameters. The fertility model of Coale and Trussell (1974) is perhaps the best among this second group because the parameters in the model have demographic meanings. The relational Gompertz model developed by Brass (1980), however, involves only two parameters, one less than in the Coale and Trussell model, which is an important consideration when data are given in five-year age groups rather than by single years of age.

4.2 Data and Definitions

Before embarking on a comparative analysis, we must first determine how comparable the available data are. The most important discrepancies are the differences in time periods of data bases and in sizes of regions among the 17 countries. The data span almost a decade (1970–1978), and because fertility was declining during this period, international comparisons of observations at different periods cannot be very meaningful. This problem suggests that we should therefore put more emphasis on interregional comparisons within a country, but the degree of regional fertility disparities is affected by the way regions are defined as well as by existing fertility differentials.

The number of regions in each country and the size of populations or area of these regions vary greatly. For example, the US is divided into only four large regions, whereas small countries such as Czechoslovakia and Finland are divided into 10 and 12 regions, respectively, and in extreme cases, large cities such as Vienna and Warsaw exist as single regions in their respective national case studies. International comparisons of regional fertility differentials should also be viewed with caution because the degree of regional disparities increases, other things being equal, as the number of regions increases and the size of each region decreases.

The second source of incomparability is more specific to birth statistics. What is included in the statistics and the degree to which all national births are registered vary from country to country. The definition of a live birth is not uniformly applied, even among developed countries, and in some countries live births that result in early deaths are routinely excluded from the count. Births that occur to parents temporarily out of the country are included in the count in some countries, but not in others. Further, at the regional level, births are tabulated by place of usual residence in most countries, but by place of occurrence in others. Births may also be tabulated by year of occurrence or by year of registration. The degree of underregistration varies not only by region but also by age of mother. And even among registered births, when information on the age of the mother is missing and is estimated, the adopted method of allocation by age affects the age-specific measures of fertility. Since birth rates are a function of population stocks as well as the birth statistics, variation in population coverage is another factor to be considered. Differing degrees of underenumeration in census counts and of accuracy in the postcensal estimates of population for noncensus years produce biased rates. This problem is even more pronounced when the population is classified both by region and by age.

With these points in mind, let us examine the data that are available for our comparative analysis. Population data are enumerated in five-year age groups and birth data are tabulated by age of mother, also in five-year age groups, and by region of each country. In the Migration and Settlement Study these data are disaggregated by sex in seven of the 17 countries (Canada, the

Federal Republic of Germany, Finland, France, Japan, Sweden, and the UK). In the remaining 10 countries the case studies use data for both sexes combined, which obviously prevents us from calculating conventional measures of fertility, because these measures are based on female populations (except for the crude birth rate). To calculate such rates as the general or age-specific fertility rates, population data should be disaggregated by sex as well as by age. Since we do not have such data for more than half of the countries in our study, we must adopt an alternative strategy.

We recall that the age-specific fertility rate is the ratio of the number of births to mothers of a given age group to the number (in thousands) of females in that age group and that the sum of these rates over all ages results in the total fertility rate. Paralleling these measures of replacement are those defined with female births along: the gross maternity function (although the term "function" connotes a continuous form, we maintain this terminology) and the gross reproduction rate, respectively. The GRR represents the number of daughters a woman would have by the end of her childbearing years if she were to live through those years. Because fertility is a component of spatial population dynamics and the model for the process is essentially a one-sex model, it is natural to introduce these single-sex measures in the analysis. The measure, therefore, that was called the ASFR in the series of 17 national case studies was actually the gross maternity function either for females or for both sexes combined, depending on the availability of sex-specific data.

Because births are tabulated by age of mother, the two sets of rates — females alone and both sexes combined — are not compatible with each other for a given population. The discrepancy between the two sets depends on how different the sex ratios are among births and in successive age groups. In order to see just how distorted this picture might be, we computed the age schedules of fertility for females alone, where available, and for both sexes combined.

We compared age patterns of $^{(F)}f_X$, the gross maternity function for females alone, and $^{(F+M)}f_X$, the function for both sexes combined. We calculated the mean, standard deviation, and skewness as well as the gross reproduction rate of the available age schedules. For the seven countries that have sex-specific data, little difference was found between the female and the both-sexes-combined schedules. Consequently, we shall use the rates for combined sexes for all countries, even for those for which sex-specific data are available. For convenience and the consistency with the earlier national case studies, we shall henceforth call $^{(F+M)}f_X$ the age-specific fertility rate. The sum of the ASFRs defined in this way over all age groups, multiplied by the width of the age interval (in our case five years), gives the gross reproduction rate (GRR):

$$\text{GRR} = 5 \sum_{X}^{(F+M)} f_X \, .$$

We emphasize again that the ASFR in the remainder of this chapter is the gross maternity function, that is, the component of the measure of replacement of the population, and is therefore approximately half the value of the usual age-specific fertility rate.

4.3 Comparisons of Fertility Levels

Although we have reservations concerning the appropriateness of comparing national fertility levels observed at different times, we nevertheless examine international differentials among the IIASA nations for the respective reference years. Then we examine the prevailing trend in fertility levels during the 1970s in these countries to account for the differences in the reference years.

4.3.1 Comparisons Between Countries

We use the crude birth rate and the gross reproduction rate for our comparison; the CBR is examined because of its simplicity and popularity as a fertility measure, whereas the GRR is examined in order to obtain a better comparison of fertility levels without the confounding effects of differing age and sex distributions.

To do this, we follow the numerical and graphical procedures of explanatory data analysis introduced by Tukey (1977). In this form of analysis, the basic numbers that are easy to find and that tell us something about a collection, a *batch*, of numbers as a whole are the two extremes (minimum and maximum values) and a middle value. The middle value of a batch is called the *median* and is used as a measure of location. In addition to these three numbers, the *lower* and *upper quartiles* add more information about the batch of numbers; the range between them is called the *midspread*. These numbers will be used to summarize and compare the CBRs and GRRs of the 17 IIASA countries.

Table 4.1 gives, for the 17 countries, values of the CBR and GRR and their respective ranks in ascending order for the reference years and values of the GRR for 1975. Let us first summarize the fertility levels in the reference years. Values of the CBR range from a low of 10.1 in the Federal Republic of Germany to a high of 19.6 in Czechoslovakia. The median value is 16.1, with a midspread of 4.7. Values of the GRR range from a low of 0.73 in the Federal Republic of Germany to a high of 1.33 in the Soviet Union, giving a range of 0.6 (equivalent to 1.2 babies per woman). The median value of the GRR is 1.09 and the midspread is 0.27. In seven countries, the Federal Republic of Germany, the German Democratic Republic, Finland, the Netherlands, Italy, Sweden, and France, in ascending order, the GRR is less than unity, that is, the fertility

Table 4.1 The crude birth rate in the reference year and gross reproduction rates in the reference year and in 1975 by country, and their ranks.

Country (reference year)	CBR[a]	Rank order	GRR[a,b]	Rank order	GRR in 1975[c]	Rank order
Austria (1971)	14.6	8	1.09	9	0.90	9
Bulgaria (1975)	16.6	10	1.10	10	1.10	13
Canada (1971)	17.6	11	1.23	15	0.88	8
Czechoslovakia (1975)	19.6	17	1.21	14	1.21	17
FRG (1974)	10.1	1	0.73	1	0.70	1
Finland (1974)	13.3	4	0.79	3	0.82	4
France (1975)	14.2	7	0.94	7	0.94	11
GDR (1975)	10.9	2	0.76	2	0.75	2
Hungary (1974)	17.8	12	1.14	12	1.16	15
Italy (1978)	12.7	3	0.91	5	1.03[d]	12
Japan (1970)	18.7	15	1.05	8	0.92	10
Netherlands (1974)	13.8	6	0.87	4	0.81	3
Poland (1977)	19.4	16	1.10	11	1.10	14
Soviet Union (1974)	18.1	13	1.33	17	1.17	16
Sweden (1974)	13.4	5	0.92	6	0.87	5
United Kingdom (1970)	16.1	9	1.18	13	0.87	6
United States (1970)	18.4	14	1.26	16	0.88	7

[a]In reference years.
[b]The GRRs and mean age of fertility schedules for each region in the study are given in Appendix 4.
[c]Data are from United Nations (1979).
[d]This value was obtained by interpolating values for 1972 and 1978.

rate is below replacement level. Japan's GRR of 1.05, when combined with the rate of mortality, would also be near or below replacement level.

Another, and perhaps better, way of displaying the distribution of a set of numbers is the box-plot. A box-plot is obtained by plotting the lower and upper quartile values of a batch of numbers and drawing a box to identify the length of the midspread. A vertical bar in the box represents the location of the median. Crosses at the end of the horizontal line drawn outwards from the lower and upper quartiles are the last data points that lie within 1 midspread from the quartiles. This is a modified version by McNeil (1977) of the original rule by Tukey, who put crosses at 1.5 midspreads from the quartiles. We chose the modified rule because when the data have a normal distribution, the proportion of numbers in the batch outside the crosses, on average, approaches the familiar level of 0.05. Numbers that lie outside these crosses are called *outliers*. The box-plots of the distribution of CBRs and GRRs among IIASA countries are given in Figure 4.1. Both distributions for the reference years (the first two) are skewed to the left, and there are no outliers. (Since the scales

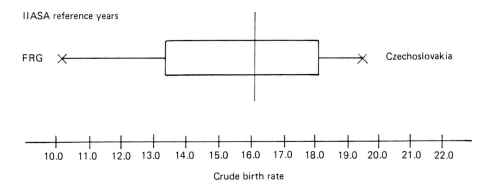

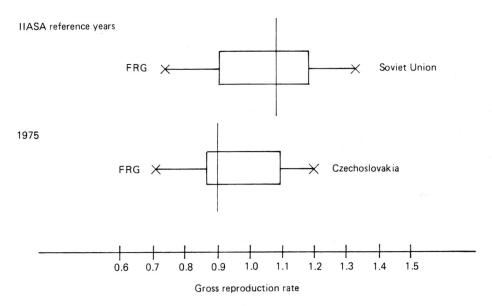

Figure 4.1 Box-plots of the distributions of the crude birth rates and gross reproduction rates among the 17 IIASA countries.

of the two plots are arbitrarily set, the relative lengths of the two measures
should not be compared with each other.)

   Because the levels of fertility have been shifting in recent years, however, more meaningful comparisons of national levels can be made by looking at
the fertility in each country at a fixed point in time. We first examine the time
trend in fertility levels in the 17 IIASA countries. Figures 4.2 and 4.3 show the

time trends observed between 1950 and 1980 in the total fertility rates in selected West European countries plus Canada and in Eastern Europe. Values of the gross reproduction rate for countries that are not included in these figures are presented for the 1970s in Figure 4.4.

The decline in fertility started around 1965 in West European countries (and around 1960 in Canada), but the trend in Eastern Europe since that time is less clear except for the German Democratic Republic. By noting that a TFR of 2.0 corresponds roughly to a GRR of 1.0, we see first that below-replacement fertility is the phenomenon of the 1970s, and second that there is a recent sign of increasing fertility in most West European countries and the German Democratic Republic, where the TFR fell below 2.0. How long these below-replacement levels of fertility will be sustained in the future is a matter of speculation.

To see how the comparison at a fixed point in time differs from the earlier comparison for the various reference years, values of the GRR in 1975 are also presented in Table 4.1, and the distribution is plotted in Figure 4.1. Because fertility in most countries declined between the reference years (usually in the early 1970s) and 1975, we see a decline of about 0.2 in the median value of the GRR to 0.9, and the distribution is now right-skewed on our boxplot. Canada, the US, the UK, and Japan were the largest contributors to this shift. Eleven of the 17 countries had a below-replacement level of GRR in 1975.

We now examine, in somewhat greater detail, national differentials in the levels of fertility as measured by the CBR and GRR. To show the relationship between the two indices graphically, values of the CBR are plotted against those of the GRR in a scatter diagram in Figure 4.5. The coefficient of correlation between the two indices is 0.77, and the dispersion around the fitted line (CBR = 0.97 + 14.14 GRR) tends to be larger for countries with higher fertility levels. Inspection of the graph reveals the implied age distribution of a country. For example, the values of the CBR are higher than might be expected from the values of the GRR in Japan and Poland because of the effect of age distributions: a relatively large proportion of females are of childbearing age. It is the other way around in Austria and the Soviet Union.

To summarize, the GRRs are below unity in seven countries in their respective reference years: the Federal Republic of Germany (1974), the German Democratic Republic (1975), Finland (1974), the Netherlands (1974), Italy (1978), Sweden (1974), and France (1975), in ascending order. At the other end of the range, the Soviet Union (1974), the US (1970), Canada (1971), and Czechoslovakia (1975), listed in descending order, have relatively high fertility levels compared with the other countries, the GRR being 1.2 or above (the highest value being 1.33 for the Soviet Union), but these are still low compared with fertility levels prevailing in the rest of the world. Note that fertility in Canada and the US declined to 0.88 by 1975.

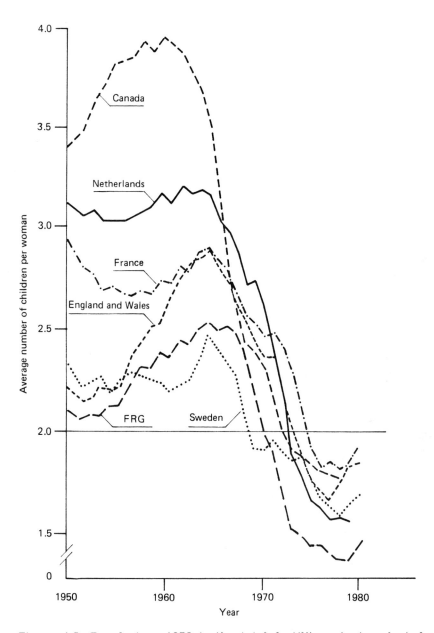

Figure 4.2 Trend since 1950 in the total fertility rate in selected countries of Western Europe and in Canada.
Reproduced with permission from Bourgeois-Pichat (1981).

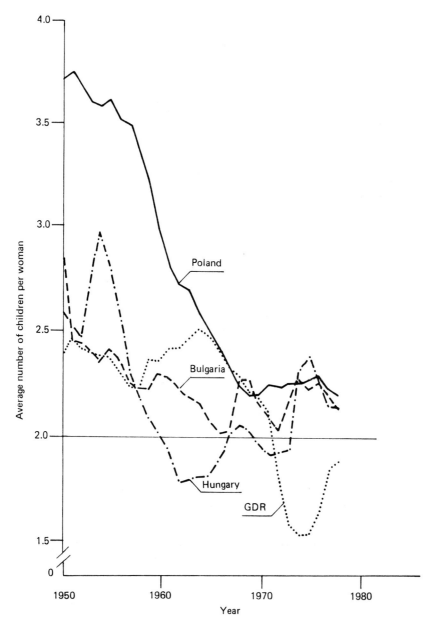

Figure 4.3 Trend since 1950 in the total fertility rate in selected countries of Eastern Europe.
Reproduced with permission from Bourgeois-Pichat (1981).

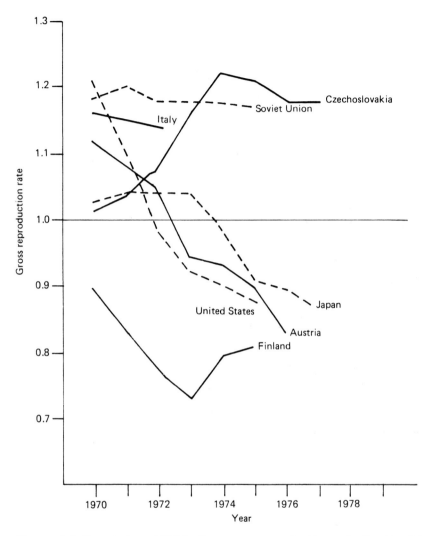

Figure 4.4 Trend since 1970 in the gross reproduction rate for the IIASA countries that are not included in Figures 4.2 and 4.3. Note change in scale from Figures 4.2 and 4.3.
Source: United Nations (1979).

4.3.2 Comparisons Between Regions

As mentioned previously, each of the 17 IIASA countries in the study was disaggregated into regions by the individual authors of the national reports. Because of this, the numbers and sizes of the regions vary considerably from

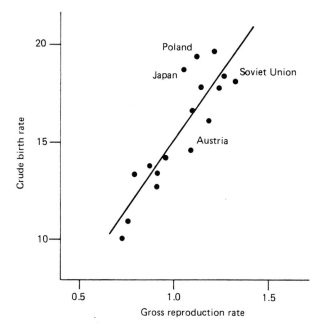

Figure 4.5 Values of the CBR plotted against the GRR in the 17 IIASA study countries.

country to country. Keeping this in mind, we now examine the regional differentials of CBRs in each country. Table 4.2 presents the median and the
midspread of the regional distribution of CBRs together with the extreme
values. They are also set out graphically as box-plots in Figure 4.6. In a box-
plot, a data point that lies between 1.0 and 1.5 times the midspread from
either end of the box is denoted by O, which will be called an *outside* value
following Tukey (1977), and a data point that lies beyond 1.5 times the
midspread from the box is denoted by ⊙ and will be called a *far-out* value. The
cross (×) at the end of the line represents the last data point that lies within
1.0 midspread from the quartiles, as explained in Section 4.3.1.

      We first notice that the median CBR for each country is very close to its
national CBR presented in Table 4.1. The median is the value around which half
of the regions have larger values and half have smaller values, regardless of
the size of the population in each region. The national CBR, on the other hand,
is a weighted average of the regional CBRs, where the weights are the relative
population sizes of the regions. Considering this relationship between the
median CBR and the national CBR, and the diverse manner in which the regions
were defined, the closeness of the two numbers in each country is comforting.
Because the national comparison was made in Section 4.3.1, we do not discuss
the national levels but instead go on to compare regional fertility variations.

Table 4.2 Summary statistics for the regional distribution of the crude birth rate in each IIASA country.

Country (reference year: number of regions)	Crude birth rate (CBR)			
	Median	Midspread	Minimum	Maximum
Austria (1971:9)	15.9	2.2	10.7	19.5
Bulgaria (1975:7)	17.3	2.3	13.6	18.5
Canada (1971:10)	18.5	1.3	16.5	25.5
Czechoslovakia (1975:10)	19.7	1.4	16.5	22.4
FRG (1974:11)	9.8	1.2	7.8	11.1
Finland (1974:12)	12.9	1.7	11.3	15.6
France (1975:8)	14.7	2.3	11.5	17.0
GDR (1975:5)	10.9	0.6	10.2	12.5
Hungary (1974:6)	17.6	1.7	16.4	20.2
Italy (1978:5)	11.2	5.6	10.4	16.8
Japan (1970:8)	17.2	3.0	15.7	20.8
Netherlands (1974:5)	14.0	0.7	12.9	15.1
Poland (1977:13)	19.8	1.5	15.0	21.2
Soviet Union (1974:8)	19.5	4.7	15.8	27.1
Sweden (1974:8)	13.5	1.3	11.9	14.1
United Kingdom (1970:10)	16.1	1.3	15.1	17.3
United States (1970:4)	18.6	1.4	16.9	19.2

The regional variation of the CBR measured by the midspread (unless mentioned otherwise, the variation will always be measured by the midspread) is largest in Italy (5.6), the Soviet Union (4.7), and Japan (3.0). In the rest of the countries, the regional variation in the CBR is small (of the order of 2 per thousand or less). Seven countries have at least one region that has a CBR value far removed (either very low or very high) from those for the rest of the country. Newfoundland in Canada, Eastern Slovakia in Czechoslovakia, the North region of the German Democratic Republic, and the rural areas in the Soviet Union have high far-out values, whereas Vienna in Austria and Warsaw in Poland exhibit low far-out values. Overall, the rural areas of the Soviet Union have the highest CBR (27.1), whereas Hamburg in the FRG has the lowest (7.8) among all regions in the IIASA countries.

Finally, in order to see how the magnitude of these regional variations compares with the national variation, the distribution of national CBRs plotted at the top of Figure 4.1 is presented at the bottom of Figure 4.6. It is interesting to note that the midspread for Italy is larger than the all-IIASA-countries midspread, which is about the same as that of the Soviet Union.

The same summary statistics that were given for the CBR are presented for the GRR in Table 4.3, and the associated box-plots are given in Figure 4.7. Again, the median value of the GRR for each country is extremely close to the value of the national GRR presented in Table 4.1. Countries with large regional variations of the GRR are the Soviet Union (0.66), Italy (0.34), and Canada (0.25). Although the regions in the Soviet Union are defined for this study in a

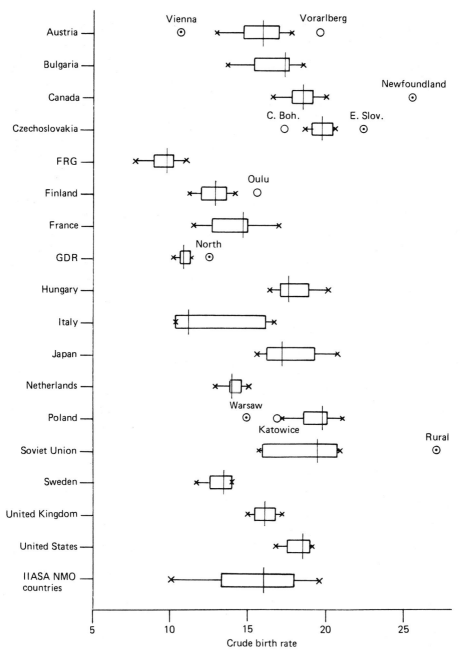

Figure 4.6 Box-plots of the regional distribution of crude birth rates in the IIASA countries, and national distribution among these countries.

rather unusual manner (urban areas of seven geographical regions plus all rural areas for the eighth region), the large regional variation in the Soviet Union is not due to this disaggregation. A large variation in fertility exists between urban areas of geographical regions as well as between urban and rural areas. The GRR ranges from below 1 to almost 2 (a range of two to four children per woman) in different regions. Regional differentials of the GRR in Canada are much smaller than those in the Soviet Union, when measured by the midspread, but the far-out value in Newfoundland makes the range almost as large (0.80) in the former as in the latter. Countries that have small regional variations are Austria, Czechoslovakia, the Federal Republic of Germany, the German Democratic Republic, Hungary, Japan, Sweden, and the US, where the midspread of the CRR is below 0.10. Among these countries, however, Czechoslovakia, Finland, and Hungary have far-out values, which give them a larger range than exists for the Netherlands and the UK, where the distances between the quartiles and extreme values are small. When the interregional variations of fertility are compared with the international variation, we see that the interregional variations in Canada, Italy, and the Soviet Union are larger than the international variation among all IIASA countries.

Table 4.3 Summary statistics for the regional distribution of the gross reproduction rate in each IIASA country.

Country (reference year: number of regions)	Gross reproduction rate (GRR)			
	Median	Midspread	Minimum	Maximum
Austria (1971:9)	1.17	0.08	0.82	1.31
Bulgaria (1975:7)	1.11	0.11	0.96	1.22
Canada (1971:10)	1.35	0.25	1.10	1.90
Czechoslovakia (1975:10)	1.21	0.05	1.08	1.39
FRG (1974:11)	0.72	0.07	0.58	0.81
Finland (1974:12)	0.78	0.06	0.73	0.96
France (1975:8)	0.93	0.16	0.83	1.12
GDR (1975:5)	0.78	0.05	0.74	0.80
Hungary (1974:6)	1.18	0.05	0.99	1.36
Italy (1978:5)	0.82	0.34	0.76	1.17
Japan (1970:8)	1.06	0.05	1.01	1.15
Netherlands (1974:5)	0.98	0.11	0.81	0.98
Poland (1977:13)	1.09	0.18	0.81	1.41
Soviet Union (1974:8)	1.17	0.66	0.97	1.92
Sweden (1974:8)	0.93	0.06	0.86	0.97
United Kingdom (1970:10)	1.20	0.11	1.11	1.26
United States (1970:4)	1.26	0.05	1.22	1.30

When we compare the regional distributions of the CBR (Figure 4.6) with those of the GRR (Figure 4.7), we notice that there is a larger variation between countries in the regional fertility differentials when the GRR is used than when

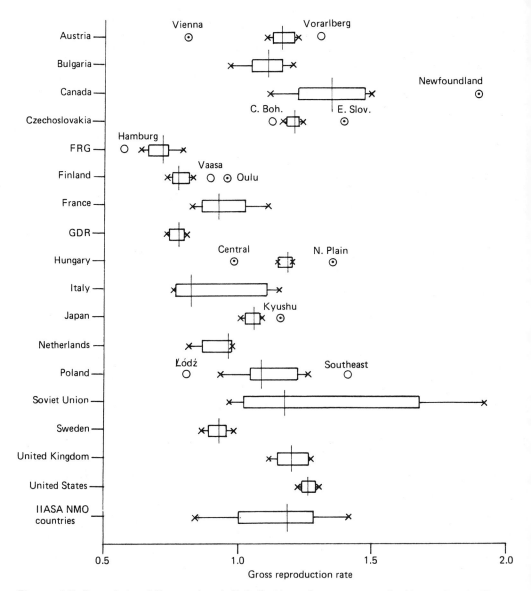

Figure 4.7 Box-plots of the regional distribution of gross reproduction rates in the
IIASA countries, and national distribution among these countries.

the CBR is used. For example, the regional variation of the GRR in the Soviet
Union is more than 10 times that of countries with small regional variations; on
the other hand, the regional variation of the CBR in the Soviet Union is only
about four times that of countries with small regional variations. We also notice

that the relative regional dispersion for a country varies greatly depending on which of the two measures of fertility is used. For example, the regional dispersion is small for the CBR but is large for the GRR in Canada, whereas the opposite is true in Japan. This implies that the fertility behavior is similar but the age—sex structure of the population is different across regions in Japan, whereas in Canada the age—sex structure of regional populations somehow compensates for the differing fertility levels to produce less variable CBRs across regions.

4.4 A Linear Model for Location- and Age-Specific Fertility Rates

In the previous section our interest was in comparing the level of fertility without regard to its age pattern. We now examine age patterns as well as fertility levels in different locations (countries or regions). When we look at the ASFR in various locations, we have a "response" arising as a function of two kinds of factors: location and age. Thus we can imagine a two-way table of responses, with ages of mothers along the columns and locations along the rows. We then fit a linear model to this table using the "median polish" technique developed by Tukey (1977). In this procedure the response in each cell of a two-way table is expressed as:

response = fit + residual,

where

fit = common value + row effect + column effect.

To carry out a median polish of the responses, we first remove row medians from the data and then remove column medians from the resulting residuals. The medians that are removed identify the row effects, the column effects, and the common value.

This procedure is illustrated in Table 4.4 by using the age-specific fertility rates in three broad age categories (15—24, 25—34, and 35—44) in three countries (the Federal Republic of Germany, Poland, and the Soviet Union). The data are presented in Table 4.4 (a). Removing row medians from the data gives the residuals in Table 4.4(b), where the removed medians in the first column are separated from the second column by a vertical line. Next, removing column medians from Table 4.4(b) gives Table 4.4(c), where the removed medians are presented in the first row above the horizontal line. In Table 4.4(c), the number 49.8 is the number taken out of every response and is therefore the effect common to all. The numbers −19.7 and 6.8 are row effects for the Federal Republic of Germany and the Soviet Union, whereas 0.4 and −39.4 are column effects for age groups 25—34 and 35—44. Numbers in the rest of the table are the residuals. For example, the data for age group 35—44 in

Table 4.4 Illustrative example of a median polish: age-specific fertility rates (ASFR) in three age groups in three countries.

Country	Age group		
	15–24	25–34	35–44
(a)			
FRG	30.1	34.7	7.5
Poland	49.8	50.2	9.9
Soviet Union	58.9	56.6	17.2
(b)			
30.1	0	4.6	−22.6
49.8	0	0.4	−39.9
56.6	2.3	0	−39.4
(c)			
49.8	0	0.4	−39.4
−19.7	0	4.2	16.8
0	0	0	−0.5
6.8	2.3	0.4	0

the Soviet Union satisfy

$$17.2 = 49.8 + 6.8 + (−39.4) + 0.$$
$$\text{data} = \text{common} + \text{row} + \text{column} + \text{residual.}$$
$$\text{value} \quad \text{effect} \quad \text{effect}$$

The procedure of removing row and column medians is repeated until the sum of the magnitudes of the residuals is reduced to less than a preassigned value (e.g., 1%) between two successive iterations. In this example, we stopped at the first iteration.

Having carried out the median polish, we may wish to see how well the row-plus-column model fits the data. Since the median of a batch of numbers minimizes the sum of absolute values of the residuals, it is clear that a median polish reduces the sum of the magnitudes of the values in Table 4.4. Therefore, following McNeil (1977), we compare the average size of the residuals with the average deviation of the original data from their median values. We call this measure G (for goodness-of-fit) and define it as

$$G = 1 - \frac{\text{sum of absolute values of residuals}}{\text{sum of absolute values of deviations of the data from the median}},$$

that is, G is the proportionate reduction in the sum of the absolute deviations from the median. It represents the proportion of variation in the data accounted for by the median polish. For the example given in Table 4.4, the sum of the absolute values of the residuals is 24.2 and the sum of the absolute deviations of the data from their median is 150.8, thus

$$G = 1 - \frac{24.2}{150.8} = 0.84 \quad,$$

that is, 84% of the variation in the data is accounted for by the row-plus-column model.

To perform these calculations with fertility data, FORTRAN programs written by McNeil were used with one modification. We adjusted the row effects and column effects to sum to zero, following the familiar rule used in the analysis of variance.

4.4.1 *National Age-Specific Fertility Rates*

We first consider the ASFR in each country and median-polish the fertility data, after setting out the countries as rows and the age groups as columns. Because the ASFR in age group 45–49 in most IIASA study countries is extremely low, this age group has been dropped from the analysis.

The results of the median polish are presented in Table 4.5. The country effects are shown in the second column, and the age effects are shown in the row under the age group identification. The common value is given at the upper left-hand corner and is underlined. The rest of the table shows the pattern of residuals. The ASFR in any cell may be obtained by combining the common value, the country effect, and the row effect with the residual.

We first consider the fitted values of age and country effects, leaving the pattern of residuals to be examined later. As expected, the age effect accounts for most of the variation in the two-way table. The overall age pattern, which may be viewed as an average pattern for the 17 countries, shows a "typical" fertility pattern in which fertility is concentrated in the age group 20–24. The fitted age pattern is presented graphically in Figure 4.8. The scale on the left indicates the deviation (the set of which sums to zero) from the typical value. The largest relative age effect is 35.7 in age group 20–24, and the lowest is −30.2 in age group 40–44, giving a range of 65.9. The relative effect added to the common value of 34.1 gives the absolute value of the fitted ASFR, and this scale is indicated on the right-hand side of the graph. The height from the horizontal line at zero of the absolute scale to the end of the bar in each age group depicts the visual shape of the fitted ASFR.

The country effects range from a low of −6.7 in the Federal Republic of Germany to a high of 8.2 in the Soviet Union, giving a range of 14.9. Since the country effect is expected to represent the relative level of fertility in each country, the country effect from the median polish is plotted against the value of the GRR in Figure 4.9. The data points fall around a straight line (country effect = − 22.81 + 22.02 GRR) except for a few outliers. The most notable outlier is Bulgaria. The coefficient of correlation between the country effect and the GRR is 0.70. Because the deviations of the data points from the expected line seem to be related to the pattern of residuals in the median

Table 4.5 Common value, country effects, and age effects from the median polish of national ASFRs, with the pattern of residuals.[a]

Country (reference year)	Country effects	Age group					
		15–19	20–24	25–29	30–34	35–39	40–44
	34.1	−15.6	35.7	30.9	−0.7	−20.1	−30.2
Austria (1971)	3.3	•	•	–	•	•	•
Bulgaria (1975)	−5.0	++	+++	•	•	•	•
Canada (1971)	7.8	•	•	•	•	•	•
Czechoslovakia (1975)	1.1	•	+++	•	•	•	•
FRG (1974)	−6.7	•	––	–	•	•	•
Finland (1974)	−5.4	•	–	•	•	•	•
France (1975)	−2.0	•	•	•	•	•	•
GDR (1975)	−5.8	+	•	–	–	•	•
Hungary (1974)	−1.3	+	++	•	•	•	•
Italy (1978)	−0.9	–	––	•	•	•	•
Japan (1970)	−3.2	•	•	+++	+	•	•
Netherlands (1974)	−2.6	•	––	•	•	•	•
Poland (1977)	1.4	•	+	•	•	•	•
Soviet Union (1974)	8.2	•	++	+	–	•	•
Sweden (1974)	−1.2	•	–	•	•	•	•
United Kingdom (1970)	5.8	•	•	•	•	•	•
United States (1970)	6.5	•	+	•	•	•	•

[a] • residual lies within 1.0 midspread from the quartiles.
+,– residual lies between 1.0 and 1.5 times the midspread from the quartiles.
++,–– residual lies between 1.5 and 3.0 times the midspread from the quartiles.
+++,––– residual lies more than 3.0 times the midspread from the quartiles.

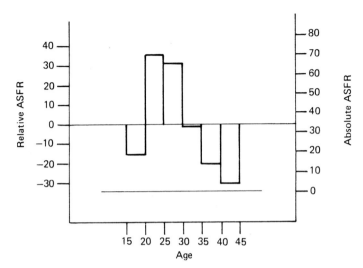

Figure 4.8 Relative and absolute age effects of the national ASFRs obtained by a median polish.

polish, we examine the residuals next, and then come back to the discussion of the deviations of the country effect from the regression line.

Before examining the residuals, however, let us first determine how much variation in the national ASFRs is accounted for by the row-plus-column model. As was explained before, a median polish minimizes the sum of the absolute deviations of the residuals from the median. The procedure is iterated until the improvement in the sum of the magnitudes of the residuals is less than 1%. The sum of the absolute deviations of the 102 original fertility rates (six age groups in 17 countries) from their median is 2334.0 and, after three iterations, the sum of the absolute values of the residuals (since the median of the residuals is zero) reduces to 658.9. Thus the reduction in the residual size is

$$G = 1 - \frac{658.9}{2334.0} = 0.72 \ ,$$

or 72%. Therefore about three-quarters of the variation in the national ASFR is accounted for by the linear model of country effect plus age effect.

Having examined the overall fit of the model, we now inspect the pattern of its residuals in Table 4.5. The median of the residuals is zero, as mentioned above, and the midspread is 7.13. The distribution of the residuals is symmetric, except for a few large positive outliers. Residuals that lie within 1.0 midspread away from either quartile are represented by O and residuals that lie between 1.0 and 1.5 times the width of the midspread from the quartile are represented by − if they are located below the lower quartile, or by + if they are located above the upper quartile to depict the magnitude as well as the

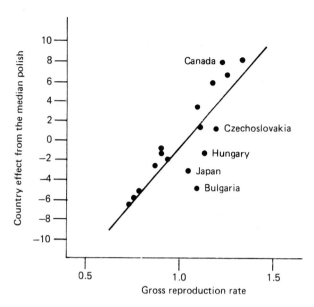

Figure 4.9 The country effect from the median polish of the national ASFRs plotted against the GRR.

sign. Residuals that lie between 1.5 and 3.0 times the width of the midspread from the lower or upper quartile are denoted by −− or ++, and outliers more than 3.0 times the width of the midspread from the quartiles are denoted by −−− and +++. The three largest outlier residuals are all positive and are associated with Bulgaria, Czechoslovakia, and Japan. Of these countries, Bulgaria and Czechoslovakia have a large residual in age group 20–24, whereas Japan exhibits it in age group 25–29. In addition, Hungary and the Soviet Union also show a large positive residual in age group 20–24, indicating more concentrated fertility. In Bulgaria and Hungary, fertility in age group 15–19 is also elevated, implying high fertility in early ages. The structure of residuals in the German Democratic Republic, with a positive residual in age group 15–19 and negative residuals in age groups 25–29 and 30–34, reveals a highly skewed age pattern of childbearing concentrated at early ages. On the other hand, Japan's peak fertility appears in age group 25–29, with negative residuals in early age groups 15–19 and 20–24. This implies that Japan's fertility is extremely concentrated in age group 25–29 and has a narrow spread. On the other hand, the Federal Republic of Germany, Finland, Italy, the Netherlands, and Sweden have a negative residual in age group 20–24, which implies a flatter age pattern in these countries than the overall age pattern shown in Figure 4.8.

Going back to the relative country effect, it is now clear from an inspection of Figure 4.9 that four of the five countries having large positive residuals (Bulgaria, Czechoslovakia, Japan, and Hungary) have lower country effects in the median polish than would be predicted by their GRRs. In retrospect, this could have been expected because the GRR is the sum of the ASFRs over all ages in a country, whereas in the median polish the country effect and the residual together are components of the ASFR. Why the country effect for Canada is larger then expected in the absence of any large negative residuals is not clear.

4.4.2 Regional Age-Specific Fertility Rates

Setting regions out as rows and age groups as columns, we now examine the regional ASFRs within each country by median-polishing them. The results of the 17 separate median polishes are summarized in Table 4.6. The second column presents the common value derived from the median polish, denoted here as the "typical" ASFR value for each country. One can see from the table that the Federal Republic of Germany has the lowest typical value, followed by the German Democratic Republic and Finland. The highest typical value is in Canada, followed by the Soviet Union. Since the typical ASFR value represents an average fertility for the country, we may compare it with the value of the GRR by plotting the two values on a graph (Figure 4.10). The correlation between the two measures is very high, the correlation coefficient being 0.96. As was the case with the country effect, Canada's typical value again deviates from the straight line (typical value $= -1.25 + 35.14$ GRR). A comparison of Figures 4.9 and 4.10 suggests that the typical value for each country from the median polish of *regional* ASFRs represents the relative level of fertility far more accurately than the country effect obtained from the median polish performed on the *national* ASFRs.

Table 4.6 also gives the age effects obtained from the median polish of the regional ASFRs in each country. These age effects represent the relative age pattern of fertility for the country from the regional data, that is, they are deviations from their respective typical values. Figure 4.11 shows these age patterns graphically, where the zero line represents the typical ASFR value for each country. As was shown in Figure 4.8, a visual shape of the fitted absolute ASFR may be obtained by connecting the end of the bar in each age group from the horizontal line drawn near the end of the bar for the last age group. This line represents the absolute level of zero for each country. The bar graphs in Figure 4.11 illustrate, therefore, the level as well as the age pattern of fertility.

Among the 17 IIASA countries, the highest fertility in early ages (age groups 15–19 and 20–24) is shown in Bulgaria; it is one of the two countries where the level of fertility in age group 15–19 is as high as the average level of fertility for the country (the other being the German Democratic Republic).

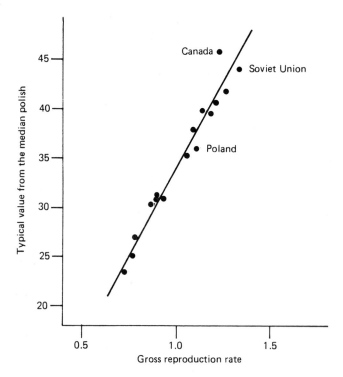

Figure 4.10 The typical value from the median polish of the regional ASFR in each country plotted against the GRR.

In addition, Czechoslovakia, the German Democratic Republic, and Hungary also show high fertility at early ages. (Although the German Democratic Republic follows this age pattern of early fertility, its fertility level is low.) In contrast to this pattern, Italy, Japan, the Netherlands, and Sweden have the highest fertility in age group 25–29. In addition to these countries, the Federal Republic of Germany, Finland, France, the Soviet Union, and the UK exhibit a flat age pattern, where the fertility in age groups 20–24 and 25–29 are about equal. These results are consistent with the observation inferred from the structure of residuals of the age-plus-country effect model fitted to the national ASFRs.

Let us next examine the regional effects in each country. Because the numbers and sizes of regions vary widely from country to country, and because our interest is in international comparison of the degree of interregional variation within a country, we focus on summary statistics of the variation; the midspread and range of the regional effects are given in Table 4.6. The highest regional variation as measured by the range is to be found in the Soviet Union, which shows a range of 34.3; this is followed by Canada, Poland, Austria, and

Table 4.6 The typical value, age effects, and regional effects from a median polish of the regional ASFRs, by country.

Country (reference year: number of regions)	Typical ASFR value	Age effects						Regional effects		Goodness-of-fit
		15–19	20–24	25–29	30–34	35–39	40–44	Midspread	Range	
Austria (1971:9)	38.0	−12.5	38.6	21.7	1.9	−17.0	−32.7	3.4	17.0	0.84
Bulgaria (1975:7)	37.5	−1.3	65.6	19.3	−17.3	−31.0	−35.2	2.5	4.7	0.91
Canada (1971:10)	45.9	−19.7	40.0	34.4	1.9	−20.1	−36.5	7.6	26.3	0.88
Czechoslovakia (1975:10)	40.6	−13.0	65.5	27.5	−11.1	−30.7	−38.2	2.2	6.8	0.88
FRG (1974:11)	23.6	−8.8	23.3	20.6	−0.7	−13.6	−20.8	2.5	6.6	0.91
Finland (1974:12)	26.9	−13.7	24.5	26.2	1.8	−15.0	−23.6	1.8	9.3	0.91
France (1975:8)	31.0	−18.4	29.8	30.1	1.6	−16.6	−26.7	3.4	6.7	0.91
GDR (1975:5)	25.2	−1.6	43.8	12.1	−10.4	−20.1	−23.8	0.8	1.2	0.94
Hungary (1974:6)	39.8	−6.6	58.6	24.7	−9.7	−29.7	−37.2	1.2	8.1	0.91
Italy (1978:5)	30.9	−13.5	19.4	26.9	5.7	−14.9	−23.7	11.0	14.1	0.89
Japan (1970:8)	35.4	−33.0	20.5	69.8	3.8	−27.2	−34.0	0.5	3.3	0.92
Netherlands (1974:5)	30.3	−21.6	23.5	42.2	1.4	−18.6	−27.0	2.4	4.1	0.92
Poland (1977:13)	36.0	−18.9	47.0	26.5	−1.8	−21.2	−31.6	5.2	18.0	0.85
Soviet Union (1974:8)	44.0	−23.1	47.2	43.8	−15.3	−17.4	−35.2	16.8	34.3	0.08
Sweden (1974:8)	30.9	−19.8	25.6	34.0	6.1	−18.0	−27.9	1.2	2.3	0.94
United Kingdom (1970:10)	39.7	−14.1	39.2	35.5	−2.0	−23.0	−35.6	2.6	4.6	0.93
United States (1970:4)	41.9	−9.3	44.9	32.5	−4.5	−25.8	−37.8	1.4	1.8	0.90

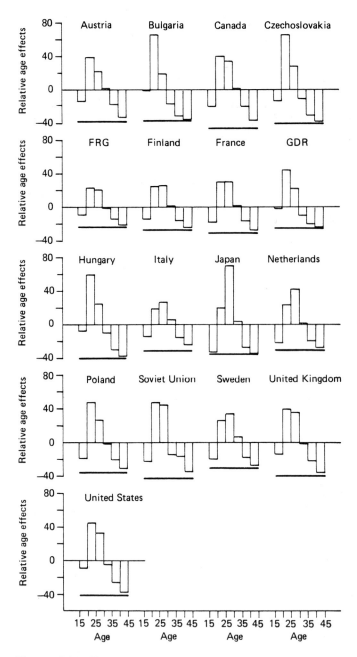

Figure 4.11 The relative age effects for the six age groups from the median polishes of the regional ASFRs, by country.

Italy. In terms of the midspread, the Soviet Union and Italy continue to have large relative values, but the relative values for Austria, Poland, and Canada are much less prominent. Large ranges of variation in the latter group of countries were caused by extreme levels of fertility in just one or two regions relative to the rest of their respective countries, whereas countries in the former group have large overall fertility differentials between regions. Countries that show the smallest interregional variation in the level of fertility are the German Democratic Republic, the US, and Sweden. The small regional variation in the US might be due to the country being divided into only four vast regions. Again, these results are consistent with the observations made in terms of the regional distribution of the GRR in each country presented in Figure 4.7.

Finally, we examine the goodness-of-fit of the region-plus-age model for each country. Each of the 17 median polishes produced a structure of residuals similar to those presented in Table 4.5. Because it is impractical to set out 17 such tables, they are not presented here. Instead, the measure G, which represents the proportion of interregional variation explained by the model and, hence, summarizes the degree of regional uniformity in the age pattern of fertility, is presented in the last column of Table 4.6. The value of G in most countries hovers around 0.90; the highest value is 0.94 for Sweden and the German Democratic Republic, which indicates a small regional variation in age patterns of fertility, and the lowest value is about 0.80 for the Soviet Union, which is a negative outlier, indicating a large regional variation in age patterns of fertility. Austria and Poland also show high variations, although they are not as high as those in the Soviet Union.

The last two points of the above discussion deal with interregional variation in fertility levels and age patterns of childbearing. Variation in fertility levels is summarized by the midspread or range of the regional effects, whereas variation in age patterns is summarized by the measure G. We notice that a country with large (small) variation in fertility levels also tends to exhibit large (small) variation in age patterns of childbearing. Because fertility decline usually results from a decline in young ages (through later age at marriage or postponement of the first birth after marriage) or in old ages (by limiting family size), the decline in overall fertility level accompanies shifts in the age pattern of childbearing. Sweden and the German Democratic Republic have extremely small interregional variations in both fertility levels and age patterns. Although the US has a comparably small variation in fertility levels, age pattern differentiation is larger than those in the aforementioned two countries. The UK, Japan, and the Netherlands also show small interregional variations. At the other end of the scale, the Soviet Union has by far the largest interregional variation in fertility, both in level and age pattern. High variability among the rest of the countries is shown in Austria and Poland but, as noted earlier, it is mainly because of the outlier regions in these countries. Canada shows a relatively higher variation in fertility level than in age pattern.

4.5 A Relational Gompertz Fertility Model

In this section we are interested only in the age pattern of childbearing, without regard to differing levels of fertility. Hence in this part of the analysis the ASFRs are adjusted for the value of the GRR, so that when the age distribution is cumulated to the end of childbearing ages, the cumulated value at the end is always unity. Therefore, terms like age pattern or age distribution in this section refer to density functions.

It has been pointed out in the literature that the cumulative distribution function of the ASFR closely follows a Gompertz curve, with a fit that is good over the central range of childbearing ages but less satisfactory over the tails (Brass 1980, Murphy and Nagnur 1972). In the following we briefly summarize the properties of the Gompertz function and then explain how the poor fit at lower and upper ages of child bearing is improved by the relational model.

If a cumulative distribution function $F(x)$ obeys a Gompertz function

$$F(x) = \exp\{-\exp[-\lambda(x - \mu)]\} \ ,$$

then the density function is given by

$$f(x) = \lambda \exp\{-\lambda(x - \mu)\exp[-\lambda(x - \mu)]\} \ ,$$

where λ and μ are positive parameters. This density function is a double-exponential function similar to that used by Coale and McNeil (1972) for first marriages and by Rogers and Castro (1981c) for migration schedules. This density function has one less parameter than the more general double-exponential functions used for first marriages and migration schedules. Because

$$\frac{df(x)}{dx} = 0 \quad \text{at } x = \mu$$

and

$$\frac{d^2 f(x)}{dx^2} = -\frac{\lambda^3}{e} \quad \text{at } x = \mu \ ,$$

the density function $f(x)$ is unimodal with a peak at $x = \mu$. It is clear the μ is a location parameter, while λ is a shape parameter. A large value of μ is associated with a later peak in the childbearing ages, whereas a large value of λ is associated with a narrow spread of the age distribution.

For the Gompertz function $F(x)$, there exists a linearizing transformation:

$$Y(x) = -\ln[-\ln F(x)] = \lambda(x - \mu) \ .$$

Since a linear transformation of a linear function is again linear, the $-\ln(-\ln)$ transformations of several Gompertz curves are related linearly to each other. For example, if we relate the transform $Y(x)$ to a standard transform $Y_s(x) = \lambda_s(x - \mu_s)$ linearly by

$$Y(x) = A + BY_s(x) ,$$

then the parameters A and B represent

$$A = \lambda(\mu_s - \mu) \quad B = \frac{\lambda}{\lambda_s} .$$

Therefore, a large A implies an earlier age of childbearing, whereas a value of B larger than unity implies a more peaked fertility schedule than the standard density function.

The relational Gompertz model is a generalization of the above. Even when the distribution functions do not obey the Gompertz function exactly, if they deviate from it in much the same way, the transformed nonlinear functions still may be related linearly. For example, the nonlinear transformation $Y(x)$ given by

$$Y(x) = -\ln[-\ln F(x)]$$

is related linearly to the transformation $Y_s(x)$ of a standard distribution function $F_s(x)$ that belongs to the same family by the expression

$$Y(x) = A + BY_s(x) ,$$

where A and B are constants. The standard function presented by Brass (1980) is used as our standard $Y_s(x)$ in this analysis, and the parameters A and B are estimated for each age pattern using the least-squares method. The cumulative distribution function is obtained by the inverse transformation

$$F(x) = \exp[-\exp(-Y(x))]$$

and the density function is obtained by differencing the cumulative values at adjacent ages,

$$f(x) = F(x) - F(x-1) .$$

The standard density function generated in this way from the standard function $Y_s(x)$ had a dip at age 39; this was corrected to give a smooth curve. The role of parameters A and B in the relational model when $Y(x)$ is nonlinear is not as simple as that described earlier in the linear case. When $Y(x)$ is nonlinear, a change in A not only shifts the location of the curve along the age axis, but also affects the peakedness and skewness of the density function. A change in B also changes the location and skewness in addition to the peakedness. These properties are shown in Figures 4.12 and 4.13.

In applying the relational model to our fertility data in five-year age groups, cumulated fertility rates at ages 20, 25, 30, 35, 40, and 45 are used (the value at age 50 being unity by definition). Because of the low fertility rate in age group 45–49, however, the cumulated value at age 45 is nearly 1, which makes $Y(45)$ unstable. Therefore, the cumulative value at age 45 is excluded and only five values up to age 40 are used in the analysis.

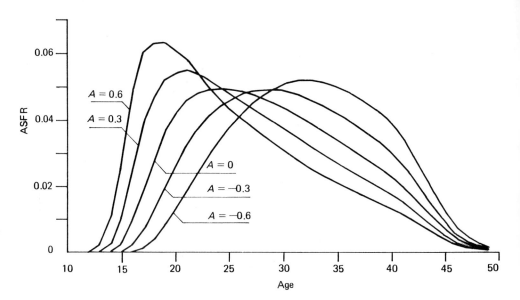

Figure 4.12 Standard age-specific fertility pattern ($A = 0$), and patterns for selected values of A in the relational model.

4.5.1 *Patterns of National Age-Specific Fertility Rates*

Before fitting the relational Gompertz model, whose parameters will not
be familiar to most readers, we calculate more familiar measures for the purpose of easy reference. The mean, standard deviation, and skewness of the
ASFR for each country are presented in Table 4.7. The mean age at childbearing
ranges from a low of 24.5 years in Bulgaria to a high of 27.9 years in Japan, giving a spread of 3.4 years. The range of the standard deviation of the childbearing pattern is 2.1 years, from a low of 4.3 years in Japan to a high of 6.4
years in Austria. In general, early mean age is associated with large standard
deviation and skewness, but there are irregularities. Next, each of the 17
national age patterns of fertility will be fitted by the relational Gompertz
model, and the estimated parameters A and B in the relational model will be
compared with the mean and standard deviation of the age schedule of fertility.

Estimated values of A and B are presented in Table 4.8 together with
values of R^2 (proportion of variance explained by the linear fit). Values of R^2
are extremely high for all countries,,but we shall see later that the almost
perfect linear fit (e.g., $R^2 = 0.999$) of $Y(x)$ to $Y_s(x)$ does not necessarily generate a good fit of the density function. We first examine the estimated values
of A and B for each country. The values of A range from a low of -0.22 to a

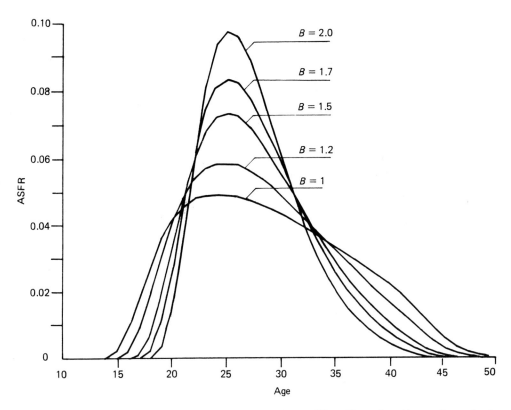

Figure 4.13 Standard age-specific fertility pattern ($B = 1$), and patterns for selected values of B in the relational model.

high of 0.67. Bulgaria, the German Democratic Republic, Hungary, and
Czechoslovakia have high values of A, whereas Japan has by far the lowest
value, -0.22. In addition to Japan, the Netherlands also has a negative value of
A. As mentioned earlier, a high (low) value of A shifts the age distribution to
younger (older) ages and, hence, implies higher (lower) fertility at early ages.
The estimated value of A reflects our earlier observation of the national age
pattern; childbearing is high at young ages, with consequently a low mean age
of childbearing, in such East European countries as Bulgaria, Czechoslovakia,
the German Democratic Republic, and Hungary, whereas childbearing at young
ages is low in Japan, Italy, and the Netherlands. In order to show how well the
estimated A in the relational model depicts the timing of childbearing more
systematically, values of A are plotted against the mean ages (μ) of the ASFR in
Figure 4.14. There is an almost perfect linear relationship between the two
measures ($A = 6.267 - 0.229\mu$; $R^2 = 0.979$). The only point that deviates from
the regression line at the bottom right depicts the values for Japan.

Table 4.7 The mean, standard deviation, and skewness of the age pattern of fertility, by country.

Country (reference year)	Mean	Standard deviation	Skewness
Austria (1971)	26.7	6.4	0.55
Bulgaria (1975)	24.5	5.1	0.80
Canada (1971)	27.3	6.1	0.53
Czechoslovakia (1975)	25.4	5.2	0.71
FRG (1974)	26.9	5.9	0.55
Finland (1974)	27.0	5.7	0.52
France (1975)	27.1	5.7	0.60
GDR (1975)	24.6	5.1	0.84
Hungary (1974)	25.4	5.4	0.64
Italy (1978)	27.5	6.0	0.40
Japan (1970)	27.9	4.3	0.51
Netherlands (1974)	27.4	5.2	0.58
Poland (1977)	26.7	5.7	0.70
Soviet Union (1974)	27.0	6.0	0.81
Sweden (1974)	27.3	5.4	0.43
United Kingdom (1970)	26.7	5.8	0.52
United States (1970)	26.1	5.9	0.58

Table 4.8 The estimated coefficients in the relational model fitted to the national fertility age pattern, by country.

Country (reference year)	Parameter		
	A	B	R^2
Austria (1971)	0.190	1.276	0.9998
Bulgaria (1975)	0.671	1.683	0.9969
Canada (1971)	0.060	1.310	0.9991
Czechoslovakia (1975)	0.428	1.678	0.9995
FRG (1974)	0.132	1.391	0.9987
Finland (1974)	0.109	1.467	0.9993
France (1975)	0.061	1.436	0.9981
GDR (1975)	0.636	1.636	0.9970
Hungary (1974)	0.438	1.592	0.9995
Italy (1978)	0.032	1.380	0.9989
Japan (1970)	−0.216	1.993	0.9974
Netherlands (1974)	−0.016	1.585	0.9962
Poland (1977)	0.156	1.432	0.9972
Soviet Union (1974)	0.103	1.324	0.9897
Sweden (1974)	0.027	1.581	0.9993
United kingdom (1970)	0.171	1.441	0.9995
United States (1970)	0.300	1.434	0.9996

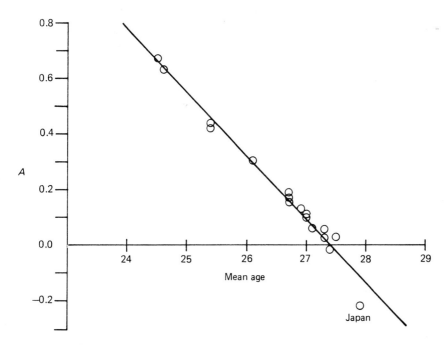

Figure 4.14 Estimated coefficient A in the relational model plotted against the mean of the age schedule of fertility.

The estimated value of B ranges from a minimum of 1.28 in Austria to a maximum of 1.99 in Japan. The values of B in all 17 IIASA countries are larger than 1, indicating that the age pattern in these countries has a smaller variance than the variance of the adopted standard age pattern. To confirm the seemingly good indication of B representing the spread of the ASFRs, values of B are plotted against standard deviations of the age-specific schedules in Figure 4.15. Again, the parameter B is almost perfectly linearly related to the standard deviation σ ($B = 3.456 - 0.349\sigma$; $R^2 = 0.967$). The point at the upper left represents Japan, which has an extremely narrow spread in the age schedule of childbearing, as noted earlier.

Having established that the estimated parameters A and B correspond closely to the mean and standard deviation of the age pattern of fertility, we now examine A and B for a country simultaneously. Inspection of A and B simultaneously reveals that, except for Japan, countries with a high value of A tend also to have a high value of B. The value of B is plotted against that of A in Figure 4.16. The one outstanding point at the top left represents Japan with its unusual fertility pattern of a late beginning and a small spread. Points at the upper right represent Bulgaria, Czechoslovakia, the German Democratic Republic, and Hungary. In these countries, the values of both A and B are

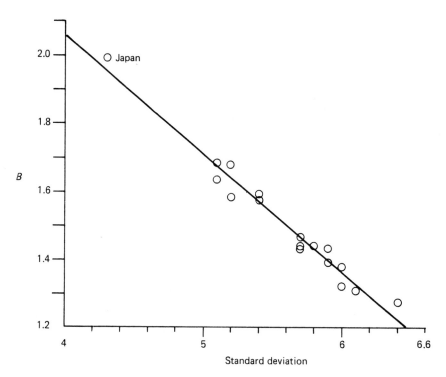

Figure 4.15 Estimated coefficient B in the relational model plotted against the standard deviation of the age schedule of fertility.

high, characterizing high fertility in the first two age groups with much reduced fertility in subsequent age groups. Among these four countries, Bulgaria and the German Democratic Republic are depicted by the rightmost points, indicating an earlier age of childbearing. The remaining countries form the rest of the group. The points for two of these countries are somewhat removed to the upper left. These represent the Netherlands and Sweden, where childbearing starts relatively late and ends early. The lowest point on the plot reflects Austria's largest age variance in fertility among all IIASA countries.

In summary, the horizontal position in Figure 4.16 represents the timing of childbearing (earlier childbearing as one moves to the right), whereas the vertical position represents the age variation of childbearing (larger age variability as one moves downward).

Next, using the estimated A and B for each country, the cumulative distribution function $F(x)$ is generated by the double-exponential transformation; finally, the density function $f(x)$ is generated by differencing $F(x)$. Figure 4.17 represents both the original data (country ASFR normalized to unit

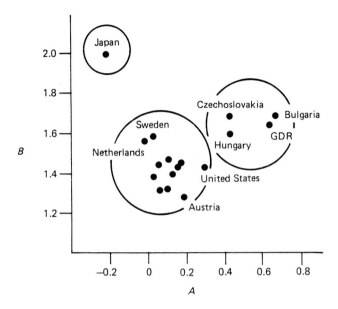

Figure 4.16 The value of B plotted against the value of A in the relational Gompertz model.

area) and the density curve generated by the relational model. Tests of the goodness-of-fit are not performed; instead, the fit is inspected by comparing the area under the curve and the area occupied by the bar in each five-year age interval. The fits seem remarkably good, especially for the West European countries, Canada, and the US, but they are less satisfactory for the East European countries and Japan. This is because of the particular pattern of the standard curve used, which depicts an age pattern with the highest fertility in age group 20–24 and a slowly declining fertility thereafter. (Recall the curve with $A = 0$ in Figure 4.12 or $B = 1$ in Figure 4.13.) Considering that fertility data in five-year age groups (cumulative values at only five points) are used with only one standard age pattern, the results are encouraging. The two parameters A and B of the relational Gompertz model clearly highlight the characteristics of a given age pattern and reproduce a continuous age pattern associated with it from only five data points.

4.5.2 Patterns of Regional Age-Specific Fertility Rates

Before summarizing the regional distributions of A and B of the relative Gompertz model, we present in Table 4.9 the regional distributions of the mean and standard deviation of the ASFRs as summarized by the midspread and range.

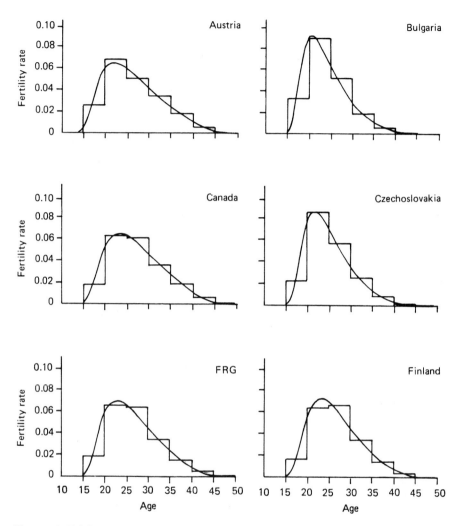

Figure 4.17(a) The age-specific fertility rates and the relational fit, by country.

In Austria, Canada, Czechoslovakia, and the Soviet Union, there are large regional variations in the mean age at childbearing (ranges of about two years, and midspreads of about one year). In Bulgaria and Poland, regional variation in timing of childbearing is large when measured by the range (almost two years) but is small when measured by the midspread. The regional variation in the standard deviation of age at childbearing is large in the Soviet Union, Italy, and Canada. Thus the age pattern of childbearing varies markedly in the Soviet Union in terms of both the timing and spread, whereas only the timing

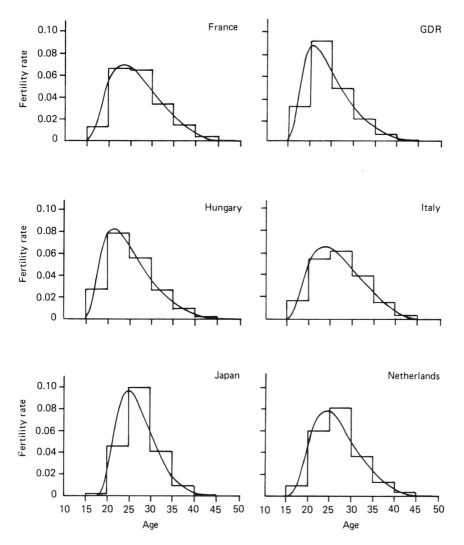

Figure 4.17(b) The age-specific fertility rates and the relational fit, by country.

varies in Austria and Czechoslovakia, while only the spread in age pattern varies widely in Italy.

The relational Gompertz model, using the same standard as that used for the national patterns, is then fitted to the regional ASFRs in each country. As in Section 4.4.2, instead of presenting all values for each region in each country, which would be too cumbersome for any meaningful comparison, the results are summarized in Table 4.10. To permit examination of the regional

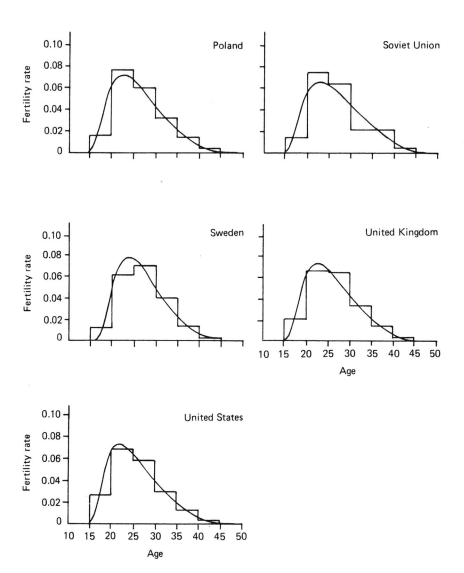

Figure 4.17(c) The age specific fertility rates and the relational fit, by country.

variations in estimated A and B within each country, the midspread and range of the regional values are presented.

The regional variation in A, which summarizes the timing of childbearing, is large in Austria, Canada, Czechoslovakia, and the Soviet Union; the regional variation in B, which summarizes the age spread of childbearing, is large in Czechoslovakia, Italy, and the Soviet Union. If the variation in A is large for a

Table 4.9 The midspread and range of the mean and standard deviation of the regional age pattern of fertility, by country.

Country (reference year)	Mean		Standard deviation	
	Midspread	Range	Midspread	Range
Austria (1971)	0.8	2.1	0.2	0.6
Bulgaria (1975)	0.2	1.5	0.2	0.5
Canada (1971)	1.0	1.7	0.4	0.5
Czechoslovakia (1975)	0.9	1.6	0.2	0.6
FRG (1974)	0.4	1.0	0.2	0.4
Finland (1974)	0.7	1.1	0.2	0.7
France (1975)	0.2	0.5	0.2	0.4
GDR (1975)	0.4	0.5	0.1	0.4
Hungary (1974)	0.4	0.9	0.2	0.4
Italy (1978)	0.7	0.8	0.5	0.7
Japan (1970)	0.6	1.2	0.2	0.3
Netherlands (1974)	0.2	0.7	0.2	0.2
Poland (1977)	0.5	1.9	0.1	0.5
Soviet Union (1974)	0.9	2.1	0.7	1.1
Sweden (1974)	0.3	0.6	0.1	0.2
United Kingdom (1970)	0.4	0.7	0.2	0.3
United States (1970)	0.6	1.0	0.1	0.2

Table 4.10 The midspread and range of the estimated regional parameters of the relational Gompertz model, by country.

Country (reference year: number of regions)	A		B	
	Midspread	Range	Midspread	Range
Austria (1971:9)	0.16	0.40	0.05	0.20
Bulgaria (1975:7)	0.06	0.38	0.06	0.18
Canada (1971:10)	0.17	0.33	0.10	0.21
Czechoslovakia (1975:10)	0.23	0.38	0.19	0.36
FRG (1974:11)	0.08	0.20	0.08	0.18
Finland (1974:12)	0.14	0.20	0.12	0.27
France (1975:8)	0.06	0.14	0.08	0.12
GDR (1975:5)	0.09	0.13	0.01	0.09
Hungary (1974:6)	0.09	0.21	0.05	0.17
Italy (1978:5)	0.07	0.12	0.17	0.22
Japan (1970:8)	0.14	0.28	0.14	0.21
Netherlands (1974:5)	0.05	0.14	0.09	0.11
Poland (1977:13)	0.10	0.41	0.06	0.25
Soviet Union (1974:8)	0.15	0.38	0.29	0.43
Sweden (1974:8)	0.05	0.12	0.03	0.14
United Kingdom (1970:10)	0.07	0.14	0.05	0.10
United States (1970:4)	0.13	0.23	0.04	0.07

country, the variation in B is also large in general, but this pattern is not regular. For example, Austria has an extremely small variation in B without having a corresponding small variation in A, whereas Italy has a large variation in B without a large variation in A. It is suspected that a relatively large variation in B in Japan, in the light of its small variation in the standard deviation of the age pattern, is an artifact due to the poor fit of the Japanese age pattern to the standard chosen for this study. Because the estimated values of A and B in a region are not independent of each other, they perhaps should be compared as a pair rather than separately as two numbers. The midspreads and ranges of A and B for a country nevertheless reflect differing degrees of regional variation (as do the mean and variance), and they identify countries with large or small regional variations in the age pattern of childbearing that are consistent with both Table 4.9 and the results given in Section 4.4.2. Finally, we note that a "large" regional variation in fertility age patterns refers to a dispersion of about one year in midspread or two years in range for the mean age, and about half of those figures for the standard deviation.

4.6 Conclusion

Fertility differentials between IIASA countries have been studied systematically in this chapter. However, it should be kept in mind that observations made here are contingent upon the data that were used in the analyses. Some problems with the data include differing reference years for the countries in a period when fertility was shifting rather rapidly, and differing ways in which regions were defined in each country.

Comparisons were made at two levels throughout the chapter. The first involved international comparison of national measures and the second involved two steps: interregional comparison of regional measures in each country and international comparison of the degree of interregional variation. The midspread and range of the distribution were used as measures of variation of the distribution. We were interested in two aspects of fertility differentials: the overall level and the age pattern.

As a first step, only the level of fertility was considered without regard to differing age patterns in Section 4.3. Although parallel comparisons were made with regard to both CBRs and GRRs, emphasis was given to the GRR as a measure of fertility level. The GRR in the reference years is below unity in seven countries: in ascending order, the Federal Republic of Germany (1974), the German Democratic Republic (1975), Finland (1974), the Netherlands (1974), Italy (1978), Sweden (1974), and France (1975); at the other end of the scale, it is highest in the Soviet Union (1974), with a GRR of 1.33. The effect of rather dramatic fertility decline in the Western countries since around 1965 is reflected in the comparatively high fertility levels for Canada (1971), the UK (1970), and the US (1970), in contrast to data in other countries that describe conditions around 1975. Collectively, the median value of the GRR is 1.09 with a midspread of 0.27, showing that fertility levels in the 17 countries are much lower than those prevailing in the rest of the world. When we examine the fertility data for 1975 for all IIASA countries to account for the effect of the difference in the reference years, we see that the GRRs in Austria, Canada, Japan, the UK, and the US all went down to below one, while Italy's GRR went up to above one (because Italy's reference year was 1978). Thus 11 of the 17 IIASA countries had a GRR value less than 1.0 in 1975 with the median value of 0.9.

Interregional variation in the GRR, as measured by the midspread of the regional distribution, is by far the largest in the Soviet Union (0.66). Countries that show small regional variations are Austria, Czechoslovakia, the Federal Republic of Germany, Finland, the German Democratic Republic, Hungary, Japan, Sweden, and the US, where the midspread is below 0.10. This large variation between countries in regional fertility differentials of the GRR (more than 10-fold) is much reduced when the regional differentials of the CBR are compared between countries (Figures 4.6 and 4.7).

To investigate the level and age pattern of fertility simultaneously, the ASFRs in different locations (countries in the case of international comparison, and regions in the case of interregional comparison) were considered as a two-way table in Section 4.4. The age effects and location effects in the linear model were estimated by Tukey's median polish together with the magnitude and pattern of residuals. Seventy-two percent of the variation in the national ASFRs is accounted for by the age-plus-country effect model, in which age effects contribute about four times as much variation as country effects. The relative country effects represent relative levels of fertility (studied in Section 4.3), whereas the relative age effects represent the overall age pattern of childbearing in all 17 IIASA countries. The magnitude and pattern of residuals in each country represent a departure of that country's age pattern from the overall pattern, thus indicating a difference in national age patterns. The distinct age pattern in Japan, where fertility is concentrated in age group 25–29, as well as the East European pattern, in which fertility is high at early ages (in age groups 15–19 and 20–24) in Bulgaria, Czechoslovakia, the German Democratic Republic, and Hungary, is separated from that of the rest of the countries. It is interesting to note that very different fertility patterns appear in the Federal Republic of Germany than in the German Democratic Republic; the former exhibits a typically Western pattern and the latter shows a typically East European pattern.

From the median polish of the regional ASFRs in each country, we obtained the typical value that summarizes the overall country level, the age effects that represent an average age pattern for that country, and the regional effects that give relative levels of fertility in each region. The magnitude and pattern of residuals in the resultant table represent the degree of inter-regional variation in the age pattern of childbearing: the measure G of goodness-of-fit of the model summarizes this. We found that the typical value for a country from the analysis of regional ASFRs correlates better with the GRR than does the country effect from the analysis of national ASFRs. The relative magnitude of interregional variation in the fertility level in each country obtained from this analysis is consistent with the results in Section 4.3: small in Sweden, the German Democratic Republic, and the US, and large in Canada, Italy, Austria, and Poland with the largest in the Soviet Union. Differing national age patterns of childbearing, which were suggested by the structure of residuals in the median polish of national ASFRs, were confirmed by the estimated age effects in this analysis. Finally, interregional variation in the age pattern (measured by G) is small in Sweden, the German Democratic Republic, and the UK, large in Austria and Poland, and largest in the Soviet Union. Thus countries that have large interregional variations in fertility levels tend also to have large interregional variations in their age patterns of fertility.

Finally, after adjusting for differing levels, the age pattern of fertility was studied in more detail (Section 4.5), taking both the timing and age dispersion into account. The fertility age distribution was fitted using Brass's relational Gompertz fertility model. Estimated values of the parameters A and B in the model characterize the timing and age spread that are consistent with the mean and standard deviation of the ASFRs in five-year age groups. Parameters from the national age pattern distinctly differentiate the early childbearing East European pattern, the late childbearing and centrally concentrated Japanese pattern, and the more typical Western pattern. In general, early age at childbearing is associated with a small spread of the age distribution, but Japan is an exception. When the single-year age distribution is generated using the estimated parameters A and B, the fit of the generated curve to the five-year ASFRs is more satisfactory for the Western than for the Eastern pattern or for Japan. This is because the standard age pattern of fertility used in this analysis is similar to that found in Western Europe.

Interregional variation in the age pattern of fertility was obtained by fitting the regional age patterns and comparing the estimated regional parameters of timing (A) and age spread (B). Interregional variation in the timing is large in Austria, Canada, Czechoslovakia, and the Soviet Union, and small in France, the German Democratic Republic, Italy, the Netherlands, Sweden, and the UK. On the other hand, interregional variation in age dispersion is large in Czechoslovakia, Italy, Japan, and the Soviet Union, and small in the German Democratic Republic, Sweden, the UK, and the US. Large (small) interregional variation in timing of childbearing is usually accompanied by a correspondingly large (small) interregional variation in age dispersion, but the correspondence is not regular. It is suspected that when the chosen standard fits poorly to the given age schedule, the estimated B is less reliable as a measure of the spread of the age distribution.

To summarize, a country with a high fertility level tends to have a large interregional variation in fertility levels, which is also accompanied by a large interregional variation in age schedules of fertility, again in terms of both the timing and age dispersion. The Soviet Union exhibits by far the largest variations, followed by Canada and Italy. Countries with the lowest and most uniform fertility include Sweden and the German Democratic Republic. Countries with outlier regions (e.g., Austria) present conflicting pictures, depending on whether the midspread or range is used as a criterion. Countries that are not mentioned specifically in the discussion fall into the middle-of-the-road category by implication.

APPENDIX 4:   The Gross Reproduction Rates (total, under 30, and over 30 years of age) and the Mean Age of Fertility Schedule for Each Region in the Migration and Settlement Study

Country (reference year) and region	Population (1)	GRR (2)	Fertility Mean age of fert.sched. (3)	GRR(<30) (4)	GRR(>30) (5)
Austria (1971)					
Burgenland	272119.	1.16	25.96	0.882	0.274
Carinthia	525728.	1.22	27.12	0.853	0.363
Lower Austria	1414161.	1.10	26.34	0.810	0.293
Upper Austria	1223444.	1.19	27.00	0.832	0.359
Salzburg	401766.	1.17	26.96	0.823	0.344
Styria	1192100.	1.13	26.77	0.806	0.329
Tyrol	540771.	1.23	27.94	0.792	0.437
Vorarlberg	271473.	1.31	27.66	0.888	0.423
Vienna	1614841.	0.82	25.77	0.618	0.199
Austria	7456403.	1.09	26.72	0.776	0.312
Bulgaria (1975)					
North West	1042803.	1.10	24.06	0.977	0.119
North	1400117.	1.01	24.25	0.888	0.123
North East	1486719.	1.20	24.43	1.050	0.154
South West	696466.	1.11	24.60	0.959	0.153
South	2164076.	1.13	24.45	0.989	0.141
South East	866834.	1.22	24.36	1.065	0.152
Sofia	1069975.	0.96	25.44	0.780	0.182
Bulgaria	8726990.	1.10	24.49	0.957	0.146
Canada (1971)					
Newfoundland	507750.	1.90	28.01	1.258	0.643
Prince Edward Island	110085.	1.51	28.13	0.981	0.524
Nova Scotia	772500.	1.33	27.16	0.935	0.392
New Brunswick	625674.	1.41	27.49	0.965	0.443
Quebec	5904307.	1.10	28.16	0.728	0.373
Ontario	7331987.	1.22	26.99	0.881	0.344
Manitoba	975655.	1.33	27.33	0.932	0.397
Saskatchewan	940790.	1.47	27.30	1.036	0.438
Alberta	1545537.	1.37	26.79	1.002	0.368
British Columbia	2029147.	1.19	26.54	0.886	0.301
Canada	20743436.	1.23	27.33	0.866	0.367
Czechoslovakia (1975)					
Central Bohemia	2300705.	1.13	25.37	0.937	0.198
Southern Bohemia	667998.	1.17	25.11	0.991	0.179
Western Bohemia	872796.	1.20	24.87	1.014	0.184
Northern Bohemia	1135800.	1.21	24.72	1.028	0.185
Eastern Bohemia	1224599.	1.21	24.93	1.034	0.180
Southern Moravia	1985174.	1.22	25.26	1.021	0.200
Northern Moravia	1875294.	1.21	25.08	1.023	0.192
Western Slovakia	1966889.	1.18	25.84	0.953	0.231
Central Slovakia	1455491.	1.25	25.94	0.996	0.251
Eastern Slovakia	1316921.	1.39	26.32	1.081	0.313
Czechoslovakia	14801667.	1.21	25.41	0.998	0.212

		Fertility			
Country (reference year) and region	Population (1)	GRR (2)	Mean age of fert.sched. (3)	GRR(<30) (4)	GRR(>30) (5)

Fed.Rep.of Germany(1974)

Region	Population	GRR	Mean age	GRR(<30)	GRR(>30)
Schleswig-Holstein	2584343.	0.73	26.52	0.552	0.176
Hamburg	1733802.	0.58	26.61	0.432	0.145
Lower Saxony	7265539.	0.81	27.25	0.575	0.232
Bremen	723990.	0.68	26.23	0.521	0.156
N. Rhine-Westphalia	17218626.	0.72	26.81	0.534	0.186
Hessen	5576082.	0.70	26.76	0.516	0.180
Rhineland-Palatinate	3687561.	0.73	26.62	0.553	0.180
Baden-Wuerttemberg	9226239.	0.77	26.98	0.559	0.212
Bavaria	10849123.	0.75	27.23	0.532	0.215
Saarland	1103325.	0.65	26.51	0.490	0.164
West Berlin	2034366.	0.65	26.34	0.490	0.161
Fed.Rep. of Germany	62002996.	0.73	26.91	0.537	0.196

Finland (1974)

Region	Population	GRR	Mean age	GRR(<30)	GRR(>30)
Uusimaa	1073485.	0.76	26.76	0.568	0.195
Turku and Pori	691672.	0.76	26.54	0.581	0.182
Ahvenanmaa	22009.	0.80	26.60	0.618	0.184
Hame	657049.	0.75	26.64	0.566	0.187
Kymi	345985.	0.73	26.64	0.553	0.176
Mikkeli	212200.	0.75	27.41	0.540	0.212
Pohjois-Karjala	177870.	0.79	27.57	0.535	0.251
Kuopio	251320.	0.77	27.27	0.550	0.219
Keski-Suomi	238814.	0.80	27.31	0.568	0.230
Vaasa	423043.	0.90	27.25	0.644	0.253
Oulu	400853.	0.96	27.57	0.667	0.293
Lappi	196232.	0.83	27.25	0.589	0.241
Finland	4690532.	0.79	26.96	0.581	0.211

France (1975)

Region	Population	GRR	Mean age	GRR(<30)	GRR(>30)
Paris Region	9876665.	0.88	27.28	0.630	0.250
Paris Basin	9647540.	0.99	26.86	0.734	0.253
North	3913250.	1.12	27.08	0.815	0.303
East	4905810.	0.94	27.13	0.681	0.258
West	6889705.	1.06	27.14	0.777	0.280
Southwest	5553655.	0.84	27.20	0.614	0.227
Middle East	6129105.	0.91	27.44	0.654	0.260
Mediterranean	5464635.	0.83	27.34	0.594	0.231
France	52380364.	0.94	27.15	0.686	0.255

German Dem.Rep.(1975)

Region	Population	GRR	Mean age	GRR(<30)	GRR(>30)
North	2085383.	0.79	24.50	0.684	0.110
Berlin	1098174.	0.80	24.85	0.686	0.111
Southwest	2529805.	0.78	24.97	0.636	0.141
South	7134846.	0.74	24.54	0.635	0.101
Middle	3972041.	0.74	24.50	0.646	0.097
German Dem.Rep.	16820250.	0.76	24.61	0.648	0.108

Hungary (1974)

Region	Population	GRR	Mean age	GRR(<30)	GRR(>30)
Central	2968109.	0.99	25.80	0.776	0.210
North Hungary	1357973.	1.20	25.15	0.989	0.208
North Plain	1543604.	1.36	25.53	1.087	0.269
South Plain	1451260.	1.15	25.30	0.939	0.210
North Trans-Danubia	1823844.	1.19	25.40	0.980	0.214
South Trans-Danubia	1303694.	1.17	24.90	0.984	0.183
Hungary	10448484.	1.14	25.42	0.929	0.216

			Fertility		
Country (reference year) and region	Population (1)	GRR (2)	Mean age of fert.sched. (3)	GRR(<30) (4)	GRR(>30) (5)

Italy (1978)

North West	15424582.	0.77	27.22	0.546	0.221
North East	10394756.	0.76	27.31	0.531	0.227
Center	10790837.	0.82	27.25	0.582	0.239
South	13471822.	1.17	28.03	0.750	0.420
Islands	6518288.	1.11	27.90	0.714	0.398
Italy	56600292.	0.91	27.47	0.625	0.286

Japan (1970)

Hokkaido	5184287.	1.01	27.24	0.800	0.213
Tohoku	11392179.	1.08	27.38	0.840	0.242
Kanto	30257930.	1.02	28.43	0.705	0.319
Chubu	17401128.	1.07	27.44	0.832	0.234
Kinki	16511391.	1.03	27.90	0.764	0.271
Chugoku	6996961.	1.05	27.26	0.837	0.215
Shikoku	3904014.	1.06	27.17	0.842	0.219
Kyushu	13017290.	1.15	27.92	0.842	0.313
Japan	104665176.	1.05	27.85	0.777	0.273

Netherlands (1974)

North	1473611.	0.98	27.18	0.728	0.248
East	2592786.	0.98	27.61	0.713	0.268
West	6150477.	0.81	27.35	0.598	0.209
South-West	322891.	0.98	26.94	0.749	0.227
South	2948600.	0.86	27.41	0.645	0.218
Netherlands	13488365.	0.87	27.39	0.647	0.227

Poland (1977)

Warsaw	2207161.	0.83	26.41	0.640	0.195
Łódź	1099132.	0.81	25.86	0.644	0.163
Gdansk	1287689.	1.04	26.70	0.778	0.267
Katowice	3557261.	0.92	25.77	0.737	0.187
Cracow	1143864.	0.94	26.68	0.691	0.248
East-Central	2930837.	1.22	26.71	0.923	0.297
Northeast	2398497.	1.27	27.18	0.921	0.346
Northwest	2106814.	1.09	26.19	0.846	0.240
South	2505722.	1.11	26.74	0.832	0.283
Southeast	4208485.	1.41	27.74	0.975	0.432
East	2479828.	1.25	26.99	0.926	0.327
West-Central	4712562.	1.14	26.76	0.850	0.288
West	4059724.	1.05	26.25	0.813	0.238
Poland	34697580.	1.10	26.69	0.826	0.275

Soviet Union (1974)

Urban areas of the:

RSFSR	88230272.	1.00	26.07	0.830	0.172
Ukrainian+Mold.SSRs	29527222.	1.03	26.08	0.833	0.200
Byelorussian SSR	4549020.	1.08	26.56	0.865	0.220
Central Asian Rep.s	8681624.	1.92	28.33	1.318	0.604
Kazakh SSR	7348350.	1.26	27.14	0.955	0.300
Caucasian Republics	6918171.	1.47	27.09	1.146	0.326
Baltic Republics	4334008.	0.97	26.75	0.724	0.241
Rural areas of USSR	101280288.	1.88	27.40	1.375	0.510
Soviet Union	250868944.	1.33	27.00	1.014	0.320

Fertility				
Country (reference year) and region	Population (1)	GRR (2)	Mean age of fert.sched. (3)	GRR(<30) (4)	GRR(>30) (5)

Country (reference year) and region	Population (1)	GRR (2)	Mean age of fert.sched. (3)	GRR(<30) (4)	GRR(>30) (5)
Sweden (1974)					
Stockholm	1486821.	0.86	27.52	0.599	0.260
East Middle	1397129.	0.95	26.96	0.694	0.252
South Middle	763793.	0.97	27.38	0.695	0.278
South	1157556.	0.92	27.31	0.660	0.262
West	1603323.	0.93	27.32	0.670	0.263
North Middle	853655.	0.89	26.95	0.651	0.243
Lower North	400292.	0.90	27.35	0.631	0.266
Upper North	494569.	0.96	27.41	0.679	0.286
Sweden	8157138.	0.92	27.26	0.658	0.262
United Kingdom (1970)					
North	3359700.	1.16	26.40	0.881	0.278
Yorkshire + Humbers.	4811900.	1.26	26.41	0.953	0.306
North West	6788700.	1.26	26.61	0.938	0.324
East Midlands	3362800.	1.21	26.45	0.923	0.286
West Midlands	5178000.	1.21	26.82	0.891	0.324
East Anglia	1673500.	1.11	26.43	0.853	0.256
South East	17315502.	1.12	26.91	0.822	0.298
South West	3763700.	1.15	26.49	0.878	0.271
Wales	2733900.	1.19	26.42	0.900	0.285
Scotland	5199100.	1.26	27.07	0.907	0.358
United Kingdom	54186800.	1.18	26.70	0.881	0.304
United States (1970)					
Northeast	49040708.	1.24	26.64	0.926	0.316
North Central	56571668.	1.30	26.15	0.999	0.298
South	62795372.	1.27	25.60	1.003	0.272
West	34804200.	1.22	26.02	0.946	0.277
United States	203211920.	1.26	26.07	0.974	0.290

CHAPTER FIVE

Migration

Andrei Rogers and Luis J. Castro

Declining fertility levels and generally stable mortality patterns in the more developed industrialized nations have elevated the relative importance of migration as a contributor to regional population change. Migration not only affects the size of an area's population, but also alters the composition of that population by selectively adding and subtracting people with distinctive characteristics. Because of its growth and compositional impacts, few governments are indifferent to the patterns of migration that evolve within and across their borders.

The label "migration" has in the past been applied to two related, but different, indicators of mobility: a population of *moves* and a population of *movers*. The first concept views migration as an *event* much like birth and death; the second treats migration as a *transition* – a transfer of status analogous to a change in marital or employment status. Thus one of the central problems in migration measurement arises as a consequence of the different sources of migration data.

5.1 Migration Data, Rates, and Schedules

Most information regarding migration is obtained from population censuses or registers that report migration data, for a given time interval, in terms of counts of migrants or of moves, respectively. Migration data produced by censuses are usually in the form of transitions; population registers treat migration as an event and generate data on moves. Yet another source of migration data is the sample survey, which may be designed to provide information both about migrants and about moves.

A mover is an individual who has made a move at least once during a given interval. A migrant, on the other hand, is an individual who at the end of a given interval no longer inhabits the same community of residence as at the start of the interval.[1] Thus, paradoxically, a multiple mover can be a non-migrant, if after moving several times he returns to his initial place of residence before the end of the unit time interval.

Migration data collected by population censuses usually come from responses to four typical questions that ask about place of birth, duration of residence, place of last residence, and place of residence at a fixed prior date (United Nations 1970). From the answers to these questions it is possible to establish the count of surviving migrants living in a region at the time of the census, disaggregated by different retrospective time intervals. The longer the time interval, the less accurate becomes the migration measure as an indicator of mobility level.

Because population registers focus on moves and not on transitions, differences will arise between data obtained from registers and from population censuses. This inconsistency is examined in the annex to the UN *Manual on Methods of Measuring Internal Migration*, where it is stated:

> Since at least some migrants, by census definition, will have been involved, by registration definition, in more than one migratory event, counts from registers should normally exceed those from censuses.... . Only with Japanese data has it so far been possible to test the correspondence between migrations, as registered during a one-year period and migrants enumerated in the census in terms of fixed-period change in residence. (United Nations 1970, p.50)

Table 5.1, taken from the UN analysis, illustrates how the ratio of register-to-census migration data is in general greater than unity, increasing with decreasing distance, as for example, in the case of intra- versus inter-prefectural migration in Japan. In general, the ratio of register-to-census migration data should tend to unity as longer distances are involved. It should be greater than unity when shorter distances are considered, because the probability of moving across long distances several times is expected to be less than the probability of moving the same number of times across short distances.

Finally, migration occurs both over time and across space; therefore, studies of its patterns must trace its occurrence with respect to a time interval, as well as over a system of geographical areas. In general, the longer the time interval, the larger the number of return movers and nonsurviving migrants; hence, the more the count of *migrants* will understate the number of interarea *movers* (and moves). Rees (1977a), for example, after examining the ratios of one-year to five-year migrants between the Standard Regions of

---

[1]In some countries (e.g., Canada and the US) a mover is officially defined as a person who has different residences *within* a single local community between two points in time, whereas a migrant is a person who resides in different local communities between two points in time.

Table 5.1 Comparison of migration by sex and type based on the population register and the census for the one-year period between October 1959 and October 1960 in Japan.

Sex and type of migration	Register data	Census data	Ratio × 100
Both sexes			
Intraprefectural	2,966,621	1,998,171	148.47
Interprefectural	2,625,135	2,590,751	101.33
Males			
Intraprefectural	1,488,935	1,001,745	148.63
Interprefectural	1,450,817	1,466,898	98.90
Females			
Intraprefectural	1,477,686	996,426	148.30
Interprefectural	1,174,318	1,123,853	104.49

Source: United Nations (1970, table 42, p.50).

Great Britain, found that

> The number of migrants recorded over five years in an interregional flow varies from four times to two times the number of migrants recorded over one year. (Rees 1977a, p.247)

A fundamental aspect of migration is its change over time. As Ryder (1964) pointed out for the case of fertility, period and cohort reproduction rates will differ whenever the age distribution of childbearing varies from one cohort to another. The usefulness of a cohort approach in migration, as in fertility analysis, lies in the importance of historical experience as an explanation of current behavior. Morrison (1970) has argued that migration is induced by transitions from one stage of the life cycle to another, and "chronic" migrants may artificially inflate the migration rates of origin areas that are heavily populated with migration-prone individuals. Both influences on period migration are readily assessed by a cohort analysis.

The simplest and most common measure of migration is the crude outmigration rate: the ratio of the *number of migrants*, leaving a particular population located in space and time, to the average *number of persons* (person-years) "exposed to the risk" of becoming migrants. Data on nonsurviving migrants are generally unavailable; therefore the numerator in this ratio generally excludes them.

Because migration is highly age-selective, with a large fraction of migrants being young, our understanding of migration patterns and dynamics is aided by computing migration rates for each single year of age. Summing these rates over all ages of life gives the *gross migraproduction rate* (GMR), the migration analog of fertility's gross reproduction rate. This rate reflects the level at which migration occurs out of a given region.

The age-specific migration schedules of multiregional populations exhibit remarkably persistent regularities. For example, when comparing the age-specific annual rates of residential migration among whites and blacks in the United States during 1966–1971, one finds a common profile (Figure 5.1). Migration rates among infants and young children mirrored the relatively high rates of their parents, young adults in their late twenties. The mobility of adolescents was lower but exceeded that of young teens, with the latter showing a local low point around age 15. Thereafter migration rates increased, attaining a high peak at about age 22, and then declined monotonically until the ages of retirement. The migration *levels* of both whites and blacks were roughly similar, with whites showing a GMR of about 14 and blacks one of approximately 15.

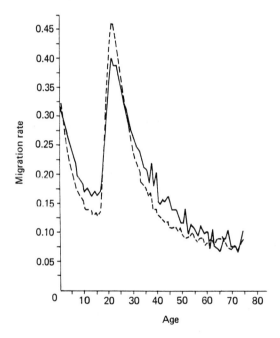

Figure 5.1 Observed annual migration rates by color (––– whites, — blacks) and single years of age in the United States, 1966–1971.
Source: Long (1973).

Although it has frequently been asserted that migration is strongly sex-selective, with males being more mobile than females, recent research indicates that sex selectivity is much less pronounced than age selectivity and is less uniform across time and space. Nevertheless, because most models and studies of population dynamics distinguish between the sexes, most migration measures do also.

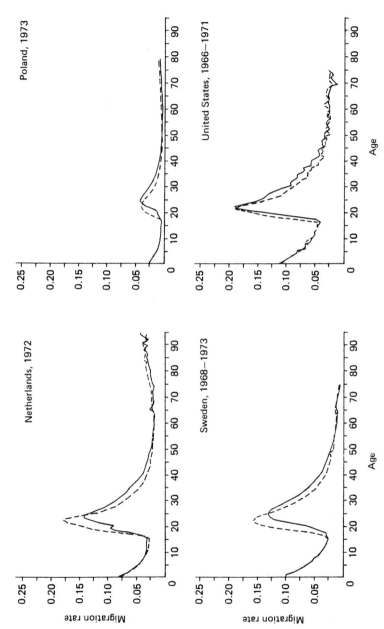

Figure 5.2 Observed annual migration rates by sex (– – – females, —— males) and single years of age in the Netherlands (intercommunal), Poland (*intervoivodship*), Sweden (intercommunal), and the US (intercounty) around 1970.

Sources: (Netherlands) P. Drewe (1978, personal communication); (Poland) Polish Central Bureau of Statistics (1973); (Sweden) Swedish Central Bureau of Statistics (1974); (US) Long (1973).

Figure 5.2 illustrates the age profiles of male and female migration schedules in four different countries at about the same time between roughly comparable areal units: communes in the Netherlands and Sweden, *voivodships* in Poland, and counties in the US. The migration levels for all but Poland are similar, varying between 3.5 and 5.3 migrations per lifetime; and the levels for males and females are roughly the same. The age profiles, however, show a distinct, and consistent, difference. The high peak of the female schedule precedes that of the male schedule by an amount that appears to approximate the difference between the average ages at marriage of the two sexes.

Under normal statistical conditions, point-to-point movements are aggregated into streams between one civil division and another; consequently, the level of interregional migration depends on the size of the areal unit selected. Thus a minor civil division, such as a county or commune, would have a greater proportion of residential relocation included as migration than would a major civil division, such as a state or province.

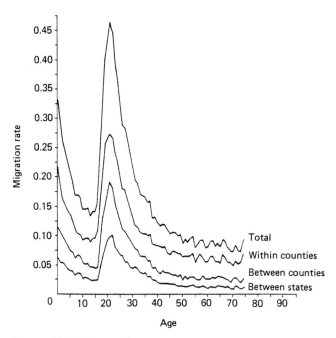

Figure 5.3 Observed average annual migration rates of females by levels of areal aggregation and single years of age in the United States, 1966–1971.
Source: Long (1973).

Figure 5.3 presents the age profiles of female migration schedules as measured by different sizes of areal units: (1) all migrations from one residence to another, (2) changes of residence within county boundaries, (3) migration between counties, and (4) migration between states. The respective four GMRs are 14.3, 9.3, 5.0, and 2.5. The four age profiles appear to be remarkably similar, indicating that the regularity in age pattern persists across areal delineations of different sizes.

5.2 Regional Comparative Analysis of Migration: Levels

Despite the growing availability of statistics on migration among various administrative areas within the more developed nations, the unresolved problem of how to standardize areal units to reflect different sizes and shapes has hampered international comparisons of geographical mobility levels. To avoid this problem, a few studies have resorted to comparisons of counts of all changes of residence during a specified interval of time (e.g., Long and Boertlein 1976). Table 5.2 sets out such a comparison by way of illustration.

Table 5.2 The residentially mobile population in six countries around 1970.

Country	Percent are moving in one year[a]	
	Including movers from abroad	Excluding movers from abroad
Australia	NA[b]	15.7
Great Britain	11.8	11.1
Ireland	5.1	4.3
Japan	12.0	12.0
Taiwan	NA	9.1
United States	19.2	18.6

[a]Persons one year old and over. [b]NA: not available.
Source: Long and Boertlein (1976, p.3).

According to the last column of Table 5.2, about 18.6% of the US population moved from one residence to another within the country during a 12-month period around 1970, compared with about 11.1% in Great Britain and 12.0% in Japan. These data lend support to the hypothesis that rates of geographical mobility are relatively high in the US.

The migration data collected for the Migration and Settlement Study have a number of deficiencies that make them unsuitable for international comparisons of this sort. Not only do they describe flows of people between areas of different sizes and shapes, but also they do so for different moments in time, using time intervals of different widths, and relying on data collected in different ways. Therefore, in this chapter, we focus only on comparisons of differences *within* (and not *between*) countries. In this way we hope to reduce, as much as possible, the unknown impacts of these deficiencies in the data and to carry out some guarded and rough assessments of *intra*national differentials in migration patterns.

The shape, or *profile*, of an age-specific schedule of migration rates is a feature that may be usefully studied independently of its intensity, or *level*. This is because there is considerable empirical evidence that although the latter tends to vary significantly from place to place, the former is remarkably similar in various communities. Regional differentials in migration levels are examined in this section; a comparison of regional differentials in migration age profiles is made in the next section. We begin with an examination of differentials among regional populations and then consider disaggregations by sex and age.

5.2.1 *Differentials Among Regional Populations*

To examine regional differentials in outmigration levels, we must first adopt an aggregate measure of such levels. A convenient indicator is the gross migraproduction rate (GMR): the sum of all age-specific outmigration rates from a region multiplied by the number of years in the age interval (five in our case). It is evident from this definition that a region's gross migraproduction rate is calculated in a way analogous to its gross death rate and its gross reproduction rate. Because equal weight is given to each age-specific outmigration rate, this measure avoids the dependence on a particular population's age composition that is exhibited by alternative indicators such as the crude outmigration rate.

The 17 countries of IIASA's Migration and Settlement Study were divided into a total of 139 regions. Gross migraproduction rates for each country and for each region may be found in Appendix 5. Since the main purpose of this section is to analyze national patterns of regional differentials, we shall focus only on a summary indicator of regional variation within each country. Following the example set by the study of regional differentials in mortality in Chapter 3, we adopt the mean absolute deviation (MAD) as our principal indicator, that is, the sum of the differences between each regional value and the national figure, divided by the number of regions. To control for differences in aggregate levels among nations, we express the mean absolute deviation as a percentage of the national value (MAD/N%).

Table 5.3 sets out the lowest and highest regional gross migraproduction rates for each of the 17 IIASA countries, including the corresponding national figure. In Austria, for example, the national rate in 1971 was 0.35. Among the nine regions into which the country was divided, the lowest rate was 0.22, the highest was 0.51, and the difference between 0.51 and 0.35, 0.16, was the "highest absolute deviation". Adding to this figure the other eight absolute deviations and then dividing by nine gives 0.09, the entry at the top of the fourth column of numbers. Expressing this as a percentage of the national gross migraproduction rate yields the 27.0% found in the last column.

An examination of the last column in Table 5.3 reveals that considerable

Table 5.3 Regional differentials in gross migraproduction rates.

Country (reference year: number of regions)	National (N)	Lowest	Highest	MAD	MAD/N(%)
Austria (1971:9)	0.35	0.22	0.51	0.09	27.0
Bulgaria (1975:7)	0.31	0.23	0.46	0.07	23.5
Canada (1971:10)	0.77	0.48	2.14	0.57	74.2
Czechoslovakia (1975:10)	0.52	0.31	0.87	0.15	29.6
FRG (1974:11)	1.19	0.74	3.30	0.68	56.8
Finland (1974:12)	1.62	0.85	2.47	0.35	21.9
France (1975:8)	0.84	0.64	1.35	0.19	22.2
GDR (1975:5)	0.44	0.37	0.53	0.07	15.5
Hungary (1974:6)	2.36	1.77	3.19	0.48	20.4
Italy (1978:5)	0.43	0.26	0.54	0.11	25.1
Japan (1970:8)	1.35	0.76	2.37	0.56	41.3
Netherlands (1974:5)	1.10	0.82	1.62	0.22	19.6
Poland (1977:13)	0.66	0.44	1.05	0.12	18.2
Soviet Union (1974:8)	2.20	1.06	3.53	0.70	31.8
Sweden (1974:8)	1.20	0.82	1.47	0.22	18.3
United Kingdom (1970:10)	1.20	0.87	1.84	0.25	20.5
United States (1970:4)	1.31	1.12	1.45	0.10	7.6
Additional aggregation					
Austria (1971:4)	0.16	0.11	0.23	0.04	25.0
Italy (1978:20)	0.54	0.32	0.80	0.16	30.1

regional differentials in levels of outmigration exist in a number of the IIASA countries. Foremost are the high-differential countries of Canada (74.2%) and the Federal Republic of Germany (56.8%), with Japan not far behind (41.3%). At the other extreme are the low-differential countries of the German Democratic Republic (15.5%), Poland (18.2%), and Sweden (18.3%).[2] The remaining 10 countries exhibit a range of MAD/N values lying between 20 and 40%.

The particular regional disaggregation adopted for each country has an obvious influence on migration levels and on the degree of regional differences observed. In two cases, we have an indication of the impact of regional delineation: Austria and Italy. In the Austrian case study a four region disaggregation was also studied, and the Italian case study also considered spatial population dynamics in a system of 20 regions. The last two rows of Table 5.3 indicate that, for these two countries, an increase in the number of regions led to an increase in the degree of spatial differentials in regional migration levels, which is to be expected. What is somewhat surprising is that the amount of the increase was relatively small: from 25.0 to 27.0% in the Austrian case and from 25.1 to 30.1% in the Italian case.

---

[2]The US, with its four very large regions, naturally exhibits an unusually low degree of regional disparity (7.6%); however, the coarseness of the regional disaggregation makes its inclusion unsuitable for our study. Consequently we do not include it in our analysis.

Several city regions are included in the case studies of the Federal Republic of Germany and Poland. If outmigration from such geographically small regions is higher than the average, then of course the degree of a country's regional differentials is inflated relative to that of nations without city regions. The data on the sample of city regions presented in Table 5.4, however, suggest that no such simple pattern is evident. In the Federal Republic of Germany outmigration from city regions was about twice as high as the national figure, whereas in Poland they were about the same, with four out of five city regions showing a *lower* than national value. No regularities are evident in the other countries either, except for an apparent association between the level of a city region's gross migraproduction rate and its crude net inmigration rate. All city regions with low GMRs (≤ 0.75) gained population through net migration; those with high GMRs (≥ 1.50) lost, with two exceptions: Helsinki and Budapest. The latter, however, is a member of a class of city regions exhibiting positive net inmigration: all East European cities.

To summarize, regional differentials in outmigration levels are roughly twice as strong in some IIASA countries as in others. Apparently these differences are not simply a consequence of different regionalizations. (Austria and Italy stayed in the 20—40% category despite significantly different degrees of disaggregation.) Nor do they simply reflect the presence or absence of city regions.

Among city regions few generalizations are apparent. Those with low outmigration levels gained from migration exchanges with the rest of the country, whereas those with high GMRs generally lost. City regions in Eastern Europe gained from net migration, whereas those in Western Europe gained or lost, depending on their level of outmigration.

5.2.2 *Differentials Among Sex- and Age-Specific Regional Populations*

A study of regional differentials among populations without regard to sex- and age-specific details may hide patterns that are identifiable only at finer levels of resolution. Male and female migration patterns may vary, and infants may exhibit migration rates that differ from those of the elderly.

Table 5.5 repeats the calculations set out in Table 5.3 for the seven IIASA countries for which a disaggregation by sex could be made. These figures indicate that regional differentials in migration levels among females are slightly higher than among males in high-differential countries, with Japan being the only country in which males show greater regional differentials than females. Regional differentials for the two sexes in low-differential countries are about the same.

Do females migrate more than males? According to Table 5.5 they do not. Differences in national levels of the GMR between the sexes are small; nevertheless it does seem that males migrate more than females in high-differential countries.

Table 5.4 Regional differentials in gross migraproduction rates: city regions.

Country/city (reference year)	National (N)	Urban (U)	Difference (U − N)	Net migration rate (per thousand)
Austria (1971)	0.35			
Vienna		0.43	0.08	1.89
Bulgaria (1975)	0.31			
Sofia		0.30	−0.01	5.64
FRG (1974)	1.19			
Hamburg		2.87	1.68	−5.90
Bremen		3.30	2.11	−4.80
Finland (1974)	1.62			
Uusimaa − Helsinki		1.46	−0.16	6.21
France (1975)	0.84			
Paris		1.35	0.51	−2.91
GDR (1975)	0.44			
Berlin		0.50	0.06	11.13
Hungary (1974)	2.36			
Central − Budapest		2.77	0.41	3.66
Japan (1970)	1.35			
Kanto − Tokyo		0.76	−0.59	15.36
Poland (1977)	0.66			
Warsaw		0.50	−0.16	7.78
Lódź		0.59	−0.07	3.23
Gdańsk		0.71	0.05	4.57
Katowice		0.44	−0.22	6.84
Krakow		0.63	−0.03	3.09
Sweden (1974)	1.20			
Stockholm		1.45	0.25	−2.99
United Kingdom (1970)	1.20			
South East − London		1.06	−0.14	−0.85
Additional aggregation				
Czechoslovakia (1975)	0.62			
Prague		0.83	0.21	5.26
Bratislavia		0.78	0.16	12.24
Italy (1978)	0.35			
Lazio − Rome		0.52	0.17	1.48
Netherlands (1974)	1.66			
North − Amsterdam		1.75	0.09	−5.82

Tables 5.6, 5.7, and 5.8 present data on regional migration differentials for three distinct age groups: infants (0–4 years), young adults (15–29 years), and the elderly (65 years and over). Recalling the age profiles of migration set out earlier in this chapter, one might reasonably expect these groups to capture the range of diverse patterns of migration behavior. Migration levels should be relatively high among young adults, low among the elderly, and somewhere between these two extremes among infants.

Table 5.5 Regional differentials in gross migraproduction rates: males and females.

Country (reference year: number of regions)	National (N)	Lowest	Highest	MAD	MAD/N(%)
Males					
Canada (1971:10)	0.77	0.49	2.12	0.56	72.7
FRG (1974:11)	1.36	0.87	3.68	0.74	54.7
Finland (1974:12)	1.60	0.75	2.33	0.34	21.0
France (1975:8)	0.83	0.62	1.36	0.18	22.1
Japan (1970:8)	1.58	0.88	2.79	0.66	42.0
Sweden (1974:8)	1.18	0.81	1.47	0.22	18.3
United Kingdom (1970:10)	1.23	0.93	1.90	0.25	20.2
Females					
Canada (1971:10)	0.74	0.46	2.13	0.58	78.4
FRG (1974:11)	1.02	0.61	2.89	0.60	58.7
Finland (1974:12)	1.64	0.96	2.63	0.39	23.7
France (1975:8)	0.84	0.65	1.33	0.19	22.2
Japan (1970:8)	1.17	0.63	2.01	0.46	39.6
Sweden (1974:8)	1.21	0.82	1.48	0.23	18.8
United Kingdom (1970:10)	1.17	0.81	1.80	0.24	20.7

Table 5.6 Regional differentials in gross migraproduction rates: infants (0–4 years).

Country (reference year: number of regions)	National (N)	Lowest	Highest	MAD	MAD/N(%)
Austria (1971:9)	0.022	0.012	0.041	0.008	36.4
Bulgaria (1975:7)	0.021	0.014	0.034	0.006	30.6
Canada (1971:10)	0.085	0.048	0.228	0.059	69.1
Czechoslovakia (1975:10)	0.056	0.038	0.096	0.016	29.3
FRG (1974:11)	0.083	0.053	0.287	0.058	69.6
Finland (1974:12)	0.202	0.099	0.276	0.036	17.8
France (1975:8)	0.088	0.069	0.126	0.014	16.1
GDR (1975:5)	0.055	0.045	0.076	0.010	18.5
Hungary (1974:6)	0.110	0.086	0.135	0.017	15.3
Italy (1978:5)	0.027	0.017	0.037	0.006	20.7
Japan (1970:8)	0.077	0.062	0.099	0.015	19.2
Netherlands (1974:5)	0.077	0.049	0.105	0.015	19.7
Poland (1977:13)	0.060	0.033	0.086	0.013	21.9
Soviet Union (1974:8)	0.070	0.029	0.099	0.019	26.4
Sweden (1974:8)	0.134	0.093	0.180	0.025	18.6
United Kingdom (1970:10)	0.104	0.082	0.191	0.027	26.2
United States (1970:4)	0.123	0.091	0.148	0.019	15.7
Additional aggregation					
Austria (1971:4)	0.010	0.008	0.013	0.002	15.0
Italy (1978:20)	0.033	0.018	0.062	0.011	32.1

Table 5.7 Regional differentials in gross migraproduction rates: young adults (15—29 years).

Country (reference year: number of regions)	National (N)	Lowest	Highest	MAD	MAD/N(%)
Austria (1971:9)	0.165	0.109	0.246	0.040	24.1
Bulgaria (1975:7)	0.164	0.107	0.284	0.054	33.0
Canada (1971:10)	0.216	0.119	0.756	0.218	101.1
Czechoslovakia (1975:10)	0.202	0.137	0.289	0.048	24.0
FRG (1974:11)	0.521	0.343	1.390	0.281	53.9
Finland (1974:12)	0.772	0.426	1.270	0.204	26.4
France (1975:8)	0.251	0.200	0.287	0.028	11.3
GDR (1975:5)	0.206	0.179	0.246	0.024	11.7
Hungary (1974:6)	1.239	0.866	1.797	0.292	23.5
Italy (1978:5)	0.169	0.086	0.245	0.058	34.6
Japan (1970:8)	0.679	0.269	1.385	0.396	58.3
Netherlands (1974:5)	0.417	0.341	0.698	0.124	29.8
Poland (1977:13)	0.240	0.104	0.402	0.075	31.2
Soviet Union (1974:8)	1.357	0.607	2.443	0.486	35.8
Sweden (1974:8)	0.517	0.341	0.724	0.120	23.3
United Kingdom (1970:10)	0.463	0.360	0.749	0.108	23.4
United States (1970:4)	0.506	0.398	0.568	0.057	11.2
Additional aggregation					
Austria (1971:4)	0.084	0.054	0.125	0.021	25.0
Italy (1978:20)	0.201	0.099	0.489	0.077	38.4

Of the three high-differential countries in Table 5.3, the German Democratic Republic and Sweden exhibit relatively low differentials in all three age groups, with MAD/N not exceeding 25% in all cases. But Poland, which in Table 5.3 had a MAD/N value under 20%, now shows a slightly higher figure for infants and significantly higher values for young adults and the elderly (31.2 and 35.6%).

Within each of the three age groups considered, no distinct patterns of differentials are evident. France and the Soviet Union show high regional differentials among the elderly, but exhibit, respectively, low and moderate differentials in the other two age groups. Seven countries have MAD/N values under 20% for infant migration and four countries have scores this low for the elderly. Yet no pattern emerges. It appears that it might be more profitable to search for regularities using the entire age profile, viewed independently of any particular migration level.

5.3 Regional Comparative Analysis of Migration: Age Profiles

Most human populations experience rates of age-specific fertility and mortality that exhibit remarkably persistent regularities. Consequently, demographers have found it possible to summarize and codify such regularities by

Table 5.8 Regional differentials in gross migraproduction rates: elderly (65 years and over).

Country (reference year: number of regions)	National (N)	Lowest	Highest	MAD	MAD/N(%)
Austria (1971:9)	0.030	0.017	0.041	0.008	28.1
Bulgaria (1975:7)	0.018	0.015	0.025	0.004	20.6
Canada (1971:10)	0.107	0.063	0.253	0.056	52.2
Czechoslovakia (1975:10)	0.090	0.051	0.161	0.027	30.4
FRG (1974:11)	0.139	0.064	0.368	0.077	55.2
Finland (1974:12)	0.060	0.024	0.093	0.015	25.6
France (1975:8)	0.104	0.055	0.283	0.055	52.8
GDR (1975:5)	0.020	0.016	0.028	0.005	25.0
Hungary (1974:6)	0.274	0.214	0.306	0.022	8.2
Italy (1978:5)	0.047	0.037	0.055	0.005	10.6
Japan (1970:8)	0.110	0.085	0.221	0.026	23.9
Netherlands (1974:5)	0.196	0.144	0.253	0.035	17.8
Poland (1977:13)	0.151	0.104	0.317	0.054	35.6
Soviet Union (1974:8)	0.191	0.132	0.471	0.090	47.2
Sweden (1974:8)	0.063	0.039	0.112	0.016	25.0
United Kingdom (1970:10)	0.136	0.061	0.185	0.027	19.9
United States (1970:4)	0.106	0.102	0.113	0.003	3.1
Additional aggregation					
Austria (1971:4)	0.012	0.009	0.015	0.003	22.9
Italy (1978:20)	0.066	0.042	0.154	0.021	32.3

means of mathematical expressions called model schedules. Although the development of model fertility and mortality schedules has received considerable attention in demographic studies, the construction of model migration schedules has not, even though the techniques that have been successfully applied to treat the former can be readily extended to deal with the latter.

We began this chapter with an examination of regularities in age profiles exhibited by empirical schedules of migration rates; we now adopt the notion of model migration schedules to express these regularities in mathematical form. We then use model schedules to examine patterns of variation present in a large number of such schedules. Drawing on this comparative analysis of "observed" model schedules, we develop several families of schedules and define a standard migration schedule. We then disaggregate age profiles by cause and by family status in an effort to account for their apparent universality.

5.3.1 *Model Migration Schedules*

The most prominent regularity found in empirical schedules of age-specific migration rates is the selectivity of migration with respect to age. Young adults in their early twenties generally show the highest migration rates and young teenagers the lowest. The migration rates of children mirror those of their parents; hence the migration rates of infants exceed those of adolescents. Finally, migration streams directed toward regions with warmer climates and into or out of large cities with relatively high levels of social services and cultural amenities often exhibit a retirement peak at ages in the mid-sixties or beyond.

Figure 5.4 illustrates a typical *observed* age-specific migration schedule (the jagged outline) and its graduation by a *model schedule* (the superimposed smooth outline) defined as the sum of four components:

(1)   A single negative exponential curve of the *pre-labor force ages*, with its descent parameter α_1

(2)   A left-skewed unimodal curve of the *labor force* ages positioned at μ_2 on the age axis and exhibiting parameters of ascent λ_2 and descent α_2

(3)   An almost bell-shaped curve of the *post-labor force* ages positioned at μ_3 on the age axis and exhibiting parameters of ascent λ_3 and descent α_3

(4)   A constant curve c, the inclusion of which improves the fit of the mathematical expression to the observed schedule.

The decomposition described above suggests the definition of the migration rate as the following simple sum of four curves (Rogers *et al.* 1978):[3]

$$m_x = a_1 \exp(-\alpha_1 x)$$
$$+ a_2 \exp\{-\alpha_2(x - \mu_2) - \exp[-\lambda_2(x - \mu_2)]\}$$
$$+ a_3 \exp\{-\alpha_3(x - \mu_3) - \exp[-\lambda_3(x - \mu_3)]\}$$
$$+ c, \qquad x = 0,1,2,\dots \ . \tag{5.1}$$

The labor force and the post-labor force components in equation (5.1) adopt the "double exponential" curve formulated by Coale and McNeil (1972) for their studies of nuptiality patterns.

The full model schedule in equation (5.1) has 11 parameters: a_1, α_1, a_2, μ_2, α_2, λ_2, a_3, μ_3, α_3, λ_3, and c. The *profile* of the full model schedule is defined by seven of the 11 parameters: α_1, μ_2, α_2, λ_2, μ_3, α_3, and λ_3. Its *level* is determined by the remaining four parameters: a_1, a_2, a_3, and c. A change in the value of the GMR of a particular model schedule alters proportionally the values of the latter, but does not affect the former. As we shall see later in this chapter, however, certain aspects of the profile also depend on the allocation of the schedule's level among the pre-labor, labor, and post-labor force age components and on the share of the total level accounted for by the constant term c. Finally, migration schedules without a retirement peak may be

---

[3]When fitted to empirical data, the age variable x is taken at the midpoint of the observed age interval, e.g., $x = 0.5, 1.5, 2.5\dots$.

α_1 = descent parameter of pre-labor force component
λ_2 = ascent parameter of labor force component
α_2 = descent parameter of labor force component
λ_3 = ascent parameter of post-labor force component
α_3 = descent parameter of post-labor force component
c = constant
x_ℓ = low point
x_h = high peak
x_r = retirement peak
Z = labor force shift
A = parental shift
B = jump

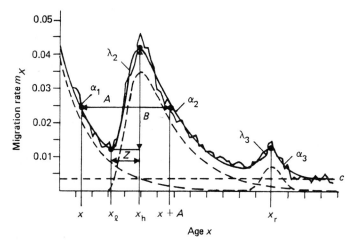

Figure 5.4 Observed and model migration schedules for males in Stockholm, 1974.
Source: Rogers and Castro (1981b).

represented by a "reduced" model with seven parameters, because in such
instances the third component of equation (5.1) is omitted.

Table 5.9 sets out estimated values for the basic and derived measures of
the model schedule presented in Figure 5.4. The method chosen for fitting the
model schedule to the data is a functional-minimization procedure known as the
modified Levenberg–Marquardt algorithm (Appendix A of Rogers and Castro
1981b, Brown and Dennis 1972, Levenberg 1944, Marquardt 1963). Minimum
chi-square estimators are used to give more weight to age groups with smaller
rates of migration.

To assess the goodness-of-fit that the model schedule provides when it is
applied to observed data, we may calculate E, the mean of the absolute differences between estimated and observed values expressed as a percentage of
the average observed value:

$$E = \left[\left(\sum_X |\hat{m}_X - m_X| \right) \Big/ \sum_X m_X \right] 100 \qquad (5.2)$$

Table 5.9 Parameters and variables defining observed model migration schedules: outmigration of males from the Stockholm region, 1974; observed data by single years of age.

Parameter or variable	Value	Parameter or variable	Value
GMR^a	1.45	$\bar{x}_m$	31.02
a_1	0.033	$\%(0-14)$	25.61
α_1	0.097	$\%(15-64)$	64.49
a_2	0.059	$\%(65+)$	9.90
μ_2	20.80	δ_{1c}	13.56
α_2	0.077	δ_{12}	0.716
λ_2	0.374	δ_{32}	0.003
a_3	0.000	β_{12}	1.26
μ_3	76.55	σ_2	4.86
α_3	0.776	σ_3	0.187
λ_3	0.145	x_1	16.39
c	0.003	x_h	24.68
		x_r	64.80
		Z	8.29
		A	27.87
		B	0.029

^{a}The GMR, its percentage distribution across the three major age categories (0–14, 15–64, 65+), and the mean age $\bar{x}_m$ are all calculated with a model schedule spanning an age range of 95 years.

This measure indicates that the fit of the model to the Stockholm data in Figure 5.4 is reasonably good, the index of goodness-of-fit, E, being 6.87%.

Model migration schedules of the form specified in equation (5.1) may be classified into *families* according to the ranges of values taken by their principal parameters. For example, we may order schedules according to their migration levels as defined by the values of the four level parameters in equation (5.1), that is, a_1, a_2, a_3, and c (or by their associated GMRs). Alternatively, we may distinguish schedules with a retirement peak from those without one, or we may refer to schedules with relatively low or high values for the parameter of ascent of the labor force curve, λ_2, or for the mean age $\bar{x}_m$. In many applications, it is also meaningful to characterize migration schedules in terms of several of the fundamental measures illustrated in Figure 5.4, such as the *low point* x_1, the *high peak* x_h, and the *retirement peak* x_r. Associated with the first pair of points is the *labor force shift* Z, which is defined to be the difference in years between the ages of the high peak and the low point, that is $Z = x_h - x_1$. The increase in the migration rate of individuals aged x_h over those aged x_1 will be called the *jump B*.

The close correspondence between the migration rates of children and those of their parents suggests another important shift in observed migration schedules. If, for each point x on the post-high-peak part of the migration curve, we obtain by interpolation the age (where it exists), $x - A_x$ say, with the identical rate of migration on the pre-low-point part of the migration curve, then the average of the values of A_x, calculated incrementally for the number of years between zero and the low point x_1, will be defined as the observed *parental shift A*.

An observed (or a graduated) age-specific migration schedule may be described in a number of useful ways. For example, references may be made to the heights at particular ages, to locations of important peaks or troughs, to slopes along the schedule's age profile, to ratios between particular heights or slopes, to areas under parts of the curve, and to both horizontal and vertical distances between important heights and locations. The various descriptive measures characterizing an age-specific model migration schedule may be conveniently grouped into the following categories and subcategories:

(1) Basic measures (the 11 fundamental parameters and their ratios)

heights: a_1, a_2, a_3, c

locations: μ_2, μ_3

slopes: $\alpha_1, \alpha_2, \lambda_2, \alpha_3, \lambda_3$

ratios: $\delta_{1c} = a_1/c$, $\delta_{12} = a_1/a_2$, $\delta_{32} = a_3/a_2$,
$\beta_{12} = \alpha_1/\alpha_2$, $\sigma_2 = \lambda_2/\alpha_2$, $\sigma_3 = \lambda_3/\alpha_3$

(2) Derived measures (properties of the model schedule)

areas: GMR, %(0–14), %(15–64), %(65+)

locations: $\bar{x}_m, x_1, x_h, x_r$

intervals: Z, A, B

A convenient approach for characterizing an observed model migration schedule (i.e., an empirical schedule graduated by equation (5.1) is to begin with the central labor force curve and then to "add on" the pre-labor force, post-labor force, and constant components. This approach is represented graphically in Figure 5.5.

One can imagine describing a decomposition of the model migration schedule along the vertical and horizontal dimensions; for example, allocating a fraction of its level to the constant component and then dividing the remainder among the other three (or two) components. The ratio $\delta_{1c} = a_1/c$ measures the former allocation, and $\delta_{12} = a_1/a_2$ and $\delta_{32} = a_3/a_2$ reflect the latter division.

The heights of the labor force and pre-labor force components are reflected in the parameters a_2 and a_1, respectively; therefore the ratio a_2/a_1 indicates the degree of "labor dominance", and its reciprocal, $\delta_{12} = a_1/a_2$, the index of child dependency, measures the rate at which children

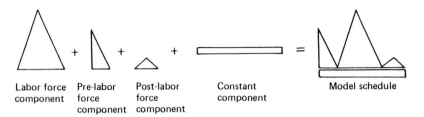

Figure 5.5 A schematic diagram of the fundamental components of the full migration model schedule.

migrate with their parents. Thus the lower the value of δ_{12}, the lower the degree of child dependency exhibited by a migration schedule and, correspondingly, the greater its labor dominance. This suggests a dichotomous classification of migration schedules into *child-dependent* and *labor-dominant* categories.

An analogous argument applies to the post-labor force curve, and $\delta_{32} = a_3/a_2$ suggests itself as the appropriate index. It will be sufficient for our purposes, however, to rely simply on the value taken by the parameter α_3, with positive values pointing out the presence of a retirement peak and a zero value indicating its absence.

Labor dominance reflects the relative migration levels of those in the working ages relative to those of children and pensioners. *Labor asymmetry* refers to the shape of the left-skewed unimodal curve describing the age profile of labor force migration. A convenient indicator of the degree of asymmetry of the curve is the ratio $\sigma_2 = \lambda_2/\alpha_2$.

Again, an analogous argument applies to the post-labor force curve, and $\sigma_3 = \lambda_3/\alpha_3$ may be defined as the index of retirement asymmetry.

When adding a pre-labor force curve of a given *level* on to the labor force component, it is also important to indicate something of its *shape*. For example, if the migration rates of children mirror those of their parents, then α_1 should be approximately equal to α_2, and $\beta_{12} = \alpha_1/\alpha_2$, the index of parental-shift regularity, should be close to unity.

Large differences in GMRs give rise to slopes and vertical relationships among schedules that are noncomparable when examined visually. Recourse then must be made to a standardization of the areas under the migration curves, for example, a general rescaling to a GMR of unity. The principal slope and location parameters and ratios used to characterize model migration schedules are not affected by changes in levels. Only heights, areas, and vertical distances, such as the jump, are level-dependent measures.

5.3.2 *A Comparative Analysis*

Section 5.3.1 demonstrated that age-specific rates of migration exhibit a fundamental age profile, which can be expressed in mathematical form as a model migration schedule defined by a total of 11 parameters. In this section we seek to establish the range of values typically assumed by each of these parameters and their associated derived variables. This exercise is made possible by the availability of the relatively large data base on migration flows collected in the Migration and Settlement Study.

The age-specific migration rates that were used to demonstrate the fit of the model migration schedule in the last section were single-year rates. Such data are scarce at the regional level and, in our analysis, were available only for Sweden. All other region-specific migration data were reported for five-year age groups only and, therefore, must be interpolated to provide the necessary input data by single years of age. In all such instances the region-specific migration schedules were first scaled to a GMR of unity (GMR = 1) before being subjected to a cubic-spline interpolation (McNeil *et al.* 1977). Starting with a migration schedule with a GMR of unity and rates by single years of age, the nonlinear parameter estimation algorithm ultimately yields a set of estimates for the model schedule's parameters.

Table 5.9 referred to results for rates of male migration from the Stockholm region to the rest of Sweden, that is, to the aggregate of the other seven regions that were defined in the Swedish case study. If these rates were to be disaggregated by region of destination, then $8 \times 7 = 56$ interregional and eight intraregional schedules would need to be examined for each sex, which would complicate comparisons with other nations. To resolve this difficulty we shall associate a "typical" schedule with each collection of national rates by calculating the mean of each parameter and derived variable. [The median, mode, ratio of standard deviation to mean, and lower and upper bounds are also of interest and are included as part of the more detailed computer outputs reproduced in Appendix B of Rogers and Castro (1981b).]

To avoid the influence of unrepresentative outlier observations in the computation of averages defining a typical national schedule, it was decided to delete approximately 10% of the extreme schedules. Specifically, the parameters and derived variables were ordered from low value to high value; the lowest 5% and the highest 5% were defined to be extreme values. Schedules with the largest number of low and high extreme values were discarded, in sequence, until only about 90% of the original number of schedules remained. This reduced set then served for the calculation of various summary statistics. Table 5.10 illustrates the average parameter values obtained with the Swedish data.

The availability of the same Swedish data aggregated by both one-year and five-year age intervals allowed us to test whether the interpolation procedure gives satisfactory results. To investigate this, the results of Table 5.10

Table 5.10 Mean values of parameters defining the reduced set of observed model migration schedules: Sweden, 8 regions, 1974 observed data by single years of age until 84 years and over.[a]

Parameter	Males		Females	
	Without retirement peak (48 schedules)	With retirement peak (9 schedules)	Without retirement peak (54 schedules)	With retirement peak (3 schedules)
a_1	0.029	0.026	0.026	0.024
α_1	0.124	0.085	0.108	0.093
a_2	0.067	0.051	0.076	0.055
μ_2	20.50	21.25	19.09	18.87
α_2	0.104	0.093	0.127	0.106
λ_2	0.448	0.416	0.537	0.424
c	0.003	0.002	0.003	0.003
a_3		0.0006		0.0001
μ_3		76.71		74.78
α_3		0.847		0.938
λ_3		0.158		0.170

[a]Region 1 (Stockholm) is a single-commune region; hence there exists no intraregional schedule for it, leaving $8^2 - 1 = 63$ schedules, of which 6 were deleted.

were replicated using an aggregation with five-year age intervals. The results, set out in Table 5.11, indicate that although the interpolation procedure is adequate, the parameter λ_2 is consistently underestimated with five-year data. This tendency should be noted and kept in mind.

It is also important to note the erratic behavior of the retirement peak, apparently a result of its extreme sensitivity to the loss of information arising from the aggregation. Thus, although we shall continue to present results relating to the post-labor force ages, they will not be a part of our search for families of schedules.

Tables 5.10 and 5.11 summarize average parameter values for 57 male and 57 female Swedish model migration schedules. We now expand our analysis to include a much larger data base, adding to the 114 Swedish model schedules another 164 schedules from the UK (Table 5.12), 114 from Japan, 20 from the Netherlands (Table 5.13), 58 from the Soviet Union, eight from the US, and 32 from Hungary (Table 5.14). Summary statistics for these 510 schedules are set out in Appendix B of Rogers and Castro (1981b); 206 are male schedules, 206 are female schedules, and 98 are for males plus females.[4]

---

[4]This total does not include the 56 schedules excluded as outliers. During the process of fitting the model schedule to these more than 500 interregional migration schedules, a frequently encountered problem was the occurrence of a negative value for the constant c. In all such instances the initial value of c was set equal to the lowest observed migration rate, and the nonlinear estimation procedure was started once again.

Table 5.11 Mean values of parameters defining the reduced set of observed model migration schedules: Sweden, 8 regions, 1974 observed data by five years of age until 80 years and over.[a]

Parameter	Males		Females	
	Without retirement peak (49 schedules)	With retirement peak (8 schedules)	Without retirement peak (54 schedules)	With retirement peak (3 schedules)
a_1	0.028	0.026	0.026	0.026
α_1	0.115	0.088	0.108	0.077
a_2	0.068	0.052	0.080	0.044
μ_2	20.61	20.26	19.52	19.18
α_2	0.105	0.084	0.133	0.089
λ_2	0.396	0.390	0.374	0.341
c	0.002	0.001	0.002	0.002
a_3		0.0017		0.0036
μ_3		77.47		77.72
α_3		0.603		0.375
λ_3		0.148		0.134

[a]Region 1 (Stockholm) is a single-commune region; hence there exists no intraregional schedule for it, leaving $8^2 - 1 = 63$ schedules, of which 6 were deleted.

Table 5.12 Mean values of parameters defining the reduced set of observed model migration schedules: the United Kingdom, 10 regions, 1970.[a]

Parameter	Males		Females	
	Without retirement peak (59 schedules)	With retirement peak (23 schedules)	Without retirement peak (61 schedules)	With retirement peak (21 schedules)
a_1	0.021	0.016	0.021	0.018
α_1	0.099	0.080	0.097	0.089
a_2	0.059	0.053	0.063	0.048
μ_2	22.00	20.42	21.35	21.56
α_2	0.127	0.120	0.151	0.153
λ_2	0.259	0.301	0.327	0.333
c	0.003	0.004	0.003	0.004
a_3		0.007		0.002
μ_3		71.11		71.84
α_3		0.692		0.583
λ_3		0.309		0.403

[a]No intraregional migration data were included in the United Kingdom data; hence $10^2 - 10 = 90$ schedules were analyzed, of which 8 were deleted.

Table 5.13 Mean values of parameters defining the reduced set of observed model migration schedules: Japan, 8 regions, 1970; the Netherlands, 12 regions, 1974.[a]

Parameter	Japan		Netherlands	
	Males	Females	Males	Females
	Without retirement peak (57 schedules)	With retirement peak (57 schedules)	Without retirement peak (10 schedules)	With retirement peak (10 schedules)
a_1	0.014	0.021	0.013	0.012
α_1	0.095	0.117	0.080	0.098
a_2	0.075	0.085	0.063	0.084
μ_2	17.63	21.32	20.86	20.10
α_2	0.102	0.152	0.130	0.174
λ_2	0.480	0.350	0.287	0.307
c	0.002	0.004	0.003	0.004
a_3			0.00001	0.00004
α_3			0.077	0.071

[a]Region 1 in Japan (Hokkaido) is a single-prefecture region; hence there exists no intraregional schedule for it, leaving $8^2 - 1 = 63$ schedules, of which 6 were deleted. The only migration schedules available for the Netherlands were the migration rates out of each region without regard to destination; hence only 12 schedules were used, of which 2 were deleted.

A significant number of schedules exhibited a pattern of migration in the post-labor force ages that differed from that of the 11-parameter model migration schedule defined in equation (5.1). Instead of a retirement peak, the age profile took on the form of an "upward slope". In such instances the following nine-parameter modification of the basic model migration schedule was introduced:

$$m_x = a_1 \exp(-\alpha_1 x)$$
$$+ a_2 \exp\{-\alpha_2(x - \mu_2) - \exp[-\lambda_2(x - \mu_2)]\}$$
$$+ a_3 \exp(\alpha_3 x)$$
$$+ c, \qquad x = 0,1,2,\dots \ . \tag{5.3}$$

The right-hand side of Table 5.13, for example, sets out the mean parameter estimates of this modified form of the model migration schedule for the Netherlands.

Tables 5.10–5.14 present a wealth of information about national patterns of migration by age. The parameters define a wide range of model migration schedules. Four refer only to migration level: a_1, a_2, a_3, and c. Their values are for a GMR of unity; to obtain corresponding values for other levels of migration, these four numbers need to be multiplied by the desired level of GMR. For example, the observed GMR for male migration out of the Stockholm region in

Table 5.14 Mean values of parameters defining the reduced set of observed total (males plus females) model migration schedules: the Soviet Union, 8 regions, 1974; the United States, 4 regions, 1970; Hungary, 6 regions, 1974.[a]

Parameter	Soviet Union	United States	Hungary	
	Without retirement peak (58 schedules)	With retirement peak (8 schedules)	Without retirement slope (7 schedules)	With retirement slope (25 schedules)
a_1	0.005	0.021	0.010	0.015
α_1	0.302	0.075	0.245	0.193
a_2	0.126	0.060	0.090	0.099
μ_2	19.14	20.14	17.22	18.74
α_2	0.176	0.118	0.130	0.159
λ_2	0.310	0.569	0.415	0.274
c	0.004	0.002	0.004	0.003
a_3		0.002		0.00032
μ_3		81.80		
α_3		0.430		0.033
λ_3		0.119		

[a]Intraregional migration was included in the Soviet Union and Hungarian data but not in the United States data; hence there were $8^2 = 64$ schedules for the Soviet Union, of which 6 were deleted, $6^2 = 36$ schedules for Hungary, of which 4 were deleted, and $4^2 - 4 = 12$ schedules for the United States, of which 2 were deleted because they lacked a retirement peak and another 2 were deleted because of their extreme values.

1974 was 1.45. Multiplying $a_1 = 0.023$ by 1.45 gives 0.033, the appropriate value of a_1 with which to generate the migration schedule having a GMR of 1.45.

The remaining model schedule parameters refer to migration age profile: $\alpha_1, \mu_2, \alpha_2, \lambda_2, \mu_3, \alpha_3,$ and λ_3. Their values remain constant for all levels of the GMR. Taken together, they define the age profile of migration from one region to another. Schedules without a retirement peak yield only four profile parameters: $\alpha_1, \mu_2, \alpha_2,$ and λ_2, and schedules with a retirement slope have an additional profile parameter α_3.

A detailed analysis of the parameters defining the various classes of schedules is beyond the scope of this study. Nevertheless a few basic contrasts among national average age profiles may be usefully highlighted.

Let us begin with an examination of the labor force component defined by the four parameters a_2 (level), μ_2 (position), α_2 (descent parameter), and λ_2 (ascent parameter). The national average values for these parameters generally lie within the following ranges:

$$0.05 < a_2 < 0.10$$

$$17 < \mu_2 < 22$$

$$0.10 < \alpha_2 < 0.20$$

$0.25 \ < \lambda_2 \ < 0.60$.

In all but two instances, the values of a_2, α_2, and λ_2 are larger for females than for males. The reverse is the case for μ_2, with two exceptions, the most important of which is exhibited by Japan's females, who consistently show an older value for μ_2 than do males. This apparently is a consequence of the tradition in Japan that girls leave the family home at a later age than boys.

The two parameters defining the pre-labor force component, a_1 and α_1, generally lie within the ranges 0.01–0.03 and 0.08–0.12, respectively. The exceptions are the Soviet Union and Hungary, which exhibit unusually high values for α_1. Unlike the case of the labor force component, consistent sex differentials are difficult to identify.

Average national migration age profiles, like most aggregations, hide more than they reveal. Some insight into the ranges of variations that are averaged out may be found by consulting the lower and upper bounds and standard-deviation-to-mean ratios (i.e., coefficients of variation) for each set of national schedules listed in Appendix B of Rogers and Castro (1981b). Table 5.15 illustrates how parameters vary in several *unaveraged* national schedules, by way of example. The model schedules presented there described migration flows out of and into the capital regions of each of six countries: Helsinki, Finland; Budapest, Hungary; Tokyo, Japan; Amsterdam, the Netherlands; Stockholm, Sweden; and London, the UK. All are illustrated in Figure 5.6.

The most apparent difference between the age profiles of the outflow and inflow migration patterns of the six national capitals is the dominance of young labor force migrants in the inflows; that is, proportionately more migrants in the young labor force ages appear in the flows destined for the capital regions. The larger values of the product $a_2\lambda_2$ in the inflow profiles and of the ratio $\delta_{12} = a_1 / a_2$ in the outflow schedules indicate this labor dominance.

A second profile attribute is the degree of asymmetry in the labor force component of the migration schedule, that is, the ratio of the ascent parameter λ_2 to the descent parameter α_2, defined as σ_2. In all but the Japanese case, the labor force curves of the capital region outmigration profiles are more asymmetric than those of the corresponding reverse flows. We refer to this characteristic as labor asymmetry.

Examining the observed descent parameters of the labor (α_2) and pre-labor force (α_1) curves, we find, for example, that they are close to being equal in the outflow schedules of Helsinki and Stockholm and are highly unequal in the cases of Budapest, Tokyo, and Amsterdam. In four of the six capital region inflow profiles α_2 is greater than α_1. Profiles with significantly different values for α_2 and α_1 are said to be irregular.

In conclusion, the empirical migration data of six industrialized nations suggest the following hypothesis. *The age profile of a typical migration schedule associated with flows into a capital region is, in general, more labor-dominant and more labor-symmetric than the age profile of the*

Table 5.15 Parameters defining observed total (males plus females) model migration schedules for flows from and to capital cities: Finland, 1974; Hungary, 1974; Japan, 1970; the Netherlands, 1974; Sweden, 1974; the United Kingdom, 1970.

Parameter	Finland		Hungary		Japan	
	From Helsinki	To Helsinki	From Budapest	To Budapest	From Tokyo	To Tokyo
a_1	0.037	0.024	0.015	0.008	0.019	0.008
α_1	0.127	0.170	0.239	0.262	0.157	0.149
a_2	0.081	0.130	0.082	0.094	0.064	0.096
μ_2	21.42	22.13	17.10	17.69	20.70	15.74
α_2	0.124	0.198	0.130	0.152	0.111	0.134
λ_2	0.231	0.321	0.355	0.305	0.204	0.577
c	0.000	0.003	0.003	0.003	0.003	0.002
a_3	0.00027		0.00001	0.00005	0.00002	0.00131
μ_3	99.32					
α_3	0.204					
λ_3	0.042		0.072	0.059	0.061	0.000

Parameter	Netherlands		Sweden		United Kingdom	
	From Amsterdam	To Amsterdam	From Stockholm	To Stockholm	From London	To London
a_1	0.015	0.012	0.028	0.018	0.015	0.014
α_1	0.085	0.108	0.098	0.102	0.090	0.072
a_2	0.050	0.093	0.046	0.093	0.048	0.067
μ_2	21.62	19.66	20.48	19.20	19.65	18.81
α_2	0.141	0.150	0.095	0.134	0.111	0.123
λ_2	0.284	0.288	0.322	0.323	0.327	0.320
c	0.002	0.003	0.003	0.002	0.005	0.004
a_3	0.00229	0.00002	0.00004	0.00003	0.00003	
μ_3			80.32	73.19	81.13	
α_3			0.616	1.359	0.676	
λ_3	0.012	0.066	0.105	0.255	0.112	

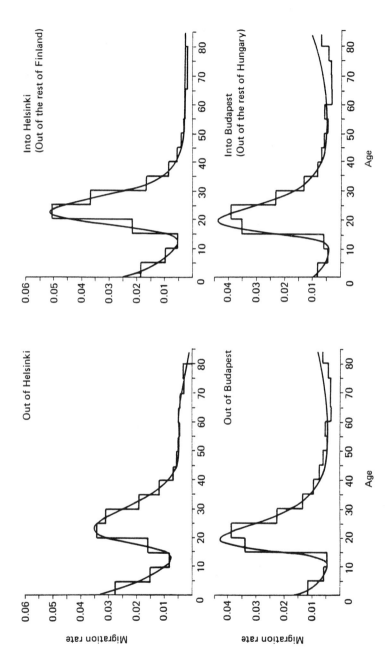

Figure 5.6(a) Migration schedules of flows from and to capital cities: Helsinki and Budapest.
Source: Rogers and Castro (1981b).

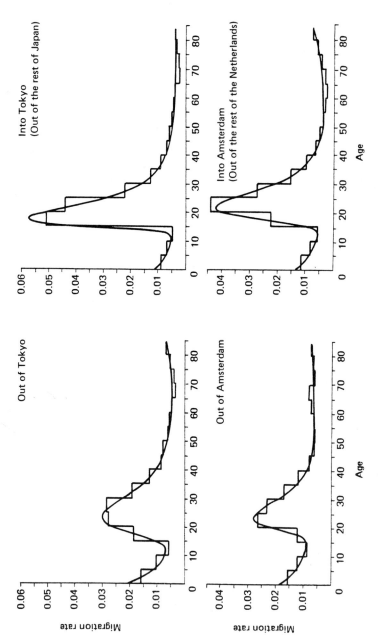

Figure 5.6(b) Migration schedules and flows from and to capital cities: Tokyo and Amsterdam.
Source: Rogers and Castro (1981b).

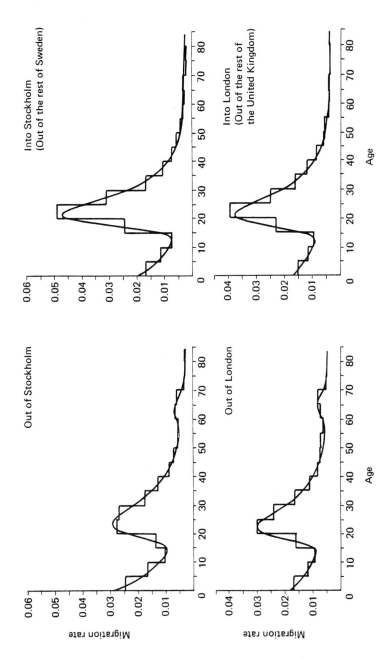

Figure 5.6(c) Migration schedules and flows from and to capital cities: Stockholm and London.
Source: Rogers and Castro (1981b).

corresponding capital region outmigration schedule. No comparable hypothesis can be made regarding its anticipated degree of irregularity.

5.3.3 *Families of Schedules and a Basic Standard Schedule*

Three sets of model migration schedules have been defined in this chapter: the 11-parameter schedule with a retirement peak, the alternative nine-parameter schedule with a retirement slope, and the simple seven-parameter schedule with neither a peak nor a slope. Thus we have at least three broad families of schedules.

Additional dimensions for classifying schedules into families are suggested by the above comparative analysis of national migration age profiles and the basic measures and derived variables defined in Section 5.3.1. These dimensions reflect different locations on the horizontal and vertical axes of the schedule, as well as different ratios of slopes and heights.

Of the 510 model migration schedules studied in this section, 412 are sex-specific and, of these, 336 exhibit neither a retirement peak nor a retirement slope. Because the parameter estimates describing the age profile of post-labor force migration behave erratically, we shall restrict our search for families of schedules to these 164 male and 172 female model schedules.

An examination of the parametric values exhibited by the 336 migration schedules summarized in Rogers and Castro (1981c) suggests that a large fraction of the variation shown by these schedules is a consequence of changes in the values of the following four parameters and derived variables: μ_2, δ_{12}, σ_2, and β_{12}.

Migration schedules may peak early or late, depending on the location of μ_2 on the horizontal (age) axis. Although this parameter generally takes on a value close to 20, roughly three out of four observations fall within the range 17–25. We shall call those below age 19 early-peaking schedules and those above 22 late-peaking schedules.

The ratio of the two basic vertical parameters, a_1 and a_2, is a measure of the relative importance of the migration of children in a model migration schedule. The index of child dependence, $\delta_{12} = a_1/a_2$, tends to exhibit a mean value of about one-third, with 80% of the values falling between one-fifth and four-fifths. Schedules with an index of one-fifth or less will be said to be labor-dominant; those above two-fifths will be called child-dependent.

Migration schedules with labor force components that take the form of a relatively symmetrical bell shape will be said to be *labor-symmetric.* These schedules tend to exhibit an index of labor asymmetry ($\sigma_2 = \lambda_2/\alpha_2$) that is less than 2. Labor-asymmetric schedules, on the other hand, usually assume values for σ_2 value of about 4, with approximately five out of six schedules exhibiting a σ_2 within the range 1–8.

Finally, the index of parental-shift regularity, $\beta_{12} = \alpha_1/\alpha_2$, in many schedules is close to unity, with approximately 70% of the values lying between one-third and four-thirds. Values of β_{12} that are lower then four-fifths or higher than six-fifths will be called irregular.

We may imagine a 3 × 4 cross-classification of migration schedules that defines a dozen "average families" (Table 5.16). Introducing a low and a high value for each parameter gives rise to 16 additional families for each of the three classes of schedules. Thus we may conceive of a minimum set of 60 families, equally divided among schedules with a retirement peak, schedules with a retirement slope, and schedules with neither a retirement peak nor a retirement slope (a reduced form).

Table 5.16 A cross-classification of migration schedules.

Schedule	Measure (average value)			
	Peaking $(\mu_2 = 20)$	Dominance $(\delta_{12} = \frac{1}{3})$	Asymmetry $(\sigma_2 = 4)$	Regularity $(\beta_{12} = 1)$
Retirement peak	+	+	+	+
Retirement slope	+	+	+	+
Reduced form	+	+	+	+

The comparative analysis of national and interregional migration patterns carried out in Section 5.3.2 identified at least three distinct families of age profiles. First, there was the 11-parameter *basic model migration schedule* with a retirement peak that adequately described a number of interregional flows, such as the age profiles of outmigrants leaving capital regions such as Stockholm and London. The elimination of the retirement peak gave rise to the seven-parameter *reduced form* of this basic schedule, a form that was used to describe a large number of labor-dominant profiles and the age pattern of migration schedules with a single open-ended age interval for the post-labor force population, such as Japan's migration schedules. Finally, the existence of a monotonically rising tails in migration schedules such as those exhibited by the Dutch data led to the definition of a third profile, the nine-parameter *model migration schedule with an upward slope*.

Within each family of schedules, a number of key parameters or variables may be put forward in order to further classify different categories of migration profiles. For example, in Section 5.3.2 we noted the special importance of the following aspects of shape and location along the age axis:

(1)   Peaking: early peaking versus late peaking (μ_2)
(2)   Dominance: child dependency versus labor dominance (δ_{12})
(3)   Asymmetry: labor symmetry versus labor asymmetry (σ_2)

(4) Regularity: parental-shift regularity versus parental-shift irregularity (β_{12}).

These fundamental families and four key parameters give rise to a large variety of standard schedules. For example, even if the four key parameters are restricted to only dichotomous values, one already needs $2^4 = 16$ standard schedules. If, in addition, the sexes are to be differentiated, then 32 standard schedules are a minimum. A large number of such schedules would make the notion of a standard curve somewhat unworkable. Hence we propose only a single standard for both sexes and assume that the shape of the post-labor force part of the schedule may be determined exogenously.

The similarity of the male and female median parameter values set out in Rogers and Castro (1981b) (for Sweden, the UK, and Japan) suggests that one could use the average of the values for the two sexes to define a unisexual standard. A rough rounding of these averages would simplify matters even more. Table 5.17 presents the simplified basic standard parameters obtained in this way. The values of a_1, a_2, and c are initial values only and need to be scaled proportionately to ensure a unit GMR. Figure 5.7 illustrates the age profile of this simplified basic standard migration schedule.

Table 5.17 The simplified basic (Rogers–Castro) standard migration schedule.

Fundamental parameter	Fundamental ratio
$a_1 = 0.02$	$\delta_{12} = \dfrac{1}{3}$
$\alpha_1 = 0.10$	$\sigma_2 = 4$
$a_2 = 0.06$	$\beta_{12} = 1$
$\mu_2 = 20$	$\delta_{1c} = 6$
$\alpha_2 = 0.10$	
$\lambda_2 = 0.40$	
$c = 0.003$	

5.3.4 *Accounting for the Age Profile: Migration by Cause*

Studies have shown that the age pattern of deaths varies systematically with the level of mortality. For example, as the expectation of life at birth increases, the largest absolute declines in mortality generally occur at ages below 5 and above 65. This is a consequence of the dramatic reduction in the contribution to overall deaths made by infectious diseases, which have a U-shaped age profile of mortality. Are there analogous systematic variations in age patterns of migration? Does the age pattern of migration vary with the level of migration? For example, if divorce is a reason for migration, and if the level of migration and the number of divorces per capita both increase with

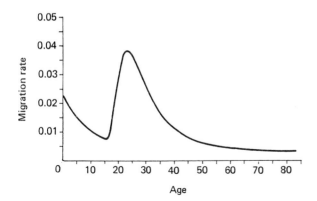

Figure 5.7 The simplified basic (Rogers–Castro) standard migration schedule.
Source: Rogers and Castro (1981b).

economic development, should one then expect a particular shift in the age profile of aggregate migration?

Why people move is a question that needs to be considered with respect to (1) those characteristics of potential migrants that condition receptivity to migration, and (2) those environmental factors that stimulate migration from one community to another. Nevertheless, some insight into motivations for migration may be obtained simply by asking people why they moved. This approach has been adopted, for example, in nationwide surveys conducted by the US Bureau of the Census (Long and Hansen 1979) and in national migration registers maintained in such countries as Czechoslovakia (Kühnl 1978).

Studies of reported causes for migration within a given country are subject to a number of serious limitations. First, usually only the "main" cause is tabulated and examined, yet multiple interdependent causes underlie migration behavior. Second, the alternative causes listed in migration questionnaires are typically broad aggregations of a much wider range of causes and therefore may inadequately reflect the true importance of motivations connected with migration. Finally, problems arise when the causes are not separately classified for the initiators of migration (e.g., household heads) and for their dependents (e.g., children). In short, reported causes of migration are often mutually interdependent, usually insufficient in number, and generally not linked directly to the true decision maker. However, analogous limitations also appear in studies of mortality disaggregated by cause, without presenting insuperable obstacles. As noted by Preston (1976, p.2):

> Causes are undoubtedly recorded with considerable inaccuracy and inter-population incomparability, and these problems have discouraged the exploitation of cause-of-death statistics. But demographic data are

never perfectly accurate, and the choice is between neglecting them altogether and producing qualified statements about the tendencies they suggest.

Table 5.18 Migration data disaggregated by cause: the United States[a], Hungary[b], and Czechoslovakia[c], various years.

Country (years)	Percentage of migrants citing the cause				
	Employment	Education	Marriage	Housing	Other
(a) *Household heads only*					
United States (1974–76)	56.6	5.4	1.6	8.1	28.3
Hungary (1958)	49.7	2.5	15.4	12.0	20.4
Hungary (1968)	43.8	1.7	21.5	14.1	18.9
(b) *All migrants*					
United States (1974–76)	59.8	3.9	1.4	8.0	26.9
Czechoslovakia (1973)	28.1	1.0	17.0	41.8	12.1

[a]US data are taken from Long and Hansen (1979) and refer to interstate migration.
[b]Hungarian data are taken from Compton (1971) and refer to all intercommunal migration.
[c]Czechoslovakian data are taken from Kühnl (1978) and refer to all intercommunal migration.

Table 5.18 gives the percentage of migrants moving for each of five causes in the US and in Hungary. These data confirm that it is a great oversimplification to explain migration solely in terms of job-related motivations. For example, although approximately half of the migrating household heads cited employment as the main reason for moving, a combination of education, marriage, housing, and other reasons provided the motivation for the other half to migrate. Moreover, Hungarian data indicate that employment as a cause of migration has been declining in relative importance over time.

Only 36% of all migrants were found to be household heads in the US survey (Long and Hansen 1979); in Hungary the corresponding proportion ranged from 55% in 1958 to 63% in 1968 (Compton 1971). The data for Czechoslovakia do not distinguish between household heads and their accompanying dependents.

Housing reasons accounted for over 40% of all migration between communities (communes) in Czechoslovakia in 1973; this total is about five times as high as the figure for the US. Data for the US, however, refer to *interstate* migration, and one would expect housing reasons to decline in importance relative to employment reasons when considering migrations over such relatively greater distance.

Less than 30% of migration within Czechoslovakia was caused by changes in employment. This relatively low share of the total is somewhat surprising and apparently reflects a leveling of regional economic differences (Kühnl 1978).

Causes of migration are related to a person's age and sex. For example, migration motivated by health reasons is a phenomenon characteristic of old persons, whereas education-related migration is predominantly associated with young people. Wives tend to be younger than their husbands; therefore the age profile of female migration peaks at an earlier age than the corresponding profile for males. Thus, in order to understand better why people move, it is important to disaggregate cause-specific migration data by age and sex.

If the age pattern of migration is influenced by its cause-specific structure, then it should be possible to attribute differences in age patterns of migration in two or more populations, at least partially, to differences in their cause-specific structures. Unfortunately, detailed age-specific migration data that are disaggregated by cause are extremely scarce, and we have been able to find only one source for this study: the Czechoslovakian migration register.[5]

Figure 5.8 displays histograms and their associated model migration schedules for age-specific male and female migration rates in Czechoslovakia. Figure 5.9 presents the age-specific cause-of-migration structures that underlie these rates. For ease of visual comparison all age profiles have been scaled so that the area under the curve is unity.

The model schedule defined in equation (5.1) may be used to fit all of the cause-specific profiles illustrated in Figure 5.9. The profiles associated with change of employment, moving closer to the place of work, and marriage may be described by the reduced seven-parameter model. Profiles of education-motivated migration follow the model schedule with both the first and the third components omitted ($a_1 = a_3 = 0$). The age pattern of health-related migration can be described by the model schedule with both the first and the second components omitted ($a_1 = a_2 = 0$). Finally, migration for housing reasons and for the remaining "all other causes" (including divorce) takes on the profile of the full 11-parameter model, as does the aggregate schedule. More detailed numerical outputs are described in Rogers and Castro (1981a).

The age profiles reveal that the causes of migration have quite different age patterns. Of the seven causes illustrated, the age profile of *housing* reasons is most similar to that of the aggregate migration schedule, exhibiting roughly the same peaks: during infancy, during the early years of labor force participation, and at retirement.

Migrations due to marriage and education, on the other hand, are concentrated between the ages of 10 and 30 and are essentially unimodal in age profile. Migrations caused by change of employment and moving closer to the place of work have profiles that are bimodal, with local peaks during infancy and

---

[5]Identification of causes of migration has been a part of the regular internal migration register of Czechoslovakia since 1966. The data are based on responses given by migrants at the time that they notify local authorities of their change of address. Dependents are not distinguished from household heads in these data.

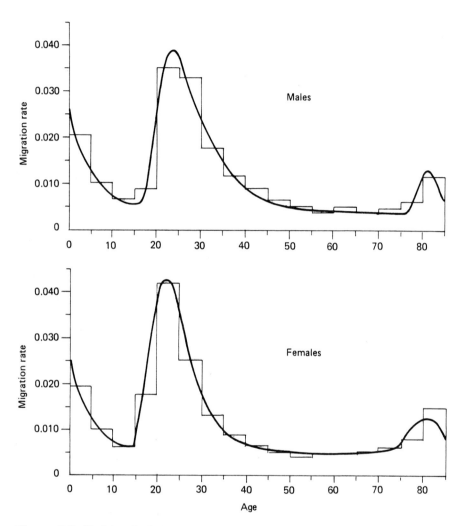

Figure 5.8 Model schedules of observed migration rates for all causes combined: Czechoslovakia, males and females, 1973.

during the early years of labor force participation. Finally, health is apparently an important cause of migration only for the elderly. (The residual category "all other causes" is aggregated with divorce in Figure 5.9 in order to give it a profile that is more amenable to our analysis.)

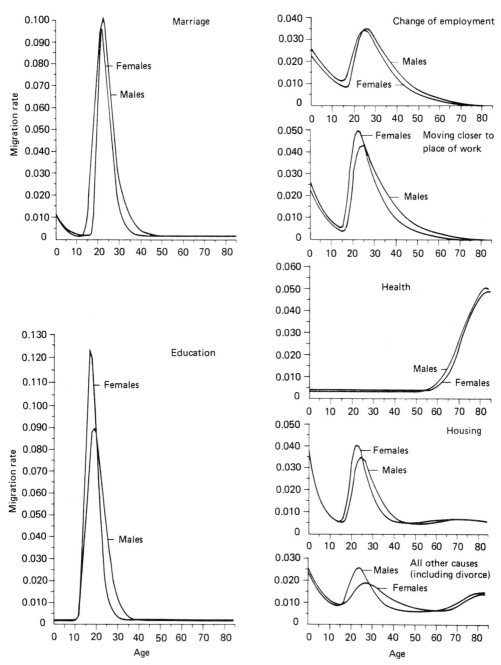

Figure 5.9 Model schedules of observed cause-specific migration rates: Czechoslovakia, males and females, 1973.

The different cause-specific age patterns may be interpreted within a life-cycle framework in which individuals pass through different states of existence. Starting with birth and then entry into the educational system at the elementary level, the "passage" may also include entry into military service or university, marriage, multiple entries into and withdrawals from the labor force, perhaps divorce and remarriage, retirement, death of spouse, and moves to enter sanatoria or to rejoin relatives.

Associated with this individual life-cycle perspective is a family life cycle, which begins with marriage, passes on to procreation and child rearing (possibly interrupted by divorce or death), continues with child "launching", and ends with the "empty nest" and ultimately with the death of both spouses. Such a perspective suggests an alternative means of accounting for the migration age profile: family status. We take up this idea next.

5.3.5 *Accounting for the Age Profile: Migration by Family Status*

A population pyramid graphically displays the age composition of a population — a composition that reflects the past history of fertility and mortality to which the population has been exposed. For example, high rates of natural increase give rise to age pyramids that taper more rapidly with age, and zero growth rates ultimately produce age pyramids that are nearly rectangular until ages 50 and 60 and that decline rapidly thereafter as death rates increase among the aged. Thus one may conclude that the age composition of a population tells us something about past patterns of fertility and mortality. What does the age composition of migrants tell us?

The age profile of a schedule of migration rates reflects the influences of two age distributions: the age composition of migrants and that of the population of which they were a part (Rogers 1976c). This can be easily demonstrated by decomposing the numerator and denominator of the fraction that defines an age-specific migration rate.

If $O(x)$ denotes the number of outmigrants at age x, leaving a region with a population of $K(x)$ at that age, then

$$m_x = \frac{O(x)}{K(x)} = \frac{O\,N(x)}{K\,C(x)} = o\,\frac{N(x)}{C(x)} \quad , \tag{5.4}$$

where

m_x = migration rate for individuals at age x at time of migration
O = total number of outmigrants
$N(x)$ = proportion of migrants at age x at the time of migration
K = total population
$C(x)$ = proportion of total population at age x
o = crude outmigration rate.

We define the collection of $N(x)$ values to be the *migration proportion schedule* and the set of m_x values to be the *migration rate schedule*.[6]

We have shown that observed age-specific migration rate schedules exhibit a common shape. The same shape also characterizes the shape of migration proportion schedules. That is, the migration proportion schedule may be divided into young-dependent, adult, and elderly components. We confine our attention in this section to only the first two; but our argument is equally valid for profiles showing a retirement peak or an upward retirement slope.

The observed age distribution of migrants, $N(x)$, may be described by a function of the form:

$$N(x) = N_1(x) + N_2(x) + c \ ,$$ (5.5)

where

$$N_1(x) = a_1 \exp(-\alpha_1 x)$$

for the young-dependent component,

$$N_2(x) = a_2 \exp\{-\alpha_2(x - \mu_2) - \exp[-\lambda_2(x - \mu_2)]\}$$

for the adult (independent) component, and c is the constant term that improves the fit when migration distributions at older ages are relatively high. Figure 5.10 illustrates the female model migration proportion schedules of the observed data for Mexico and Sweden, which by definition show an area of unity under each curve.

An alternative way of expressing equation (5.5) is as a weighted linear combination of the density functions representing the above-mentioned three components (Castro and Rogers 1983a):

$$N(x) = \varphi_1 f_1(x) + \varphi_2 f_2(x) + \varphi_c (1/\omega) \ ,$$ (5.6)

where ω is the last age included in the schedule, φ_1 and φ_2 are the relative shares of the child and adult components, φ_c is the relative share of the constant term, and $f_1(x)$ and $f_2(x)$ are the single- and double-exponential density functions, respectively;

$$f_1(x) = \alpha_1 \exp(-\alpha_1 x)$$ (5.7)

$$f_2(x) = \frac{\lambda_2}{\Gamma(\alpha_2/\lambda_2)} \exp\{-\alpha_2(x - \mu_2) - \exp[-\lambda_2(x - \mu_2)]\} \ ,$$ (5.8)

---

[6]To be consistent with conventional statistical notation for probability density functions and cumulative distribution functions, used later in this chapter, we express the age variable x as an argument of the function and not as a subscript.

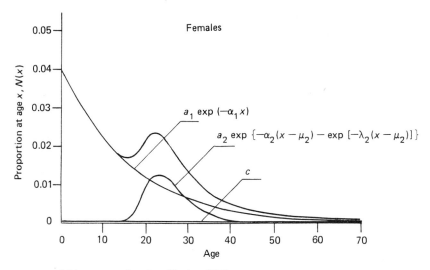

(a) Interstate migration: Mexico, 1970

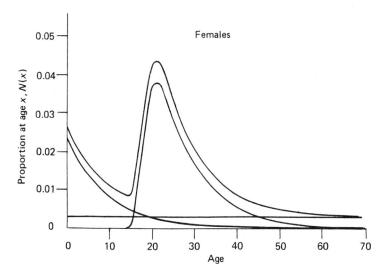

(b) Interregional migration: Sweden, 1974

Figure 5.10 Components of the model migration proportion schedule.

and $\Gamma(\alpha_2/\lambda_2)$ represents the gamma function value of α_2/λ_2. Note that $\varphi_1 + \varphi_2 + \varphi_c = 1$ by definition.

Equations (5.6–5.8) imply that

$$a_1 = \varphi_1\,\alpha_1\ ,\tag{5.9}$$

$$a_2 = \varphi_2 \frac{\lambda_2}{\Gamma(\alpha_2 / \lambda_2)} , \qquad (5.10)$$

and

$$c = \frac{\varphi_c}{\omega} . \qquad (5.11)$$

The six parameters a_1, α_1, a_2, α_2, λ_2, and μ_2 do not seem to have demographic interpretations. (Both a_1 and a_2 reflect the heights of their respective parts of the profile; α_1 and α_2 refer to the descending slopes; λ_2 reflects the ascending slope; and μ_2 positions the adult component on the age axis.) Taken as a group, these parameters suggest a number of useful and robust measures for describing an observed migration proportion schedule. For example, the ratio $D_0 = \varphi_1 / \varphi_2$, the dependency migration ratio, is one of several important ratios that may be used to interpret particular patterns of dependency among migrants. It assumes a central role as an indicator of family dependency structure by defining the number of dependents per adult migrant (Castro and Rogers 1983a).

It is widely recognized that a large fraction of total migration is accounted for by individuals whose moves are dependent on those of others. Indeed family migration is such a well established phenomenon that Ryder (1978) has even suggested its use as a criterion for identifying family membership: a family comprises those individuals who would migrate together.

To understand the influences that family and dependency relationships have on migration age compositions, it is useful to examine how such profiles respond to fundamental changes in dependency patterns (Castro and Rogers 1983b). To illustrate this, consider a single-sex population that is divided into two groups: dependents and heads, where dependents are simply individuals who have not left home to become heads. (Included as heads are independent single individuals who may be viewed as one-person families.) Thus the age distribution of the female population $C(x)$ may be composed by weighting the density functions of dependents and heads:

$$C(x) = \varphi_{1c} f_{1c}(x) + \varphi_{2c} f_{2c}(x) ,$$

where φ_{1c} and φ_{2c} are the proportions of dependents and heads in the total female population, and $f_{1c}(x)$ and $f_{2c}(x)$ are the respective age distributions.

To investigate analytically some of the underlying patterns of "head formation" requires some mathematical theorizing. Let y_0 denote the age at which an appreciable number of females first leave home to establish their own households. Since marriage is an important reason for leaving the family home, it is likely that the probability density function describing the pattern of head formation by age is similar to the one found in studies of nuptiality — the double-exponential function defined in equaton (5.8). If $g(y)$ is such a function then

$$G(x) = \int_{y_0}^{x} g(y)\,dy$$

defines the proportion of females who have ever left home by age x, that is, who are heads according to our definition.

Since $f_{2c}(x)$ defines the proportion of the population of heads of age x, and $G(x)$ defines the proportion of the population who are heads by age x, it is evident that in a stable population growing at an intrinsic rate of growth r,

$$f_{2c}(x) = \frac{\exp(-rx)\,l_x\,G(x)}{\int_0^{\infty} \exp(-ry)\,l_y\,G(y)\,dy} \quad ,$$

where l_x denotes the probability of surviving from birth to age x. For similar reasons,

$$f_{1c}(x) = \frac{\exp(-rx)\,l_x\,[1 - G(x)]}{\int_0^{\infty} \exp(-ry)\,l_y\,[1 - G(y)]\,dy} \quad .$$

Figure 5.11 illustrates the above argument with hypothetical data. It presents the survivorship curve, l_x, which is that of the Brass standard with $\alpha = -0.80$ and $\beta = 1.75$ and an expectation of life at birth of approximately 69 years (Brass 1971); and the head formation curve, $G(x)$, which is the Coale–McNeil double-exponential (Coale and McNeil 1972) expressed by the Rodriguez and Trussell (1980) standard with mean (22 years) and variance (five years) of age of becoming a head. Figure 5.12 shows the resulting dependent, head, and population (dependents plus heads) distributions of stable populations growing at intrinsic rates $r = 0$ and $r = 0.03$, respectively.

To derive the corresponding age compositions of migrants we introduce the probabilities $p_1(x)$ and $p_2(x)$ that a dependent and a head, respectively, migrate at age x in an interval of time. The age distribution of migrants is defined as before:

$$N(x) = \varphi_1 f_1(x) + \varphi_2 f_2(x) \quad ,$$

where

$$f_1(x) = \frac{\exp(-rx)\,l_x\,[1 - G(x)]p_1(x)}{\int_0^{\infty} \exp(-ry)\,l_y\,[1 - G(y)p_1(y)]\,dy} \quad .$$

and

$$f_2(x) = \frac{\exp(-rx)\,l_x\,G(x)p_2(x)}{\int_0^{\infty} \exp(-ry)l_y\,G(y)p_2(y)\,dy} \quad .$$

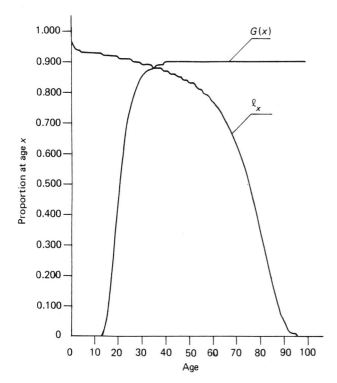

Figure 5.11 Proportion surviving to age x, l_x, and proportion of individuals who have ever left home by age x, $G(x)$.

To specify correctly the probabilities $p_1(x)$ and $p_2(x)$ from different sources of migration data, it is necessary to identify first the frequency distribution that takes into account the number of moves a person undertakes during a unit interval. For our purposes, however, we may assume that both dependents and heads follow a negative-exponential propensity to migrate with respect to age, with the function's parameter reflecting the average rate of moving per unit of time. Formally, we have then

$$p_1(x) = o_1 \exp(-o_1 x)$$

and

$$p_2(x - y_0) = o_2 \exp[-o_2(x - y_0)] \ ,$$

where y_0 denotes, as before, the age at which an appreciable number of females first leave home to establish their own household, and o_1 and o_2 denote the average rates of moving per unit of time for dependents and heads,

Figure 5.12 (landscape)

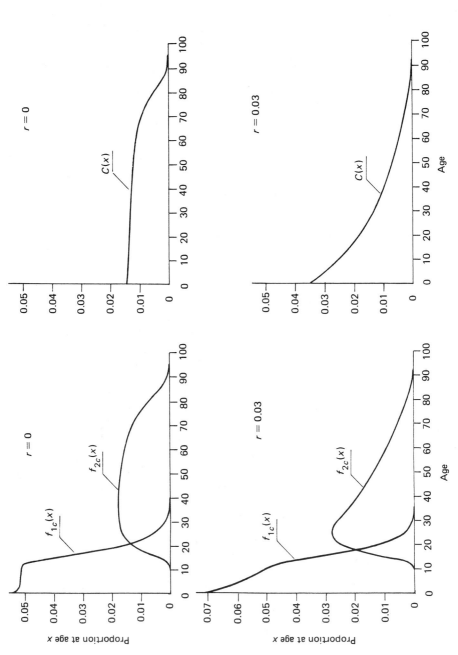

Figure 5.12 Proportion of dependents at age x, $f_{1c}(x)$, proportion of heads at age x, $f_{2c}(x)$, and the resulting population age composition, $C(x)$, for intrinsic rates of growth r of 0 and 0.03, respectively.

respectively. One might expect that the average rate of moving per unit of time for dependents, o_1, should not exceed o_2, the corresponding rate for heads.

The parameters defining the mobility conditions may be used to set out a typology of migration profiles that helps to identify how a particular family migration pattern may be reflected in a migration age composition and how important the migration propensities among heads and dependents are in structuring that age composition. Figures 5.13 and 5.14 present a set of profiles classified according to two distinctly different rates of natural increase. For each of the hypothetical populations, we show three alternative combinations of propensities to migrate among heads and dependents. First, Figure 5.13 sets out, for low head migration propensities ($o_2 = 0.08$), profiles showing a significant degree of family migration ($o_1 = o_2$) and also low family dependency ($o_1 = 0.10 o_2$ and $o_1 = 0.20 o_2$). In a similar format, Figure 5.14 presents the corresponding profiles for high head migration propensities ($o_2 = 0.16$). With the aid of these two figures we can see that patterns such as those of Sweden in Figure 5.10 indicate a relatively low family migration dependency with high head migration propensities and low population growth rates, whereas profiles such as those of Mexico present characteristics that correspond to high family migration dependency and relatively high dependent and head migration propensities.

In conclusion, it appears that the regularities that occur among migration age compositions can be summarized in a useful manner and that they may tell us something about patterns of natural increase, family relationships, and mobility levels among migrants.

A disaggregation of migrants into dependent and independent categories, and the adoption of model migration proportion schedules, illuminates the ways in which the age profile of migration is sensitive to relative changes in dependency levels and in rates of natural increase and mobility. Viewing the migration process within a framework of dependent and independent movements allows one to observe that if the independent component is mainly comprised of single persons, the associated dependent migration may be insignificant in terms of its relative share of the total migration. On the other hand, if migration tends to consist principally of family migration, then the share of dependent children may become an important part of total migration.

The degree of propensity to migrate among independent migrants is also evident from observed age profiles. Strongly skewed distributions in the adult ages, corresponding to high values for λ_2 and α_2, indicate relatively higher migration propensities for the independent component. Profiles with high dependency levels show much more weakly skewed adult migration compositions, owing to lower propensities for individual moves among heads.

Just as population age compositions reflect particular characteristics of fertility and mortality regimes, so observed migration age compositions reflect key aspects of family structure and migration patterns. Although many of the

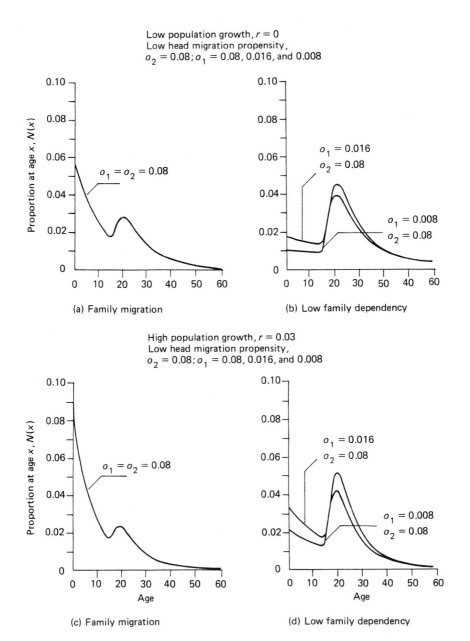

Figure 5.13 A typology of age migration distributions for different rates of population growth and family migration dependencies, and low head migration propensities.

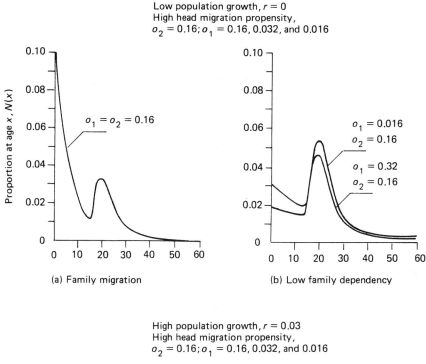

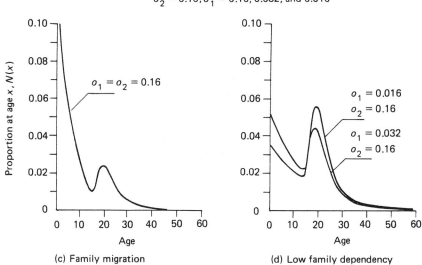

Figure 5.14 A typology of age migration distributions for different rates of population growth and family migration dependencies, and high head migration propensities.

relationships set out in this section are still conjectural, a modest start has been made. A framework for assessing the impacts of natural increase, family dependencies, and differing migration propensities has been outlined.

5.4 Conclusion

The two principal conclusions that arise as a consequence of the findings presented in this chapter are that significant spatial differences in migration levels exist in a number of IIASA countries and that remarkably stable age profiles characterize the patterns of internal migration flows in all of these countries. Because differences in levels are so directly associated with differences in the areal delineations adopted, we emphasized the analysis of differentials in age profiles over differentials in levels. It appears that the former exhibit surprisingly stable regularities across areal delineations of substantially different scale.

Among the data examined in this study, Canada and the Federal Republic of Germany showed the highest degrees of regional variation in migration levels; the German Democratic Republic and Sweden exhibited the lowest. City regions in Eastern Europe gained from net migration, whereas those in Western Europe gained only if their outmigration levels were relatively low. Differentials by sex were generally insignificant, but differentials by age were important. In some countries, such as Japan, a narrow age bracket (young adults) accounted for much of the aggregate regional differentials; in other countries, such as the German Democratic Republic and Sweden, the same general pattern of regional differences was reflected by all age groups.

The data analyzed in this study confirmed the observation that although migration levels vary substantially from region to region, the shape of an age-specific schedule of migration rates seems to be quite similar across a wide range of communities. Young adults in their early twenties generally exhibit the highest regional outmigration rates and young teenagers show the lowest. Because children migrate with their parents, infant migration rates are higher than those of adolescents. And retirement migration may give rise to a bell-shaped protrusion in the migration age profile around the ages of retirement.

Model migration schedules may be used to capture the regularities in age pattern exhibited by observed age-specific rates of migration. The particular mathematical form used in this study successfully represented over 600 such schedules. It suggested a disaggregation of observed schedules into families and the designation of a standard schedule. Efforts to account for this age profile led to a decomposition of migration flows by cause and then to a disaggregation of migrants by family status. Although exploratory in nature, these efforts indicate that considerable insight is afforded by such techniques borrowed from mortality and fertility analysis.

Appendix 5: Gross Migraproduction Rates and Mean Age of the Outmigration Schedule for Each Region in the Migration and Settlement Study

Migration

Country (reference year) and region	Population (1)	GMR (2)	mean age of migr. sched. (3)	GMR(0-4) (4)	GMR(15-29) (5)	GMR(65+) (6)	GMR(70-74) (7)
Austria (1971)							
Burgenland	272119.	0.51	26.32	0.029	0.246	0.028	0.007
Carinthia	525728.	0.33	27.02	0.016	0.184	0.021	0.005
Lower Austria	1414161.	0.49	29.05	0.030	0.243	0.037	0.009
Upper Austria	1223444.	0.22	30.23	0.012	0.109	0.020	0.005
Salzburg	401766.	0.35	30.25	0.022	0.172	0.030	0.007
Styria	1192100.	0.26	27.89	0.016	0.136	0.017	0.004
Tyrol	540771.	0.22	30.45	0.013	0.110	0.018	0.004
Vorarlberg	271473.	0.25	29.24	0.015	0.137	0.018	0.005
Vienna	1614841.	0.43	31.83	0.041	0.160	0.041	0.010
Austria	7456403.	0.35	30.14	0.022	0.165	0.030	0.007
Bulgaria (1975)							
North West	1042803.	0.46	21.91	0.032	0.284	0.015	0.003
North	1400117.	0.30	23.35	0.020	0.157	0.018	0.002
North East	1486719.	0.25	23.62	0.014	0.138	0.016	0.003
South West	696466.	0.39	23.90	0.020	0.213	0.025	0.004
South	2164076.	0.23	25.06	0.014	0.122	0.016	0.003
South East	866834.	0.43	23.59	0.026	0.242	0.025	0.004
Sofia	1069975.	0.30	28.44	0.034	0.107	0.023	0.004
Bulgaria	8726990.	0.31	24.13	0.021	0.164	0.018	0.003
Canada (1971)							
Newfoundland	507750.	1.03	31.01	0.100	0.424	0.080	0.013
Prince Edward Island	110085.	1.61	29.00	0.178	0.628	0.103	0.019
Nova Scotia	772500.	1.28	29.26	0.151	0.449	0.090	0.016
New Brunswick	625674.	1.33	30.76	0.154	0.470	0.118	0.021
Quebec	5904307.	0.49	37.31	0.048	0.119	0.086	0.013
Ontario	7331987.	0.48	33.20	0.059	0.131	0.063	0.011
Manitoba	975655.	1.70	34.03	0.176	0.460	0.225	0.041
Saskatchewan	940790.	2.14	32.45	0.228	0.756	0.251	0.049
Alberta	1545537.	1.33	38.31	0.125	0.302	0.253	0.046
British Columbia	2029147.	0.66	32.30	0.078	0.191	0.080	0.015
Canada	20743436.	0.77	34.14	0.085	0.216	0.107	0.019
Czechoslovakia (1975)							
Central Bohemia	2300705.	0.53	35.61	0.061	0.204	0.106	0.011
Southern Bohemia	667998.	0.70	31.63	0.079	0.282	0.092	0.015
Western Bohemia	872796.	0.87	33.72	0.096	0.289	0.139	0.014
Northern Bohemia	1135800.	0.84	36.50	0.081	0.282	0.161	0.018
Eastern Bohemia	1224599.	0.66	34.02	0.072	0.271	0.109	0.011
Southern Moravia	1985174.	0.44	33.88	0.048	0.186	0.075	0.009
Northern Moravia	1875294.	0.44	33.78	0.046	0.162	0.070	0.009
Western Slovakia	1966889.	0.31	33.04	0.038	0.137	0.051	0.007
Central Slovakia	1455491.	0.49	33.90	0.055	0.204	0.080	0.011
Eastern Slovakia	1316921.	0.38	33.71	0.038	0.159	0.057	0.006
Czechoslovakia	14801667.	0.52	34.46	0.056	0.202	0.090	0.010

Migration

Country (reference year) and region	Population (1)	GMR (2)	mean age of migr.sched. (3)	GMR(0-4) (4)	GMR(15-29) (5)	GMR(65+) (6)	GMR(70-74) (7)
Fed.Rep.of Germany(1974)							
Schleswig-Holstein	2584343.	1.84	31.23	0.127	0.897	0.165	0.026
Hamburg	1733802.	2.87	33.51	0.265	1.043	0.364	0.050
Lower Saxony	7265539.	1.35	32.42	0.088	0.647	0.149	0.025
Bremen	723990.	3.30	32.05	0.287	1.390	0.368	0.051
N. Rhine-Westphalia	17218626.	0.83	34.58	0.060	0.347	0.112	0.019
Hessen	5576082.	1.38	33.45	0.101	0.561	0.157	0.026
Rhineland-Palatinate	3687561.	1.77	32.12	0.115	0.852	0.187	0.031
Baden-Wuerttemberg	9226239.	1.05	32.30	0.070	0.479	0.099	0.018
Bavaria	10849123.	0.74	31.64	0.053	0.343	0.064	0.012
Saarland	1103325.	1.49	30.58	0.090	0.797	0.129	0.019
West Berlin	2034366.	2.00	35.43	0.160	0.676	0.275	0.052
Fed.Rep. of Germany	62002996.	1.19	33.33	0.083	0.521	0.139	0.023
Finland (1974)							
Uusimaa	1073485.	1.46	26.59	0.205	0.599	0.070	0.022
Turku and Pori	691672.	1.25	25.40	0.162	0.596	0.043	0.015
Ahvenanmaa	22009.	0.85	24.19	0.099	0.426	0.024	.
Hame	657049.	1.75	25.80	0.225	0.817	0.064	0.019
Kymi	345985.	1.56	25.76	0.200	0.727	0.052	0.017
Mikkeli	212200.	2.47	26.05	0.276	1.270	0.093	0.029
Pohjois-Karjala	177870.	2.18	25.73	0.235	1.170	0.074	0.024
Kuopio	251320.	2.03	25.78	0.244	1.033	0.078	0.026
Keski-Suomi	238814.	2.00	25.33	0.245	1.009	0.061	0.022
Vaasa	423043.	1.29	24.95	0.159	0.682	0.036	0.011
Oulu	400853.	1.63	26.26	0.183	0.822	0.055	0.017
Lappi	196232.	1.84	27.22	0.208	0.897	0.074	0.024
Finland	4690532.	1.62	25.89	0.202	0.772	0.060	0.019
France (1975)							
Paris Region	9876665.	1.35	39.62	0.126	0.261	0.283	0.065
Paris Basin	9647540.	0.89	31.58	0.092	0.287	0.092	0.018
North	3913250.	0.65	31.49	0.071	0.212	0.064	0.012
East	4905810.	0.68	30.94	0.072	0.204	0.058	0.010
West	6889705.	0.64	29.32	0.072	0.254	0.055	0.011
Southwest	5553655.	0.73	29.05	0.087	0.278	0.061	0.012
Middle East	6129105.	0.65	31.81	0.069	0.200	0.068	0.014
Mediterranean	5464635.	0.76	29.76	0.090	0.264	0.070	0.014
France	52380364.	0.84	33.06	0.088	0.251	0.104	0.022
German Dem.Rep. (1975)							
North	2085383.	0.53	25.59	0.076	0.246	0.028	0.007
Berlin	1098174.	0.50	26.15	0.062	0.199	0.024	0.007
Southwest	2529805.	0.39	25.29	0.045	0.192	0.017	0.005
South	7134846.	0.37	24.87	0.047	0.179	0.016	0.005
Middle	3972041.	0.51	25.53	0.060	0.239	0.026	0.008
German Dem.Rep.	16820250.	0.44	25.20	0.055	0.206	0.020	0.006

Migration

Country (reference year) and region	Population (1)	GMR (2)	mean age of migr.sched. (3)	GMR(0-4) (4)	GMR(15-29) (5)	GMR(65+) (6)	GMR(70-74) (7)
Hungary (1974)							
Central	2968109.	2.77	32.54	0.135	1.451	0.306	0.056
North Hungary	1357973.	2.27	31.60	0.096	1.232	0.214	0.044
North Plain	1543604.	3.19	30.93	0.128	1.797	0.288	0.054
South Plain	1451260.	1.91	33.08	0.105	0.954	0.260	0.045
North Trans-Danubia	1823844.	1.77	34.70	0.086	0.866	0.270	0.045
South Trans-Danubia	1303694.	1.84	33.65	0.095	0.924	0.263	0.045
Hungary	10448484.	2.36	32.57	0.110	1.239	0.274	0.049
Italy (1978)							
North West	15424582.	0.48	33.34	0.037	0.155	0.050	0.010
North East	10394756.	0.26	35.67	0.017	0.086	0.037	0.006
Center	10790837.	0.32	35.04	0.021	0.113	0.043	0.008
South	13471822.	0.54	32.58	0.026	0.245	0.055	0.011
Islands	6518288.	0.53	31.59	0.028	0.232	0.047	0.009
Italy	56600292.	0.43	33.17	0.027	0.169	0.047	0.009
Japan (1970)							
Hokkaido	5184287.	1.86	32.71	0.099	0.820	0.221	0.034
Tohoku	11392179.	1.98	29.45	0.070	1.209	0.112	0.020
Kanto	30257930.	0.76	33.65	0.062	0.269	0.089	0.015
Chubu	17401128.	1.08	29.53	0.063	0.581	0.085	0.015
Kinki	16511391.	1.09	32.10	0.094	0.424	0.119	0.019
Chugoku	6996961.	1.70	27.79	0.089	1.021	0.103	0.019
Shikoku	3904014.	2.18	27.96	0.086	1.385	0.120	0.022
Kyushu	13017290.	2.37	29.04	0.099	1.364	0.135	0.023
Japan	104465176.	1.35	30.50	0.077	0.679	0.110	0.019
Netherlands (1974)							
North	1473611.	1.08	34.14	0.075	0.464	0.169	0.025
East	2592786.	1.36	35.01	0.085	0.589	0.225	0.034
West	6150477.	1.10	37.00	0.087	0.341	0.205	0.035
South-West	322891.	1.62	33.76	0.105	0.698	0.253	0.044
South	2948600.	0.82	35.39	0.049	0.371	0.144	0.021
Netherlands	13488365.	1.10	36.03	0.077	0.417	0.196	0.032
Poland (1977)							
Warsaw	2207161.	0.50	50.19	0.033	0.104	0.195	0.040
Lodz	1099132.	0.59	46.35	0.050	0.154	0.208	0.034
Gdansk	1287689.	0.71	49.69	0.049	0.175	0.287	0.043
Katowice	3557261.	0.44	42.90	0.035	0.128	0.125	0.022
Cracow	1143864.	0.63	41.96	0.061	0.196	0.180	0.035
East-Central	2930837.	0.90	33.23	0.086	0.402	0.137	0.025
Northeast	2398497.	0.74	33.43	0.067	0.333	0.118	0.021
Northwest	2106814.	1.05	42.11	0.086	0.311	0.317	0.052
South	2505722.	0.71	37.84	0.072	0.256	0.151	0.023
Southeast	4208485.	0.62	34.79	0.053	0.291	0.104	0.019
East	2479828.	0.68	33.77	0.063	0.321	0.111	0.017
West-Central	4712562.	0.53	36.69	0.051	0.196	0.106	0.018
West	4059724.	0.74	40.64	0.067	0.229	0.212	0.031
Poland	34697580.	0.66	38.29	0.060	0.240	0.151	0.026

| | | Migration | | | | | |
Country (reference year) and region	Population (1)	GMR (2)	mean age of migr. sched. (3)	GMR(0-4) (4)	GMR(15-29) (5)	GMR(65+) (6)	GMR(70-74) (7)
Soviet Union (1974)							
Urban areas of the:							
RSFSR	88230272.	1.38	31.61	0.060	0.788	0.146	0.029
Ukrainian+Mold.SSRs	29527222.	1.76	31.41	0.066	1.023	0.176	0.035
Byelorussian SSR	4549020.	2.33	35.17	0.084	1.178	0.343	0.067
Central Asian Rep.s	8681624.	2.13	35.54	0.045	1.141	0.296	0.058
Kazakh SSR	7348350.	3.23	35.44	0.099	1.688	0.471	0.094
Caucasian Republics	6918171.	1.06	33.88	0.029	0.607	0.132	0.026
Baltic Republics	4334008.	1.57	30.73	0.055	0.931	0.143	0.027
Rural areas of USSR	101280288.	3.53	29.17	0.080	2.443	0.208	0.041
Soviet Union	250868944.	2.20	30.92	0.070	1.357	0.191	0.037
Sweden (1974)							
Stockholm	1486821.	1.45	29.26	0.180	0.495	0.112	0.024
East Middle	1397129.	1.47	27.34	0.164	0.627	0.072	0.017
South Middle	763793.	1.38	26.83	0.143	0.654	0.064	0.016
South	1157556.	0.86	26.87	0.098	0.383	0.040	0.009
West	1603323.	0.82	27.12	0.093	0.341	0.039	0.009
North Middle	853655.	1.28	26.61	0.131	0.622	0.058	0.014
Lower North	400292.	1.40	26.26	0.138	0.724	0.057	0.016
Upper North	494569.	1.14	27.31	0.104	0.588	0.054	0.011
Sweden	8157138.	1.20	27.42	0.134	0.517	0.063	0.015
United Kingdom (1970)							
North	3359700.	1.2_	31.69	0.106	0.504	0.140	0.019
Yorkshire + Humbers.	4811900.	1.34	30.82	0.119	0.539	0.139	0.028
North West	6788700.	1.06	32.92	0.082	0.411	0.131	0.026
East Midlands	3362800.	1.57	30.63	0.146	0.611	0.162	0.034
West Midlands	5178000.	1.16	30.89	0.091	0.448	0.093	0.015
East Anglia	1673500.	1.84	30.47	0.191	0.690	0.185	0.047
South East	17315502.	1.06	33.98	0.089	0.373	0.144	0.028
South West	3763700.	1.84	30.91	0.161	0.749	0.185	0.035
Wales	2733900.	1.21	31.82	0.105	0.508	0.145	0.029
Scotland	5199100.	0.87	28.56	0.085	0.360	0.061	0.010
United Kingdom	54186800.	1.20	31.96	0.104	0.463	0.136	0.026
United States (1970)							
Northeast	49040708.	1.12	31.02	0.091	0.398	0.105	0.027
North Central	56571668.	1.31	29.99	0.117	0.494	0.113	0.032
South	62795372.	1.38	28.37	0.137	0.568	0.105	0.033
West	34804200.	1.45	29.08	0.148	0.550	0.102	0.030
United States	203211920.	1.31	29.46	0.123	0.506	0.106	0.030

PART THREE

Multiregional Analysis

CHAPTER SIX

Population Projections

Andrei Rogers

The populations of IIASA's NMO countries are currently experiencing dramatic changes in patterns of demographic behavior. The consequences of these changes are likely to be profound, and their impacts are already being felt in labor and housing markets, in health care demand levels, in retirement income maintenance programs, and in what might generally be referred to as the service needs of "changing lifestyles". Yet the underlying processes producing these new patterns are imperfectly understood, and any assessments of future prospects therefore could be founded on false expectations. Nevertheless, planning for social service requirements of necessity requires assessments of future levels of demand, and population projections traditionally have served as a driving force in such assessments.

6.1 The Populations of the IIASA Nations: Retrospect and Prospect

Though differing in cultures, socioeconomic systems, and languages, the 17 IIASA nations share a central characteristic: low levels of fertility. In 1982, 13 of the 17 countries exhibited below-replacement levels of fertility; the other four countries (Bulgaria, Czechoslovakia, Poland, and the Soviet Union) showed fertility levels at or barely above the 2.1 babies per woman that are necessary for one generation to replace itself with another (Table 6.1). Moreover, past trends suggest that sometime during the 1980s the total fertility rates in *all* of the IIASA nations probably will fall below the 2.1 figure.

For a number of IIASA countries, notably Canada and the US, the foremost feature of recent demographic history has been the bulge introduced into the national age structures by the unusually large birth cohorts born after World War II — the so-called baby boom. This boom has created problems that change as the bulge moves upward in the years. From nurseries to nursing homes, smaller birth cohorts have easier lives as they enter structures

Table 6.1 Total fertility rates per woman in the IIASA countries, 1950–1982.

Year	Country								
	Austria	Bulgaria	Canada	Czecho- slovakia	FRG	Finland	France	GDR	Hungary
1950	2.1	2.9	3.5	3.0	2.1		2.9	2.3	2.6
1955	2.2	2.4	3.8	2.8	2.1		2.7	2.4	2.8
1960	2.6	2.3	3.9	2.4	2.4	2.7	2.7	2.3	2.0
1965	2.7	2.1	3.1	2.4	2.5	2.4	2.8	2.5	1.8
1970	2.3	2.2	2.3	2.1	2.0	1.8	2.5	2.2	2.0
1975	1.8	2.2	1.8	2.5	1.4		1.9	1.5	2.4
1978	1.6	2.2	1.8	2.4	1.4		1.8	1.6	2.1
1981	1.6	2.1	1.8	2.3	1.4	1.6	1.9	1.9	2.0
1982	1.7	2.2	1.8	2.1	1.5	1.6	2.0	1.9	1.9

Year	Italy	Japan	Nether- lands	Poland	Soviet Union	Sweden	UK	US
1950	2.5	3.6	3.1	3.7	2.9	2.3	2.2	3.1
1955	2.3	2.4	3.0	3.6	2.9	2.2	2.2	3.6
1960	2.4	2.0	3.1	3.0	2.8	2.2	2.7	3.6
1965	2.6	2.1	3.0	2.5	2.5	2.4	2.9	2.9
1970	2.4	2.1	2.6	2.2	2.4	1.9	2.4	2.5
1975	2.2	1.9	1.7	2.3	2.4	1.8	1.8	1.8
1978	1.9	1.8	1.6	2.2	2.3	1.6	1.7	1.8
1981	1.7	1.8	1.6	2.3	2.3	1.7	1.9	1.8
1982	1.7	1.8	1.6	2.3	2.3	1.7	1.9	1.9

Sources: Data for 1950–1978 are taken from US Bureau of the Census (1980). All 1981 (and 1982) data are taken from Population Reference Bureau (1982). Data on Finland are taken from Economic Commission for Europe (1975).

designed for the larger cohorts that preceded them, whereas the baby boom cohorts have to adjust to structures designed for the smaller cohorts that they followed.

During the 1960–1980 period many IIASA nations entered a period of transition to zero growth. According to the most recent estimates and projections published by the United Nations (1981), the total population of these countries grew by 160 million persons during this 20-year period to approximately 980 million in 1980. This population is expected (in the medium variant projection) to increase by another 120 million to reach 1.1 billion by the year 2000 (Table 6.2). Three of the 17 countries were already experiencing negative population growth in 1980 (Austria, the Federal Republic of Germany, and the UK) and a fourth (Sweden) is projected to enter this group by the end of this century. The German Democratic Republic was essentially at zero growth in 1980, and Finland, Hungary, and Italy are projected to join it by the year 2000. Thus the populations of eight of the 17 countries are expected to cease growing within the span of the next two decades, and no IIASA country is projected to exhibit an annual population growth rate of as much as 1% by the end of this period.

The UN projections may be compared with the 17 national multiregional population projections contained in the individual reports of the Migration and Settlement Study. These simple, fixed-coefficient extrapolations, which were produced with the same computer program but with data for different reference years in the 1970s, are summarized in Table 6.3 and Appendix 6A. Linear interpolation was used to bring the different reference years to the common 1980 starting point, and to obtain the projections for the years 2000 and 2030. For example, Austria's population in 1980 was obtained by interpolating four years into the projection period 1976–1981.

The IIASA projections foresee an increase of 125 million people between 1980 and the end of the century. About 75% of this increase is expected to take place in the two most populous countries: the Soviet Union (36.5%), and the US (36.6%). One out of every two persons residing in an IIASA country in 1980 lived in one of these two nations. This fraction is projected to increase slightly (by 2.6%) by the year 2000.

The process of generating national and regional population projections was greatly simplified in the study by the assumption that no international migration would occur during the projection period. This assumption is incorrect, of course, particularly for Canada, Sweden, and the US. In the US, for example, *legal* net immigration in 1980 accounted for over one-quarter of annual population growth; *illegal* immigration contributed an additional unknown amount. The relative contribution of net immigration has been about the same in Canada (see Table 7.18) and much higher in Sweden, where its share has ranged from 50 to 80% of total growth in recent years.

A comparison of IIASA's constant-coefficient projections for the year 2000 with those produced by the United Nations indicates a reasonably close

Table 6.2 Population size and average annual rates of increase for the world and for IIASA countries, UN medium variant, 1960—2000, as assessed in 1980.

Region	Population (millions)			Average annual rate of growth (%)		
	1960	1980	2000	1960–1965	1975–1980	1995–2000
World total	3037	4432	6119	1.99	1.72	1.50
More developed regions	945	1131	1272	1.19	0.70	0.48
Less developed regions	2092	3301	4847	2.34	2.08	1.77
IIASA countries						
Total	819.7	979.6	1098.9	—	—	—
Austria	7.0	7.5	7.4	0.58	−0.10	−0.04
Bulgaria	7.9	9.0	9.7	0.83	0.64	0.29
Canada	17.9	24.5	34.8	1.85	1.49	0.93
Czechoslovakia	13.7	15.3	16.8	0.73	0.71	0.49
FRG	55.4	60.9	58.8	1.25	−0.29	−0.16
Finland	4.4	4.9	5.1	0.60	0.63	0.04
France	45.7	53.5	56.3	1.30	0.30	0.22
GDR	17.2	16.9	16.9	−0.26	0.01	0.00
Hungary	10.0	10.8	11.0	0.33	0.40	0.08
Italy	50.2	56.9	59.1	0.67	0.39	0.08
Japan	94.1	116.6	129.3	0.99	0.88	0.49
Netherlands	11.5	14.1	15.2	1.37	0.60	0.30
Poland	29.6	35.8	41.2	1.27	1.02	0.54
Soviet Union	214.3	265.5	310.2	1.49	0.93	0.64
Sweden	7.5	8.3	8.1	0.67	0.20	−0.12
United Kingdom	52.6	55.9	55.2	0.73	−0.05	−0.06
United States	180.7	223.2	263.8	1.45	0.89	0.67

Source: United Nations (1981).

agreement for most countries, with the notable exception of Canada. The UN projection of 34.8 million for Canada seems to be unrealistically high; the IIASA projection of 28.6 million is possibly too low, because it ignores international migration. Projections carried out by Statistics Canada, for example, give a low of 28 million and a high of close to 35 million. The former assumes a total fertility rate of 1.8 and a net immigration of 60,000 per year, the latter assumes a total fertility rate of 2.6 in 1985 and a net immigration of 100000 per year (Beaujot 1978).

Two other IIASA national population projections differ significantly from those of the United Nations: for the UK and the US. In both cases, IIASA's use of 1970 as the reference year led to the adoption of a fertility level that was much too high; by 1980 it already had declined by over 25% in the two countries. The use of the higher fertility levels, of course, raised the projected population totals, while ignoring the international migration lowered them.

Table 6.3 Population prospects in IIASA countries as assessed in 1970–1980: IIASA and United Nations data.

Country (reference year)	Life expectancy at birth			Gross reproduction rate			Population (millions)			
	IIASA	UN		IIASA	UN		IIASA		UN	
	Reference year	1975–1980	1995–2000	Reference year	1975–1980	1995–2000	1980	2000	1980	2000
Austria (1971)	70.5	71.7	74.2	1.09	0.80	0.82	7.6	8.0	7.5	7.4
Bulgaria (1975)	70.9	72.0	73.8	1.10	1.09	1.02	9.0	9.6	9.0	9.7
Canada (1971)	72.5	73.5	75.0	1.23	0.91	0.91	23.0	28.6	24.5	34.8
Czechoslovakia (1975)	70.3	70.2	73.0	1.21	1.15	1.04	15.4	17.2	15.3	16.8
FRG (1974)	71.9	71.8	74.2	0.73	0.70	0.80	61.3	57.6	60.9	58.8
Finland (1974)	71.7	72.7	74.3	0.79	0.80	0.82	4.8	4.8	4.9	5.1
France (1975)	73.5	73.7	75.2	0.94	0.91	0.88	53.3	55.7	53.5	56.3
GDR (1975)	71.7	71.8	74.8	0.76	0.88	0.86	16.6	15.7	16.9	16.9
Hungary (1974)	69.0	69.9	72.9	1.14	1.03	0.91	10.8	11.3	10.8	11.0
Italy (1978)	74.1	72.5	74.6	0.91	0.93	0.83	57.0	59.5	56.9	59.1
Japan (1970)	72.2	75.6	77.3	1.05	0.88	0.95	116.4	129.4	116.6	129.3
Netherlands (1974)	74.7	74.8	75.8	0.87	0.77	0.85	13.9	15.1	14.1	15.2
Poland (1977)	70.6	70.8	73.2	1.10	1.10	1.02	35.7	40.7	35.8	41.2
Soviet Union (1974)	69.3	69.6	71.5	1.33	1.16	1.14	266.0	311.6	265.5	310.2
Sweden (1974)	75.2	75.3	76.0	0.92	0.80	0.80	8.3	8.2	8.3	8.1
United Kingdom (1970)	71.9	72.3	74.5	1.18	0.84	0.85	56.5	61.8	55.9	55.2
United States (1970)	70.8	72.9	73.9	1.26	0.94	1.02	225.0	270.7	223.2	263.8
Total							980.6	1105.5	979.6	1098.9

Sources: Appendix 6B and United Nations (1981), medium variant.

Aggregate national population totals conceal the diversity of age compositions that exist among the 17 IIASA countries and, at an even more spatially
disaggregated level of detail, among their principal subnational populations. At
this level additional difficulties arise. Mortality levels probably will not change
significantly in the future and, in any case, the impact of changes in mortality
patterns on population projections is relatively small. The effect of different
levels of fertility can be considerable, but unless radical changes in current
lifestyles occur, it is unlikely that dramatic deviations from replacement-level
fertility will take place between today and the year 2000. Internal migration
patterns, however, have changed substantially during the past two decades
and could continue to shift in the future. Moreover, their impact on regional
population growth can be significant. Yet the IIASA projections assume migration rates to remain fixed. The regional projections, therefore, must be interpreted with great caution.

6.2 Observed Components of Change and Age Structures

The age composition of a population reflects the impacts of past patterns
of fertility, mortality, and migration. In a growing population, the number of
individuals in any age group will normally be smaller than in the immediately
younger age group. But past fluctuations in the components of change, notably
variations in birth rates at the national and regional levels and in migration at
the local level, may distort this pattern. Such regional variations were substantial in the 17 IIASA populations during the 1970s.

6.2.1 *Natural Increase and Net Migration at the Regional Level*

In the 1970s, the populations of the 139 regions of the Migration and Settlement Study were growing at an average rate of less than 0.9%. But this
growth was spread unevenly across the 17 national landscapes. For example, a
few regions were growing at unusually high rates (Appendix 6B). Three regions
in the Soviet Union (the urban areas of the Byelorussian, the Central Asian,
and the Baltic Republics) and the Kanto region in Japan all were growing by
more than 3% a year. The Kinki region in Japan, British Columbia in Canada,
and three more regions in the Soviet Union (the urban areas of the RSFSR, the
Ukrainian—Moldavian, and the Kazakh Republics) were increasing at annual
rates above 2%.

A number of regions in IIASA countries were also exhibiting moderately
high rates of population *decline*. The Tohoku, Shikoku, and Kyushu regions in
Japan, West Berlin, Hamburg, and the Saarland region in the Federal Republic
of Germany, and the rural parts of the Soviet Union all were showing annual
rates of population decline of 1% or more.

The above-mentioned nine regions of growth and seven regions of decline are identified in the scatter diagram of Figure 6.1. (This diagram is included for illustration only, because differences in the reference years make an international comparison problematic.) They may be found to the right and left, respectively, of the downward-sloping lines running from left to right that delineate different rates of population growth. The remaining 123 regions are represented by dots located at the intersections of their respective values for net migration on the horizontal axis and for natural increase or decrease on the vertical axis. The four quadrants separate the 139 observations according to the signs of the two components of change: net inmigration or outmigration (+,−) and natural increase or decrease (+,−). Thus, for example, all populations represented in the upper right quadrant are growing as a consequence of both natural increase and net inmigration, whereas those in the lower right quadrant are declining as a result of both natural decrease and net outmigration.

Fertility declines have elevated the relative importance of migration as a contributor to regional population growth. Migration produces changes that are felt both at the local and at the national level. It transfers labor from labor-surplus areas to areas with labor deficits, but this adjustment of the national labor market has local consequences with regard to equity. Because of these potentially negative consequences, and because of its interrelatedness with emerging economic, social, and environmental problems, population movement has attracted growing attention in recent years.

According to Figure 6.1 (and Appendix 6B) a few regions were attracting migrants at unusually high rates in the 1970s. The nine "growth" regions listed above plus East Anglia in the UK and Berlin in the German Democratic Republic all were *gaining* migrants at net rates of more than 1%. Four regions in Japan (Kyushu, Tohoku, Shikoku, and Hokkaido), the province of Saskatchewan in Canada, and the rural areas of the Soviet Union were *losing* migrants at net rates in excess of 1%.

Figure 6.1 also identifies the relative contributions of net migration and natural increase to regional population growth. A 45° counter clockwise rotation of the horizontal and vertical axes partitions the 139 observations into four quadrants marked A, B, C, an D in the illustration. All populations in quadrant A were growing primarily as a consequence of net inmigration and those in B because of natural increase. Regional populations in quadrant C were declining mainly because of net outmigration and those in D because of natural decrease.

Canada's province of British Columbia, located in quadrant A, was growing at an annual rate of 2.3% at the start of the 1970s (ignoring the impact of international migration). This rate was the sum of a 0.9% rate of natural increase and a 1.4% rate of net inmigration. Thus net inmigration accounted for about 62.3% of regional population growth. British Columbia's sister provinces, Newfoundland and Saskatchewan, located in quadrants B and C,

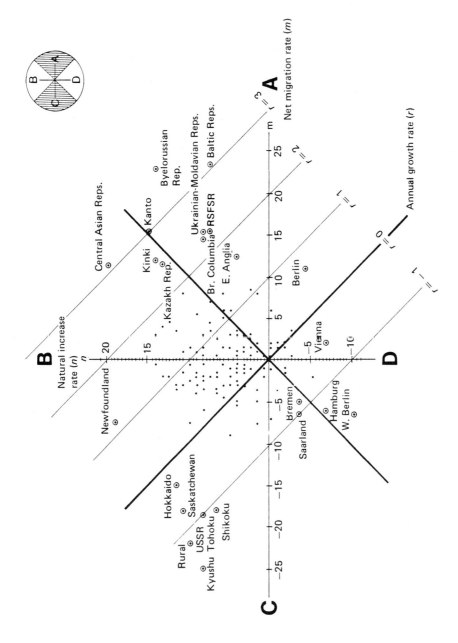

Figure 6.1 Rates of natural increase (*n*) and net migration (*m*) in the 139 IIASA regions at the time of each country's reference year.
Source: Appendix 6B.

respectively, illustrate alternative combinations. Newfoundland's rate of natural increase was the principal contributor to its population growth, more than compensating for its losses due to outmigration. Not so with Saskatchewan, whose net outmigration rate of 1.8% swamped the contribution of its natural increase rate of 1.1% to give the region a rate of decline of 0.7% per annum.

A few IIASA regions were experiencing population decline in the 1970s because of both an excess of deaths over births and outflows over inflows. Nine regions fell into this category, including city regions such as Bremen, Hamburg, and West Berlin. The last two city populations lost more people from natural decrease than from net outmigration and therefore are located in quadrant D in Figure 6.1. Joining them there is the city population of Vienna, whose growth because of net inmigration was not sufficient to counter the losses resulting from natural decrease, giving the city a negative population growth rate of −0.5%.

Figure 6.1 and Appendix 6B show that a significant fraction of all regional growth in IIASA nations during the 1970s, and a large proportion of net migration contributing to that growth, was confined to a comparatively small number of regions. The spatial evolutions of national populations, however, are also tightly linked with the age compositions of their regional populations. Prospects for future growth depend not only on the components of change but also on the starting age distributions that are to experience these regimes of fertility, mortality, and migration.

6.2.2 Age Structures

Population age structures in the 17 IIASA nations in 1980 exhibited discernible signs of aging, showing age pyramids that were narrowing at the base and widening at the apex. The young populations (those under 15 years) seldom accounted for more than one-quarter of the national total, and the share of the elderly population (those 65 and over) generally exceeded 10%. For the national populations taken as a whole, these two percentages were 24.0 and 11.8, respectively (Table 6.4).

Despite the generality of these broad patterns, significant national differences in degrees of population aging were evident in 1980. Population aging is here defined as an increase in the ratio of old people (65 years and over) to young people (less than 15 years of age) or alternatively of old people to the adult population (those 15–64 years of age), a ratio we call the *elderly dependency ratio*.

According to Table 6.4, Sweden and the German Democratic Republic were the "oldest" IIASA populations in 1980, with elderly dependency ratios of 0.26 and 0.25, respectively; Japan (0.13) and Canada (0.14) were the "youngest". When the older part of the elderly population is considered (those 75 years and older), France joins the German Democratic Republic and Sweden as

Table 6.4 Population structure in the IIASA countries in 1980.

Country (reference year)	Population (millions)	Age group (%)				Elderly dependency ratio
		0–14	15–64	65+	75+	
Austria (1971)	7.6	22.6	62.8	14.6	5.7	0.23
Bulgaria (1975)	9.0	22.4	65.9	11.7	3.8	0.18
Canada (1971)	23.0	26.7	64.6	8.8	3.3	0.14
Czechoslovakia (1975)	15.4	24.5	63.1	12.5	4.2	0.20
FRG (1974)	61.3	18.2	66.7	15.1	5.8	0.23
Finland (1974)	4.8	20.0	67.6	12.4	4.7	0.18
France (1975)	53.3	21.2	64.3	14.5	6.4	0.22
GDR (1975)	16.6	18.6	65.2	16.2	6.7	0.25
Hungary (1974)	10.8	21.8	65.1	13.0	4.5	0.20
Italy (1978)	57.0	22.4	64.6	13.0	4.8	0.20
Japan (1970)	116.4	24.5	67.1	8.4	2.8	0.13
Netherlands (1974)	13.9	23.0	65.6	11.5	4.5	0.17
Poland (1977)	35.7	24.3	65.9	9.9	3.5	0.15
Soviet Union (1974)	266.0	25.0	63.0	12.0	4.2	0.19
Sweden (1974)	8.3	20.2	63.6	16.3	6.4	0.26
United Kingdom (1970)	56.5	23.5	62.4	14.1	5.3	0.23
United States (1970)	225.0	26.1	63.3	10.7	4.2	0.17
Total	980.6	24.0	64.2	11.8	4.4	0.18

the only other country with over 6% of the national population in that age category.

Our earlier examination of annual growth rates among the 17 nations revealed significant differences between the countries. For example, toward the end of the 1970s the population of the Soviet Union was growing at an annual rate of 0.9%, whereas that of the Federal Republic of Germany was declining at a rate of 0.3% per annum (Table 6.2). But the growth differentials inside these 17 countries were even more divergent. The population of the Kanto region in Japan, for example, was growing at an annual rate of 2.2% per year in 1980, at the same time that the population of a sister region, Kyushu, was declining by 1.5% per year (Appendix 6A).

Regional disparities in growth rates, reflecting differentials in fertility, mortality, and migration, give rise to regional differentials in the prominence of particular age groups in subnational population totals. For example, according to Table 6.5 (and Appendix 6A) one out of every five residents (20.4%) in Vienna, Austria, was 65 years or older in 1980; yet only one in ten residents of the province of Vorarlberg was in that age group at that time (10.1%). Roughly one in six people in the former region was under 15 years of age (16.5%); whereas more than one out of every four of the latter's population was in this age group in 1980 (27.6%).

As much as one-third of the population of Newfoundland in Canada and of the Central Asian Republics in the Soviet Union was younger than 15 years of age in 1980; less than half of that fraction was found in the same population

Table 6.5 Regional differentials in age composition in 1980.

Country (reference year: number of regions)	Age group (%)							
	0–14				65+			
	National	Lowest	Highest	MAD/N(%)	National	Lowest	Highest	MAD/N(%)
Austria (1971:9)	22.6	16.5	27.6	11.2	14.6	10.1	20.4	17.7
Bulgaria (1975:7)	22.4	19.9	24.6	7.8	11.7	9.1	16.7	17.8
Canada (1971:10)	26.7	25.6	35.3	7.9	8.8	6.7	11.7	15.8
Czechoslovakia (1975:10)	24.5	21.1	28.4	5.3	12.5	9.3	15.9	15.0
FRG (1974:11)	18.2	14.2	19.6	7.2	15.1	13.9	21.7	9.8
Finland (1974:12)	20.0	19.0	23.3	4.4	12.4	9.5	14.8	9.9
France (1975:8)	21.2	18.4	24.3	7.7	14.5	12.1	18.3	12.6
GDR (1975:5)	18.6	17.6	20.4	4.2	16.2	13.3	18.2	9.9
Hungary (1974:6)	21.8	19.0	25.2	7.1	13.0	11.7	14.5	7.3
Italy (1978:5)	22.4	20.1	26.7	12.5	13.0	10.9	14.2	9.6
Japan (1970:8)	24.5	22.7	25.1	2.9	8.4	6.5	12.5	22.5
Netherlands (1974:5)	23.0	21.4	24.8	5.2	11.5	9.2	14.4	14.0
Poland (1977:13)	24.3	18.3	26.9	8.2	9.9	6.4	11.6	12.8
Soviet Union (1974:8)	25.0	20.3	33.2	15.6	12.0	7.1	15.4	25.3
Sweden (1974:8)	20.2	19.3	21.5	3.4	16.3	14.2	18.1	7.6
United Kingdom (1970:10)	23.5	22.5	24.8	3.5	14.1	12.6	16.2	5.6
United States (1970:4)	26.1	24.9	26.8	2.1	10.7	9.5	11.5	5.7
Total	24.0	18.2	26.7	9.1	11.8	8.4	16.3	16.8

age group in the Hamburg city region of the Federal Republic of Germany (14.2%). Only 6.5% of the population of the Kanto region in Japan was aged 65 and over in 1980; the corresponding percentage in the sister region of Shikoku was almost twice as large (12.5%).

A convenient summary measure of regional differentials is the mean absolute deviation expressed as a percentage of the national measure (MAD/N). This indicator was previously used to examine regional differentials in mortality (Chapter 3) and migration (Chapter 5). It is calculated by summing the absolute deviations of the regional measures from the national one, dividing the sum by the number of regions, and expressing the result as a percentage of the national figure.

According to the MAD/N(%) measures set out in Table 6.5, the countries exhibiting the greatest degrees of regional differences in the prevalence of elderly people were the Soviet Union (25.3%), Japan (22.5%), Bulgaria (17.8%), and Austria (17.7%). Those with the greatest spatial variation in fractions of young populations were the Soviet Union (15.6%), Italy (12.5%), and Austria (11.2%). These three countries showed larger values for the MAD/N index than the corresponding value calculated for the 17 countries taken as a single "nation". Thus regional variation *within* these IIASA countries was more pronounced than *between* them.

The age structure of a population has important consequences for its future growth. Because fertility rates in past years have exhibited more fluctuations than mortality rates, accurate projections of future births and the number of young persons are more difficult to carry out than projecting the number who will survive among those already born. Moreover, the age composition of a recently growing population has a built-in "momentum" for further population growth even if birth rates suddenly fall to bare replacement levels (Keyfitz 1971).

6.3 Multiregional Population Projections

Population *projections* trace out the consequences of a set of assumptions regarding fertility, mortality, and migration. Population *forecasts*, on the other hand, are unconditional statements about the future population of a given area at some future date. Both need to take into account population processes and determinants in order to achieve results that improve on crude extrapolation procedures.

For many, the forecasting of future populations is seen as the principal justification for the art and science of demography. Yet most demographers will only accept responsibility for the formal exercise of projection; they, understandably, are not eager to take the further step of commenting extensively on the plausibility of their assumptions and thereby to turn their projections into predictions.

The now standard method for generating population projections relies on a recognition of the contribution made by each component of population change, and assesses this contribution by the application of age-specific rates – a procedure that allows producers and users of population projections to take explicit account of the age dependence of demographic events.

6.3.1 *The Multiregional Model*

Multiregional generalizations of the classical models of mathematical demography project the numerical consequences, to an initial (single-sex) multiregional population, of a particular set of assumptions regarding future fertility, mortality, and internal migration. They introduce multiple populations and thereby permit the association of *gross flows* with the *populations at risk* of experiencing these flows.

The fundamental difference between the uniregional and the multiregional approaches to population analysis is illustrated in Figure 6.2. Imagine a barrel containing a continuously fluctuating level of water. At any moment the water level is changing as a consequence of losses because of two outflows, identified by the labels *deaths* and *outmigrants*, and as a result of gains introduced by two inflows, labeled *births* and *inmigrants*.

If it is assumed that during a unit period of time, the migration outflow and migration inflow of the barrel vary in direct proportion to the average water level in the barrel at that time, then the two flows may be consolidated into a single *net* flow (which may be positive or negative), and the ratio of this net flow to the average water level defines the appropriate rate of net inmigration. Such a perspective of the problem reflects a uniregional approach.

Now imagine an interconnected system of three barrels, say, where each barrel is linked to the other two by a network of flows, as in Figure 6.2(b). In this system the migration outflows from two barrels define the migration inflow of the third. A uniregional analysis of the evolution of water levels in this three-barrel system focuses on the changes in the outflows and inflows in each barrel, one at a time. A multiregional perspective, on the other hand, regards the three barrels as a system of three interacting bodies of water, with a pattern of outflows and inflows to be examined as a simultaneous system of relationships. Moreover, the multiregional approach focuses on migration outflows; hence the associated migration rates are always positive, and refer to the appropriate population exposed to the possibility of outmigrating.

Two fundamental features, then, distinguish the multiregional from the uniregional perspective: the population being examined and the definition of rates of flow. The multiregional approach considers the entire population as an interacting system; the uniregional approach examines each subpopulation one at a time. Moreover, the multiregional approach employs rates of flow that always refer to the appropriate at-risk populations; the uniregional approach, by relying on *net* rates, cannot do that.

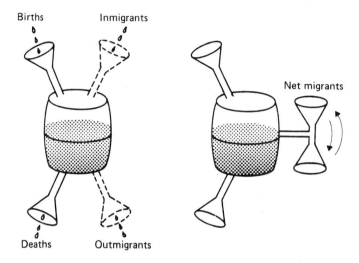

Births   Inmigrants

Net migrants

Deaths   Outmigrants

(a) Uniregional model

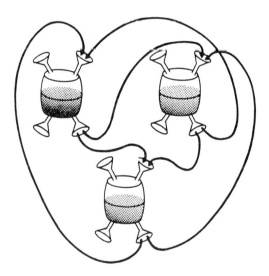

(b) Multiregional model

Figure 6.2 Contrasting the uniregional and the multiregional perspectives.

The mechanics of multiregional projections typically revolve around three basic steps. The first ascertains the starting age—region distributions and the age-specific regional schedules of fertility, mortality, and migration to which the multiregional population has been subject during a past period; the second adopts a set of assumptions regarding the future behavior of such schedules; and the third derives the consequences of applying these schedules to the initial population.

The discrete model of multiregional demographic growth expresses the population projection process by means of a matrix operation in which a multiregional population, set out as a vector, is multiplied by a growth matrix that develops the surviving population over time. The projection calculates the region- and age-specific survivors of a multiregional population of a given sex and adds to this total the new births that survive to the end of the unit time interval. As in the uniregional model, survival of individuals from one moment to another, say five years later, is calculated by diminishing each regional population to take into account the decrement due to mortality. In the multiregional model, however, we also need to include the decrement resulting from outmigration and the increment contributed by inmigration. An analogous problem is presented by surviving children born during the five-year interval. Some of these migrate with their parents; others are born after their parents have migrated but before the time interval has elapsed.

6.3.2 *The Uniregional and Multiregional Perspectives Contrasted*

A multiregional perspective in demographic analysis focuses simultaneously on several interdependent population *stocks*, on the *events* that alter the levels of such stocks, and on the gross *flows* that connect these stocks, to form a system of interacting populations. The perspective deals with rates that refer to populations truly at risk, and it considers the dynamics of multiple populations exposed to multiregional growth regimes defined by such rates. All of these attributes are absent in a uniregional perspective of growth and change in multiple interacting populations.

To deal with the linkages that connect one population's dynamics to that of another, the uniregional perspective generally must resort to the use of *ad hoc* procedures and unsatisfactory concepts such as the statistical fiction of the invisible net migrant. But does it really matter? What are the drawbacks of a view that ignores gross flows in favor of a focus on net changes in stocks? In what respects is a multiregional perspective superior to a regional one?

A focus on gross flows more clearly identifies the regularities, illuminates the dynamics, and enhances the understanding of demographic processes that occur within multiple interacting populations. Distinguishing between flows and changes in stocks reveals regularities that otherwise may be obscured; focusing on flows into and out of a region-specific stock exposes dynamics that otherwise may be hidden; and linking explanatory variables to disaggregated gross flows permits a more appropriately specified causal analysis.

Net rates express differences between arrivals and departures as a fraction of the single population experiencing both. But net rates also reflect sizes of population stocks. For example, if the gross rates of migration between urban and rural areas of a nation are held constant, the net migration rate will change over time with shifts in the relative population totals in each area. Accordingly, one's inferences about changes in net migration patterns over time will confound the impacts of migration propensities with those of changing population stocks, hiding regularities that may prevail among gross migration flows (Rogers 1982b).

Gross flow data permit the construction of improved population projection models. It can be demonstrated that multiregional projection models based on gross flow statistics are superior to uniregional models in at least three respects. First, uniregional models can introduce a bias into the projections, and they can produce inconsistent results in a long-term prognosis. Second, the impacts of changes in age compositions on movement patterns can be important, yet a uniregional perspective fixes these impacts at the start of a projection and thereby can introduce a potentially serious bias into the projection. Third, multiregional projection models have a decisive advantage over uniregional models in that they alone can follow subpopulations over time. Thus they can produce disaggregated projections that are impossible to obtain with uniregional models (Rogers 1982a).

Finally, causal explanations brought forth by studies of population redistribution all too often have been founded on models of population dynamics that reflect inadequate statistical perspectives. For example, no reliable inferences about migration behavior can be made on the basis of cross-sectional tabulations of changing fractions of a population defined to be net migrants. Data on gross flows are essential, and increasingly it is being recognized that such data must be available in disaggregated form.

But simple (Markovian-based) multiregional demographic models also are inadequate in several respects, largely because they generally adopt three assumptions that are violated by the empirical process generating the data. First, the population is not a homogeneous one; the same parameter values to not hold for all members of the population. Second, the observed parameter values do not remain constant over time. And third, an individual's propensity to leave a particular region is not independent of his or her past migration patterns and also may not be independent of the migration patterns of others.

In other words the empirical process being studied is *inhomogeneous, nonstationary,* and *temporally dependent.* Tests for the empirical validity of each of these assumptions must establish either that the other two assumptions are invalid or that controls for their effects are incorporated into the tests.

Heterogeneous populations exhibiting temporally dependent, changing patterns contain subgroups whose demographic behavior is diverse. To the extent that their differing propensities to experience events and movements can be incorporated in a formal macrodemographic analysis, illumination of the aggregate patterns of behavior is enhanced. For instance, our understanding of migration is enriched by information on the degree to which such movements occur among those who have previously migrated. In generating such information, a multiregional analysis can identify, for example, how much of a change in levels of migration in a country can be attributed to "chronic" migrants as opposed to "first" migrants.

Multiregional demography is a young branch of formal demography, and its potential contributions are only now coming to be recognized. Further progress in the field will depend to a large extent on the experiences gained in investigations such as the Migration and Settlement Study.

6.4 Projected Patterns of Growth and Decline: 1980—2000

The growth, spatial distribution, and regional age compositions of a national multiregional population undisturbed by international migration are completely determined by its recent history of fertility, mortality, and internal migration. The current crude regional birth, death, migration, and growth rates are all governed by the interaction of the prevailing regime of growth with the current regional age compositions and regional shares of the total population. The projections produced by the Migration and Settlement Study assume a fixed regime of growth and an absence of international migration. The resulting patterns of population growth and decline during the 1980—2000 period are examined in this section.

6.4.1 *Growth, Decline, and Redistribution*

The total population of the 17 IIASA countries increased at an annual rate of 0.9% during the 20-year period from 1960—1980. According to the projections produced by the Migration and Settlement Study, this rate of growth should decline to about 0.6% during the following 20-year period (Table 6.6). Contributing to this aggregate rate are national rates as diverse as Canada's 1.1% and the negative 0.3% rates of the two Germanies. Lying within this range are the zero-growth rates of Finland and Sweden. In addition to Canada, above-average growth rates are exhibited by Poland (0.7%), the Soviet Union (0.8%), and the US (0.9%).

Disaggregating the growth rates by age groups, one finds that the elderly population in the 17 countries should increase at twice the rate of the young population and that the very old (75 years and over) should increase even more rapidly. These aggregate figures, however, conceal wide national

Table 6.6 Average annual population growth rates for subgroups from 1980 to 2000.

Country (reference year)	Age group				
	All ages	0–14	15–64	65+	75+
Austria (1971)	0.003	0.004	0.005	−0.007	−0.007
Bulgaria (1975)	0.003	0.002	0.002	0.012	0.014
Canada (1971)	0.011	0.010	0.010	0.019	0.022
Czechoslovakia (1975)	0.006	0.005	0.007	−0.001	0.003
FRG (1974)	−0.003	−0.010	−0.002	−0.001	−0.003
Finland (1974)	−0.000	−0.008	0.001	0.004	0.008
France (1975)	0.002	−0.001	0.003	0.003	0.001
GDR (1975)	−0.003	−0.010	0.000	−0.010	−0.018
Hungary (1974)	0.002	0.002	0.002	0.003	0.005
Italy (1978)	0.002	−0.005	0.003	0.010	0.014
Japan (1970)	0.005	−0.003	0.005	0.025	0.022
Netherlands (1974)	0.004	−0.004	0.005	0.010	0.013
Poland (1977)	0.007	0.003	0.006	0.014	0.014
Soviet Union (1974)	0.008	0.008	0.008	0.009	0.012
Sweden (1974)	−0.000	−0.005	0.001	−0.000	0.010
United Kingdom (1970)	0.004	0.006	0.005	−0.002	0.004
United States (1970)	0.009	0.009	0.010	0.007	1.014
Total	0.006	0.004	0.006	0.008	0.010

variations. The elderly populations in the presently "older" countries such as Austria, the two Germanies, Sweden, and the UK are not expected to show any increase during the period 1980–2000; the highest rates of increase for this age group are projected for the currently "young" countries such as Canada (1.9%) and Japan (2.5%) − a veritable "population explosion", when one recalls that India's population has been growing at an annual rate of 2.5% during the past two decades.

A serious drawback of the IIASA projections is their reliance on fertility patterns that prevailed during a single reference period. In cases where the reference year is as far back as 1970 or 1971 and where fertility declined substantially during the following decade (Austria, Canada, Japan, the UK, and the US), no effort was made to incorporate this decline in the fixed-coefficient projections. The impact of excluding such declines in birth rates could be considerable.

Table 6.7 sets out the average annual growth rates obtained from an alternative set of population projections for the four countries that, according to Table 6.3, experienced the largest percentage fertility declines during the decade of the 1970s: Austria (27%), Canada (26%), the UK (29%), and the US (25%). In these projections all birth rates were reduced proportionately for the second five-year projection interval to the 1975–1980 levels reported by the United Nations and presented in Table 6.3. From that point on, the respective fertility regimes remained unchanged.

Table 6.7 Average annual population growth rates for subgroups from 1980 to 2000: alternative projection with reduced fertility levels.

Country (reference year)	Age group		
	All ages	0–14	15–64
Austria (1971)	−0.001	−0.009	0.002
Canada (1971)	0.006	−0.003	0.007
United Kingdom (1970)	−0.001	−0.008	0.002
United States (1970)	0.004	−0.002	0.006

The impacts of the fertility reductions on the average annual growth
rates were quite remarkable. Aggregate rates for all four countries declined,
of course, but for Austria and the UK they turned negative, as did all of the
rates for the 0–14 age group. Corresponding impacts were felt in aggregate
population totals and age compositions. The widely recognized sensitivity of
population projections to variations in fertility levels, demonstrated once
again in this experiment, underscores the need to interpret the outcomes of
such exercises with great caution.

The diversity of growth rates revealed by a disaggregation by age is
further amplified by a disaggregation across regions. Table 6.8 shows the
lowest and highest regional values in each country for the projected annual
rates of increase for the young and the elderly populations. Also included are
the corresponding MAD/N measures.[1] Comparing the national MAD/N percentages with those calculated for the collection of 17 IIASA nations taken as a
whole reveals that regional differences in growth rates within several IIASA
countries are higher than between them. Those countries showing high
regional differentials in growth rates tend to have one or more regions exhibiting negative growth rates.

Countries with high projected regional differentials in aggregate growth
rates are Austria, the two Germanies, Japan, and the Soviet Union. Among
these, Austria and the Soviet Union also show high regional differences in both
the growth rates of the young and the elderly populations, whereas Japan
shows large differences only for the young population, and the Federal Republic of Germany for the elderly population. A few other countries also exhibit
high regional differentials only for a particular age group: Bulgaria, France,
and the Netherlands for the young population, and Czechoslovakia and the UK
for the elderly population.

Regional differentials in aggregate growth rates are manifested in changing spatial distributions of the national population. In a few IIASA countries

[1]The latter were not computed for Finland and Sweden in those three instances where the
national measure indicated near-zero growth rates, and negative national growth rates
were treated as positive values to produce positive values for MAD/N.

Table 6.8 Regional differentials in average annual population growth rates for subgroups from 1980 to 2000.

Country (reference year: number of regions)	Age group							
	All ages				0–14			
	National	Lowest	Highest	MAD/N(%)	National	Lowest	Highest	MAD/N(%)
Austria (1971:9)	0.003	−0.004	0.011	148.0	0.004	−0.002	0.011	105.6
Bulgaria (1975:7)	0.003	−0.002	0.008	91.8	0.002	−0.004	0.005	127.2
Canada (1971:10)	0.011	−0.003	0.020	41.2	0.010	−0.003	0.018	44.8
Czechoslovakia (1975:10)	0.006	0.003	0.009	29.8	0.005	0.002	0.008	25.2
FRG (1974:11)	−0.003	−0.012	−0.001	107.2	−0.010	−0.021	−0.007	33.8
Finland (1974:12)	−0.000	−0.006	0.005	—	−0.008	−0.014	−0.001	45.2
France (1975:8)	0.002	−0.000	0.004	68.1	−0.001	−0.004	0.002	118.7
GDR (1975:5)	−0.003	−0.006	0.008	129.7	−0.010	−0.014	0.005	45.0
Hungary (1974:6)	0.002	0.001	0.004	49.1	0.002	0.001	0.004	53.2
Italy (1978:5)	0.002	−0.001	0.005	93.0	−0.005	−0.010	0.001	88.8
Japan (1970:8)	0.005	−0.005	0.013	196.2	−0.003	−0.025	0.005	343.5
Netherlands (1974:5)	0.004	−0.001	0.008	97.1	−0.004	−0.009	0.001	100.9
Poland (1977:13)	0.007	0.000	0.012	31.4	0.003	−0.002	0.008	73.3
Soviet Union (1974:8)	0.008	−0.010	0.022	129.6	0.008	−0.009	0.025	140.8
Sweden (1974:8)	−0.000	−0.002	0.002	—	−0.005	−0.008	−0.002	29.1
United Kingdom (1970:10)	0.004	0.002	1.011	43.1	0.006	0.004	0.011	26.6
United States (1970:4)	0.009	0.005	0.015	27.2	0.009	0.007	0.014	21.2
Total	0.006	−0.003	0.011	88.2	0.004	−0.010	0.010	158.8

Table 6.8 (*continued*)

Country (reference year: number of regions)	Age group			
	65+			
	National	Lowest	Highest	MAD/N(%)
Austria (1971:9)	−0.007	−0.019	0.006	108.1
Bulgaria (1975:7)	0.012	0.003	0.023	44.0
Canada (1971:10)	0.019	0.006	0.025	30.0
Czechoslovakia (1975:10)	−0.001	−0.009	0.010	817.1
FRG (1974:11)	−0.001	−0.033	0.003	456.8
Finland (1974:12)	0.004	−0.002	0.011	63.6
France (1975:8)	0.003	0.000	0.006	45.5
GDR (1975:5)	−0.010	−0.013	−0.003	29.3
Hungary (1974:6)	0.003	−0.001	0.007	63.7
Italy (1978:5)	0.010	0.007	0.013	21.1
Japan (1970:8)	0.025	0.011	0.034	26.2
Netherlands (1974:5)	0.010	0.003	0.021	48.9
Poland (1977:13)	0.014	0.008	1.031	33.0
Soviet Union (1974:8)	0.009	−0.005	0.023	128.7
Sweden (1974:8)	−0.000	−0.003	0.004	−
United Kingdom (1970:10)	−0.002	−0.007	0.005	127.4
United States (1970:4)	0.007	0.002	0.015	58.8
Total	0.008	−0.010	0.025	101.5

the projected changes in regional shares are significant (Appendix 6A). For example, during the 20-year period 1980–2000, Quebec in Canada can expect to see its share of the national population drop by more than 2%, approximately the increase that is projected for its sister province British Columbia.[2] The West region in the Netherlands, during the same period, is expected to lose more than 4%, the Kyushu region in Japan more than 3%, and the rural parts of the Soviet Union 10.5%. Larger shares of the national total population are projected for the Uusimaa (Helsinki) region in Finland (2%), Berlin in the German Democratic Republic (1.6%), the Kanto and Kinki regions in Japan (5.6 and 1.8%, respectively), and the West region of the US (2.1%).

6.4.2 *Changing Settlement Patterns*

Since the late 1960s and early 1970s many of the IIASA nations have shown a surprising uniformity in their spatial patterns of population redistribution. In most, the historical processes leading to population concentration have been weakened or reversed, producing a turnabout — a decentralization of national populations away from their large metropolitan agglomerations. Discussing this trend, Vining and Kontuly (1978, p.66) observed:

---

[2]More recent data, however, reveal that the growth experienced by British Columbia in 1966–1971 slowed down during the 1971–1976 period (see Table 7.24).

Of the eighteen countries studied here, eleven (Japan, Sweden, Italy, Norway, Denmark, New Zealand, Belgium, France, West Germany, East Germany, and the Netherlands) show either a reversal in the direction of net population flow from periphery to core or a drastic reduction in the level of this net flow. In the first seven of these eleven countries, this reduction or reversal first became evident in the 1970s; in the last four, its onset was recorded in the 1960s. Six countries (Hungary, Finland, Spain, Poland, Taiwan, and South Korea) have yet to show an attenuation in the movement of persons into their core regions. Some ... British data likewise fail to reveal a slackening in the growth of the regions surrounding London ... migration continues heavily into the capital regions of three of the Eastern European countries that publish annual migration data (Poland, Hungary, and East Germany). However, the low rates of natural increase in these regions has blunted their expansion.

Although the regionalizations adopted in the Migration and Settlement Study are ill-suited to deal with questions of metropolitan deconcentration, nevertheless it is instructive to examine the projected shares of national populations that are associated with several city regions. Table 6.9 indicates that, even with the assumption of unchanging fertility, mortality, and origin–destination-specific migration rates, a number of city regions such as Vienna, Hamburg, Bremen, Paris, Łódź, and Stockholm are projected to show declining shares of their national populations over the next 20 years and beyond. At the same time, almost all East European city regions, together with Helsinki and Tokyo, are expected to experience increases in their allocation

Table 6.9 Changes in the shares (%) of the national total populations projected for selected city regions in IIASA countries.

Country: city region		Regional share of national total		
		1980	2000	2030
Austria:	Vienna	20.36	17.89	15.88
Bulgaria:	Sofia	12.73	13.91	15.06
FRG:	Hamburg	2.64	2.34	2.21
	Bremen	1.13	1.05	1.03
Finland:	Uusimaa (Helsinki)	23.90	25.86	27.10
France:	Paris	18.79	18.35	17.77
GDR:	Berlin	6.87	8.50	10.62
Hungary:	Central (Budapest)	28.70	29.18	29.33
Japan:	Kanto (Tokyo)	33.28	38.91	43.41
Poland:	Warsaw	6.42	6.71	7.02
	Łódź	3.14	2.92	2.63
	Gdańsk	3.78	4.19	4.60
	Katowice	10.39	11.14	11.86
	Krakow	3.31	3.38	3.45
Sweden:	Stockholm	18.07	17.58	16.86
UK:	South East (London)	31.72	31.56	31.60

of the national population total. The South East region centered on London is projected to continue to maintain its stable 32% of the UK's population.

Translating changing regional shares into numbers of people reveals that a few city regions are projected to gain or lose substantial numbers. The Kanto region centered on Tokyo, for example, is projected to grow by more than 11 million residents, an increase of 30% in 20 years. Gdańsk, Katowice, and Warsaw in Poland should increase by 26, 22, and 19%, respectively, Sofia in Bulgaria and Berlin in the German Democratic Republic by 17% each, and Krakow in Poland by 16%.

Major declines in city-region growth are expected for the populations of West Berlin (−17%), Hamburg (−17%), Bremen (−13%), and Vienna (−7%).

6.5 Age Structures in the Year 2000

Transformations of the 1980 age structures into those of the year 2000 reflect variations in projected national and regional growth rates during the 1980–2000 period. The principal results of the previous section, therefore, reappear in a different guise in this one. For example, the 0.8% annual growth rate of the elderly population in the 17 IIASA nations (Table 6.6) produces a very small aggregate aging effect, increasing the fraction of persons 65 years and older from 11.8% in 1980 (Table 6.4) to a projected 12.2% in the year 2000 (Table 6.10), thus raising the elderly dependency ratio from 0.18 to 0.19. The decline in the rate of growth of the elderly population in the German Democratic Republic displaces it from the second to the fifth "oldest" IIASA population, lowering its elderly percentage from 16.2 in 1980 to 14.1 in the year 2000. Japan's corresponding fraction grows from 8.4 to 12.5%, reflecting a population increase of over 6 million persons (two-thirds of the 1980 total) during the 20-year interval. Sweden is once again projected to be the "oldest" IIASA national population in the year 2000 with an unchanging elderly fraction of 16.3%. That elderly population, however, will become older in average age. Whereas in 1980, 6.4% of Sweden's population was aged 75 years and over, by the year 2000 this share is projected to increase to 7.8%.

Changes in population size are a major driving force behind shifts in demands for public services and in revenues to support such services. But many service demands increase or decline in proportion to the pattern of population growth in certain age groups. The need for elementary schools falls with declines in the numbers of children. Demands for police forces and prisons increase with the growth of young adults in the ages of peak criminal activity. Health care requirements grow with the rise in the number of persons in the pensionable age groups.

An important anticipated shift in the age structures of a number of the 17 national populations is a sharp decline in the fraction accounted for by young people. Between 1980 and the year 2000, the number of children under 15 years of age is expected to fall by more than 2 million in the Federal

Table 6.10 Population structure in the IIASA countries in the year 2000.

Country (reference year)	Population (millions)	Age group (%)				Elderly dependency ratio
		0–14	15–64	65+	75+	
Austria (1971)	8.0	23.0	65.0	12.1	4.7	0.19
Bulgaria (1975)	9.6	21.8	64.2	13.9	4.7	0.22
Canada (1971)	28.6	26.0	63.7	10.3	4.2	0.16
Czechoslovakia (1975)	17.2	24.3	64.7	11.0	4.0	0.17
FRG (1974)	57.6	15.9	68.5	15.6	5.9	0.23
Finland (1974)	4.8	17.2	69.3	13.5	5.6	0.19
France (1975)	55.7	19.8	65.4	14.7	6.2	0.23
GDR (1975)	15.7	16.2	69.7	14.1	4.9	0.20
Hungary (1974)	11.3	21.7	65.0	13.3	4.8	0.20
Italy (1978)	59.5	19.5	65.3	15.2	6.1	0.23
Japan (1970)	129.4	20.5	67.0	12.5	3.9	0.19
Netherlands (1974)	15.1	19.6	67.5	12.9	5.4	0.19
Poland (1977)	40.7	22.7	65.8	11.5	4.1	0.18
Soviet Union (1974)	311.6	25.2	62.5	12.2	4.6	0.20
Sweden (1974)	8.2	18.4	65.2	16.3	7.8	0.25
United Kingdom (1970)	61.8	24.2	63.5	12.3	5.3	0.19
United States (1970)	270.7	26.0	63.7	10.2	4.6	0.16
Total	1105.5	23.3	64.5	12.2	4.8	0.19

Republic of Germany, a drop of almost 20%. Declines of 17 and 14% are projected for the German Democratic Republic and Finland, respectively. Italy and Sweden are each expected to lose 9%, Japan and the Netherlands approximately 7%. These developments, of course, have direct consequences for the demand for teachers and for the educational system in general. The uncertainties for educational planning at the regional level are even greater because of the impact of shifting patterns of internal migration.

The relatively high birth rates of the late 1950s and early 1960s in a number of IIASA countries have been affecting the sizes of their labor force since 1970 and have continued to do so until the 1980s. During the 1980s those reaching the pensionable ages (here approximated by the population aged 65 and over) will be survivors of the relatively smaller birth cohorts of the post-World War I era. Thus the size of the population in the labor force ages should increase slightly during the 1980–2000 projection period.

Changes in the size of the population of working age, taken here to consist of persons aged 15–64, are only crude approximations of changes in the labor force, because the latter figures of course also depend on the proportions in those age groups that are economically active — those working or seeking work. And in recent years these proportions have been growing for married women and declining for young workers and older males. Nevertheless, changes in the size of this broad age group suggest corresponding changes in the working population brought about by demographic factors. During 1980–2000, the *fraction* of the 17-nation total population that is in this category remains virtually constant, because the rates of growth of both this subgroup and the aggregate population are approximately equal (0.6%). But the *size* of the population of working age is projected to increase from 630 to approximately 713 million persons, an increase of 13% (Appendix 6A). Only in the Federal Republic of Germany is this population subgroup expected to decline slightly.

Beyond simple extrapolations of national and regional populations in the labor force lies a system of interdependent relationships that are poorly understood and whose future development is difficult to project. Foremost among these is the question of labor force participation of married women and the relationship between such participation and fertility. Women are entering the labor force and remaining longer, and are therefore caught between the desire for and need to work and the desire for and responsibilities of child-bearing. No projection of the evolution of such interdependencies in the 17 countries was attempted in the Migration and Settlement Study.

Finally, the relative size of the elderly population is projected to increase dramatically during the next few decades in several IIASA countries and to decline in others. Elderly dependency ratios are projected to decline, for example, in Austria, Czechoslovakia, the German Democratic Republic, Sweden, the UK, and the US. They are expected to increase in Bulgaria, Canada, Finland, France, Italy, Japan, the Netherlands, Poland, and the Soviet Union. The most significant decline is projected for the German Democratic Republic (20%) and the sharpest increase for Japan (46%).

Although the actuarial problems of pensions are serious, they may be dwarfed by those of social service provision, particularly health care. Leaving aside the problems of inflation, the drain on the working population of a growing dependent population of the elderly is calculable, and total expenditures can be projected with some confidence using alternative assumptions regarding economic growth. The health service needs of the elderly, on the other hand, are more difficult to forecast. But they will undoubtedly increase at least in proportion to the advancing mean age of the elderly population.

The number of people aged 75 and over in the IIASA nations is projected to grow from 43 to 53 million during the 20-year period from 1980 to 2000. This is a prospective increase of 23% in a population subgroup that makes particularly heavy demands on a nation's health and service system — demands that generally increase faster than population size. The proportion of people requiring regular attention increases sharply above age 75. Stays in hospitals for acute or long-term illness increase, as do numbers of doctors' visits and of persons entering nursing homes; costs related to health care increase dramatically.

The projected aggregate increase by almost one-quarter of the population of the 75-and over age group hides large variations at the national level. In Canada and in Japan, for example, the expected increase is much higher: 56 and 57%, respectively. However, in Austria and in the German Democratic

Republic and populations in this subgroup should *decline* by about 12 and 30%, respectively.

Extrapolation of current trends identifies important differences in the "graying" of IIASA's national populations; also revealed are significant regional differences. In a number of countries, one can already find spatial concentrations of the aged, for example, in Vienna, Austria, the Southwest and the Mediterranean regions in France, and the Shikoku and Kyushu regions in Japan. If current migration patterns remain constant, some regions will experience a considerable further aging of their populations. The number of elderly persons in the Kanto region of Japan, for example, is projected to almost double in size between 1980 and 2000 (Appendix 6A). Because of the higher than average rate of natural increase in the region, however, the share accorded to the elderly population will continue to be lower in Kanto than in the rest of Japan. Regions in other countries that are projected to experience large increases in the numbers of elderly persons between 1980 and 2000 are, for example, British Columbia (166%) in Canada, Sofia (158%) in Bulgaria, and the Kazakh Republics (156%) in the Soviet Union. A few regions centered on large cities may expect substantial declines in the numbers of their aged. In West Berlin, for example, the elderly population will decrease by about one-half and in Vienna by almost one-third. Whereas in 1980, about one out of every five persons in Vienna was 65 years or older, this fraction is projected to be only one out of every seven by the year 2000.

Patterns of regional differentiation in age composition in the year 2000 are summarized in Table 6.11. A comparison of these figures with the corresponding data for 1980, set out in Table 6.5, shows that Italy and the Soviet Union continue to exhibit the highest degrees of regional differences in the prevalence of young populations, with the former country overtaking the latter by the year 2000. Japan and the Soviet Union once again lead the IIASA countries in the amount of regional variations in the concentration of elderly people. In this indicator too, the Soviet Union is overtaken by Japan by the year 2000. In both 1980 and 2000, Austria and Bulgaria show higher than average degrees of variation in regional concentrations of the elderly.

For the 17 nations as a whole, it appears that differences in the fractions of regional populations found in the young and elderly categories by the year 2000 are likely to rise for the young and decline for the elderly. The MAD/N value for the former increases from 9.1 to 13.3%, whereas that for the latter decreases from 16.8 to 12.6%.

6.6 Conclusion: Population Processes, Prospects, and Issues

Social concern with population processes arises when the acts of individuals affect the welfare of others and combine demographically in ways that produce a sharp divergence between the sum of individual (private)

Table 6.11 Regional differentials in age composition in the year 2000.

Country (reference year: number of regions)	Age group (%)							
	0–14				65+			
	National	Lowest	Highest	MAD/N(%)	National	Lowest	Highest	MAD/N(%)
Austria (1971:9)	23.0	16.9	27.2	9.6	12.1	9.2	15.0	13.6
Bulgaria (1975:7)	21.8	19.5	23.9	6.4	13.9	12.2	18.4	13.1
Canada (1971:10)	26.0	24.2	35.4	10.1	10.3	7.3	14.2	11.9
Czechoslovakia (1975:10)	24.3	21.7	27.8	3.8	11.0	9.5	12.4	6.4
FRG (1974:11)	15.9	12.3	17.5	7.1	15.6	14.2	18.1	4.6
Finland (1974:12)	17.2	16.0	21.0	5.9	13.5	11.6	15.3	8.0
France (1975:8)	19.8	17.0	23.5	8.5	14.7	12.1	18.5	12.3
GDR (1975:5)	16.2	15.3	17.7	5.3	14.1	10.4	15.9	11.1
Hungary (1974:6)	21.7	19.0	24.8	6.4	13.3	12.2	14.0	4.1
Italy (1978:5)	19.5	16.5	24.3	17.1	15.2	12.6	17.2	11.9
Japan (1970:8)	20.5	18.2	21.2	5.6	12.5	9.8	20.1	31.8
Netherlands (1974:5)	19.6	18.1	21.4	5.7	12.9	12.0	14.8	6.8
Poland (1977:13)	22.7	16.4	27.3	10.0	11.5	9.1	13.6	9.1
Soviet Union (1974:8)	25.2	21.6	35.4	15.5	12.2	6.9	16.9	24.4
Sweden (1974:8)	18.4	17.1	19.9	3.4	16.3	14.7	17.5	5.4
United Kingdom (1970:10)	24.2	22.8	25.7	3.9	12.3	11.3	14.4	5.8
United States (1970:4)	26.0	25.6	27.1	2.2	10.2	9.5	10.9	5.8
Total	23.3	15.9	26.0	13.3	12.2	10.2	16.3	12.6

preferences and social well-being. In such instances, population processes properly become the subject of public debate and the object of public policy.

Population policies are actions undertaken by public bodies with the aim of affecting processes of demographic growth and change. Family planning programs, investments in health care facilities and services, and government-assisted migration are examples of public actions taken, respectively, to reduce fertility levels, to promote health and longevity, and to foster personal betterment through geographical mobility.

6.6.1 *Fertility and Migration*

Among national population policies in the less developed world, the problem of fertility reduction has been of paramount importance. The negative consequences of rapid population growth for socioeconomic development are becoming widely recognized and this has led many developing countries to undertake serious efforts to control fertility.

Among the more developed countries, the perceived negative consequences of population *decline* have generated a fear of possible future labor shortages, "stagnating" non-innovative aging populations, and reduced national influence in international affairs ("demographic suicide"). A few countries have responded with pronatalist measures; others have adopted policies on egalitarian grounds that reduce the burdens for childbearing and childrearing. Free medical care before, during, and after delivery; child grants; paid maternity leave; tighter controls on abortion; free infant, preschool, and school health care; educational grants; low-interest loans; and family and housing allowances are some of the measures that have been adopted.

Concern with national population growth or decline necessarily has been a concern about levels of fertility. Spatial population policies, on the other hand, tend to focus primarily on internal migration and its contribution to human settlement growth and structure. The potential negative impacts of rapid rates of urban growth on socioeconomic development have led to the adoption of policies to curtail growth in certain localities, while at the same time stimulating it in others. Generally, such national urbanization or human settlement policies have been defended on the grounds either of national efficiency or of regional equity. They may seek to encourage some underemployed people in declining regions to migrate and shift to more productive occupations, for example. Or they might strive to divert migrants away from major overcrowded metropolitan areas. They might also try to make it possible for an economically depressed region to attract the skilled and professional manpower that it needs for its growth and development.

During the past two decades shifts in long-standing demographic patterns of fertility and migration in the IIASA countries have brought about a growing debate about the long-range implications of current trends. Declining rates of national population growth, continuing differential levels of regional economic activity, and shifts in the migration patterns of people and jobs are changing the sizes, age compositions, and spatial distributions of the 17 national populations, thereby altering the well-being of particular population groups and regions. Major declines in fertility have dramatically changed prospects for future population growth at the same time that new patterns of internal migration have rearranged the territorial structures of national populations. The combination has brought forward two major policy issues: the consequences of changing age profiles and the impacts of changing spatial distributions.

6.6.2 *Slowing Population Growth and Changing Age Profiles*

By 1980 almost all of the 17 IIASA populations had entered a period of transition to nongrowth. Population increase averaged less than 1% per year during the preceding 20 years and is projected to drop to slightly over half that rate during the following two decades. Eight of the 17 national populations will cease to grow by the end of this century if current fertility rates remain unchanged. Another four or five are likely to be growing at near-zero rates at that time.

Fertility rates in these nations have been declining for most of the past two decades and are now at below replacement levels in 13 of the 17 countries. A sharp reversal of this historical pattern is not a likely prospect. About 10% of the women in several European countries go through life without bearing any children and another 20% have only one. If bare replacement-level fertility is to occur in such countries, 50% have to have three children each. Past and current trends suggest that this is not likely to happen soon.

The impacts of declining birth rates are felt in population age compositions: reducing the proportion in the youngest age groups, increasing the proportion aged 65 and over, and leaving approximately the same fraction in the working ages. Changing age compositions will affect school enrolments, demands for health care and particular categories of housing units, and the sizes of the beneficiary and donor populations involved in social security systems.

School enrolments are correlated with the number of children. Health care facilities and nursing homes expand or contract with changes in the sizes of the elderly population. Housing demand varies with, among other things, the number of persons in the ages of principal home ownership, usually young and middle-aged adults.

Of particular concern is the projected increase in the number and proportion of older people, especially of the very old populations. In most IIASA nations, a major part of the costs of ensuring the well-being of the elderly is borne by those in the labor force by means of payroll taxes or income taxes. If these countries decide to continue current levels of health care and income maintenance (social security) benefits to their elderly citizens, then fertility declines imply rising per capita support burdens on the workforce.

Nongrowth at the national level does not imply a corresponding halt of population growth for local areas and regions, since migration will continue to cause some regions to grow and others to decline. Thus problems of expansion and contraction will continue to confront national and regional decision makers.

6.6.3 *Migration Shifts and Changing Spatial Distributions*

Shifts in the patterns of migration flows, together with the emergence of low fertility levels at the regional scale, are altering national territorial arrangements. The attractiveness of large urban centers has diminished in a number of IIASA's market economy countries and regional redistributions of populations and economic activity are signaling altered regional fortunes and giving rise to a variety of regional conflicts of interest.

Rearrangements of national territorial structures are contributing to political and economic imbalances in the distribution of employment, income, and wealth. In the US, the Northeast shows declining rates of population growth, while the South continues to maintain its share of the national population. In Canada, Quebec is projected to experience a sharp decline in relative population size, while British Columbia is expected to increase its share of the national population total. In Japan, the Kanto region centered on Tokyo continues to attract migrants and could account for almost 40% of Japan's population by the year 2000, at the same time that the Kyushu and Shikoku regions continue to lose their populations to other parts of the nation. Social infrastructure will need to be expanded in the growing regions and obsolescent physical plants will need to be revitalized or replaced in the regions of decline.

A region's political representation in national bodies and its claims on national resources are generally linked to its population size. Shrinking populations imply reduced influence and reduced claims. Moreover, declining regions may lose much of their scarce human capital, receiving less skilled inmigrants in exchange. Population groups that are heavily dependent on public support may grow in relative size, raising the per capita public burden. Outdated public facilities, inadequate transportation systems, and other symptoms of decline emerge at a time of eroding local tax bases and sharply escalating service demands.

APPENDIX 6A: Regional Population Projections, Annual Rates of Increase (R), and Percentage Shares (Perc.), and Mean Ages for the 139 IIASA Regions, for Total Populations for All Ages Combined, and for Major Age Groups

All ages

Country (reference year) and region	1980 Population (1)	f (2)	Perc. (3)	Mean age (4)	2000 Population (5)	f (6)	Perc. (7)	Mean age (8)	2030 Population (9)	f (10)	Perc. (11)	Mean age (12)	Stable f (13)	Perc. (14)	Mean age (15)
Austria (1971)															
Burgenland	269.	-0.001	3.55	35.95	263.	-0.002	3.28	36.08	252.	-0.002	2.85	37.12	0.005	0.77	36.04
Carinthia	544.	-0.004	7.18	34.33	593.	0.004	7.37	34.60	654.	0.002	7.41	35.97	0.005	6.37	35.48
Lower Austria	1404.	-0.001	18.53	36.68	1410.	0.000	17.54	36.43	1412.	0.001	16.00	37.64	0.005	5.84	36.84
Upper Austria	1277.	0.005	16.85	34.21	1435.	0.006	17.85	34.18	1665.	0.004	18.86	35.44	0.005	14.76	35.37
Salzburg	437.	0.009	5.77	33.83	525.	0.009	6.53	33.94	658.	0.006	7.45	35.25	0.005	8.99	35.65
Styria	1213.	0.002	16.01	35.24	1280.	0.002	15.92	35.23	1367.	0.001	15.48	36.49	0.005	9.56	35.81
Tyrol	589.	0.009	7.77	32.95	717.	0.009	8.91	33.19	920.	0.007	10.41	34.57	0.005	24.77	35.08
Vorarlberg	301.	0.011	3.98	31.87	378.	0.011	4.70	33.47	500.	0.008	5.66	33.65	0.005	21.54	34.43
Vienna	1543.	-0.005	20.36	41.40	1438.	-0.002	17.89	39.73	1402.	-0.001	15.88	39.96	0.005	7.40	38.80
Austria	7577.	0.002	100.00	36.16	8038.	0.003	100.00	35.64	8830.	0.003	100.00	36.55	0.005	100.00	35.52
Bulgaria (1975)															
North West	1040.	-0.001	11.59	39.38	1003.	-0.001	10.45	39.14	985.	0.001	9.64	37.74	0.002	8.47	37.37
North	1417.	0.002	15.79	38.04	1447.	0.001	15.07	38.23	1507.	0.002	14.74	37.63	0.002	15.49	37.46
North East	1540.	0.007	17.16	34.14	1705.	0.005	17.76	35.20	1908.	0.004	18.67	35.16	0.002	24.26	35.51
South West	705.	0.002	7.85	35.08	703.	-0.002	7.32	37.47	642.	-0.003	6.28	38.16	0.002	2.83	36.35
South	2247.	0.008	25.04	34.12	2502.	0.004	26.07	36.60	2759.	-0.003	27.00	35.93	0.002	26.67	36.09
South East	884.	-0.004	9.84	34.95	902.	0.000	9.40	36.88	879.	-0.000	8.60	36.24	0.002	6.39	35.51
Sofia	1143.	0.013	12.73	34.91	1335.	0.006	13.91	36.75	1539.	0.004	15.06	36.78	0.002	15.88	37.23
Bulgaria	8976.	0.006	100.00	35.61	9596.	0.003	100.00	36.71	10220.	0.002	100.00	36.59	0.002	100.00	36.42
Canada (1971)															
Newfoundland	573.	0.014	2.49	27.23	749.	0.012	2.62	27.95	1048.	0.010	2.87	28.99	0.007	4.71	29.09
Prince Edward Island	119.	0.009	0.52	31.61	145.	0.009	0.51	32.02	188.	0.008	0.51	33.63	0.007	0.52	33.59
Nova Scotia	836.	0.009	3.64	30.46	1008.	0.008	3.52	32.48	1275.	0.007	3.49	34.10	0.007	3.56	33.86
New Brunswick	683.	0.010	2.97	30.46	833.	0.009	2.91	31.72	1048.	0.007	2.87	33.59	0.007	2.68	33.33
Quebec	6340.	0.008	27.56	31.30	7274.	0.005	25.42	34.09	7999.	0.002	21.91	36.61	0.007	12.10	35.51
Ontario	8226.	0.013	35.75	32.08	10442.	0.010	36.50	33.50	13649.	0.008	37.39	35.09	0.007	37.67	34.98
Manitoba	1013.	-0.005	4.40	32.40	1119.	0.004	3.91	33.09	1301.	0.005	3.56	34.14	0.007	3.48	33.78
Saskatchewan	895.	-0.005	3.89	32.94	838.	-0.003	2.93	33.05	847.	0.003	2.32	34.30	0.007	2.23	33.75
Alberta	1823.	0.018	7.92	30.03	2506.	0.013	8.76	31.23	3520.	0.010	9.65	32.88	0.007	11.96	33.17
British Columbia	2500.	0.023	10.87	32.74	3700.	0.017	12.93	34.07	5525.	0.012	15.41	35.96	0.007	21.09	36.39
Canada	23008.	0.012	100.00	31.63	28612.	0.009	100.00	33.29	36500.	0.007	100.00	35.03	0.007	100.00	34.69
Czechoslovakia (1975)															
Central Bohemia	2354.	0.005	15.32	37.58	2521.	0.005	14.64	36.29	3015.	0.006	14.52	35.52	0.006	14.43	35.41
Southern Bohemia	692.	0.007	4.50	35.38	774.	0.007	4.50	34.54	950.	0.007	4.58	34.14	0.006	4.63	34.54
Western Bohemia	895.	0.005	5.83	34.34	953.	0.004	5.54	34.13	1080.	0.005	5.20	33.80	0.006	4.69	33.76
Northern Bohemia	1172.	0.006	7.63	33.86	1263.	0.005	7.34	34.98	1459.	0.005	6.99	33.90	0.006	6.37	33.51
Eastern Bohemia	1254.	0.005	8.16	35.76	1346.	0.005	7.82	34.67	1582.	0.006	7.62	34.62	0.006	7.23	34.40
Southern Moravia	2054.	0.007	13.37	35.38	2288.	0.006	13.29	34.04	2804.	0.007	13.51	34.37	0.006	14.39	34.34
Northern Moravia	1955.	0.008	12.73	33.50	2212.	0.006	12.85	34.20	2648.	0.006	12.76	34.17	0.006	12.39	34.00
Western Slovakia	2070.	0.010	13.47	33.46	2412.	0.007	14.02	34.38	2959.	0.006	14.26	35.06	0.006	13.51	34.99
Central Slovakia	1525.	0.009	9.92	32.50	1758.	0.009	10.21	31.98	2173.	0.006	10.18	34.34	0.006	9.10	34.10
Eastern Slovakia	1395.	0.012	9.08	31.14	1686.	0.013	9.80	31.98	2157.	0.008	10.39	32.87	0.006	13.34	32.92
Czechoslovakia	15366.	0.007	100.00	34.40	17212.	0.006	100.00	34.34	20757.	0.006	100.00	34.42	0.006	100.00	34.25

All ages

Country (reference year) and region	1980 Population (1)	r (2)	Perc. (3)	Mean age (4)	2000 Population (5)	r (6)	Perc. (7)	Mean age (8)	2030 Population (9)	r (10)	Perc. (11)	Mean age (12)	Stable r (13)	Perc. (14)	Mean age (15)
Fed.Rep.of Germany (1974)															
Schleswig-Holstein	2589.	0.000	4.22	38.06	2487.	-0.004	4.32	40.87	1966.	-0.011	4.36	45.23	-0.013	4.27	45.49
Hamburg	1616.	-0.012	2.64	41.26	1348.	-0.009	2.34	42.84	997.	-0.012	2.21	46.09	-0.013	2.16	46.16
Lower Saxony	7266.	-0.000	11.85	37.67	7021.	-0.003	12.19	40.03	5664.	-0.010	12.55	43.88	-0.013	12.77	44.28
Bremen	691.	-0.008	1.13	39.39	604.	-0.007	1.05	41.32	463.	-0.012	1.03	44.60	-0.013	1.03	44.83
N. Rhine-Westphalia	16934.	-0.003	27.63	37.97	15608.	-0.006	27.09	40.47	11836.	-0.012	26.23	44.82	-0.013	24.53	44.98
Hessen	5605.	-0.000	9.08	38.33	5551.	-0.004	9.29	41.17	4248.	-0.011	9.41	45.22	-0.013	9.38	45.50
Rhineland-Palatinate	3605.	-0.004	5.88	38.18	3256.	-0.006	5.65	41.58	2449.	-0.010	5.43	45.71	-0.013	5.09	45.82
Baden-Wuerttemberg	9274.	0.001	15.13	37.01	9071.	-0.003	15.74	40.24	7308.	-0.010	16.20	44.25	-0.013	16.98	44.62
Bavaria	10864.	0.009	17.72	37.80	10571.	-0.003	18.35	40.68	8595.	-0.010	19.05	44.67	-0.013	20.54	45.02
Saarland	1039.	-0.010	1.69	38.28	831.	-0.012	1.44	42.52	539.	-0.016	1.20	46.29	-0.013	0.97	45.54
West Berlin	1854.	-0.015	3.03	41.80	1469.	-0.011	2.55	41.21	1057.	-0.013	2.34	44.10	-0.013	2.27	44.04
Fed.Rep. of Germany	61298.	-0.002	100.00	38.03	57618.	-0.004	100.00	40.81	45124.	-0.011	100.00	44.71	-0.013	100.00	44.96
Finland (1974)															
Uusimaa	1153.	0.012	23.90	35.26	1245.	0.001	25.86	38.55	1114.	-0.010	27.10	43.08	-0.010	27.57	43.06
Turku and Pori	720.	0.007	14.93	36.62	739.	0.000	15.35	39.44	655.	-0.010	15.93	43.64	-0.010	16.36	43.57
Ahvenanmaa	23.	0.009	0.48	36.73	26.	-0.003	0.54	37.92	26.	-0.006	0.62	42.04	-0.010	0.78	42.91
Hame	687.	0.007	14.24	36.22	707.	0.000	14.68	39.49	621.	-0.010	15.10	43.86	-0.010	15.23	43.68
Kymi	347.	0.009	7.19	36.63	324.	-0.004	6.74	40.00	261.	-0.012	6.36	43.94	-0.010	6.08	43.39
Mikkeli	205.	-0.006	4.24	36.64	180.	-0.006	3.74	39.34	141.	-0.012	3.43	43.45	-0.010	3.29	42.83
Pohjois-Karjala	173.	-0.004	3.59	35.93	154.	-0.006	3.21	39.25	122.	-0.012	2.96	42.95	-0.010	2.84	42.25
Kuopio	249.	-0.002	5.15	35.78	228.	-0.005	4.74	39.47	182.	-0.012	4.42	43.40	-0.010	4.23	42.72
Keski-Soomi	240.	0.001	4.98	35.64	229.	-0.003	4.77	39.08	188.	-0.011	4.58	42.88	-0.010	4.49	42.43
Vaasa	423.	-0.000	8.76	35.96	392.	-0.005	8.14	38.95	316.	-0.011	7.69	42.26	-0.010	7.48	41.83
Oulu	411.	-0.004	8.52	32.96	413.	-0.001	8.58	36.28	350.	-0.009	8.51	40.05	-0.010	8.55	39.78
Lappi	194.	-0.002	4.01	33.31	176.	-0.005	3.65	37.81	136.	-0.011	3.31	41.75	-0.010	3.10	39.93
Finland	4825.	0.005	100.00	35.62	4815.	-0.001	100.00	38.87	4111.	-0.010	100.00	42.98	-0.010	100.00	42.75
France (1975)															
Paris Region	10023.	0.003	18.79	35.84	10227.	-0.000	18.35	37.47	9712.	-0.003	17.77	39.54	-0.003	17.77	39.46
Paris Basin	9868.	0.005	18.50	35.80	10489.	0.002	18.82	37.49	10465.	-0.002	19.15	40.52	-0.003	19.36	40.63
North	3941.	0.001	7.39	34.03	3996.	-0.003	7.17	35.07	3826.	-0.003	7.00	37.24	-0.003	6.79	37.26
East	4957.	0.002	9.29	34.94	5034.	-0.001	9.03	37.18	4664.	-0.004	8.53	40.34	-0.003	7.12	40.09
West	7065.	0.005	13.24	34.98	7626.	0.003	13.68	37.21	7873.	-0.001	14.40	39.77	-0.003	16.61	40.04
Southwest	5574.	0.001	10.45	39.23	5549.	-0.001	9.96	40.75	5221.	-0.003	9.55	43.74	-0.003	8.82	43.52
Middle East	6271.	0.005	11.76	36.29	6693.	0.002	12.01	38.03	6676.	-0.002	12.21	40.99	-0.003	12.28	41.02
Mediterranean	5643.	0.006	10.58	36.20	6123.	0.003	10.99	41.02	6223.	-0.001	11.39	44.20	-0.003	11.34	44.38
France	53342.	0.004	100.00	36.41	55738.	0.001	100.00	38.02	54660.	-0.002	100.00	40.77	-0.003	100.00	40.78
German Dem.Rep.(1975)															
North	2087.	0.000	12.54	35.21	2051.	-0.000	13.04	38.27	1710.	-0.006	13.36	43.43	-0.012	13.45	43.07
Berlin	1143.	0.008	6.87	36.84	1337.	0.007	8.50	37.53	1359.	-0.002	10.62	41.62	-0.012	18.21	42.82
Southwest	2520.	-0.001	15.14	37.23	2433.	0.000	15.46	39.23	2030.	-0.007	15.86	43.57	-0.012	16.22	43.48
South	6945.	-0.005	41.75	35.24	6107.	-0.004	38.82	40.91	4571.	-0.010	35.72	45.24	-0.012	27.24	43.38
Middle	3945.	-0.001	23.70	36.75	3802.	-0.000	24.17	39.36	3128.	-0.007	24.45	44.36	-0.012	24.88	44.62
German Dem.Rep.	16642.	-0.002	100.00	37.58	15730.	-0.001	100.00	39.64	12798.	-0.007	100.00	44.14	-0.012	100.00	43.69

Country (reference year) and region	All ages 1980 Population (1)	f (2)	Perc. (3)	Mean age (4)	2000 Population (5)	f (6)	Perc. (7)	Mean age (8)	2030 Population (9)	f (10)	Perc. (11)	Mean age (12)	Stable f (13)	Perc. (14)	Mean age (15)
Hungary (1974)															
Central	3093.	0.007	28.70	37.44	3297.	0.003	29.18	37.71	3567.	0.003	29.33	37.42	0.003	29.29	37.23
North Hungary	1389.	0.004	12.89	35.53	1429.	0.001	12.65	36.45	1509.	0.002	12.49	35.84	0.003	12.32	35.64
North Plain	1581.	0.004	14.67	34.55	1641.	0.002	14.52	36.94	1761.	0.002	14.48	36.28	0.003	14.44	34.59
South Plain	1472.	0.002	13.66	36.97	1489.	0.001	13.17	35.94	1575.	0.003	12.95	35.28	0.003	12.87	36.05
North Trans-Danubia	1911.	0.008	17.74	34.82	2079.	0.004	18.40	35.50	2295.	0.003	18.87	35.26	0.003	19.11	35.15
South Trans-Danubia	1330.	0.003	12.34	36.38	1365.	0.002	12.08	35.64	1455.	0.002	11.97	36.04	0.003	11.97	35.87
Hungary	10775.	0.005	100.00	36.11	11301.	0.002	100.00	36.55	12162.	0.003	100.00	36.12	0.003	100.00	35.94
Italy (1978)															
Northwest	15427.	0.000	27.09	37.57	15239.	-0.001	25.62	40.12	13747.	-0.004	23.89	42.37	-0.002	21.51	41.85
Northeast	10423.	0.004	18.31	37.52	10515.	-0.001	17.68	40.44	9499.	-0.005	16.51	43.54	-0.002	11.20	43.08
Central	10868.	0.004	19.08	37.40	11355.	0.001	19.09	40.28	10816.	-0.003	18.79	42.79	-0.002	16.60	42.77
South	13638.	0.006	23.95	32.98	15140.	0.004	25.45	35.05	15967.	0.001	27.74	37.34	-0.002	36.35	37.62
Islands	6591.	0.006	11.57	33.78	7235.	0.004	12.16	35.82	7522.	-0.000	13.07	38.29	-0.002	14.33	38.59
Italy	56954.	0.003	100.00	35.99	59484.	0.001	100.00	38.39	57551.	-0.002	100.00	40.71	-0.002	100.00	40.13
Japan (1970)															
Hokkaido	5027.	-0.003	4.32	35.92	4395.	-0.007	3.40	39.59	3421.	-0.007	2.55	40.27	0.000	2.11	39.01
Tohoku	10472.	-0.008	8.99	35.63	8849.	-0.008	6.84	40.91	7274.	-0.004	5.43	41.19	0.000	5.12	40.70
Kanto	38752.	0.022	33.28	31.49	50364.	0.010	38.91	35.05	58128.	0.003	43.41	36.91	0.000	46.58	37.39
Chubu	19923.	0.012	17.11	33.44	22759.	0.005	17.58	37.27	23638.	0.000	17.65	38.74	0.000	17.19	37.78
Kinki	20375.	0.018	17.50	34.34	25031.	0.008	19.34	35.87	27067.	0.001	20.21	37.62	0.000	19.55	37.82
Chugoku	7150.	0.002	6.14	35.89	6879.	-0.002	5.31	40.20	6109.	-0.004	4.56	40.76	0.000	4.06	40.82
Shikoku	3538.	-0.009	3.04	37.24	2867.	-0.010	2.21	42.14	2254.	-0.006	1.68	41.36	0.000	1.49	40.30
Kyushu	11188.	-0.015	9.61	35.77	8299.	-0.014	6.41	40.78	6017.	-0.007	4.49	39.73	0.000	3.89	38.43
Japan	116425.	-0.010	100.00	33.30	129441.	0.004	100.00	36.95	133908.	0.000	100.00	38.07	0.000	100.00	38.11
Netherlands (1974)															
North	1569.	0.010	11.25	34.52	1840.	0.006	12.19	37.00	1965.	-0.001	13.38	41.21	-0.005	15.15	41.74
East	2771.	0.011	19.86	33.45	3244.	0.006	21.48	36.54	3353.	-0.002	22.82	40.84	-0.005	24.01	41.19
West	6123.	-0.001	43.94	35.45	5994.	-0.002	39.69	38.41	5322.	-0.006	36.23	42.28	-0.005	33.43	41.97
South-West	349.	0.010	2.46	35.93	304.	0.005	2.61	38.23	407.	-0.002	2.89	42.68	-0.005	2.78	43.05
South	3136.	0.010	22.48	33.00	3629.	0.005	24.03	37.41	3643.	-0.003	24.89	42.22	-0.005	24.64	42.44
Netherlands	13949.	0.006	100.00	34.41	15102.	0.002	100.00	37.59	14691.	-0.003	100.00	41.80	-0.005	100.00	41.89
Poland (1977)															
Warsaw	2296.	0.013	6.42	35.87	2734.	0.007	6.71	37.52	3190.	0.004	7.02	39.10	0.003	6.36	39.16
Lodz	1122.	0.007	3.14	36.41	1190.	0.001	2.92	38.35	1196.	-0.001	2.63	40.68	0.003	1.74	39.79
Gdansk	1353.	0.017	3.78	31.88	1708.	0.009	4.19	34.47	2089.	0.005	4.60	36.79	0.003	4.34	36.98
Katowice	3711.	0.014	10.39	33.39	4537.	0.008	11.14	35.74	5389.	0.004	11.86	37.63	0.003	14.18	37.73
Cracow	1183.	0.011	3.31	34.15	1377.	0.006	3.38	36.66	1568.	0.003	3.45	33.66	0.003	4.98	38.40
East-Central	2976.	0.005	8.33	33.69	3137.	0.002	7.70	35.19	3262.	0.001	7.18	36.53	0.003	5.45	36.24
Northeast	2461.	0.009	6.89	32.05	2774.	0.004	6.81	34.26	3046.	0.002	6.70	36.15	0.003	5.03	36.13
Northwest	2191.	0.013	6.13	30.93	2568.	0.006	6.31	34.46	2823.	0.001	6.21	36.99	0.003	4.77	36.70
South	2576.	0.009	7.21	32.83	2931.	0.005	7.20	34.85	3263.	0.002	7.18	36.65	0.003	7.25	36.52
Southeast	4318.	0.009	12.08	32.76	4954.	0.006	12.17	33.03	5914.	0.005	13.01	33.61	0.003	23.33	33.64
East	2524.	0.006	7.06	34.00	2702.	0.002	6.64	35.35	2874.	0.002	6.32	36.36	0.003	5.64	36.06
West-Central	4841.	0.009	13.55	32.84	5452.	0.005	13.39	34.68	6026.	-0.000	13.26	36.82	0.003	9.38	36.65
West	4185.	0.010	11.71	31.97	4656.	0.003	11.43	35.84	4812.	-0.002	10.59	38.32	0.003	7.56	37.88
Poland	35735.	0.010	100.00	33.06	40719.	0.005	100.00	35.15	45451.	0.002	100.00	36.88	0.003	100.00	36.43

Country (reference year) and region	All ages 1980 Population (1)	f (2)	Perc. (3)	Mean age (4)	2000 Population (5)	f (6)	Perc. (7)	Mean age (8)	2030 Population (9)	f (10)	Perc. (11)	Mean age (12)	Stable f (13)	Perc. (14)	Mean age (15)
Soviet Union (1974)															
Urban areas of the:															
RSFSR	100770.	0.022	37.89	34.29	134783.	0.010	43.25	35.35	169291.	0.006	44.75	36.91	0.006	44.03	37.04
Ukrainian+Mold.SSRs	33815.	0.022	12.71	34.12	45630.	0.011	14.64	34.66	58062.	0.007	15.35	36.17	0.006	15.08	36.35
Byelorussian SSR	5567.	0.033	2.09	30.63	8273.	0.013	2.65	31.64	10707.	0.006	2.83	33.83	0.006	2.76	34.07
Central Asian Rep.s	10449.	0.030	3.93	27.83	16227.	0.016	5.21	27.91	23516.	0.010	6.22	28.82	0.006	7.19	29.01
Kazakh SSR	8475.	0.023	3.19	30.22	11534.	0.010	3.70	31.71	14521.	0.006	3.84	33.10	0.006	3.85	33.21
Caucasian Republics	7729.	0.018	2.91	30.64	10411.	0.012	3.34	31.69	13983.	0.008	3.70	32.66	0.006	4.34	32.96
Baltic Republics	5146.	0.028	1.93	34.26	7415.	0.013	2.38	35.24	9757.	0.007	2.58	37.33	0.006	2.55	37.68
Rural areas of USSR	94021.	-0.012	35.35	34.22	77350.	-0.006	24.82	34.84	78495.	0.004	20.75	32.79	0.006	20.21	32.74
Soviet Union	265972.	0.010	100.00	33.68	311623.	0.007	100.00	34.38	378331.	0.006	100.00	35.06	0.006	100.00	35.10
Sweden (1974)															
Stockholm	1492.	0.001	18.07	37.78	1444.	-0.002	17.58	39.77	1305.	-0.004	16.86	41.47	-0.004	16.22	41.18
East Middle	1409.	0.001	17.06	37.91	1384.	-0.002	16.84	39.29	1282.	-0.004	16.57	41.08	-0.004	16.15	40.94
South Middle	767.	0.001	9.28	38.84	745.	-0.002	9.07	39.89	693.	-0.003	8.96	41.47	-0.004	8.91	41.41
South	1182.	0.003	14.31	38.75	1206.	0.000	14.68	40.15	1163.	-0.002	15.03	41.95	-0.004	15.47	42.06
West	1636.	0.003	19.81	38.21	1669.	0.000	20.31	39.36	1618.	-0.002	20.91	41.18	-0.004	21.68	41.36
North Middle	860.	0.001	10.41	39.63	843.	-0.002	10.26	40.27	792.	-0.003	10.23	41.92	-0.004	10.08	41.88
Lower North	403.	0.001	4.88	39.70	395.	-0.001	4.81	40.41	371.	-0.003	4.79	42.06	-0.004	4.72	42.02
Upper North	510.	0.005	6.17	36.94	530.	-0.001	6.45	38.44	514.	-0.002	6.64	40.31	-0.004	6.77	40.46
Sweden	8259.	0.002	100.00	38.36	8216.	-0.001	100.00	39.67	7738.	-0.003	100.00	41.41	-0.004	100.00	41.40
United Kingdom (1970)															
North	3463.	0.003	6.13	35.96	3710.	0.004	6.01	35.27	4252.	0.005	5.85	35.41	0.005	5.68	35.34
Yorkshire + Humbers.	4884.	0.001	8.65	35.87	5123.	0.003	8.29	34.80	5837.	0.005	8.03	34.66	0.005	7.88	34.60
North West	6938.	0.002	12.29	35.53	7439.	0.004	12.04	34.09	8684.	0.005	11.95	34.10	0.005	11.88	34.11
East Midlands	3628.	0.007	6.42	35.43	4173.	0.007	6.76	34.69	5097.	0.005	7.01	35.07	0.005	7.23	35.23
West Midlands	5423.	0.004	9.61	35.16	5922.	0.005	9.59	34.71	6912.	0.007	9.51	34.73	0.005	9.57	34.75
East Anglia	1937.	0.013	3.43	36.51	2464.	0.010	3.89	35.17	3066.	0.007	4.22	37.01	0.005	4.42	37.31
South East	17908.	0.003	31.72	36.46	19493.	0.005	31.56	35.57	22969.	0.005	31.60	35.74	0.005	31.96	35.79
South West	4159.	0.009	7.37	37.19	4868.	0.007	7.88	36.49	5999.	0.006	8.26	36.98	0.005	8.50	37.14
Wales	2818.	0.003	4.99	36.69	3020.	0.004	4.89	35.81	3500.	0.005	4.82	35.96	0.005	4.78	35.94
Scotland	5306.	0.002	9.40	34.85	5617.	0.003	9.09	34.00	6357.	0.004	8.75	34.40	0.005	8.10	34.24
United Kingdom	56463.	0.004	100.00	35.99	61769.	0.005	100.00	35.13	72664.	0.005	100.00	35.34	0.005	100.00	35.39
United States (1970)															
Northeast	51450.	0.005	22.86	33.78	57207.	0.005	21.13	33.59	69196.	0.006	19.86	34.16	0.007	18.82	33.93
North Central	61677.	0.009	27.41	32.29	73081.	0.008	27.00	32.37	93811.	0.008	26.92	33.29	0.007	27.12	33.28
South	69924.	0.011	31.08	32.67	84306.	0.009	31.15	33.57	109364.	0.008	31.10	34.82	0.007	31.10	34.76
West	41965.	0.018	18.65	32.60	56086.	0.012	20.72	33.01	77102.	0.009	22.13	34.58	0.007	22.96	34.78
United States	225016.	0.011	100.00	32.70	270681.	0.008	100.00	33.13	348473.	0.008	100.00	34.22	0.007	100.00	34.21

	Ages 0-14										
	1980			2000			2030			Stable	
Country (reference year) and region	Population (1)	f (2)	Perc. (3)	Population (4)	f (5)	Perc. (6)	Population (7)	f (8)	Perc. (9)	f (10)	Perc. (11)
Austria (1971)											
Burgenland	62.	-0.009	23.06	61.	-0.006	23.22	56.	-0.003	22.37	0.005	23.08
Carinthia	135.	-0.007	24.81	147.	-0.000	24.83	154.	0.001	23.62	0.005	23.94
Lower Austria	316.	-0.012	22.48	318.	-0.002	22.57	304.	-0.002	21.50	0.005	21.98
Upper Austria	315.	-0.008	24.67	357.	0.003	24.89	395.	0.003	23.71	0.005	23.71
Salzburg	109.	-0.002	24.92	130.	0.007	24.72	155.	0.006	23.58	0.005	23.32
Styria	286.	-0.010	23.54	302.	-0.001	23.58	307.	0.001	22.47	0.005	22.86
Tyrol	154.	-0.004	26.12	186.	0.008	25.90	227.	0.007	24.67	0.005	24.33
Vorarlberg	83.	0.001	27.56	103.	0.009	27.15	131.	0.008	26.11	0.005	25.60
Vienna	254.	-0.010	16.46	243.	0.000	16.93	233.	-0.001	16.64	0.005	17.11
Austria	1713.	-0.008	22.61	1847.	0.001	22.98	1962.	0.002	22.22	0.005	23.57
Bulgaria (1975)											
North West	208.	0.001	20.02	207.	0.001	20.63	212.	0.001	21.56	0.002	21.79
North	282.	0.009	19.90	289.	0.002	19.94	310.	0.003	20.56	0.002	20.64
North East	379.	0.009	24.59	407.	0.005	23.87	461.	0.004	24.14	0.002	23.85
South West	164.	-0.006	23.26	151.	-0.005	23.55	136.	-0.003	21.15	0.002	22.42
South	534.	0.004	23.76	573.	-0.002	22.91	629.	0.003	22.81	0.002	22.71
South East	208.	0.004	23.58	205.	-0.001	22.75	207.	0.001	23.60	0.002	24.19
Sofia	236.	0.028	20.67	260.	0.005	19.50	308.	0.005	20.02	0.002	19.75
Bulgaria	2011.	0.007	22.41	2093.	0.002	21.81	2263.	0.003	22.15	0.002	22.20
Canada (1971)											
Newfoundland	202.	0.006	35.25	265.	0.008	35.40	360.	0.009	34.36	0.007	34.30
Prince Edward Island	35.	-0.003	29.11	43.	0.004	29.48	52.	0.006	27.94	0.007	27.99
Nova Scotia	234.	-0.004	27.95	278.	0.003	27.62	334.	0.006	26.19	0.007	26.44
New Brunswick	200.	-0.004	29.29	241.	0.002	28.88	286.	0.005	27.25	0.007	27.50
Quebec	1622.	-0.013	25.58	1762.	-0.003	24.22	1786.	0.000	22.33	0.007	23.25
Ontario	2155.	-0.001	26.20	2677.	0.004	25.64	3318.	0.006	24.31	0.007	24.42
Manitoba	272.	-0.007	26.88	303.	-0.001	27.09	339.	0.004	26.06	0.007	26.41
Saskatchewan	246.	-0.020	27.52	234.	-0.007	27.89	232.	0.001	27.44	0.007	27.99
Alberta	530.	0.006	29.08	718.	0.007	28.65	958.	0.006	27.21	0.007	27.07
British Columbia	639.	0.010	25.56	923.	0.010	24.94	1218.	0.010	23.43	0.007	23.21
Canada	6135.	-0.004	26.66	7442.	0.003	26.01	8983.	0.005	24.61	0.007	25.13
Czechoslovakia (1975)											
Central Bohemia	497.	0.026	21.10	546.	0.008	21.66	692.	0.009	22.96	0.006	23.01
Southern Bohemia	164.	0.021	23.70	184.	0.007	23.80	233.	0.009	24.55	0.006	24.51
Western Bohemia	217.	0.016	24.26	228.	0.005	23.96	269.	0.007	24.92	0.006	25.16
Northern Bohemia	292.	0.019	24.95	308.	0.007	24.36	367.	0.007	25.28	0.006	25.41
Eastern Bohemia	297.	0.020	23.68	329.	0.007	23.82	392.	0.008	24.78	0.006	24.87
Southern Moravia	489.	0.020	23.83	552.	0.007	24.15	702.	0.009	25.03	0.006	25.01
Northern Moravia	494.	0.015	25.28	544.	0.006	24.61	664.	0.008	25.08	0.006	25.17
Western Slovakia	514.	0.015	25.81	579.	0.002	24.01	707.	0.007	23.88	0.006	24.08
Central Slovakia	400.	0.009	26.21	447.	0.001	25.42	530.	0.006	25.07	0.006	25.34
Eastern Slovakia	396.	0.010	28.37	458.	0.003	27.76	590.	0.007	27.35	0.006	27.41
Czechoslovakia	3760.	0.017	24.47	4178.	0.005	24.27	5145.	0.008	24.79	0.006	24.96

Country (reference year) and region	Ages 0-14									
	1980			2000			2030			Stable
	Population (1)	r (2)	Perc. (3)	Population (4)	r (5)	Perc. (6)	Population (7)	r (8)	Perc. (9)	r (10)	Perc. (11)
Fed.Rep.of Germany (1974)											
Schleswig-Holstein	489.	-0.031	18.87	398.	-0.009	16.00	261.	-0.014	13.26	-0.013	13.08
Hamburg	229.	-0.046	14.16	166.	-0.012	12.31	104.	-0.014	10.48	-0.013	10.37
Lower Saxony	1421.	-0.028	19.56	1225.	-0.008	17.45	841.	-0.012	14.86	-0.013	14.61
Bremen	115.	-0.041	16.60	88.	-0.012	14.58	58.	-0.012	12.52	-0.013	12.38
N. Rhine-Westphalia	3044.	-0.035	17.98	2426.	-0.012	15.54	1551.	-0.014	13.10	-0.013	12.95
Hessen	975.	-0.029	17.52	810.	-0.010	15.13	541.	-0.013	13.06	-0.013	12.57
Rhineland-Palatinate	665.	-0.037	18.45	512.	-0.014	15.71	320.	-0.015	12.95	-0.013	12.95
Baden-Wuerttemberg	1781.	-0.028	19.21	1513.	-0.009	16.68	1037.	-0.012	14.19	-0.013	13.98
Bavaria	2000.	-0.029	18.41	1701.	-0.009	16.09	1174.	-0.012	13.65	-0.013	13.47
Saarland	179.	-0.049	17.27	119.	-0.022	14.32	64.	-0.018	11.93	-0.013	12.16
West Berlin	274.	-0.028	14.75	203.	-0.013	13.84	130.	-0.014	12.25	-0.013	12.17
Fed.Rep. of Germany	11171.	-0.032	18.22	9161.	-0.010	15.90	6081.	-0.013	13.48	-0.013	13.33
Finland (1974)											
Uusimaa	223.	-0.003	19.34	203.	-0.010	16.32	156.	-0.011	14.03	-0.010	14.02
Turku and Pori	139.	-0.009	19.31	122.	-0.011	16.57	94.	-0.010	14.31	-0.010	14.32
Ahvenanmaa	5.	-0.003	20.00	5.	-0.003	17.91	4.	-0.007	15.46	-0.010	14.99
Hame	133.	-0.009	19.38	116.	-0.012	16.41	88.	-0.011	14.11	-0.010	14.17
Kymi	66.	-0.021	18.98	52.	-0.016	15.99	36.	-0.012	13.90	-0.010	14.17
Mikkeli	39.	-0.029	19.28	30.	-0.018	16.71	21.	-0.012	14.74	-0.010	15.05
Pohjois-Karjala	34.	-0.027	19.71	27.	-0.018	17.50	19.	-0.012	14.76	-0.010	15.73
Kuopio	49.	-0.029	19.89	39.	-0.017	16.93	27.	-0.012	15.10	-0.010	15.10
Keski-Suomi	48.	-0.020	20.10	40.	-0.015	17.39	29.	-0.012	15.26	-0.010	15.47
Vaasa	89.	-0.016	21.15	73.	-0.014	18.57	52.	-0.012	16.59	-0.010	16.81
Oulu	96.	-0.015	23.30	87.	-0.013	21.01	65.	-0.011	18.61	-0.010	18.73
Lappi	43.	-0.035	21.97	33.	-0.019	18.84	22.	-0.013	16.42	-0.010	16.85
Finland	965.	-0.014	20.00	827.	-0.013	17.17	613.	-0.011	14.91	-0.010	15.00
France (1975)											
Paris Region	2032.	-0.004	20.27	1938.	-0.007	18.95	1731.	-0.005	17.82	-0.003	17.87
Paris Basin	2220.	-0.010	22.49	2180.	-0.006	20.78	1952.	-0.005	18.74	-0.003	18.72
North	956.	-0.010	24.25	938.	-0.007	23.47	834.	-0.005	21.81	-0.003	21.84
East	1097.	-0.016	22.14	1023.	-0.009	20.32	849.	-0.007	18.21	-0.003	18.45
West	1595.	-0.008	22.58	1649.	-0.005	21.62	1554.	-0.003	19.74	-0.003	19.61
Southwest	1040.	-0.016	18.65	960.	-0.009	17.29	806.	-0.006	15.43	-0.003	15.60
Middle East	1331.	-0.016	21.23	1311.	-0.004	19.59	1183.	-0.004	17.72	-0.003	17.63
Mediterranean	1036.	-0.012	18.36	1039.	-0.005	16.96	935.	-0.005	15.02	-0.003	14.94
France	11307.	-0.010	21.20	11037.	-0.006	19.80	9854.	-0.005	18.03	-0.003	18.07
German Dem.Rep.(1975)											
North	426.	-0.032	20.40	358.	-0.018	17.45	243.	-0.014	14.22	-0.012	14.48
Berlin	213.	-0.019	18.65	237.	-0.005	17.73	204.	-0.009	15.01	-0.012	14.48
Southwest	479.	-0.026	19.02	409.	-0.014	16.81	285.	-0.013	14.06	-0.012	14.13
South	1221.	-0.031	17.57	932.	-0.019	15.26	578.	-0.015	12.65	-0.012	13.15
Middle	752.	-0.033	19.07	620.	-0.017	16.31	414.	-0.015	13.24	-0.012	13.50
German Dem.Rep.	3091.	-0.030	18.57	2556.	-0.016	16.25	1725.	-0.014	13.48	-0.012	13.82

Ages 0-14

Country (reference year) and region	1980 Population (1)	r (2)	Perc. (3)	2000 Population (4)	r (5)	Perc. (6)	2030 Population (7)	r (8)	Perc. (9)	Stable r (10)	Perc. (11)
Hungary (1974)											
Central	587.	0.033	18.99	626.	-0.001	18.98	706.	0.004	19.80	0.003	19.98
North Hungary	317.	0.011	22.83	321.	-0.001	22.45	354.	0.004	23.49	0.003	23.64
North Plain	398.	0.012	25.19	406.	-0.001	24.76	453.	0.004	25.74	0.003	25.90
South Plain	313.	0.017	21.28	321.	-0.001	21.54	356.	0.004	22.63	0.003	22.81
North Trans-Danubia	446.	0.021	23.36	480.	0.000	23.07	550.	0.005	23.97	0.003	24.11
South Trans-Danubia	290.	0.015	23.11	299.	-0.001	21.91	334.	0.004	22.96	0.003	23.11
Hungary	2352.	0.020	21.83	2452.	-0.001	21.70	2754.	0.004	22.65	0.003	22.81
Italy (1978)											
Northwest	3100.	-0.024	20.09	2527.	0.002	16.59	2069.	-0.004	15.05	-0.002	15.28
Northeast	2107.	-0.023	20.21	1731.	0.001	16.46	1369.	-0.005	14.41	-0.002	14.60
Central	2225.	-0.018	20.47	1955.	0.002	17.22	1677.	-0.003	15.50	-0.002	15.47
South	3640.	-0.008	26.69	3680.	0.003	24.30	3581.	0.000	22.43	-0.002	22.27
Islands	1690.	-0.007	25.65	1677.	0.003	23.18	1600.	-0.001	21.27	-0.002	21.11
Italy	12762.	-0.016	22.41	11570.	0.002	19.45	10296.	-0.002	17.89	-0.002	18.61
Japan (1970)											
Hokkaido	1196.	-0.010	23.80	823.	-0.011	18.71	646.	-0.003	18.87	0.000	19.64
Tohoku	2452.	-0.015	23.42	1652.	-0.012	18.67	1371.	-0.001	18.85	0.000	19.17
Kanto	9708.	0.027	25.05	10686.	0.007	21.22	12036.	0.004	20.70	0.000	20.64
Chubu	4890.	0.013	24.55	4690.	0.004	20.61	4789.	0.003	20.26	0.000	20.32
Kinki	5023.	0.021	24.65	5233.	0.007	20.91	5522.	0.003	20.40	0.000	20.40
Chugoku	1656.	0.002	23.16	1305.	-0.003	18.97	1176.	0.000	19.26	0.000	19.76
Shikoku	802.	-0.013	22.68	522.	-0.009	18.21	437.	-0.001	19.38	0.000	19.07
Kyushu	2746.	-0.020	24.55	1669.	-0.015	20.11	1289.	-0.003	21.42	0.000	22.36
Japan	28474.	0.011	24.46	26580.	0.002	20.53	27260.	0.003	20.36	0.000	20.46
Netherlands (1974)											
North	380.	-0.007	24.22	388.	0.002	21.07	357.	-0.003	18.16	-0.005	17.82
East	687.	-0.008	24.81	695.	0.001	21.43	620.	-0.004	18.48	-0.005	18.21
West	1309.	-0.023	21.36	1084.	-0.007	18.08	832.	-0.007	15.64	-0.005	15.69
South-West	80.	-0.004	23.33	80.	0.000	20.30	70.	-0.005	17.32	-0.005	17.08
South	749.	-0.016	23.88	709.	-0.002	19.54	599.	-0.005	16.45	-0.005	16.24
Netherlands	3206.	-0.016	22.98	2956.	-0.003	19.57	2479.	-0.005	16.87	-0.005	16.80
Poland (1977)											
Warsaw	432.	0.034	18.82	490.	-0.004	17.91	559.	-0.002	17.52	0.003	17.61
Lodz	205.	0.023	18.26	196.	-0.010	16.45	191.	-0.002	15.98	0.003	16.52
Gdansk	332.	0.024	24.56	379.	-0.000	20.27	442.	0.004	21.17	0.003	21.14
Katowice	821.	0.021	22.13	920.	-0.001	22.22	1054.	0.003	19.55	0.003	21.54
Cracow	258.	0.018	21.77	271.	-0.003	19.65	296.	0.002	18.85	0.003	19.09
East-Central	745.	0.011	25.03	754.	-0.006	24.04	761.	-0.000	23.31	0.003	23.62
Northeast	656.	0.007	25.66	700.	-0.004	25.22	730.	0.000	23.95	0.003	24.09
Northwest	569.	0.017	25.97	586.	-0.005	22.82	609.	0.001	21.57	0.003	21.79
South	635.	0.009	24.64	679.	-0.003	23.15	721.	0.001	22.11	0.003	22.29
Southeast	1161.	0.013	26.89	1354.	-0.001	27.33	1593.	0.004	26.93	0.003	27.03
East	628.	0.012	26.90	653.	-0.004	24.18	681.	0.000	23.69	0.003	24.01
West-Central	1215.	0.012	25.03	1270.	-0.004	23.31	1336.	0.001	22.18	0.003	22.40
West	1018.	0.016	24.32	998.	-0.008	21.44	978.	-0.001	20.32	0.003	20.69
Poland	8674.	0.015	24.27	9250.	-0.004	22.72	9349.	0.001	21.89	0.003	22.53

	Ages 0-14										
	1980			2000			2030			Stable	
Country (reference year) and region	Population (1)	f (2)	Perc. (3)	Population (4)	f (5)	Perc. (6)	Population (7)	f (8)	Perc. (9)	f (10)	Perc. (11)
Soviet Union (1974)											
Urban areas of the:											
RSFSR	20469.	0.015	20.31	29077.	0.002	21.57	34726.	0.004	20.51	0.006	20.54
Ukrainian+Mold.SSRs	7240.	0.017	21.41	10391.	0.004	22.77	12617.	0.004	21.73	0.006	21.73
Byelorussian SSR	1329.	0.029	23.87	2132.	0.005	25.77	2586.	0.004	24.16	0.006	24.12
Central Asian Rep.s	3471.	0.024	33.22	5746.	0.012	35.41	8170.	0.009	34.74	0.006	34.93
Kazakh SSR	2252.	0.013	26.57	3166.	0.004	27.45	3833.	0.004	26.40	0.006	26.42
Caucasian Republics	2177.	0.007	28.17	3020.	0.005	29.00	3942.	0.006	28.19	0.006	28.26
Baltic Republics	1102.	0.022	21.42	1625.	0.008	21.92	1994.	0.004	20.44	0.006	20.31
Rural areas of USSR	28339.	-0.026	30.14	23513.	-0.007	30.40	24733.	0.003	31.51	0.006	31.52
Soviet Union	66380.	-0.003	24.96	78669.	0.000	25.24	92602.	0.004	24.48	0.006	24.63
Sweden (1974)											
Stockholm	290.	-0.008	19.42	248.	-0.003	17.14	212.	-0.004	16.27	-0.004	16.39
East Middle	294.	-0.004	20.90	263.	-0.002	18.97	230.	-0.004	17.93	-0.004	17.97
South Middle	158.	-0.003	20.58	142.	-0.002	19.03	125.	-0.003	18.07	-0.004	18.08
South	235.	-0.001	19.90	219.	-0.000	18.13	193.	-0.002	17.13	-0.004	17.02
West	334.	-0.002	20.43	313.	-0.001	18.75	286.	-0.002	17.66	-0.004	17.52
North Middle	166.	-0.003	19.29	153.	-0.003	18.19	136.	-0.003	17.19	-0.004	17.19
Lower North	78.	-0.001	19.39	72.	-0.003	18.12	64.	-0.003	17.16	-0.004	17.16
Upper North	110.	-0.002	21.54	105.	-0.002	19.91	97.	-0.003	18.85	-0.004	18.74
Sweden	1666.	-0.003	20.17	1514.	-0.002	18.43	1349.	-0.003	17.43	-0.004	17.42
United Kingdom (1970)											
North	796.	-0.007	22.99	888.	0.003	23.94	1004.	0.004	23.62	0.005	23.66
Yorkshire + Humbers.	1177.	-0.003	24.09	1285.	0.004	25.08	1458.	0.004	24.98	0.005	24.99
North West	1691.	-0.003	24.37	1910.	0.005	25.67	2208.	0.005	25.42	0.005	25.40
East Midlands	875.	0.000	24.11	1030.	0.007	24.69	1235.	0.006	24.23	0.005	24.10
West Midlands	1326.	0.000	24.45	1467.	0.006	24.77	1700.	0.005	24.59	0.005	24.54
East Anglia	440.	0.009	22.72	548.	0.010	22.82	677.	0.006	22.10	0.005	21.88
South East	4050.	-0.001	22.62	4518.	0.006	23.18	5246.	0.005	22.85	0.005	22.79
South West	934.	-0.003	22.46	1122.	0.008	23.04	1349.	0.006	22.49	0.005	22.38
Wales	641.	-0.004	22.74	713.	0.004	23.60	816.	0.005	23.30	0.005	23.30
Scotland	1313.	-0.004	24.76	1443.	0.002	25.69	1602.	0.003	25.19	0.005	25.29
United Kingdom	13243.	-0.001	23.45	14923.	0.005	24.16	17294.	0.005	23.80	0.005	23.74
United States (1970)											
Northeast	12801.	0.002	24.88	14633.	-0.001	25.58	17452.	0.005	25.22	0.007	25.49
North Central	16519.	0.007	26.78	19823.	0.002	27.12	24970.	0.007	26.62	0.007	26.74
South	18367.	0.007	26.27	21695.	0.003	25.73	27153.	0.007	25.06	0.007	25.18
West	10940.	0.014	26.07	14335.	0.006	25.56	19022.	0.008	24.67	0.007	24.65
United States	58627.	0.007	26.05	70487.	0.002	26.04	88597.	0.007	25.42	0.007	25.54

Country (reference year) and region	Ages 15-64 — 1980 Population (1)	f (2)	Perc. (3)	2000 Population (4)	f (5)	Perc. (6)	2030 Population (7)	f (8)	Perc. (9)	Stable f (10)	Perc. (11)
Austria (1971)											
Burgenland	169.	0.002	62.91	167.	0.000	63.24	158.	-0.004	62.71	0.005	64.15
Carinthia	341.	0.008	62.64	377.	0.007	63.57	410.	-0.001	62.64	0.005	63.44
Lower Austria	871.	0.004	62.06	907.	0.003	64.29	895.	-0.003	63.37	0.005	64.04
Upper Austria	805.	0.011	63.08	923.	0.008	64.31	1059.	0.002	63.56	0.005	63.99
Salzburg	276.	0.013	63.27	342.	0.011	65.11	422.	0.005	64.09	0.005	64.04
Styria	765.	0.006	63.04	827.	0.011	64.57	870.	-0.001	63.65	0.005	64.59
Tyrol	368.	0.015	62.57	462.	0.011	64.47	583.	0.005	63.43	0.005	63.22
Vorarlberg	188.	0.016	62.35	241.	0.002	63.70	314.	0.007	62.73	0.005	62.32
Vienna	974.	-0.003	63.17	979.	0.006	68.06	944.	-0.003	67.29	0.005	68.54
Austria	4759.	0.006	62.81	5222.	0.006	64.97	5653.	0.000	64.02	0.005	63.83
Bulgaria (1975)											
North West	659.	-0.003	63.31	611.	-0.004	60.93	623.	0.001	63.23	0.002	63.49
North	927.	-0.001	65.42	929.	-0.000	64.22	979.	0.003	64.97	0.002	65.17
North East	1000.	-0.004	64.90	1090.	-0.003	63.93	1218.	0.004	62.99	0.002	63.67
South West	461.	0.002	65.41	446.	-0.004	63.55	405.	-0.004	64.38	0.002	64.22
South	1485.	0.000	66.10	1614.	-0.003	64.50	1776.	0.003	62.60	0.002	64.40
South East	581.	0.001	65.70	564.	-0.004	62.56	550.	0.000	62.56	0.002	63.20
Sofia	802.	0.005	70.19	911.	0.006	68.20	1041.	0.006	67.64	0.002	67.20
Bulgaria	5914.	0.003	65.89	6165.	0.001	64.25	6592.	0.003	64.51	0.002	64.63
Canada (1971)											
Newfoundland	333.	0.017	58.04	429.	0.015	57.34	596.	0.009	56.88	0.007	57.00
Prince Edward Island	71.	0.015	59.70	87.	0.013	59.79	111.	0.006	58.88	0.007	59.36
Nova Scotia	521.	0.014	62.34	626.	0.011	62.18	780.	0.005	61.17	0.007	61.69
New Brunswick	421.	0.016	61.65	512.	0.012	61.47	632.	-0.005	60.25	0.007	60.88
Quebec	4225.	0.015	66.65	4779.	0.006	65.71	5052.	-0.000	63.16	0.007	64.48
Ontario	5336.	0.018	64.87	6676.	0.012	63.93	8570.	0.006	62.79	0.007	63.26
Manitoba	634.	0.008	62.61	689.	0.007	61.57	796.	0.004	61.18	0.007	61.84
Saskatchewan	544.	-0.002	60.77	485.	-0.001	57.89	494.	0.001	58.31	0.007	59.12
Alberta	1155.	0.024	63.35	1575.	0.010	62.87	2178.	0.008	61.86	0.007	61.92
British Columbia	1613.	0.027	64.52	2364.	0.019	63.91	3513.	0.010	62.44	0.007	62.41
Canada	14853.	0.017	64.56	18224.	0.011	63.69	22720.	0.005	62.25	0.007	62.49
Czechoslovakia (1975)											
Central Bohemia	1483.	-0.003	63.03	1663.	0.007	65.96	1969.	0.008	65.31	0.006	65.43
Southern Bohemia	431.	0.002	62.25	502.	0.008	64.81	607.	0.008	63.91	0.006	64.08
Western Bohemia	573.	-0.000	64.01	620.	0.004	65.08	693.	0.006	64.14	0.006	64.50
Northern Bohemia	750.	-0.001	61.61	826.	0.006	65.41	934.	0.006	64.41	0.005	64.67
Eastern Bohemia	773.	-0.001	62.16	864.	0.006	64.24	1004.	0.007	63.46	0.006	63.77
Southern Moravia	1277.	0.005	63.71	1470.	0.008	64.27	1778.	0.008	63.77	0.006	63.59
Northern Moravia	1246.	0.007	63.96	1438.	0.007	65.01	1689.	0.007	63.82	0.006	64.02
Western Slovakia	1324.	0.008	63.29	1574.	0.010	65.25	1889.	0.007	62.98	0.006	64.17
Central Slovakia	965.	0.011	62.31	1128.	0.009	64.19	1331.	0.006	61.82	0.006	63.39
Eastern Slovakia	869.	0.011	61.82	1058.	0.011	62.74	1334.	0.007	61.82	0.006	61.98
Czechoslovakia	9691.	0.003	63.07	11143.	0.008	64.74	13226.	0.007	63.72	0.006	63.90

Ages 15-64

Country (reference year) and region	1980 Population (1)	f (2)	Perc. (3)	2000 Population (4)	f (5)	Perc. (6)	2030 Population (7)	f (8)	Perc. (9)	Stable f (10)	Perc. (11)
Fed.Rep.of Germany (1974)											
Schleswig-Holstein	1689.	0.009	65.21	1706.	-0.004	68.61	1233.	-0.017	62.70	-0.013	62.61
Hamburg	1082.	-0.005	66.93	959.	-0.008	71.15	661.	-0.018	66.27	-0.013	66.52
Lower Saxony	4723.	0.008	65.00	4718.	-0.004	67.20	3544.	-0.016	62.57	-0.013	62.30
Bremen	459.	-0.001	66.44	420.	-0.007	69.56	303.	-0.017	65.29	-0.013	65.23
N.Rhine-Westphalia	11448.	0.005	67.61	10741.	-0.007	68.82	7586.	-0.018	64.09	-0.013	64.36
Hessen	3746.	0.006	67.32	3698.	-0.004	69.10	2701.	-0.017	63.58	-0.013	63.55
Rhineland-Palatinate	2383.	0.004	66.09	2181.	-0.007	66.97	1517.	-0.018	61.95	-0.013	62.30
Baden-Wuerttemberg	6205.	0.008	66.91	6180.	-0.004	68.13	4592.	-0.016	62.84	-0.013	62.64
Bavaria	7244.	0.007	66.68	7228.	-0.004	68.37	5413.	-0.016	62.98	-0.013	62.81
Saarland	707.	-0.002	68.05	562.	-0.014	67.57	338.	-0.023	62.73	-0.013	64.63
West Berlin	1179.	-0.011	63.56	1058.	-0.009	72.00	710.	-0.017	67.10	-0.013	67.52
Fed.Rep. of Germany	40865.	0.005	65.67	39450.	-0.005	68.47	28598.	-0.017	63.38	-0.013	63.36
Finland (1974)											
Uusimaa	797.	0.012	69.07	894.	0.003	71.81	721.	-0.010	64.75	-0.010	65.17
Turku and Pori	482.	0.006	66.94	511.	0.002	69.13	413.	-0.010	63.02	-0.010	63.55
Ahvenanmaa	15.	0.010	65.23	18.	0.006	69.14	16.	-0.010	64.26	-0.010	63.27
Hame	464.	0.007	67.50	491.	0.001	69.41	390.	-0.010	62.81	-0.010	62.50
Kymi	235.	0.001	67.69	225.	-0.003	69.33	166.	-0.012	63.42	-0.010	64.65
Mikkeli	138.	-0.003	67.29	123.	-0.005	68.07	89.	-0.012	63.11	-0.010	64.52
Pohjois-Karjala	117.	-0.003	67.46	105.	-0.003	68.07	76.	-0.012	62.82	-0.010	64.42
Kuopio	168.	0.001	67.66	156.	-0.003	68.47	114.	-0.012	62.91	-0.010	64.44
Keski-Suomi	163.	0.001	67.79	158.	-0.001	68.77	119.	-0.011	63.30	-0.010	64.45
Vaasa	277.	-0.001	65.67	259.	-0.003	66.10	195.	-0.011	61.68	-0.010	62.67
Oulu	276.	0.007	67.07	279.	0.001	67.44	220.	-0.010	62.74	-0.010	63.66
Lappi	133.	0.004	68.50	120.	-0.005	68.13	86.	-0.013	63.01	-0.010	64.73
Finland	3264.	0.006	67.65	3338.	0.000	69.33	2605.	-0.010	63.37	-0.010	64.17
France (1975)											
Paris Region	6216.	0.005	67.66	7026.	0.001	68.70	6409.	-0.004	65.99	-0.003	66.34
Paris Basin	6216.	0.010	62.99	6772.	0.003	64.56	6460.	-0.004	61.73	-0.003	61.88
North	2505.	0.006	63.57	2573.	0.002	64.39	2409.	-0.004	62.96	-0.003	63.28
East	3232.	0.008	65.20	3335.	0.000	66.25	2945.	-0.007	63.14	-0.003	63.89
West	4408.	0.009	62.39	4841.	0.005	63.48	4839.	-0.003	61.46	-0.003	61.49
Southwest	3517.	0.004	63.10	3562.	0.000	64.20	3192.	-0.006	61.13	-0.003	61.73
Middle East	4057.	0.009	64.70	4420.	0.003	66.05	4216.	-0.004	63.16	-0.003	63.29
Mediterranean	3602.	0.009	63.82	3950.	0.004	64.51	3790.	-0.005	60.89	-0.003	61.05
France	34319.	0.008	64.34	36480.	0.002	65.45	34259.	-0.004	62.68	-0.003	62.91
German Dem.Rep.(1975)											
North	1384.	0.012	66.33	1433.	-0.002	69.87	1086.	-0.017	63.50	-0.012	64.71
Berlin	761.	0.020	66.55	961.	0.006	71.83	906.	-0.009	66.69	-0.012	65.60
Southwest	1646.	0.007	65.30	1689.	-0.001	69.42	1296.	-0.012	63.87	-0.012	64.55
South	4464.	0.001	64.25	4205.	-0.006	68.86	2870.	-0.018	62.79	-0.012	64.37
Middle	2599.	0.010	65.87	2670.	-0.003	70.22	1991.	-0.017	63.63	-0.012	64.73
German Dem.Rep.	10853.	0.007	65.21	10958.	-0.003	69.66	8149.	-0.016	63.68	-0.012	64.75

Ages 15-64

Country (reference year) and region	1980 Population (1)	r (2)	Perc. (3)	2000 Population (4)	r (5)	Perc. (6)	2030 Population (7)	r (8)	Perc. (9)	Stable r (10)	Perc. (11)
Hungary (1974)											
Central	2078.	-0.002	67.18	2217.	0.004	67.23	2361.	0.005	66.20	0.003	66.53
North Hungary	905.	-0.001	65.15	918.	0.001	64.19	957.	0.005	63.44	0.003	63.80
North Plain	988.	-0.001	62.53	1027.	0.003	62.59	1085.	0.005	61.63	0.003	61.93
South Plain	945.	-0.004	64.18	969.	0.002	64.48	1005.	0.005	63.78	0.003	64.17
North Trans-Danubia	1241.	0.002	64.95	1346.	0.004	64.71	1457.	0.005	63.51	0.003	63.73
South Trans-Danubia	880.	-0.001	64.83	880.	0.002	64.46	929.	0.005	63.86	0.003	64.23
Hungary	7019.	-0.001	65.14	7347.	0.003	65.01	7795.	0.005	64.09	0.003	64.42
Italy (1978)											
Northwest	10172.	0.007	65.94	10248.	-0.004	67.25	9071.	-0.007	65.99	-0.002	66.06
Northeast	6837.	0.008	65.56	7021.	-0.002	66.77	6145.	-0.009	64.70	-0.002	64.86
Central	7143.	0.008	65.73	7449.	-0.001	65.60	6932.	-0.006	64.09	-0.002	63.79
South	8513.	0.012	62.42	9552.	0.003	63.09	9915.	-0.002	62.10	-0.002	61.63
Islands	4119.	0.010	62.49	4600.	0.003	63.58	4680.	-0.003	62.21	-0.002	61.76
Italy	36785.	0.009	64.59	38871.	-0.001	65.35	36744.	-0.005	63.85	-0.002	63.32
Japan (1970)											
Hokkaido	3420.	-0.005	68.04	2884.	-0.013	65.62	2173.	-0.005	63.54	0.000	64.62
Tohoku	6953.	-0.009	66.40	5649.	-0.013	63.84	4596.	-0.002	63.19	0.000	62.50
Kanto	26526.	0.019	63.45	34750.	0.008	69.00	38409.	0.003	66.08	0.000	64.92
Chubu	13315.	0.010	66.83	15181.	0.001	66.70	15155.	0.001	64.11	0.000	63.54
Kinki	13822.	0.016	67.84	17048.	0.004	68.11	17089.	0.001	65.35	0.000	64.58
Chugoku	4699.	-0.001	65.72	4413.	-0.008	64.15	3814.	-0.002	62.43	0.000	62.72
Shikoku	2292.	-0.012	64.70	1768.	-0.017	61.69	1386.	-0.003	61.47	0.000	62.16
Kyushu	7141.	-0.017	63.83	4997.	-0.021	60.22	3635.	-0.005	60.42	0.000	61.37
Japan	78168.	0.008	67.14	86691.	0.001	66.97	86858.	0.001	64.86	0.000	64.27
Netherlands (1974)											
North	991.	0.016	63.14	1207.	0.007	65.61	1215.	-0.004	61.83	-0.005	61.21
East	1784.	0.017	64.38	2148.	0.006	66.21	2085.	-0.005	62.17	-0.005	61.83
West	4057.	0.005	66.19	4098.	-0.001	68.36	3427.	-0.009	64.39	-0.005	64.93
South-West	214.	0.014	62.24	256.	0.007	64.86	246.	-0.006	60.49	-0.005	60.06
South	2099.	0.018	66.93	2484.	0.005	68.45	2310.	-0.006	63.39	-0.005	63.29
Netherlands	9144.	0.011	65.56	10193.	0.003	67.49	9282.	-0.007	63.18	-0.005	63.08
Poland (1977)											
Warsaw	1608.	0.010	70.02	1919.	0.009	70.18	2145.	0.005	67.25	0.003	67.58
Lodz	789.	0.003	70.32	834.	0.004	70.06	799.	0.001	66.81	0.003	68.27
Gdansk	908.	0.015	67.13	1172.	0.011	68.63	1365.	0.005	65.33	0.003	65.43
Katowice	2552.	0.014	68.75	3177.	0.009	70.03	3595.	0.005	66.71	0.003	66.98
Cracow	805.	0.009	68.07	947.	0.007	68.82	1031.	0.004	65.73	0.003	66.29
East-Central	1892.	0.002	63.57	1966.	0.003	62.66	2001.	0.001	61.35	0.003	61.99
Northeast	1564.	0.010	63.54	1735.	0.005	62.56	1804.	0.002	60.92	0.003	61.30
Northwest	1482.	0.011	67.62	1719.	0.007	66.94	1854.	0.002	63.92	0.003	64.51
South	1688.	0.010	65.55	1922.	0.006	65.59	2075.	0.002	63.59	0.003	64.04
Southeast	2680.	0.007	62.07	3028.	0.007	65.12	3393.	0.006	60.83	0.003	61.99
East	1604.	0.003	63.55	1680.	0.004	62.19	1758.	0.002	61.16	0.003	61.77
West-Central	3114.	0.007	64.32	3577.	0.007	65.62	3801.	0.002	63.07	0.003	63.55
West	2849.	0.007	68.09	3100.	0.004	65.58	3047.	0.004	63.32	0.003	64.23
Poland	23534.	0.008	65.86	26777.	0.006	65.76	28873.	0.003	63.53	0.003	63.83

Ages 15-64

Country (reference year) and region	1980			2000			2030			Stable	
	Population (1)	f (2)	Perc. (3)	Population (4)	f (5)	Perc. (6)	Population (7)	f (8)	Perc. (9)	f (10)	Perc. (11)
Soviet Union (1974)											
Urban areas of the:											
RSFSR	69532.	0.020	69.00	90360.	0.010	67.04	110755.	0.004	65.42	0.006	65.64
Ukrainian+Mold.SSRs	22885.	0.033	67.68	30201.	0.011	66.18	37595.	0.004	64.75	0.006	64.87
Byelorussian SSR	3831.	0.033	68.82	5492.	0.013	66.38	6929.	0.005	64.72	0.006	64.69
Central Asian Rep.s	6232.	0.032	59.64	9361.	0.017	57.69	13308.	0.009	56.59	0.006	56.16
Kazakh SSR	5591.	0.025	65.97	7389.	0.010	63.99	9097.	0.005	62.64	0.005	62.79
Caucasian Republics	4895.	0.020	63.32	6410.	0.011	61.57	8458.	0.007	60.48	0.006	60.16
Baltic Republics	3471.	0.028	67.45	4960.	0.012	66.89	6349.	0.005	64.97	0.006	64.89
Rural areas of USSR	51216.	-0.015	54.47	40729.	-0.010	52.66	42998.	0.003	54.78	0.006	55.36
Soviet Union	167652.	0.010	63.03	194894.	0.006	62.54	235479.	0.004	62.24	0.006	62.37
Sweden (1974)											
Stockholm	986.	-0.001	66.05	974.	-0.000	67.46	848.	-0.005	64.95	-0.004	65.96
East Middle	890.	-0.000	63.16	900.	0.001	65.05	805.	-0.004	62.81	-0.004	62.71
South Middle	474.	-0.002	61.80	473.	0.002	63.51	428.	-0.004	61.75	-0.004	61.57
South	747.	0.001	63.19	781.	0.002	64.73	726.	-0.003	62.42	-0.004	62.00
West	1036.	0.001	63.32	1086.	0.003	65.11	1020.	-0.003	63.07	-0.004	62.59
North Middle	538.	-0.001	62.57	543.	0.002	64.42	496.	-0.004	62.62	-0.004	62.45
Lower North	252.	-0.002	62.52	255.	0.002	64.57	232.	-0.003	62.65	-0.004	62.48
Upper North	328.	-0.002	64.29	347.	0.003	65.42	324.	-0.003	63.11	-0.004	62.79
Sweden	5250.	-0.000	63.57	5360.	0.001	65.23	4880.	-0.004	63.06	-0.004	62.82
United Kingdom (1970)											
North	2190.	0.005	63.25	2362.	0.005	63.68	2719.	0.003	63.95	0.005	64.21
Yorkshire + Humbers.	3023.	0.002	61.90	3205.	0.005	62.59	3685.	0.004	63.12	0.005	63.29
North West	4284.	0.003	61.75	4686.	0.006	62.99	5508.	0.004	63.43	0.005	63.55
East Midlands	2272.	0.008	62.64	2654.	0.009	63.59	3246.	0.005	63.68	0.005	63.63
West Midlands	3416.	0.004	62.98	3752.	0.006	63.35	4403.	0.004	63.70	0.005	63.75
East Anglia	1207.	0.014	62.33	1535.	0.011	63.85	1941.	0.005	63.32	0.005	63.12
South East	11255.	0.003	62.85	12537.	0.007	64.32	14820.	0.004	64.55	0.005	64.60
South West	2550.	0.010	61.32	3045.	0.010	62.58	3751.	0.005	62.52	0.005	62.46
Wales	1760.	0.004	62.45	1911.	0.006	63.29	2224.	0.004	63.55	0.005	63.73
Scotland	3282.	0.003	61.86	3536.	0.007	62.95	4004.	0.003	62.98	0.005	63.36
United Kingdom	35241.	0.005	62.41	39225.	0.007	63.50	46390.	0.004	63.72	0.005	63.81
United States (1970)											
Northeast	32712.	0.006	63.58	36355.	0.010	63.55	43537.	0.006	62.92	0.007	63.51
North Central	38660.	0.010	62.68	46171.	0.013	63.18	58193.	0.007	62.03	0.007	62.42
South	43948.	0.011	62.85	53567.	0.012	63.54	66990.	0.007	61.82	0.007	62.31
West	27053.	0.020	64.47	36418.	0.016	64.93	48504.	0.008	62.91	0.007	63.11
United States	142373.	0.011	63.27	172511.	0.013	63.73	217225.	0.007	62.34	0.007	62.75

Country (reference year) and region	Ages 65+										
	1980			2000			2030			Stable	
	Population (1)	f (2)	Perc. (3)	Population (4)	f (5)	Perc. (6)	Population (7)	f (8)	Perc. (9)	f (10)	Perc. (11)
Austria (1971)											
Burgenland	38.	-0.000	14.04	36.	-0.002	13.54	38.	0.007	14.92	0.005	12.77
Carinthia	68.	0.009	12.55	69.	-0.005	11.59	90.	0.013	13.74	0.005	12.62
Lower Austria	217.	-0.004	15.46	185.	-0.006	13.14	214.	0.011	15.13	0.005	13.65
Upper Austria	156.	0.003	12.25	155.	0.000	10.80	212.	0.018	12.73	0.005	12.25
Salzburg	52.	0.010	11.81	53.	-0.001	10.16	81.	0.018	12.33	0.005	12.70
Styria	163.	0.003	13.43	152.	-0.006	11.84	190.	0.013	13.88	0.005	12.55
Tyrol	67.	0.011	11.31	69.	0.003	9.63	109.	0.020	11.91	0.005	12.46
Vorarlberg	30.	0.012	10.09	35.	0.012	9.15	56.	0.019	11.17	0.005	12.08
Vienna	314.	-0.010	20.37	216.	-0.021	15.02	225.	0.006	16.08	0.005	14.36
Austria	1105.	-0.001	14.59	969.	-0.007	12.06	1215.	0.013	13.75	0.005	12.60
Bulgaria (1975)											
North West	173.	0.007	16.67	185.	0.003	18.44	150.	-0.003	15.22	0.002	14.72
North	208.	0.008	14.68	229.	0.006	15.83	218.	-0.003	14.46	0.002	14.18
North East	162.	0.020	10.51	208.	0.013	12.19	229.	-0.000	12.01	0.002	12.48
South West	80.	0.026	11.34	105.	0.015	14.90	102.	-0.001	15.86	0.002	13.35
South	228.	0.025	10.14	315.	0.018	12.59	354.	0.004	12.82	0.002	12.89
South East	95.	0.021	10.72	133.	0.018	14.69	121.	-0.006	13.80	0.002	12.70
Sofia	104.	0.048	9.13	164.	0.009	12.30	190.	-0.010	12.35	0.002	13.05
Bulgaria	1050.	0.020	11.70	1338.	0.012	13.95	1364.	-0.002	13.35	0.002	13.17
Canada (1971)											
Newfoundland	38.	0.027	6.70	54.	0.009	7.26	92.	0.021	8.76	0.007	8.70
Prince Edward Island	13.	0.013	11.19	16.	0.005	10.74	25.	0.021	13.19	0.007	12.65
Nova Scotia	81.	0.018	9.72	103.	0.005	10.21	161.	0.020	12.64	0.007	11.86
New Brunswick	62.	0.019	9.05	80.	0.006	9.64	131.	0.020	12.51	0.007	11.62
Quebec	493.	0.027	7.77	733.	0.014	10.08	1161.	0.016	14.51	0.007	12.27
Ontario	735.	0.021	8.94	1090.	0.015	10.43	1761.	0.020	12.90	0.007	12.32
Manitoba	107.	0.021	10.52	127.	0.001	11.34	166.	0.017	12.75	0.007	11.75
Saskatchewan	105.	0.016	11.71	119.	-0.002	11.22	121.	0.013	14.24	0.007	12.89
Alberta	138.	0.023	7.57	212.	0.017	8.48	385.	0.024	10.92	0.007	11.01
British Columbia	248.	0.029	9.92	412.	0.019	11.15	795.	0.025	14.13	0.007	14.38
Canada	2020.	0.023	8.78	2947.	0.013	10.30	4796.	0.020	13.14	0.007	12.38
Czechoslovakia (1975)											
Central Bohemia	374.	0.007	15.87	312.	-0.009	12.38	353.	-0.009	11.72	0.006	11.56
Southern Bohemia	97.	0.010	14.05	88.	-0.001	11.39	110.	-0.004	11.54	0.006	11.40
Western Bohemia	105.	0.013	11.74	104.	-0.000	10.96	118.	-0.008	10.94	0.006	10.34
Northern Bohemia	129.	0.020	11.04	129.	-0.006	10.23	149.	-0.010	10.31	0.006	9.92
Eastern Bohemia	184.	0.008	14.70	161.	-0.006	11.94	186.	-0.006	11.76	0.006	11.37
Southern Moravia	288.	0.011	14.02	265.	-0.003	11.58	325.	-0.003	11.57	0.006	11.40
Northern Moravia	215.	0.016	11.01	230.	-0.002	10.38	295.	-0.002	11.15	0.006	10.81
Western Slovakia	232.	0.020	11.22	259.	0.004	10.73	364.	-0.003	12.30	0.006	11.75
Central Slovakia	160.	0.019	10.59	183.	0.008	10.39	252.	-0.005	11.95	0.006	11.27
Eastern Slovakia	130.	0.010	9.33	160.	0.013	9.50	234.	0.009	10.83	0.006	10.61
Czechoslovakia	1915.	0.013	12.46	1891.	-0.000	10.98	2387.	-0.002	11.50	0.006	11.13

Ages 65+

Country (reference year) and region	1980 Population (1)	f (2)	Perc. (3)	2000 Population (4)	f (5)	Perc. (6)	2030 Population (7)	f (8)	Perc. (9)	Stable r (10)	Perc. (11)
Fed.Rep.of Germany (1974)											
Schleswig-Holstein	412.	0.006	15.92	383.	0.005	15.39	473.	0.007	24.04	-0.013	24.31
Hamburg	306.	-0.007	18.91	223.	-0.007	16.54	232.	0.006	23.25	-0.013	23.11
Lower Saxony	1122.	0.007	15.44	1077.	0.005	15.35	1279.	0.009	22.57	-0.013	23.09
Bremen	117.	0.000	16.96	96.	-0.004	15.86	103.	0.008	22.19	-0.013	22.39
N. Rhine-Westphalia	2442.	0.007	14.42	2441.	0.006	15.64	2699.	0.008	22.80	-0.013	22.70
Hessen	844.	0.006	15.16	844.	0.005	15.76	1006.	0.008	23.68	-0.013	23.87
Rhineland-Palatinate	557.	0.008	15.46	564.	0.006	17.32	612.	0.007	25.00	-0.013	24.75
Baden-Wuerttemberg	1288.	0.012	13.88	1379.	0.011	15.20	1679.	0.008	22.97	-0.013	23.38
Bavaria	1620.	0.009	14.91	1643.	0.007	15.54	2008.	0.008	23.36	-0.013	23.72
Saarland	152.	0.005	14.68	151.	0.003	18.11	137.	0.003	25.34	-0.013	23.21
West Berlin	402.	-0.020	21.69	208.	-0.018	14.16	218.	0.002	20.65	-0.013	20.31
Fed.Rep. of Germany	9262.	0.006	15.11	9007.	0.005	15.63	10445.	0.008	23.15	-0.013	23.31
Finland (1974)											
Uusimaa	134.	0.037	11.59	148.	0.011	11.87	236.	-0.010	21.22	-0.010	20.81
Turku and Pori	99.	0.032	13.76	106.	-0.007	14.30	148.	-0.003	22.67	-0.010	22.13
Ahvenanmaa	3.	0.025	14.78	3.	-0.006	12.95	5.	-0.003	20.27	-0.010	21.73
Hame	90.	0.038	13.13	100.	0.008	14.18	143.	-0.010	23.08	-0.010	22.32
Kymi	46.	0.029	13.33	48.	0.004	14.68	59.	-0.011	22.69	-0.010	21.18
Mikkeli	27.	0.018	13.43	27.	0.002	15.03	31.	-0.010	22.15	-0.010	20.43
Pohjois-Karjala	22.	0.033	12.83	22.	0.000	14.43	26.	-0.009	21.79	-0.010	19.85
Kuopio	31.	0.028	12.44	33.	0.004	14.54	41.	-0.008	21.44	-0.010	20.46
Keski-Suomi	29.	0.033	12.11	32.	0.005	13.84	40.	-0.010	21.73	-0.010	20.08
Vaasa	56.	0.031	13.18	60.	-0.001	14.54	69.	-0.011	21.73	-0.010	20.52
Oulu	40.	0.035	9.62	48.	0.008	11.55	65.	-0.004	18.66	-0.010	17.61
Lappi	18.	0.039	9.53	23.	0.010	13.03	28.	-0.003	20.57	-0.010	18.43
Finland	596.	0.033	12.35	650.	0.006	13.49	893.	-0.009	21.73	-0.010	20.83
France (1975)											
Paris Region	1210.	0.002	12.07	1263.	0.006	12.35	1572.	0.004	16.18	-0.003	15.79
Paris Basin	1432.	0.000	14.52	1537.	0.006	14.66	2044.	0.008	19.53	-0.003	19.40
North	480.	0.005	12.18	485.	0.002	12.14	583.	0.008	15.24	-0.003	14.87
East	627.	0.010	12.66	676.	0.008	13.43	870.	0.007	18.65	-0.003	17.66
West	1061.	0.006	15.02	1137.	0.005	14.90	1480.	0.010	18.80	-0.003	18.89
Southwest	1017.	0.006	18.25	1027.	0.001	18.51	1224.	0.007	23.44	-0.003	22.67
Middle East	882.	0.006	14.06	961.	0.007	18.36	1277.	0.009	19.13	-0.003	19.07
Mediterranean	1006.	0.016	17.82	1134.	0.006	18.52	1499.	0.010	24.08	-0.003	24.00
France	7716.	0.007	14.47	8221.	0.005	14.75	10548.	0.008	19.30	-0.003	19.02
German Dem.Rep. (1975)											
North	277.	-0.004	13.27	260.	0.042	12.67	381.	0.032	22.28	-0.012	20.89
Berlin	169.	-0.009	14.80	140.	0.041	10.44	249.	0.037	18.30	-0.012	19.91
Southwest	395.	-0.001	15.68	335.	0.026	13.77	448.	0.023	22.07	-0.012	21.32
South	1263.	-0.003	18.18	970.	0.023	15.89	1122.	0.019	24.56	-0.012	22.48
Middle	594.	-0.004	15.06	512.	0.035	13.47	724.	0.031	23.13	-0.012	21.77
German Dem.Rep.	2698.	-0.003	16.21	2217.	0.030	14.09	2923.	0.026	22.84	-0.012	21.42

	Ages 65+										
	1980			2000			2030			Stable	
Country (reference year) and region	Population (1)	f (2)	Perc. (3)	Population (4)	f (5)	Perc. (6)	Population (7)	f (8)	Perc. (9)	f (10)	Perc. (11)
Hungary (1974)											
Central	428.	0.018	13.83	454.	0.001	13.78	500.	-0.011	14.01	0.003	13.49
North Hungary	167.	0.014	12.03	191.	0.007	13.35	197.	-0.012	13.07	0.003	12.56
North Plain	194.	0.010	12.28	208.	0.005	12.66	223.	-0.011	12.64	0.003	12.17
South Plain	214.	0.014	14.54	208.	-0.000	13.98	214.	-0.012	13.59	0.003	13.02
North Trans-Danubia	224.	0.014	11.70	254.	0.007	12.22	287.	-0.010	12.53	0.003	12.16
South Trans-Danubia	178.	0.007	13.37	186.	0.004	13.63	192.	-0.011	13.18	0.003	12.66
Hungary	1404.	0.013	13.03	1501.	0.004	13.29	1613.	-0.011	13.26	0.003	12.77
Italy (1978)											
Northwest	2155.	0.007	13.97	2463.	0.007	16.17	2606.	0.005	18.96	-0.002	18.66
Northeast	1485.	0.011	14.23	1763.	0.004	16.77	1984.	0.008	20.89	-0.002	20.53
Central	1500.	0.015	13.80	1951.	0.008	17.18	2207.	0.007	20.40	-0.002	20.74
South	1485.	0.011	10.89	1908.	0.011	12.61	2471.	0.012	15.48	-0.002	16.10
Islands	782.	0.010	11.87	957.	0.009	13.23	1242.	0.011	16.51	-0.002	17.13
Italy	7407.	0.010	13.01	9043.	0.008	15.20	10511.	0.008	18.26	-0.002	18.07
Japan (1970)											
Hokkaido	410.	0.030	8.17	688.	0.023	15.66	602.	-0.018	17.59	0.000	15.73
Tohoku	1066.	0.018	10.18	1548.	0.019	17.49	1306.	-0.015	17.96	0.000	17.33
Kanto	2518.	0.035	6.50	4927.	0.037	9.78	7689.	-0.003	13.23	0.000	14.45
Chubu	1718.	0.026	8.62	2888.	0.029	12.69	3694.	-0.007	15.63	0.000	16.13
Kinki	1530.	0.032	7.51	2749.	0.034	10.98	3857.	-0.005	14.25	0.000	15.02
Chugoku	795.	0.019	11.12	1161.	0.020	16.88	1119.	-0.013	18.31	0.000	17.52
Shikoku	443.	0.011	12.53	576.	0.010	20.10	432.	-0.019	19.16	0.000	17.77
Kyushu	1301.	0.014	11.63	1632.	0.010	19.67	1093.	-0.021	18.16	0.000	16.27
Japan	9782.	0.026	8.40	16171.	0.028	12.49	19791.	-0.007	14.78	0.000	15.27
Netherlands (1974)											
North	198.	0.019	12.64	245.	0.007	13.32	393.	0.013	20.01	-0.005	20.97
East	300.	0.023	10.82	401.	0.011	12.36	649.	0.012	19.35	-0.005	19.96
West	763.	0.012	12.45	813.	-0.001	13.56	1063.	0.007	19.98	-0.005	19.38
South-West	50.	0.019	14.43	59.	0.004	14.84	90.	0.012	22.19	-0.005	22.85
South	288.	0.029	9.19	436.	0.018	12.01	735.	0.011	20.16	-0.005	20.47
Netherlands	1599.	0.018	11.46	1953.	0.007	12.93	2930.	0.010	19.95	-0.005	20.12
Poland (1977)											
Warsaw	256.	0.003	11.16	326.	0.013	11.91	496.	-0.001	15.23	0.003	14.81
Lodz	128.	0.004	11.42	161.	0.005	13.49	206.	-0.007	17.22	0.003	15.21
Gdansk	112.	0.012	8.31	156.	0.019	9.15	282.	0.001	13.50	0.003	13.43
Katowice	338.	0.005	9.16	440.	0.021	9.70	741.	0.001	13.74	0.003	13.48
Cracow	120.	0.010	11.40	159.	0.013	11.53	242.	0.000	15.42	0.003	14.62
East-Central	339.	0.011	9.80	417.	0.007	13.30	500.	0.002	15.34	0.003	14.39
Northeast	241.	0.005	6.40	339.	0.019	10.24	461.	0.006	15.13	0.003	14.61
Northwest	140.	0.021	9.81	263.	0.025	11.25	410.	0.001	14.52	0.003	13.70
South	253.	0.005	11.04	330.	0.018	11.55	467.	0.005	14.30	0.003	13.67
Southeast	477.	0.004	11.55	572.	0.010	13.63	724.	0.007	12.24	0.003	11.96
East	292.	0.009	10.58	368.	0.008	11.08	435.	0.002	15.15	0.003	14.23
West-Central	512.	0.007	7.59	604.	0.009	11.98	839.	0.002	14.75	0.003	14.05
West	318.	0.020	10.58	558.	0.020	11.98	787.	-0.001	16.36	0.003	15.08
Poland	3527.	0.008	9.87	4692.	0.014	11.52	6629.	0.002	14.59	0.003	13.64

Ages 65+

Country (reference year) and region	1980 Population (1)	f (2)	Perc. (3)	2000 Population (4)	f (5)	Perc. (6)	2030 Population (7)	f (8)	Perc. (9)	Stable f (10)	Perc. (11)
Soviet Union (1974)											
Urban areas of the:											
RSFSR	10769.	0.049	10.69	15347.	0.030	11.39	23810.	0.020	14.06	0.006	13.81
Ukrainian+Mold.SSRs	3690.	0.046	10.91	5038.	0.025	11.04	7850.	0.022	13.52	0.006	13.40
Byelorussian SSR	407.	0.043	7.32	649.	0.035	7.85	1191.	0.024	11.12	0.006	11.19
Central Asian Rep.s	745.	0.049	7.13	1120.	0.035	6.90	2037.	0.025	8.66	0.006	8.92
Kazakh SSR	632.	0.047	7.46	988.	0.038	6.96	1592.	0.020	10.96	0.006	10.79
Caucasian Republics	657.	0.046	8.51	981.	0.038	8.56	1584.	0.022	11.33	0.006	11.58
Baltic Republics	573.	0.042	11.13	830.	0.031	9.42	1423.	0.022	14.59	0.006	14.80
Rural areas of USSR	14466.	0.028	15.39	13108.	0.008	11.20	10764.	0.007	13.71	0.006	13.12
Soviet Union	31940.	0.038	12.01	38061.	0.022	16.95	50251.	0.018	13.28	0.006	13.00
Sweden (1974)											
Stockholm	217.	0.022	14.52	222.	-0.011	15.40	245.	-0.003	18.77	-0.004	18.55
East Middle	225.	0.016	15.95	221.	-0.010	15.97	247.	-0.002	19.26	-0.004	19.32
South Middle	135.	0.015	17.62	130.	-0.007	17.46	140.	-0.001	20.18	-0.004	20.35
South	200.	0.017	16.90	207.	-0.007	17.14	238.	-0.001	20.45	-0.004	20.97
West	266.	0.017	16.25	269.	-0.008	16.14	312.	0.000	19.27	-0.004	19.89
North Middle	156.	0.013	18.14	147.	-0.012	17.39	160.	-0.001	20.19	-0.004	20.36
Lower North	73.	0.013	18.09	68.	-0.011	17.32	75.	-0.002	20.19	-0.004	20.36
Upper North	72.	0.021	14.17	78.	-0.004	14.68	93.	-0.001	18.04	-0.004	18.47
Sweden	1343.	0.017	16.26	1343.	-0.009	16.34	1509.	-0.001	19.50	-0.004	19.76
United Kingdom (1970)											
North	476.	0.009	13.75	460.	-0.005	12.39	529.	0.014	12.44	0.005	12.13
Yorkshire + Humbers.	684.	0.008	14.01	632.	-0.009	12.33	695.	0.012	11.91	0.005	11.72
North West	963.	0.007	13.88	843.	-0.010	11.34	968.	0.014	11.15	0.005	11.05
East Midlands	481.	0.011	13.25	489.	-0.004	11.73	616.	0.014	12.09	0.005	12.27
West Midlands	682.	0.014	12.57	703.	-0.005	11.87	810.	0.012	11.71	0.005	11.70
East Anglia	290.	0.018	14.95	321.	-0.002	13.34	447.	0.015	14.58	0.005	15.00
South East	2602.	0.010	14.53	2438.	-0.007	12.51	2894.	0.013	12.61	0.005	12.61
South West	675.	0.015	16.22	700.	-0.003	14.38	899.	0.014	14.99	0.005	15.16
Wales	417.	0.007	14.81	396.	-0.008	13.11	460.	0.013	13.15	0.005	12.97
Scotland	710.	0.009	13.39	638.	-0.009	11.36	751.	0.013	11.82	0.005	11.35
United Kingdom	7979.	0.010	14.13	7620.	-0.007	12.34	9070.	0.013	12.48	0.005	12.45
United States (1970)											
Northeast	5936.	0.011	11.54	6219.	-0.008	10.87	8207.	0.012	11.86	0.007	11.00
North Central	6498.	0.011	10.54	7087.	-0.005	9.70	10647.	0.014	11.35	0.007	10.85
South	7610.	0.019	10.88	9044.	-0.000	10.73	14221.	0.014	13.12	0.007	12.51
West	3972.	0.023	9.46	5334.	-0.004	9.51	9576.	0.016	12.42	0.007	12.24
United States	24016.	0.015	10.67	27683.	-0.003	10.23	42652.	0.014	12.24	0.007	11.71

Country (reference year) and region	Ages 75+ 1980 Population (1)	r (2)	Perc. (3)	2000 Population (4)	r (5)	Perc. (6)	2030 Population (7)	r (8)	Perc. (9)	Stable r (10)	Perc. (11)
Austria (1971)											
Burgenland	14.	0.018	5.28	13.	0.013	4.94	13.	0.018	5.22	0.005	4.68
Carinthia	25.	0.026	4.53	26.	0.010	4.45	31.	0.018	4.77	0.005	4.76
Lower Austria	86.	0.017	6.15	71.	0.001	5.02	76.	0.001	5.36	0.005	5.16
Upper Austria	58.	0.021	4.54	57.	0.010	3.95	70.	0.012	4.18	0.005	4.49
Salzburg	19.	0.033	4.32	20.	0.009	3.90	28.	0.009	4.27	0.005	4.83
Styria	61.	0.020	4.99	58.	0.008	4.53	65.	0.006	4.75	0.005	4.64
Tyrol	24.	0.028	4.15	26.	0.005	3.63	38.	0.007	4.14	0.005	4.83
Vorarlberg	11.	0.035	3.66	12.	0.012	3.19	20.	0.007	3.91	0.005	4.67
Vienna	131.	0.014	8.50	93.	-0.010	6.48	86.	-0.022	6.14	0.005	5.48
Austria	429.	0.020	5.67	376.	0.003	4.68	426.	0.002	4.83	0.005	4.79
Bulgaria (1975)											
North West	76.	0.055	7.32	76.	0.035	7.62	65.	-0.002	6.62	0.002	6.18
North	82.	0.042	5.81	87.	0.034	6.05	90.	0.005	5.98	0.002	5.57
North East	48.	0.024	3.13	67.	0.036	3.95	86.	0.009	4.51	0.002	4.46
South West	23.	0.025	3.23	34.	0.032	3.86	38.	0.002	5.89	0.002	4.84
South	62.	0.020	2.76	96.	0.036	3.84	121.	0.019	5.33	0.002	4.51
South East	28.	0.026	3.21	41.	0.039	4.50	47.	-0.000	4.39	0.002	4.58
Sofia	18.	-0.000	1.60	48.	0.062	3.56	67.	0.017	4.36	0.002	4.04
Bulgaria	338.	0.033	3.77	450.	0.038	4.69	514.	0.006	5.03	0.002	4.74
Canada (1971)											
Newfoundland	14.	0.020	2.45	23.	0.019	3.02	34.	0.033	3.23	0.007	3.55
Prince Edward Island	6.	0.011	4.98	7.	0.011	5.07	10.	0.031	5.38	0.007	5.75
Nova Scotia	32.	0.012	3.81	45.	0.015	4.48	61.	0.031	4.82	0.007	5.01
New Brunswick	24.	0.015	3.56	35.	0.016	4.16	50.	0.034	4.78	0.007	4.90
Quebec	169.	0.029	2.67	276.	0.021	3.80	429.	0.026	5.36	0.007	4.91
Ontario	282.	0.021	3.43	430.	0.023	4.12	661.	0.027	4.85	0.007	5.13
Manitoba	42.	0.010	4.15	56.	0.012	5.04	65.	0.026	4.97	0.007	5.03
Saskatchewan	43.	0.006	4.76	56.	0.010	6.65	50.	0.016	5.90	0.007	5.86
Alberta	52.	0.018	2.88	85.	0.024	3.38	142.	0.033	5.02	0.007	4.62
British Columbia	101.	0.020	4.02	177.	0.028	4.78	312.	0.034	5.55	0.007	6.40
Canada	765.	0.020	3.32	1190.	0.022	4.16	1814.	0.028	4.97	0.007	5.24
Czechoslovakia (1975)											
Central Bohemia	128.	0.029	5.43	117.	0.018	4.64	148.	0.014	4.91	0.006	4.05
Southern Bohemia	35.	0.027	5.00	33.	0.015	4.28	45.	0.019	4.75	0.006	4.17
Western Bohemia	34.	0.031	3.75	36.	0.026	3.79	47.	0.011	4.31	0.006	3.51
Northern Bohemia	39.	0.036	3.32	47.	0.034	3.71	60.	0.012	4.16	0.006	3.34
Eastern Bohemia	67.	0.029	5.31	60.	0.015	4.48	72.	0.017	4.98	0.006	4.18
Southern Moravia	100.	0.030	4.89	100.	0.017	3.71	133.	0.017	4.74	0.006	4.19
Northern Moravia	71.	0.035	3.64	82.	0.031	3.97	116.	0.015	4.40	0.006	3.84
Western Slovakia	79.	0.039	3.79	96.	0.034	3.76	141.	0.037	4.76	0.006	4.37
Central Slovakia	54.	0.035	3.57	66.	0.035	3.32	95.	0.035	4.50	0.006	4.21
Eastern Slovakia	45.	0.041	3.20	56.	0.041	4.03	85.	0.035	3.95	0.006	3.93
Czechoslovakia	651.	0.033	4.23	694.	0.026		949.	0.022	4.57	0.006	4.03

Ages 75+

Country (reference year) and region	1980			2000			2030			Stable	
	Population (1)	f (2)	Perc. (3)	Population (4)	f (5)	Perc. (6)	Population (7)	f (8)	Perc. (9)	f (10)	Perc. (11)
Fed.Rep.of Germany (1974)											
Schleswig-Holstein	167.	0.026	6.46	150.	0.002	6.04	181.	-0.008	9.23	-0.013	10.84
Hamburg	126.	0.015	7.80	90.	-0.009	6.69	88.	-0.012	8.89	-0.013	10.07
Lower Saxony	445.	0.031	6.12	415.	-0.006	5.90	482.	-0.005	8.50	-0.013	10.22
Bremen	45.	0.023	6.54	38.	-0.003	6.35	38.	-0.007	8.26	-0.013	9.74
N. Rhine-Westphalia	920.	0.036	5.43	894.	-0.009	5.73	991.	-0.004	8.37	-0.013	9.79
Hessen	327.	0.033	5.87	320.	0.009	5.99	381.	-0.003	8.96	-0.013	10.48
Rhineland-Palatinate	212.	0.036	5.29	211.	0.012	6.49	230.	-0.002	9.40	-0.013	10.86
Baden-Wuerttemberg	490.	0.039	5.71	514.	0.009	5.67	646.	-0.004	8.84	-0.013	10.46
Bavaria	620.	0.034	5.22	625.	0.011	5.91	758.	-0.003	8.82	-0.013	10.43
Saarland	54.	0.036	5.22	54.	0.015	6.52	49.	-0.007	9.11	-0.013	9.64
West Berlin	173.	0.003	9.31	86.	-0.037	5.84	84.	-0.012	7.93	-0.013	8.62
Fed.Rep. of Germany	3579.	0.032	5.84	3398.	0.007	5.90	3927.	-0.004	8.70	-0.013	10.23
Finland (1974)											
Uusimaa	54.	0.078	4.66	62.	0.016	4.99	107.	-0.011	9.61	-0.010	9.42
Turku and Pori	39.	0.071	5.41	45.	0.019	6.02	66.	-0.006	10.08	-0.010	9.77
Ahvenanmaa	1.	0.039	6.05	2.	-0.001	5.93	2.	-0.004	9.10	-0.010	9.94
Hame	35.	0.080	5.08	42.	0.019	5.96	64.	-0.008	10.31	-0.010	9.89
Kymi	17.	0.069	4.90	19.	0.015	5.76	25.	-0.009	9.54	-0.010	8.82
Mikkeli	10.	0.044	4.74	10.	0.015	5.68	13.	-0.006	8.88	-0.010	8.82
Pohjois-Karjala	8.	0.068	4.42	9.	0.011	5.65	11.	-0.002	9.00	-0.010	8.12
Kuopio	11.	0.058	4.53	13.	0.018	5.89	17.	-0.001	9.45	-0.010	8.58
Keski-Suomi	10.	0.070	4.33	13.	0.020	5.47	17.	-0.006	8.93	-0.010	8.28
Vaasa	21.	0.059	4.92	26.	0.014	6.52	30.	-0.008	9.42	-0.010	8.78
Oulu	14.	0.060	3.40	19.	0.022	4.58	27.	0.005	7.79	-0.010	7.39
Lappi	7.	0.080	3.67	10.	0.027	5.46	12.	-0.005	9.07	-0.010	8.22
Finland	227.	0.070	4.70	263.	0.018	5.56	391.	-0.007	9.51	-0.010	9.09
France (1975)											
Paris Region	552.	0.026	5.51	516.	0.014	5.04	703.	0.011	7.24	-0.003	7.21
Paris Basin	637.	0.029	6.46	644.	0.018	6.14	896.	0.018	8.56	-0.003	9.01
North	202.	0.022	5.11	188.	0.024	4.71	230.	0.020	6.02	-0.003	6.30
East	264.	0.031	5.32	258.	0.020	5.13	357.	0.017	7.67	-0.003	7.75
West	452.	0.029	6.39	480.	0.019	6.29	631.	0.019	8.91	-0.003	8.66
Southwest	454.	0.027	8.15	453.	0.015	8.17	551.	0.017	10.56	-0.003	10.77
Middle East	387.	0.027	6.17	392.	0.021	5.86	552.	0.015	8.27	-0.003	8.70
Mediterranean	450.	0.036	7.97	507.	0.016	8.29	691.	0.017	11.11	-0.003	11.76
France	3397.	0.029	6.37	3439.	0.018	6.17	4613.	0.016	8.44	-0.003	8.79
German Dem.Rep. (1975)											
North	111.	0.025	5.32	81.	0.066	3.97	138.	0.084	8.08	-0.012	8.18
Berlin	67.	0.020	5.84	40.	0.040	3.03	79.	0.058	5.85	-0.012	7.50
Southwest	158.	0.033	6.26	121.	0.058	4.96	164.	0.055	8.09	-0.012	8.43
South	534.	0.034	7.68	363.	0.050	5.95	433.	0.050	9.47	-0.012	9.23
Middle	240.	0.026	6.09	169.	0.060	4.44	263.	0.076	8.40	-0.012	8.63
German Dem.Rep.	1109.	0.030	6.67	775.	0.061	4.92	1077.	0.061	8.42	-0.012	8.49

	Ages 75+										
	1980			2000			2030			Stable	
Country (reference year) and region	Population (1)	r (2)	Perc. (3)	Population (4)	r (5)	Perc. (6)	Population (7)	r (8)	Perc. (9)	r (10)	Perc. (11)
Hungary (1974)											
Central	149.	0.031	4.82	173.	0.017	5.26	209.	0.019	5.85	0.003	5.16
North Hungary	57.	0.025	4.11	67.	0.024	4.70	80.	0.015	5.27	0.003	4.64
North Plain	69.	0.023	4.35	74.	0.022	4.52	91.	0.018	5.16	0.003	4.54
South Plain	75.	0.027	5.08	77.	0.015	5.18	88.	0.016	5.56	0.003	4.87
North Trans-Danubia	78.	0.034	4.07	89.	0.024	4.30	115.	0.020	5.00	0.003	4.49
South Trans-Danubia	62.	0.030	4.64	64.	0.024	4.72	75.	0.018	5.13	0.003	4.55
Hungary	489.	0.029	4.54	546.	0.020	4.83	656.	0.018	5.39	0.003	4.77
Italy (1978)											
Northwest	786.	0.038	5.09	959.	0.001	6.30	1079.	-0.004	7.85	-0.002	8.06
Northeast	544.	0.042	5.21	730.	0.006	6.94	833.	-0.002	8.77	-0.002	9.16
Central	555.	0.041	5.11	809.	0.012	7.13	948.	0.003	8.77	-0.002	9.47
South	536.	0.036	3.93	734.	0.010	4.85	978.	0.016	6.13	-0.002	6.97
Islands	292.	0.032	4.43	380.	0.006	5.26	504.	0.015	6.70	-0.002	7.55
Italy	2713.	0.038	4.76	3613.	0.007	6.07	4343.	0.005	7.55	-0.002	7.95
Japan (1970)											
Hokkaido	127.	0.038	2.53	217.	0.027	4.94	276.	-0.015	8.06	0.000	6.18
Tohoku	353.	0.031	3.37	491.	0.021	5.55	577.	-0.014	7.93	0.000	6.68
Kanto	796.	0.042	2.06	1469.	0.032	2.92	3275.	-0.002	5.63	0.000	5.66
Chubu	570.	0.033	2.86	902.	0.025	3.96	1676.	-0.003	6.88	0.000	6.42
Kinki	492.	0.044	2.42	838.	0.027	3.35	1625.	-0.003	6.19	0.000	5.95
Chugoku	287.	0.024	4.01	399.	0.021	5.81	527.	-0.012	8.63	0.000	7.22
Shikoku	164.	0.019	4.63	202.	0.017	7.04	208.	-0.021	9.23	0.000	7.36
Kyushu	474.	0.023	4.23	591.	0.013	7.12	531.	-0.022	8.82	0.000	6.82
Japan	3263.	0.034	2.80	5110.	0.025	3.95	8695.	-0.004	6.49	0.000	6.05
Netherlands (1974)											
North	81.	0.029	5.18	109.	0.012	5.90	168.	0.019	8.56	-0.005	9.76
East	116.	0.031	4.19	165.	0.016	5.10	269.	0.018	8.03	-0.005	9.00
West	305.	0.024	4.97	353.	0.005	5.59	453.	0.012	8.51	-0.005	8.79
South-West	21.	0.031	6.08	27.	0.010	6.83	40.	0.018	9.86	-0.005	10.97
South	105.	0.041	3.35	168.	0.022	4.63	298.	0.017	8.17	-0.005	9.05
Netherlands	628.	0.029	4.50	822.	0.012	5.44	1228.	0.016	8.36	-0.005	9.11
Poland (1977)											
Warsaw	97.	0.049	4.24	118.	0.012	4.32	208.	0.041	6.53	0.003	6.19
Lodz	46.	0.045	4.07	59.	0.019	4.97	88.	0.038	7.34	0.003	6.14
Gdansk	38.	0.062	2.83	54.	0.013	3.17	115.	0.043	5.50	0.003	5.42
Katowice	118.	0.045	3.19	142.	0.009	3.12	289.	0.033	5.36	0.003	5.19
Cracow	44.	0.052	3.69	57.	0.013	3.16	102.	0.035	6.51	0.003	5.99
East-Central	120.	0.046	4.03	157.	0.011	5.00	203.	0.032	6.23	0.003	5.98
Northeast	93.	0.050	3.79	120.	0.018	4.32	187.	0.032	6.14	0.003	6.33
Northwest	48.	0.056	2.21	85.	0.039	3.30	163.	0.041	5.77	0.003	5.55
South	91.	0.052	3.54	112.	0.011	3.83	182.	0.032	5.59	0.003	5.56
Southeast	172.	0.054	3.99	207.	0.008	4.19	277.	0.030	4.68	0.003	4.79
East	104.	0.050	4.11	137.	0.013	5.07	177.	0.030	6.16	0.003	5.89
West-Central	183.	0.052	3.77	225.	0.005	4.13	364.	0.038	6.05	0.003	5.82
West	109.	0.060	2.60	191.	0.036	4.10	326.	0.039	6.78	0.002	6.31
Poland	1264.	0.051	3.54	1565.	0.015	4.09	2682.	0.036	5.90	0.003	5.55

	Ages 75+										
	1980			2000			2030			Stable	
Country (reference year) and region	Population (1)	f (2)	Perc. (3)	Population (4)	f (5)	Perc. (6)	Population (7)	f (8)	Perc. (9)	f (10)	Perc. (11)
Soviet Union (1974)											
Urban areas of the:											
RSFSR	3569.	0.071	3.54	5497.	-0.011	4.08	8897.	0.022	5.26	0.006	5.91
Ukrainian+Mold.SSRs	1255.	0.069	3.71	1855.	-0.012	4.07	2941.	0.022	5.07	0.006	5.74
Byelorussian SSR	151.	0.077	2.71	227.	-0.001	2.75	445.	0.027	4.15	0.006	4.87
Central Asian Rep.s	261.	0.079	2.50	414.	-0.007	2.55	774.	0.027	3.29	0.006	3.94
Kazakh SSR	216.	0.076	2.55	337.	-0.006	2.92	598.	0.020	4.12	0.006	4.60
Caucasian Republics	226.	0.072	2.92	339.	-0.010	3.26	606.	0.019	4.34	0.006	5.48
Baltic Republics	218.	0.076	4.23	307.	-0.008	4.13	552.	0.019	5.66	0.006	6.55
Rural areas of USSR	5365.	0.061	5.71	5359.	-0.035	6.93	4569.	-0.009	5.82	0.006	5.93
Soviet Union	11261.	0.066	4.23	14336.	-0.020	4.60	19383.	0.015	5.12	0.006	5.65
Sweden (1974)											
Stockholm	82.	0.029	5.48	108.	0.004	7.47	115.	-0.003	8.84	-0.004	8.34
East Middle	88.	0.026	6.24	105.	0.002	7.56	114.	-0.002	8.86	-0.004	8.56
South Middle	54.	0.025	7.08	63.	-0.001	8.40	65.	0.000	9.45	-0.004	9.24
South	80.	0.026	6.76	99.	0.002	8.22	113.	0.000	9.72	-0.004	9.68
West	106.	0.026	6.45	129.	-0.003	7.73	144.	0.002	8.93	-0.004	9.02
North Middle	61.	0.025	7.09	69.	-0.001	8.21	72.	0.002	9.05	-0.004	8.91
Lower North	29.	0.025	7.18	32.	-0.001	8.13	34.	0.002	9.13	-0.004	8.94
Upper North	27.	0.035	5.24	34.	0.003	6.47	41.	0.005	7.98	-0.004	8.00
Sweden	526.	0.027	6.37	639.	0.002	7.78	698.	0.000	9.03	-0.004	8.87
United Kingdom (1970)											
North	172.	0.023	4.96	185.	0.006	5.00	191.	0.000	4.49	0.005	4.56
Yorkshire + Humbers.	253.	0.019	5.18	266.	0.002	5.19	258.	-0.002	4.43	0.005	4.47
North West	352.	0.017	5.07	351.	-0.000	4.72	346.	-0.002	3.98	0.005	4.10
East Midlands	182.	0.022	5.01	205.	0.008	4.92	233.	-0.002	4.56	0.005	4.80
West Midlands	247.	0.026	4.56	298.	0.009	5.03	311.	-0.002	4.50	0.005	4.57
East Anglia	113.	0.026	5.84	142.	0.010	5.91	180.	0.004	5.89	0.005	6.26
South East	1009.	0.017	5.63	1096.	0.001	5.62	1146.	0.000	4.99	0.005	5.13
South West	263.	0.026	6.33	312.	0.007	6.41	359.	0.003	5.98	0.005	6.26
Wales	155.	0.025	5.52	164.	0.007	5.45	170.	0.001	4.85	0.005	4.92
Scotland	257.	0.021	4.85	264.	-0.004	4.70	270.	0.003	4.25	0.005	4.25
United Kingdom	3003.	0.020	5.32	3284.	0.004	5.32	3464.	0.000	4.77	0.005	4.91
United States (1970)											
Northeast	2344.	0.011	4.56	2812.	0.006	4.92	3189.	0.029	4.61	0.007	4.49
North Central	2616.	0.008	4.24	3214.	0.009	4.40	4172.	0.034	4.45	0.007	4.51
South	3012.	0.026	4.31	4087.	0.011	4.85	5753.	0.031	5.31	0.007	5.34
West	1555.	0.020	3.71	2391.	0.020	4.26	3846.	0.035	4.99	0.007	5.26
United States	9527.	0.016	4.23	12504.	0.011	4.62	16960.	0.032	4.87	0.007	4.94

APPENDIX 6B: Annual Regional Rates of Growth (r), Natural Increase (n), and Net Migration (m)

Country (ref.year) and region	r (1)	n (2)	m (3)
Austria (1971)			
Burgenland	-1.695	1.878	-3.573
Carinthia	3.347	5.131	-1.784
Lower Austria	-0.923	-0.019	-0.904
Upper Austria	4.277	4.574	-0.297
Salzburg	9.502	6.836	2.666
Styria	1.686	2.953	-1.267
Tyrol	9.386	8.133	1.253
Vorarlberg	11.780	10.841	0.939
Vienna	-4.589	-6.483	1.894
Austria	1.599	1.599	0.
Bulgaria (1975)			
North West	-0.058	0.744	-0.802
North	2.964	1.929	1.035
North East	7.907	8.382	-0.475
South West	2.823	6.761	-3.938
South	7.899	7.936	-0.037
South East	4.615	8.206	-3.591
Sofia	14.726	9.091	5.635
Bulgaria	6.263	6.263	0.
Canada (1971)			
Newfoundland	11.939	19.338	-7.399
Prince Edward Island	7.335	9.468	-2.133
Nova Scotia	7.224	9.686	-2.462
New Brunswick	8.271	11.263	-2.992
Quebec	7.059	9.780	-2.721
Ontario	11.913	10.177	1.736
Manitoba	2.591	10.098	-7.507
Saskatchewan	-7.096	10.814	-17.910
Alberta	17.492	13.625	3.867
British Columbia	23.162	8.723	14.439
Canada	10.439	10.439	0.
Czechoslovakia (1975)			
Central Bohemia	5.452	2.707	2.745
Southern Bohemia	7.710	5.982	1.728
Western Bohemia	6.142	8.058	-1.916
Northern Bohemia	7.668	9.184	-1.516
Eastern Bohemia	5.528	6.245	-0.717
Southern Moravia	7.501	7.051	0.450
Northern Moravia	9.252	9.667	-0.415
Western Slovakia	10.447	9.544	0.903
Central Slovakia	9.286	10.853	-1.567
Eastern Slovakia	11.411	13.542	-2.131
Czechoslovakia	8.098	8.098	0.
Fed.Rep.of Germany (1974)			
Schleswig-Holstein	1.156	-2.533	3.689
Hamburg	-12.683	-6.787	-5.896
Lower Saxony	0.594	-1.325	1.919
Bremen	-8.535	-3.739	-4.796
N. Rhine-Westphalia	-2.508	-1.679	-0.829
Hessen	0.040	-1.680	1.720
Rhineland-Palatinate	-3.377	-2.064	-1.313
Baden-Wuerttemberg	1.368	0.982	0.386
Bavaria	0.637	-0.917	1.554
Saarland	-9.746	-3.058	-6.688
West Berlin	-16.494	-9.954	-6.540
Fed.Rep. of Germany	-1.630	-1.630	0.

Country (ref.year) and region	r (1)	n (2)	m (3)
Finland (1974)			
Uusimaa	11.783	5.577	6.206
Turku and Pori	5.805	2.859	2.946
Ahvenanmaa	9.132	1.272	7.860
Hame	6.511	3.499	3.012
Kymi	-0.616	1.211	-1.827
Mikkeli	-7.337	-0.377	-6.960
Pohjois-Karjala	-5.774	1.557	-7.331
Kuopio	-3.025	1.770	-4.795
Keski-Suomi	-0.063	3.145	-3.208
Vaasa	-1.286	4.260	-5.546
Oulu	3.623	7.058	-3.435
Lappi	-3.486	5.407	-8.893
Finland	3.794	3.794	0.
France (1975)			
Paris Region	3.180	6.093	-2.913
Paris Basin	4.299	3.930	0.369
North	1.339	5.752	-4.413
East	1.998	4.450	-2.452
West	4.787	3.889	0.898
Southwest	0.522	-0.836	1.358
Middle East	4.467	3.191	1.276
Mediterranean	6.161	0.129	6.032
France	3.529	3.529	0.
German Dem.Rep.(1975)			
North	-0.986	0.046	-1.032
Berlin	6.571	-4.562	11.133
Southwest	-1.986	-2.478	0.492
South	-6.673	-4.907	-1.766
Middle	-2.535	-2.858	0.323
German Dem.Rep.	-3.421	-3.421	0.
Hungary (1974)			
Central	7.450	3.795	3.655
North Hungary	4.532	6.483	-1.951
North Plain	4.843	8.850	-4.007
South Plain	2.922	4.116	-1.194
North Trans-Danubia	8.578	8.021	0.557
South Trans-Danubia	3.797	4.792	-0.995
Hungary	5.798	5.798	0.
Italy (1978)			
Northwest	0.247	-0.254	0.501
Northeast	1.825	0.090	1.735
Central	3.747	1.890	1.857
South	6.069	8.588	-2.519
Islands	5.549	7.367	-1.818
Italy	3.200	3.200	0.
Japan (1970)			
Hokkaido	-3.216	11.567	-14.783
Tohoku	-10.088	8.238	-18.326
Kanto	30.241	14.883	15.358
Chubu	15.381	11.776	3.605
Kinki	26.503	14.281	12.222
Chugoku	2.170	8.345	-6.175
Shikoku	-11.711	6.438	-18.149
Kyushu	-16.700	8.633	-25.333
Japan	11.854	11.854	0.

Country (ref.year) and region	r (1)	n (2)	m (3)
Netherlands (1974)			
North	10.777	5.741	5.036
East	11.674	7.182	4.492
West	-0.744	4.415	-5.159
South-West	10.818	4.714	6.104
South	10.726	7.101	3.625
Netherlands	5.686	5.686	0.
Poland (1977)			
Warsaw	13.518	5.734	7.784
Lodz	7.533	4.300	3.233
Gdansk	16.923	12.350	4.573
Katowice	14.602	7.764	6.838
Cracow	11.360	8.274	3.086
East-Central	5.215	9.227	-4.012
Northeast	8.307	11.694	-3.387
Northwest	13.626	14.141	-0.515
South	9.245	9.739	-0.494
Southeast	8.244	11.032	-2.788
East	5.898	8.900	-3.002
West-Central	9.159	10.428	-1.269
West	10.776	12.528	-1.752
Poland	10.034	10.034	0.
Soviet Union (1974) Urban areas of:			
RSFSR	23.053	7.564	15.489
Ukrainian+Mold.SSRs	23.648	8.259	15.389
Byelorussian SSR	36.731	13.931	22.800
Central Asian Rep.s	31.457	20.042	11.415
Kazakh SSR	25.190	13.608	11.582
Caucasian Republics	17.610	14.545	3.065
Baltic Republics	30.993	7.547	23.446
Rural areas of USSR	-12.432	9.603	-22.035
Soviet Union	9.386	9.386	0.
Sweden (1974)			
Stockholm	1.518	4.506	-2.988
East Middle	2.284	3.428	-1.144
South Middle	1.306	2.246	-0.940
South	4.343	2.730	1.613
West	4.213	3.293	0.920
North Middle	1.964	-0.279	2.243
Lower North	1.671	-0.477	2.148
Upper North	5.941	4.641	1.300
Sweden	2.882	2.882	0.
United Kingdom (1970)			
North	3.288	3.595	-0.307
Yorkshire + Humbers.	1.688	4.805	-3.117
North West	2.172	3.856	-1.684
East Midlands	8.171	5.293	2.878
West Midlands	5.178	6.732	-1.554
East Anglia	16.768	4.181	12.587
South East	3.270	4.121	-0.851
South West	11.180	2.504	8.676
Wales	3.202	2.740	0.462
Scotland	1.785	4.557	-2.772
United Kingdom	4.300	4.300	0.
United States (1970)			
Northeast	3.154	6.768	-3.614
North Central	6.720	8.793	-2.073
South	9.921	9.794	0.127
West	18.768	10.536	8.232
United States	8.912	8.912	0.

CHAPTER SEVEN

National Case Studies: The United Kingdom, The Soviet Union, and Canada

7.1 The United Kingdom

Philip Rees

Where you live has always influenced the quality of your life and your behavior. If you live in Scotland you can expect to live three years less than if you live in the South East or East Anglia regions of England. If you are raising a family in Northern Ireland you are likely to have one more child than the average family in the South East or East Anglia. If you live in Northern Ireland or Scotland you are unlikely to meet a fellow resident who has immigrated from abroad, whereas in the South East this will be an everyday occurrence. Those who live in East Anglia and the South West experience the stimulation and pressures of living in regions of population growth; in the North West and North East people experience the problems of regions with declining shares of the national population.

These are some of the contrasts in regional demographic patterns within the United Kingdom of Great Britain and Northern Ireland that are discussed in this chapter. On a world scale, of course, the differences among the regions of the UK are rather small. Population growth has virtually ceased nationally and was composed of seven regions of increase and four of decrease in the 1976–1981 period. The differences between regions in life expectancy, fertility, and migration propensity are mitigated by the movement of people from their place of birth to other regions. Although population redistribution from northern to southern regions has continued apace in the last three decades, the current shares of the national population are not far removed from their stable equivalents. Thus the British live in a country experiencing near-zero national population growth, interregional migration that serves to level the quality of life a little, and a regional population distribution that is fairly close to equilibrium.

Evidence for these broad-brush statements follows in a variety of ways. Section 7.1 considers the patterns of spatial population change in UK regions over a three-decade period, 1951–1981, using conventional, single-region methods. Shifting to analyses that incorporate the age-disaggregated gross migration flows between regions requires a number of choices regarding data and methods to be used. These options in the *multiregional* population analysis of the UK are explored in Section 7.2. Results from the chosen multiregional population analysis are then presented in Section 7.3: the life table, fertility expectancies, and migration expectancies. A more complex picture of demographic behavior emerges that identifies the variety of people's migration experiences. For example, as an individual I have spent portions of my life in four UK regions – Wales, the West Midlands, East Anglia, and Yorkshire and Humberside; multiregional population analysis takes cognizance of this kind of individual history.

This case study constitutes an example of the application of methods described elsewhere in the book. It also serves as a complete revision of the story told in the UK Migration and Settlement Research Report (Rees 1979a), updating the picture of regional population change and developing an alternative set of multiregional statistics for UK regions.

7.1 Patterns of Spatial Population Change

In the UK, standard regions for which many governmental statistical series are published have been redefined on two separate occasions since World War II. Some analyses in this chapter use the regional boundaries that existed between 1 April 1965 and 1 April 1974, referred to as the "old" regions. Other analyses use data for the current regions, redefined on 1 April 1974 as a consequence of local government reorganization, here called "new" regions. The differences between the two sets of regions are not great and involve exchanges of territory between the North and Yorkshire and Humberside, and between Yorkshire and Humberside and the East Midlands and North West.

Table 7.1 gives the total population figures at five-year intervals from 1951–1981. Over the 30 years the population of the UK has grown relatively little – by just 12% at annual rates varying between 1 and 6 per thousand, very low on a world scale. Between 1974 and 1978 the UK population decreased marginally.

The relative sizes and ranks of individual regions have also shifted little over the 30-year period. Up to 1966 these shifts were primarily to the southern regions of the country – a phenomenon known as the "drift to the South

Table 7.1 Populations[a] of UK regions, 1951–1981.

Region	Year						
	1951	1956	1961	1966	1971	1976	1981
North	2.98	3.03	3.11	3.13	3.14	3.12	3.11
Yorks. and Humb.[b]	4.63	4.62	4.68	4.81	4.87	4.89	4.91
North West	6.28	6.30	6.41	6.54	6.60	6.55	6.46
East Midlands	3.11	3.20	3.33	3.50	3.64	3.74	3.84
West Midlands	4.42	4.55	4.76	4.95	5.12	5.17	5.18
East Anglia	1.38	1.43	1.49	1.58	1.69	1.80	1.90
South East	14.97	15.42	16.07	16.72	16.99	16.89	17.03
South West	3.38	3.52	3.71	3.92	4.09	4.26	4.36
Wales	2.60	2.61	2.64	2.69	2.72	2.77	2.81
Scotland	5.10	5.12	5.18	5.20	5.22	5.21	5.15
Northern Ireland	1.37	1.40	1.43	1.48	1.54	1.54	1.54
United Kingdom[c]	50.23	51.18	52.81	54.50	55.61	22.89	56.29

[a]Populations are in millions and were estimated on the basis of the new regions.
[b]Yorks. and Humb. refers to Yorkshire and Humberside throughout this chapter.
[c]Slight differences between the sum of regional populations and that shown for the United Kingdom are due to rounding.
Sources: 1951 census populations were estimated from the Office of Population Censuses and Surveys (1974b); 1956 midyear populations were estimated from the General Register Office (1957); and 1961–1981 midyear estimates were taken from the Office of Population Censuses and Surveys (1982, table 3).

East". The South West shared in this drift, as did the East Midlands, West Midlands, and East Anglia. Conversely, the northern and Celtic regions lost shares, although only marginally in Northern Ireland.

In the next decade, 1966–1976, the pattern changed in nature. The South East lost some of its share of the national population (substantially in the 1970s), as did the West Midlands in 1975–1976. The South West, East Anglia, and the East Midlands gained more significant shares, as did Wales. In the 1976–1981 period the South East ceased to lose population, and the shift out of Scotland and the North West and into the East Midlands, East Anglia, and the South West continued.

The change in pattern over the last 15 years in the southern half of the UK can be interpreted as a result of the metropolitan decentralization of London beyond the boundaries of the South East region because of the extension of London's commuting field, the decentralization of jobs from London, and the independent growth of employment in peripheral regions (Drewett *et al.* 1975, East Anglian Economic Planning Council 1978).

At the simplest level, population change can be divided into two components: natural increase and net migration. Between 1951 and 1981 net migration, by and large, determined the pattern of population change. The correlation between the rate of population change and the net migration rate was above 0.80 throughout this period, whereas the correlation of the total rate with the natural increase rate was low and negative in five out of the six quinquennia. The relationship between natural increase and net migration was negative; those regions with the highest natural increase also had the highest rates of net outmigration.

The pattern of change in natural increase was relatively uniform over the 30 years. There was a slight rise in the average annual rate in the first three quinquennia, followed by a sharper fall to almost zero natural increase in 1976–1981 in the UK as a whole. Differences among the regions of mainland Britain were not marked — only 2.8 per thousand per year on average; the highest (West Midlands) and the lowest (South West) natural increase regions were separated by 3.0 points. The natural increase rate for Northern Ireland remained substantially higher throughout the period.

Net migration, on the other hand, shows no such uniform pattern over time over all regions. During 1951–1966 there was a strong division between the North and West regions and the Midlands and South East regions. The former experienced net outmigration, the latter net inmigration. Then in 1966–1976 the pattern changed to one in which the northern regions experienced lower net losses, Wales experienced small net gains, the West Midlands and South East suffered net outmigration, and the net gains of the South West and East Anglia were pronounced. Between 1976 and 1981 this pattern continued except for a discontinuation of losses from the South East.

At the regional scale external migration was quantitatively almost as important as internal migration. Some 40–50% of the gross flows involved external migration compared with 50–60% involving internal migration. However, the variation in the total net migration rate was due mainly to variations in internal net migration. The correlation between the total and the internal net migration rate was high, whereas that between the total and the external migration rate was low or negative. Most regions experienced losses from external migration in most periods, the only exceptions being the South East in both 1970–1971 and 1975–1976 and East Anglia in 1975–1976.

The 11 UK regions can be divided into four categories: consistent losers, losers most of the time, mixed losers and gainers, and gainers. Those regions that lost population consistently throughout the 1965–1981 period as a result of both internal and external migration were the North West, West Midlands, and (excluding any troop movements) Northern Ireland. The other northern regions — Scotland, the North, and Yorkshire and Humberside — also lost population through internal and external migration, though not quite as heavily and not in every year. Wales falls in the third group, because of its consistent moderate gains from internal migration that were offset by external losses in 1965–1966 and 1970–1971. Also in this mixed group is the South East, which experienced internal losses in all years except 1980–1981 and external gains in 1970–1971 and 1975–1976, which were not enough to prevent an overall migration loss; the 1976–1981 period was one of modest overall net migration gain. In the final group of regions are the East Midlands, the South West, and

East Anglia, whose recorded net internal and overall gains in all years were only partially reduced by net external loss.

7.2 Multiregional Population Analysis: Choices

Conventional single-region analyses such as those reported in Section 7.1 are, however, inadequate. Multiregional population analysis has been developed to answer a number of demographic questions that a uniregional analysis leaves unanswered.

Consider the traditional life table. Applied at the regional scale this set of calculations assumes that people die in their region of birth at a rate consistent with that of the region. But how many of the expected (in 1970) 73.2 years of life are actually spent in the South East region, for example, given the substantial outmigration experienced by the population?

Consider the net reproduction rate. If potential mothers migrate, the children they are likely to have will be born in a region different from that in which they themselves were born.

Consider the conventional method of single-region population projection with allowance made for migration by assumptions about net migrants or net migration rates. This can lead to substantial errors in projection (Rogers 1976b, Rees 1977b).

The set of computer programs adopted in this study has been used to investigate the dynamics of population and migration patterns in a variety of countries (Rogers 1976a, Willekens 1978); data from each country have been entered in the spatial population analysis programs at IIASA and the results analyzed by participating national investigators. In this section the data and the results of a multiregional analysis of Great Britain's population are described.

7.2.1 *The Data Used*

The UK data required for the multiregional analysis programs were extracted from the available censuses and vital statistics. The key data are interregional migration flows disaggregated by age. At the time the UK case study (Rees 1979c) was written, the only source of such data was the 1971 census. Migrant data were available for two periods: the year before the 1971 census and the five years prior to that date. Comparisons were made based on those one-year/five-year migrant data.[1]

The procedures involved in transforming the one-year migrant data (Office of Population Censuses and Surveys 1974a, tables 2A and 3A) into model

---

[1] Northern Ireland was not included, because although data on the flows from Northern Ireland to Great Britain regions were available, data on the reverse flows were not.

variables are described in detail in Rees (1979c). Similar methods were needed
to adjust the five-year migrant data.

The first step was to solve the "three-face" migration estimation problem
(see Chapter 2 for details and references) in order to break down into 5-year
age groups the 10- or 15-year age groups for which interregional migrations
were reported. The second step was to convert the migrant figures so obtained
into the age–time plan of the Willekens and Rogers (1978) program using:

$$\mathrm{P}K_X^{ij} = \frac{1}{2}\left[K_{X-5}^{ij} + K_X^{ij}\right] , \tag{7.1}$$

where $\mathrm{P}K_X^{ij}$ is the estimated number of migrants between regions i and j
recorded in the model (or period, p) age–time plan, K_{X-5}^{ij} is the recorded
number of migrants from i to j who are in age group $(x-5, x)$ at time $t-5$ and
in age group $(x-5, x)$ at time t, and K_X^{ij} is the number of recorded migrants
who are in age group $(x-5, x)$ at time $t-5$ and in age group $(x+5, x+10)$ at
time t. This equation embodies the assumption that migrations are evenly distributed within census data age–time parallelograms and the assumption that
transition data (which are what census migrant tables are) can be reasonably
used in a movement-based model (see Chapter 10 for further discussion of this
point).

Migrants in the last age group, 75+, were further deconsolidated into
those in age groups 75–79, 80–84, and 85+, using the ratios previously calculated for the one-year migrants:

$$\mathrm{P}K_X^{ij} = \left[0.5K_{70,5}^{ij} + K_{75+,5}^{ij}\right] \mathrm{P}K_{X,1}^{ij} \Big/ \mathrm{P}K_{75+,1}^{ij} , \tag{7.2}$$

where the subscripts 5 and 1 refer to the length of the period of observation
of the variable concerned. The ratios were based on proportions of the population in age groups 75–79, 80–84, and 85+ (Rees 1979c). This, in effect,
involved the assumption of a uniform migration rate at these older ages.

The number of infant migrants (those born during the five-year period
1966–1971) was not tabulated. The estimation method used assumed that the
observed ratio of 1–4-year-old to 5–9-year-old migrants in the one-year period
also held for the five-year period, so that

$$\mathrm{P}K_{0,5}^{ij} = 0.5\,K_{0,5}^{ij}\frac{\mathrm{P}K_{0,1}^{ij}}{\mathrm{P}K_{5,1}^{ij}} + 0.5\,K_{0,5}^{ij} , \tag{7.3}$$

where $K_{0,5}^{ij}$ is the estimated number of i-to-j five-year migrants from age
group 0–4 to age group 5–9, and $\mathrm{P}K_{0,1}^{ij}$ and $\mathrm{P}K_{5,1}^{ij}$ are the previously estimated
(Rees 1979c) numbers of one-year migrants between regions i and j at ages 0
(0–4) and 5 (5–9). Initially, the multiregional population analysis was carried
out with a version of equation (7.3) in which the last term on the right-hand
side was missing. In this case, however, the first set of terms was not multiplied by one-half. The results of this erroneous run are considered below

since they provide some idea of the magnitude of possible estimation errors in the analysis.

The data described above refer to the 10 regions of Great Britain, with Northern Ireland excluded. Similar data were available for a three-region set based on population accounts for East Anglia, the South East, and the Rest of Britain for 1966–1971 (Rees 1977b), which were also used in a comparative analysis.

7.2.2 The Sources of Variation

It is clear from our discussion of the data inputs to the multiregional model that there exist a number of alternative ways of carrying out the multiregional population analysis for the UK. We can, in fact, identify five dimensions of choice, which can be explored using the 1971 UK census data. Further comparisons (for example, of movement versus transition data) could be carried out using 1981 census migrant tabulations and National Health Service Central Register migration tables, but these will be reported elsewhere.

We begin by selecting the type of probability estimation equation to be used. For the Migration and Settlement Study a standard linear equation was applied to compute the life table transition probability matrices $\mathbf{p}_x$, by age, from the usual matrices of observed annual mortality and mobility rates $\mathbf{m}_X$:

$$\mathbf{p}_x = [\mathbf{I} + (h/2)\,\mathbf{m}_X]^{-1}\,[\mathbf{I} - (h/2)\,\mathbf{m}_X] \ , \qquad (7.4)$$

where $\mathbf{I}$ is the identity matrix and h is the age interval of the mortality and mobility data. An alternative to this equation, which avoids some of its awkward properties at extreme mortality and mobility rates, is a power equivalent:

$$\mathbf{p}_x = \{[\mathbf{I} + (1/2)\,\mathbf{m}_X]^{-1}\,[\mathbf{I} - (1/2)\,\mathbf{m}_X]\}^{h/u} \ , \qquad (7.5)$$

where u is the length of the time interval of the mortality and mobility data. At observed levels of mortality and mobility does the use of this revised equation make any significant difference?

A second choice concerns regional aggregation. Just as census migration data fail to aggregate cumulatively over time, so do they fail over space. Rogers (1976b) has shown that systematic differences could result between population projections carried out using alternative regional aggregations in the model. Does this effect also show up in the other products of multiregional population analysis?

Third, we consider the period of measurement of migration data. Two migration questions were asked in the 1971 UK census: "Where did you live one year ago?" and "Where did you live five years ago?" Comparisons of the migration volumes and rates generated by these two questions and theoretical analysis (Courgeau 1973a, Rees 1977a, Kitsul and Philipov 1981, Long 1981) suggested that they measured migration in different ways; the five-year migration volumes were always systematically less than the one-year migration volumes multiplied by five. What effect do these differences have on the products of multiregional population analysis?

Temporal trends and fluctuations in mortality data must be taken into account. Most official life table analyses in the UK use data averaged over three calendar years to smooth fluctuations in mortality resulting from severe winter weather or influenza epidemics in any one calendar year. It would be useful to check whether 1970 exhibited unusual mortality compared with preceding years.

Finally, errors in estimating model inputs are considered. National systems of demographic statistics rarely produce, in their published tabulations, the precise variables required by population models. Thus some variables have to be estimated with greater or lesser degrees of accuracy.

7.2.3 *The Analyses*

Given these five dimensions of choice and two choices per dimension, we could have run 32 separate analyses. In fact, we only carried out six multiregional analyses, but by careful pairwise comparison the rough effects of the various choices can be identified.

Table 7.2 The characteristics of the multiregional population analyses.

Run	Type of transition probability estimation equation[a]	Regional aggregation (number of regions)[b]	Period of measurement of migration data[c] (years)	Temporal period of deaths data[c]	Infant migrant estimation equation[e]
1	Power	10	1	1970	Correct
2	Linear	10	1	1970	Correct
3	Linear	3	1	1970	Correct
4	Linear	3	5	1966–1971	Correct
5	Linear	10	5	1970	Incorrect
6	Linear	10	5	1970	Correct

[a]Power equation refers to equation (7.5) where $h = 5$, $u = 1$. Linear equation refers to equation (7.4) where $h = 5$, $u = 1$ in Runs 2 and 3 and $h = 5$, $u = 5$ in Runs 4, 5, and 6.
[b]The 10 regions are North, Yorkshire and Humberside, North West, East Midlands, West Midlands, East Anglia, South East, South West, Wales, and Scotland ("old" regions). The 3 regions are East Anglia, South East, and the Rest of Great Britain ("new" regions in Run 4, otherwise "old" regions).
[c]1 refers to the one year prior to the census on 25/26 April 1971. 5 refers to the five years prior to the census on 25/26 April 1971.
[d]1970 is the calendar year. 1966–1971 is the intercensal period 24/25 April 1966 to 25/26 April 1971.
[e]The correct equation is equation (7.3). The incorrect equation is equation (7.3) without the last term on the right-hand side.

Table 7.2 gives the characteristics of each analysis. For each, the full set of products of multiregional population analysis was produced, but here we focus on just the life expectancy matrix. This matrix for run 4 is presented in Table 7.3. It shows, for example, that our estimate in this analysis is that, under 1966–1971 mortality and mobility conditions, persons born in East Anglia can expect to live a total of 72.79 years of which 40.85 will be spent in their natal region, 14.41 in the South East, and 17.52 in the Rest of Britain. The conventional, single-region life expectancy for a population experiencing East Anglian mortality conditions throughout life is 73.65 years.

Table 7.3 Life expectancy by region of birth and region of residence for three British regions.[a]

Region of residence	Region of birth			Life expectancy by place of birth
	East Anglia	South East	Rest of Britain	
East Anglia	40.85	2.56	1.32	73.65
South East	14.41	53.59	8.33	72.97
Rest of Britain	17.52	16.37	62.06	71.42
Life expectancy by place of residence[b]	72.79	72.51	71.70	72.34

[a]This is the Run 4 life expectancy matrix.
[b]Columns may not sum to totals because of rounding errors.

For comparative purposes we focus only on life expectancies for East Anglia and the South East, because comparison for the Rest of Britain is difficult when it consists of one region in two analyses (Runs 3 and 4) and of eight regions in four analyses (Runs 1, 2, 5, and 6). Table 7.4 sets out these selections from the life expectancy matrices of Runs 1–6, arranged for convenient comparisons between adjacent columns.

7.2.4 The Comparisons

The Effect of the Choice of the Transition Probability Equation: Run 1 versus Run 2. Comparison of the life expectancies in Table 7.4 for Runs 1 and 2 shows that the choice of the probability estimation equation has some effect on the analysis but not a great one. This confirms the similar conclusions of Rees (1978) and Ledent (1978a) for regional systems in which the probabilities of migration were reasonably low (see also Chapter 10). The intra-regional values in the life expectancy matrix are marginally higher in Run 1 than in Run 2, in line with the expected behavior of the power equation compared with the linear equation. The linear equation was, however, retained to maintain comparability with results from other countries in the Migration and Settlement Study.

Table 7.4 A comparison of the results of a variety of multiregional life tables for Great Britain.

Element in the multiregional life expectancy matrix (three-region version)			Choice combinations[a]					
		(A)	Power	Linear	Linear	Linear	Linear	Linear
		(B)	10	10	3	3	10	10
		(C)	1	1	1	5	5	5
		(D)	1970	1970	1970	1966–1971	1970	1970
		(E)	Correct	Correct	Correct	Correct	Incorrect	Correct
Born in	Resident in	Row	Run 1	Run 2	Run 3	Run 4	Run 5	Run 6
East Anglia	East Anglia	(1)	29.88	29.80	29.72	40.85	43.10	41.64
East Anglia	South East	(2)	19.11	19.14	18.67	14.41	13.66	14.25
East Anglia	Rest of Britain	(3)	23.61[b]	23.62[b]	24.04	17.52	16.07[b]	16.92[b]
East Anglia	All regions	(4)	72.60	72.56	72.43	72.79	72.83	72.81
South East	East Anglia	(5)	3.03	3.04	2.97	2.56	2.49	2.58
South East	South East	(6)	47.47	47.41	46.76	53.59	55.54	54.45
South East	Rest of Britain	(7)	22.13[b]	22.14[b]	22.71	16.37	15.05[b]	15.74[b]
South East	All regions	(8)	76.63	72.59	72.45	72.51	72.78	72.77
All regions	East Anglia	(9)	–[c]	73.51	73.51	73.65	73.51	73.51
All regions	South East	(10)	–[c]	73.19	73.19	72.97	73.19	73.19

[a] Choice dimensions: (A) type of transition probability estimation equation, (B) number of regions, (C) period of migration measurement, (D) period of deaths data, and (E) infant migration estimation equation.

[b] This figure is worked out as a residual by subtracting the sum of the first 2 rows from the 4th.

[c] Not computed in Run 1.

Source: Computed using the British data sets described in Subsection 7.2.1 and the computer program documented.

The Effect of Regional Aggregation: Run 2 versus Run 3. A comparison of Run 2 with Run 3 shows what effect the spatial aggregation of the system has on the resulting life expectancies. The effect is to change expectancies by an average of about 0.38 of a year (compared with a change of about 0.03 of a year from Run 1 to Run 2). These figures are the absolute difference between elements in the columns in rows (1)–(3) and (5)–(7) summed and averaged. The effect of aggregation is to increase life expectancy in the aggregated region (Rest of Britain) at the expense of the other regions for persons born in East Anglia and the South East. The more disaggregated run, Run 2, would be the preferred one.

The Effect of the Choice of the Period of Measurement on the Migration Data: Run 3 versus Run 4. This third comparison reveals the effect of the choice of the period of migration measurement on the life expectancy matrix. The period length does not affect mortality data; the life expectancies for all regions in rows (4), (8), (9), and (10), which depend largely on mortality information, differ by only small amounts (0.2 on average). The other life expectancies, which depend crucially on the level of migration, are profoundly affected. The average difference between the Run 3 and Run 4 off-diagonal life expectancies is 5.92 years. At the extreme, persons born in East Anglia can expect to live 11 years more there when the five-year probabilities are used than when the one-year probabilities are employed.

This results principally from violations of the Markovian assumption inherent in the multiregional life table model; people return more readily to their previous places of residence than the one-step Markov chain model predicts. Hence when measured over five years, the migration data pick up the return migrants left out when the one-year data are expanded to "model" five-year transitions. Disturbing questions may then be posed: Does this effect repeat itself at longer time scales? Would lifetime migration data be better to use? These questions are further discussed in Chapter 10. No definitive answers are yet available for the simple reason that no one has yet constructed, say from migration histories of a total population, observed life expectancy matrices against which our models can be compared. At present we can only agree with Ledent (1978a, b, 1980c) that if five-year migrant data are available they should be used in preference to one-year figures.

The Effect of Temporal Fluctuations in Mortality Data: Run 4 versus Run 5 and Run 6. The view that five-year migration data are preferable was adopted, and Run 5 for all 10 regions was prepared using births and deaths data for 1970 and migration data for 1966–1971. The expectation was that the elements of the life expectancy matrix would differ, because of the greater spatial disaggregation, to the same degree as Run 2 and Run 3. In fact, the life expectancy elements differed by considerably more, an average of 1.25 years compared with 0.38 of a year.

A careful examination of the estimation equations involved revealed that the numbers of infant migrants had probably been underestimated in Run 5. Run 5 was therefore repeated with a corrected version of the estimation equation to form Run 6. The average absolute difference between Run 4 and Run 6 life expectancies was 0.51 of a year, much closer to the Run 2/Run 3 variation. The reason for the slightly higher difference in the Run 4/Run 6 case is that the mortality data as well as the migration data vary across time. Some of this difference must be accounted for by the secular improvement in life expectancy noted in Section 7.1.

The Effect of Errors in Infant Migrant Estimation: Run 5 versus Run 6. The life expectancy elements for these two runs differ by an average of 0.69 of a year. The discrepancy gives us an estimate of the possible error involved and of the penalty imposed by the nontabulation of infant migrants by the Office of Population Censuses and Surveys.

Conclusions. In order of magnitude, the effects line up as follows. The period of measurement of migration is by far the most important influence on the estimates of the distribution of life expectancies across regions. The incorrect estimation of infant migrants and the effect of temporal trends and fluctuations on deaths are a distant second and third. Regional aggregation and the choice of a transition probability equation bring up the rear. Thus the choices involved with data selection and estimation have a much more serious effect on outcomes than the more theoretical choices of regional aggregation and probability equation. These comparisons made from this limited set of analyses are not ideal (not all effects are "pure"), but the broad conclusions are confirmed in the more carefully controlled analysis discussed in Chapter 10 of this volume.

7.3 Multiregional Population Analysis: Results

As a consequence of the exploration of the variety of multiregional life tables described above, the Run 2 results given in Rees (1979c) are now replaced by the Run 6 results. This updated multiregional population analysis is described below.

7.3.1 *The Multiregional Life Table*

The first stage in the development of the multiregional life table is the computation from population, mortality, and migration data of the transition probability matrices at each age, $\mathbf{p}_x$, using the linear equation. This series of transition probability matrices combines the spatial- and age-related behavior examined separately in Section 7.1.

If the $\mathbf{p}_x$ matrices are multiplied together, multistep transition probabilities are obtained. The most useful of these are the probabilities of location at age x given the location at birth:

$$_0\mathbf{l}_x = \prod_{y=0}^{x-5} \mathbf{p}_y ,\tag{7.6}$$

where $_0\mathbf{l}_x$ is a matrix of such probabilities (see Chapter 9).

As persons migrate between regions over their lifetime they cumulate residence time in the various regions. The duration-of-residence matrices $\mathbf{L}_X$ are computed on the assumption that persons making a transition spend half their time in the origin region and half in the destination (including death). The numbers in the $\mathbf{L}_X$ matrices are summed backwards and cumulatively, starting at age 85, to yield the $\mathbf{T}_x$ matrices of years lived beyond age x by region of birth and residence.

If the variables for the total years lived beyond age x are divided by the appropriate survival proportion variables then life expectancies conditional on survival to age x are obtained $(T_x / l_x = e_x)$. Table 7.5 presents the most

Table 7.5 Expectations of life at birth, $\mathbf{e}_0$, by region of birth and of residence in Great Britain.

Region of residence		Region of birth									
		I	II	III	IV	V	VI	VII	VIII	IX	X
I	North	46.0	3.0	1.3	1.6	1.1	1.2	1.1	1.2	0.9	1.5
II	Yorks. and Humb.	4.0	46.0	2.3	4.0	1.6	2.4	1.6	1.6	1.4	1.5
III	North West	3.3	3.8	50.5	2.6	3.0	2.0	2.1	2.2	3.2	2.3
IV	East Midlands	2.3	3.6	1.5	44.3	3.1	3.4	2.1	1.9	1.5	1.5
V	West Midlands	2.2	2.2	2.3	3.4	48.5	2.0	2.0	3.0	3.1	1.6
VI	East Anglia	1.2	1.3	0.8	2.1	1.0	41.6	2.6	1.5	1.0	0.8
VII	South East	7.7	7.3	6.9	8.8	7.7	14.3	54.4	15.3	8.6	6.9
VIII	South West	2.0	2.0	2.1	2.8	3.1	3.2	4.3	42.3	3.4	1.6
IX	Wales	0.8	0.9	2.0	1.0	1.7	1.2	1.1	1.8	47.4	0.6
X	Scotland	2.2	1.4	1.3	1.5	1.1	1.6	1.5	1.7	1.1	52.5
	Total	71.6	71.5	71.2	72.1	71.9	72.8	72.7	72.6	71.6	70.9
Single-region $\mathbf{e}_0$		71.1	71.2	70.5	72.0	71.6	73.5	73.1	72.8	71.1	70.2

Source: Run 6 of the Willekens and Rogers (1978) program.

used life expectancy matrix, that of age 0 or birth. The table is the multi-regional equivalent of single-region life expectancies and provides an overview of the effects of migration. The table indicates that substantial portions of a person's life are likely to be spent outside his or her region of birth, and that for all regions of birth a great deal of the lifetimes of the cohort are likely to be spent in the country's capital region, the South East.

Multiregional expectancies estimate the probable experience of the region's sons and daughters given that they migrate, whereas the conventional life expectancies estimate the mortality "environment" of the region experienced by the persons who live there. The two measures have an almost identical spatial pattern and a high correlation, but the variance of the multiregional life expectancies is less than that of the uniregional. The slope of the regression line relating the multiregional measure to the uniregional measure is substantially less than unity. Thus there is a regression toward the mean: those regions with higher or lower than average uniregional life expectancies have multiregional life expectancies closer to the mean. For example, East Anglia's uniregional life expectancy of 73.5 years becomes a multiregional expectation of 72.8 years. Conversely, Scotland's conventional expectation of 70.2 years becomes 70.9 years when migration of the Scots-born is taken into account.

7.3.2 *Multiregional Fertility Analysis*

In the same way that the multiregional life table generates tables of deaths and transitions so can the equivalent tables of births be calculated; these are births in all regions to mothers classified by region of origin (birth), assuming that the mothers who migrate to another region experience the fertility and mortality rates of that region. Then the results are consolidated to yield a matrix of spatial fertility expectancies.

The results for Great Britain are shown in Table 7.6. The table gives an indication of the likely genetic mixture across regions of a nation's population. For example, parents in East Anglia will have, under the conditions of mortality and migration in the multiregional life table estimated here, only 59% of their children born in their region of birth, just under 19% in the South East, and between 1 and 6% in each of the other regions. The children will themselves migrate among the regions, producing an even greater genetic mixture after two generations.

The rank ordering of the regions in the diagonal elements of Table 7.6 gives some indication of the degree of "endogamy" involved over a generation. The regions that retain their offspring the most are Scotland, the South East, and the North West; the most open regions are East Anglia, the South West, and the East Midlands, with the other regions lying between.

Table 7.6 Spatial fertility expectancies (net reproduction rate matrix) in Great Britain.

Region of birth of child	Region of birth of parent									
	I	II	III	IV	V	VI	VII	VIII	IX	X
I North	0.763	0.043	0.018	0.021	0.014	0.015	0.014	0.017	0.012	0.021
II Yorks. and Humb.	0.063	0.832	0.034	0.063	0.022	0.037	0.023	0.024	0.020	0.022
III North West	0.051	0.058	0.916	0.039	0.044	0.029	0.030	0.032	0.051	0.034
IV East Midlands	0.033	0.054	0.021	0.769	0.045	0.052	0.030	0.027	0.022	0.022
V West Midlands	0.033	0.032	0.034	0.053	0.846	0.030	0.029	0.047	0.048	0.023
VI East Anglia	0.015	0.017	0.010	0.027	0.012	0.652	0.032	0.018	0.012	0.009
VII South East	0.110	0.101	0.095	0.122	0.103	0.205	0.851	0.219	0.122	0.097
VIII South West	0.026	0.025	0.026	0.036	0.039	0.041	0.054	0.688	0.045	0.020
IX Wales	0.010	0.012	0.026	0.013	0.022	0.015	0.014	0.025	0.802	0.007
X Scotland	0.034	0.022	0.018	0.023	0.016	0.025	0.022	0.026	0.016	0.941
Total	1.136	1.195	1.198	1.165	1.163	1.102	1.099	1.124	1.149	1.196
Single-region NRR	1.122	1.214	1.218	1.172	1.175	1.075	1.087	1.115	1.147	1.220

Table 7.7 Net migraproduction rates in Great Britain.

Region of outmigration	Region of birth									
	I	II	III	IV	V	VI	VII	VIII	IX	X
I North	0.5159	0.0257	0.0109	0.0131	0.0088	0.0094	0.0087	0.0101	0.0073	0.0127
II Yorks. and Humb.	0.0366	0.0531	0.0206	0.0371	0.0138	0.0219	0.0139	0.0143	0.0122	0.0135
III North West	0.0236	0.0274	0.4428	0.0185	0.0213	0.0140	0.0146	0.0158	0.0237	0.0161
IV East Midlands	0.0229	0.0364	0.0148	0.5730	0.0308	0.0353	0.0210	0.0188	0.0151	0.0151
V West Midlands	0.0189	0.0190	0.0199	0.0304	0.5045	0.0178	0.0176	0.0269	0.0275	0.0140
VI East Anglia	0.0126	0.0185	0.0085	0.0224	0.0102	0.6208	0.0274	0.0157	0.0101	0.0079
VII South East	0.0558	0.0522	0.0494	0.0629	0.0543	0.1042	0.4540	0.1114	0.0621	0.0499
VIII South West	0.0214	0.0212	0.0222	0.0299	0.0330	0.0346	0.0460	0.6279	0.0369	0.0168
IX Wales	0.0060	0.0077	0.0151	0.0077	0.0126	0.0088	0.0080	0.0143	0.4905	0.0040
X Scotland	0.0121	0.0083	0.0067	0.0083	0.0059	0.0088	0.0079	0.0093	0.0058	0.3742
Total	0.7258	0.7413	0.6110	0.8033	0.6951	0.8757	0.6191	0.8645	0.6912	0.5243
Single-region NMR	0.7283	0.7575	0.5854	0.8486	0.7028	0.9693	0.5852	0.9743	0.6777	0.4706

Source for Tables 7.6 and 7.7: Run 6 of the Willekens and Rogers (1978) program.

7.3.3 *Multiregional Mobility Analysis*

In the previous section births were analyzed; migrations can be analyzed similarly and a net migraproduction rate (NMR) matrix defined (Willekens and Rogers 1978). This matrix contains the expected number of outmigrations that an individual makes from different locations during his or her lifetime.

The net migraproduction matrix for the regions of Great Britain is shown in Table 7.7. We must be careful in interpreting these migraproduction rates. They record the number of outmigrations expected over a lifetime, classified by the region of birth and by the regions from which the outmigration takes place. These outmigrations are the number of five-year transitions made, allowing for mortality over a lifetime. Since by definition only one transition can be made over a five-year interval, the migraproduction rates underestimate severely the number of interregional moves that take place. The previous calculations (Rees 1979c) involving one-year transitions produce a more accurate measure of the number of moves made.

If the multiregionally derived value of the net migraproduction rate is compared with a single-region value, the same kind of regression to the mean relationship is observed as in the cases of mortality and fertility. The variance in the migratory behavior of birth cohorts is reduced by the very act of migration. We can put forward the hypothesis for further investigation that migration acts within a national system of regions as a force of social equalization. Whatever differences exist among regions in levels of living or quality of life are reduced for the cohorts born in those regions through migration. The greater the migration the greater the leveling up or down. Of course, these conclusions depend on the assumption that the migrant adopts the behavior patterns of the region of destination instantaneously, whereas in reality there is a lag in this adoption.

7.3.4 *Multiregional Population Projections*

Although one of the most useful products of multiregional population analysis is the projection of the population (see Chapters 6 and 11), it is discussed only briefly here.

Not too much notice should be taken of the absolute numbers projected [Table 7.8(a)]. More up-to-date forecasts would show much lower projected numbers given the fall in fertility since the 1970 base year; internal migration rates and external migration flows have also fallen (Ogilvy 1980b, Rees and Stillwell 1982). In addition, external migration is not incorporated in the projections, thus causing the forecasts for the South East to be underestimated and those for the rest of the country to be overestimated.

Table 7.8(b) gives the population shares projected using the Run 6 data. It shows the effect of internal migration on regional population distribution within Great Britain from 1970 to 2020. If the projection model is allowed to

Table 7.8 The multiregional population projections for the regions of Great Britain 1970–2020.

Region	1970	1975	1980	1985	1990	2000	2010	2020	SE[a]
(a) Population numbers (thousands)									
North	3360	3393	3422	3456	3495	3572	3676	3805	2562
Yorks. and Humb.	4812	4878	4938	5005	5084	5270	5509	5795	4413
North West	6789	6888	6991	7115	7266	7621	8060	8567	6952
East Midlands	3363	3491	3616	3745	3884	4175	4492	4834	4103
West Midlands	5178	5312	5433	5553	5683	5964	6277	6630	5212
East Anglia	1674	1783	1886	1986	2087	2287	2493	2704	2285
South East	17316	17621	17912	18227	18579	19358	20286	21361	16197
South West	3764	3925	4078	4231	4386	4694	5032	5398	4382
Wales	2734	2777	2816	2857	2903	3005	3138	3295	2461
Scotland	5199	5282	5374	5478	5595	5845	6148	6489	4665
Total	54187	55350	56466	57653	58962	61791	65111	68879	53230
(b) Population shares (percentage of Great Britain total)									
North	6.20	6.13	6.06	5.99	5.93	5.78	5.64	5.52	4.81
Yorks. and Humb.	8.88	8.81	8.75	8.68	8.62	8.53	8.46	8.41	8.29
North West	12.53	12.45	12.38	12.34	12.32	12.33	12.38	12.43	13.06
East Midlands	6.21	6.31	6.40	6.50	6.59	6.76	6.90	7.02	7.71
West Midlands	9.36	9.60	9.62	9.63	9.64	9.65	9.64	9.63	9.79
East Anglia	3.09	3.22	3.34	3.44	3.54	3.70	3.83	3.93	4.29
South East	31.96	31.84	31.72	31.62	31.51	31.33	31.16	31.01	30.43
South West	6.95	7.09	7.22	7.34	7.44	7.60	7.73	7.84	8.23
Wales	5.05	5.02	4.99	4.96	4.92	4.86	4.82	4.78	4.62
Scotland	9.59	9.54	9.52	9.50	9.49	9.46	9.44	9.42	8.76
Total[b]	100.00	100.00	100.00	100.00	100.00	100.00	100.00	100.00	100.00

[a]SE refers to the stable equivalent.
[b]Columns may not sum to totals because of rounding errors.
Source: Run 6 of the Willekens and Rogers (1978) program.

continue for a long time, the shares of the population among regions and age groups reach stability; these shares are noted in the last column of the table. The distribution of the population among the regions at stability is very close to that observed in 1970. There is only one change in the size ranking of the regions: Scotland and the West Midlands exchange third and fourth places. This is in marked contrast to the Canadian provincial system (see later in this Chapter, Table 7.24) in which drastic shifts from the 1971 distribution are suggested. For example, Quebec's share declines from 27.5 to 10.7%; Alberta's share rises from 7.8 to 15.1%; and British Columbia's moves from 10.5 to 18.5%. In comparison with such shifts, Britain can be regarded as a nation at spatial equilibrium.

7.4 Conclusion

The concerns of this discussion have been of three kinds: empirical, methodological, and analytical. A number of tentative conclusions can be drawn from each.

The dominant pattern across regions in terms of fertility and mortality, whether measured by single- or multiregional methods, was one of a gradient of demographic development from a low-mortality, low-fertility South and East to a high-mortality, high-fertility North and West. At the start of the 1960s this was also a gradient from conditions of net inmigration to those of heavy net outflows.

Since 1964 fertility has declined in all regions and life expectancy has improved uniformly. Dramatic reduction in the projected populations of regions has resulted from the necessity to adopt ever lower fertility scenarios. The pattern of migration has shifted in kind from one of drift to the South East from the northern and western regions to one of occasional loss from the nation's core (the South East), substantial gains to the margins of the core in the South West, East Anglia, East Midlands, and Wales, and lesser losses in the northern and West Midlands regions. Some would see the shift in migration and population trends as the product of policy; others might view it as the natural course of decentralization from the national metropolis.

A variety of experimental runs of the multiregional population models were carried out with different data sets. It was shown that the choice of the equation used for estimating transition probabilities had little effect on multiregional life expectancies. Selecting a three-region rather than a 10-region system had a small effect on the distribution of life expectancy. The choice of the equation used to estimate missing information on infant migrants had a slightly larger influence than the other four dimensions of choice — mistakes here could have serious consequences.

The most dramatic changes in the distribution of life expectancies among regions, however, were effected by substituting migration measured by the five-year question. Five-year migrant data, it was argued, were the more appropriate to use in a multiregional population model employing a five-year age and time interval. The second British multiregional life table therefore looks very different from the first (Rees 1979c). The second table predicts that substantially smaller portions of people's lives would be spent outside their regions of birth than does the first. The root cause of the difference between the two life tables is the inadequate representation of return and repeat migration. More work is needed to represent and account for this behavior in the methodology of multiregional population analysis.

A series of comparisons of uniregional and multiregional measures of life expectancy, net reproduction, and migraproduction rates were carried out. The degree of regression to the mean showed that uniregional and multi-regional indicators were not alternative measures of the same concept, but rather related measures of different concepts. The single-region measures were applied to a regional population unchanged by the flux of migrants over time; the multiregional measures were applied to regional cohorts, which were assumed to adopt instantaneously the behavior of their current residence region. Finally, the multiregional measures were regressions of the single-region measures toward the national mean.

Population projections using the multiregional model were carried out based on 1970 births and deaths data and on 1966–1971 internal migrant data. The most important conclusion was that, although the populations of the North, Yorkshire and Humberside, and Scotland regions together with the South East would lose relative to the populations of East Anglia, the South West, and the East Midlands, the regional distribution of the population at stability was not far removed from the 1970 situation.

Much remains to be done before we can be satisfied that our methods of description and analysis match the complexity of the processes being described and analyzed. Work is currently under way (Rees and Stillwell 1982, 1984, Rees 1984, Stillwell 1984) to develop descriptions and projections of multiregional population change using accounting and migration modeling methods as well as life table models at a scale more in tune with the settlement geography of the UK. Much better information is now becoming available on annual migration that should make possible a substantial updating of the results of this analysis in the near future.

7.II The Soviet Union[2]

Svetlana Soboleva

The Soviet Union has the third largest population in the world, after China and India. On 1 January 1979 it had a population of 262.4 million people. This number might have been reached much earlier had it not been for the deaths of many millions of people in World War II; more than 20 million lost their lives during the war, but the country's total loss, including the indirect losses resulting from higher mortality and reduced fertility, was closer to 50 million. It took 10 postwar years for the nation's population to grow back to its prewar numbers.

7.5 Historical Overview

The most important aspects of the dynamics and distribution of the Soviet Union's population are connected with urbanization. In 1920 the urban population was 15% of the total, while in 1975 it was 60% (Table 7.9). The average annual rate of increase of the country's urban population has slowed somewhat during the last 15 years and will continue to decrease as a higher level of urbanization is achieved.

In the postwar years, the urban population has grown, while the rural population has declined. In a period of only 10 years, from 1940 to 1950, the rural population was reduced by 22.1 million. This sharp decline is connected not only with wartime casualties and with the drop in the levels of natural increase, but also with the intensive rural-to-urban flow of the population. In the following decade, 1950–1960, the comparatively high natural increase of the rural population was counteracted by a high level of outmigration. As a result, the rural population in this period hardly changed in size, whereas the urban population grew by more than 34 million. This pattern did not continue, however. Beginning in the mid-1960s, the growing migration losses were no longer compensated for because of a sharp drop in the rural birth rate. From

---

[2]This part of Chapter 7 is an abridged version of the Migration and Settlement case study of the Soviet Union (Soboleva 1980).

Table 7.9 Population of the Soviet Union (thousands) for the 1920–1979 period.

Year	Population			Percentage	
	Total	Urban	Rural	Urban	Rural
1920	136810	20855	115925	15	85
1926	147028	26314	120714	18	82
1939	190678	60409	130269	32	68
1940	194352	63100	131252	32	68
1950	178547	69414	109133	39	61
1955	194415	86261	108154	44	56
1960	212372	103618	108754	49	51
1961	216286	107883	108403	50	50
1962	220003	111244	108759	51	49
1963	223457	114365	109092	51	49
1964	226669	117720	108949	52	48
1965	229628	120730	108898	53	47
1966	232243	123720	108523	53	47
1967	234823	126910	107913	54	46
1968	237165	129758	107407	55	45
1969	239468	132893	106575	55	45
1970	241720	135991	105729	56	44
1971	243873	139025	104848	57	43
1972	246293	142537	103756	58	42
1973	248625	146099	102526	59	41
1974	250869	149589	101280	60	40
1975	253261	153110	100151	60	40
1979	262442	163600	98800	62	38

Sources: Central Statistical Office (1975, p.7) and *Izvestiya*, April 1979.

1966 to 1975, the rural population declined by 8.4 million, while the urban population grew by more than 29 million.

7.6 Components of Spatial Population Growth

Population change is a complex process that is influenced by a wide range of social, economic, demographic, and political factors, which are reflected in the variations in patterns of fertility, mortality, and migration.

7.6.1 *Fertility*

Differences among the crude birth rates of individual union republics are the result of socioeconomic development and national traditions and customs. [The locations of the regions used in this study are given in Figure 2.5(a).] In 1940 the Soviet Union had a comparatively high birth rate (over 30 per thousand).

From 1960 to 1969, however, a significant decrease took place, which affected all of the republics except Tadzhik in Central Asia, where the crude birth rate increased from 33.5 to 34.7 per thousand. The national birth rate decreased until 1969 when it was 17.0 per thousand, at which point it began to increase and in 1975 reached 18.0 per thousand.

A detailed analysis by Pankrat'eva (1977) described the dependence of the crude birth rates in the individual regions on the age composition of the female population. This study showed that in some republics the decline in this rate was because of a change in the number of women of childbearing age, while in other regions the decline was connected with a change in age-specific fertility rates.

World War II left a substantial mark on fertility dynamics. The fertility curve for the country as a whole shows two "waves" caused by the war: the first in the 1940s and the second in the 1960s — the generation born after the war. Today high birth rates persist in the Central Asian Republics, where a strong influence of national traditions and customs favoring large families prevails. Marriage is encouraged and there is little family planning. By contrast, among the populations of the Russian Soviet Federated Socialist Republic (RSFSR) and the Baltic Republics (as well as Ukraine and Byelorussia) the birth rate is lower than the country's national average.

Geographical and national variations still play an important role in fertility levels. In 1975 the birth rate in Tadzhik, the highest in the Soviet Union, was 2.6 times higher than the birth rate in the Baltic region of Latvia. These distinctions turn out to be even more significant when one considers the mix of nationalities in these republics. The birth rate of the native populations of the Central Asian Republics was almost four times that of the Baltic peoples. Thus the birth rate for the country as a whole is an aggregation of two different levels of population reproduction. On the one hand, there are the below-average birth rates in the Baltic Republics, the RSFSR, the Ukraine, and Byelorussia; on the other hand, there are the high birth rates in the Central Asian and Caucasian Republics.

The fluctuation of age-specific fertility rates among the territories of the Soviet Union is also significant, not only for a comparison of the levels of fertility among women of the same age groups in different regions, but also because of the distribution of births within the entire reproductive period. While the reproductive period of women in the majority of regions in the RSFSR and the Ukrainian and Baltic Republics virtually ends before 40 years of age, in most of the Central Asian and Caucasian Republics it lasts considerably longer. The fertility rate of the 40–44 age group in some of these republics is more than 100 births per 1000 women. These significant fluctuations among the republics is reflected in the overall fertility rates. In the RSFSR the average number of births per woman is 1.7; for the Central Asian Republics of Uzbek, Tadzhik, and Turkmen the average number is 6.0 — that is, 3.5 times higher than in the RSFSR (Kurman 1976).

Examining the dynamics of age-specific fertility rates for the Soviet Union as a whole, one finds that the total fertility rate was 1.6 times lower by the end of the 1950s than it was in prewar years. In 1960–1970, fertility rates continued to fall in all age groups; however, in 1970–1975 these rates began to increase in the pre-30 age groups only. It should be mentioned that since 1935 no generation of women has had a higher birth rate for the 25-years-and-under age groups than the generation born in the 1950s. This was due primarily to young marriages and a shift to a younger mean-age of childbearing.

In any country, fertility depends on an intricate combination of socioeconomic factors. The change in the pace of life of the Soviet people, the growth of prosperity, the social demands for an increased level of educational and cultural resources, the changing needs of the population in connection with urbanization and growth, the change of value orientations in the use of leisure time, the growing employment of women in the labor force – all of these factors have contributed to the decrease in the fertility of the population.

Table 7.10 Age-specific fertility rates in the urban and rural areas of the Soviet Union (per thousand women), 1960–1973.

Age group	1960–1961			1965–1966		
	Urban	Rural	$\%^a$	Urban	Rural	$\%^a$
15–19	28.9	42.4	146.7	25.8	25.1	97.3
20–24	143.4	193.7	135.1	137.5	198.1	144.1
25–29	131.9	195.2	148.0	111.0	177.6	160.0
30–34	83.0	143.0	172.3	69.6	135.0	194.0
35–39	40.5	85.4	210.8	31.3	77.3	247.0
40–44	11.5	37.3	324.3	9.4	32.2	342.6
45–49	1.4	7.3	521.4	1.3	8.4	646.2
15–49	73.5	111.2	151.3	57.0	90.4	158.6
	1969–1970			1972–1973		
	Urban	Rural	$\%^a$	Urban	Rural	$\%^a$
15–19	28.5	33.8	118.6	30.5	35.4	116.1
20–24	144.2	209.5	145.3	147.3	236.5	160.6
25–29	108.8	163.2	150.0	115.3	184.5	160.0
30–34	68.6	121.9	177.7	64.1	115.1	179.6
35–39	29.6	75.5	255.1	31.3	76.5	244.4
40–44	7.3	27.0	369.9	6.5	25.8	396.9
45–49	1.1	5.5	500.0	0.6	3.8	633.3
15–49	55.7	82.3	147.8	57.5	82.7	143.8

[a]The rural fertility rate as a percentage of the urban fertility rate.
Source: Central Statistical Office (1975, p.136).

As is apparent from Table 7.10, the age-specific fertility levels of urban and rural populations in the Soviet Union are quite different; fertility is

higher for rural than for urban populations. In 1960, the number of births per
thousand women in the rural areas was 51.3% higher than in the urban areas.
Such differences are generated by the contrasting conditions and ways of life
between urban and rural populations, which have developed historically. With
each passing year, these differences are declining but even so they are still
significant, the rural birth rate in 1972 still being 43.8% higher than the
urban.

7.6.2 *Mortality*

The crude death rate (CDR) in the Soviet Union has shown a tendency to
fall in the past four decades; in 1973 it was 48.3% of the 1940 level. The average life expectancy during this time increased from 44 years to 70 years (64
for men and 74 for women). The fall in the death rate and the increase in average life expectancy were a result of the increased standard of living and the
improvement of labor conditions, as well as a consequence of achievements in
health care and medicine.

Table 7.11   Age-specific mortality rates (per thousnad) in the Soviet Union,
1958–1975.

Age group	Year						
	1958–1959	1965–1966	1969–1970	1972–1973	1973–1974	1974–1975	$\%^a$
0–4	11.9	6.9	6.9	7.2	7.7	8.2	68.9
5–9	1.1	0.8	0.7	0.7	0.7	0.7	63.6
10–14	0.8	0.6	0.6	0.5	0.5	0.5	62.5
15–19	1.3	1.0	1.0	1.0	1.0	1.0	76.9
20–24	1.8	1.6	1.6	1.6	1.6	1.7	94.4
25–29	2.2	2.0	2.2	2.1	2.0	2.1	95.5
30–34	2.6	2.6	2.8	2.8	2.8	3.0	115.4
35–39	3.1	3.2	3.7	3.6	3.6	3.7	119.4
40–44	4.0	3.9	4.7	4.8	4.9	5.2	130.0
45–49	5.4	5.1	6.0	6.2	6.4	6.7	124.1
50–54	7.9	7.9	8.7	8.6	8.8	9.0	113.9
55–59	11.2	11.1	11.7	12.5	12.3	13.0	116.1
60–64	17.1	17.2	18.0	18.0	18.2	18.3	107.0
65–69	25.2	25.5	27.5	27.2	27.0	27.4	108.7
70+	63.8	65.8	75.7	75.5	73.5	73.3	114.9
Crude death rate	7.4	7.3	8.2	8.6	8.7	9.0	121.6

[a]The 1974–1975 mortality rate as a percentage of the 1958–1959 mortality rate.
Sources: Central Statistical Office (1975, p.141 and 1976, p.43).

The age-specific mortality rate (Table 7.11) provides an even more precise description of the mortality trends in a country. As the calculations

conducted by Pankrat'eva (1977) on the influence of age on the crude death rate showed, the increased rates were a consequence of changes in the population's age structure. Between 1958–1959 and 1973–1974 there was an increase in the crude death rate of 17.6%. The increase due to rises in age-specific rates was only 2.0%, while the increase resulting from changes in the age structure was 15.6%. As the proportion of the population in the older age groups grew, the crude death rate rose.

As well as being a function of the age distribution, death rates are dependent on the sex structure of the population. In all age groups the mortality level is lower among women than men. As child mortality falls, deaths from causes affecting men more than women seem to play a larger role. Among men, there is a higher mortality rate from cardiovascular diseases, malignant tumors, and accidents.

There are wide variations in the difference between mortality rates for men and women, however, among the individual regions. For example, in the Kazakh Republic in 1973 the difference between the crude death rate for men and that for women was 2.0 per thousand, while in the Baltic Republic of Estonia it was only 0.1 per thousand.

Many of the differences in the death rates of the individual republics may be explained by differences in population age structure. The highest crude death rate was found in the Baltic Republics (in Estonia and Latvia) where the birth rate was low and the share of population over 60 was high. The lowest mortality rates of 5.2–6.4 per thousand occurred in the republics where the birth rate was high and a large share of the population was young.

7.6.3 *Migration*

In discussing migration it is useful to differentiate between urban-to-urban migration and rural-to-urban migration. These two flows are particularly interesting because of their recent trends, which result from the difference between life in the city and life in the country: industrial versus agricultural labor, collective versus state ownership of the means of production, and urban versus rural quality of life.

The principal source of migration data used in this chapter is the continuously updated national register of each individual's permanent place of residence. These unpublished data and special tabulations, carried out for other purposes, are the sources of the age-specific migration flows used here. The standard definition of an internal migrant in the Soviet Union states two conditions: first, that the change of permanent residence involves a change in community (commune) of residence and second, that the duration of stay in the new place of permanent residence must exceed a minimum of two years. At the present time, there is more information available for urban than for rural populations because of the quality of registration. We therefore have more accurate data on the urban than the rural populations.

Table 7.12 Crude migration rates (per thousand) of urban and rural
populations in the Soviet Union, based on the 1970 census.

Republic	Crude migration rate		
	Urban	Rural	%[a]
RSFSR	55.4	83.9	151.4
Ukrainian Republic	41.7	51.2	123.5
Moldavian Republic	48.2	42.2	87.6
Byelorussian Republic	50.2	51.6	102.8
Central Asian Republics[b]	46.7	25.1	53.7
Kazakh Republic	75.5	85.5	113.2
Caucasian Republics[c]	28.1	23.9	85.1
Baltic Republics[d]	41.7	63.2	151.6
Total Soviet Union	51.8	64.7	124.9

[a]The rural crude migration rate as a percentage of the urban crude migration rate.
[b]Uzbek, Kirgiz, Tadzhik, and Turkmen SSRs. (The Kazakh Republic is considered separately.)
[c]Georgian, Azerbaijan, and Armenian SSRs.
[d]Estonian, Latvian, and Lithuanian SSRs.
Source: Khorev and Moiseyenko (1976, p.56).

Differences in urban and rural migration in the Soviet Union are listed in
Table 7.12. As the table shows, migration of the rural population, at the
national level, exceeds that of the urban population by 24.9%. The highest
ratios of rural to urban migration rates occur in the RSFSR and the Baltic and
Ukrainian Republics. The outmigration rate of the rural populations in these
republics is higher than the rate of natural increase, causing an absolute
decrease in the number of people living in these rural areas. In the Byelorussian Republic the level of migration is approximately identical for both urban
and rural populations. In the Moldavian, Caucasian, and Central Asian Republics, the migration rate of the rural population is lower than that of the urban.

The total number of in- and outmigrants in the Soviet Union grew by 23.2%
between 1961 and 1973 (Khorev and Moiseyenko 1976) and the flow from rural
areas to urban increased by more than 80%. The increase in migration from
rural areas is a direct result of high rates of urban industrialization, which
cause a concentration of industrial production in the big cities and release the
labor force from agricultural work. Many specialists studying the question of
migration in the Soviet Union feel that the migratory flow from rural to urban
areas will have a tendency to decline, whereas intercity (urban-to-urban)
migration will increase in importance.

The growth of migration to urban areas has been influenced by a further
deepening of labor division in urban and rural areas, caused by the growing
demand for nonagricultural labor. The most important source of labor force
growth in cities has been the inmigration of the rural population, which contributed almost half of the total increase of labor force in 1959–1970.

Socioeconomic differences between urban and rural areas play an important role in the redistribution of the population between cities and villages. A significant gap in the development of the productive forces in industry and in agriculture has been the basic reason for differences in the conditions, levels, and ways of life of the urban and rural populations. Because of this gap, the rural population has a lower level of income; a lag in the improvement of living and housing conditions; a different domestic economy; a need to organize a personal, secondary economy; and a different correlation between free time and work time (Khorev and Moiseyenko 1976).

Migration of the rural population into the cities fulfills an important economic and social function — the redistribution of labor — thus raising the welfare of the rural-to-urban migrants by means of specialized education and of allotting work according to ability and inclination. Migration, by redistributing manpower throughout the country, substantially influences different aspects of social and economic development in the individual regions. This movement of the rural population to nonagricultural activities in urban areas, however, often deviates from the interests of society.

As stated above, the exchange between city and village is not equal in many regions. Rural areas lose several times more people than they receive in return. By far the majority of migrants entering the rural areas are those people who, having moved to the city, could not become acclimatized to the new environment and chose to return to the conditions to which they were accustomed. More often, however, migrants from rural areas do not return. Skilled personnel whose education level is above that needed for the demands of the village leave the rural area along with the young. Having received training in technical schools, skilled workers find employment easily and quickly adapt themselves to city life.

Migration from the village to the city also has a substantial impact on the rate of natural increase in the rural areas. The outmigration of young, healthy villagers lowers the demographic potential of the village. Fertility levels drop and so do the rates of natural increase. Furthermore, the village is left with a predominantly older and less healthy population as a result of the "selective" migration from village to city.

The disproportion of the economic—geographic distribution of the population and manpower inherited from prerevolutionary times still persists to a certain extent in the Soviet Union. This disproportion leads to a lack of manpower in some regions and a surplus in others. Since the Revolution, much has been done to overcome this imbalance, particularly in Kazakhstan. Before the Revolution, Kazakhstan was an outlying colonial district of the Russian Empire, regarded by Russian manufacturers as a source of raw materials and as a commodity market. The population of this region was made up primarily of the native population. In the post-revolutionary period, the increased industrialization of this region encouraged a significant inflow of people from other areas of the Soviet Union. Between 1959 and 1970 alone, the Kazakh Republic experienced a positive net inmigration of around 0.75 million people, which amounted to an increase of more than 6% in its population during this period.

The level of intraregional migration is high in all regions. For example, in 1968–1969 the percentage of outmigrants that left for other communes in the same economic region was 54.6% for the Central Asian Republics, 74.5% for the Ukrainian Republic, and 87.9% for the RSFSR. This tendency also holds for the inmigrants of individual economic regions. Intraregional population redistribution is, therefore, the most important tendency of the total migration among all regions.

In this population exchange, the majority of the observed regions interact primarily with a limited number of other regions. Those regions losing significant numbers of people to other regions generally receive the bulk of the migrants from these same regions; that is, the population exchange is usually symmetric. This is mainly due to territorial, economic, and cultural proximity.

The RSFSR and the Kazakh Republic are regions with a broad and dispersed range of migratory interaction. Conversely, there are regions with a highly limited sphere of migration interaction: the Baltic, Caucasian, Byelorussian, and Moldavian Republics. In view of the significant number of migrants over the country as a whole (more than 11% of the total population in the 1968–1969 period), the "efficiency" of migration is not high. For example, the Ukrainian Republic received only 102 inmigrants for every 100 outmigrants, and in the Byelorussian Republic the number of inmigrants almost equaled the number of outmigrants.

The intensity of migration depends on a multitude of diverse factors — economic, geographical, sociological, ethnic, cultural, and legal. It is also well known that identical conditions evoke varying intensities of migration in different age–sex groups.

Data on the age structure of migrants show that the age distribution of those migrating to urban areas of each republic has approximately the same structure for all republics. The fraction of migrants in each age group fluctuates only slightly between migration flows. The most mobile groups are those aged 16–25 years. The territorial redistributions in these groups are connected with the move to study in educational institutions and the attraction of newly developed regions.

7.6.4 *Age Composition*[3]

The history of demographic development in the Soviet Union during the past several decades has been characterized by a gradual decrease in the fraction of children in the total population and an increase in the fraction of the pension-age population. (Pension age in the Soviet Union begins at 55 for

---

[3]This section is taken largely from the results of research conducted by Kalinjuk (1975).

women and 60 for men.) This "aging" process is taking place as a consequence of the lowering of the birth rate, especially evident in the postwar years.

The decline in the birth rate has had a profound effect on the age composition of the population of the Soviet Union. The enormous human losses during World War II must also be considered, however. According to the 1959 census, the war primarily reduced the number of people in the 35–44 age groups, but also had an effect on the number of 10–14-year-olds (born in 1944–1948) and 15–19-year-olds (born in 1939–1943). The base of the population age pyramid for 1959 is significantly narrower than that for the prewar period.

With respect to reproductive potential, these pyramids are of two different types. The female population of 1959 relates to a stationary type, whereas the male population still relates to a growing one, characterized by a high fraction of children and a low fraction of population older than 60. By 1970 the age structure had undergone substantial changes. The war was largely responsible for the decline in the number of people aged 50–54 years as well as for the fall in the 20–24 age group (those born in 1945–1949) and the 25–29 age group (those born in 1940–1944). By 1970 the share of the population aged 20–39 had dropped significantly, causing a decrease in the relative size of the working-age population. In 1959 the 15–59 age groups made up 61.1% of the population, while in 1970 their share was 59.3%. At the same time, the fraction of the population older than 60 increased.

A basic feature of the change in the age structure of the postwar population is that the increase in the number of older people is greater than the total population growth. This aging process also affects the working-age population; the share of older people capable of working increased, while the share of the younger, 20–39 age groups declined. (After 1970, however, this tendency was checked somewhat by the entry to the labor market of a large number of youths born in 1955–1959.) Together with the fall of the share of children, the share of females over 60 years of age increased. In 1974 the fraction of women aged 60 or older was almost twice that of men of this age.

The urban population of the Soviet Union is characterized by a rather high share of elderly and middle-aged people, which in the period between the 1959 and 1970 censuses increased by 32% and made up 10.3%, as opposed to 7.8%, of the total population. The fraction in the 0–14 age group dropped to 25.6%. The fraction of the working-age population (those in the 20–59 age group) also dropped; in 1959 it made up 57.3% of the population, but by 1970 this figure had fallen to 54.9%. Nevertheless, the fraction of the working-age urban population remained high. Because of heavy migration from the country to the city, populations having low fractions of children and elderly people and a high fraction of working-age people evolved in the urban areas.

In rural areas the proportion of people in the 0–4 age group remained rather high, as did the middle-aged and elderly groups. At the same time, the fraction of the working-age population gradually decreased.

7.7 Multiregional Analysis of Soviet Urbanization in the 1970s

Multiregional population analysis serves as an instrument for estimating the dynamics of interregional population change. Along with traditional indices showing the demographic development of an individual region, this analysis permits one to estimate the population characteristics that can only be calculated by taking into account the entire system of regions.

7.7.1 *Data Preparation*

Taking into consideration the difficulties of obtaining information, the relative homogeneity of demographic development in the union republics, and their territorial proximity, we aggregated the 15 republics of the Soviet Union into seven territorial regions for the Migration and Settlement Study. All regions were then further divided into urban and rural areas for the purposes of a more detailed analysis.

The urban areas of each of the seven regions were defined as independent territorial units, whereas all rural areas were aggregated into a single eighth region because of the absence of age-specific data on rural-to-rural migration between republics. Thus the following eight regions were defined:

I   Urban areas of the Russian Soviet Federal Socialist Republic (the RSFSR)
II   Urban areas of the Ukrainian and Moldavian Republics
III   Urban areas of the Byelorussian Republic
IV   Urban areas of the Central Asian Republics except the Kazakh Republic (Uzbek, Kirgiz, Tadzhik, and Turkmen)
V   Urban areas of the Kazakh Republic
VI   Urban areas of the Caucasian Republics (Georgia, Azerbaijan, and Armenia)
VII   Urban areas of the Baltic Republics (Estonia, Latvia, and Lithuania)
VIII All rural areas of the USSR.

In addition to our division into eight territorial regions, we also made an aggregation involving only two regions, with all rural areas as one region and all urban areas as the other.

For the multiregional population analysis, the following 1974 input data — with both sexes added together — were used for each region of the observed territorial system:

(1)   Population by age and region at midyear
(2)   Number of deaths by age and region

(3)   Number of births by age of mother and by region
(4)   Number of migrants by age, region of origin, and region of destination.

The base year for our study was 1974. The data on population by age groups (from the beginning of 1970 through 1974) and for births, deaths, and migrations (1973–1974) were compiled from the nation's official statistics (Central Statistical Office 1973, 1974, 1975), supplemented by other statistical sources.

The population distribution in individual regions was disaggregated into five-year age groups, the last including people 70 years and over. For the purposes of this study, however, it was believed to be important to include the age distribution in older age groups − between the ages of 70 and 85. Because of a lack of information on these groups in 1974, we used for all eight regions 1974 age profiles obtained in Poland. These data were acceptable because the age structure and mortality patterns in the older age-specific mortality rates were recorded according to five-year groups between the ages of 0 and 70.

Age-specific migration rates were calculated from data on the total in-migration to the urban areas of each republic of the Soviet Union (for urban regions) and on the migration rate of the rural population for the Soviet Union as a whole. Again the age-specific migration rates for the older age groups (70–85) were assumed to follow the age profile of corresponding rates for Poland.

All preliminary information for the urban areas was collected separately for each union republic, whereas the data for rural areas were collected for the Soviet Union as a whole. In the final stage of preparation, the aggregation of republics was carried out as shown above, with an eight-region aggregation and an urban–rural dimension.

7.7.2 *Analysis of Observed Population Characteristics*

Appendix A of Soboleva (1980) presents the mortality, fertility, and migration rates for all regions in the system, including both the eight-region and the two-region divisions. Along with the observed five-year age-specific birth, death, and migration rates are included other rates, for example, the gross and crude mortality, fertility, and outmigration rates, as well as the mean ages of death, childbearing, and outmigration.

The crude rate in demographic analysis, defined as the total number of births, deaths, or outmigrants divided by the total midyear population, characterizes the aggregate level of births, deaths, and outmigrations. For example, the crude death rate for urban areas of the RSFSR is estimated to be 0.0083 (or 8.3 per thousand) and 0.0079 for the urban areas of the Ukrainian

Republic. The lowest CDR occurs in the urban areas of Byelorussia and the highest in the rural areas of the country.

The fertility level may be expressed in terms of the gross reproduction rate (GRR). The GRR is usually calculated for the female population only; it is the sum of the age-specific fertility rates multiplied by the length of the age interval (five years in this case). For this study, sex-specific data were not available and the GRR was computed for the total of both sexes. It ranges from 1.00 in the RSFSR to 1.92 in the Central Asian Republics. In the rural areas the GRR is estimated to be 1.88.

Analogous to the GRR is the gross migraproduction rate (GMR). It is an index of the migration level between two regions and is the sum of age-specific migration rates multiplied by five, in the case of five-year age intervals. With it, one can compare the total level of outmigration from one region with that of another at a certain period of time; it is a period and not a cohort index.

Table 7.13 Gross migraproduction rates (including intraregional migration) for the eight regions of the Soviet Union, 1974.

Region of destinations[a]		Region of outmigration							
		I	II	III	IV	V	VI	VII	VIII
I	RSFSR	4.17	0.79	0.92	0.88	1.55	0.54	0.50	2.16
II	Ukrainian and Moldavian Republics	0.28	3.43	0.28	0.12	0.29	0.13	0.13	0.66
III	Byelorussian Republic	0.04	0.04	3.63	0.01	0.04	0.01	0.05	0.16
IV	Central Asian Republics	0.08	0.03	0.03	2.44	0.28	0.05	0.02	0.16
V	Kazakh Republic	0.11	0.06	0.05	0.22	3.56	0.03	0.02	0.20
VI	Caucasian Republics	0.02	0.02	0.01	0.02	0.02	1.78	0.01	0.07
VII	Baltic Republics	0.04	0.03	0.16	0.01	0.02	0.01	3.46	0.12
VIII	Rural areas of the Soviet Union	0.80	0.79	0.87	0.86	1.05	0.29	0.84	2.16
	Total	5.54	5.18	5.96	4.57	6.79	2.84	5.03	5.69

[a]Only urban areas are included in regions I–VII.

Table 7.13 shows the results of GMR calculations for each region. As is apparent from the table, the total GMR is highest for regions V (6.79), III (5.96), VIII (5.69), and I (5.54). By comparing the data in the columns of this table, it is possible to analyze the interregional migration relationships. For example, the "strongest" links of region I are with region VIII ($GMR_{18} = 0.80$), and the strongest links of region VI are with region I ($GMR_{61} = 0.54$).

The elements of this table arranged on the main diagonal represent intraregional migration indices. The highest level of such migrations occurs in the RSFSR with an index of 4.17, more than 75% of the total. The level of intraregional migration is of course related to the size of a given region. The lowest level is observed in region VI.

Once these intraregional flows have been excluded, one can estimate the level of interregional streams. The GMRs representing migration from the rural areas to the other regions are among the highest in the country.

The mean age is an important demographic indicator characterizing the peculiarities of an age profile. In 1974 the population of region VII (urban areas of the Baltic Republics) had the highest mean age among the eight regions of the Soviet Union. The mean age of the population in this region was 34 years. Other regions with a high mean age were regions II (33.96 years) and I (33.84 years). As the previous description of demographic trends in the country's individual regions showed, the high level of the mean age of the population, typical for these regions, is the result of low birth rates over a long period of time.

The lowest mean ages were exhibited by the urban populations of the Central Asian and Caucasian Republics, where high birth rates have existed for a long time. The difference between the highest and the lowest mean ages among the country's regions was 6.29 years in 1974.

7.7.3 Multiregional Life Table Analysis

The life table is an important element in demographic analysis. Such indices as probability of survival, expected number of survivors, and life expectancy make it possible to observe the evolution of a hypothetical cohort born at some fixed moment in time. The multiregional life table, a generalization of the concept of the single-region life table, introduces interregional migration flows. By using death and migration probabilities it is possible to estimate the probabilities that individuals at given ages reach subsequent ages and stay in a given region or move to any other region.

Within the two-region urban—rural system of the Soviet Union, for example, the mobility of the urban population is lower than that of the rural population for almost all age groups. Thus the probabilities of the urban population staying in urban regions between the ages 15—19 and 20—24 are 0.90 and 0.88, respectively; for the rural population staying in rural regions the corresponding figures are 0.58 and 0.26. For every 100 thousand people living in urban areas at the age of 20, only 11.5 thousand will have moved to rural areas by the age of 24, but the flow from rural to urban areas constitutes 72.5 thousand people. There are large discrepancies in the size of in- and outflows in all age groups. These data confirm clearly the unequal character of urban—rural population exchange in the individual age groups.

The index of life expectancy according to place of birth and future residence is an important measure in multiregional population analysis. Table 7.14 presents life expectancies at birth by place of residence for all eight regions of the system. The table shows, for example, that people born in the urban areas of the RSFSR are expected to live 46.32 years out of a total of 69.55 years in the region of birth, 6.91 years in region II, 1.08 years in region III, and so on.

Table 7.14 Life expectancies at birth for the eight regions of the Soviet Union.

Region of residence		Region of birth							
		I	II	III	IV	V	VI	VII	VIII
I	RSFSR	46.32	20.39	20.86	19.40	23.97	14.49	17.81	25.53
II	Ukrainian and Moldavian Republics	6.91	34.92	6.82	4.91	6.66	4.29	5.52	8.52
III	Byelo-russian Republic	1.08	1.10	28.15	0.77	1.04	0.55	1.33	1.68
IV	Central Asian Republics	1.89	1.44	1.40	29.58	2.95	1.27	1.22	2.12
V	Kazakh Republic	1.81	1.45	1.41	2.33	22.80	0.93	1.14	1.95
VI	Caucasian Republics	0.80	0.77	0.67	0.73	0.74	42.44	0.64	1.11
VII	Baltic Republics	1.10	1.04	2.19	0.75	0.90	0.58	33.57	1.53
VIII	Rural areas of the Soviet Union	9.64	9.72	9.92	9.31	10.00	5.93	9.96	26.67
	Total	69.55	70.84	71.42	67.77	69.07	70.48	71.20	69.12

Note: Columns may not agree with totals because of rounding errors.

The main diagonal shows how many years a person born in a given region can expect to live in that region. By comparing these figures with the total life expectancy, the relative "immobility" of each regional population can be clearly identified. As is apparent from this table, the highest immobilities in the Soviet Union exist in region I (46.32 years) and in region VI (42.44 years), and the lowest in region VIII (26.67 years) and region V (22.80 years).

The life expectancy index, by place of birth and future residence, is a useful measure for assessing the migration levels between individual regions. The migration level or proportional allocation of life expectancy is the fraction of total life expectancy that a person born in region i might expect to live in region j. For example, one-third of the average lifetime of a baby born in the urban areas of the RSFSR is expected to be lived outside that region (and two-thirds within it). These fractions are reversed for a baby born in the urban areas of the Kazakh Republic.

The multiregional life table allows for a more complete analysis of fertility patterns in different regions of the country by introducing the impact of internal migration. Spatial net reproduction rates and net reproduction allocations are the relevant multiregional indices.

Table 7.15 Net reproduction rates for the eight regions of the Soviet Union.

Region of residence		Region of birth							
		I	II	III	IV	V	VI	VII	VIII
I	RSFSR	0.62	0.28	0.28	0.26	0.34	0.18	0.24	0.39
II	Ukrainian and Moldavian Republics	0.10	0.48	0.10	0.06	0.09	0.05	0.08	0.13
III	Byelorussian Republic	0.02	0.02	0.39	0.01	0.02	0.01	0.02	0.03
IV	Central Asian Republics	0.05	0.04	0.04	0.71	0.09	0.03	0.03	0.07
V	Kazakh Republic	0.04	0.03	0.03	0.05	0.33	0.02	0.02	0.04
VI	Caucasian Republics	0.02	0.01	0.01	0.01	0.01	0.85	0.01	0.02
VII	Baltic Republics	0.01	0.01	0.03	0.01	0.01	0.01	0.42	0.02
VIII	Rural areas of the Soviet Union	0.25	0.25	0.25	0.23	0.26	0.13	0.27	0.49
	Total	1.10	1.13	1.13	1.34	1.16	1.28	1.09	1.20

Note: Columns may not agree with totals because of rounding errors.

Table 7.15 gives net reproduction rates (NRR) for all regions of the Soviet Union. The bottom row of this table shows the total expected number of births per parent born in a particular region, given the multiregional regime of fertility, mortality, and migration. The elements in each column represent the distribution of this total among the different regions of birth of the child. The NRR matrix as a whole shows the regional distribution of the expected number of births by region of birth of parent and child. For example, of the expected 1.10 births per parent born in region I, 0.62 will occur in region I, 0.10 will occur in region II, 0.02 in region III, and so on.

As is apparent from Table 7.15, the NRR for each region is greater than unity, indicating a rate of reproduction that is higher than bare replacement level for all regions. The highest NRRs are recorded in the republics of Central Asia and Caucasus, the lowest in the RSFSR and the Baltic Republics. For the urban and rural populations of the Soviet Union as a whole, the NRRs are 1.12 and 1.20, respectively.

The spatial net reproduction allocation provides another way of looking at the net reproduction rate. It is simply the fraction of each column total in

Table 7.15 that is allocated to each row. Such allocations of the total regional net reproduction rates show, for example, that 32.8% of the births to parents born in the rural areas of the USSR will occur in region I.

Along with spatial net reproduction rates and allocations, one can also calculate spatial net migraproduction rates and allocations. These are given in Table 7.16.

Table 7.16 Net migraproduction rates for the eight regions of the Soviet Union.[a]

Region of outmigration		Region of birth							
		I	II	III	IV	V	VI	VII	VIII
I	RSFSR	3.35	1.28	1.31	1.17	1.56	0.85	1.10	1.74
II	Ukrainian and Moldavian Republics	0.40	2.56	0.39	0.25	0.38	0.23	0.31	0.54
III	Byelorussian Republic	0.08	0.08	2.42	0.05	0.07	0.03	0.10	0.13
IV	Central Asian Republics	0.11	0.08	0.07	1.76	0.18	0.07	0.06	0.13
V	Kazakh Republic	0.15	0.12	0.11	0.20	1.98	0.07	0.09	0.17
VI	Caucasian Republics	0.03	0.02	0.02	0.02	0.02	1.60	0.02	0.04
VII	Baltic Republics	0.06	0.05	0.13	0.03	0.04	0.03	2.41	0.09
VIII	Rural areas of the Soviet Union	0.68	0.69	0.69	0.63	0.71	0.35	0.74	1.87
	Total	4.85	4.89	5.15	4.13	4.95	3.23	4.82	4.71

Note: Columns may not agree with totals because of rounding errors.
[a]These migraproduction rates are high relative to those of other Migration and Settlement case studies (cf. Table 7.7 for the UK and Table 7.20 for Canada). This is because the particular regionalization and period used here captures an extremely vigorous urbanization process.

The elements in Table 7.16 represent the number of outmigrations that a person born in region i can expect to make from region j during a lifetime. (In contrast to the GMR discussed in the section on observed population characteristics, the NMR includes the effects of mortality and interregional migration.) The elements of the main diagonal of this table reflect the pattern of interregional migration out of the region of birth. The high interregional outmigration levels in the first row of the table represent the flow from the urban areas of the RSFSR. Of the total 4.85 migrations per person born in the RSFSR, 3.35 originate in this region. The lowest rate represents migration from the urban areas of the Caucasus (region VI).

7.7.4 *Multiregional Population Projection*

The consistent projection of regional population growth is one of the most important contributions of multiregional demographic analysis. In this section, the projection of the 1974 populations of all eight regions is described and extended to the urban—rural dimensions. All age-specific fertility, mortality, and migration rates for this projection were held constant at their 1974 levels.

Table 7.17 presents the aggregate totals of the population projection and the percentage of the total population in the individual regions of the country for the 1984—2024 period. According to this table, the assumption of constant rates of fertility, mortality, and migration implies that the population will increase in all regions except region VIII during the projection period. Contributing to a total increase of 88 246 thousand in the Soviet Union population are a growth in the urban population of 100 830 thousand and a decrease in the rural population of 12 585 thousand.

The largest percentage increase in the population is expected in region IV: during the 1984—2024 period, the Central Asian population is expected to increase almost twofold. The populations in region III and region VII should grow considerably, increasing by 64.8 and 64.6%, respectively. The rural population is expected to decrease by 14.1%.

The regional shares will also change considerably. The share of the national population residing in region I will increase substantially. In 1974 it was 35.2%; by 1984 it will approach 39.5%; and by 2024 it will converge to 44.7%. The share of the population living in region II will grow by 2.0% for 1984—2024 and that living in region IV by 1.8%. The rural population will decrease to about 21.0% of the total.

The mean age of the population will increase along with the growth in size of the older age groups, confirming that the population is aging. Thus, even though the fertility rates are assumed to remain constant, the proportion of the population in the older age groups will change.

By the end of the projection period (1974—2024), along with the increase in the mean age of the country's population (1.94 years), the mean ages in the urban regions will increase, but that of the rural population will decline (from 34.9 to 32.9 years). The populations of the Central Asian and the Caucasian Republics will continue to be the "youngest" in the country. The mean age of the urban population of these regions is projected to lie in the range 28.6—32.5 years. The "oldest" age structure will be found in the urban areas of the Baltic Republics and the RSFSR, with mean ages of 37.0 and 36.6, respectively.

Table 7.17 Multiregional population projection for the Soviet Union with 1974 fertility, mortality, and migration rates.

Region[a]		1984	1994	2004	2014	2024
Population (thousands)						
I	RSFSR	109168.5	126828.8	139760.8	152497.7	162998.4
II	Ukrainian and Moldavian Republics	36683.3	42799.1	47413.8	51989.1	55795.0
III	Byelorussian Republic	6244.8	7656.7	8652.4	9570.2	10294.1
IV	Central Asian Republics	11694.6	14683.8	17218.7	19776.4	22141.8
V	Kazakh Republic	9226.4	10829.3	11968.5	13059.9	13974.4
VI	Caucasian Republics	8309.5	9700.1	10872.2	12125.7	13285.4
VII	Baltic Republics	5680.6	6849.6	7765.5	8633.1	9349.5
VIII	Rural areas of the Soviet Union	89263.7	80281.6	75937.5	75480.3	76678.4
	Total	276271.7	299629.2	319589.5	343132.6	364517.0
Population share (%)						
I	RSFSR	39.51	42.33	43.73	44.44	44.72
II	Ukrainian and Moldavian Republics	13.28	14.28	14.84	15.15	15.31
III	Byelorussian Republic	2.26	2.56	2.71	2.79	2.82
IV	Central Asian Republics	4.23	4.90	5.39	5.76	6.08
V	Kazakh Republic	3.34	3.61	3.74	3.81	3.83
VI	Caucasian Republics	3.01	3.24	3.40	3.53	3.64
VII	Baltic Republics	2.06	2.29	2.43	2.52	2.56
VIII	Rural areas of the Soviet Uniion	32.31	26.79	23.76	22.00	21.04
	Total	100.00	100.00	100.00	100.00	100.00

[a]Only urban areas are included in regions I–VII.

7.8 Conclusion

Migration within a country can have positive or negative effects on its overall economic development. For example, there can be an undesirable redistribution of population from regions of labor shortage to regions of labor surplus, an excessive outward flow of rural population to cities, or an inadequate proportion of migrants moving to regions of new development. Thus the need for a population policy is apparent.

The planned redistribution of labor is a particularly important component of population policy in the Soviet Union, and various regions have addressed the problem differently. The alternative approaches to this problem appear to have been the results of social, economic, practical, and technical decisions made on the basis of a particular region's history of development.

The problem of maintaining a stable labor force in the less developed regions of the country occupies a particular place in the decision making tha The stimulation of the material welfare of the population of the country's less developed regions is principally carried out by means of allocation of incentives, of which there are two kinds. First, there are incentives that release migrants from any expenditures (for example, the abolition of debts, the repeal of obligatory deliveries and agricultural taxes, the reduction of rents on apartments retained in the region of origin by temporary outmigrants, exemption from service in the armed forces or a shortening of the call-up period, and free or low-cost transportation for persons and goods). Second, there are incentives in the form of supplementary incomes and advantages obtained by migrants (for example, wage and salary supplements, additional leave without loss of pay, grants, large traveling expenses, and loans). This system of incentives has the aim of encouraging people to live permanently in less developed regions of the nation.

The policy of incentives for migration and hence population stabilization is carried out in concert with general economic development in the less developed regions. In addition to incentives, moral persuasion plays an important role. The enthusiasm and patriotism of the Soviet people shown in the development of new lands are well known: for example, the Komsomol drives in the 1930s, the development of the northern regions during the war (when all incentives were canceled), and the social directives to youth to work in the new regions today.

The migration flow from the rural to the urban areas poses an important problem concerning labor force redistribution in the country. This problem affects both the economic interests of agriculture, industry, and construction and the broader interest of the population. It is impossible to study the problem of rural-to-urban migration, particularly of the young, without also taking into consideration the existing cultural setting of the Soviet Union. Sociological research carried out in some regions of the country shows that today it is not only the level of wages that is important to young people in rural areas, but also factors such as the availability and type of employment and the amount of leisure time. The growing contradictions between these demands and the facilities that the thousands of small villages are able to offer is the main force behind the migrations of the young to urban areas. According to the data, outmigration is most intensive from rural settlements with less favorable cultural and welfare conditions. In some cases, this migration is so intense that the settlement disappears altogether.

The policy problem, then, is to reorganize the existing system of rural settlements, eliminate the small villages, and encourage migration to regions that will foster acceptable working and living conditions. This rural settlement reconstruction requires long-term planning in which the industrial, housing, cultural, and welfare conditions are made sufficient to accommodate almost the entire rural population, considerably decreasing the number of existing villages.

At the same time, much attention is being given to the problem of educating the village youth for the more sophisticated agricultural production requirements (in particular, to produce young, skilled machine operators and personnel with a higher level of education for the agricultural economy). It is also important to provide the conditions necessary for the residential stability of skilled workers in their villages.

Migration in the Soviet Union, however, is not restricted to rural-to-urban flows. Migration is also dependent to a large extent on general inter-urban population mobility. The share of urban inmigration attributable to migration from other *urban* areas was 60–65% in the 1960s.

The nation's urban migration policy is aimed at restricting the growth of large cities, developing cities of medium size, constructing new regional centers, and distributing these centers uniformly throughout the country. All these measures should equalize urbanization levels and improve the migration situation, whereby the Soviet Union will approach more closely the desired levels of socioeconomic development in urban and rural areas throughout the country.

7.III Canada

Marc Termote

In a society like Canada, where the rate of natural increase is dropping markedly, one may expect that the contribution of migration to the growth and spatial redistribution of the population will increase. The problem is that migration, among all demographic phenomena, is the one that shows the largest variability over time.

Canada has recently been experiencing noticeable changes in migration patterns. Along with a considerable drop in fertility in all provinces, a remarkable reversal in interprovincial migration flows occurred between the 1960s and the 1970s, which favored those provinces that for decades had been losing population because of migration. Thus a multiregional analysis, measuring the amplitude and impact of these important changes in demographic behavior, is of interest here. To what extent are the results and conclusions obtained from a previous study (Termote 1980), based on 1966–1971 data affected by these changes?

To answer this question we begin with a brief presentation of the data, a description of the 1971–1976 pattern of spatial population growth, and a comparison of this with the pattern observed in 1966–1971. Section 7.10 is devoted to the multiregional life table and to spatial life and reproduction expectancies, as they change from one period to the next. Finally, we examine the results of the population projections and the stable population equivalent.

7.9 Comparing the 1966–1971 and 1971–1976 Regional Growth Patterns

Almost all basic data used in this brief report are of the same kind as those used in our previous Migration and Settlement case study (Termote 1980). Recall that the spatial units are the 10 provinces (because of small numbers and data unreliability, the Yukon and Northwest Territories are not included); that the choice of the period is determined by the date of the census, the only age/sex-disaggregated migration data available being those obtained from the census question on the individual's place of residence five years earlier; that the number of births and deaths are obtained from the vital registers; and that the provincial population data (by age and sex) used for obtaining the rates and probabilities are derived from the 1966, 1971, and 1976 censuses.

There are, however, a few minor differences in the sources and the quality of the data used for each of the two periods. The rates of under-registration (underenumeration), and of incomplete registration (enumeration), of births, deaths, and migration are not exactly the same over time. Moreover, for migration in 1971–1976 we had to disaggregate some large age groups (5–14, 35–44, 45–64, and 65 and over) into five-year age groups, whereas in 1966–1971 only the 65-and-over group had to be disaggregated. The migration data for the 0–4 age group had to be estimated for 1971–1976, while data were directly available (from birth–residence data) for 1966–1971. Finally, the rate of underenumeration of the census populations did slightly vary from one census to another. These differences led, of course, to rates that were not strictly comparable over time, but their impact appears to be so small that they do not significantly affect our comparisons. (Some of these temporal differences may actually be canceled out.)

By looking at the relative importance of each component of growth in each province, one may obtain a first indication of the main changes in the regional growth pattern. The values presented in Table 7.18 clearly show that the new regional pattern is characterized by an important decline in the "demographic power" of the two central provinces (Quebec and Ontario), which until the 1960s occupied most of Canada's demographic picture. Today, both provinces represent only 54% of Canada's total increase (down from 64% in the previous five-year period), this reversal being obviously in favor of the four eastern (Atlantic) provinces and of the four western provinces. The difference between Quebec and Ontario, in this respect, is that Ontario's decline is quite recent, while Quebec's decline is mainly the continuation of a long-term process.

In 1966–1971, natural growth was the only source of growth in each of the four Atlantic provinces (except for Nova Scotia, which benefited from international migration as well), but in 1971–1976, three of these provinces also had a positive net interprovincial migration. (Only Newfoundland was still losing population because of interprovincial migration, but by a relatively small amount.) In 1966–1971, Manitoba and Saskatchewan were in a situation close to the one observed in the Atlantic provinces during that period, and still in 1971–1976 natural growth remained their main source of growth. It should nevertheless be mentioned that Saskatchewan's negative interprovincial migration balance was reduced by 60%, resulting in a decline in total population that is now very small.

Quebec experienced a sizable decrease in total growth, mainly because of a sharp drop in its natural increase (more than 20% over five years). In contrast to Quebec, Ontario's decline in total growth was the result not so much of

Table 7.18 Components of Canadian multiregional demographic growth: 1966–1971 and 1971–1976.

Province	Total increase		Natural growth	
	1966–1971	1971–1976	1966–1971	1971–1976
Newfoundland	28708	35621	49096	43386
Prince Edward Island	3106	6588	5211	4509
Nova Scotia	32921	39611	37411	32141
New Brunswick	17769	42692	35233	32909
Quebec	246919	206681	288727	229321
Ontario	742236	561359	373072	325549
Manitoba	25181	33259	49259	44866
Saskatchewan	−29102	−4919	50868	38156
Alberta	164671	210163	105295	95851
British Columbia	310947	281987	88494	82830
Total	1543356	1413042	1082666	929518

Province	Net interprovincial migration		Net international migration	
	1966–1971	1971–1976	1966–1971	1971–1976
Newfoundland	−17589	−6745	−2799	−1020
Prince Edward Island	−1114	2675	−991	−596
Nova Scotia	−8745	6688	4255	782
New Brunswick	−8804	11628	−8660	−1845
Quebec	−78144	−62221	36336	39581
Ontario	60792	−63498	308372	299308
Manitoba	−34240	−28592	10162	16985
Saskatchewan	−78369	−32323	−1601	−10752
Alberta	27453	67651	31923	46661
British Columbia	138760	104737	83693	94420
Total	−	−	460690	483524

its decreasing natural growth as of the complete reversal of its interprovincial migration balance (from a gain of 61000 in 1966–1971 to a loss of 63000 in 1971–1976). Finally, if we exclude Nova Scotia (which had a negligible gain from international migration), there are only two provinces that benefited from all three sources of growth – Alberta and British Columbia – but the former experienced a doubling in its gain from interprovincial migration, while British Columbia suffered a sharp decline in these gains. Demographic growth in these two provinces was mainly a result of migration (which represented 54 and 71%, respectively, of total growth), with interprovincial migration accounting for a little more than half of these gains from migration.

The main conclusion to be drawn from these changes is that interprovincial migration is now more balanced; there are now equal numbers of losers and gainers, with losers losing less and gainers gaining less.

Of course, these changes in net migration do not tell much about modifications in migration behavior. Let us look at Table 7.19, which presents the total (crude) migration rates between provinces. This table shows how much the annual *propensity* to outmigrate may vary from one province to another. The range goes from 5.4 per thousand (Quebec) to 21.6 per thousand (Saskatchewan). Compared with 1966–1971, this range has been reduced significantly. In the previous period, the lowest rate was 6.3 per thousand (Quebec) and the highest 28.1 per thousand (Saskatchewan).

It should be recalled that these rates refer to five-year (census) migrants, thus excluding multiple migration as well as emigration and mortality among migrants. From what is known about the ratio between migrations and migrants over a five-year period in Canada, these rates should be multiplied by about two in order to obtain an estimate of the annual rate of outmigration.

Just as for the 1966–1971 period, we may distinguish three groups of regions for the 1971–1976 period. A first group contains those provinces that had a rate of outmigration below the average (9.9 per thousand); there are now only two provinces in this group — Quebec and Ontario — and no longer British Columbia. A second group contains those provinces that had middle-range outmigration rates (British Columbia, Newfoundland, New Brunswick, Nova Scotia, and Alberta). Finally, three provinces had relatively high rates, as they did in the 1966–1971 period: Prince Edward Island, Manitoba, and Saskatchewan.

Only two provinces experienced an increase in their annual outmigration rate between the two periods: Ontario (from 6.6 to 8.0 per thousand) and British Columbia (from 8.9 to 10.5 per thousand). All eight remaining provinces showed a decline in the overall propensity of their population to outmigrate. This decline was particularly important in the case of Saskatchewan (from 28.1 to 21.6 per thousand) and New Brunswick (from 18.5 to 14.2 per thousand). The more balanced pattern of interprovincial migration mentioned before was thus accompanied by a generally lower propensity to migrate. But on the whole, the overall rate of interprovincial migration dropped only slightly, from 10.3 to 9.9 per thousand.

To interpret the reversal in the interprovincial migration pattern observed between 1966–1971 and 1971–1976, it is worth investigating whether the change in the propensity to outmigrate from a specific province is caused by a modification of a few particular flows, or whether it is a general phenomenon, that is, experienced with respect to most of the regions of destination.

Ontario underwent an increase in its outmigration rates to all provinces of destination (except Quebec, for which the rate remained stable); the increase was particularly marked for Alberta. But all provinces of origin also had a lower rate of outmigration to Ontario. This decline was particularly important in the case of the four Atlantic provinces (whose rates dropped by half, from 8–9 to 4–5 per thousand). Ontario thus showed simultaneously a lower capacity to attract people from all over the Canadian territory and a

Table 7.19 Crude migration rates (per thousand) between Canadian provinces, 1971–1976.

Province of origin	Province of destination										Total, 1971–1976	Total, 1966–1971
	I	II	III	IV	V	VI	VII	VIII	IX	X		
I Newfoundland	–	0.2	2.1	1.1	1.0	5.5	0.7	0.2	0.7	0.9	12.2	14.8
II Prince Edward Island	0.8	–	5.1	3.3	0.7	5.2	0.8	0.3	2.2	1.4	19.7	22.2
III Nova Scotia	1.0	0.7	–	2.9	1.2	5.5	0.6	0.3	1.5	1.7	15.2	18.1
IV New Brunswick	0.5	0.7	3.1	–	2.6	4.3	0.5	0.3	1.1	1.2	14.2	18.5
V Quebec	0.1	0.0	0.3	0.4	–	3.4	0.2	0.1	0.4	0.6	5.4	6.3
VI Ontario	0.4	0.2	0.8	0.6	1.8	–	0.7	0.3	1.4	1.8	8.0	6.6
VII Manitoba	0.1	0.1	0.5	0.3	0.7	5.1	–	3.4	5.3	4.8	20.3	22.4
VIII Saskatchewan	0.0	0.0	0.2	0.2	0.3	2.2	2.9	–	10.1	5.7	21.6	28.1
IX Alberta	0.1	0.1	0.4	0.2	0.5	2.5	1.1	2.4	–	8.6	15.8	16.8
X British Columbia	0.1	0.0	0.4	0.2	0.5	2.5	0.9	1.0	4.9	–	10.5	8.9

Note: Migration rates are obtained by dividing one-fifth of the number of 1971–1976 migrants enumerated at the 1976 census by the arithmetic mean of the population enumerated in 1971 and 1976 in the province of origin. Because of rounding, the total outmigration rate does not necessarily equal the sum of the destination-specific rates.

Table 7.20 Gross migraproduction rates between Canadian provinces, 1971–1976.

Province of origin	Region of destination										Total, 1971–1976	Total, 1966–1971
	I	II	III	IV	V	VI	VII	VIII	IX	X		
I Newfoundland	–	0.01	0.15	0.07	0.07	0.38	0.04	0.01	0.05	0.07	0.84	1.03
II Prince Edward Island	0.05	–	0.38	0.23	0.06	0.37	0.05	0.02	0.14	0.10	1.42	1.61
III Nova Scotia	0.07	0.05	–	0.20	0.09	0.39	0.04	0.02	0.10	0.12	1.07	1.28
IV New Brunswick	0.04	0.05	0.22	–	0.18	0.30	0.03	0.02	0.07	0.08	1.00	1.33
V Quebec	0.01	0.00	0.02	0.03	–	0.27	0.01	0.00	0.03	0.05	0.43	0.49
VI Ontario	0.03	0.01	0.06	0.04	0.14	–	0.05	0.02	0.09	0.14	0.58	0.48
VII Manitoba	0.01	0.01	0.03	0.02	0.06	0.46	–	0.24	0.37	0.39	1.59	1.70
VIII Saskatchewan	0.00	0.00	0.01	0.01	0.02	0.16	0.22	–	0.73	0.48	1.65	2.14
IX Alberta	0.01	0.00	0.02	0.02	0.03	0.17	0.08	0.16	–	0.70	1.20	1.33
X British Columbia	0.00	0.00	0.03	0.01	0.04	0.18	0.07	0.08	0.36	–	0.77	0.66

lower capacity to retain its own people. Considering the demographic weight of this province, and its central location within Canada, one may conclude that Ontario has played a crucial role in the reversal of the Canadian internal migration pattern. It should, however, be mentioned that Alberta too has played a role in this reversal. Indeed, people of all provinces (except Saskatchewan) showed a higher propensity to migrate to Alberta – a result of the energy crisis, which gave this oil- and gas-rich province a privileged position within the Canadian economic system.

A useful way to summarize the present level of migration is to calculate the gross migraproduction rate (GMR), by summing the age-specific migration rates and multiplying by five, the length of the age interval. Table 7.20 presents these rates for each migration flow and for the total outmigration of each province.

The results clearly show that despite the reversal in the traditional migration pattern and despite the increasing propensity of Ontario's population to outmigrate, by 1976 this province still occupied a dominant position in the interprovincial migration system. Its GMR to each province of destination was always much lower than that of the corresponding counterflow. And despite the remarkable decline in the propensity to outmigrate from the four Atlantic provinces, these provinces still had in most cases (for Prince Edward Island in each case) destination-specific GMRs that were larger than those of the corresponding counterflows.

The GMRs produced in Table 7.20 also demonstrate the high geographical mobility of the Canadian population, notwithstanding the considerable distances separating the provinces. Even in 1971–1976, which was a period of low mobility (all GMRs declined except those of Ontario and British Columbia), the Canadian GMRs were still much larger than those observed in other countries. For instance, the lowest Canadian GMR (0.43 in Quebec) was of the same magnitude as the highest CMRs observed in Bulgaria, even though the interregional distances in Canada are much larger.

This high geographical mobility of the Canadian population is thus a characteristic of most provinces. In 6 of the 10 provinces, the "average" individual born in 1971–1976 is expected to make at least one migration out of his or her province during a lifetime. But only a few provinces will receive these expected migrants. If we take 0.25 as a threshold (i.e., we need four individuals to get one "expected" migrant), then almost nobody is expected to outmigrate from any of the 10 provinces to Newfoundland, Prince Edward Island, New Brunswick, Quebec, Manitoba, and Saskatchewan. At the other extreme, Ontario is quite attractive for individuals leaving each of the five provinces east of it, plus contiguous Manitoba.

Each of the four Atlantic provinces shows a higher migraproduction rate with respect to Ontario than to Quebec, which is closer. Even with respect to British Columbia the rate of these four provinces is significantly larger. This shows that, at least in Canada, physical distance does not play a dominant role in migration behavior. Once the decision has been made to move over a long distance, the distance itself is of little importance. Cultural distances, however, may affect the choice of the province of destination; migrants from the English-speaking Atlantic provinces tend to bypass the predominantly French-speaking Quebec.

The age—sex profile of Canada's interprovincial migration flows did not significantly change between the two periods. Since this profile is similar to the one generally observed in other countries, we do not discuss it here.

Before concluding this section, we briefly discuss regional fertility and mortality differentials. Between 1966–1971 and 1971–1976, fertility rates declined in all provinces and for all age groups (except in three provinces for the 15–19 age group, for which the numbers involved were small). The Canadian population does not reproduce itself any more, and only three provinces still have a gross reproduction rate (GRR) that implies a self-reproducing population: Newfoundland, Prince Edward Island, and Saskatchewan. If we had considered end-of-period data, only Newfoundland would have shown a gross reproduction rate significantly above replacement level. Fertility conditions are now much more homogeneous between provinces, but this is mainly because Newfoundland experienced an above-average decline in fertility (its GRR dropped from 1.9 to 1.4 in five years). Quebec still has the lowest fertility level (with a GRR of 0.87). On the whole, there is some room for a decline in fertility; if, for each age group, each province adopted the lowest existing provincial fertility rate, Canada's GRR would be 0.8 instead of 1.0.

Finally, as far as regional mortality differentials are concerned, not much has changed. Quebec is still the province where life expectancy is the lowest, for males as well as for females, and the Prairie provinces (Manitoba, Saskatchewan, and Alberta) have the highest. Actually, gains to male life expectancy by 1976 were marginal in most provinces (except in Ontario, which gained 7/10 of a year), while female life expectancy showed a significant increase (about one year in each province). Most provinces experienced a significant increase in the mortality rate for young (15–24) males and for males aged 70–74, but mortality among children of both sexes in the 0–4 age group decreased markedly in all provinces. Regional disparities may not appear important if we consider only life expectancy at birth. (The range was 68.6–71.0 for males and 76.1–78.3 for females.) But if we measure these disparities by computing the percentage of excess (or missing) deaths because of the region's level (and age profile) of death rates being different from the national standard, then we observe that Quebec had a 10% over-mortality (i.e. where "excess" deaths represent 10% of deaths registered in this province), while in Saskatchewan there were 9% "missing" deaths. (Similar figures were obtained for both periods.) The range, therefore, is far from negligible.

7.10 Analyzing Changes in Demographic Behavior Through Multi-regional Analysis

The main feature of a multiregional demographic model is that it allows us to take into account simultaneously all interdependencies between the three basic demographic phenomena (fertility, migration, and mortality) and between all regions. In other words, the multiregional model allows us to summarize the impact of a change in demographic behavior across the multiregional demographic system.

Let us first consider the relation between migration and life expectancy. We begin by analyzing the probabilities of surviving (to some exact age) in the region of birth. That is, we summarize in one figure the propensities to outmigrate and survive, as they are observed for a given period (e.g. 1966–1971 or 1971–1976). Table 7.21 gives these combined probabilities for each of the 10 provinces by sex. In this table we show the probabilities that an individual born in a particular province will still be there at the exact ages 20, 35, and 65. These ages were chosen to represent the three most significant stages in a working lifetime: entry into the labor market, midterm job mobility, and retirement. Thus it is possible to see, for example, whether a boy born in a given province is likely to spend most of his working life in the province of his birth.

The data reproduced in Table 7.21 show that, despite the important reversal in Canada's interprovincial migration flows, not much has changed between 1966–1971 and 1971–1976 as far as the capacity of each province to retain its own natives is concerned. Some provinces (Saskatchewan, Manitoba, and Prince Edward Island) will have lost from 33 to 40% of their potential labor force before this potential reaches working age. Things become even worse for these provinces when these cohorts go through the 20–35 age span; between one-third and one-half of those who remain until the age of 20 will leave before reaching 35. And finally, only about 20% of those born in these provinces will still be there at the age of 65. At the other extreme, Quebec, Ontario, and British Columbia are able to retain about 50% of their natives until age 65.

The next step is to consider the impact of migration on life expectancies, or more precisely, to disaggregate these expectancies by province of residence while assuming that inmigrants are exposed to the probabilities of dying and outmigrating that exist in the region of inmigration. Table 7.22 shows the evolution, between 1966–1971 and 1971–1976, of life expectancies at birth with and without migration and presents the percentage of total life expectancy spent in the province of birth.

As expected, the range of life expectancies is narrower with migration than without. The difference between the extreme values is 1.3 (for males as well as females) in the first case and about 2.3 in the second case. On the whole, however, taking migration into account only slightly affects life expectancies, except for provinces with high life expectancy and heavy

Table 7.21 Probabilities (%) of surviving at the exact ages 20, 35, and 65 in the Canadian province of birth: 1966–1971[a] and 1971–1976.

Province of birth	At age 20		At age 35		At age 65	
	Males	Females	Males	Females	Males	Females
Newfoundland	77	78	55	56	34	40
	(74)	(75)	(46)	(49)	(27)	(33)
Prince Edward Island	65	65	35	35	19	23
	(61)	(63)	(29)	(31)	(15)	(19)
Nova Scotia	70	70	46	18	26	33
	(67)	(66)	(40)	(40)	(22)	(26)
New Brunswick	72	73	49	50	29	35
	(67)	(67)	(39)	(40)	(21)	(26)
Quebec	86	87	75	77	49	59
	(85)	(86)	(73)	(75)	(46)	(56)
Ontario	81	82	67	69	45	54
	(84)	(85)	(72)	(75)	(48)	(59)
Manitoba	62	63	38	40	20	25
	(60)	(60)	(35)	(36)	(18)	(21)
Saskatchewan	62	61	36	34	20	22
	(55)	(54)	(24)	(24)	(13)	(15)
Alberta	69	71	53	54	31	36
	(69)	(70)	(50)	(51)	(28)	(33)
British Columbia	75	77	60	63	41	50
	(80)	(81)	(64)	(66)	(44)	(53)

[a]Values in parentheses refer to the 1966–1971 period.

outmigration. (For instance, in Saskatchewan male life expectancy drops by almost one year when migration is taken into consideration.) For most provinces, gains in male life expectancy between 1966–1971 and 1971–1976 were much higher when migration was accounted for than when no migration was considered. The reverse is true for female life expectancy.

The total number of years that a newborn baby may expect to live in his or her province of birth varies considerably. A boy born in 1971–1976 in Prince Edward Island or Saskatchewan may expect to live only 33 years in his province of birth, whereas a boy born in Quebec may expect to live 56 years in Quebec. For females the corresponding figures are 34 and 61 years. Actually, migration propensities observed in 1971–1976 imply that the average individual born in seven of the 10 provinces will spend more than one-third of his or her life outside the province of birth. When 1966–1971 propensities are considered, the percentage of life expectancy spent in the province of birth is in most cases even lower. But the most (less) "absorbing" provinces in 1971–1976 were also the most (less) absorbing ones in the previous period. Again, the reversal in migration flows does not significantly affect the hierarchy of the provinces in their capacity for retaining their natives.

Although the values for each province of residence by province of birth are not reproduced here, it is worth noting that, based on the 1971–1976 data,

Table 7.22 Life expectancies at birth in Canada, with and without migration: 1966–1971 and 1971–1976.

Province of birth	With migration (multiregional)		Without migration (uniregional)		Percentage spent in province of birth	
	1966–1971	1971–1976	1966–1971	1971–1976	1966–1971	1971–1976
(a) *Males*						
Newfoundland	69.1	69.8	69.5	69.9	58	64
Prince Edward Island	68.8	69.3	69.1	69.3	44	48
Nova Scotia	68.9	69.5	68.6	68.9	52	56
New Brunswick	69.0	69.4	69.1	69.3	51	59
Quebec	68.7	69.0	68.4	68.6	79	81
Ontario	69.5	70.1	69.3	70.0	79	74
Manitoba	69.7	70.2	70.1	70.3	46	48
Saskatchewan	69.7	70.2	70.8	71.0	38	47
Alberta	70.0	70.3	70.7	70.7	58	60
British Columbia	69.7	69.9	69.7	70.0	73	69
(b) *Females*						
Newfoundland	75.7	76.8	75.3	76.5	57	64
Prince Edward Island	76.2	77.1	76.5	77.7	42	48
Nova Scotia	76.1	77.0	75.7	76.9	49	56
New Brunswick	75.9	77.0	75.8	76.9	49	59
Quebec	75.4	76.4	75.0	76.1	79	81
Ontario	76.4	77.3	76.4	77.3	79	74
Manitoba	76.6	77.4	76.8	77.5	44	48
Saskatchewan	76.6	77.6	77.5	78.3	36	47
Alberta	76.8	77.7	77.2	78.0	57	60
British Columbia	76.7	77.5	76.8	77.6	73	69

a baby born in one of the four Atlantic provinces or in Manitoba may expect to spend about 10 years in Ontario. And a baby born in another Canadian province outside Ontario may expect to live no less than six years in the latter province. The socioeconomic and demographic consequences of such a phenomenon obviously are considerable. When 1966–1971 migration propensities are taken into account, the number of years a person born in the Atlantic provinces is likely to live in Ontario is between 15 and 19, instead of the 10 years based on the 1971–1976 data. Life expectancy by region of residence thus captures the important decline in Ontario's attractivity, and more generally (as may be seen from the last two columns of Table 7.22) the variation in the capacity of a region to retain its natives.

Now let us turn to the indirect impact of migration – the relation between migration and reproduction. The ages of highest mobility also are the ages of highest fertility. The question we now ask is: To what extent did the changes in migration behavior, combined with the drop in fertility (and mortality), affect the reproduction rate of each province? Table 7.23 presents for 1966–1971 and 1971–1976 the net reproduction rates for each province of birth (of the parents), and compares the rates obtained when migration is accounted for with the traditional single-region rates as well as the percentage of births expected in the province of birth of the parents.

Table 7.23 Net reproduction rates in Canada, with and without migration: 1966–1971 and 1971–1976.

Province	Net reproduction rate					
	With migration (multiregional)		Without migration (uniregional)		In province of birth of parents	
	1966–1971	1971–1976	1966–1971	1971–1976	1966–1971	1971–1976
Newfoundland	1.5	1.2	1.8	1.4	1.1	0.9
Prince Edward Island	1.3	1.0	1.4	1.1	0.6	0.6
Nova Scotia	1.2	1.0	1.3	1.0	0.7	0.6
New Brunswick	1.3	1.0	1.3	1.1	0.7	0.7
Quebec	1.1	0.8	1.1	0.8	0.9	0.7
Ontario	1.2	0.9	1.2	0.9	1.0	0.7
Manitoba	1.2	1.0	1.3	1.1	0.6	0.6
Saskatchewan	1.3	1.0	1.4	1.1	0.6	0.6
Alberta	1.3	1.0	1.3	1.0	0.8	0.7
British Columbia	1.2	0.9	1.1	0.9	0.9	0.7

Again, as for life expectancies, migration reduces the range of net reproduction rates (NRRs). In the case of Canada, this is true mainly because of Newfoundland, which, being a region of high fertility, experiences a significant drop in its NRR when migration is taken into account. For all other provinces, however, the difference between the multiregional and the single-region NRRs is marginal. But the capacity for a region to reproduce itself with its own (native) population is markedly affected. Indeed, for some provinces, an important percentage of the expected births will actually take place outside the province of birth of the parents because of migration.

Once migration is taken into account, there is not a single Canadian provincial population that is able, according to the demographic behavior observed in 1971–1976, to reproduce itself with only the fertility of its own native population (last column of Table 7.23). The most striking situations are, of course, to be found in the four Atlantic provinces and in Manitoba and Saskatchewan, that is, in provinces of (relatively) high fertility and high mobility. In Newfoundland, the NRR without migration is 1.4; with migration, it drops to 1.2 but its local NRR (i.e., the rate of reproduction of its natives) is only 0.9. In the case of the five other provinces just mentioned, the NRR drops from 1.0–1.1 without migration to 0.6–0.7 (local NRR). Of course, when the 1966–1971 demographic behavior is considered, the impact of migration is even higher, because the previous period is characterized by higher fertility and mobility levels. The decline in the local NRR is particularly impressive in the case of Ontario and British Columbia, which combined a declining fertility with an increasing propensity to outmigrate. In the other provinces, the local NRRs dropped only slightly, because a lower propensity to outmigrate from these regions partly neutralized the decline in the fertility level.

The values in Table 7.23 also show that, whereas Quebec and Ontario may count on retaining about 80% of the births expected from the cohorts born in these provinces in 1966–1976, some other provinces, like Prince Edward Island, Saskatchewan, and Manitoba may count on keeping only about half of them. Of course, if there are "missing" births in some provinces, there also will be "imported" births in others. Data not shown here demonstrate that imported births may represent as much as 40–50% of total expected births in provinces like Ontario, Alberta, and British Columbia, but less than 10% in Newfoundland and Prince Edward Island. Again, despite the important changes in migration behavior between the 1960s and 1970s, the provincial hierarchy in terms of ability to retain expected births and of dependency upon imported births has not been noticeably modified.

7.11 Confronting Population Projections and Stability

The multiregional demographic growth model is, as such, not a forecasting model. It is interesting, however, to extrapolate the present demographic behavior of a population in order to look for medium- and long-term implications. Table 7.24 presents the following characteristics of the projected population: total population in absolute numbers and provincial distribution, rate of growth, mean age, percentage under 20 years of age, and percentage aged 65 years and over.

In interpreting the figures reproduced in Table 7.24, we emphasize that they should by no means be considered a forecast of the future evolution of the population of Canada and its provinces. On the other hand, we may compare our projections for 1981 with the results of the 1981 census. In making such a comparison, one should bear in mind that our projections do not take international migration into account. When due consideration is given to this form of migration, it appears that our projections based on the 1966–1971 demographic behavior have significantly overestimated the growth rate of the Canadian population in the 1970s. If we add to the projected total population (24 108 000) estimates of net international migration based on the data presented in Table 7.18, the total is well above the observed 24 274 000 figure. This overprojection is mainly a result of the important drop in fertility during the 1970s. Since this decline in fertility was much more pronounced in the first half of the decade, a projection based on the 1971–1976 observed demographic behavior gives a total 1981 population close to the observed one. By adding to the projected 23 749 000 figure, half (because the projection starts with the population at midperiod) of the 1971–1976 net international migration figure (Table 7.18), and the 1976–1981 figure estimated by Statistics Canada (300 000), one obtains a total of 24 291 000, only 17 000 (0.07%) above the observed figure. At the provincial level, a comparison between the results of the second projection (based on 1971–1976) and the enumerated 1981 population shows that indeed the provinces for which there was underprojection (Ontario, Alberta, and British Columbia) are those that usually benefit the most from international migration.

On the whole, the provincial shares projected from the 1971–1976 behavior are close to those observed in 1981. There are only two exceptions. In Quebec, losses from interprovincial migration were much greater in 1976–1981 than could be anticipated from the 1971–1976 behavior, so that the observed share is markedly below the projected one. The reverse is true for Alberta. If the multiregional behavior observed in 1971–1976 were to remain constant during the last quarter of the century, the latter province would contain about 10% of Canada's population in 2001 (up from 7.5% in 1966–1976), while British Columbia would contain close to 13%. Simultaneously, Quebec would continue its decline, from 28.4% in 1966–1971 to about 25% in 2001, and Ontario would experience a slight decline in its share, which, however, is underprojected here because of the exclusion of international migration.

It is obvious, from the values of Table 7.24, that projecting growth rates is much more difficult than projecting the evolution of total populations. For all provinces, there are important differences in the rate of growth observed between 1976 and 1981 and the projected rates. Even the projections based on the most recent period (1971–1976) produced growth rates far from reality. Mainly because of the persistent decline in fertility, the growth rate in each

Table 7.24 The observed, projected[a], and stable[a] equivalents of Canadian provincial populations.

Characteristic		Province[b]										Total
		NFD	PEI	NS	NB	QUE	ONT	MAN	SAS	ALB	BC	
Share (%) (total in thousands)	Obs. 1966–1971	2.5	0.5	3.8	3.0	28.4	35.3	4.7	4.6	7.5	9.7	20743
	Obs. 1971–1976	2.4	0.5	3.7	2.9	27.5	35.9	4.6	4.2	7.8	10.5	22222
	Obs. 1981	2.4	0.5	3.5	2.9	26.5	35.5	4.2	4.0	9.2	11.3	24274
	Proj. 1981 (I)	2.5	0.5	3.6	3.0	27.2	35.9	4.3	3.7	8.1	11.2	24018
	Proj. 1981 (II)	2.5	0.5	3.7	3.0	27.0	35.4	4.3	4.0	8.4	11.1	23749
	Proj. 2001 (I)	2.7	0.5	3.5	2.9	25.0	36.6	3.9	2.8	8.9	13.2	29508
	Proj. 2001 (II)	2.9	0.6	3.8	3.4	25.2	33.9	4.0	3.7	9.9	12.6	27016
	Stable (I)	4.7	0.5	3.5	2.7	12.1	37.7	3.5	2.2	12.0	21.1	20986
	Stable (II)	9.3	0.8	5.2	4.8	10.7	27.2	4.2	4.2	15.1	18.5	20221
Growth rate (over five years) (%)	Obs. 1981	1.8	3.6	2.3	2.8	3.3	4.4	0.5	5.1	21.8	11.3	5.9
	Proj. 1981 (I)	7.5	5.1	5.1	5.5	4.3	6.8	2.7	-2.0	9.6	11.8	6.3
	Proj. 1981 (II)	7.5	7.0	5.4	7.5	2.9	3.4	1.9	1.4	10.1	8.6	4.5
	Proj. 2001 (I)	6.1	4.6	4.1	4.3	2.1	5.1	2.2	-1.2	6.6	8.4	4.5
	Proj. 2001 (II)	5.2	4.8	3.4	4.5	0.2	1.1	0.8	0.8	5.6	5.2	2.1
	Stable (I)	3.8	3.8	3.8	3.8	3.8	3.8	3.8	3.8	3.8	3.8	3.8
	Stable (II)	-0.0	-0.0	-0.0	-0.0	-0.0	-0.0	-0.0	-0.0	-0.0	-0.0	-0.0
Mean age	Obs. 1981	29.6	33.4	33.3	32.4	33.0	33.9	34.1	33.5	30.6	34.2	33.2
	Proj. 1981 (I)	27.3	31.6	31.6	30.6	31.8	32.3	32.5	33.1	30.1	32.9	31.9
	Proj. 1981 (II)	28.4	32.4	32.5	31.4	32.8	33.5	33.3	33.4	31.1	34.0	32.9
	Proj. 2001 (I)	28.1	32.2	32.7	31.9	34.6	33.8	33.2	34.0	31.5	34.4	33.6
	Proj. 2001 (II)	30.6	34.4	35.0	33.9	37.0	37.1	35.3	34.9	34.1	37.4	36.3
	Stable (I)	29.1	33.6	33.9	33.3	35.5	35.0	33.8	33.7	33.2	36.4	34.7
	Stable (II)	33.9	38.3	38.3	37.6	40.0	39.8	37.5	37.3	38.3	41.7	39.0

Characteristic		Province										Total
		NFD	PEI	NS	NB	QUE	ONT	MAN	SAS	ALB	BC	
Percentage under 20 years	Obs. 1981	40.6	35.4	33.5	35.3	31.3	31.3	32.6	34.4	33.8	30.2	32.0
	Proj. 1981 (I)	45.7	38.8	37.0	38.8	33.9	34.5	35.6	36.9	37.9	33.7	35.2
	Proj. 1981 (II)	42.5	36.6	34.7	36.6	31.7	31.9	33.7	35.0	34.9	31.0	32.7
	Proj. 2001 (I)	45.2	38.2	35.8	37.4	31.4	33.2	35.2	36.7	36.7	32.3	33.7
	Proj. 2001 (II)	39.0	33.1	30.9	32.8	26.7	27.6	31.0	32.8	30.9	26.8	28.6
	Stable (I)	43.9	36.6	34.5	35.9	30.6	32.0	34.3	36.5	35.1	30.5	32.8
	Stable (II)	35.4	29.3	27.7	29.1	24.3	25.2	28.8	30.3	27.1	23.2	26.7
Percentage older than 65 years	Obs. 1981	7.7	12.2	10.9	10.1	8.8	10.1	11.9	12.0	7.3	10.9	9.7
	Proj. 1981 (I)	7.0	11.3	10.0	9.3	8.2	9.2	10.9	12.3	7.7	10.2	9.1
	Proj. 1981 (II)	7.1	11.3	10.3	9.5	8.8	9.9	11.0	12.0	7.9	10.8	9.5
	Proj. 2001 (I)	7.2	10.5	10.0	9.5	10.2	10.4	11.0	13.8	8.4	11.1	10.3
	Proj. 2001 (II)	7.5	10.9	10.6	9.8	11.5	12.7	11.8	12.7	9.2	12.7	11.7
	Stable (I)	8.7	12.7	11.9	11.6	12.3	12.3	11.8	12.9	11.0	14.4	12.4
	Stable (II)	12.6	17.3	16.3	15.8	17.0	17.5	15.6	16.1	16.0	20.3	17.0

[a] I represents projections and stable equivalents based on the 1966–1971 period II, the 1971–1976 period.
[b] NFD, Newfoundland; PEI, Prince Edward Island; NS, Nova Scotia; NB, New Brunswick; QUE, Quebec; ONT, Ontario; MAN, Manitoba; SAS, Saskatchewan; ALB, Alberta; BC, British Columbia.

of the Atlantic provinces has been widely overprojected (with rates two to four times larger than the observed ones). On the other side of the continent, the three most western provinces had observed rates significantly larger than the projected ones. The difference is particularly important for Saskatchewan and Alberta, mainly because of the considerable increase in the migration attractivity of these provinces. If the demographic behavior observed in 1971–1976 were to continue during the next decades, then four provinces would experience a roughly zero population growth by 2001, with Quebec growing at only about 0.04% per year.

It is no surprise that, whatever projection is considered, the population of Canada and of each of its provinces will be aging. But, mainly because of the unanticipated continuation of the decline in fertility, these projected rates of aging are lower than those observed in each province: the population of Canada and its provinces aged much faster in 1976–1981 than could be projected on the basis of the 1971–1976 behavior. This is true for the mean age as well as the percentages accounted for by the 0–19 and 65-and-over age groups. But differences between observed and projected figures are particularly obvious when the share of the 0–19 age group is considered. This is quite normal because the unexpected drop in fertility does not (in the short run) so much affect the share of the older population as it does the share of the younger age groups.

In some provinces, the aging of the population will be particularly rapid. If the 1971–1976 behavior remains constant over the next decades, in 2001 Quebec will have only about 27% of its population in the 0–19 age group (down from 42% in 1966–1971) and 12% in the 65-and-over group (up from 6.5%). The four Atlantic provinces, plus Manitoba and Saskatchewan, would age at a much lower rate than the other provinces. Alberta shows a particular pattern. The share of the 0–19 age group in this province is projected to drop by about 4 percentage points (similar to the national average), but the share of its 65-and-over age group, as well as the mean age, is projected to increase only slightly. (Actually, the 65-and-over share and the mean age observed in 1981 are lower than the projected figures.) Such an evolution is obviously related to the age selectivity of migration, which showed its impact in the share of the older population and on the mean age, while the impact of the drop in fertility was more pronounced in the share of the younger age groups. On the basis of the 1971–1976 behavior, one could expect that the provinces of Quebec, Ontario, and British Columbia would have the oldest populations at the end of this century, with Newfoundland having – by far – the youngest one.

Finally, let us consider the stable population values. One way to interpret these figures is to see them as a measure of demographic "speed". Stable population characteristics are a way of summarizing the demographic behavior of a population during a given period. If, for instance, the stable share for a given province (as obtained from the 1971–1976 fertility, migration, and mortality rates) is smaller than the share observed during this period, its demographic speed, as compared with the other provinces, is decreasing.

Before we analyze the provincial figures, however, a few comments on the national results are in order. The stable equivalent of the 1971–1976 Canadian population is 20.2 million, instead of the 22.2 million observed during the same period. On the basis of the 1966–1971 behavior, the total stable equivalent population was 21 million. We may conclude that for the whole of the 1966–1976 period, the Canadian behavior in terms of fertility, interprovincial migration, and mortality implied a stable equivalent population somewhere between 20 and 21 million (ignoring international migration). But Canada's stable growth rate (and therefore also the provincial rates) is now slightly negative.

Probably the most important conclusion that may be inferred from this stable population analysis is related to the interprovincial redistribution of the Canadian population. Whatever projection is considered, it is clear that this redistribution is dominated by a centrifugal process. At the western end of the country, Alberta and British Columbia show a demographic speed much higher than the Canadian average, so that their stable share of the population markedly exceeds their observed share; the latter was only 20% in 1981 (17% in 1966–1971), while their stable share was 33%. It is mainly because of their migration attractivity that these provinces show such a high speed. At the other end of the country, the four Atlantic provinces not only are experiencing a higher speed than the Canadian average, but also they show an acceleration. These provinces contained only 9% of the total Canadian population in 1981, but, thanks to their above-average fertility, their stable share based on 1966–1971 behavior was 11.4%. Between 1966–1971 and 1971–1976, because of the impressive increase in their migration attractivity, their stable share rose to 20%.

Correlatively to the "peripherization" of Canada's population, there is a clear lack of demographic dynamism in the central regions. Manitoba and Saskatchewan do not show a high speed, but a certain acceleration in recent years (primarily because of an increase in their migration attractivity) has allowed them to regain a stable share close to their present one. But their demographic weight in the Canadian system remains small. Finally, there are two big losers: Quebec and Ontario, the two most centrally located provinces. The demographic behavior of these provinces is, however, chronologically quite different. In the 1960s, Ontario's behavior made it a winner, with a demographic speed slightly above average so that its stable share exceeded the observed share. But in the 1970s, a considerable drop in migration attractivity reduced Ontario's speed, so that its stable share declined from 38 to 27% (compared with an observed share of 36%). Quebec also has experienced a decrease in its demographic speed, which, however, was already so low that the deceleration is much less pronounced than in Ontario. Quebec's below-average fertility, combined with a lack of migration attractivity, implies that this province's stable share is only slightly above 10%, while its observed share is 27%. The two central provinces taken together contained 62% of Canada's population in 1981 (64% in 1966–1971), but the decelaration of their demographic speed is such that their total share in the stable population is reduced to 38%.

Stable population theory requires not only that each region should have a constant share in the total population and a constant and equal rate of growth, but also that the age structure should remain constant. The present demographic behavior implies that in Quebec, Ontario, and British Columbia, the 0–19 age group would – at stability – represent only between 23 and 25% (35% in Newfoundland), while the 65-and-over age group would reach 17 to 20% (compared with 13% Newfoundland). Correlatively, the stable mean age would noticeably increase, varying between 37 and 42 years, except for Newfoundland where it reaches only 34 years. The present multiregional demographic behavior thus implies considerable regional disparities in age structures and in the rate of aging.

7.12 Conclusion

The use of multiregional analysis has helped us to emphasize the importance of the changes that have taken place in the demographic behavior of the Canadian population and to make more apparent some significant long-term implications of these changes. The marked reversal in migration flows observed between 1966–1971 and 1971–1976 (which seems to have continued at least until the end of the 1970s), combined with an unequally declining fertility, is characterized by strong centrifugal forces, particularly favoring the two most western provinces, but also benefiting the four most eastern provinces. This, along with a rapid aging of the population, obviously has many important implications, not only socioeconomic but also political. Thus one hopes that multiregional models will be increasingly applied, not only for analyzing the present demographic behavior and its short-term evolution, but also for studying the long-term policy implications of this evolution.

CHAPTER EIGHT

Migration and Urban Change[1]

Piotr Korcelli

Spatial concentration of populations was claimed in the 1950–1960 demographic literature to be increasing in both absolute and relative terms. Projections based on past trends of growing urban agglomerations and declining lower-level units showed the bulk of the population of urbanized countries to be clustered in a few megalopolises and indicated the actual disappearance of small- and medium-sized towns by the end of the century. Although some authors asserted later that the suburbanization of population and economic activity, observed in many highly urbanized countries during the previous decades, could ultimately lead to dispersal, others continued to predict concentration in the largest metropolitan areas and decline in most rural and small-town areas. Recently, however, more systematic analyses of urban growth have led a number of researchers to the conclusion that interregional population *deconcentration* represents a "normal" phenomenon – in fact, a stage in the urban transition. Still, it has been generally acknowledged that theories of urban growth and structure have yet to incorporate these observed developments.

Inadequacies in these theories are reflected in urban policies, which traditionally restrict the expansion of large urban agglomerations while promoting the growth centers within economically less active and sparsely populated regions. Hence, as Hall and Metcalf (1978) pointed out, in the case of highly urbanized countries some of these policies were addressing the past, rather than present-day issues. A reformulation of prevailing urban policies has therefore become an important issue in a number of countries. The emergence of new approaches to human settlement hinges on the development of empirical analyses and evaluations of urban trends. Accordingly, a study of the reproduction and mobility patterns of the population of a metropolitan

---

[1]A shorter version of this chapter appeared in Rogers (1982c).

area as against those of a nationwide population should answer some of the questions pertaining to recent trends in human settlement development.

This assumption forms the background of this chapter, in which several hypotheses pertaining to population development in large urban regions are examined. Such hypotheses refer to relations between population growth and urban size, the roles of migration and natural increase as components of urban population change, overall spatial mobility, hierarchical migration, and the age distributions of migrants moving out of, into, or between urban areas. Empirical material used in the analysis is derived from IIASA's Migration and Settlement Study. The discussion of individual hypotheses is preceded by a brief description of spatial units for which data were aggregated.

8.1 Regional Aggregation Units

Many authors (e.g., Boudeville 1978) postulate that at an advanced stage of urbanization the bulk of labor-oriented migrations take place between large metropolitan areas, whereas moves within such areas represent adjustments to the changing socioeconomic and family status of migrants and to the evolving urban environment. Accordingly, the adoption of functional urban regions (FURs) (Berry 1973, Hall et al. 1973) as spatial units in a multiregional demographic analysis should allow one to separate the effects of different types of moves, while focusing on labor-oriented migration.

The spatial units actually used in the Migration and Settlement Study were typically much larger than labor market regions and, depending on the country concerned, captured between 20 and 50% of registered moves that involved the crossing of local administrative boundaries. Nevertheless, most of the regional systems include one or more units whose identity, in terms of the settlement structure, can be clearly interpreted. This is true for 13 of the 17 countries covered by the study; namely, Austria, Bulgaria, Czechoslovakia, the Federal Republic of Germany, Finland, France, the German Democratic Republic, the UK, Hungary, Japan, the Netherlands, Poland, and Sweden.[2] The selected regional units are compared in Table 8.1 with functional urban regions as defined by Kawashima and Korcelli (1982), or alternatively with metropolitan regions as defined by Hall and Hay (1980).

Out of the total of 124 regions, on which this study of the 13 countries is based, 35 can be identified as urban-oriented units. They jointly represent 9.7% of the area but more than 30% of the total population and about 40% of the total urban population. All the capital regions and a number of major industrial agglomerations have been accounted for; however, whereas the areas of both "old" and "new" urbanization are represented in the sample, the balance is slightly tilted in favor of the former type. This is mainly true of France and

---

[2]The data available for Canada, Italy, the US, and the Soviet Union, at the time this chapter was written, could not be readily adapted for this analysis.

the Federal Republic of Germany, where areas of recent urban expansion, situated in the southern parts of these countries, could not be singled out using the available spatial disaggregation.

Table 8.1 begins with the functional urban region of Vienna, one of the nine *Länder* of Austria. Also included in the Migration and Settlement report by Sauberer (1981) is a more aggregated breakdown of the country into four regions: Central, South, East, and West. In this division, Vienna is included in the East region along with Lower Austria and Burgenland. For our purposes, both the Vienna city and East regions constitute relevant spatial units; the former exemplifies a large, central city, and the latter serves as an approximation of the labor market region, although admittedly it extends well beyond the daily commuting range to the region's core.

For Bulgaria, the clear choice for cross-sectional comparisons is Region 7 (Philipov 1981a), which corresponds to the administrative extent of the city of Sofia and is one of the seven regions obtained as a result of the aggregation of 28 administrative districts. Although this region includes more area than the city proper, it may be considered as the metropolitan area of Sofia. A corroboration of this can be found in a paper by Grigorev (1978), who shows that the Sofia District, which surrounds the capital, has been characterized by low population density (43.6 inhabitants per square kilometer, compared with 78.7 for the country as a whole) and an absolute population decrease (by 4% between 1946 and 1975).

The 12 upper-level administrative districts of Czechoslovakia, adopted as regions in an early version of the Migration and Settlement Study, included the city districts of Prague and Bratislava. [The final report (Kühnl 1982) merges these two cities into the surrounding Central Bohemia and Western Slovakia regions, respectively.] Unlike Sofia, the urban agglomeration of Prague extends well beyond the city's administrative boundaries into the district of Central Bohemia, which exemplifies a high urbanization level (Hampl *et al.* 1978). Hence, as in the case of Vienna, it is justifiable to consider Prague city and Central Bohemia (including Prague) as spatial units representing a central city (urban core) and a broader urban region.

Among the 10 *Länder* of the FRG, Hamburg and Bremen correspond to cores of FURs and in 1970 accounted for 63 and 58.5% of the total populations of the respective urban regions (Sherrill 1977). Another *Land* that can be considered as an urban region is North Rhine–Westphalia. Unlike the previously identified units, it is characterized by a clearly polynucleated structure and contains a number of major urban centers as well as less urbanized peripheral zones. Yet another urban unit covered in the study by Koch and Gatzweiler (1980) is West Berlin. Although included in this analysis, West Berlin displays quite specific demographic features and trends, which are largely attributable to its status as a separate political and territorial unit.

In the case of Finland (Rikkinen 1979), the Helsinki region, containing

Table 8.1 Basic characteristics of 35 urban regions included in the analysis.

Code	Region	Year	Population (thousands)	Area (sq. km)	Population density (persons per sq. km)	Population share in the multiregional systems (%)	Single or polycenter (S or P)	Degree of closure[a]			
								Metropolitan region classification		Functional urban region classification	
								Population	Area	Population	Area
1	Vienna city	1971	1615	414	3901	21.7	S			0.629	0.030
2	East Austria (incl. Vienna)	1971	3301	23543	141	44.3	S			1.286	1.731
3	Sofia city	1975	1077	953	1026	12.3	S				
4	Prague city[b]	1975	1161	291	3990	7.7	S				
5	Central Bohemia (incl. Prague)	1975	2301	11299	204	15.3	S				
6	Bratislava city	1975	331	368	700	2.3	S				
7	Bremen city	1974	724	404	1792	1.2	S			0.586	0.058
8	Hamburg city	1974	1734	753	2303	2.8	S	1.434	2.127	0.631	0.090
9	North Rhine–Westphalia	1974	17219	34044	506	27.8	P				
10	West Berlin	1974	2034	480	4238	3.3	S				
11	Uusimaa province (Helsinki region)	1974	1073	10351	97	23.8	S			0.968	1.021
12	Paris region	1975	9878	11984	824	18.8	P	0.970	0.881		
13	North France	1975	3914	12542	312	7.4	P	1.630	4.279		
14	Berlin capital district	1975	1098	403	2726	6.5	S				
15	Karl-Marx-Stadt	1975	1979	6009	329	11.8	P				
16	Leipzig–Halle	1975	3322	13737	242	19.8	P				
17	Dresden district	1975	1836	6733	273	10.9	P				
18	South GDR	1975	7135	26484	269	42.6	P				

#	Region	Year				%					
19	Central Hungary (Budapest)	1974	2968	7489	396	28.4	S			0.942	0.787
20	Kanto region	1970	30258	36742	824	28.9	S			1.373	3.087
21	Kinki region	1970	16511	23237	711	15.8	P			1.163	1.836
22	Noord-Holland (Amsterdam)	1974	2283	2654	860	16.9	S	0.972	0.884		
23	Zuid-Holland (Rotterdam)	1974	3019	2869	1053	22.4	P	1.015	0.095		
24	Utrecht province	1974	849	1328	640	6.3	S	1.314	1.175		
25	West Netherlands (Randstad)	1974	6150	6854	897	45.6	P	1.033	0.941		
26	Warsaw *voivodship*	1977	2207	3788	588	6.4	S			0.656	0.182
27	Łódź *voivodship*	1977	1099	1526	723	3.2	S			0.714	0.211
28	Gdańsk *voivodship*	1977	1288	7394	176	3.7	P			0.902	0.641
29	Katowice *voivodship* (Upper Silesia)	1977	3557	6650	538	10.3	P			0.939	0.615
30	Krakow *voivodship*	1977	1144	3255	354	3.3	S			0.676	0.372
31	Stockholm	1974	1487	6493	229	18.2	S	1.033	0.908		
32	South Sweden	1974	1159	13866	84	14.2	P	1.305	1.862		
33	South East England	1970	17316	27408	642	32.0	S	1.771	3.251		
34	West Midlands	1970	5178	13013	398	9.6	P	1.501	3.491		
35	North West England	1970	6789	7993	849	12.5	P	1.887	3.065		
	TOTALS[c]		119136	299316 (9.7%)	398	30.3 (40% of total urban population)					

Note: Metropolitan regions are defined according to Hall and Hay (1980), functional urban regions according to Kawashima and Korcelli (1982). [a]Proportion of regional population (area) in the metropolitan region (functional urban region) population (area). [b]The data here are taken from an earlier version of the Czechoslovakian case study, with 12 aggregations, the additional two being Prague and Bratislava. [c]Without double-counting of Vienna, Prague, South GDR, and West Netherlands.

the only major city in Finland and accounting for more than one-fifth of the total population, closely approximates the province of Uusimaa.

The division of France into eight planning regions offers two compact and heavily urbanized regions: Paris and the North. The Paris region as used by Ledent with Courgeau (1982) can be treated as a close approximation of the FUR of the French capital; the North region has an overall population density of more than three times the national average or that of the next most densely occupied region — the East.

The administrative division of the GDR into 15 districts basically follows the city-region principle; hence it is particularly relevant for the study of settlement structure. Boundaries of individual districts largely follow the spheres of influence of high-ranking urban centers (Krönert 1982). The main exception is the capital district of Berlin, which basically corresponds to the city's built-up area. For the Migration and Settlement Study, the districts were aggregated into 10 and then five regions, with only the latter results discussed in the GDR report (Mohs 1980). In the 10-region version, the districts of Halle and Leipzig are treated as one spatial unit, and the Dresden, Karl-Marx-Stadt, and Berlin districts constitute separate regions.

For Hungary, the main concern was to make sure that Budapest, the country's capital city and one of the largest urban centers in central Europe, was taken into account in this analysis. The task was rather straightforward since the regionalization scheme adopted in the Migration and Settlement report (Bies and Tekse 1980) followed principles basically similar to those used by Lackó et al. (1978), who analyzed FURs in Hungary. Boundaries of the Central region are identical with those of the Budapest FUR, except in the northeastern sector where the range of commuter flows extends into the western part of the North Hungary region.

The case of Japan resembles that of the UK (discussed below). Even though the spatial division in the Migration and Settlement report (Nanjo et al. 1982) was not concerned with mapping settlement systems, two of the regions — Kanto and Kinki — are almost totally urban and dominated by Japan's largest urban agglomerations. The former contains the Tokyo—Yokohama urban complex; the latter includes Osaka, Kyoto, and Kobe. These metropolises, according to Kawashima's (1982) definition, accounted for 72.8 and 86.0% of the total populations of the respective regions in 1970.

The Migration and Settlement analysis for the Netherlands used a division of 11 provinces, which, in the summary report (Drewe 1980), were aggregated into five major regions. Keeping the provinces as separate units, one observes that three of the upper-level administrative units — Noord-Holland, Zuid-Holland, and Utrecht — contain Holland's four largest cities (Amsterdam, Rotterdam, Utrecht, and The Hague). The FURs, as defined by Hall and Hay (1980), of these cities almost exhaust the territories of the respective provinces, which taken together correspond to the *Randstad* area, sometimes described as one polynucleated urban agglomeration. Therefore it is justifiable to include the entire West region of the Netherlands as a fourth spatial unit for this study.

The regionalization of Poland (Dziewoński and Korcelli 1981) was designed to permit the analysis of demographic patterns for major urban areas as well as for major planning regions. Out of the total of 49 *voivodships* (upper-level administrative units), five were treated as separate regions. Three of the five (Warsaw, Łódź, and Krakow) have the status of city *voivodships*, and the other two (Gdańsk and Katowice) are also heavily urbanized. The three city *voivodships*, although larger than the central cities themselves, fall short of encompassing daily commuting zones. The respective FURs (Korcelli 1977) are more extensive in terms of area and population. However, the FURs include rural hinterlands in addition to urban cores and their commuting zones; hence, the differences shown in Table 8.1 should be noted with some reservation.

Among the eight regions analyzed by Andersson and Holmberg (1980) for Sweden, Stockholm and the South merit closer attention. These regions correspond to the extents of counties (or groups thereof), and at the same time they can be approximated by aggregations of A-regions, which have been defined in Sweden on the basis of spatial labor market criteria. For consistency, however, the standard units in our comparisons are regions defined by Hall and Hay (1980). Therefore the Stockholm region can be considered as almost identical with the respective metropolitan region in terms of population size, although in terms of territorial extent the two units do not completely overlap. The South region, according to Hall and Hay's definition, consists of three metropolitan and two nonmetropolitan zones. Out of the former, the Malmö—Lund and Helsingborg regions represent jointly some 72% of the population of the South — over 0.8 million distributed within an area only marginally larger than that of the Stockholm region.

Finally, of the 10 regions used in the UK study (Rees 1979b), three (South East, West Midlands, and North West) broadly correspond to the densely occupied belt along the Liverpool—London axis, referred to by Hall *et al.* (1973) as Megalopolis England. The first region contains Greater London, the second the West Midlands conurbation, and the third the Merseyside and South-East Lancashire conurbations. These areas account for some 53—66% of the total populations of the respective regions. The proportions are very high, considering that a number of smaller urban nuclei, closely integrated with the London, Birmingham, Liverpool, and Manchester areas, form separate metropolitan cores.

Together these 35 regions represent a broad spectrum in terms of population size, density, and share in a multiregional system, and degree of correspondence to a metropolitan area (FUR). Since this diversity may be reflected in population trends, it ishould be taken into account in their interpretation. The initial disaggregation of spatial units into three categories is shown in Figure 8.1.

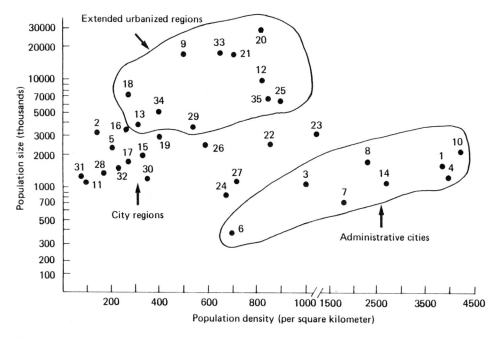

Figure 8.1 Distribution of urban regions by population size and density.

The first group, consisting of eight administrative cities, occupies low to medium ranks in terms of population size but undoubtedly has the highest intensity of settlement. The next group comprises city regions, predominantly monocentric. The third group represents larger urban agglomerations as well as more loosely interconnected, extensive urbanized regions; their overall density figures fall around the mean, whereas the absolute population numbers are clearly the largest within the whole set of regional units under analysis.

The degree of regional closure is expressed as a proportion of the regional population or area to the respective value for the metropolitan region (or FUR) aggregations (Table 8.1). The three administrative cities for which the respective quotients could be calculated have the lowest of all proportions (around 0.6 for population and 0.03–0.1 for area). The city regions, on the other hand, reveal values close to 1.0. Deviation from this figure indicates the degree to which an individual region may be considered overbounded or under-bounded when compared with an independently defined, standard urban (metropolitan) region. Finally, for the third group of regions the corresponding values are over 1.0 when these units are compared with the major regions, rather than all the standard urban (metropolitan) regions contained within their boundaries.

8.2 Five Hypotheses Concerning Patterns of Urban Change

From the descriptions and interpretations of contemporary patterns of urban change,[3] one can derive a number of hypotheses relating to their demographic aspects, which may be tested with relevant data and findings of the Migration and Settlement Study. As previously noted, the focus of this study is on developed countries — countries with low natural increase of population and advanced urbanization levels. Even within this group, however, these characteristics are not uniform; the proportion of population living in urban areas in 1975 ranged from 0.50 (Hungary) to 0.80 (Sweden). The variation of natural increase was also substantial: between −1.9 per thousand for the FRG and 10.1 for Japan and Poland in 1977.

In spite of such differences, all countries included in the sample are in advanced stages of the demographic as well as the urbanization transition. Their locations at different points within these stages may be considered as a positive feature, since it allows the implicit introduction of the time factor. Three of the hypotheses consider spatial mobility patterns, whereas the remaining two deal with total population change and its components. Some empirical evidence may refer to more than one hypothesis at a time, as the data produced with the help of multistate demographic models (Willekens and Rogers 1978) capture the effects of interaction between fertility, mobility, and mortality patterns. Most of the figures presented below are either ratios or differences calculated with respect to national figures (or mean values for respective multiregional systems). This introduces a common denominator, although it by no means solves the difficult problems involved in international comparisons of population data.

Hypothesis 1. The rate of population growth in an urban area is inversely related to the level of urbanization (at a national scale) and to city size.

The later stages of demographic and mobility transitions (Zelinsky 1971) are characterized by diminishing rates of growth of the urban population. Typically, the level of urbanization becomes stable after reaching roughly 80%. Large urban areas lead the trend. During the periods of rapid urbanization (such as the 1950s throughout most of Europe, or the present decade in the case of less developed countries) large cities expanded faster than the total urban population; such a pattern was reversed during more advanced urbanization stages. There is ample empirical evidence of this evolution, although it

---

[3]See, among others, Beale (1977), Vining and Strauss (1977), Glickman (1977a, b), Gordon (1978), Simmons (1979), Hall and Hay (1980), Bourne *et al.* (1980), Leven (1981), Kawashima (1982), and Bourne (1982).

suffers from lack of comparability among the spatial units for which data are usually available (for example, cities in their administrative boundaries). Yet the few studies that are based on comparable units point toward similar conclusions. For example, in the case of cores of FURs in 17 European countries, the relation between rate of growth and size was found either to be increasingly negative or to have evolved from positive to negative between 1950 and 1975 (Korcelli 1980). Typically, growth rates shift from a level higher to a level lower than the national rate and subsequently evolve toward absolute population decline. However, population growth tends to be a negative function of urban size, although it varies positively with the distance from the core of an urban region. Thus the relationship between growth and size can be obscured by variations in the proportion accounted for by hinterland zones within individual urban regions.

The data derived from the Migration and Settlement Study basically support the above observations. During the mid-1970s, 19 of the 35 urban regions experienced population growth slower than the national growth; half of the remaining units exceeded the respective national rates by less than 2%, whereas 13 regions suffered absolute population losses. If present fertility, mortality, and spatial interaction patterns continue, the last number may in fact increase to 16 by the year 2000 and to 21 two decades later according to multiregional population projections.

The data, however, offer only limited support to the postulated association between population growth and urban size. Perhaps this statement would not have been true if the national population increase and urbanization level had been kept constant within the data sample or if the regions had been disaggregated into cores and rings. Unfortunately, the small number of observation units prevents such comparisons from being made.

The population size of an urban region is also expected to be negatively related to its gross inmigration rate, a result of two factors: the negative association between growth and size and the greater degree of closure of migration movements in larger urban regions. Indeed, the pattern evident from the data suggests a negative association, although much weaker than anticipated.

Hypothesis 2. The roles of migration and natural increase, as components of urban population growth, evolve in the course of the urbanization process. During the advanced stages of urbanization migration becomes of secondary importance.

A substantial body of literature has recently accumulated pertaining to the changing proportions and interactions among the two major components of urban growth. Keyfitz (1980), in view of contrasting empirical evidence, attempted to put this question on a theoretical plane. Among other things, he identified conditions for the crossover point beyond which, with all rates kept constant, the urban population growth becomes predominantly endogenous. Following this argument one may conclude that, in the developed countries of today, the growth of cities should be increasingly a result of the natural increase of the urban population. Such a development is likely to occur when, at an advanced urbanization level, the core—periphery development patterns (Friedmann 1977) evolve in favor of peripheral zones. Higher investments in the countryside are translated into a lower natural increase of its population, lower outmigration to urban areas, and finally, higher urban-to-rural migration rates.[4] Keyfitz's results were extended by Ledent (1980a), who also presented detailed analyses of two alternative demographic models of urbanization: a continuous, biregional version of the Rogers model and the United Nations model (1981). Subsequently, Keyfitz and Philipov (1981) attempted to capture long-term interaction between migration and natural increase by focusing on the age structure and fertility of successive generations of rural-to-urban migrants as well as their offspring.

Consideration of aggregate national growth rates of the urban population is not sufficient for the purposes of this chapter, which is concerned with changes within settlement systems. Hypothesis 2 rests on the assumption, also reflected in Hypothesis 1, that large cities actually lead the trends generally established for the urban sector, especially since they account for a substantial share (estimated between 0.4 and 0.8, depending on the country and definition used) of the total urban population at advanced urbanization levels. Hence the larger the urban region and the higher the urbanization level, the smaller the expected contribution of migration (as compared with natural increase) to the total population change.

The empirical evidence from the Migration and Settlement Study supports the above statements. Of the 35 regions, 24 feature a positive natural increase, whereas only 18 show positive migration. Natural increase appears as the greater contributor in 19 cases, migration in 16. Out of the latter group seven regions show a negative migration balance (also less pronounced when compared with natural population decrease); in five regions with both rates positive, the migration component was just marginally larger. About half of the regions with a higher contribution from natural increase, including Paris (12), London (33), and Randstad (25), had a negative migration balance, but only one, Bremen (7), had both rates negative (Figure 8.2).

Similar net values, however, may conceal substantial differences in demographic behavior. It is therefore necessary to look at some of the theoretically postulated specific relationships. For example, the data show a rather strong negative association between the crude birth and death rates for the

---

[4]This discussion pertains to migration and natural increase measured by one-year rates. Historically, one can argue that all urban growth is attributable to migration as present-day urban populations represent the accumulation of successive generations of migrants and their offspring.

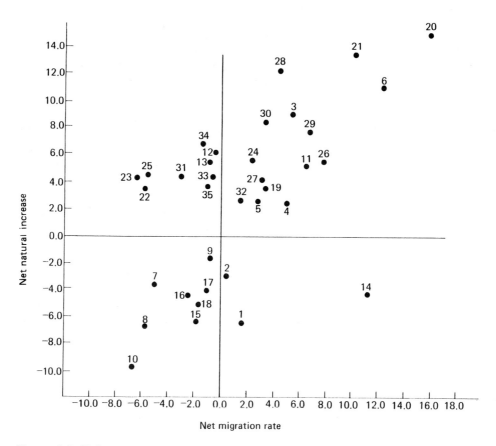

Figure 8.2 Major components of population change in 35 urban regions.

35 spatial units under analysis — a pattern typical of a late stage in demographic transition. (The majority of regions fall into the class with high death and low birth rates.) The association between gross in- and outmigration rates postulated by Cordey-Hayes (1975) and others finds limited support. Finally, the relation between birth rates and outmigration rates is of a totally symmetric nature.

None of the above conclusions disproves the earlier findings concerning the contribution of the two aggregate components of population change in the urban regions. Still, it should be noted that the greater role of natural increase as a contributor to growth is due to the poor performance of urban regions in attracting migrants from other units within the respective multiregional systems, rather than to the high fertility of their resident population. More than two-thirds of all the urban regions have rates of natural increase lower than the relevant mean multiregional rates. The patterns of net reproduction rates are even more striking; only five regions are situated above the respective multiregional values.

The decrease of net migration, both in its absolute magnitude and in its contribution to total population change, appears to be a recent phenomenon. For example, during the 1960s migration accounted for as much as 75–95% of the total urban population growth in a number of European countries (Economic Commission for Europe 1979, p.204). In the case of the cores of the largest Japanese urban regions (the urban agglomerations of Tokyo and Osaka) the ratios of natural increase to net migration have evolved from 1:2 during the late 1950s to 3:1 for Tokyo and 30:1 for Osaka during 1970–1975 (Nanjo *et al.* 1982). As has been noted, the analyses by Keyfitz (1980) are restricted to the case when the total population is disaggregated into its rural and urban parts. Still, the data just presented point to a behavior of large urban regions that tends to be similar to the expected behavior of the total urban population under the migration and natural increase regimes prevailing in highly urbanized societies — as if all urban inmigration corresponds to rural outmigration.

The approaches and findings discussed so far all pertain to the case when the contribution of natural increase or of migration is defined as the difference between respective rates for a given spatial aggregate: a city, region, or total urban population of a given country. A number of authors, however, consider the question of the components of population change in terms of their variability within a spatial system. When such a definition is preferred, migration generally appears as the greater contributor. For example, such a conclusion is reached by Kennett (1977), who studied patterns of population change for 126 Metropolitan Economic Labor Areas in Great Britain during 1961–1971. Whereas the overwhelming majority of these areas had natural increase rates approximating Britain's 6% decennial increase, the net migration rates extended over a broad range from −10.0 to 40.0. Thus the differentiating effect in the population growth pattern within an urban system can be mainly attributed to the migration component. Similar conclusions are derived by Borchert (1980) for Dutch municipalities during 1961–1973 and by Simmons (1977) for 124 urban regions in Canada. In the latter analysis net internal migration explains more of the variations in the total population change during 1966–1971 than do natural increase and net foreign inmigration combined. Although during the subsequent period (1971–1976) the variation in natural increase among the regions increased while that of net migration declined, the differentials between the two were still substantial. At the same time the rates of natural increase remained considerably higher than those of net migration for all the major hierarchical levels within the system (Simmons 1979, p.55).

One cannot expect such trends to continue for more than a few decades if current national population projections are to hold true. Once the natural increase at the national level falls toward zero, migration will gain ascendancy even in terms of rates. Definitional problems are not easily resolved, however. For example, it is not clear whether the contribution should be measured in terms of change or of growth only. As to spatial effects of such an evolution, the following generalization by Bourne (1982, p.144) seems instructive:

> During periods of rapid aggregate growth (particularly high rates of natural increase) almost all areas witness growth. During periods of high foreign immigration growth tends to become more focused spatially. Similarly, as the contribution of natural increase to aggregate growth declines, spatial variability increases.

Hypothesis 3. The population of a large city is characterized by greater spatial mobility than rural and nonmetropolitan populations.

According to the concept of mobility transition (Zelinsky 1971), spatial mobility increases during the rapid urbanization stage and remains high afterwards. As Rogers (1977) pointed out, however, the decrease of interregional welfare disparities may eventually bring about a decline in geographical mobility. Also, short-distance migration may be largely replaced by daily commuting between residence and work place.

No matter which way the overall mobility indices evolve during the later stages of the demographic and urbanization transition, the large-city population is expected to be more mobile than either the rural or the small-city (nonmetropolitan) population. This expectation stems from positive relations, found in a number of developed countries, between the propensity to move and such variables as educational level and female labor participation (Brown and Neuburger 1977). Other factors reportedly contributing to the greater spatial mobility of the large-city population include a delayed process of family formation and growth and the accumulation within cities of individuals with previous migration experience and a high repeat-migration (including return-migration) probability (DaVanzo and Morrison 1978, DaVanzo 1980). Conversely, large urban places may be sending out and attracting disproportionately fewer migrants because of the greater internal opportunities offered (Simmons 1979).

The majority of urban regions in this analysis (20 out of 35) were characterized by gross migration rates lower than aggregate values for the corresponding multiregional systems. Regions with outmigration rates higher than the aggregate rates were almost uniformly represented within the population growth and absolute decline categories. This pattern becomes even more noticeable when mobility is measured by the fraction of life that an individual is expected to spend in the region of birth, calculated on the basis of age-specific migration and mortality rates. For a typical urban region this fraction is some 3–4% higher than the mean share for the respective multiregional system (Figure 8.3). Only for eight regions are such probabilities lower than mean national values: four of these regions have experienced nega-

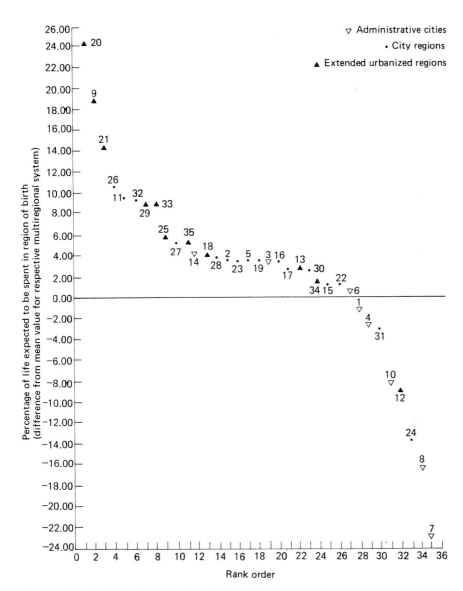

Figure 8.3 Spatial migration levels for 35 urban regions.

tive total population change and five, net migration loss. As might have been anticipated, the pattern represented in Figure 8.3 is not independent of the population size of urban regions. Among eight regions for which the fraction of life to be spent in the region of birth is highest relative to corresponding mean values, five constitute large, polynucleated regions. They include the urban agglomerations of Kanto (20), Kinki (21), North Rhine—Westphalia (9), South East England (33), and Upper Silesia (29). On the other hand, administrative cities are clustered in the interval of lowest relative values.

The distribution of the values of another summary measure of population mobility, the net migraproduction rate (Willekens and Rogers 1978), is very close to the allocation of the expected length of stay in a region.[5] Only in the case of 16 urban regions (out of 35) is a locally born individual expected to make more moves during his or her life span than an average person in the respective national or multiregional system. Six of these regions recorded absolute population losses around 1975, and seven regions experienced negative migration balance. No regularities can be found concerning the relation between net migraproduction rate and population size of urban regions.

In sum, large-city populations seem to be less rather than more mobile when compared with the total national population. This is at least what the interregional migration patterns suggest. Even though a causal interpretation is not attempted at this point, various explanatory factors may be relevant in different national contexts. Some of these factors may be related to settlement policies (for example, restrictions on inmigration tend to discourage outmigration), others may be related to substitution between migration and daily travel. The initial hypothesis, however, should not be totally discarded since the evidence is positive for regions (basically administrative cities) with highest population losses. Still, a typical urban region, one with a slowly growing or slowly decreasing population, is characterized by relatively low overall mobility.

Hypothesis 4. The dominant migration flows within highly urbanized countries are those among major urban regions. The traditional configuration of interurban moves, which correspond to an urban hierarchy, evolves toward a pattern characterized by a lack of interdependence between net inflow and city size.

This hypothesis, unlike the previous one, is concerned with directional mobility. It refers to the third stage in Zelinsky's scheme of mobility transition, during which rural-to-urban migration is gradually replaced by urban-to-urban flows and by commuting within urban regions, as well as by an increasing population shift outwards from the large cities and toward smaller communities.

The structure of national settlement systems in highly urbanized societies has been described as a combination of vertical (hierarchical) and

---

[5]This rate describes the average number of migrations a person will make during his or her lifetime.

horizontal linkages (e.g., Bourne 1975). The latter component is mainly represented by interconnections among the large cities that perform high-level service and decision-making functions. This is the basis for Pred's (1975) model of city-systems development and of Dziewoński's (1980) concept of the system of main urban centers. Translated into population-related terms, such concepts suggest that the origin- and destination-specific migration rates, spatial migraproduction rates, and other demographic mobility measures attain higher levels among urban regions than among nonurban regions or between urban and nonurban regions.

Looking at in- and outmigration rates region by region would not be a helpful exercise in view of the divergences in population size and the role played by physical distance. Instead the data are arranged so as to permit a comparison of demographic interaction occurring between a given urban region and an aggregate of other urban regions *vis-à-vis* "nonurban" regions within the multiregional system. Figure 8.4 shows the spatial allocation of life expectancy at birth for 29 urban regions (the remaining six, i.e., Vienna, East Austria, the *Randstad* area of Holland, Helsinki, Sofia, and Budapest, have no urban counterparts within the respective systems). One of the regularities to be observed pertains to the importance of the gravity factors, that is, mass and distance. Strong interactions among urban regions occur typically when the units in question are situated close to each other and have large population potential compared with other regions. Relatively weak linkages are characteristic of smaller regions (including administrative cities) and of those urban regions whose urban counterparts represent much smaller potential. For example, an individual born in the West Midlands region (34) of England is expected to spend an average of 7.41% of his or her life span in each of the two other urban regions, South East and North West England, but only an average of 2.82% in each of the seven nonurban regions. A person born in Prague (4), however, would live only 0.24% of his or her life in Bratislava (the only other urban region in the multiregional system), as opposed to an average of 2.95% in each of the nonurban regions. This case is also illustrative of data inadequacies; the latter proportion may be heavily accounted for by flows toward such cities as Brno and Ostrava, which in this study constitute cores of nonurban regions. Note also that because of variations in the number of regions, only proportions between the urban and nonurban components, and not the percentage figures, are of any comparative value.

The pattern of spatial net migraproduction rates conforms to the life expectancy pattern. Regions with strong nonurban connections are somewhat more numerous than those with predominantly urban-oriented linkages. As indicated earlier, however, the nonurban category is not uniform; it may include traditional nodal regions and city hinterlands as well as remote rural peripheries. Generally speaking, those urban regions characterized by relatively high outmigration rates display stronger interactions with the nonurban units. For example, according to observed migration patterns, a person born in

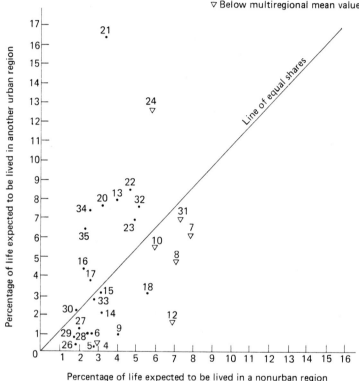

Figure 8.4 Spatial allocation of life expectancy at birth for 29 urban regions.

Bremen (7) may be expected to move out of an average nonurban region more frequently than out of an average urban region within the multiregional system. In fact, a substantial fraction of the former moves are accounted for by the neighboring region of Lower Saxony, the main destination of Bremen-born migrants. The average share of urban regions as origins of outmigration by the natives of Bremen is lower than their respective life expectancy share, because of higher average outmigration rates experienced by nonurban as compared with urban regions. (In the calculations, individuals assume the mobility rates of the region of destination.)

Somewhat similar results can be found in a detailed study of in- and outmigration patterns of Poland's 11 major urban centers (Rykiel and Żurkowa 1981). Migrations between those cities accounted for only 9% of the total number of moves, and 13% were between the cities and their satellite towns. The other 78% were moves between the cities and the rest of the country (both its rural and urban parts).

The second part of Hypothesis 4 relates to interdependence between net migration and urban size. Traditional theories of settlement structure imply that population flows among urban places represent a reversal of innovation diffusion patterns, that is, the direction of the predominant numbers of moves is up the urban size hierarchy. During the earlier stages of urbanization transition, typical moves are those from rural to urban communities (both small and large), whereas the more advanced stages witness concentration within the settlement network, with smaller towns losing their population to metropolitan areas. This process may involve a number of generations of moves as well as of migrants.

Thus, according to the concept of hierarchical migration, categories of urban places record net migration gains in their interaction with each of the smaller-sized groups of cities. This is true not only of net migration rates, but also of the absolute size of flows.

This regularity found in growing urban systems, such as those of Japan (Kawashima 1982) and Poland (Rykiel and Zurkowa 1981), is not likely to hold true when the largest cities register absolute population losses (although it is still possible because of variations in the natural increase). Such a situation, however, may arise under various interurban and urban—nonurban (core—hinterland) patterns of population movements. As Alonso (1978a) pointed out, under low levels of natural increase and rural outmigration, the flows among metropolitan areas represent a zero-sum game, in which individual urban units may fall into the category of net losers as a consequence of their relatively poor economic base and environmental quality — characteristics not necessarily related to overall population potential.

The concept of hierarchical migration has been questioned by Simmons (1977, 1979) and Drewett et al. (1975). Their analyses of migration flows among urban regions in Canada and Great Britain, respectively, take account of population deconcentration from large urban cores to peripheral areas and subcenters. From 1966 to 1971 the net migration among 124 urban regions in Canada, aggregated into five hierarchical groups, showed moderate net losses for regions of order 5 (composed of the two largest metropolitan areas of Montreal and Toronto) and order 3 (regions centered on medium-sized towns), and heavier losses for regions of order 1 (regions with small towns as cores). Net gains were made by regions centered on cities with some 100 000 to 1 000 000 inhabitants (order 2), as well as by regions of order 4, in particular those located in the proximity of large urban centers. When regions were re-arranged so as to form 11 spatial subsystems centered on metropolitan areas of the two upper levels, the net migration patterns were dominated by inter-regional population shifts from eastern to central and from central to western provinces (Simmons 1977). In the subsequent period of 1971—1976 the relation between the urban size (hierarchical level) and net migration became more pronouncedly negative, with increasing losses in the two largest metropolitan areas, declining gains in the remaining large urban regions, and a change from a heavy loss to a nominal gain in regions centered on the smallest towns in the system. In the 11-region breakdown the most visible changes, compared with the previous period, were shifts from a positive to a negative internal migration balance for the metropolitan region of Toronto and a decline in the gains of Vancouver, the third largest urban region.

Drewett *et al.* (1975) have demonstrated that flows from bigger to smaller Metropolitan Economic Labor Areas in Britain accounted for a higher proportion of total moves within short distances than over long distances. This implies that hierarchical migration patterns are still characteristic of an interregional scale; however, deconcentration from large city cores to metropolitan rings renders this generalization inadequate when intraregional population shifts are examined. Migration patterns of the seven largest urban regions of Great Britain (each with over one million inhabitants) reveal a positive association between urban population size and net migration loss from 1966 to 1971. Still, the London region maintained a positive migration balance with each of the remaining six large metropolitan areas (Kennett 1977).

The data on migration between pairs of urban regions do not disprove the hierarchical migration concept. To the contrary, in 30 cases the destination-specific outmigration rates are higher for urban regions with a smaller population size (Table 8.2).[6] The size and direction of net flows, as measured by the index of migration effectiveness, reveal a somewhat different pattern, however. Although smaller regions recorded a net migration gain in only 12 out of 33 cases, this reversal was typical of countries (multiregional systems) with 75–85% urban population, including the Netherlands, the FRG and West Berlin, the GDR, and Sweden. Some of these flows (for example, Stockholm to South Sweden and Noord-Holland to Utrecht) can be attributed to environmental factors. Vienna and Prague maintained positive migration balances with their hinterlands, but the effectiveness values were small. This is also true of interactions among the three urban regions of England. In any event the size of net flows cannot be explained by differences in population size between the origin and destination.

While the material presented falls short of providing consistent evidence against the concept of intermetropolitan linkages, it offers little to support it. Intensive migration takes place mostly among those urban regions that form a contiguous territory (the *Randstad* area, South GDR, and Hall's Megalopolis

---

[6]Because of its function as a capital, Berlin was treated as a larger unit than the Leipzig–Halle, Karl-Marx-Stadt, and Dresden districts. Similarly, Warsaw was considered larger than the Katowice region, despite a smaller population size. Such exceptions would not have had to be made had regional size been measured by the aggregate population of the main urban center.

England) or that are situated fairly close to each other. Similarly, the concept of hierarchical migration cannot be disproved with the help of the available data, although it is clearly no longer applicable under conditions of urban contraction, as expressed by absolute population loss.

In support of the hypothesis one may argue (as many authors have) that the importance of intermetropolitan migration rests not so much on volume as on composition and "quality". Such flows tend to be highly selective in social, economic, and demographic terms. The data allow us to take a closer look at one of the crucial characteristics of the structure of migrant populations.

Hypothesis 5. The age profile of interurban migration is typical of the outflow schedule for a capital region, that is, it is less labor-dominant and less labor-symmetric than the corresponding inflow schedule.

This statement paraphrases the hypothesis identified by Rogers and Castro, in Chapter 5 of this book, concerning differences between inflow and outflow profiles for capital regions. Their data relate to eight of the 35 urban regions analyzed in this chapter.

The age structure of migrants represents perhaps the most important characteristic of population flows, from the point of view of both economic and demographic change. Its relation with labor force formation and service demand is equally as strong as its fertility and mortality implications. The large cities have traditionally benefited from a heavy concentration of migrants within the early labor force and reproductive age groups as well as from sending more of their elderly and mid-career members of the labor force to smaller urban and nonurban places. However, as interurban moves become a major component of interregional migration and the positive association between migration patterns and urban hierarchy tends to disappear, the differences between the inflow and outflow schedules will also diminish. This trend would have pronounced and (largely negative) long-term effects on the economic and demographic development of large metropolitan areas.

Such a hypothesis may not apply on an intraregional scale, in particular to migration between cores and peripheries within urban regions. The typical pattern is one in which moves toward large-city cores are dominated by young individuals, whereas families prevail among the outmigrating population (Borchert 1980, Ley and Mercer 1980, van der Knaap and Sleegers 1981). There are no indications that such a pattern may undergo major change under conditions of interregional deconcentration of settlements.

As a preliminary step in the study of interurban migration profiles, the model migration-by-age schedule, described in Chapter 5, was fitted to the data for urban regions of the FRG, Poland, and Japan. The resulting generalized profiles are compared with conclusions set out in that chapter concerning aggregate migration in to and out of selected capital regions.

Table 8.2 Interurban migration between 33 pairs of urban regions: rates and net flows.

Pairs of regions (A/B)[a]	Migration flows		Migration effectiveness[b]	Difference in population size (A − B)	Mean age of migrants (A − B)
	Outmigration rate from A to B	Outmigration rate from B to A			
Vienna/Austria	0.0035	0.0048	9.07	6.64	32.64 − 28.81
Prague/ Central Bohemia	0.0044	0.0056	12.12	0.91	38.02 − 34.48
Prague/Bratislava	0.0001	0.0004	23.76	55.63	42.06 − 46.18
Hamburg/Bremen	0.0006	0.0014	-3.43	41.09	31.64 − 33.11
North Rhine−Westphalia/ Hamburg	0.0003	0.0029	-6.21	81.70	32.60 − 33.21
West Berlin/Hamburg	0.0009	0.0007	-18.74	7.96	33.21 − 30.49
North Rhine−Westphalia/ Bremen	0.0002	0.0041	-6.37	91.93	31.91 − 32.23
North Rhine−Westphalia/ West Berlin	0.0005	0.0051	7.43	78.87	31.56 − 34.57
West Berlin/Bremen	0.0004	0.0009	-6.85	47.50	32.01 − 32.79
Paris/North	0.0005	0.0026	38.68	43.24	34.22 − 29.23
Berlin/Leipzig−Halle	0.0007	0.0009	42.15	-50.32	25.54 − 25.67
Berlin/Karl-Marx-Stadt	0.0004	0.0006	41.53	-28.63	26.11 − 23.98
Berlin/Dresden	0.0004	0.0009	55.39	-25.15	25.66 − 24.59
Leipzig−Halle/ Karl-Marx-Stadt	0.0008	0.0015	3.41	25.33	26.86 − 24.59
Leipzig−Halle/ Dresden	0.0007	0.0011	-6.90	28.80	26.68 − 25.02
Karl-Marx-Stadt/ Dresden	0.0011	0.0009	-13.70	7.23	26.73 − 26.00
Kanto/Kinki	0.0026	0.0057	17.13	29.39	33.79 − 31.24

Zuid-Holland/					
Noord-Holland	0.0040	0.0051	-1.58	13.68	33.67 – 36.56
Zuid-Holland/Utrecht	0.0030	0.0084	-11.16	56.10	36.03 – 34.50
Noord-Holland/Utrecht	0.0045	0.0084	-17.95	45.78	38.08 – 33.56
Warsaw/Łódź	0.0001	0.0005	29.65	33.51	53.02 – 36.43
Warsaw/Gdańsk	0.0002	0.0004	18.96	26.29	42.81 – 55.68
Warsaw/Katowice	0.0002	0.0002	14.87	-23.42	45.32 – 35.24
Warsaw/Krakow	0.0001	0.0003	29.45	31.72	51.89 – 38.45
Katowice/Łódź	0.0001	0.0003	30.66	52.79	41.96 – 30.46
Katowice/Gdańsk	0.0001	0.0003	-5.88	46.83	35.53 – 39.34
Katowice/Krakow	0.0004	0.0022	25.94	51.33	43.21 – 34.48
Gdańsk/Krakow	0.0001	0.0001	10.30	5.52	52.14 – 34.00
Cracow/Łódź	0.0001	0.0001	6.06	2.00	38.27 – 34.26
Stockholm/South Sweden	0.0023	0.0025	-9.31	12.40	32.18 – 27.96
South East England/					
North West England	0.0008	0.0026	11.92	43.67	32.07 – 30.89
South East England/					
West Midlands	0.0008	0.0031	8.05	53.96	30.86 – 33.06
North West England/					
West Midlands	0.0009	0.0013	4.36	13.46	31.31 – 32.17

[a] A represents regions with larger population size, and B represents regions with smaller population size (see footnote on p. 342).

[b] Effectiveness of migration is defined as the net exchange between two regions divided by total migration between them, or $[(M_{AB} - M_{BA})/(M_{AB} + M_{BA})] \times 100$.

Table 8.3 shows values of selected parameters of the age schedules for moves to and from the city of Hamburg. The parameters refer to one part of the generalized profile known as the labor force component. The aggregate-flow profiles are very similar to those identified for the eight capital regions. Contrary to expectations, however, the origin–destination-specific schedules do not differ greatly from the aggregate-inflow schedules. The outmigration profiles from Hamburg to North Rhine–Westphalia and from Hamburg to Bremen are more interesting in this respect as they show a shift in the labor peak, also reflected in the higher mean age of migrants, when compared with the total out-of-Hamburg schedule (Figure 8.5).

Table 8.3 Selected parameters defining observed total model schedules of urban region-oriented and interurban flows: the FRG, 1974; Japan, 1970; and Poland, 1977.

Flows	Parameters[a]			Mean age
	a_2	α_2	λ_2	
Out of Hamburg (total)	0.049	0.076	0.634	36.04
In to Hamburg (total)	0.074	0.099	0.635	30.26
From Hamburg to Bremen	0.089	0.111	0.394	33.55
From Hamburg to North Rhine–Westphalia	0.069	0.097	0.320	35.85
In to Hamburg from Bremen	0.092	0.123	0.459	33.37
In to Hamburg from North Rhine–Westphalia	0.077	0.099	0.476	30.76
Out of Kanto (total)	0.064	0.111	0.204	34.83
In to Kanto (total)	0.096	0.134	0.577	33.51
From Kanto to Kinki	0.057	0.106	0.326	35.96
In to Kanto from Kinki	0.066	0.115	0.245	35.10
From Kinki to Kanto	0.069	0.109	0.281	33.07
In to Kinki from Kanto	0.064	0.108	0.321	34.00
Out of Warsaw (total)	0.001	0.653	0.126	54.24
In to Warsaw (total)	0.091	0.158	0.216	31.04
From Warsaw to four other urban regions	0.001	0.599	0.114	52.49
In to Warsaw from four other urban regions	0.065	0.148	0.242	43.13
Out of Katowice (total)	0.059	0.289	0.224	46.34
In to Katowice (total)	0.110	0.213	0.283	33.25
From Katowice to 4 urban regions	0.068	0.171	3.332	44.36
In to Katowice from 4 urban regions	0.079	0.319	0.213	41.80

[a] a_2 = level of labor force component
α_2 = descent parameter of labor force component
λ_2 = ascent parameter of labor force component (see Chapter 5).

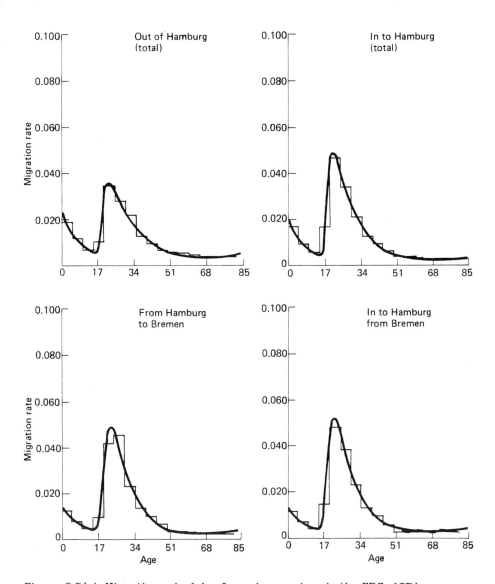

Figure 8.5(a) Migration schedules for urban regions in the FRG, 1974.

A different pattern emerges when migration profiles for the two Japanese urban regions are examined (Table 8.3 and Figure 8.6). In this case the origin—destination-specific flows closely resemble the aggregate out-of-Kanto (Tokyo) schedule and sharply contrast with the aggregate in-to-Kanto migration. This is true of the height of the labor peak as well as of the rate of ascent and descent of the labor force curve.

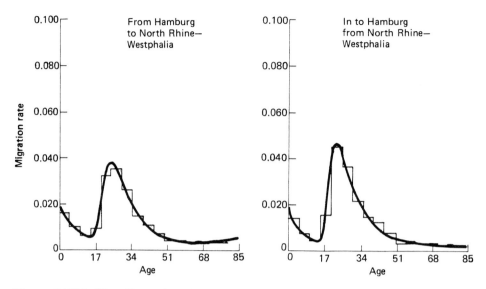

Figure 8.5(b) Migration schedules for urban regions in the FRG, 1974.

The age profiles for flows in to, out of, and between the five urban regions of Poland display some peculiar characteristics. As to the initial hypothesis the evidence is mixed, with some of the parameter values for origin–destination-specific flows being typical of either the aggregate in- or outmigration schedules (Table 8.3 and Figure 8.7). A striking feature of the observed schedules is a large difference between the mean age of in- as opposed to outmigrants, a consequence of both the underrepresentation of younger migrants from the large cities and the prominence of outmigration by the elderly. This phenomenon has been documented and interpreted in the sociological literature (Latuch 1970).

The age profiles for migrations between the five urban regions of Poland show a secondary peak in the 45–50 age group. It is especially noticeable in the case of total outflows from Warsaw, but can also be found in the outmigration profiles for the Katowice (Upper Silesia) region. This elevation in the profiles can be attributed to such factors as mid-career moves by senior executives from the main administrative and industrial centers toward provincial capitals and smaller cities. An introduction of longitudinal data would be required to test the viability of this irregularity in the age profiles. So far it gives results that are rather poor fits of the model curves to observed patterns.

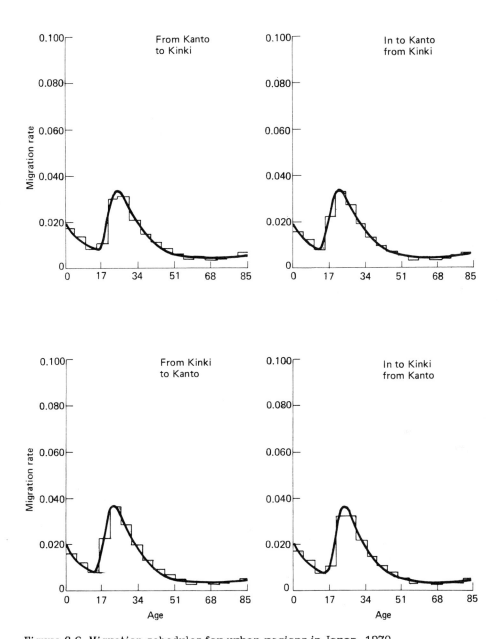

Figure 8.6 Migration schedules for urban regions in Japan, 1970.

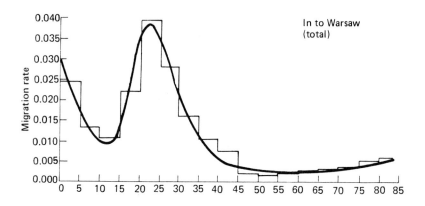

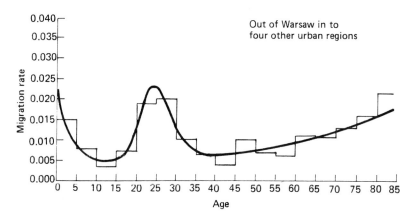

Figure 8.7(a) Migration schedules for urban regions in Poland, 1977.

Thus the hypothesis concerning age composition of interurban migrations finds a partial confirmation in the reviewed material. When compared with aggregate inmigration flows, the flows from and between urban regions are characterized both by a shift of the labor-force-related peak toward higher age groups and to some extent by a mid-career migration peak.

8.3 Conclusion

Several social sciences have contributed to the study of spatial migration patterns by focusing on different aspects and determinants of moves. Thus the sociological approach assumes the importance of family and kinship ties; the geographical hypothesis refers to the role of distance, area, and size of the

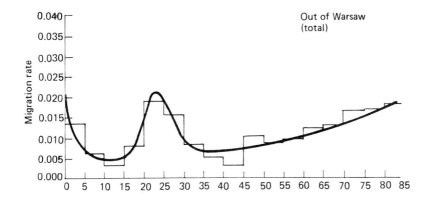

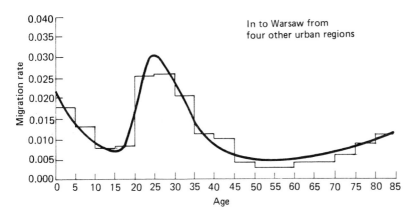

Figure 8.7(b) Migration schedules for urban regions in Poland, 1977.

interacting centers; the demographic framework explores the impacts of the
age and sex structure of the population at risk; and the economic approach
refers to variations in income, labor demand, education, housing, or environmental quality. Finally, the policy approach is concerned with ways in which
interaction between all the factors and variables can be translated into normative terms.

This chapter has examined migration as a correlate of, and a proxy for,
the changing place of large cities within national and multiregional settlement
systems. It emphasizes relationships between the population composition of
urban regions and spatial mobility. The nature of the data used only allowed
the description of observed patterns and the exploration of their implications
for future development. A rigorous economic or policy interpretation would not
be possible at the chosen comparative scale even if much richer data were

available.

Two limitations of the background material should be noted: (a) the set of urban regions was not large and homogeneous enough to allow extended statistical analysis; and (b) population shifts between cores and peripheries of urban regions could not be accounted for because of the large size of the spatial units. Bearing these restrictions in mind, the findings derived from the Migration and Settlement Study are basically in accord with the first, second, and fifth hypotheses. When the analysis is limited to those urban regions that have actually experienced population decline during the 1970s, the fourth hypothesis is also partially supported. The only case in which there is basically no positive evidence pertains to the interregional mobility level of the population living in large urban areas.

PART FOUR

Multiregional Mathematical Demography

CHAPTER NINE

A Short Course on Multiregional
Mathematical Demography

Andrei Rogers and Frans Willekens

The evolution of every regional human population is governed by the interaction of births, deaths, and migration. Individuals are born into a population, age, perhaps reproduce, and ultimately leave the population because of death or outmigration. Individuals from other regions arrive, joining the resident population. These events and flows enter into an accounting relationship in which the growth of a regional population is determined by the combined effects of natural increase (births minus deaths) and net migration (inmigrants minus outmigrants). Multiregional demography focuses on such relationships and seeks to identify and clarify some of the more fundamental spatial population dynamics that are involved by considering how fertility, mortality, and migration combine to determine the growth, age composition, and spatial distribution of a multiregional population.

Two classes of models are commonly used to examine how the growth and structure of a multiregional population evolve from particular regimes of fertility, mortality, and migration. The life table model and the stable population (projection) model both allow one to separate out the impacts, on population growth and structure, of the demographic parameters prevailing during a particular moment and of the age composition and spatial distribution of the multiregional population at that moment. Consequently, a common application of such models is standardization. The first section of this chapter highlights some common features of standardization and life table and stable population analyses.

Section 9.2 reviews the regularities that can be observed in age-specific schedules of, respectively, mortality, fertility, and migration. The regularities have induced demographers to describe such schedules using only a few parameters. For instance, if only two parameters are to be considered, one could describe the level of the schedule and the other its shape. Section 9.3 focuses on data for multiregional population analysis. Several observation plans are distinguished, illustrating the diversity of data systems with which a demographer may have to work. Each data system calls for a different method for estimating the parameters of demographic models (Chapter 10). The parameters considered in this chapter are occurrence/exposure rates. A selection of formulas to calculate such rates are presented in Section 9.4. The multiregional life table model is presented in Section 9.5, and formulas to calculate the various life table statistics are developed therein. The multiregional population projection model is presented next, and several features of the multiregional stable population are reviewed.

9.1 The Components of Multiregional Demographic Change

The allocation of a multiregional population among its constituent regions and the age compositions of its regional populations are determined by the recent history of fertility, mortality, and migration to which it has been subjected. At any given moment its crude regional rates of birth, death, migration, and growth are all governed by the interaction of its regional age compositions and regional shares with the prevailing regime of growth, defined by the current regional age-specific schedules of fertility, mortality, and migration.

Crude rates are weighted sums of age-specific rates and therefore confound patterns of population composition with those of age-specific rates. To clarify the significance of the latter, demographers generally have followed two approaches: direct standardization and stable and stationary population analysis.

Direct standardization is carried out by applying different population compositions to a given schedule, in order to clarify thereby the impact of different compositional patterns on crude rates. The crude birth rate (CBR), for example, is the weighted sum of age-specific fertility rates, the weights being the observed age composition of the population. The total fertility rate (TFR) is the sum of age-specific fertility rates with weights of unity.

Projection of a given population age distribution forward under a fixed regime of growth (i.e., using constant age- and region-specific rates of fertility, mortality, and migration) ultimately produces a *stable* population with fixed regional age compositions and regional shares and constant stable crude rates of birth, death, migration, and growth. The influence of the initial composition disappears entirely, a consequence of the so-called strong ergodicity theorem in mathematical demography.

Crude rates in a stable population are called *intrinsic* rates, and their calculation can be regarded as a form of direct standardization, the weights used being the age–region composition of the stable population. An advantage of intrinsic rates is that they resemble crude rates but are independent of the initial observed population; they are a function only of the age-specific schedules themselves.

Of particular interest to demographers is the stationary population, a stable population with a zero growth rate. Since its characteristics (except for total size) are independent of the initial observed population, and depend only on the various age-specific schedules, the stationary population is useful in the study of these schedules. Because births are equal to deaths in the aggregate population, a set of regional mortality schedules and the set of interregional migration schedules are sufficient to generate a stationary population.

A stationary population is derived from sets of mortality and migration schedules by calculating a multiregional life table. The multiregional life table may therefore be viewed as a model for obtaining the population composition by age and region implied by sets of mortality and migration schedules and by a fixed regional distribution of births. The usual life table contains information not only on the composition and size of the stationary population but also on some important characteristics of this population, such as the distribution of deaths, the probability of surviving to a given age, and the number of years a person may expect to live beyond a fixed age.

9.2 Age Patterns in Multiregional Demographic Change

A search for regularities underlies much of demographic research. The regularity of mortality schedules motivated Coale and Demeny (1966) to construct model life tables, and induced Brass (1971) to develop simple models relating the survival probabilities of a population to a standard survival function and Heligman and Pollard (1980) to develop a parameterized description of the mortality curve. The regularity of fertility curves stimulated research on their graduation (Coale and McNeil 1972, Hoem *et al.* 1981). Finally, the regularities exhibited by migration schedules led Rogers and Castro (1981b and Chapter 5) to describe them with graduation models and also with relational models.

In the simple case, an age-specific schedule may be characterized by two parameters, one pertaining to the level, or intensity, of the curve and the other to its age pattern. The summary indices treated in this section are entirely determined by the schedule, implying a uniform weight function. We consider the area under the curve to be the *level* variable. It is the sum of the age-specific rates multiplied by the width of the age interval. This measure is meaningful for repeatable events, such as birth and migration. If μ_x denotes the age-specific intensity of the schedule considered and if dx represents an infinitesimally small age interval, then the set of all μ_x values constitutes a function and the area under the curve is (gross rate) $\text{GR} = \int_0^\omega \mu_x \mathrm{d}x$, with ω being the highest attainable age.

We consider the mean age of the schedule to be a *pattern* variable, with

$$\bar{x}_\mu = \frac{\int_0^\omega x\,\mu_x \mathrm{d}x}{\int_0^\omega \mu_x \mathrm{d}x} \quad . \tag{9.1}$$

Note that the level and pattern variables are independent of the age–region composition of the population. They are unweighted sums, implying weights of unity.

9.2.1 *Mortality*

Observed age-specific death rates of both high- and low-mortality populations exhibit a remarkably regular pattern. They normally show a moderately high mortality immediately after birth, after which they drop to a minimum between ages 10 and 15, then increase slowly until about age 50, and thereafter rise at an increasing rate. Moreover, in each mortality schedule the death rates experienced at different ages are highly intercorrelated, because if health conditions, for example, are good or poor for one age group in a population they will also tend to be good or poor for all other age groups in that population. Hence if mortality at a particular age in one schedule exceeds that of the same age in another, the first is likely to also have higher death rates at every other age as well. Because of this property, demographers normally find it sufficient to represent the shape of the mortality schedule and its level by a single parameter. This parameter often is the expectation of life at birth, e_0, or at a higher age, say 10 years. The life expectancy at birth represents the mean age of dying in a stationary population.

The life expectancy at birth differs from other level variables in that it is not the sum of age-specific mortality rates but is a sum of age-specific survival probabilities. The sum of age-specific death rates has no clear interpretation, but the sum of survival probabilities can be interpreted unambiguously. If l_x denotes the probability that a person survives until age x, then the life expectancy at age 0 is simply

$$e_0 = \int_0^\omega l_x \mathrm{d}x \quad . \tag{9.2}$$

The calculation of a life table is one way of deriving the probabilities l_x from observed age-specific death rates.

9.2.2 *Fertility*

Age-specific curves of childbearing intensities, μ_x^b, in human populations are shaped by both biological and social factors. The capacity to bear children generally begins at an age α of about 15 and ends by age β, which is normally close to 50. Between these ages the fertility curve is unimodal, attaining its peak somewhere between ages 20 and 35. The precise form of this curve depends on a number of variables, among which age at marriage and the degree of contraception practiced are of paramount importance.

Fertility schedules exhibit a general pattern that persists across a wide variety of regional populations. In all, childbearing begins early in the teenage years, rises to a peak in the twenties or thirties, and then declines regularly to zero by age 50. The *level* of fertility is given by the area under the curve, which is called the *total fertility rate* (TFR) if the schedule refers to live births of both sexes and the *gross reproduction rate* (GRR) if to female births alone, where

$$\text{GRR} = \int_\alpha^\beta \mu_x^b \, dx \ .$$

This level may be interpreted as the number of children an "average" woman would have if a particular fertility schedule prevailed during her lifetime and if the effects of mortality were absent. (If the effects of mortality are introduced, then one obtains the associated *net reproduction rate*, NRR = $\int_\alpha^\beta l_x \mu_x^b \, dx$). Useful summary measures of the associated pattern are the *mean age*

$$\bar{x}_b = \frac{\displaystyle\int_\alpha^\beta x \, \mu_x^b \, dx}{\displaystyle\int_\alpha^\beta \mu_x^b \, dx} \tag{9.3}$$

and the *standard deviation* of the schedule

$$v_b = \left\{ \frac{\displaystyle\int_\alpha^\beta (x - \bar{x}_b)^2 \, \mu_x^b \, dx}{\displaystyle\int_\alpha^\beta \mu_x^b \, dx} \right\}^{1/2}$$

9.2.3 *Migration*

Demographers have long recognized the strong regularities that persist among age-specific schedules of migration, the most prominent being the high concentration of migration among young adults. Rates of migration are also high among children, starting with a peak during the first year of life and then dropping to a low point at about age 16. Beyond that age the curve turns sharply upward to another peak near age 22, declining regularly thereafter, except for possibly a slight hump around 60 through 65, or an upward-sloping curve at the post-retirement ages.

The empirical regularities are not surprising. Young adults exhibit the highest migration rates because they are much less constrained by ties to their community. They are more likely to be renters than home owners, their children generally are not yet in school, and job seniority is not an important consideration. Since children normally move only as members of a family, their migration patterns mirror those of their parents. Inasmuch as younger children generally have younger parents, the migration rates of infants are higher than those of adolescents. Finally, when it exists, the small hump in the age profile between ages 60 and 65 describes migration upon retirement and often reflects moves made to areas with more favorable living conditions.

Two alternative ways of formally specifying the *level* of migration from one region to another are immediately suggested by our discussion of fertility and mortality schedules. The first adopts the frequency concept, used in fertility studies, and defines the migration level from region i to region j in terms of the area under the relevant migration schedule, designating it as the *gross migraproduction rate*, GMR^{ij} say, a period measure specific to the two regions involved. The second adopts a duration perspective and defines the same migration level in terms of the fraction of an average person's lifetime that is spent in the region of destination, a cohort measure specific to an average individual. Specifically,

$$\text{GMR}^{ij} = \int_0^\omega \mu_x^{ij} \, dx \ , \tag{9.4}$$

where μ_x^{ij} is the rate of migration from i to j for x- to $(x + dx)$-year-old persons, and

$$^{i}\vartheta^{j} = \frac{^{i}_{0}e^{j}_{\cdot}}{^{i}_{0}e^{\cdot}_{\cdot}}$$

is said to be the migration level with respect to region j of individuals born in region i.

The numerator in the fraction defining $^{i}\vartheta^{j}$ represents the number of years expected to be lived in region j, on the average, by individuals born in region i and having a total life expectancy of $^{i}_{0}e_{\cdot}$ years. It is the sum, over all ages x, of probabilities that an individual born in i is in j at age x. If we denote the probability for exact age x by ${}_0^i l_x^j$, the number of years spent in j by an i-born individual is

$$
{}_0^i e_{\cdot}^j = \int_0^\omega {}_0^i l_x^j \, dx \ .
\tag{9.5}
$$

The ${}_0^i l_x^j$ values are generally obtained as part of the calculation of a multi-regional life table.

As in the case of fertility, the introduction of the impacts of mortality transforms the gross rate measure GMR into the net rate. The number of migrations out of j by persons born in i is:

$$
{}^i \text{NMR}^j = \int_0^\omega {}_0^i l_x^j \, \mu_x^j \, dx \ .
$$

The fundamental age pattern of migration remains essentially unchanged across populations, with peaks occurring at infancy, during the young adult ages, and occasionally at retirement. Variations in the location of the principal peak and in the levels of migration to major retirement areas indicate that, as in the case of mortality, age patterns of migration may usefully be disaggregated into families that are distinguished by the positions and relative heights of their peaks. Alternatively, such a disaggregation may be carried out, in the manner of fertility schedules, by using the mean age of the migration schedule:

$$
\bar{x}_\mu^{ij} = \frac{\displaystyle\int_0^\omega x \, \mu_x^{ij} \, dx}{\displaystyle\int_0^\omega \mu_x^{ij} \, dx} \ ,
\tag{9.6}
$$

which readily may be used to classify migration schedules into "young" and "old" categories, perhaps with suitable gradations in between.

9.2.4 Regional Age Compositions and Regional Shares

Regional age compositions and regional shares, together with age schedules of fertility, mortality, and migration, determine the main regional component rates of multiregional population growth and change. A single set of such age schedules can produce quite different crude regional rates of birth, death, and migration if combined with different sets of regional age compositions and regional shares. Consequently such rates may be unsatisfactory summary measures of the components of multiregional population growth.

Changes in regional shares, like changes in age compositions, help to shape regional component rates. Regional shares serve as weights in the consolidation process. Hence the same outmigration rate from a region that is twice the size of another will develop twice the impact on the size of the population in the destination region. Moreover, since any idiosyncrasies in the age profile of a sending region's migration schedule are transmitted to the receiving region's population, large sources of heavy outmigration can have a substantial impact on the values assumed by all of the component rates in a destination region.

Let us consider a regional female population for which the regional intensities of fertility, mortality, and migration at age x and time t are denoted by μ_{xt}^{bj}, μ_{xt}^{jd}, and μ_{xt}^{jk}, respectively. If c_{xt}^{j} is the population's age composition and SHA_t^{j} is its regional share of the total multiregional female population, we may define

$$
b_t^j = \int_0^\omega c_{xt}^j \, \mu_{xt}^{bj} \, \mathrm{d}x
$$

$$
d_t^j = \int_0^\omega c_{xt}^j \, \mu_{xt}^{jd} \, \mathrm{d}x
$$

$$
o_t^j = \sum_{\substack{k=1 \\ k \neq j}}^{N} o_t^{jk} = \sum_{\substack{k=1 \\ k \neq j}}^{N} \int_0^\omega c_{xt}^j \, \mu_{xt}^{jk} \, \mathrm{d}x
$$

$$
i_t^j = \sum_{\substack{k=1 \\ k \neq j}}^{N} i_t^{kj} = \sum_{\substack{k=1 \\ k \neq j}}^{N} \frac{\text{SHA}_t^k}{\text{SHA}_t^j} \, o_t^{kj}
$$

$$
r_t^j = b_t^j - d_t^j - o_t^j + i_t^j
$$

$\quad$ (9.7)

to be its instantaneous crude rates of birth, death, outmigration, inmigration, and growth, respectively.

The mean age of a regional population, like the mean ages of fertility and migration schedules, is a summary measure of pattern and is defined as

$$
\bar{x}_t^j = \frac{\displaystyle\int_0^\omega x c_{xt}^j \, \mathrm{d}x}{\displaystyle\int_0^\omega c_{xt}^j \, \mathrm{d}x} = \int_0^\omega x c_{xt}^j \, \mathrm{d}x \quad .
$$

$\quad$ (9.8)

While it is important to underscore the powerful influence that regional age compositions and regional shares have in shaping regional component rates, one must also recognize that past records of fertility, mortality, and migration play an important role in the determination of present regional age compositions and shares, inasmuch as the latter arise out of a history of regional births, deaths, and migrations. For example, a region experiencing high levels of fertility will have a relatively younger population, but if it also is the origin of high levels of outmigration a large proportion of its young adults will move to other regions, producing a higher growth rate in the destination regions while increasing the average age of its own population. This suggests that inferences made about regional fertility, say, on the basis of a model that ignores migration may be seriously in error.

9.3 Data for Multiregional Demographic Analysis

The data used in a multiregional demographic analysis are products of some observation plan. Such a plan describes whether the data were obtained for individuals or only for aggregates; whether for life history segments or for entire lifetimes; whether cohort or period data were collected; and whether observations were complete or fragmentary (Hoem and Funck-Jensen 1982). In short, the observation plan provides a complete description of how the data were collected.

Many observation plans have been treated in the demographic literature. Following Pressat (1969), a distinction may be made between prospective and retrospective observation. An observation is *prospective* if the members of a cohort are observed and their demographic experience is recorded as soon as it occurs. An observation is *retrospective* if people are asked at a certain time about their experience in the past.

9.3.1 *Prospective Observation*

The ideal observation plan is a complete, continuous-time recording of all demographic flows and events as well as all persons in a population that are "at risk" of experiencing such flows and events. In this chapter our attention is focused on the demographic events that imply transfers to the state of death or to other regions of residence.

An event is represented by the letter A in the Lexis diagram set out in Figure 9.1 (Pressat 1969, p.77). In the ideal observation plan, we can associate with each such event a list of characteristics of the event and of the person experiencing it. For a demographic analysis, the important characteristics are the exact time t at which the event occurs, the exact seniority x of the person, and the cohort c to which the individual belongs. Seniority is the duration elapsed since the occurrence of some initial event or event-origin (e.g., birth, entrance into the labor force, marriage, etc.). So $A(x,t,c)$ denotes that a person of cohort c and seniority x experienced event A at time t.

The three characteristics are not independent. If two of them are known, the third can be derived. This is easily shown in Figure 9.1, where t represents the calendar date and x the seniority. The cohort c is simply $t - x$ in the case of a birth cohort. The event A is shown on the lifeline of person a. If all events are recorded as they occur, they may be marked on this lifeline. A complete, continuous-time observation of all events therefore allows one to draw a complete set of individual lifelines.

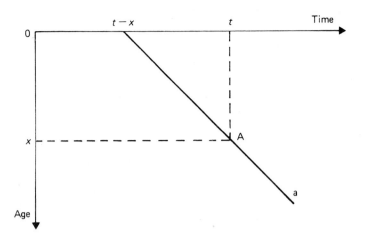

Figure 9.1 Coordinates of a demographic event.

A complete, continuous-time observation of all events is not always available because it requires a continuous registration system. Examples of such observation plans are medical follow-up studies. Other examples are the registration systems that exist in several countries of Europe and which record births, deaths, marital status changes, and residential relocations.

Demographers generally do not have data at the level of the individual. Even if all events are recorded, the data available generally are aggregate, grouped data. For reasons of privacy and manageability, the individual-level data obtained by registration systems, for example, are aggregated over discrete time, seniority, and cohort intervals. Consequently, individual lifelines can no longer be drawn, and the exact times and seniorities at which events occur can only be approximated. For instance, seniority may only be measured in completed years. It also may be impossible to identify the persons who have experienced the events recorded, implying that the interdependence between events, such as their timing, can no longer be examined. Such is the case in the Dutch population registration system. In Scandinavian registration systems, however, each individual is identified by a number and demographic events therefore can be linked to each other. Ledent and Rees make use of this feature to compare movement and transition data for Sweden in Chapter 10.

The aggregation of individual-level data influences its subsequent statistical and demographic analysis. The introduction of discrete time, seniority, and cohort intervals generates observation intervals. The size and shape of the observation interval affect the appropriate formula for the computation of transition probabilities. In the theoretical model, the observation interval is usually assumed to be small enough such that only one event can occur in the interval. (The associated time, seniority, and cohort intervals may be denoted by dt, dx, and dc, respectively.) In many practical situations, however, these intervals are one year or five years wide. These discrete intervals can be visualized in a Lexis diagram, as in Figure 9.2, which shows three lifelines: a, b, and c. Four events are shown on lifeline b: A, B, C, and D. The figure shows a seniority interval $(x, x+h)$, a time interval $(t, t+h)$, and a cohort interval $(t-x-h, t-x)$. Each of these intervals is assumed to be h years wide (hence the time interval u is equal to the age interval h). The cohort consists of the group of people who experienced the initial event in the time period from $t-x-h$ to $t-x$. By fixing two of the three component intervals, the observation interval is fixed. There are therefore three types of observations, depending on the observation interval: period observations, cohort observations, and period–cohort observations. For ease of presentation, we assume in this section that $h = 1$.

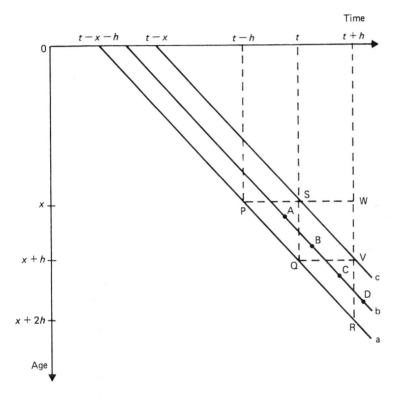

Figure 9.2 Lexis diagram.

A period observation plan records the calendar year in which an event occurs as well as the seniority of the person at the time of the event. The

seniority is recorded in completed years. In Figure 9.2, the period observation interval is represented by SQVW. This interval covers *two cohorts*.

A cohort observation plan records, for a person experiencing an event,
the cohort to which the person belongs as well as the seniority (in completed
years) at the time of the event (i.e., the parallelogram PQVS). The observation
interval extends over *two calendar years* (or two time intervals if $h \neq 1$).

Finally, a period—cohort observation plan records the calendar year in
which the event occurs as well as the cohort to which the person belongs (i.e.,
the parallelogram SQRV). The observation interval covers *two seniority
classes*. Recording the cohort in a period—cohort observation is equivalent to
recording the seniority at the beginning of the time interval (i.e., at time t) or
at the end of the interval (i.e., at time $t + h$) and is also equivalent to recording seniority as a period difference. The latter is obtained by subtracting the
year of occurrence of the event of study from the year of occurrence of the
initial event, or event-origin (Wunsch and Termote 1978, p.10).

By way of summary, each observation is now described on the assumption
that the events of interest are migrations from region i to region j and that
the cohorts are birth cohorts. Then the period observation plan measures the
number of persons who migrate at age x (in completed years) in year $(t, t + 1)$.
The cohort observation plan measures how many members of the cohort
$(t - x - 1, t - x)$ move at age x in completed years (i.e., between ages x and
$x + 1$). The period—cohort observation plan measures how many members of the
cohort $(t - x - 1, t - x)$ move in calendar year $(t, t + 1)$, that is, it records the
number of migrations by year of birth or by age on January 1 of the calendar
year considered. (Recall that the period observation plan records age at the
time of migration.)

9.3.2 *Retrospective Observation*

In retrospective observation, individuals are asked about past experiences. A major difference from prospective observation is that only a
subcohort's demographic experiences can be recorded. Some persons are
excluded from observation because of death or of emigration out of the country.

The subcohort observed therefore consists of a group of persons who did
not experience terminating events (Feichtinger 1979, p.154). Retrospective
observations approximate observations in a pure state under certain conditions (Wunsch and Termote 1978, p.40). Events are said to be observed in a
pure state if the occurrence of the event observed is not disturbed by the
influence of other events, such as mortality and international migration. In
other words, measurement in a pure state is a measurement of an event in the
absence of competing risks.[1] Other problems of retrospective observation,

---

[1]The concept of a pure state was developed by Henry (1972, p.76). For an extensive treatment, see Wunsch and Termote (1978). Some interesting observations on this and other

such as memory lapse, are not considered here, but they may be important in empirical studies.

In retrospective surveys, there are basically two approaches to measuring migration. In the first approach, migrations are measured directly. People may be asked about the last migration, the first and last migration, or about all the migrations made since a particular age (migration histories). In the second approach, migrations are measured indirectly by comparing the current region of residence with one at some previous point in time. The point in time may be a variable (e.g., region of birth) or it may be fixed (e.g., residence exactly one year prior to the survey).

The first approach focuses on events (migrations), while the second approach focuses on the persons experiencing the events (migrants). The character of life history data is similar to the character of data from prospective observation provided that no terminating events have occurred. Both types of data fall in the category of *movement* data (Ledent 1980c). The indirect measurement of transfers leads to what Ledent calls *transition* data. The distinction between movement and transition data is important for the calculation of transition probabilities, as Ledent and Rees demonstrate in Chapter 10 of this book.

In prospective observation, differences in the measurement of age lead to different observation plans and to different formulas for estimating the corresponding transition probabilities. The same is true for retrospective surveys. In retrospective surveys the age group at the time of enumeration is measured. It can be seen in the Lexis diagram that this age measurement is equivalent to the measurement of the period of birth; consequently the observation is a period–cohort observation.

9.4 Estimation of Occurrence/Exposure Rates and Transition Probabilities: Mathematical Theory

Life tables and population projections are normally generated from sets of age-specific probabilities of survival, migration, and childbearing. These transition probabilities, in turn, need to be estimated from the data available to the demographer.

The observation plans presented in the previous section illustrate the diversity of data types with which a demographer may have to work. The parameters (probabilities) derived from the data (i.e., the *empirical measures*) frequently differ in character from the parameters used in the demographic models (the *model measures*). For instance, life table analysis is basically a cohort analysis and the probabilities used are cohort measures. These

---

concepts, and on some resulting inconsistencies in the language demographers use, are made by Feichtinger (1979, pp.42–43).

relate the status of a person at exact age $x + h$ to his status at exact age x (e.g., the lifelines crossing QV in Figure 9.2 are related to lifelines crossing PS). In population projections, different probabilities are used; namely, period—cohort probabilities. They relate the status of a person aged $x + h$ in completed years at time $t + 1$ to the status of a person aged x in completed years at time t (lifelines crossing RV are related to lifelines crossing QS).

The mathematical theory for the derivation of transition probabilities is based on a continuous-time formulation of the dynamics of multiregional population systems and adopts a cohort perspective of transition probabilities. The theory leads to the estimation of discrete-time probabilities that are functions of continuous-time intensities. Since obtaining complete, continuous-time observations of all events is generally not a feasible strategy, the theoretical formulation often must be adapted to conform with the data available for the analysis. In addition, available data may not allow a calculation of the appropriate type of probabilities. Such a situation calls for approximations that involve certain simplifying assumptions in order to relate transition probability calculations to specific observation plans. In Chapters 2 and 10, such assumptions are spelled out.

To facilitate the exposition, we distinguish three steps in the derivation of transition probabilities. First, the population at age $x + dx$ is expressed as a function of the population at age x and of the events that occurred in the ensuing interval dx. It will be assumed that the population is undisturbed by international migration. Second, a set of instantaneous rates of transition (called intensities) are defined. Finally, transition probabilities are derived for discrete age—time intervals. The first two steps are equivalent to postulating that the evolution of the multiregional system is described by a continuous-time Markov process, representable by the Kolmogorov equation.

Let l_x^i be the number of people of exact age x in region i, and let the number of people in i of exact age $x + dx$ be[2]

$$l_{x+dx}^i = l_x^i - l_x^{id} - \sum_{j \neq i} l_x^{ij} + \sum_{k \neq i} l_x^{ki} \, , \tag{9.9}$$

where l_x^{id} is the number of persons of exact age x in region i who die before reaching age $x + dx$ (i.e., who die during the interval dx), and l_x^{ij} is the number of migrations from i to j in the interval dx.

We now introduce transition intensities. Let μ_x^{id} be the intensity of mortality at age x in region i and μ_x^{ij} be the rate of transition from i to j at age x. The intensity is the ratio of the number of occurrences of events in the interval dx to the total length of exposure experienced by the l_x^i persons in the interval dx. This total is equal to $l_x^i dx$. Equation (9.9) therefore may be

---

[2] The number of people is expressed in terms of a unit birth cohort. Therefore, l_x^i coincides with the probability that a new born baby survives to exact age x and resides in region i.

reexpressed as follows:

$$l^i_{x+dx} = l^i_x - \mu^{id}_x l^i_x dx - \sum_{j \neq i} \mu^{ij}_x l^i_x dx + \sum_{k \neq i} \mu^{ki}_x l^k_x dx \; ,$$

from which

$$\frac{l^i_{x+dx} - l^i_x}{dx} = -\hat{\mu}^{i\cdot}_x l^i_x + \sum_{k \neq i} \mu^{ki}_x l^k_x \; , \tag{9.10}$$

where

$$\hat{\mu}^{i\cdot}_x = \mu^{id}_x + \sum_{j \neq i} \mu^{ij}_x \; .$$

Equation (9.10) yields the Kolmogorov differential equation for Markov chains,

$$\frac{d}{dx} l^{i\cdot}_x = -\hat{\mu}^{i\cdot}_x l^i_x + \sum_{k \neq i} \mu^{ki}_x l^k_x \; , \tag{9.11}$$

an equation that describes the changes in l^i_x as a function of the instantaneous rates of mobility and mortality and of the initial condition, that is, the region of residence at exact age x. The equation may be written for all i and the system of equations may be expressed in matrix form as:

$$\frac{d}{dx} \mathbf{l}_x = -\boldsymbol{\mu}_x \mathbf{l}_x \; , \tag{9.12}$$

where $\boldsymbol{\mu}_x$ is the matrix of instantaneous rates, set out as

$$\boldsymbol{\mu}_x = \begin{bmatrix} \hat{\mu}^{1\cdot}_x & -\mu^{21}_x & \cdots & -\mu^{N1}_x \\ -\mu^{12}_x & \hat{\mu}^{2\cdot}_x & \cdots & -\mu^{N2}_x \\ \vdots & \vdots & & \vdots \\ -\mu^{1N}_x & -\mu^{2N}_x & \cdots & \hat{\mu}^{N\cdot}_x \end{bmatrix} \; , \tag{9.13}$$

where N is the number of regions.

Equation (9.12) describes the evolution of a cohort by region of residence at age x. In multiregional analysis, it also may be of interest to relate the region of residence at age x to the region of residence at a previous age y. Let $^m_y l^i_x$ be the number of people in i at age x who were in m at age y. The age y defines a cohort. If $y = 0$, the cohort is the birth cohort or *radix*. The values of $^m_y l^i_x$ for a given y and x may be arranged as the following matrix:

$$_y\mathbf{l}_x = \begin{bmatrix} ^1_y l^1_x & ^2_y l^1_x & \cdots & ^N_y l^1_x \\ ^1_y l^2_x & ^2_y l^2_x & \cdots & ^N_y l^2_x \\ \vdots & \vdots & & \vdots \\ ^1_y l^N_x & ^2_y l^N_x & \cdots & ^N_y l^N_x \end{bmatrix} \; . \tag{9.14}$$

The evolution of a population disaggregated by region of residence at age x and region of residence at age y is governed by the Kolmogorov equation

$$\frac{\mathrm{d}}{\mathrm{d}x}\,_y\mathbf{l}_x = -\,\mu_x\,_y\mathbf{l}_x \; , \tag{9.15}$$

where it is assumed that the intensities depend only on the (current) region of residence at age x and are independent of the region of residence at age y. (Note that $_y\mathbf{l}_y$ is a diagonal matrix, with the diagonal elements denoting the regional distribution of the cohort's members.)

Following the standard approach used when μ_x is a scalar, one might try to solve equation (9.15) with

$$_y\mathbf{l}_x = \exp\left(-\int_y^x \mu_t\,\mathrm{d}t\right)\,_y\mathbf{l}_y \; . \tag{9.16}$$

However, this approach does not work when μ_x is a matrix. For the above function to be a solution of equation (9.12) the μ_x matrices must be commutative, and in general they are not. Therefore other approaches must be adopted.

To solve equation (9.15), we may follow two avenues. Both introduce age intervals of equal width, h say. The first avenue postulates a piecewise constant intensity function, assuming that μ_x is fixed in the interval $(x, x+h)$. This implies an exponential distribution of demographic events within each age interval, and the survival function that results is therefore referred to as the exponential model. The assumption of constant intensities within age intervals not only helps solve equation (9.12), but it is also needed to equate μ_x to observed occurrence/exposure rates and hence to calculate $\mathbf{l}_x$ from the data.

The second avenue postulates a piecewise linear survival function $_y\mathbf{l}_x$. A piecewise linear function is obtained if demographic events are uniformly distributed within the age intervals of length h. The survival function that results is referred to as the linear model. Although the first avenue is simpler and leads to transition probabilities with useful properties, the second avenue also has its merits. The assumption of a uniform distribution of events over the observation interval enables one to derive the life table directly from a set of simple accounting equations, clarifying the choices that arise in life table construction if different observation plans are available. It also clarifies some of the similarities and differences between life table and projection models in uniregional and multiregional population systems.

The first avenue of solution is preferred by mathematical statisticians, because it focuses on the Kolmogorov equation. The second avenue may be preferred by demographers since it foquses more directly on the data and on familiar accounting relationships. Both avenues are presented below.

9.4.1 *The Exponential Model (Piecewise Constant Intensity Function).*

If μ_x is constant within the interval $(x, x + h)$, the solution to equation (9.12) for this interval is

$$_y l_{x+h} = e^{-h\, m_X} {}_y l_x \quad , \qquad (9.17)$$

where $m_X = \mu_x$ is the matrix of occurrence/exposure rates for the age interval $X = (x, x + h)$.

We define the matrix of conditional probabilities

$$\mathbf{p}_x = \begin{bmatrix} p_x^{11} & p_x^{21} & \cdots & p_x^{N1} \\ p_x^{12} & p_x^{22} & \cdots & p_x^{N2} \\ \vdots & \vdots & & \vdots \\ p_x^{1N} & p_x^{2N} & \cdots & p_x^{NN} \end{bmatrix}, \qquad (9.18)$$

where p_x^{ij} denotes $p_{x,x+h}^{ij}$ and is the probability that an individual alive in region i at exact age x will be in region j, h years later, at age $x + h$. If we assume that this probability is independent of region of residence at any prior age y and that it depends only on the region at the beginning of the interval h, then the transition probability matrix may be seen to be

$$\mathbf{p}_x = e^{-h\, m_X} \quad . \qquad (9.19)$$

This solution of the set of differential equations in equation (9.12) has been followed by Hoem and Fong (1976), Krishnamoorthy (1979), and Ledent (1980c).

The probability of dying may be obtained by subtraction: $q_x^i = p_x^{id} = 1 - \sum_{j=1}^{N} p_x^{ij}$, and the survival function $_y l_x$ in equation (9.17) decreases exponentially in the interval.

9.4.2 *The Linear Model (Piecewise Linear Survival Function)*

To solve the system of linear time-inhomogeneous differential equations in equation (9.15), we may replace it by the following system of differential equations (Willekens *et al.* 1982):

$$_y l_x = {}_y l_y - \int_0^n \mu_{y+t}\, {}_y l_{y+t}\, dt \quad , \qquad (9.20)$$

where $n = x - y$. This transforms the problem of solving the system of Kolmogorov differential equations into that of evaluating

$$\int_0^n \mu_{y+t}\, {}_y l_{y+t}\, dt \quad .$$

Let the interval (y, x) be divided into subintervals of length h:

$$_y\mathbf{l}_{y+h} = {}_y\mathbf{l}_y - \int_0^h \mu_{y+t} \, {}_y\mathbf{l}_{y+t} \, dt$$

$$_y\mathbf{l}_{y+2h} = {}_y\mathbf{l}_{y+h} - \int_0^h \mu_{y+h+t} \, {}_y\mathbf{l}_{y+h+t} \, dt \tag{9.21}$$

$$\vdots$$

$$_y\mathbf{l}_{x+h} = {}_y\mathbf{l}_x - \int_0^h \mu_{x+t} \, {}_y\mathbf{l}_{x+t} \, dt$$

If $_y\mathbf{l}_x$ is nonsingular, $\mathbf{p}_x$ is given by

$$\mathbf{p}_x = {}_y\mathbf{l}_{x+h} \, {}_y\mathbf{l}_x^{-1} . \tag{9.22}$$

Equation (9.22) implies that $_y\mathbf{l}_{x+h} = \mathbf{p}_x \, {}_y\mathbf{l}_x$. A comparison of this expression with equation (9.21) yields

$$\mathbf{p}_x = \mathbf{I} - \int_0^h \mu_{x+t} \, {}_y\mathbf{l}_{x+t} \, {}_y\mathbf{l}_x^{-1} \, dt . \tag{9.23}$$

We have obtained the expression for $\mathbf{p}_x$ without making any assumption about the behavior of the instantaneous rates in the intervals of width h. This derivation does not at the outset approximate the μ_t function by a set of step functions.

From equation (9.21) one may also derive an expression for the annual age-specific rates in the multiregional life table:

$$_y\mathbf{l}_{x+h} - {}_y\mathbf{l}_x = - \int_0^h \mu_{x+t} \, {}_y\mathbf{l}_{x+t} \, dt \left[\int_0^h {}_y\mathbf{l}_{x+t} \, dt \right]^{-1} \left[\int_0^h {}_y\mathbf{l}_{x+t} \, dt \right] . \tag{9.24}$$

The expression $\int_0^h {}_y\mathbf{l}_{x+t} \, dt$ represents the number of years lived in each region, between ages x and $x+h$, per person in each region at age y. We define this quantity by

$$_y\mathbf{L}_X = \int_0^h {}_y\mathbf{l}_{x+t} \, dt . \tag{9.25}$$

The matrix $_y\mathbf{L}_X$ also may be looked upon as representing the number of people by region in age group x to $x+h$, per person in each region at age y. Hence it gives the age distribution of the life table population. The expression

$$\left[\int_0^h \mu_{x+t} \, {}_y\mathbf{l}_{x+t} \, dt \right] \left[\int_0^h {}_y\mathbf{l}_{x+t} \, dt \right]^{-1} = \mathbf{m}_X \tag{9.26}$$

is then the matrix of age-specific life table rates. These rates are occurrence/exposure rates and are cohort rates because they are derived from the life table model.

Equation (9.26) expresses the occurrence/exposure rate of the life table population (cohort rate) in terms of the intensities. It permits us to express equation (9.24) as follows:

$$_y l_{x+h} - {}_y l_x = - m_X \, {}_y L_X \ .$$

To derive an expression for p_x in terms of life table rates, recall that $_y l_{x+h} = p_x \, {}_y l_x$. Hence

$$(p_x - I) \, {}_y l_x = - m_X \, {}_y L_X$$

and

$$p_x = I - m_X \, {}_y L_X \, {}_y l_x^{-1} \ . \tag{9.27}$$

To solve this equation, one must find an approximation for the integral in equation (9.25). The simplest approximation derives from the assumption that all events are uniformly distributed over the interval $(x, x + h)$, implying that $\int_0^h {}_y l_{x+t} \, dt$ may be approximated by the linear integration

$$_y L_X = (h/2)({}_y l_x + {}_y l_{x+h}) \ . \tag{9.28}$$

Introducing equation (9.28) into the expression for p_x gives

$$\begin{aligned}
p_x &= I - (h/2) \, m_X ({}_y l_x + {}_y l_{x+h}) \, {}_y l_x^{-1} \\
&= I - (h/2) \, m_X (I + p_x) \\
&= [I + (h/2) \, m_X]^{-1} [I - (h/2) \, m_X] \ . \tag{9.29}
\end{aligned}$$

With empirical data the elements m_X^{ij} may be estimated using equations presented in Chapter 10.

9.5 The Multiregional Life Table

The life table is a model devised to study the demographic implications of applying a particular schedule of mortality to a birth cohort. A birth cohort, or radix, is a hypothetical group of children born at the same moment. Frequently, this hypothetical cohort is assumed to consist of 100 000 persons. The consequences are expressed in terms of survival probabilities, numbers of years lived, number of persons in each group, and number of deaths by age. A life table thus describes the evolution of a hypothetical group of babies born at the same time and exposed to a particular schedule of mortality.

A multiregional life table is a model for evaluating the demographic implications of applying a particular set of mortality and migration schedules to a multiregional birth cohort. The consequences are expressed in terms of such indices as migration and survival probabilities, numbers of years lived in each region, and numbers of migrants.

The simple mortality table and the multiregional life table are the two extremes among a number of alternative life table models. The simplest model recognizes only one class of decrement, such as death. It is referred to as a *single-decrement* (uniregional) life table. Life tables that recognize several modes of exit from the population are known as *multiple-decrement* life tables (Keyfitz 1968). They have been applied, for example, in studies of mortality by cause of death and in analyses of first marriage and of death.

A further generalization of the life table concept arises with the recognition of entries as well as exits. Such *increment–decrement life tables* (Schoen 1975) allow for multiple movements between several states, for example, transitions between marital statuses (single, married, divorced, widowed) and death, or between labor force statuses (employed, unemployed, out of labor force) and death. In uniradix, increment–decrement life tables, there is a single birth cohort or radix, which implies complete homogeneity in the hypothetical initial population.

Multiple-radix increment–decrement life tables recognize heterogeneity in the birth cohort. Tables that simultaneously consider several regional populations, each with its own region-specific schedule of mortality and several destination-specific schedules of internal migration, are called *multiregional life tables* (Rogers 1973a, b). They represent the most general class of life tables and were developed for the study of interregional migration flows between interacting multiregional populations.

Several useful statistics of the life table may be derived from the matrices of probabilities $_y\mathbf{l}_x$ and $\mathbf{p}_x$. For example, the matrix $_y\mathbf{L}_X$ represents the number of years lived in each region between ages x and $x + h$, per person in each region at age y [equation (9.25)]. It may also be interpreted as the number of persons in age group $(x, x + h)$ in each region, per person at age y in each region. The elements of the $_y\mathbf{L}_X$ matrices therefore give the age composition of the life table or stationary population. In this perspective, $_0^j l_0^j$ is unity and an element $_0^j L_X^i$ denotes the number of j-born people in region i of age x to $x + h$ per birth in j. To obtain the number of people aged x to $x + h$ in region i, $_0^j L_X^i$ must be multiplied by the number of births in j in the stationary population.

For $y = 0$, $_y\mathbf{L}_X$ denotes the average number of years lived between x and $x + h$ in each region by the birth cohort. This quantity may be approximated by linear interpolation to give

$$_0\mathbf{L}_X = (h/2)\,(_0\mathbf{l}_x + {_0\mathbf{l}_{x+h}})_0\mathbf{l}_0^{-1} \;,$$

where $_0\mathbf{l}_0$ is a diagonal matrix containing the regional radices in the diagonal. In other words, $_0\mathbf{L}_X$ represents the *relative* population distribution by places of current and previous residences. Instead of being expressed in percentages or in some other manner, the distribution is given with respect to a single birth. This is a logical procedure in demography since it separates the fertility component from the survivorship (mortality and migration) component. $_0\mathbf{L}_X$ depends on two components: the probability of surviving to age x, and the average time spent in each region during the h-year interval by a person of age x at the beginning of the interval. The latter component is the number of person-years lived between x and $x + h$ by region of residence at age x.

If $y = x$, $_y\mathbf{L}_X$ represents the number of years lived in each region per person aged x and present in each of the regions at exact age x. It is equal to:

$$_x\mathbf{L}_X = {_0\mathbf{L}_X}\,{_0\mathbf{l}_x^{-1}} \,, \tag{9.30}$$

where $_x\mathbf{L}_X$ is the $_0\mathbf{L}_X$ matrix expressed per unit *regional* cohort. Using the linear approximation of $_0\mathbf{L}_X$, we may reduce this expression to

$$_x\mathbf{L}_X = (h/2)\,({_0\mathbf{l}_{x+h}} + {_0\mathbf{l}_x})\,{_0\mathbf{l}_x^{-1}} = (h/2)\,(\mathbf{p}_x + \mathbf{I}) \,. \tag{9.31}$$

The matrix $_0\mathbf{l}_x$ is an *unconditional* measure, whereas $_x\mathbf{L}_X$ is *conditional* on reaching age x. These two matrices are, respectively, the matrix of duration of residence *by region of birth*, and the corresponding matrix by *region of residence*. These expressions of residence duration provide a logical basis for population-based and region-based measures of numbers of years lived and of life expectancies.

Before proceeding to derive the matrix of life expectancies, we must develop expressions for $_y\mathbf{L}_X$ and $_x\mathbf{L}_X$ for $X = \Omega$, the last, open-ended age group. Setting $\mathbf{p}_x = 0$ in equation (9.27) shows that the number of years lived in the last age group is given by

$$_y\mathbf{L}_\Omega = \mathbf{m}_\Omega^{-1}\,{_y\mathbf{l}_\omega} \,. \tag{9.32}$$

Summing the $_y\mathbf{L}_X$ matrices over all ages greater than x yields the total number of person-years lived beyond age x by members of the cohort aged y:

$$_y\mathbf{T}_x = \sum_{Z=X}^{\Omega} {_y\mathbf{L}_Z} \,.$$

A particularly interesting life table function is the expectation of life. As mentioned earlier, two measures of life expectancy may be distinguished in multiregional analysis: those based on populations (irrespective of residence status) and those based on regions of residence (irrespective of birth status).

9.5.1 *Population-Based Measure of Life Expectancy*

The population-based measure of life expectancy gives the number of years spent in each region beyond age x and the expectation of life at age x without reference to an individual's region of residence at age x or at some previous age. To compute the population-based measure of life expectancy, we must determine the average probability of surviving to age x. Let R^k be the proportion of children that are born in region k in the stationary population $(\sum_k R^k = 1)$. The average probability of surviving to age x is therefore:

$$_0\dot{l}_x^{\cdot} = \sum_i \sum_k R^k \, _0^k l_x^i \, .$$

The number of years lived beyond age x in each of the regions by an average person is

$$_0\dot{T}_x^i = \sum_{Z=X}^{\Omega} \sum_k R^k \, _0^k L_Z^i \, .$$

The population-based measure of life expectancy at age x by region of future residence is therefore

$$_0\dot{e}_x^i = \frac{_0\dot{T}_x^i}{_0\dot{l}_x^{\cdot}} \, . \tag{9.33}$$

The total number of years lived beyond age x by an average person of age x is

$$_0\dot{e}_x^{\cdot} = \sum_i {_0\dot{e}_x^i} \, .$$

9.5.2 Residence-Based Measure of Life Expectancy

The residence-based measure of life expectancy gives the average time spent in the various regions beyond age x by an individual who resides in a particular region at age $y\,(y \leq x)$. If $y = x$, this status-based measure refers to a person's current residential status and the formula becomes particularly simple and illuminating. For example, the total number of years a person of age y in region k may expect to spend in the same region is

$$_y^k e^k = \int_0^{\omega-y} {_y^k l_{y+t}^k} \, \mathrm{d}t \, ,$$

with $_y^k l_{y+t}^k$ being the probability that a person aged y in region k will also be alive there t years later, and where ω is the highest attainable age. In general, we may write

$$_y\mathbf{e}_y = \int_0^{\omega-y} {_y\mathbf{l}_{y+t}} \, \mathrm{d}t$$

or, in discrete form,

$$_y\mathbf{e}_y = \sum_{z=0}^{\Omega-Y} {_y\mathbf{L}_{Y+Z}} = {_y\mathbf{T}_y} \, . \tag{9.34}$$

Equation (9.34) refers to the life expectancy beyond age y of persons currently aged y years. What is the life expectancy beyond age x of persons in a given region at any previous age y? Their state of residence at age x is of no importance here. The life expectancy beyond age x by future region of residence and location at age y is

$$_y\mathbf{e}_x = \left[\int_0^{\omega-x} {}_y\mathbf{l}_{x+t}\,dt\right]_y\hat{\mathbf{l}}_x^{-1}$$

$$= {}_y\mathbf{T}_x\,_y\hat{\mathbf{l}}_x^{-1} , \tag{9.35}$$

where $_y\hat{\mathbf{l}}_x$ is a diagonal matrix with elements $_y^i l_x^{\cdot} = \sum_k {}_y^i l_x^k$ that denote the probability that a person aged y in region i will survive to age x. If $y = 0$, we obtain the life expectancy by regions of future residence and of birth.

The life expectancy matrix has a form similar to $_y\mathbf{l}_x$. An element $_y^i e_x^j$ denotes the number of years a person in region i at age y may expect to spend in region j after birthday x. The total expectation of life beyond age x of a person in region i at age y is given by the column sum. The numbers of years lived in each region are represented by the column elements. These life expectancy measures are region-specific.

Two remarks may be made at this point. First, equation (9.34) is a special case of equation (9.35) since, for $x = y$, $_y\hat{\mathbf{l}}_x$ is the identity matrix. Second, given values for $_y\mathbf{T}_x$ and $_y\mathbf{l}_x$ one can derive the matrix of life expectancies for any age $x \geq y$:

$$_x\mathbf{e}_x = {}_y\mathbf{T}_x\,_y\mathbf{l}_x^{-1} . \tag{9.36}$$

The notion of expectancy is a common demographic measure of level. Besides life expectancies, demographers also refer to reproduction expectancies when discussing fertility levels and to migraproduction expectancies when describing mobility levels. The continuous formulation of the net reproduction rate is given in Subsection 9.2.2. The discrete version is:

$$\text{NRR} = \sum_{X=0}^{\Omega} L_X m_X^b ,$$

where m_X^b is the age-specific fertility rate. The corresponding formula for migration is

$$\text{NMR} = \sum_{X=0}^{\Omega} L_X m_X^{\cdot} ,$$

where $m_X^{\cdot}$ is the total migration rate for age group X. Both measures represent the average number of occurrences of a recurrent event over an individual's lifetime. Only the latter measure, however, is influenced by the spatial extent of the territorial units.

Spatial expectancies introduce a disaggregation by place of birth and place of occurrence, using superscripts. Thus

$$^i\text{NRR}^j = \sum_{X=0}^{\Omega} {}_0^iL_X^j\, m_X^{bj}$$

and

$$^i\text{NMR}^j = \sum_{X=0}^{\Omega} {}_0^iL_X^j\, m_X^{j\cdot} \ .$$

The spatial net reproduction rate describes the number of births experienced in region j by an average individual born in region i over the expected lifetime. The spatial net migraproduction rate describes the number of migrations made out of region j by an average individual born in region i over the expected lifetime.

Finally, a statistic that is generally calculated in a life table is the survivorship proportion. It is the probability that a person aged x to $x+h$ in region i at time t will be in region j and aged $x+h$ to $x+2h$ at time $t+1$.[3] The survivorship proportion is a period–cohort transition probability. If period–cohort data are available it can directly be derived from the data by using equation (9.34). The life table transforms the cohort transition probability matrix $\mathbf{p}_x$ into the period–cohort survivorship proportion matrix $\mathbf{s}_x$.

The matrix of survivorship proportions has the same configuration as the $\mathbf{p}_x$ matrix given in equation (9.18):

$$\mathbf{s}_X = \begin{bmatrix} s_X^{11} & s_X^{21} & \cdots & s_X^{N1} \\ s_X^{12} & s_X^{22} & \cdots & s_X^{N2} \\ \vdots & \vdots & & \vdots \\ s_X^{1N} & s_X^{2N} & \cdots & s_X^{NN} \end{bmatrix} \tag{9.37}$$

where s_X^{ij} is the proportion of x- to $(x+h)$-year-old residents of region i at time t who are alive and aged $x+h$ to $x+2h$ in region j, h years later at time $t+1$. It is a period–cohort transition probability that may be derived from cohort probabilities:

$$\mathbf{s}_X = {}_y\mathbf{L}_{X+H}\ {}_y\mathbf{L}_X^{-1}$$

or

$$\mathbf{s}_X = (\mathbf{I} + \mathbf{p}_{x+h})\mathbf{p}_x(\mathbf{I} + \mathbf{p}_x)^{-1} \ . \tag{9.38}$$

The survivorship matrix for the next-to-last age group may be obtained form

$$\mathbf{s}_{\Omega} - H = \mathbf{L}_{\Omega}\,\mathbf{L}_{\Omega-H}^{-1}$$

---

[3] For convenience we shall henceforth define unit time intervals to be h years long. This will allow us to raise the matrix $\mathbf{G}$ in equation (9.52) to powers that are sequential integers.

$$= (2/h)\mathbf{m}_{\Omega}^{-1}\,\mathbf{p}_{\omega-h}\,(\mathbf{I} + \mathbf{p}_{\omega-h})^{-1} \tag{9.39}$$

or

$$\mathbf{s}_{\Omega-H} = (1/h)\mathbf{m}_{\Omega}^{-1}[\mathbf{I} - (h/2)\mathbf{m}_{\Omega-H}] \ . \tag{9.40}$$

However, it has been shown by Just and Liaw (1983) that equations (9.39) and (9.40) can yield a highly unrealistic result for the last, open-ended age group. To obtain an improved result with such a model, one could proceed by setting

$$\mathbf{s}_{\Omega-H} = (\mathbf{I} - e^{-h\,\mathbf{m}_{\Omega}})\,\mathbf{m}_{\Omega}^{-1}\mathbf{p}_{\omega}\mathbf{m}_{\Omega-H}\,(\mathbf{I} - \mathbf{p}_{\omega-h})^{-1} \tag{9.41}$$

and

$$\mathbf{s}_{\Omega} = e^{-h\,\mathbf{m}_{\Omega}} \ . \tag{9.42}$$

Equations (9.41) and (9.42) are derived from the relation

$$\mathbf{L}_{\Omega} = \mathbf{s}_{\Omega-H}\mathbf{L}_{\Omega-H} + \mathbf{s}_{\Omega}\mathbf{l}_{\Omega} \ , \tag{9.43}$$

which recognizes that some individuals in $\mathbf{L}_{\Omega}$ may still remain in the system after h years have gone by.

The survivorship proportions may also be estimated directly from the data, if data on transitions are available. Chapter 10 gives an exposition of the transition approach to estimating survivorship proportions and transition probabilities.

9.6 Multiregional Population Projection

Until about two decades ago, the contribution of internal migration to population growth was generally assessed in nonspatial terms. The evolution of regional populations affected by migration was examined by adding the contribution of *net* migration to that of natural increase. The dynamics of redistribution were therefore expressed over time but not over space; the evolution of a system of interacting regional populations was studied one region at a time.

Beginning in the mid-1960s, efforts to express the dynamics of spatial change in matrix form began to appear in the demographic literature and had considerable success in describing processes of geographical redistribution in multiregional population systems. Such studies have viewed the spatial distribution of a multiregional population across its constituent regions and the age compositions of its regional populations as being determined by the interactions of fertility, mortality, and interregional migration.

9.6.1 *Projecting with the Multiregional Growth Matrix*

The multiregional growth process for a closed population may be expressed in matrix form as

$$K_{t+1} = \mathbf{G}_T K_t \; , \tag{9.44}$$

where K_t is the age and regional distribution of the population at time t, and $\mathbf{G}_T$ is the multiregional growth matrix, which applies to the period $(t, t+h)$. In this section the growth matrix is viewed as being time-independent, namely $\mathbf{G}_T = \mathbf{G}$, and the projection is for unit time intervals that are u years in length (five years, say) and equal to the width h of the age interval. (The assumption of time independence is not essential, but it is convenient for deriving the characteristics of the stable population.) The vector K_t is partitioned as follows:

$$K_t = \begin{bmatrix} K_{0t} \\ K_{Ht} \\ \vdots \\ K_{\Omega t} \end{bmatrix} \text{ and } K_{Xt} = \begin{bmatrix} K_{Xt}^1 \\ K_{Xt}^2 \\ \vdots \\ K_{Xt}^N \end{bmatrix}, \tag{9.45}$$

where K_{Xt} is the regional distribution of the population in age group x to $x+h$, and K_{Xt}^i denotes the number of people in region i at time t who are x to $x+h$ years of age.

The arrangement of the submatrices in the multiregional growth matrix is

$$\mathbf{G} = \begin{bmatrix} \mathbf{0} & \mathbf{0} & \mathbf{b}_{\alpha-h} & \cdots & \mathbf{b}_{\beta-h} & \cdots & \mathbf{0} & \mathbf{0} \\ \mathbf{s}_O & \mathbf{0} & & & & & & \cdot \\ \mathbf{0} & \mathbf{s}_H & & & & & \cdot & \cdot \\ \vdots & \vdots & & \ddots & & & \cdot & \\ \mathbf{0} & \mathbf{0} & & & & & \mathbf{s}_{\Omega-H} & \mathbf{s}_{\Omega} \end{bmatrix}, \tag{9.46}$$

where α and β are the first and last ages of childbearing, respectively.[4]

The first row of $\mathbf{G}$ is composed of matrices $\mathbf{b}_X$:

$$\mathbf{b}_X = \begin{bmatrix} b_X^{11} & b_X^{21} & \cdots & b_X^{N1} \\ b_X^{12} & b_X^{22} & \cdots & b_X^{N2} \\ \vdots & \vdots & & \vdots \\ b_X^{1N} & b_X^{2N} & \cdots & b_X^{NN} \end{bmatrix}, \tag{9.47}$$

---

[4] In the projections reported in Chapter 6, the submatrix $\mathbf{s}_{\Omega-H}$ was computed according to eqn. (9.40) with the submatrix $\mathbf{s}_{\Omega}$ set equal to zero. The new IIASA projection program has been modified so that these two submatrices are now computed according to eqns. (9.41) and (9.42).

where b_X^{ij} is the average number of babies born during the unit time interval, *and alive* in region j at the end of that interval, per x- to $(x + h)$-year-old resident of region i at the beginning of the interval. The off-diagonal elements of $\mathbf{b}_X$ reflect the mobility of children 0 to h years old who were born to x- to $(x + h)$-year-old parents.

If fertility rates are derived from period data, then the number of births in a period of h years contributed by those aged x to $x + h$ at time t, is

$$(h / 2) (\mathbf{m}_X^b K_{Xt} + \mathbf{m}_{X+H}^b K_{X+H,t+1})$$
$$= (h / 2) (\mathbf{m}_X^b + \mathbf{m}_{X+H}^b \, \mathbf{s}_X) \, K_{Xt} \; .$$

Of these births, a proportion $_0\mathbf{l}_0 \, (h_0 \mathbf{l}_0)^{-1}$ will survive to the end of the time interval in the various regions.

It can be shown that $\mathbf{b}_X$ obeys the relationship (Rogers 1975a, pp.120–121):

$$\mathbf{b}_X = (h / 2) \, _0\mathbf{l}_0 \, (h_0 \mathbf{l}_0)^{-1} (\mathbf{m}_X^b + \mathbf{m}_{X+H}^b \, \mathbf{s}_X) \; ,$$

whence

$$\mathbf{b}_X = (h / 4) \, (\mathbf{p}_0 + \mathbf{I}) \, (\mathbf{m}_X^b + \mathbf{m}_{X+H}^b \, \mathbf{s}_X) \tag{9.48}$$

since

$$_0\mathbf{l}_0 = (h / 2) \, (\mathbf{p}_0 + \mathbf{I}) \; ,$$

where $_0\mathbf{l}_0$, $\mathbf{p}_0$, and $\mathbf{s}_X$ are life table functions, $\mathbf{I}$ is the identity matrix, and $\mathbf{m}_X^b$ is a diagonal matrix containing the annual regional birth rates of persons aged x to $x + h$. The matrix $\mathbf{b}_{\alpha-h}$ is not zero because it depends on the fertility rate in the age group α to $\alpha + h$ [see equation (9.48)].

If cohort or period–cohort data are available, $\mathbf{b}_X$ and $\mathbf{s}_X$ may be derived in a simpler way (Willekens 1983).

Because of the special structure of the multiregional growth matrix set out in equation (9.46), the demographic projection model may be expressed in the form of the following systems of equations:

$$K_{0,t+1} = \sum_{X=\alpha-h}^{\beta-h} \mathbf{b}_X \, K_{Xt} \tag{9.49}$$

$$K_{X+H,t+1} = \mathbf{s}_X \, K_{Xt} \qquad \text{for } H \le X \le \Omega - 2H \tag{9.50}$$

$$K_{\Omega,t+1} = \mathbf{s}_{\Omega-H} K_{\Omega-H,t} + \mathbf{s}_\Omega K_{\Omega t} \; . \tag{9.51}$$

The age- and region-specific population may be projected forward over time by these equations with constant coefficients. The initial population is the observed base-year population.

Projection should not be confused with forecasting. Forecasting requires the consideration of the effects that possible future events may have on demo-graphic parameters. The purpose of projecting a population with a constant growth matrix is to study the future impacts of *current* patterns of behavior. A study of the population that would arise if such patterns were to be continued indefinitely is particularly helpful to the understanding of the significance of current demographic patterns. The population that would then evolve is called a *stable* population.

9.6.2 *The Stable Equivalent Population*

A population undisturbed by migration will, if subjected to an unchanging regime of mortality and fertility, ultimately achieve a stable constant age distribution that increases at a constant stable growth ratio, λ say. This same property is obtained in the case of a multiregional population system that is closed to external migration and subjected to an unchanging multiregional regime of mortality, fertility, and internal migration. Knowledge of the asymptotic properties of such a population projection helps us to understand the meaning of observed age-specific birth, death, and migration rates.

If one projects a population with a constant growth matrix for a long enough time, then the ultimate (stable) growth ratio λ and the associated ultimate (stable) distribution become independent of the current population distribution. For constant growth matrices, we may write

$$K_t = G^t K_0 \ . \tag{9.52}$$

Increasing t, we obtain K_s, the stable population disaggregated by age and region of residence.

Once stability is achieved, the age-by-region composition of the population remains constant. All regions grow at the same constant ratio, λ. (The stable growth ratio is the so-called dominant eigenvalue of G.) The relative stable distribution ξ is the right eigenvector of G associated with λ. In other words, ξ is the solution of the system of equations

$$G\,\xi = \lambda\,\xi \ . \tag{9.53}$$

The eigenvector ξ is unique up to a scalar; therefore we may scale it such that its elements sum to unity,

$$1'\,\xi = 1 \ ,$$

where 1 is a column vector of ones, and 1' is its (row vector) transpose.

The population for large values of t equal to n, say, may be expressed as

$$K_s \doteq G^n K_0 = G^n Y\xi$$

$$= \lambda^n Y\xi = \lambda^n Y \ , \tag{9.54}$$

where $Y = Y\xi$.

The scalar Y is called the *stable equivalent* of the observed population (Keyfitz 1969, Rogers 1975a, p.38). It is the total population that, if distributed as the stable population ξ, would increase at a constant rate and converge toward the same population as would, in the long run, the observed population under the projection defined by equation (9.53). The vector Y is the stable equivalent population disaggregated by age and region.

From equation (9.54) it follows that

$$1' G^n K_0 = \lambda^n Y 1' \xi ,$$

where

$$Y = (1/\lambda^n) 1' G^n K_0 \qquad \text{for } n \to \infty . \tag{9.55}$$

A percentage distribution is but one of the several possible ways of expressing the age composition of a stable population. An alternative expression is in terms of a single birth, that is, stable birth cohorts of a single person. This approach is analogous to that followed in multiregional life tables. In such tables $_0l_x$ denotes the number of people at exact age x by place of birth and place of residence, and $_0L_X$ gives the number of people in age group $(x, x + h)$ by place of birth and residence. In both measures, the number of people is expressed in terms of unit births. Analogously, we may define matrices $_0l_x(r)$ and $_0L_X(r)$ to represent, respectively, the number of people at exact age x and in age group $(x, x + h)$ by place of birth and residence in stable populations (both expressed in terms of the unit birth cohort).

The alternative expression of the stable population in terms of unit births has an important advantage: its self-evident relation to the life table population. The stable population by place of birth and place of residence, per unit birth, is given by

$$_0l_x(r) = e^{-rx} {}_0l_x \tag{9.56}$$

and

$$_0L_X(r) = e^{-r(x+h/2)} {}_0L_X , \tag{9.57}$$

where r is the annual growth rate of the stable population, or intrinsic growth rate. The rate r depends only on the observed schedules and is independent of the observed population distribution. It is computed as

$$r = (1/h) \ln \lambda ,$$

with h being the age interval and λ the dominant eigenvalue associated with the population growth matrix G.

The absolute number of people in each age group by place of residence is

$$K_{Xs} = e^{-r(x+h/2)} {}_0L_X Q , \tag{9.58}$$

where Q is the stable distribution of births. Equation (9.58) may be interpreted as the numerical evaluation of the continuous-time model,

$$K_{xs} = e^{-rx} {}_0l_x Q . \tag{9.59}$$

The life table population distribution is a special case of equations (9.56) and (9.57), that is, when $r = 0$, and any stable population with a zero growth rate (i.e., a stationary population) is distributed as the life table population. Its *relative* distribution in terms of unit births is therefore independent of how fertility is reduced to replacement level.

The stable equivalent number of births may be obtained from equation (9.59):

$$Q = [_0\mathbf{l}_X(r)]^{-1} K_{Xs}$$

because the relation between the number of births and the number of people in the first age group is $Q = [_0\mathbf{l}_0(r)]^{-1} K_{0s}$. Equivalently, Q may be derived by means of the expression

$$\bar{Y} = \sum_x K_{Xs} = \sum_X {}_0\mathbf{l}_X(r)Q \quad , \tag{9.60}$$

where $\bar{Y}$ is the regional distribution of the stable equivalent population. Therefore

$$Q = \left[\sum_X {}_0\mathbf{l}_X(r) \right]^{-1} \bar{Y}$$

$$= [\mathbf{e}_0(r)]^{-1} \bar{Y} \quad , \tag{9.61}$$

a multiregional and stable population generalization of the well-known fundamental relationship in a stationary life table population:

$$e_0 = \frac{T_0}{l_0} \quad ,$$

or

$$l_0 = \frac{T_0}{e_0} = \frac{\text{Total population}}{\substack{\text{Life expectancy} \\ \text{at birth}}} = \text{Annual number of births} \quad .$$

CHAPTER TEN

Life Tables

Jacques Ledent and Philip Rees

In this chapter we review systematically the consequences of using different data types, rate definitions, and probability estimation methods in the construction of multiregional life tables. We do this by applying various methods to the same data set and then examining the effects. Out of these experiments with a variety of national data sets emerge recommendations for the most reliable estimation methods, given available data, the most reliable data to seek, and the data set that should ideally be collected.

In a sense our search for optimum data and an optimum methodology resembles the search of the surfer for the perfect wave. There is always a better wave to be found on the next beach on the next day. However, choices have to be made from the waves and beaches available. Our series of experiments is intended to provide constructors of multiregional life tables with advice based on information available today.

Although our experiments are with multiregional population systems, most of our methods and conclusions carry over into other multistate population systems: the movement of people between marital states, the transfer of workers in to and out of the labor force, the movement of students through an educational system. We first review the principal steps involved in constructing a multiregional life table and then identify particular steps about which choices can be made.

The multiregional life table is a demographic device that extends the life table model to the case of a population experiencing migration in a system of regions (Rogers 1973a, 1975a). As demonstrated by each of the 17 national reports of the Migration and Settlement Study, it is a most important tool for describing and analyzing spatial population change within a country.

In their short course on mathematical demography (Chapter 9), Rogers and Willekens review the theory behind the multiregional life table model and introduce the issues involved in the applied calculation of multiregional life tables. In practice, different types of migration data can be used as inputs in the construction of such a life table, and a variety of methods for converting

these data and the associated mortality data into appropriate transition probabilities have been suggested (Rogers 1973a, 1975a, Rees and Wilson 1975,
1977, Rogers and Ledent 1976, Ledent 1978a, 1980b,c, 1981, 1982a, Rees 1978,
1979c). This chapter considers in greater detail the issues and choices
involved in computing these tables.

Section 10.1 lays out possible choices for the calculation of multiregional
life tables. In particular it stresses the important distinction between mobility
data in the form of *migration* counts and those in the form of *migrant*
counts. Sections 10.2 and 10.3 present and compare the various estimation
methods that can be employed when the data available refer to migrations and
migrants, respectively. The results of these two approaches are contrasted in
Section 10.4. Finally, Section 10.5 draws conclusions that should help those
constructing multiregional life tables in the future.

10.1 Alternatives in the Construction of Multiregional Life Tables

The person who wishes to construct a multiregional life table may face
four main choices — two with respect to data and two with respect to methods
(Table 10.1). For each choice, we spell out below possible alternatives together
with a judgment about the likelihood of their occurrence.

10.1.1 *Choice 1: Data Types*

In most instances data on geographical mobility are obtained from either
a population register or a population census. In some countries each change of
address must be registered with the local authorities. A special treatment of
these registers permits the derivation of tables of *movements*, which
represent the numbers of *migrations* observed in a given period between
each pair of origins and destinations.

Countries that carry out regular population censuses often ask respondents to state their address at some earlier time. If the past and current
addresses for each of the respondents are compared, it is possible to construct tables of *transitions*, which represent numbers of *migrants*: persons
who, at the time of the census, reside in a region different from the one they
lived in at an earlier date.

The two alternative sources of data on geographical mobility — population
registers and population censuses — clearly involve different definitions of
the transfer of an individual from one region to another. As a result, they may
produce quite different observed mobility flows. It is therefore necessary to
distinguish two approaches to the construction of multiregional life tables: the
movement approach, using register data, and the *transition* approach, using
census data (Ledent 1980c).

Table 10.1 Alternatives in the construction of multiregional life tables.

Choice 1: Data Types (Data Choice)
- migration data (*movement approach*) versus migrant data (*transition approach*)
- cross-classification of mobility data by place of birth (both approaches)

Choice 2: Period Lengths and Age Intervals (Data Choice)
- period length for migrant data (transition approach)
- abridged or unabridged life tables (both approaches)

Choice 3: Input Quantities (Method Choice)
- conventional or adjusted occurrence/exposure rates for migrant data (transition approach A)
- transition proportions conditional on survival (transition approach B)

Choice 4: Transition Probability Estimators (Method Choice)
- exponential, linear, quadratic, cubic, or interpolative–iterative (movement approach)
- interpolation first or interpolation last (transition approach B)
- linear interpolation or cubic spline interpolation (transition approach B)

Note: The specific approach, given in brackets after each choice alternative, refers to the approach to multiregional life table construction in which the alternative occurs. The nature of each approach is discussed in the text.

In practice, one of the two approaches imposes itself:

- In those countries that do not maintain a population register, the only pertinent data available are census or survey data in the form of migrant counts.
- In those countries where population registers are extensively used to produce geographical mobility data, a migration question often is not included in the population census.
- Even if a country produces relevant data from both possible sources, some peculiar conditions (such as data accuracy or level of spatial aggregation) often lead to the choice of one of the two data types, apart from any methodological considerations.

Given that the multiregional life table is formulated as a simple Markov chain model, its application to real data should be carried out for populations that are as homogeneous as possible. In particular, since an individual's migration propensity strongly depends on his birthplace (see, e.g., Long and Hansen 1975), more meaningful life table statistics are likely to be obtained if they are derived from mobility data cross-classified by place of birth.

In practice, such data are rarely available; we know of only one country (the US) where the necessary tabulations (in the form of migrant counts) have

been produced. In many countries, however, appropriate treatment of the
questions on birthplace and place of residence at some prior fixed date, usually asked in a population census, makes it possible to produce similar tabulations, which prospective builders of multiregional life tables should seek.
(Section 10.4 contrasts life table statistics generated from place-of-birth-
dependent and place-of-birth-independent data.)

10.1.2 *Choice 2: Period Lengths and Age Intervals*

Movement data from registration systems are collected for monthly, quarterly, or annual periods. For the purpose of constructing a multiregional life
table, it is advisable to use data for at least annual periods since these are
less likely to be influenced by seasonal patterns. The length of the observation period, in fact, does not have an effect on the measurement of annual-
equivalent migration rates as long as migration is stable in level and pattern
over the interval.

This is not the case when migrant data are used. The annual-equivalent
migrant rates generally decrease with the length of the period over which
they are retrospectively observed (Long and Boertlein 1976, Rees 1977a,
Kitsul and Philipov 1981). What value should the researcher choose for the
period length?

In the majority of situations, in fact, the researcher has no choice
because period length is determined by the migration question posed in
national censuses, which usually refers to two points in time that are a fixed
interval apart. In the UK censuses of 1961 and 1981, a one-year question only
was employed; in the Soviet census of 1970 a two-year question was asked; in
the last three Canadian censuses (1971, 1976, and 1981) and the US censuses
of 1940, 1960, 1970, and 1980 a five-year question was used; in the French censuses of 1962, 1968, 1975, and 1982 a question for a period of a varying length
(six to eight years) was posed in order to allow a linkage with the previous
census. There are, nevertheless, some instances in which mobility information
from a population census is available for more than one period of observation:
in the UK censuses of 1966 and 1971, in the Japanese census of 1970, and in
the Australian census of 1976, both one-year and five-year migrant data are
tabulated. The question of which data to use is discussed in Section 10.4 on the
basis of some Swedish evidence drawn from a recent study by Ledent and Just
(1985).

Migration data and migrant data are usually collected using a single-year-
of-age classification; but, in many instances, they are aggregated over five-
year age groups before being released. Would single-year age groups be
preferable? Owing to the intricate roles of time and age, these questions are
also considered in Section 10.4.

10.1.3 *Choice 3: Input Quantities*

The third choice involves the selection of the quantities to be used as inputs to the multiregional life table calculations. If migration data are available, the definition and measurement of the inputs readily follow from the classical demographic approach focusing on events. For each possible observation plan, occurrence/exposure rates can be ascertained in the usual way.

The data that have generally been used up to now for calculating a multiregional life table have been either period data or data treated as period data. The reason for this is simply that the observation plan yielding such data coincides with the plan implicit in the theoretical presentation of the multiregional life table; as a result, period rates can be directly linked to the transition probabilities from which all multiregional life table statistics originate. If cohort data on migrations are available, then the estimation of migration rates can be considerably improved. If period–cohort data only are available, then survivorship proportions must first be estimated and transition probabilities computed from them.

Where migrant data are available, we consider two alternative ways of defining the input quantities. In the first alternative we derive rates, using the available mobility data, that are similar in nature to migration-based mobility rates. The second alternative relies on different quantities: transition probabilities conditional on survival. The derivation of the latter is made possible by the consideration not only of migrants but also of "stayers" (persons residing in the same region at the beginning and end of the observation period); such information is either known from census enumerations or estimated indirectly using accounting equations. The two alternatives naturally give rise to two versions of the transition approach, which we examine in Section 10.3.

10.1.4 *Choice 4: Transition Probability Estimators*

The final choice that needs to be made concerns the selection of the estimation equations linking transition probabilities to input quantities. This choice is always available to the builder of a multiregional life table since, given the type of mobility data available, nothing constrains the selection of any set of desired estimation equations from among those available.

In the case of the *movement* approach, the researcher may pick either of the two estimation methods already introduced by Rogers and Willekens in Chapter 9 or the alternative methods illustrated in Section 10.2 using a data set for the Netherlands in order to compare results.

Similarly, several probability equations are available for each of the two transition subapproaches to *migrant* data. On the basis of data for Great Britain, in Section 10.3 we first compare the various estimation equations available within each subapproach and then provide a comparison of the subapproaches themselves.

10.2 The Movement Approach: The Effects of Alternative Transition Probability Estimators

We begin this section by reviewing the various methods that have been suggested for dealing with mobility data in the form of migration counts. For each method, the discussion focuses on the transition probability estimators and, when necessary, on the function assumed for the calculation of the stationary population.

10.2.1 The Alternative Methods

First, we consider the two "basic" methods that have already been discussed in Chapter 9: the exponential and the linear methods. We then continue the discussion with a brief review of three "complex" methods that are available to the builder of a multiregional life table: the quadratic, cubic, and interpolative—iterative methods.

The *exponential* method readily follows from the Kolmogorov forward differential equation underlying the life table [equation (9.12)] when it is assumed that the intensities of mortality and mobility, μ, are piecewise constant; that is, $\mu = \mathbf{m}_X$ for all y, $x \leq y < x + h$, where $\mathbf{m}_X$ is the matrix of age-specific rates relating to ages $(x, x + h)$. The matrix $\mathbf{p}_x$ of transition probabilities between ages x and $x + h$ is given by (Krishnamoorthy 1979, Schoen and Land 1979)

$$\mathbf{p}_x = e^{-h\,\mathbf{m}_X} . \tag{10.1}$$

This matrix may be evaluated by using the matrix equivalent of the Taylor expansion for computing $e^{-\mu}$, that is,

$$\mathbf{p}_x = \mathbf{I} - h\,\mathbf{m}_X + \frac{h^2}{2!}\,\mathbf{m}_X^2 - \frac{h^3}{3!}\,\mathbf{m}_X^3 + \frac{h^4}{4!}\,\mathbf{m}_X^4 \cdots . \tag{10.2}$$

In practice, we used as many terms as were necessary to obtain $\mathbf{p}_x$ probabilities accurate to the sixth decimal place.

Once the transition probability matrices $\mathbf{p}_x$ are determined, the calculation of the multiregional life table continues with the computation of the survival functions

$$\mathbf{l}_{x+h} = \mathbf{p}_x\,\mathbf{l}_x . \tag{10.3}$$

The ij^{th} element of the survival function matrix $\mathbf{l}_x$ represents the probability that a person born in j survives to be in i at age x. If multiplied by the radix, the survival function expresses the number of people at exact age x by region of birth and region of residence. The number of person-years lived, $\mathbf{L}_X$, may be derived next using the discrete equivalent of the Kolmogorov forward differential equation

$$\mathbf{l}_x - \mathbf{l}_{x+h} = \mathbf{m}_X\,\mathbf{L}_X . \tag{10.4}$$

Multiplying both sides of this equation by the inverse of the matrix of age-specific rates yields

$$L_X = m_x^{-1} (l_x - l_{x+h}) \ . \tag{10.5}$$

In the case of the last age group, this equation becomes

$$L_\Omega = m_\Omega^{-1} l_\omega \ , \tag{10.6}$$

an expression general enough to be applicable to all of the alternative methods considered below.

The *linear* method is derived from the assumption of a uniform distribution of events over the age–time interval and thus represents the stationary population L_X as an arithmetic average of the l_x and l_{x+h} matrices:

$$L_X = (h/2)(l_x + l_{x+h}) \ . \tag{10.7}$$

As shown by Rogers and Ledent (1976), this leads to

$$P_x = [I + (h/2)m_X]^{-1} [I - (h/2)m_X] \ . \tag{10.8}$$

The two basic methods described above treat each age interval separately. The following three methods allow for some degree of continuity over the age continuum by considering each age group along with the previous and subsequent age groups.

Land and Schoen (1982) have developed a *quadratic* estimation method based on quadratic flows, which makes use of an algorithm originally devised by Schoen (1979).

The crucial concept in this estimation method is the mean duration a_X^{ij} to transfer between each pair of regions i and j. This statistic is assumed to be a weighted sum of the total numbers of survivors in region i at ages x and $x+h$, where the weights f_X^{ij} and g_X^{ij} are such that the curve of instantaneous forces of transition from region i to region j passes through the observed values of the corresponding age-specific rates at ages $x-h$, x, and $x+h$. The weights f_X^{ij} and g_X^{ij} are weighted sums of the mobility rates at ages $x-h$, x, and $x+h$. Details of the weighting functions and derivation are given in Schoen (1979).

In this approach, the stationary population L_X is defined by

$$L_X = f_X l_x + (hI + g_X) l_{x+h} \ , \tag{10.9}$$

where f_X and g_X contain the various f_X^{ij} and g_X^{ij} coefficients. Combining this with the identity in equation (10.4) then yields

$$P_x = [I + m_X(hI + g_X)]^{-1} (I - m_X f_X) \ . \tag{10.10}$$

In practice, this method is implemented through the successive applications of equations (10.10), (10.3), and, for the calculation of L_X, either (10.9) or (10.5). Expression (10.10), however, needs to be amended in the case of the first and the last-but-one age groups. In our numerical application below, we used, for the last-but-one age group, the amended equation proposed by Schoen (1979), and for the first age group, the linear estimation equation (10.8).

Initially suggested by Schoen and Nelson (1974) and revised by Ledent (1978a), the *cubic* method involves calculating L_X on the basis of a curve of degree three through four successive values of the survivor matrices:

$$L_X = \frac{13h}{24}(l_x + l_{x+h}) - \frac{h}{24}(l_{x+h} + l_{x+2h}) . \qquad (10.11)$$

Following the procedure of the corresponding ordinary life table method (Keyfitz 1968), which can be generalized to the multiregional case, this method is applied to all closed age intervals except the second and the last-but-one age groups. For those age groups, as well as for the first age group, the linear method is introduced.

This complex method is implemented through an iterative procedure. First, initial values of l_x are derived using the linear or exponential method. (In our numerical application below, we have adopted the former.) These values are then entered into equation (10.11) to produce initial estimates of L_X. From there , a new set of l_x is obtained from equation (10.4) rewritten as

$$l_{x+h} = l_x - m_X L_X . \qquad (10.12)$$

The procedure is repeated until stable l_x values are obtained. At the end of each iteration, fresh estimates of p_x can be assessed from

$$p_x = l_{x+h} l_x^{-1} . \qquad (10.13)$$

In our numerical application described below, we considered the iteration procedure complete when the sixth decimal figure for each element of p_x did not change with successive iterations.

The last complex method considered here extends the calculation of a graduated life table (Keyfitz 1968, pp.234–236) to the multiregional case. The *interpolative–iterative* method permits one to calculate a multiregional life table using small age intervals in order to estimate more accurate life table statistics for aggregated, wider age intervals. As indicated by its name, the method displays two essential features. First, it is an interpolative method: the necessary mortality and mobility information that is normally lacking is derived by means of a graduation procedure. Second, it is an iterative method: the graduated rates are adjusted, in successive steps, to match the subsequent life table rates for the original age groups with the observed rates. In this section, m_X refers to the matrix of life table rates. The matrix of observed rates is denoted by M_X.

The calculation begins with the graduation of the mortality and mobility curves to small intervals of width q (here q equals 0.2 of a year) by interpolating through the observed rate values. This interpolation uses a cubic spline function (McNeil *et al.* 1977), which is passed through the cumulative values of the observed mortality and mobility rates. This offers the advantage of producing a sensible graduation between age zero and the middle age in the first interval, and it improves the quality of the interpolation around the turning points.

Next, the linear estimation method is used to derive the matrices of survivors, $\hat{\mathbf{l}}_y$, and the matrices of person-years lived, $\hat{\mathbf{L}}_Y$, relating to all small intervals within each initial interval $(x, x + h)$. Selecting the $\mathbf{l}_x$ and $\mathbf{l}_{x+h}$ matrices from the more detailed $\hat{\mathbf{l}}_x$, $\hat{\mathbf{l}}_{x+q}$, $\hat{\mathbf{l}}_{x+2q}$, ..., $\hat{\mathbf{l}}_{x+h}$ series and calculating

$$\mathbf{L}_X = \sum_{Y=X}^{X+H-Q} \hat{\mathbf{L}}_Y \qquad (10.14)$$

yields the implied mortality and mobility rates for age intervals x to $x + h$ derived from equation (10.4) rewritten as

$$\mathbf{m}_X^* = (\mathbf{l}_x - \mathbf{l}_{x+h}) \mathbf{L}_X^{-1} \ . \qquad (10.15)$$

Generally, the $\mathbf{m}_X^*$ estimates thus obtained do not agree with the observed $\mathbf{m}_X$. Improved estimates of the h-year mortality rates m_Y^{id} and migration rates m_Y^{ij} are derived from

$$\hat{m}_Y^{id}(k + 1) = \hat{m}_Y^{id}(k) \frac{m_X^{id}}{m_X^{id*}(k)} \qquad (10.16)$$

and

$$\hat{m}_Y^{ij}(k + 1) = \hat{m}_Y^{ij}(k) \frac{m_X^{ij}}{m_X^{ij*}(k)} \qquad (10.17)$$

for all y, $x \le y < x + h - q$, where k and $k + 1$ refer to successive iterations of the procedure.

The procedure is repeated until satisfactory values of $\mathbf{m}_X^*$ are obtained. In our numerical application below, the procedure was repeated until the sixth decimal figure for the elements of $\mathbf{p}_x$ remained unchanged in successive iterations.

10.2.2 *The Effects of Alternative Methods*

To ascertain the importance of the choice of the probability estimator, we applied each method to data on the Netherlands (Drewe 1980). The mobility data are register-derived migration data that have been aggregated, for convenience of presentation, from a five- to a four-region system by combining the South-West and South regions into one.

There is no "true" multiregional life table against which we can evaluate the alternative methods; thus we are reduced to a comparison among methods. The principal feature of such a comparison is that all of the five estimation methods introduced above are in very close general agreement. On a fine scale, however, there are some interesting differences.

A first assessment of the discrepancies between methods is carried out at the level of the transition probabilities. Figure 10.1 shows the variations with age of the migration, retention, and mortality probabilities relating to the North region of the Netherlands as obtained with the five estimation methods. Because of the closeness of these statistics, the diagrams do not show the variations of the probabilities themselves but rather their differences.

The three graphs on the left-hand side of Figure 10.1 show, respectively, the (total out-) migration, the (within-region) retention, and the mortality probabilities for the North region using the iterative—interpolative method. The corresponding three graphs on the right-hand side show the deviations of the exponential, linear, quadratic, and cubic probabilities from those of the iterative—interpolative method.

Juxtaposition of the migration probability graphs indicates that, across the age continuum, the disparities observed are closely related to the migration intensity. They are wider around ages where migration propensity varies rapidly (between ages 10 and 40) and almost zero where the migration probabilities are relatively stable (between ages 40 and 60). Compared with the interpolative—iterative method, the other methods tend to underestimate migration probabilities around the low point in migration propensity and to overestimate them around the high peak. The related converse pattern is observed among retention probabilities.

The deviations from the reference (interpolative—iterative) method are similar except at the older ages, where the exponential and quadratic methods fare less favorably than do the linear and cubic methods.

The disparities between alternative methods are, however, rather small. Such small differences in the transition probabilities naturally result in small differences at the level of summary statistics such as life expectancies. For example, as Table 10.2 shows, the total life expectancy of a five-year-old resident of the North region ranges from 70.50 years (exponential method) to nearly 70.59 years (all complex methods), taking on the intermediate value of 70.54 years in the case of the linear method. Such small discrepancies are also observed at the regional distribution level of the total expectations of life.

Nevertheless, not all multiregional life table statistics are so insensitive to the choice of the estimation method. A particularly interesting exception concerns the set of mean durations to transfer (from the start of each age interval); that is, the average of the times a_X^{id} (or a_X^{ij}) elapsed at the time of death in (or migration from) region i since the time that age x was reached. [For the calculation of these mean duration statistics, see Ledent (1978a,

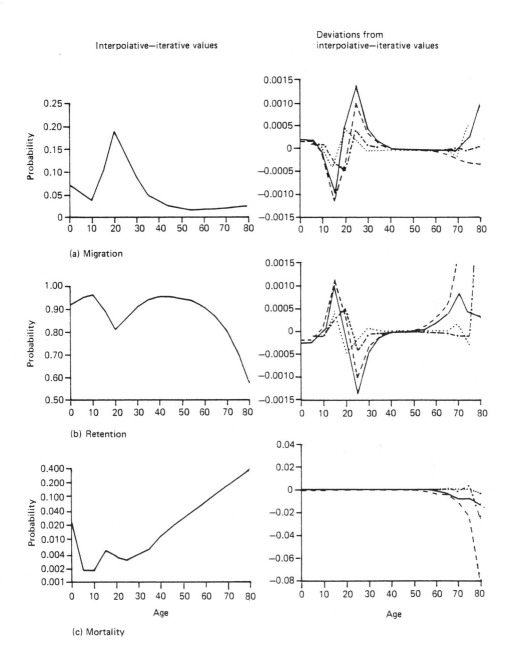

Figure 10.1 The movement approach: migration, retention, and mortality probabilities for the North region of the Netherlands, as calculated using the
interpolative—iterative method and compared with the results from other methods: —
— — — exponential, ——— linear, —·—·—·— quadratic, · · · · · cubic.

Table 10.2 The movement approach (Netherlands data set): totals[a] and regional distributions (in years) of expectations of life by place of residence at age five in the Netherlands — a comparison of alternative estimation methods.

Region of residence at age five		Method				
		Exponential	Linear	Quadratic	Cubic	Interpolative—iterative
North		70.500	70.535	70.583	70.583	70.587
Spent in	North	43.234	43.244	43.282	43.269	43.272
	East	10.084	10.101	10.098	10.105	10.104
	West	11.991	12.000	11.997	12.003	12.001
	South	5.190	5.190	5.205	5.206	5.210
East		70.421	70.458	70.507	70.506	70.506
Spent in	North	6.029	6.038	6.037	6.040	6.039
	East	40.359	40.354	40.414	40.395	40.402
	West	14.691	14.711	14.695	14.705	14.699
	South	9.342	9.354	9.361	9.366	9.366
West		70.652	70.688	70.737	70.737	70.740
Spent in	North	4.736	4.739	4.744	4.745	4.746
	East	9.337	9.347	9.353	9.357	9.358
	West	46.974	46.990	47.012	47.006	47.005
	South	9.605	9.611	9.627	9.629	9.632
South		70.302	70.338	70.386	70.387	70.388
Spent in	North	2.341	2.341	2.346	2.347	2.348
	East	6.867	6.875	6.876	6.881	6.880
	West	11.574	11.584	11.579	11.586	11.582
	South	49.519	49.537	49.586	49.575	49.578

[a]The life expectancy totals for regions may not exactly equal the sum of the constituent figures because of rounding.

Note: Since the linear estimators are used, in implementing the quadratic and cubic approaches, to calculate p_x in the first age group, expectations of life at age five (rather than at birth) are chosen here to ensure better comparability of the methods.

pp.39—40).] Such statistics are necessarily equal to half the width of the age interval ($h/2$) in the case of the linear method because this method is equivalent to assuming a time-homogeneous distribution of movements (deaths and migrations). In the alternative methods, however, these statistics can exhibit rapid age variations that differ somewhat from one method to another.

Figure 10.2 contrasts the five alternative methods of estimating (a) the mean duration to transfer from the North region to the East region and (b) the mean duration to death in the North region of the Netherlands. Not surprisingly, we find again the pattern of deviations observed in transition probabilities and life expectancies. The curves relating to the quadratic and cubic methods follow closely those of the interpolative—iterative method over virtually the entire age spectrum (exhibiting a somewhat larger discrepancy for age 10 in the case of death and age 15 in the case of migration), whereas the curves arising from the linear and exponential methods are further away. Yet

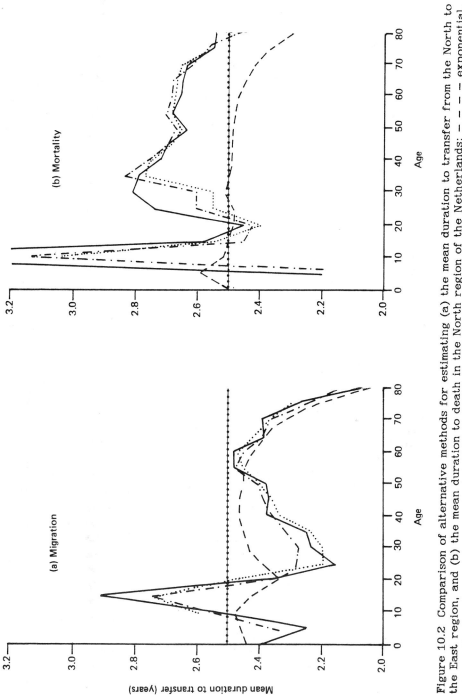

Figure 10.2 Comparison of alternative methods for estimating (a) the mean duration to transfer from the North to the East region, and (b) the mean duration to death in the North region of the Netherlands: – – – exponential, – · – · – linear, – · · – · · – quadratic, · · · · · cubic, —— interpolative–iterative.

the magnitudes of the differences between methods are much larger than observed earlier; they amount to about 10% in relative terms.

In general, the values of the mean duration statistics are in broad agreement with our expectations. The only exception concerns the mean duration to death in the case of the exponential method, which is less than $h/2$ for older ages. (A value greater than $h/2$ was expected because of the increasing propensity to die in those ages.) This observation is naturally related to the deteriorating performance of the exponential method toward the older ages, which was noted earlier with respect to retention and death probabilities (Figure 10.1).

10.2.3 *Further Contrasts Between the Exponential and Linear Methods*

The empirical analysis above has revealed very small differences between the alternative estimation methods. Since the complex methods are more demanding in terms of programming and computer time than the simpler methods, we would argue for the generalized use of either the exponential or the linear method. Moreover, since the linear method appears to perform slightly better (with respect to the treatment of mortality in the older age groups) than the exponential method, on balance we would recommend the linear method on empirical grounds. This was the method used in virtually all of the Migration and Settlement studies.

However, this conclusion relies on an empirical analysis based on a given selection of the mortality and migration rates. Would the conclusion be identical with any other set of rates? Unfortunately, unlike the exponential estimators [derived directly from the Kolmogorov forward differential equation (9.12)], the linear estimators may produce improper transition probability matrices at extreme levels of mobility and mortality. Specifically, the observation was made by Schoen (personal communication) and later by Rees (1978) that the linear method can produce negative probability estimates, typically on the diagonal, if high annual migration rates are observed.

To gain an understanding of how the discrepancies between the linear and exponential methods are influenced by changes in the input rates, imagine a simple hypothetical two-region system in which the mortality and mobility rates are multiples of one per thousand, so that the rate matrix **m** can be expressed as

$$\mathbf{m} = v \begin{bmatrix} 0.001 & 0 \\ 0 & 0.001 \end{bmatrix} + w \begin{bmatrix} 0.001 & -0.001 \\ -0.001 & 0.001 \end{bmatrix}, \qquad (10.18)$$

where v and w are indices of the mortality and mobility levels, respectively. Moreover, to cover all possible empirical situations, we assume that v and w can increase to values of 400. Such a value corresponds to an annual rate of 0.4, which, in the case of mortality, is about three times as high as the typical rate registered in the Migration and Settlement Study for the last closed age group (80–84 years) and, in the case of migration, is far greater than any rate normally observed. When the $\mathbf{m}_x$ matrix is used in equations (10.1) and (10.8), v and w are, in effect, multiplied by the age interval, yielding quantities we call $\bar{v}$ and $\bar{w}$ in Figure 10.3.

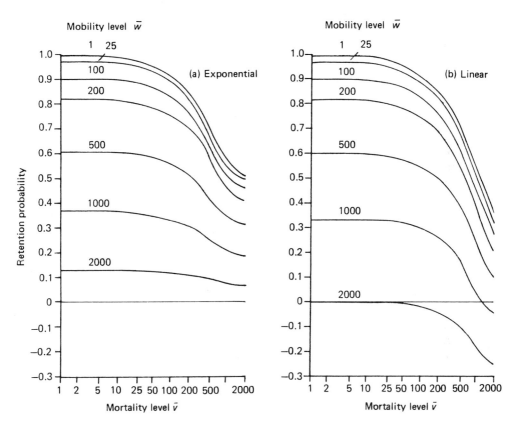

Figure 10.3 The movement approach (hypothetical data set): influence of alternative mortality and mobility levels on retention probabilities for the (a) exponential and (b) linear methods.

It turns out that, as expected, the retention probabilities (here identical for the two regions) are always positive in the case of the exponential method but may become negative in the case of the linear method. Focusing on the linear method, we see from Figure 10.3(b) that, regardless of the mortality level, the occurrence of a negative retention probability requires a high value of the mobility level $\bar{w}$ (in the neighborhood of 1 000 in the case of a high mortality level and around 2 000 in the case of a low mortality level). Given the definitions of $\bar{v}$ and $\bar{w}$, negative retention probabilities are impossible for single-year age groups. They can occur for five-year age groups, but only for migration rates much higher than those normally observed. Extrapolating from this, we conclude that the negativity problem is not a serious drawback for the linear estimation method.

How do the linear and exponential methods compare at more realistic levels of mobility and mortality? First, we observe that in Figure 10.3 the retention probability estimates from the linear method are less than the corresponding estimates from the exponential method. Second, for common values of the migration rates, the differences between the exponential and linear estimates remain low (even for $h = 5$) as long as the mortality level is low; at higher mortality levels (at older ages) the differences are more marked. Thus the linear method leads to transition probabilities as acceptable as those drawn from the exponential method, where normally observed mobility and mortality levels are experienced.

10.2.4 *Influence of the Period Length and the Age Interval Width*

As demonstrated above, choice 4 (the choice of a probability estimation method) leads to differences of limited magnitude. Does this conclusion also apply to the other two choices available whenever a multiregional life table is to be constructed from migration data? Since we deliberately restricted ourselves to the assessment of period rates from the data normally available, we need not worry here about choice 3 (the choice between input quantities); thus we only investigate the effects of choice 2, the choice of age and time intervals.

Our calculations suggest that the use of alternative observation periods apparently does not produce markedly different occurrence/exposure rates as long as mobility patterns exhibit small temporal variations. However, the choice of observation period length demands careful empirical attention when mobility rates vary sharply over time.

The impact of the age interval width on multiregional life table functions is similar to its effect on the ordinary life table. More precisely, the discrepancies observable between corresponding statistics of multiregional life tables based on single-year and five-year age groups are roughly equal to those discrepancies observed between corresponding statistics of an ordinary complete life table (usually based on single-year age groups) and the corresponding abridged life table (usually based on five-year age groups). The similarity of the life expectancy statistics observed earlier (Table 10.2) in the case of the interpolative–iterative method (based on 0.2-year intervals) with those of the alternative methods (based on five-year intervals) suggests that abridged multiregional life tables are adequate for most purposes.

However, the small impact of the age interval width essentially follows from the small magnitude of the migration rates usually observed. If much higher migration rates were to be observed, then discrepancies would occur, especially if the linear approach were used (Ledent and Rees 1980, pp.35–38).

10.3 The Transition Approach: The Effects of Alternative Mobility Inputs

We now turn to the situation in which the mobility data are in the form of one-year or five-year migrant counts from a population census. Attention is thus confined to the mobility behavior of survivors through the period. We assume that the format of the mortality data remains unchanged, yielding conventionally measured mortality rates. Two subapproaches are possible, depending on whether or not information on stayers (those who were in the same region at the beginning and end of the observation period) is available.

10.3.1 *Transition Approach A (Information on Stayers Unavailable)*

The first subapproach reflects the common practice of statistical bureaus of ignoring stayers in their published tabulations on geographical mobility, although the numbers of stayers can be derived along with those of migrants when comparing initial and final regions of residence for survivors. The subapproach owes its development to Rogers (1973a, 1975a), whose estimators, given his assumption of no multiple moves within each age/time interval, could be applied either to migration or to migrant data.

However, the ruling out of multiple moves caused problems; in particular, the exclusion of a death following a migration artificially reduced the exposure to the risk of dying. This defect was, in the case of the transition approach, corrected by Ledent (1982a, p.360). The full linear estimators, from migrant data, thus consist of

$$p_x^{ij} = \frac{h\,\hat{m}_X^{ij}}{1 + (h/2)\left[m_X^{i\,\mathrm{d}} + \sum_{k \neq i}[1 + (h/2)\,m_X^{k\,\mathrm{d}}]\,\hat{m}_X^{ik}\right]} \tag{10.19}$$

and of

$$p_x^{ii} = \frac{1 - (h/2)\left[m_x^{i\,\mathrm{d}} + \sum_{k \neq i}[1 + (h/2)\,m_X^{k\,\mathrm{d}}]\,\hat{m}_X^{ik}\right]}{1 + (h/2)\left[m_X^{i\,\mathrm{d}} + \sum_{k \neq i}[1 + (h/2)\,m_X^{k\,\mathrm{d}}]\,\hat{m}_X^{ik}\right]}, \tag{10.20}$$

where $m_X^{i\,\mathrm{d}}$ is the age-specific mortality rate in region i and $\hat{m}_X^{ij}$ is the age-specific migrant rate for transitions from region i to region j.

In practice, the calculation of these probability estimators raises the question of how to measure each migrant rate $\hat{m}_X^{ij}$. The migrant rate is assumed to be a period rate and is therefore defined as the ratio of the number of migrants from region i to region j who are of age X at the time of transition, $^p K_X^{ij}$, to the person-years lived in region i by the persons who are at risk of migrating at age X during the interval $^p K_X^i$. In the case of the numerator, it is important to note that there is no equivalence of the age–time space in which the data are gathered with that used in the model; that is, the age index X of $^p K_X^{ij}$ refers to neither the beginning nor the end of the observation period. Consequently, following Rees (1979b), the number $^p K_X^{ij}$ of migrants must be estimated from data for adjacent groups using

$$ ^p K_X^{ij} = \left[1 - \frac{T}{2h} \right] K_{X-H}^{ij} + \frac{T}{2h} K_X^{ij} \ , \tag{10.21} $$

where K_X^{ij} is the number of migrants from region i to region j who were aged x to $x + h$ at the beginning of the observation period. The denominator in the migrant rate definition initially can be estimated as the average number of person-years lived in region i between ages x and $x + h$, which can be approximated by

$$ ^p \hat{K}_X^i = \frac{u}{2} \left[K_{Xt}^i + K_{X,t+u}^i \right] \ , \tag{10.22} $$

where K_{Xt}^i is the population aged x to $x + h$ residing in region i at time t.

To illustrate the effect of measuring the $\hat{m}_X^{ij}$ rates in this way, we have calculated a multiregional life table for a three-region system of Great Britain (East Anglia, the South East, and the Rest of Britain) using five-year migrant data (1966–1971) presented in Rees (1979a). Curve A in Figure 10.4 depicts the age variations in the probability of migration out of East Anglia and the second column in Table 10.3 shows life expectancies at age five and their regional breakdowns.

There are arguments against the measurement of the migrant rate denominator using equation (10.22). The transition approach (including both subapproaches A and B) focuses on groups of people who, at the beginning of the period, reside in region i. As a result, the end-of-period term appearing in equation (10.22) should be diminished by a quantity equal to the fraction of the $K_{X,t+u}^i$ population who, at the beginning of the period, did not reside in region i. Thus

$$ \hat{K}_X^i = \frac{u}{2} \left[K_{Xt}^i + K_{X,t+u}^i - \sum_{k \neq i} K_X^{ki} \right] \ . \tag{10.23} $$

This modification leads to migrant rates higher than those derived on the basis of equation (10.22), and thus produces higher migration probabilities (curve B in Figure 10.4) and higher durations of remaining lifetime spent outside the region of current residence (the third column of Table 10.3).

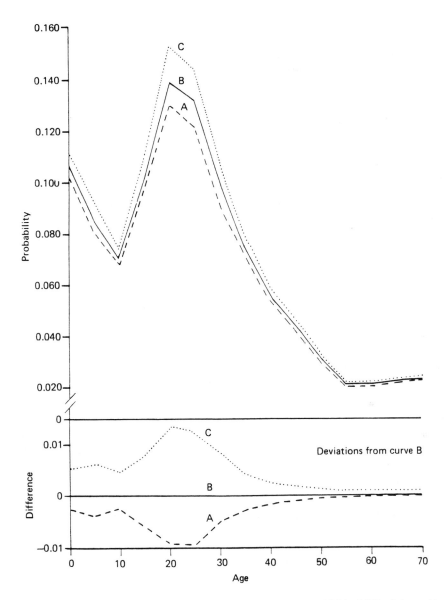

Figure 10.4 Transition approach A (Great Britain, 1966–1971 data set): probabilities of migration out of East Anglia, according to alternative measurements of migrant rates: absolute values and differentials. Migrant rates are based on: A, the conventional population at risk (PAR) [equation (10.22)]; B, reduced PAR [equation (10.23)]; and C, PAR with no external migrants [equation (10.31)].

Table 10.3 Transition approach A (Great Britain, 1966–1971 data set): totals[a] and
regional distributions (in years) of expectations of life by place of residence at age
five according to alternative measurements of the migrant rates.

Region of residence at age five	Migrant rates based on:[b]		
	Conventional PAR	Reduced PAR	No external PAR
East Anglia	69.227	69.206	69.166
Spent in East Anglia	40.840	39.797	38.234
South East	12.786	13.397	13.995
Rest of Britain	15.600	16.011	16.936
South East	69.189	69.185	69.166
Spent in East Anglia	2.406	2.431	2.491
South East	51.841	51.357	50.860
Rest of Britain	14.942	15.096	15.814
Rest of Britain	68.232	68.268	38.271
Spent in East Anglia	1.150	1.178	1.190
South East	6.535	7.866	7.984
Rest of Britain	60.547	59.224	59.098

[a]The life expectancy totals for regions may not exactly equal the sum of the constituent
figures because of rounding.
[b]PAR refers to the population at risk in person-years. Conventional PAR is defined in
equation (10.22), reduced PAR in (10.23), and PAR with no external migrants in (10.31).

10.3.2 *Transition Approach B (Information on Stayers Available)*

We now consider the situation in which the numbers of stayers, K_X^{ii} —
either obtained from a population census or estimated from an accounting
equation — are available along with the numbers of migrants, K_X^{ij}.

In the initial development of this subapproach, the leading idea was first
to assess, from the available data, observed values of the survivorship proportion matrices s_X, and second, to convert, on the basis of an adequate method,
these matrices into transition probabilities p_x. An acceptable method for carrying out such a conversion was proposed by Rees and Wilson (1977), who suggested taking p_x as the arithmetic average of the survivorship proportion
matrices associated with the two consecutive age groups located immediately
below and above age x. Ledent (1980b) proposed an extension of this procedure in which the interpolation is implemented with the help of cubic spline
functions passed through the observed survivorship proportions.

In practice, the implementation of this subapproach is hampered by the
difficulty of estimating accurately the observed survivorship proportions (or,
more exactly, the denominators appearing in the definition of such proportions).

Survivorship and nonsurvivorship proportions are best computed from a
set of multiregional population accounts. The construction of such accounts,
though fairly straightforward in principle, is rather complicated in practice

(Rees 1981). Consequently, for the purposes of this chapter, a thorough exploration of the relationship between multiregional accounts and the transition approach to life table construction is not undertaken (see Ledent and Rees 1980, pp.70–86 for a preliminary discussion). Instead we describe a methodology developed by Ledent (1980b) to allow the separate assessment of mortality and mobility inputs.

This methodology employs conventional mortality rates $m_X^{i\,\mathrm{d}}$ and transition survivorship proportions conditional on survival,

$$\bar{s}_X^{ij} = \frac{K_X^{ij}}{\sum\limits_{k} K_X^{ik}} \ , \qquad \text{for all } j \text{ including } j = i \ , \tag{10.24}$$

gathered, for convenience, into a matrix $\bar{\mathbf{s}}_X$. The summation over k in the denominator on the right-hand side of equation (10.24) is over regions within a country only. The conditional transition proportion matrices $\bar{\mathbf{s}}_X$ are converted into survivorship proportion matrices $\mathbf{s}_X$ by incorporating the effect of mortality. This is done in two steps, which actually can be implemented in either order thus giving rise to two alternative variants.

The first variant consists first of transforming $\bar{\mathbf{s}}_X$ into some unconditional transition proportions $\mathbf{s}_X$ and then of interpolating, using either a linear or a cubic spline function, through the ensuing values of $\mathbf{s}_X$ to derive the series of $\mathbf{P}_x$. By contrast, the second variant consists first of interpolating between the $\bar{\mathbf{s}}_X$ matrices to obtain a series of conditional transition probabilities $\bar{\mathbf{P}}_X$ and then of transforming these $\bar{\mathbf{P}}_x$ matrices into adequate values of $\mathbf{P}_x$. Below, these two variants are referred to as the "interpolation last" and the "interpolation first" variants.

Finally, in addition to the two choices regarding the nature and timing of the interpolation procedure, there is a third choice in the interpolation-last variant that involves the calculation of the number of person-years lived.

The Linear Versus the Cubic Spline Interpolation. The two alternative interpolation methods involve, for each pair of regions i and j ($j \neq i$), the fitting of a curve passing through consecutive values of the observed transition proportions $\mathbf{s}_X^{ij}$ or $\bar{\mathbf{s}}_X^{ij}$, plotted on a graph of such proportions against age at ages $-h/2, h/2, 3h/2, \ldots$. The mobility information referring to those born during the observation period gives rise to a survivorship matrix $\mathbf{s}_{-H}$ or $\bar{\mathbf{s}}_{-H}$. The elements of the square of this matrix (rather than those of the matrix itself) are plotted at $-h/2$ since infants were, on average, alive for only half of the observation period.

What are the consequences of selecting the linear rather than the cubic spline interpolation method? To answer this question, we employed both methods, applying the interpolation-first variant to the data set for Great Britain that we used earlier to illustrate transition approach A, but making use this time of the numbers of stayers. The variation with age of the probability of migration out of East Anglia obtained from the two methods is shown in Figure 10.5.

Substantial differences between the interpolation methods are observed only around the turning points of the migration curve, where, in principle, the cubic spline interpolation should perform better. The cubic spline values are lower than the linear values around the migration low point (0.067 against 0.076 at age 10), but higher around the migration high peak (0.165 against 0.154 at age 20). These discrepancies, which run in opposite directions, have impacts on multiregional life table functions that tend to cancel each other out. Thus the expectations of life computed from the two interpolation methods, such as those displayed in Table 10.4, do not show very large differences.

The Interpolation-First Versus the Interpolation-Last Variant. The conversion of conditional proportions into unconditional proportions (in the interpolation-last variant) and that of conditional probabilities into unconditional probabilities (in the interpolation-first variant) rely on very similar procedures. Specifically, the implementation of both conversions follows from similar relationships in the multiregional life table model that link corresponding conditional and unconditional values in the event that the numbers of person-years lived are calculated linearly according to equation (10.7).

The conditional and unconditional values of the transition proportions are linked by the relation

$$\mathbf{s}_X = \bar{\mathbf{s}}_X \, \mathbf{s}_X^\sigma \, , \tag{10.25}$$

where $\mathbf{s}_X^\sigma$ is a diagonal matrix whose ith diagonal element $s_X^{i\,\sigma}$ represents the proportion of those who, among the residents of region i aged x to $x + h$, survive in any region h years later. Ledent and Rees (1980, pp.84–85) have shown that, if the linear integration assumption holds:

$$s_X^{i\,\sigma} = \frac{1 - (h/2)m_x^{i\,\mathrm{d}}}{1 + (h/2)\sum_k \bar{s}_X^{ik} \, m_{X+H}^{k\,\mathrm{d}}} \, , \tag{10.26}$$

where $\bar{s}_K^{ik}$ is the ikth element of $\bar{\mathbf{s}}_X$ and $m_X^{k\,\mathrm{d}}$ is the mortality rate in region k for age group $x + h$ to $x + 2h$. Thus knowledge of the input quantities (mortality rates and conditional transition proportions) readily yields, on the basis of equations (10.25) and (10.26), the values of $\mathbf{s}_X$ sought in the first step of the interpolation-last variant.

The conditional and unconditional values of the transition probabilities are linked by

$$\mathbf{P}_x = \bar{\mathbf{P}}_x \, \mathbf{P}_x^\sigma \, , \tag{10.27}$$

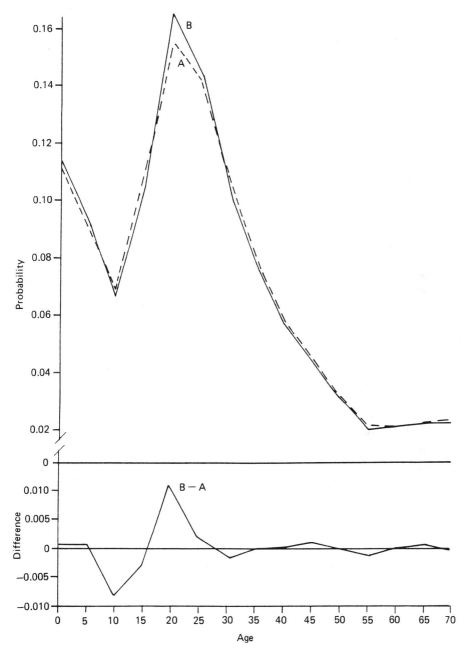

Figure 10.5 Transition approach B (Great Britain, 1966–1971 data set): a survivorship proportion profile (migration out of East Anglia) showing the difference between the cubic spline interpolation (B) and the linear interpolation (A).

Table 10.4 Transition approach B (Great Britain, 1966–1971 data set): totals and regional distributions (in years) of expectations of life by place of residence at age zero according to alternative interpolation methods.[a]

Region of residence at age zero	Transition probabilities estimated using:		
	Linear interpolation	Cubic spline interpolation	Cubic spline interpolation: direct estimate of $\mathbf{l}_x$
East Anglia	72.33	72.61	72.72
Spent in East Anglia	37.97	38.12	37.95
South East	15.42	15.42	15.61
Rest of Britain	18.94	19.07	19.16
South East	72.09	72.38	72.48
Spent in East Anglia	2.69	2.70	2.73
South East	51.98	52.16	52.12
Rest of Britain	17.42	17.52	17.63
Rest of Britain	71.34	71.63	71.12
Spent in East Anglia	1.35	1.34	1.36
South East	8.59	8.62	8.61
Rest of Britain	61.40	61.66	61.16

[a]The expectations of life were computed using the interpolation-first method. These results refer to expectation of life at age zero and are taken from Ledent and Rees (1980, table A.3.2, p.150, runs 31, 33, and 34).

where $\bar{\mathbf{p}}_x$ has an interpretation similar to $\bar{\mathbf{s}}_X$. Again, if the linear integration assumption holds, we have (Ledent 1982a)

$$p_x^{i\sigma} = \frac{1 - (h/2)\,m_X^{i\,d}}{1 + (h/2)\sum_k \bar{p}_x^{ik}\,m_X^{k\,d}}. \tag{10.28}$$

Consequently, if we know the mortality rates and can determine the conditional probabilities by interpolation through the conditional proportions, we can, on the basis of equations (10.27) and (10.28), estimate the values of $\mathbf{p}_x$ according to the interpolation-first variant.

The application of the two variants to the three-region Great Britain illustration produces small differences in migration probabilities, which this time do not appear to be linked to the intensity of migration. Table 10.5 shows the results obtained on the basis of the linear interpolation method. The differences between the two variants can, however, be more substantial for the death probabilities (and hence the retention probabilities), but only when the linear interpolation method is used. Such a finding can be attributed to the inaccurate death probabilities implicit in the matrix $\mathbf{p}_x$ obtained by an inadequate interpolation (e.g., a linear interpolation) between the values of $\mathbf{s}_X$. In conclusion, we suggest reserving the interpolation-first variant for those situations where a realistic interpolation method (such as one based on a cubic spline function) is available.

Table 10.5 Transition approach B (Great Britain): probability of migration out of East Anglia: contrast between interpolation-first and interpolation-last variants.[a]

Age	Variant		
	Interpolation first (1)	Interpolation last (2)	Difference: [(1) − (2)] × 10^6
0	0.11304	0.11263	418
5	0.09140	0.09185	−448
10	0.07550	0.07554	−39
15	0.10797	0.10796	15
20	0.15386	0.45382	40
25	0.14255	0.14260	−59
30	0.10724	0.10726	−15
35	0.08000	0.08004	−33
40	0.05883	0.05886	−29
45	0.04609	0.04608	4
50	0.03242	0.03244	−26
55	0.02227	0.00230	−33
60	0.02209	0.02223	−143
65	0.02361	0.02368	−68
70	0.02436	0.02450	−139

[a]Based on the linear interpolation method.

The Calculation of the Numbers of Person-Years Lived. Given the assumption basic to the transformation of $\bar{\mathbf{p}}_x$ to $\mathbf{p}_x$, the calculation of $\mathbf{L}_X$ in the interpolation-first variant follows readily from the linear integration assumption in equation (10.7). Another alternative, however, comes from the observation that availability of a set of observed survivorship proportions $\mathbf{s}_X$ (including a value for the set of newborns) provides a *direct* estimate of the $\mathbf{L}_X$ statistics (Ledent 1978a, Ledent and Rees 1980, pp.99−102):

$$\mathbf{l}_0 = h \, \mathbf{s}_{-H} \, \mathbf{l}_0 \; , \tag{10.29}$$

where $\mathbf{l}_0$ represents the regional allocation of the initial cohort and $\mathbf{s}_{-H}$ denotes the survivorship proportions for the newborn cohort, and

$$\mathbf{L}_{X+H} = \mathbf{s}_X \mathbf{L}_X \tag{10.30}$$

for all values of $X = 0,...,\Omega-H$. The second and fourth columns of Table 10.4 show the consequences of choosing the direct procedure rather than the linear procedure for estimating the expectations of life at birth for the three-region British illustration. The effect of switching from the linear to the direct method of estimating years lived is modest and of about the same magnitude as the difference between using linear and cubic spline interpolations of the transition probabilities.

10.3.3 The Contrast Between Transition Approaches A and B and the Closure Problem

Having illustrated the effect of choice 4 in the transition approach by comparing the alternative estimation methods available within each sub-approach, we now shift to an examination of the impacts of choice 3, which involves choosing between the two subapproaches.

If we compare the probabilities of migration out of East Anglia estimated using transition approach A with those estimated using transition approach B (the first and third columns of probabilities in Table 10.6), we observe moderate differences in the values. These differences are much larger than those between the different transition probability estimators in the movement approach, and of the same magnitude as the differences produced by the alternative methods of measuring migration rates in transition approach A.

Table 10.6 Transition approaches A and B contrasted (Great Britain 1966–1971 data set): migration probabilities out of East Anglia.

Age	Transition approach A		Transition approach B
	Revised migrant rate estimation based on:		Linear interpolation method
	eqn. (10.23)	eqn. (10.31)	
0	0.10657	0.11171	0.11304
5	0.08598	0.09202	0.09140
10	0.07095	0.07555	0.07550
15	0.10189	0.10987	0.10797
20	0.13952	0.15286	0.15386
25	0.13148	0.14366	0.14255
30	0.09896	0.10719	0.10724
35	0.07526	0.07960	0.08000
40	0.05611	0.05860	0.05883
45	0.04438	0.04630	0.04609
50	0.03093	0.03224	0.03242
55	0.02123	0.02227	0.02227
60	0.02093	0.02194	0.02209
65	0.02250	0.02353	0.02361
70	0.02292	0.02395	0.02436

The question arises whether the discrepancies just observed, moderate as they are, result solely from the different treatment of stayers in the two subapproaches or whether they are the consequences of starting with different input quantities (migrant rates versus conditional transition proportions). The answer depends on the handling of the closure problem, a problem that stems from the open nature of observed population systems.

In contrast to the population system in the theoretical model, any observed system is not closed, since it experiences population exchanges with the rest of the world. Therefore, when constructing a multiregional life table, we should add an extra geographical unit, labeled "Rest of the World". In practice, however, such an addition proves difficult though not impossible to achieve. If the focus of interest is on the behavior and life expectancies of people who remain within the system, the problem becomes one of sensibly excluding the influence of international migration on the results.

By explicitly considering stayers along with surviving migrants, transition approach B leads to input quantities (conditional transition proportions) that assume survival within the system of interest and thus that ensure a proper closure of the system. The approach "purges" any external migration effects. By contrast, this observation does not apply to transition approach A, where the existence of external migration affects the value of the migrant rate $\hat{m}_X^{ij}$ assessed on the basis of equation (10.23).

In principle, to rid the measurement of $\hat{m}_X^{ij}$ from international migration effects, it would be necessary to decrease each of the first two terms in equation (10.23) by the relevant function involved in international migration: that is, the number of emigrants ($K_X^{i,o}$) in the case of the beginning-of-period population and the number of immigrants ($K_X^{o,j}$) in the case of the end-of-period population. Thus equation (10.23) becomes

$$\hat{K}_X^i = \frac{u}{2}\left[K_{Xt}^i - K_{XT}^{io} + \sum_k K_{XT}^{ki} - K_{XT}^{oi}\right] , \tag{10.31}$$

where T denotes the time interval $(t, t + u)$ and u is the length of the interval.

From a practical point of view, the correction just suggested cannot be easily implemented as the necessary data on emigrants are lacking; a population census can only provide information on immigrants. One possibility for securing the missing information, however, would be to use a demographic accounting method (Rees 1981) or to use adjusted survey or register data.

For the three-region example for Great Britain, the missing numbers of emigrants were estimated by Rees (1977b, 1979c), along with the numbers of stayers necessary for the implementation of transition approach B. Correcting the migrant rates along the lines suggested earlier leads to a new multiregional life table with migration probabilities out of East Anglia that are shown in the third column of Table 10.6 (see also curve C in Figure 10.4) and the life expectancies set out in the final column of Table 10.3. Interestingly, these statistics take on values that are very close to those obtained by applying the linear interpolation method (interpolation-first variant) of transition approach B: for example, compare columns 3 and 4 in Table 10.6.

Applying transition approaches A and B with identical system closures (ensured, in the above illustration, by the simultaneous estimation of the quantities necessary for the implementation of each subapproach) eliminates the numerical differences found earlier between the results of the two subapproaches. Therefore, these differences apparently were not a consequence of using different input quantities; they reflected a different treatment of external migration. Our conclusion therefore must be that since the two subapproaches are more or less equivalent, the decision to use one or the other in constructing a multiregional life table from migrant data depends on the difficulty of obtaining the necessary information on stayers (transition approach B) or emigrants (transition approach A).

In practice, transition approach B can be easily implemented using stayer numbers, either observed directly (even though the corresponding numbers are not always published in printed form) or estimated as residuals from

$$K_X^{ii} = K_{X,t+u}^i - \sum_{k \neq i} K_{XT}^{ik} - K_{XT}^{oi} , \qquad (10.32)$$

where the elements on the right-hand side have the same meaning as before. Also, given the accuracy of the stayer numbers thus obtained, multiregional life tables calculated by use of transition approach B are virtually purged of external migrant effects. So implementation of the transition approach A variant, in which the impact of an improper system closure is removed, proves satisfactory only to the extent that emigrants are correctly estimated. Thus, transition approach B generally may become the preferred alternative.

10.3.4 *The Effect of the Choice of Age and Time Intervals*

To conclude with the case of migrant data, we turn our attention to choice 2. First, in the case of transition approach A, a change in the age interval width has a small impact, similar to the corresponding impact registered when dealing with the movement approach. By contrast, the choice of the period length is not a matter of indifference because, unlike migration rates, migrant rates do not vary linearly with time (Rees 1977a, 1979b). For example, multiregional life tables based on five-year data lead to higher retention probabilities and far lower shares of expected lifetimes outside the region of birth than do the corresponding one-year-based tables (see Ledent and Rees 1980, pp.64–66, and Chapter 7).

Second, the implementation of transition approach B requires that the age interval width h and the period length u be equal. What shall we do if h does not equal u? The answer is simple: construct a multiregional life table for u-year age intervals (rather than h-year age intervals); the relevant probabilities can be easily found as the ordinates of the transition proportion curves upon interpolating between the observed values. Consequently, in the case of transition approach B, it suffices to choose u, the impact of which on life table statistics is identical to the corresponding impact in transition approach A.

If the mobility data are available as counts of migrants, the choice of the period length u has a substantial influence on the statistics of a multiregional life table. A quantitative analysis of this influence is provided in the next section, which also sheds some light on its possible causes.

10.4 The Effects of Choosing Alternative Data Types

Having examined the consequences of choices 2 through 4 within both the movement and the transition approaches, we now turn to analyzing the consequences of choice 1, that is, the selection of either the movement or the transition approach. We also examine the consequences of using mobility data cross-classified by place of birth.

10.4.1 *Migrations Versus Migrants and the Contrast Between the Movement and Transition Approaches*

To investigate how mobility data types influence multiregional life table calculations, it is necessary to gather the two data types for the same population system observed over identical periods and to compare the results obtained by the application of the relevant estimation method to each data set. But, if the data come from two different sources (migration data from a population register and migrant data from a population census), the ensuing comparison may be inaccurate. The discrepancies observed could reflect, in part, the difference in the sampling procedures underlying the two data sources. Migration data and migrant data must be secured from the same source.

From a file of all individual, intercounty migration histories over a six-year period, obtained from Sweden's National Bureau of Statistics, Ledent and Just (1985) produced consistent tabulations of migrations and migrants in an eight-region system for observation periods of length u varying from one year (1 January 1970 to 31 December 1970) to six years (1 January 1970 to 31 December 1975). They constructed, for each value of u, a migration-based multiregional life table using the linear method and a migrant-based table employing the cubic spline interpolation method of transition approach B (interpolation-first variant).

Table 10.7 illustrates the magnitudes of the discrepancies between the two alternative approaches for different values of u. It indicates that, compared with migration data, migrant data generate higher retention probabilities and higher shares of the expected lifetimes spent within the region of birth. These differences increase with the period length.

Part (c) of Table 10.7 gives the ratio of the transition approach life expectancies to the movement approach life expectancies. In the column recording this ratio for life expectancy in the region of birth, all the ratios are above one. The ratio increases most between $u = 1$ and $u = 2$, rising from 3% to 10% above 1. Thereafter it increases linearly, reaching 22% above 1 when the true period is five years in length.

In addition to illustrating the relative differences between migration-based and migrant-based life tables for different time intervals, Table 10.7 provides insights into the numerical impact of the choice of u within each of

Table 10.7 The movement versus the transition approach, for Sweden: regional allocations (in years) of life expectancies at birth[a] for region 1 according to alternative lengths u of the observation period.

Period length u (years)	Region[b]							
	1	2	3	4	5	6	7	8
(a) *Movement approach (migratrion data)*								
1	37.37	10.47	3.49	5.46	6.61	4.52	2.35	2.18
2	37.54	10.09	3.38	5.52	6.35	4.71	2.54	2.34
3	37.16	10.12	3.41	5.47	6.38	4.80	2.60	2.53
4	36.55	10.30	3.50	5.43	6.43	4.88	2.66	2.70
5	36.15	10.31	3.55	5.40	6.41	5.07	2.73	2.84
6	35.75	10.34	3.55	5.27	6.36	5.38	2.78	3.00
(b) *Transition approach (migrant data)*								
1	38.65	10.24	3.39	5.26	6.21	4.36	2.28	2.07
2	41.44	9.36	3.07	4.83	5.25	4.19	2.32	1.99
3	42.60	9.09	2.96	4.51	4.95	1.10	2.25	1.99
4	43.23	9.09	2.90	4.28	4.63	4.03	2.23	2.06
5	44.15	8.79	2.80	4.09	4.28	4.03	2.23	2.08
6	44.89	8.56	2.68	3.72	4.02	4.21	2.22	2.15
(c) *Ratio* b/a								
1	1.034	0.978	0.971	0.963	0.939	0.965	0.970	0.950
2	1.104	0.928	0.908	0.875	0.827	0.890	0.913	0.850
3	1.146	0.898	0.868	0.824	0.776	0.854	0.865	0.787
4	1.183	0.882	0.829	0.788	0.720	0.826	0.838	0.763
5	1.221	0.853	0.789	0.757	0.668	0.795	0.808	0.732
6	1.256	0.828	0.755	0.706	0.632	0.782	0.799	0.717

[a]The life expectancy at birth (identical in all regions by assumption) equals 72.46 years.
[b]The eight regions are those used by Andersson and Holmberg (1980) for the Swedish case in the Migration and Settlement Study.
Source: Ledent and Just (1985).

the two approaches. Migrant-based statistics are much more sensitive than migration-based statistics to changes in the value of u. However, the observed differences not only reflect the impact of u, but also depend on temporal variations in migration patterns. In the case of migration data (movement approach), these differences also reflect the assumption that h equals u when multiregional life tables are calculated.

What accounts for the differences observed between multiregional life tables calculated from, first, migration and migrant data and, second, from migrant data for alternative values of u? The answer is the Markov specification underlying the multiregional life table model and, in particular, the assumption that the probability that an individual changes regions is independent of his or her past mobility history.

On the one hand, the movement approach resorts to estimation methods transforming migrations into migrants on the basis of a Markovian process, which is known for its inability to reproduce adequately the extent of return and chain movements. On the other hand, the transition approach avoids such a transformation since such movements are already accounted for in the data. It starts directly with some information (on transitions for people aged x to $x + h$) that already is close to the information that it seeks to develop (transitions for people of exact age x in the presence of the added impact of mortality). That is why migrant data normally are to be preferred to migration data when such a choice exists.

The Markovian assumption also intervenes when one proceeds from one age interval to the next. Therefore, even in the case of the transition approach, where the effect of this assumption is purged *within* each age interval, its impact is not entirely removed *between* age intervals. Clearly, its importance is linked to the number of age intervals (or equivalently to the age interval width h). To put it in approximate but more revealing terms, a multiregional life table based on single-year age groups (generally 85 such age groups plus one open-ended group for those aged 85 and over) uses the Markovian assumption 86 times, whereas a multiregional life table based on five-year age groups (generally 17 such age groups plus one open-ended group for those aged 85 and over) uses it only 18 times. Thus the wider the age interval, the smaller the number of intervals and the weaker the impact of the Markovian assumption.

If we take this argument to its logical conclusion, transition probabilities would best be measured directly by matching place of birth with place of death. The multiregional life expectancy statistics that such an approach generates would, however, be gross simplifications of the distribution of a population's years of life across a set of regions. To capture the detail that life histories have, the analyst is forced to return to much smaller age and time intervals, such as one-year or five-year intervals, and to seek ways of relaxing the Markovian assumption by developing measures of transition probabilities that depend not only on the state a person is in at age x but also on some prior state, such as place of birth.

10.4.2 *The Case of Place-of-Birth-Dependent Data*

Another assumption adopted for the multiregional life table model is a consequence of its underlying specification as a simple Markov chain model: the assumption of population homogeneity. All individuals represented by the initial cohort have identical demographic characteristics and the same patterns of mortality and mobility apply to them all. In the real world, however, mortality and mobility patterns vary from one individual to another. It is therefore advisable to construct separate multiregional life tables for population groups that may be distinguished according to traits such as sex and race.

The decision to move and the choice of destination are heavily influenced by the birthplace of the prospective migrant. In their study of migration flows to the South from the rest of the US, for instance, Long and Hansen (1975) present convincing evidence that the probability of moving to the South is considerably higher for those born in the South who have since moved to another region than for those born elsewhere. Therefore, to reduce the effects of the underlying population homogeneity assumption, multiregional life tables should be calculated from interregional mobility data cross-classified by place of birth.

Formally, this requirement leads to the construction of as many separate life tables as there are birthplaces. Ledent (1981) carried out such a place-of-birth-dependent study for the female populations of the four US census regions, observed over the period 1965–1970. Since the mobility data were in the form of migrant counts, with the numbers of stayers available, transition approach B was used to calculate each of the four birthplace-specific multi-regional life tables, as well as the multiregional life tables based on the same mobility information without a disaggregation

Table 10.8 Totals[a] and regional distributions (in years) of expectations of life at birth (the United States): comparison between uses of place-of-birth-independent and place-of-birth-dependent data.

Region of birth	Number of years spent in:				
	North East	North Central	South	West	Total
(a) *Place-of-birth-dependent approach*					
North East	61.78	2.53	6.06	3.87	74.24
North Central	1.44	60.21	5.22	7.43	74.30
South	2.49	5.10	62.63	3.99	74.20
West	1.10	2.71	3.52	68.51	75.85
(b) *Place-of-birth-independent approach*					
North East	52.04	5.80	10.94	5.56	74.34
North Central	4.10	50.43	11.38	8.36	74.26
South	5.55	8.83	52.64	7.23	74.25
West	4.45	9.25	12.88	48.70	75.27

[a]Totals may not exactly equal the sum of the constituent figures because of rounding.
Source: Ledent (1981, p.44).

Table 10.8 contrasts the life expectancy at birth and its regional distribution obtained from each place-of-birth-specific life table with the corresponding statistics drawn from the corresponding place-of-birth-independent table. It suggests that switching from place-of-birth-independent to place-of-birth-dependent mobility data cuts the proportion of lifetime to be spent outside the region of birth by about half, except in the case of

Western-born women, for whom the reduction amounted to slightly more than 70%.

Since the place-of-birth-dependent approach involves considerably more realistic migration patterns (essentially an explicit accounting of return migration to the birthplace) the above finding leads us to conclude that statistics on expectations of life at birth derived from commonly available data may be unreliable. Therefore, whenever possible, the use of place-of-birth-dependent migration data is to be recommended. There may well be other place-at-particular-age dependencies in migration behavior that are equally important. The impact of such dependencies still requires study.

10.5 Conclusion

This chapter has dealt with the construction of multiregional life tables from an applied point of view. The objective was to assess the impact of alternative computational choices available to the researcher. Our principal findings were as follows:

- Methodological choices concerning actual life table construction — choice 3 regarding the selection of input quantities (in the transition approach) and especially choice 4 regarding the selection of the transition probability estimators (in the movement approach) — did not affect multiregional life table statistics very much.
- By contrast, the alternative choices regarding the selection of the data set from which to calculate a multiregional life table — choice 1 regarding the nature of the mobility data and choice 2 regarding the period length in the case of migrant data — have quite sizable effects on the multiregional life table measures. When a choice of data types is possible, our recommendation is to use migrant data rather than migration data, if resources do not permit an analysis and comparison of both sets. This preference derives in part from a concern regarding the statistics of the expected distribution of the lives of regional cohorts across regions. The movement approach might be more pertinent in studies that focused instead on mobility measures.
- It is clear that multiregional life tables should be constructed using migration data or migrant data cross-classified by place of birth. The results in Section 10.4 suggest that using such data will change the distribution of life expectancies as much as a shift from migration data to migrant data.

These findings lead us naturally to the following conclusions:

- Since the researcher generally has little freedom of choice in the selection of an appropriate data set, the nature of a multiregional life table is likely to be determined at the outset by the characteristics of the available data set. The selection of a particular estimation method within the movement or transition approaches apparently has very little influence on the life table statistics.
- Given this observation, any attempt to improve our understanding of multiregional life tables should emphasize the acquisition of more pertinent data sets. For this purpose, the prospective builder of a multiregional life table should not limit him- or herself to using published data, but should try his or her best to obtain, from population registers or censuses, special tabulations on migrants and stayers cross-classified by place of birth.

CHAPTER ELEVEN

Spatial Population Dynamics

Kao-Lee Liaw

Classical renewal theory, which deals with the evolution of an age-disaggregated population subject to time-invariant schedules of fertility and mortality, is an important branch of classical mathematical demography. Such prominent scientists as Lotka (1907), Lotka with Sharpe (1911), Fisher (1930), Feller (1941), Leslie (1945), Keyfitz (1968, 1972), Coale (1972), and Samuelson (1976) have contributed to this theory, which is based on the Lotka model (an integral equation) or the Leslie model (a system of difference equations). Dynamic properties central to the population system are revealed by the analytic solution of these mathematical models.

Since classical renewal theory does not deal with space, few geographers or regional scientists have appreciated the usefulness of it. The impact of interregional migration on population redistribution has usually been analyzed separately from birth and death processes, without taking age disaggregation into account (e.g., Vining 1975), even though age selectivity in migration is a significant fact of life. The combined effect of birth, death, and migration on the evolution of age-by-region population systems was not studied until the late 1960s, when Rogers (1966) and Tabah (1968) formulated multiregional generalizations of the Leslie or uniregional model.

Our goal here is to make a spatial extension of classical renewal theory by incorporating time-invariant, age-specific interregional migration into it. To achieve this goal, we use the analytic solution of the discrete-time multiregional population growth model developed by Rogers (1975a). We also synthesize the important findings in classical renewal theory and the simple mathematical properties of column stochastic matrices by creating and analyzing the so-called factorizable and quasi-factorizable multiregional demographic models (Rogers 1968) that capture the essential properties of age-by-region population systems and are analytically tractable.

The age-by-region population system is represented by the multiregional model in Section 11.1, along with a description of the analytic solution of the model. In Section 11.2, the uniregional model is considered as a simplified

multiregional model, and important results in classical renewal theory are summarized. The following two sections specify both the factorizable and quasi-
factorizable multiregional models and perform analysis and synthesis. Section
11.5 uses the demographic data on Swedish females for 1974 as an illustration,
and Section 11.6 reports the findings of applying the general multiregional
model to four population systems. The final section summarizes and discusses
the main points of the chapter.

11.1 The Multiregional Model and its Analytic Solution

Consider a population system with N regions and a total of w age groups
(0–4, 5–9,...), with the last group open-ended. With five years as the unit
time interval, the (discrete) multiregional model (Rogers 1975a, pp.117–129) is

$$
\begin{bmatrix}
K_{1,t+1} \\
K_{2,t+1} \\
K_{3,t+1} \\
\vdots \\
K_{f,t+1} \\
K_{f+1,t+1} \\
\\
\vdots \\
K_{w,t+1}
\end{bmatrix}
=
\begin{bmatrix}
\mathbf{b}_1 & \mathbf{b}_2 & \cdots & \mathbf{b}_{f-1} & \mathbf{b}_f \\
\mathbf{s}_1 & \mathbf{0} & \cdots & \mathbf{0} & \mathbf{0} \\
\mathbf{0} & \mathbf{s}_2 & \cdots & \mathbf{0} & \mathbf{0} & & & \mathbf{0} \\
\vdots & \vdots & & \vdots & \vdots \\
\mathbf{0} & \mathbf{0} & \cdots & \mathbf{s}_{f-1} & \mathbf{0} \\
\mathbf{0} & \mathbf{0} & \cdots & \mathbf{0} & \mathbf{s}_f & \mathbf{0} & \mathbf{0} & \cdots & \mathbf{0} & \mathbf{0} \\
& & \mathbf{0} & & & \mathbf{s}_{f+1} & \mathbf{0} & \cdots & \mathbf{0} & \mathbf{0} \\
& & & & & \vdots & \vdots & & \vdots & \vdots \\
& & & & & \mathbf{0} & \mathbf{0} & \cdots & \mathbf{s}_{w-1} & \mathbf{s}_w
\end{bmatrix}
\begin{bmatrix}
K_{1t} \\
K_{2t} \\
K_{3t} \\
\vdots \\
K_{ft} \\
K_{f+1,t} \\
\\
\vdots \\
K_{wt}
\end{bmatrix}
\tag{11.1}
$$

$$\text{for } t = 0,1,2,\ldots,$$

where K_{at}, for $a = 1,2,\ldots,w$, represents the interregional population distribution of the ath age group at time t;[1] the submatrices $\mathbf{b}$ measure the birth of
babies, their survival, and their migration among regions; and the submatrices
$\mathbf{s}$ indicate how existing people in individual age groups survive and migrate
within a unit time interval.[2] The order of K_{at} is $N \times 1$, and those of $\mathbf{b}_a$ and $\mathbf{s}_a$
are $N \times N$. The index f indicates the last fertile age group. We may write the
model more compactly as

---

[1] The age indices refer to the order of the age group and not to the lowest age of the age
group, as in the other chapters. To distinguish this approach, a different age variable is
used in this chapter. Other differences in notation between this and other chapters are
made explicit as they appear.

[2] If foreign migration is important, the model can be modified to accommodate it (Liaw
1978b, 1979b). If data are available on an annual basis, the unit age and time interval can,
of course, be set to one year. Note that $\mathbf{s}_w$ need not be a zero matrix, because the last age
group is open-ended (e.g. 65+ or 85+).

$$K_{t+1} = GK_t \quad , \tag{11.2}$$

where the *growth matrix* G has the order of $wN \times wN$, and the population vectors K_{t+1} and K_t the order of $wN \times 1$.

Using the empirically valid assumption that the nonzero eigenvalues of G are distinct, Liaw (1978a) showed that the analytic solution of equation (11.2) is

$$K_t = \sum_i \lambda_i^t Q_i P_i' K_0 + R \quad , \tag{11.3}$$

where λ_i is a nonzero *eigenvalue* of G, Q_i and P_i' are, respectively, the normalized *right* and *left eigenvectors* of G associated with λ_i, and K_0 is the population in the base period. In other words, λ_i, Q_i, and P_i' are computed from the conditions

$$GQ_i = \lambda_i Q_i$$

$$P_i' G = \lambda_i P_i'$$

$$P_i' Q_i = 1$$

$$\lambda_i \neq 0 \quad .$$

The residual vector R is filled with zeros up to the last reproductive age group (f) and becomes a zero vector for $t \geq w - f$. By letting c_i equal $P_i' K_0$, the analytic solution can also be written as

$$K_t = \sum_i \lambda_i^t c_i Q_i + R \quad . \tag{11.4}$$

Ignoring the residual, we see that the age-by-region population at time t is simply a linear combination of the right eigenvectors of G, with the weights being $\lambda_i^t c_i$.[3] The relative importance of each term at $t = 0$ depends on the magnitude of the scalar c_i. Since c_i remains constant through time, however, the relative importance of each term for large t depends increasingly on the magnitude of λ_i. As t becomes very large, only the *dominant component* (i.e., the term associated with the largest eigenvalue λ_1) remains important. In other words,

$$\lim_{t \to \infty} K_t / \lambda_1^t = c_1 Q_1 \quad ,$$

where, according to the Frobenius theorem (Gantmacher 1964, pp.53–54), both c_1 and Q_1 are real and nonnegative. Clearly, the system will approach a fixed *long-run (stable) age-by-region population distribution*, which is

---

[3]The right eigenvectors can be arbitrarily scaled as long as $P_i' Q_i = 1$. For interpretative and computational convenience, the sum of the magnitudes of the elements in each real right eigenvector is set to unity, as is the sum of the squares of the elements of each complex right eigenvector.

represented by the dominant right eigenvector Q_1.[4] The annual discrete *long-run growth rate* of every subpopulation is $\lambda^{0.2} - 1$. The scalar c_1 is the *stable equivalent population size*, which is denoted by Y in Chapter 9.[5] The *momentum* of the population system equals $[(c_1 - k)/k] \times 100\%$, where k is the total population size at $t = 0$.[6] The momentum represents the percentage amplification (or deduction, if negative) of the "ultimate" population size due to the difference between the initial and the long-run age-by-region distributions. By "ultimate" we mean the time when the dominant component begins to overwhelm the remaining components in the analytic solution. It is obvious that the dominant component, as well as other components associated with positive real eigenvalues, will behave monotonically through time.

Most of the eigenvalues of the growth matrix are complex numbers, which occur necessarily in conjugate pairs because **G** is real. For substantive interpretations, we must transform all complex terms into a real form. Denoting the square root of -1 by i, let $\alpha_i + i\beta_i$ and $\alpha_i - i\beta_i$ be a pair of complex eigenvalues of **G**, with $U_i' + iV_i'$, $U_i' - iV_i'$, $X_i + iY_i$, and $X_i - iY_i$ as the associated left and right eigenvectors. Then the analytic components associated with these two eigenvalues can be changed into the real form:

$$2\delta_i \, \sigma_i^t [\cos(t\vartheta_i + \omega_i)X_i - \sin(t\vartheta_i + \omega_i)Y_i] \, , \tag{11.5}$$

where

$\sigma_i = (\alpha_i^2 + \beta_i^2)^{1/2}$ is the *magnitude* of the eigenvalue
$\vartheta_i = \tan^{-1}(\beta_i / \alpha_i)$ is the *amplitude* of the eigenvalue
$\delta_i = [(U_i' K_0)^2 (V_i' K_0)^2]^{1/2}$
$\omega_i = \tan^{-1}[V_i' K_0 / U_i' K_0]$.

The element in the combined analytic component in equation (11.5) corresponding to the ath age group and the jth region can be further simplified into

$$2\delta_i \, \gamma_{iaj} \, \sigma_i^t \cos(t\vartheta_i + \omega_i + \varphi_{iaj}) \, , \tag{11.6}$$

where

$$\gamma_{iaj} = (X_{iaj}^2 + Y_{iaj}^2)^{1/2} \tag{11.7}$$

and

$$\varphi_{iaj} = \tan^{-1}(Y_{iaj} / X_{iaj}) \, . \tag{11.8}$$

---

[4]The dominant right eigenvector Q_1 is denoted by ξ in Chapter 9.
[5]The notation used in this chapter is consistent with that used in spectral analysis, whereas that of Chapter 9 follows the traditional demographic convention (e.g., Keyfitz 1969).
[6]Some authors define momentum as c_1/k.

It is understood that X_{iaj} and Y_{iaj} are the elements of X_i and Y_i corresponding to the ath age group and jth region. Equation (11.6) shows that each pair of complex components in the analytic solution is actually a *cyclical component* with ϑ_i as the frequency (in radians per five years). The *period* (in years) of the component is

$$\tau_i = 5(2\pi / \vartheta_i) . \tag{11.9}$$

Since the cosine function assumes a value between +1 and -1 for all t, the elements in the cyclical component fluctuate below the smooth exponential *upper bounds* $2\delta_i \gamma_{iaj} \sigma_i^t$ as t increases. If the phase angles $\omega_i + \varphi_{iaj}$ are zero, then all elements start at $t = 0$ from the upper bounds; otherwise, the starting points are within $\pm 2\delta_i \gamma_{iaj}$. The number of years required to reduce the upper bounds by half of their original sizes is called the *half-life*, which is

$$t_i = 5(-\ln 2 / \ln \sigma_i) . \tag{11.10}$$

What determines what in a cyclical component? Equations (11.9) and (11.10) show that the period and half-life of a cyclical component are completely determined by a complex eigenvalue of the growth matrix $\mathbf{G}$. Equations (11.7) and (11.8) show that the *inter-age-group* and *interregional* contrasts in upper bounds and phase angles of a cyclical component are completely determined by a complex right eigenvector of $\mathbf{G}$. The initial age-by-region population distribution K_0, through its inner product with a complex left eigenvector, affects only the overall level δ_i and the overall phase direction ω_i of a cyclical component [see equation (11.5)].

The cyclical component with the longest half-life is called the *dominant cyclical component*, and its corresponding eigenvalue the *dominant complex eigenvalue*. For simplicity, we treat negative real eigenvalues as a special kind of complex eigenvalue whose amplitude is π radians per five years.

If we separate the cyclical from the monotonic components, the analytic solution for the projected population size in age group a and region j at time t is

$$K_{ajt} = \sum_{i=1}^{n_1} c_i Q_{iaj} \lambda_i^t + \sum_{i=1}^{n_2} 2\delta_i \gamma_{iaj} \sigma_i^t \cos(t\vartheta_i + \omega_i + \varphi_{iaj}) + R_{aj} , \tag{11.11}$$

where K_{ajt} and Q_{iaj} are the elements in K_t and Q_i corresponding to the ath age group and jth region; and n_1 and n_2 represent the number of monotonic and cyclical terms, respectively. For each age- and region-specific subpopulation, the relative importance of the analytic components at $t = 0$ depends on the initial *loadings* $c_i Q_{iaj}$ and $2\delta_i \gamma_{iaj} \cos(\omega_i + \varphi_{iaj})$.

For simplicity, all components are arranged in descending order of the magnitudes of the corresponding eigenvalues (e.g., $\lambda_1 > \lambda_2 > \cdots > \lambda_{n_1}$ and $\sigma_1 > \sigma_2 > \cdots > \sigma_{n_2}$). We use the notation J' to represent a *summation vector*, which is a row vector filled with ones.[7]

---

[7]In Chapter 9, a row vector of ones is denoted by $1'$.

It is the basic properties of the monotonic and cyclical components in equation (11.11) that we wish to understand by synthesizing classical renewal theory and the simple mathematical properties of column stochastic matrices.

11.2 The Uniregional Model and Classical Renewal Theory

When there is only one region, the multiregional model (Rogers 1975a) is reduced to the uniregional model (Leslie 1945):

$$\hat{K}_{t+1} = \hat{G}\hat{K}_t \ , \tag{11.12}$$

where $\hat{K}_t$, $\hat{K}_{t+1}$, and $\hat{G}$ correspond to K_t, K_{t+1}, and G in equation (11.2). The $w \times w$ matrix $\hat{G}$ is the same as G, except that the $\mathbf{b}_\alpha$ and $\mathbf{s}_\alpha$ submatrices are now reduced to scalars b_α and s_α. With realistic assumptions, it can be shown that the growth matrix $\hat{G}$ has a unique dominant eigenvalue that is real and positive (Keyfitz 1968, chapter 3). All the remaining nonzero eigenvalues are either complex or real and negative. Therefore for the α th age group the analytic solution of the uniregional model is

$$\hat{K}_{\alpha t} = \hat{c}_1 \hat{Q}_{1\alpha} \hat{\lambda}_1^t + \sum_{i=1}^{n_2} 2\hat{\delta}_i \hat{\gamma}_{i\alpha} \hat{\sigma}_i^t \cos(t\hat{\vartheta}_i + \hat{\omega}_i + \hat{\varphi}_{i\alpha}) + \hat{R}_\alpha \ , \tag{11.13}$$

where all quantities are analogous to those in equation (11.11). If we ignore the residual, the dominant component is the only monotonic term; the remaining ones are all cyclical.

The uniregional model and its continuous-time counterpart have been studied both mathematically and empirically for many decades. The resulting body of knowledge is known as classical renewal theory. There are 10 main points underlying the uniregional model.

(1)   The dominant eigenvalue of the growth matrix $\hat{G}$ and the corresponding right and left eigenvectors are relatively insensitive to alternative ways of discretizing the fertility and mortality schedules. In other words, the dominant component can actually reflect the intrinsic nature of the population system.

(2)   The dominant eigenvalue is positively related to the area under the curve of the discrete generalized net maternity function (i.e., the net reproduction rate) and negatively related to the mean age of this function.[8]

---

[8] With discrete age groups, the generalized net maternity function F_α is defined as

$$F_\alpha = b_\alpha s_{\alpha-1} \cdots s_1 \qquad \alpha = 2,3,\ldots,$$

where the right-hand-side quantities are taken from equation (11.1), with matrices being replaced by the corresponding scalars. The net reproduction rate is the sum of F_α across all age groups. We call the sum of all b_α the gross reproduction rate for simplicity,

(3)   The period of the dominant cyclical component almost equals the length of a generation and is positively and strongly related to the mean age of the net maternity function.

(4)   The half-life of the dominant cyclical component is negatively and strongly related to the dispersion of the net maternity function. In other words, a highly concentrated fertility schedule results in a small rate of attenuation for population waves that are transmitted through successive generations.

(5)   Higher-frequency eigenvalues depend on peculiarities in fertility and mortality schedules in a way that is difficult to describe and, hence, difficult to understand intuitively. Furthermore, these eigenvalues are also sensitive to alternative ways of approximating fertility and mortality schedules. Not much can be learned about a population from the components associated with these eigenvalues, except that they guarantee the "material balance" of equation (11.13) for any initial population.

(6)   The dominant cyclical component is damped, relative to the dominant component, by about 2.5–5% annually. In other words, the ratio of $\hat{\sigma}_1$ to $\hat{\lambda}_1$ is usually between 0.88 and 0.77. Cyclical components with higher frequencies are attenuated at least twice as rapidly as the dominant cyclical component.

(7)   If the initial population is heavily concentrated in the age interval 0–24, the stable equivalent population size ($\hat{c}_1$) will be much larger than the initial total population size (i.e., there will be a large momentum for the population to continue growing even if the fertility level is already below replacement level). This is because the elements of the dominant left eigenvector, which are proportional to Fisher's reproductive values, remain at a high level in the age interval 0–24 and drop sharply afterwards toward zero at the end of the reproductive age interval. The typical age pattern of the dominant left eigenvector is determined by the fertility and survival schedules of the uniregional model according to the formula

$$\hat{P}_{1,a+1} = (\hat{\lambda}_1/s_a)\hat{P}_{1,a} - (b_a/s_a)\hat{P}_{1,1} \qquad 1 \le a < f \ . \qquad (11.14)$$

For the young age groups, $\hat{\lambda}_1/s_a$ is usually close to one, and b_a/s_a equals or nearly equals zero. This explains why $\hat{P}_{1,a}$ remains more or less at the same level for young age groups. But the large values for b_a around the peak of the fertility pull $\hat{P}_{1,a+1}$ down sharply. For post-reproductive age groups, $\hat{P}_{i,a} = 0$ for any i.

---

although the b_a coefficients are affected by infant mortality (compare with Willekens and Rogers 1978, p.79).

(8)   The initial upper bound of a cyclical component $(2\hat{\delta}_i\ \hat{\gamma}_{ia})$ tends to be small, when the initial population is not highly concentrated in the youngest age group. The higher the frequency, the stronger this tendency. This relationship is a result of the elements of the left eigenvector associated with a high-frequency eigenvalue declining rapidly in magnitude as age increases. The age pattern of a complex left eigenvector can be explained by a formula like equation (11.14).[9]

(9)   For most empirical data, the time path of the 0–4 age group of the uniregional model can be quite accurately approximated by the sum of the dominant and dominant cyclical components. That is,

$$\hat{K}_{at} \doteq \hat{c}_1\hat{Q}_{1a}\hat{\lambda}_1^t + 2\hat{\delta}_1\hat{\gamma}_{1a}\hat{\sigma}_1^t\cos(t\,\hat{\vartheta}_1 + \hat{\omega}_1 + \hat{\varphi}_{1a}) \tag{11.15}$$

Thus for the youngest age group the time path of the projected population size can be visualized as a damped wave with a period of about 25–30 years, which is superimposed on a smooth exponential trend.

(10) For most empirical data, the population projected by the uniregional model 100 years into the future will be similar to the stable population that has the age profile represented by the dominant right eigenvector $\hat{Q}_1$, the intrinsic growth rate represented by ln $\hat{\lambda}_1/5$ (i.e., the annual discrete long-run growth rate of $\hat{\lambda}_1^{0.2} - 1$), and the total population size of $\hat{c}_1\hat{\lambda}_1^t$.

11.3 The Factorizable Multiregional Model and a Mathematically Simple Synthesis

In order to make the synthesis simple, in this section it is assumed that fertility and mortality schedules do not vary among the N regions, and that the level and pattern of migration are constant across all of the w age groups. In other words, it is assumed that the nonzero submatrices in equation (11.1) can be factorized in the following manner:

$$\mathbf{b}_\alpha = b_\alpha\hat{\hat{\mathbf{G}}} \tag{11.16}$$

and

$$\mathbf{s}_\alpha = s_\alpha\hat{\hat{\mathbf{G}}}\ , \tag{11.17}$$

where $\hat{\hat{\mathbf{G}}}$ is a fixed $N \times N$ column-stochastic matrix, and b_α and s_α are the birth and survival elements, respectively, of the growth matrix $\hat{\mathbf{G}}$ of the corresponding uniregional model. For simplicity, we call $\hat{\hat{\mathbf{G}}}$ a pure migration matrix and $\hat{\mathbf{G}}$ a uniregional growth matrix.

---

[9]The complex left eigenvectors of the uniregional model are discrete analogues of $Q_i(a)$ in equation (3.20) in Coale (1972, p.68).

Using the Kronecker product,[10] we find that our assumptions about the age-by-region population system lead to the *factorizable multiregional model*:

$$K_{t+1} = (\hat{G} \otimes \hat{\hat{G}})K_t \quad .$$ (11.18)

Its analytic solution the becomes

$$K_t = (\hat{G} \otimes \hat{\hat{G}})^t K_0 = (\hat{G}^t \otimes \hat{\hat{G}}^t)K_0$$

$$= \left[\sum_k \hat{\lambda}_k^t \hat{Q}_k \hat{P}_k'\right] \otimes \left[\sum_l \hat{\hat{\lambda}}_l^t \hat{\hat{Q}}_l \hat{\hat{P}}_l'\right]K_0 + \hat{R}$$ (11.19)

$$= \sum_k \sum_l (\hat{\lambda}_k \hat{\hat{\lambda}}_l)^t (\hat{Q}_k \otimes \hat{\hat{Q}}_l)(\hat{P}_k \otimes \hat{\hat{P}}_l)' K_0 + \hat{R} \quad ,$$

where $\hat{\lambda}_k$ is the kth nonzero eigenvalue of the uniregional growth matrix $\hat{G}$, and $\hat{P}_k'$ and $\hat{Q}_k$ are the left and right eigenvectors of $\hat{G}$ associated with $\hat{\lambda}_k$; and $\hat{\hat{\lambda}}_l$ is the lth nonzero eigenvalue of the pure migration matrix $\hat{\hat{G}}$, and $\hat{\hat{P}}_l'$ and $\hat{\hat{Q}}_l$ are the left and right eigenvectors of $\hat{\hat{G}}$ associated with λ_l.

Comparing equations (11.19) and (11.3) we see that for a factorizable multiregional model,

$$\lambda_i = \hat{\lambda}_k \hat{\hat{\lambda}}_l$$ (11.20)

$$Q_i = \hat{Q}_k \otimes \hat{\hat{Q}}_l$$ (11.21)

$$P_i' = \hat{P}_k' \otimes \hat{\hat{P}}_l' \quad .$$ (11.22)

In other words, each nonzero eigenvalue of G is a nonzero eigenvalue of $\hat{G}$ times an eigenvalue of $\hat{\hat{G}}$; and each left (right) eigenvector of G is a Kronecker product of a left (right) eigenvector of $\hat{G}$ and a left (right) eigenvector of $\hat{\hat{G}}$. Since we have already examined the eigenvalue and eigenvectors of $\hat{G}$ in Section 11.2, we now focus on those of $\hat{\hat{G}}$.

---

[10] Let $\hat{G} = \begin{bmatrix} b_1 & b_2 & b_3 \\ s_1 & 0 & 0 \\ 0 & s_2 & 0 \end{bmatrix}$ and $\hat{\hat{G}} = \begin{bmatrix} m_{11} & m_{12} \\ m_{21} & m_{22} \end{bmatrix}$. Then the Kronecker product of $\hat{G}$ and $\hat{\hat{G}}$ is

$$\hat{G} \otimes \hat{\hat{G}} = \begin{bmatrix} b_1 m_{11} & b_1 m_{12} & b_2 m_{11} & b_2 m_{12} & b_3 m_{11} & b_3 m_{12} \\ b_1 m_{21} & b_1 m_{22} & b_2 m_{21} & b_2 m_{22} & b_3 m_{21} & b_3 m_{22} \\ s_1 m_{11} & s_1 m_{12} & 0 & 0 & 0 & 0 \\ s_1 m_{21} & s_1 m_{22} & 0 & 0 & 0 & 0 \\ 0 & 0 & s_2 m_{11} & s_2 m_{12} & 0 & 0 \\ 0 & 0 & s_2 m_{21} & s_2 m_{22} & 0 & 0 \end{bmatrix} \quad .$$

For a brief but useful introduction, see Theil (1971, pp.303–308).

Because the pure migration matrix $\hat{\hat{\mathbf{G}}}$ is realistically taken to be an irreducible, nonnegative matrix, we know from the Frobenius theorem (Gantmacher 1964, pp.53–54) that its dominant eigenvalue and dominant right and left eigenvectors are positive. Furthermore, $\hat{\hat{\mathbf{G}}}$ being a column-stochastic matrix implies that

$$\hat{\hat{\lambda}}_1 = 1 \tag{11.23}$$

$$\hat{\hat{P}}'_1 = \mathbf{J}' = (1,1,\ldots,1) \tag{11.24}$$

$$\sum_{j=1}^{N} \hat{\hat{Q}}_{l,j} = 0 \qquad l = 2,3,\ldots,N \ . \tag{11.25}$$

Equation (11.23) is intuitively clear, because the pure migration matrix can never cause an increase or a decrease in total population size. Equation (11.24) indicates that the dominant left eigenvector of $\hat{\hat{\mathbf{G}}}$ is simply a $1 \times N$ summation vector. As a consequence of equation (11.25), we can consider every subdominant right eigenvector $\hat{\hat{Q}}_l (l > 1)$ as representing an *interregional zero-sum game*, because the sum of the positive numbers is offset by the sum of the negative ones. Finally, every subdominant left eigenvector $\hat{\hat{P}}_l (l > 1)$ must have at least one positive and one negative element, because its inner product with the dominant right eigenvector $\hat{\hat{Q}}_1$ must be zero.

There are two additional properties of $\hat{\hat{\mathbf{G}}}$ that can be easily proved in a biregional case and that have not been violated in empirically constructed migration models. First, because migration rates are always much smaller than stayer rates (i.e., $\hat{\hat{\mathbf{G}}}$ has a dominant diagonal), all eigenvalues of $\hat{\hat{\mathbf{G}}}$ are real and positive. Second, as the level of migration is increased, the subdominant eigenvalues become smaller.

We are now ready to synthesize. Consider the eigenvalues of the factorizable multiregional model. Because $\lambda_i = \hat{\lambda}_k \hat{\hat{\lambda}}_l$, we see that corresponding to each eigenvalue of the uniregional model there is a *cluster* of exactly N eigenvalues in the factorizable multiregional model. Within each cluster, all the eigenvalues have the same frequency (because all $\hat{\hat{\lambda}}_l$ are real and positive), and the eigenvalue with the largest magnitude exactly equals an eigenvalue of the uniregional model (because $\hat{\hat{\lambda}}_1 = 1$ and $\hat{\hat{\lambda}}_l < 1$ for $l > 1$). Furthermore, the difference in magnitude among the eigenvalues in each cluster increases as the level of migration is raised, because the subdominant eigenvalues of $\hat{\hat{\mathbf{G}}}$ are negatively affected by the level of migration.

The components associated with the subdominant positive and real eigenvalues (λ_2 to λ_N) are called *spatial components*, since they convey information about spatial redistribution. Each spatial component of the factorizable multiregional model represents an interregional zero-sum game for every age group, because equation (11.25) implies $\sum_{j=1}^{N} Q_{iaj} = 0$ for all spatial components. The relative importance of a spatial component at $t = 0$ depends on the relative size of the initial level $c_i = (\hat{P}'_1 \otimes \hat{\hat{P}}'_i)K_0$. Since $\hat{P}'_1$ is strictly positive, and $\hat{P}'_i$ $(i > 1)$ has both positive and negative (i.e., mutually canceling) elements, it is usually the case that the c_i $(i > 1)$ are smaller in magnitude than c_1. In other words, the spatial components are usually less important than the dominant component, even at the initial stage. The sum of all spatial components is called the *superimposed spatial component*, which is found to have smooth time paths in all known empirical applications, although this is not a necessary implication of all individual spatial components having smooth exponential time paths.

The N cyclical components associated with the most durable cluster of complex eigenvalues are called *major cyclical components* since, with the common period of one generation, they determine jointly the major features of the transmission of population waves from one generation to another. Within this group there is an important distinction between the dominant cyclical component and the remaining ones. The former represents population waves that move *synchronically* across all regions for each age group (because the dominant right eigenvector $\hat{Q}_1$ of $\hat{G}$ is real and positive), whereas each of the latter represents population waves that move in *opposite* directions simultaneously in two nonempty subsets of regions (because every subdominant right eigenvector of $\hat{G}$ has the aforementioned zero-sum nature). We call these two contrasting waves synchronical and opposite waves. Because each subdominant left eigenvector $\hat{P}'_l$ $(l > 1)$ of $\hat{G}$ has both positive and negative elements, and the dominant left eigenvector $\hat{P}'_1$ is strictly positive, the dominant cyclical component is usually more important than the other major cyclical components, even at the initial stage. In other words, we would anticipate the actual population waves to be more rather than less synchronical.

In summary, the main points we have learned about the factorizable multiregional model are (a) the existence of a cluster of N eigenvalues corresponding to each eigenvalue of the uniregional model, (b) the identification of the spatial components that control the spatial redistribution of the population, and (c) the distinction between synchronical and opposite population waves.

11.4 The Quasi-Factorizable Multiregional Model and a Substantively More Meaningful Synthesis

The quasi-factorizable multiregional model is a model in which fertility and mortality schedules do not vary among regions and the level and pattern of migration are allowed to vary among age groups. In other words, for the quasi-factorizable multiregional model, the submatrices in equation (11.1) can be written as

$$\mathbf{b}_\alpha = b_\alpha \, {}^i\mathbf{m}_\alpha \tag{11.26}$$

$$\mathbf{s}_\alpha = s_\alpha \, \mathbf{m}_\alpha \qquad \alpha = 1, 2, \ldots, w \; , \tag{11.27}$$

where the scalars b_α and s_α are the common age-specific birth and survival elements, and $^i\mathbf{m}_\alpha$ and $\mathbf{m}_\alpha$ are the infant and noninfant age-specific interregional migration matrices, respectively. By definition, $^i\mathbf{m}_\alpha$ and $\mathbf{m}_\alpha$ are $N \times N$ column-stochastic matrices. Since the migration level and pattern are allowed to differ among age groups, this model is substantively more interesting than the factorizable multiregional model. We now prove four theorems about the relationships between the quasi-factorizable multiregional model and the corresponding uniregional model.

THEOREM 1. *Any eigenvalue of the growth matrix of the corresponding uniregional model is an eigenvalue of the growth matrix of the quasi-factorizable multiregional model.*

Proof. The characteristic equation of the growth matrix $\mathbf{G}$ of the quasi-factorizable multiregional model is $g(\lambda) = |\lambda\mathbf{I} - \mathbf{G}| = 0$. From the simple structure of $\mathbf{G}$, we can write the characteristic equation as

$$g(\lambda) = |\mathbf{A}(\lambda)||\lambda\mathbf{I} - \mathbf{s}_w| = 0 \ , \tag{11.28}$$

where $\mathbf{A}(\lambda)$ is such that

$$\mathbf{A}(\lambda) = (\mathbf{I}\lambda^f - \mathbf{b}_1\lambda^{f-1} - \mathbf{b}_2\mathbf{s}_1\lambda^{f-2} - \cdots - \mathbf{b}_f\mathbf{s}_{f-1}\cdots\mathbf{s}_1)\lambda^{(w-f-1)N} \ , \tag{11.29}$$

where f is the age index of the last reproductive age group, and w is the total number of age groups in the system.

Let J' be a $1 \times N$ summation vector. Then, from equations (11.26)–(11.29) we obtain

$$J'\mathbf{A}(\lambda) = (\lambda^f - b_1\lambda^{f-1} - b_2s_1\lambda^{f-2} - \cdots - b_fs_{f-1}\cdots s_1)\lambda^{(w-f-1)N}J'$$

$$= \hat{g}_1(\lambda)\lambda^{(w-f-1)(N-1)}J' \tag{11.30}$$

and

$$J'(\lambda\mathbf{I} - \mathbf{s}_w) = (\lambda - s_w)J' = \hat{g}_2(\lambda)J' \ , \tag{11.31}$$

where

$$\hat{g}(\lambda) = \hat{g}_1(\lambda)\hat{g}_2(\lambda) \tag{11.32}$$

is the characteristic polynomial for the corresponding uniregional model. Now, $\hat{g}_1(\lambda) = 0$ implies that $J'\mathbf{A}(\lambda) = 0'$ [i.e., the row vectors of $\mathbf{A}(\lambda)$ are linearly dependent] and hence $|\mathbf{A}(\lambda)| = 0$. Similarly, $\hat{g}_2(\lambda) = 0$ implies $|\lambda\mathbf{I} - \mathbf{s}_w| = 0$. Therefore any eigenvalue of the growth matrix of the corresponding uniregional model must be an eigenvalue of the growth matrix of the quasi-factorizable multiregional model.

THEOREM 2. *Associated with each nonzero eigenvalue of the growth matrix $\mathbf{G}$ of the quasi-factorizable multiregional model that is not an eigenvalue of the growth matrix $\hat{\mathbf{G}}$ of the corresponding uniregional* *model, there is a right eigenvector of* **G** *that represents a spatial zero-sum game for every age group.*

Proof. Let λ be such that $|\lambda I - G| = 0$ and $|\lambda I - \widehat{G}| \neq 0$. Let Q be the right eigenvector of **G** associated with λ, and let Q_a $(a = 1,2,\ldots,w)$ be an $N \times 1$ subvector of Q corresponding to the ath age group. Then, by definition,

$$\sum_{a=1}^{f} \mathbf{b}_a \, Q_a = \lambda Q_1 \tag{11.33}$$

$$\mathbf{s}_{a-1} Q_{a-1} = \lambda Q_a \qquad a = 2,3,\ldots,w-1 \tag{11.34}$$

$$\mathbf{s}_{w-1} Q_{w-1} + \mathbf{s}_w Q_w = \lambda Q_w \; . \tag{11.35}$$

From equation (11.34),

$$Q_a = \mathbf{s}_{a-1} \mathbf{s}_{a-2} \cdots \mathbf{s}_1 Q_1 / \lambda^{a-1} \qquad a = 2,3,\ldots,f \; . \tag{11.36}$$

Substituting equation (11.36) into (11.33) yields

$$(\lambda^f \, I - \lambda^{f-1} \mathbf{b}_1 - \lambda^{f-2} \mathbf{b}_2 \mathbf{s}_1 - \cdots - \mathbf{b}_f \, \mathbf{s}_{f-1} \cdots \mathbf{s}_1) Q_1 = 0 \; . \tag{11.37}$$

Multiplying both sides of equation (11.37) by the summation vector J', we have

$$(\lambda^f - \lambda^{f-1} b_1 - \lambda^{f-2} b_2 s_1 - \cdots - b_f \, s_{f-1} \cdots s_1) J' \, Q_1 = 0 \; . \tag{11.38}$$

Since λ is not an eigenvalue of $\widehat{G}$ by assumption, we see that the polynomial in equation (11.38) is nonzero. Therefore it is true that

$$J' Q_1 = 0 \; , \tag{11.39}$$

which means that the sum of the N elements in Q_1 is zero. Multiplying J' by equations (11.36) and (11.35) and then substituting equation (11.39) into the results gives

$$J' Q_a = 0 \qquad a = 1,2,\ldots,w \; . \tag{11.40}$$

Therefore the right eigenvector Q represents a spatial zero-sum game for every age group.

THEOREM 3. *If λ is a common nonzero eigenvalue of the growth matrix* **G** *of the quasi-factorizable multiregional model and of the growth matrix* $\widehat{G}$ *of the corresponding uniregional model, and if $\widehat{P}'$ is the left eigenvector of $\widehat{G}$ associated with the eigenvalue λ, the $1 \times wN$ row vector $P' = \widehat{P}' \otimes J'$ is the left eigenvector of* **G** *associated with the eigenvalue λ.*

Proof. Let $\widehat{P}' = (\widehat{P}_1 \widehat{P}_2 \cdots \widehat{P}_w)$ be the left eigenvector of $\widehat{G}$ associated with the common eigenvalue λ. Then, by definition,

$$\widehat{P}_1 b_a + \widehat{P}_{a+1} s_a = \lambda \widehat{P}_a \qquad a = 1,2,\ldots,w-1 \tag{11.41}$$

and

$$\hat{P}_w s_w = \lambda \hat{P}_w .$$
(11.42)

Now, let the $1 \times N$ row vector P_a' be the ath subvector of

$$P' = \hat{P}' \otimes J' ,$$
(11.43)

where J' is a $1 \times N$ summation vector. Then we can write the product P' G in terms of individual age groups as

$$P_1' b_a + P_{a+1}' s_a = \hat{P}_1 J' b_a + \hat{P}_{a+1} J' s_a$$
$$= (\hat{P}_1 b_a + \hat{P}_{a+1} s_a) J' \qquad a < w$$
(11.44)

and

$$P_w' s_w = \hat{P}_w J' s_w = \hat{P}_w s_w J' .$$
(11.45)

Substituting equations (11.41) and (11.42) into (11.44) and (11.45) yields

$$P_1' b_a + P_{a+1}' s_a = \lambda \hat{P}_a J' = \lambda P_a' \qquad a < w$$
(11.46)

and

$$P_w' s_w = \lambda \hat{P}_w J' = \lambda P_w' .$$
(11.47)

Equations (11.46) and (11.47) imply that

$$P' G = \lambda P' .$$

In other words, $P' = \hat{P}' \otimes J'$ is the left eigenvector of G associated with the common eigenvalue λ.

THEOREM 4. *If λ is a common nonzero eigenvalue of the growth matrix G of the quasi-factorizable multiregional model and of the growth matrix $\hat{G}$ of the corresponding uniregional model, if Q and $\hat{Q}$ are the right eigenvectors of G and $\hat{G}$, respectively, associated with the common eigenvalue λ, and if Q and $\hat{Q}$ are constrained to have unit column sums, then $J'Q_a = \hat{Q}_a$ for all a, where Q_a is the ath $N \times 1$ subvector of Q and $\hat{Q}_a$ is the ath element of $\hat{Q}$.*

Proof. Rewriting the definitional equation $GQ = \lambda Q$ for individual age groups, and multiplying the resulting equations by the summation vector J', we see immediately that $J'Q_a$ is the ath element of the right eigenvector of $\hat{G}$ associated with the eigenvalue λ. But the constraints of a unit column sum make $J'Q_a$ equal $\hat{Q}_a$ for all a.

A few remarks on these theorems are useful. Theorem 1 implies that for the quasi-factorizable multiregional model, the long-run (intrinsic) growth rate of the system and the frequency and half-life of the most durable cyclical component are completely determined by the interregionally identical net maternity schedules and are independent of the migration process. However, the migration process can have a significant influence on the regional age profiles as well as on the interregional distribution of the stable population of the quasi-factorizable multiregional model. Therefore the stable regional age profiles may have lumps or hollows.

Theorem 2 implies that for the quasi-factorizable multiregional model, the transient significance of the migration process is represented in the analytic solution by a sum of many interregional zero-sum games. Although most of these games have cyclical time paths, only the few noncyclical ones are substantively important. From the spatial components representing these games, we can identify the major gainers and losers in the interregional migration transaction, and hence the general trend in the spatial redistribution of the population.

Theorem 3 implies that the dominant left eigenvector, and therefore the reproductive values and population momentum of the quasi-factorizable multiregional model, are not influenced by the migration process. From the sensitivity formulas of Liaw (1978c) it can be shown that the simple relation $P_1' = \hat{P}_1'$ $\otimes J'$ implies that

$$\frac{\partial \lambda_1}{\partial b_{al}} = \hat{P}_{1,1} Q_{1,al} \tag{11.48}$$

and

$$\frac{\partial \lambda_1}{\partial s_{al}} = \hat{P}_{1,a+1} Q_{1,al} , \tag{11.49}$$

where b_{al} and s_{al} are the effective birth and survivorship elements, respectively, of age group a and region l. Thus the sensitivity of the long-run growth factor (λ_1) to changes in regional fertility and survival schedules is indirectly related to the migration process through the dominant right eigenvector, although the reproductive values do not differ among regions.

Theorem 4 implies that for the quasi-factorizable multiregional model, the stable age profile of the whole system must be a rather smooth function of age, although the stable regional age profiles may be quite irregular.

Finally, we note that the quasi-factorizable multiregional model was studied briefly by Feeney (1970). Unfortunately, by proving incorrectly that every eigenvalue of G is an eigenvalue of $\hat{G}$ and the converse, he failed to realize the existence of the components representing the spatial zero-sum games. The analytic representation of spatial redistribution in the multiregional model remained unknown until the identification of a spatial component by Liaw (1978b, 1979a).

11.5 An Empirical Example Based on 1974 Swedish Data

Using Andersson and Holmberg's (1980) data on the age-by-region (18 × 8) Swedish female population of 1974, the IIASA staff estimated a multiregional model. (The eight regions are shown on the map of Sweden in Chapter 2.) The initial age-by-region population was then used as the weighting scheme to create a uniregional model, a factorizable multiregional model, and a quasi-factorizable multiregional model. The nonzero elements of the growth matrix $\hat{\mathbf{G}}$ of the uniregional model are shown in Table 11.1, whereas the pure migration matrix $\hat{\mathbf{G}}$ of the factorizable multiregional model is presented in Table 11.2. To save space, the age-specific migration matrices of the quasi-factorizable multiregional model are not shown in this chapter.

Table 11.1 The initial age distribution and the nonzero elements of the growth matrix of the uniregional model using 1974 Swedish female population data.

Age group	Initial population	Birth elements (b_i)	Survivorship elements (s_i)
0–4	300755	—	0.99500
5–9	289672	—	0.99883
10–14	264778	0.00003	0.99862
15–19	261624	0.02898	0.99799
20–24	282670	0.16721	0.99781
25–29	328133	0.29632	0.99725
30–34	274276	0.24907	0.99600
35–39	226512	0.12234	0.99397
40–44	221743	0.03788	0.99033
45–49	239077	0.00681	0.98509
50–54	269042	0.00036	0.97717
55–59	246333	—	0.96574
60–64	248353	—	0.94352
65–69	225571	—	0.90120
70–74	185246	—	0.82813
75–79	133952	—	0.71387
80–84	81641	—	0.81007
85+	49668	—	—

Note: The data are consolidated from the multiregional model, using the initial age-by-region population distribution as the weighting scheme.

From the data in Table 11.1, it can be shown (a) that the initial (1974) national age profile is highly irregular, reflecting mainly the low fertility of the 1930s, the brief post-World War II fertility increase, and the subsequent fertility decline; (b) that the 1974 fertility schedule has a high mean age (about 30 years), a low level (GRR = 0.91), and a small standard deviation (about six years); and (c) that the mortality level is very low, with the probability of surviving from the 0–4 to the 45–49 age group being greater than 0.95. The pure migration matrix in Table 11.2 shows that the origin–destination

Table 11.2 The pure migration matrix of the 1974 Swedish female population.

Region of destination		Region of origin			
		I	II	III	IV
I	Stockholm	0.91003	0.02916	0.01446	0.01150
II	East Middle	0.03026	0.90656	0.01840	0.00856
III	South Middle	0.00827	0.00997	0.91208	0.01268
IV	South	0.01064	0.00989	0.02273	0.94587
V	West	0.01075	0.01533	0.02328	0.01403
VI	North Middle	0.01472	0.01704	0.00482	0.00363
VII	Lower North	0.00807	0.00547	0.00158	0.00155
VIII	Upper North	0.00727	0.00657	0.00267	0.00217
	Total	0.08997	0.09344	0.08792	0.05413
		V	VI	VII	VIII
I	Stockholm	0.01007	0.02030	0.02694	0.02474
II	East Middle	0.01041	0.02528	0.01652	0.01789
III	South Middle	0.00866	0.00400	0.00338	0.00408
IV	South	0.01120	0.00441	0.00542	0.00492
V	West	0.94678	0.01589	0.01024	0.00970
VI	North Middle	0.00728	0.91930	0.01199	0.00827
VII	Lower North	0.00250	0.00591	0.91154	0.01179
VIII	Upper North	0.00309	0.00490	0.01397	0.91862
	Total	0.05322	0.08070	0.08846	0.08138

migration rates range from 0.16% (from the South to the Lower North) to 3.03% (from Stockholm to the East Middle), and that the overall outmigration rates also vary substantially between a minimum of 5.32% (West) and a maximum of 9.34% (East Middle).

11.5.1 *The Uniregional Model of the Swedish Female Population*

The dominant eigenvalue of the uniregional model is $\hat{\lambda}_1 = 0.9833$, which implies a long-run growth rate of -0.3% per year and a half-life of 205 years. The smallness of $\hat{\lambda}_1$ reflects mainly the low level of the net reproduction rate (0.90) and partly the relatively high mean age of the net maternity function (29.74 years).

The dominant cyclical component of the uniregional model has a period of 32.70 years and a half-life of 28.18 years. The period is perhaps the longest of all recorded national populations. This is, of course, because of the high mean age of the fertility schedule (29.76 years). The corresponding half-life is also unusually long, because of the strong concentration of the fertility schedule, which is the result of effective birth control. This half-life implies a damping rate, relative to the dominant component, of 2.1% per year, which is smaller than those of the 47 populations examined by Coale (1972). Because of the small damping rate, the population waves passing through the individual age groups are still visible after 100 years (Figure 11.1). The damping rates of the remaining cyclical components are shown in Table 11.3 to be greater than three times the damping rate of the dominant cyclical component.

The lack of importance of the high-frequency cyclical components in determining the projected population time path of the 0—4 age group is seen in Figure 11.1 (a), where the time path of the sum of the dominant and dominant cyclical components approximates the projected population time path quite well, even in the short run. The short-run importance of the high-frequency cyclical components for relatively old age groups is illustrated in Figure 11.1 (b). However, an attempt to make a substantive interpretation of the high-frequency cyclical component is as futile as an effort to convey the intuitive meaning of the 13th moment of a probability distribution.

The age patterns of the dominant left and right eigenvectors of the uniregional model, together with the initial and projected national age profiles, are shown in Figure 11.2. We see that the elements of the dominant left eigenvector indeed remain at a high level in the first five age groups and then drop sharply to become zero beyond the end of the reproductive range. Since there is a high concentration of the initial population in the first six age groups, it is not surprising that the stable equivalent ($\hat{c}_1 = 4\,879\,000$) is substantially greater than the initial total population size ($4\,129\,000$). The corresponding population momentum is 18%. This means that by the time the system achieves the stable growth pattern, the total population size projected from the observed distribution will be 18% greater than the total population size projected from an initial population that was rearranged in advance according to the stable age profile. Because of the positive growth momentum, the Swedish female population continues to expand from 4.13 million in 1974 until the early

Table 11.3 The nonzero eigenvalues of the uniregional model using 1974 Swedish female population data.

Real part of eigenvalue ($\hat{a}_i$)	Imaginary part of eigenvalue ($\hat{\beta}_i$)	Magnitude ($\hat{\sigma}_i$)	Half-life ($\hat{t}_i$)	Frequency ($\hat{\vartheta}_i$)	Period ($\hat{\tau}_i$)	Annual rate of change (%)
0.98325	0.00000	0.98325	205.17	0.00	∞	−0.337
0.50654	0.72482	0.88427	28.18	55.05	32.70	−2.430
−0.18255	0.59307	0.62053	7.26	107.11	16.81	−9.102
−0.15590	0.36628	0.39807	3.76	113.06	15.92	−16.825
−0.39484	0.21429	0.44925	4.33	151.51	11.88	−14.789
−0.44793	0.00000	0.44793	4.31	180.00	10.00	−14.839
−0.08181	0.00000	0.08181	1.38	180.00	10.00	−39.387

Note: Each complex conjugate pair is represented by the eigenvalue with a positive imaginary part. Half-lives and periods are in years, whereas frequencies are measured in degree per five years. The second and third pair of complex eigenvalues have periods of 17 and 16 years instead of the 21 and 13 years found in most national populations.

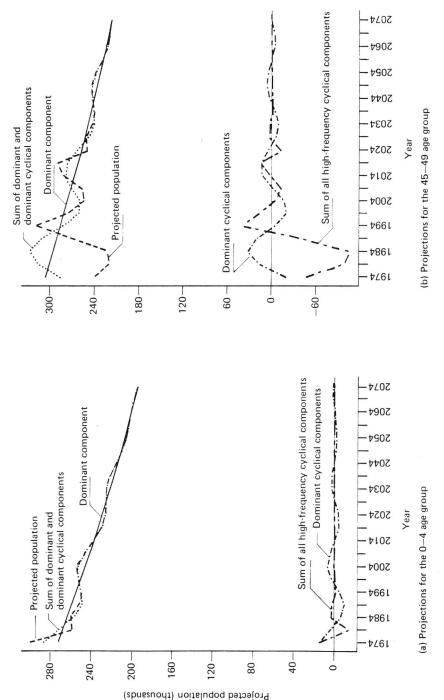

Figure 11.1 Decomposition of projected populations of the (a) 0—4 and (b) 45—49 age groups into the analytic components: uniregional model using 1974 Swedish female population data.

1990s, at which time a maximum population size of 4.23 million is reached.

Figure 11.2(b) shows that the long-run age profile (i.e., the dominant right eigenvector) starts at about 5.6% in the 0–4 age group, rises smoothly and gently toward a maximum of about 6.2% in the 50–54 age group, and then declines sharply to a minimum of about 2.7% in the 85+ age group. The shape is typical of industrialized countries, where net reproduction rates are below replacement level. The *dissimilarity index* between the 1974 and long-run age profiles is 7.9%, which means that 7.9% of the population has to be redistributed in order to make the two profiles identical. If we use a dissimilarity index of 2% to indicate the "completion" of the convergence toward the long-run distribution, then the convergence of the age profile of the uniregional model for Sweden is completed in less than 60 years. In 100 years, the age profiles of the projected and stable populations become almost identical [Figure 11.2(b)]; the projected population size becomes 3 481 800 (compared with $\hat{c}_1 \hat{\lambda}_1^t$ = 3 480 500), and the annual growth rate of the projected population is reduced to −0.3%, which is the same as that of the stable population.

11.5.2 *The Factorizable Multiregional Model of the Swedish Female Population*

The eigenvalues of the pure migration matrix $\hat{\hat{G}}$ are all positive, lying between $\hat{\lambda}_1 = 1$ and $\hat{\lambda}_8 = 0.8776$. The pattern of eigenvalues of the factorizable multiregional model of the Swedish female population is shown in Figure 11.3. It is indeed true that corresponding to each eigenvalue of the uniregional model there is a *cluster* of exactly $N = 8$ eigenvalues in the factorizable multiregional model; within each cluster all the eigenvalues have the same frequency and the eigenvalue with the largest magnitude equals an eigenvalue of the uniregional model. The difference in magnitude among the major complex eigenvalues is a result of the moderate level of interregional migration and has nothing to do with the interregional difference in the shapes of regional fertility schedules, because these schedules do not vary between regions.

The differential influences of the dominant and spatial components are indicated in Table 11.4. First, the initial regional loadings of the dominant component being much greater in magnitude than those of the spatial components suggests that the initial interregional population distribution is compatible with the migration process. The dissimilarity index between the initial and the long-run interregional population distributions is only 4.15%. Second, because the spatial components have large *positive* loadings on the Stockholm, East Middle, and South Middle regions on the one hand, and large *negative* loadings on the West and South regions on the other, the general trend of geographical redistribution tends to be *from* the Stockholm, East Middle, and South Middle regions *to* the West and South regions. Third, the spatial component with the shortest half-life (23.50 years) has the largest positive and negative loadings on the Stockholm and East Middle regions, respectively – a result of the high

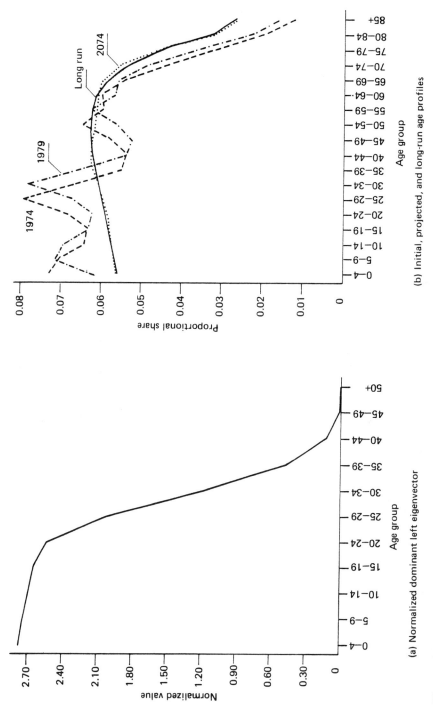

Figure 11.2 (a) The normalized dominant left eigenvector and (b) the initial, projected, and long-run age profiles of the uniregional model using 1974 Swedish female population data.

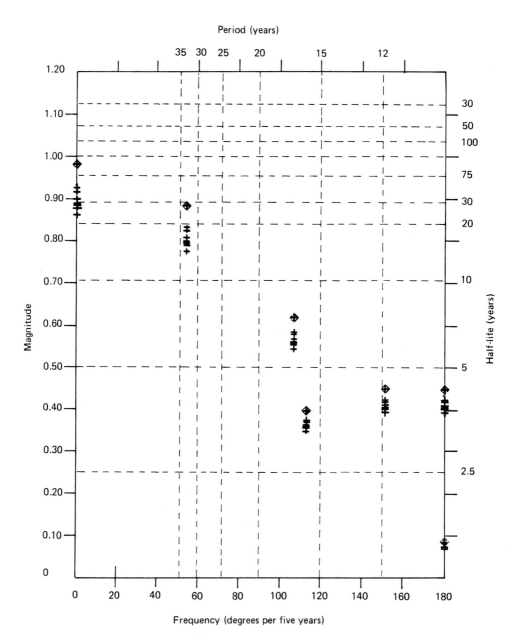

Figure 11.3 The pattern of nonzero eigenvalues of the growth matrix of the factorizable multiregional model using 1974 Swedish female population data. The eigenvalues of the corresponding uniregional model are shown as diamonds. For each
conjugate pair of complex eigenvalues, only the one with a positive imaginary part is
shown on the graph.

Table 11.4 The half-lives, initial levels, and initial regional loadings for the 0–4 age group of the dominant and spatial components of the factorizable multiregional model using 1974 Swedish female population data.[a]

Eigenvalue (λ_i)	Half-life (t_i)	Initial level (c_i)	Initial regional loadings ($c_i Q_{iaj}$)							
			Stock-holm	East Middle	South Middle	South	West	North Middle	Lower North	Upper North
λ_1	205.17	4879430	4433	43095	23719	43829	57739	29539	13663	15755
λ_2	45.89	246088	1599	4527	-862	-4376	-1620	1634	1005	1100
λ_3	40.30	60405	276	184	76	869	-1685	52	104	124
λ_4	32.90	25799	50	210	52	-29	-196	408	-149	-346
λ_5	29.84	267198	1210	1636	4256	-2376	-1235	-2993	-850	353
λ_6	28.71	20874	-88	30	-75	51	-6	188	-413	313
λ_7	27.03	198608	2798	1904	-2115	156	683	-2277	-903	-245
λ_8	23.50	34081	724	-873	67	-19	46	102	-59	13
Superimposed spatial component			3569	4619	1398	-5724	-4022	-2887	-1265	1312

[a]Half-life is measured in years, and c_i and $c_i Q_{iaj}$ in persons. Since a spatial component, relative to the dominant component, becomes less important as time increases, a positive (negative) element Q_{iaj} for $t > 1$ indicates a trend away from (toward) region j.

rates of migration between these two regions. The annual relative damping rate
is 2.57% for this component and 1.16% for the most durable spatial component.

The eight major cyclical components have a common period of 32.70 years
and have annual relative damping rates within the range of 2.09–4.61%. Since
this range overlaps with that of the damping rates of the spatial components,
it might happen that very large loadings are associated with λ_8 and σ_1 and
hence spatial convergence proceeds more rapidly than the convergence in
regional age profiles. However, we see in Tables 11.4 and 11.5 that relatively
high loadings are associated with λ_2, λ_5, λ_7, σ_1, σ_7, and σ_8. Therefore, the
Swedish interregional population system, just as the Canadian system (Liaw
1980a, b), shows the usual tendency that convergence in the regional age profiles proceeds at a higher rate than spatial convergence.

The major cyclical components are characterized in Table 11.5. Since the
initial regional phase angles of the dominant cyclical component for the 0–4
age group all equal 15.59 degrees, the *synchronical* population waves start
near their maxima at $t = 0$. The regional phase angles of each of the remaining
major cyclical components are arranged in two exactly opposite directions
(i.e., they differ by 180°). Thus each of the components represents *opposite*
population waves that involve a zero-sum type of trade-off among the regions.
Since the regional upper bounds of fluctuations are in general greater for the
dominant cyclical components than for the remaining major cyclical components, we see in Figure 11.4 that the regional time paths of the superimposed major cyclical component for the 0–4 age group appear more synchronical than opposite. The effect of the subdominant major cyclical components is shown to be the advancement of the first trough in the South Middle, North Middle, Lower North, and Upper North regions by five years and
the delay of the first trough in Stockholm by the same length of time. Since
the dominant cyclical component is much more durable than the remaining
ones, the tendency of increasing synchronization is clearly seen in Figure
11.4.

As a consequence of Q_1 being equal to $\hat{Q}_1 \otimes \hat{\hat{Q}}_1$, the factorizable multiregional model has the unattractive property of all regional long-run age profiles being identical to the smooth long-run profile of the corresponding uniregional model. To obtain substantively more meaningful stable regional age profiles, we now turn to the quasi-factorizable multiregional model.

11.5.3 *The Quasi-Factorizable Multiregional Model of the Swedish Female Population*

The nonzero eigenvalues of the quasi-factorizable multiregional model,
shown in Figure 11.5, appear in seven clusters. Within each cluster, there is
an eigenvalue identical to that of the corresponding uniregional model. This is,
of course, the implication of Theorem 1. Except for the cluster with the shortest half-lives, these common eigenvalues are the most important (i.e., most durable) within the individual clusters. In Figure 11.5 the eigenvalues in the

Table 11.5 Half-lives, periods, and regional information about the 0–4 age group of the major cyclical components of the factorizable multiregional model using 1974 Swedish female population data.

Half-life (t_i)	Period (τ_i)	Stockholm	East Middle	South Middle	South	West	North Middle	Lower North	Upper North
Initial regional upper bounds $(2\delta_i \gamma_{iaj})$									
28.18	32.70	2349	2253	1240	2291	3018	1544	714	824
19.08	32.70	113	108	61	308	115	115	71	77
18.04	32.70	141	94	39	442	857	26	53	63
16.39	32.70	72	299	73	41	279	581	213	493
15.59	32.70	162	219	569	318	165	401	114	47
15.28	32.70	103	36	87	60	7	219	483	366
14.79	32.70	2442	1662	1845	136	596	1987	788	214
13.67	32.70	2069	2495	191	54	132	290	169	37
Initial regional phase angles $(\omega_i + \varphi_{iaj})$									
28.18	32.70	15.59	15.59	15.59	15.59	15.59	15.59	15.59	15.59
19.08	32.70	-161.59	-161.59	18.41	18.41	18.41	-161.59	-161.59	-161.59
18.04	32.70	-107.67	-107.67	-107.67	-107.67	72.33	-107.67	-107.67	-107.67
16.39	32.70	-62.58	-62.58	-62.58	117.42	117.42	-62.58	117.42	117.42
15.59	32.70	-1.29	-1.29	-1.29	178.71	178.71	178.71	178.71	-1.29
15.28	32.70	-60.29	119.71	-60.29	119.71	-60.29	119.71	-60.29	119.71
14.79	32.70	-64.16	-64.16	115.84	-64.16	-64.16	115.84	115.84	115.84
13.67	32.70	-84.38	95.62	-84.38	95.62	-84.83	-84.83	95.62	-84.38
Initial regional loadings $[2\delta_i \gamma_{iaj} \cos(\omega_i + \varphi_{iaj})]$									
28.18	32.70	2262	2170	1194	2207	2907	1487	388	793
19.08	32.70	-107	-102	58	292	109	-109	-67	-73
18.04	32.70	-43	-28	-12	-134	260	-8	-16	-19
16.39	32.70	33	138	34	-19	-128	268	-98	-227
15.59	32.70	162	219	569	-318	-165	-401	-114	47
15.28	32.70	51	-18	43	-30	4	-109	239	-181
14.79	32.70	1064	724	-804	59	260	-866	-344	-93
13.67	32.70	203	-244	19	-5	13	28	-17	4
Sum	—	3626	2858	1101	2052	3258	291	272	250

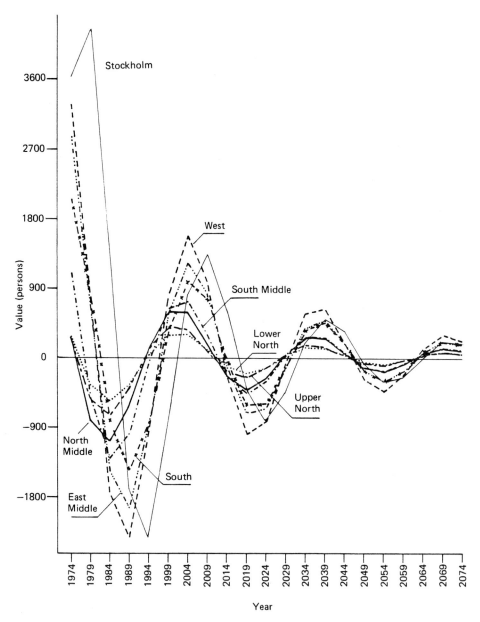

Figure 11.4 The regional time paths of the superimposed major cyclical component for the 0–4 age group of the factorizable multiregional model using 1974 Swedish female population data.

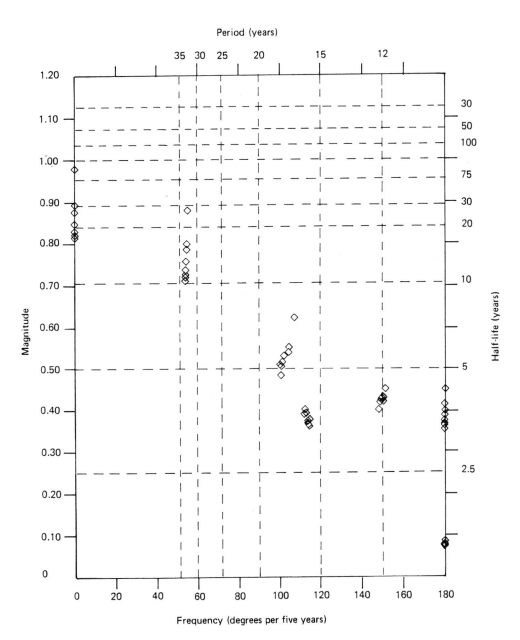

Figure 11.5 The pattern of nonzero eigenvalues of the growth matrix of the quasi-factorizable multiregional model using 1974 Swedish female population data.

two most important clusters turn out to be more dispersed than in Figure 11.3, which implies that for the Swedish population the spatial zero-sum games tend to diminish faster in the quasi-factorizable model than in the factorizable model. That is, age selectivity in the migration process somehow accelerates the spatial convergence and the synchronization of the population waves.

The patterns of the spatial zero-sum games, shown in Table 11.6, indicate that major gainers in the migration transactions are the South and West regions, whereas the major losers are the East Middle, Stockholm, and South Middle regions. Table 11.6 reflects the compatibility of the initial spatial distribution with the migration process by the smallness of the initial levels (c_i) of the spatial components relative to the stable equivalent population size (c_1). In other words, the net effect of migration on spatial distribution will be rather insignificant. As a consequence of Theorem 3, the stable equivalent population size of the quasi-factorizable multiregional model is identical to that of the corresponding uniregional and factorizable multiregional models.

Table 11.7 shows the dominance of nearly synchronical waves over waves that are nearly opposite. As a consequence of Theorem 2, the cyclical components with eigenvalues unequal to those of the corresponding uniregional model are seen to have the zero-sum nature, except for some rounding errors. Although these cyclical components do not exactly represent opposite population waves, their initial regional phase angles $(\omega_i + \varphi_{iaj})$ are shown in Table 11.7 to bunch up in two nearly opposite directions within a circle. Therefore, we describe the resulting population waves as *nearly opposite*.

The age selectivity in the migration process results in not only the nearly opposite population waves but also the irregular long-run regional age profiles shown in Figure 11.6. The long-run deficit of young adults in the three northern regions contrasts sharply with the long-run surplus of these people in the capital region of Stockholm. Figure 11.6 also shows that the convergence toward the *interregionally* different profiles of the stable age-by-region population is practically completed in 100 years. According to Theorem 4, the irregular stable regional age profiles will sum to the smooth stable national age profile shown in Figure 11.2.

Since fertility and mortality schedules do vary among regions, it is useful to have some idea of the differences in dynamic properties between the quasi-factorizable and the actual non-factorizable multiregional models. According to the 1974 Swedish data, the differences are mostly small or unnoticeable. Both models yield the same values for the population momentum (18%), the long-run growth rate (−0.3%), and the period (33 years) and half-life (28 years) of the dominant cyclical component. The long-run national age profiles generated by the two models are nearly identical; both have 17.0% in the young-dependent age group (0–14), 61.2% in the working age group (15–64), and 21.8% in the old-dependent age group (65+). Both models yield three types of long-run regional age profiles: (a) a profile with a significant surplus of young adults found in the Stockholm region, (b) three rather smooth profiles found in the

Table 11.6 The half-lives, initial levels, and initial regional loadings for the 0–4 age group of the dominant and spatial components of the quasi-factorizable multiregional model using 1974 Swedish female population data.

Half-life (t_i)	Initial level (c_i)	Initial regional loadings ($c_i Q_{iaj}$)							
		Stock-holm	East Middle	South Middle	South	West	North Middle	Lower North	Upper North
205.17	4879430	49631	44333	22475	41198	58772	26929	12279	16649
31.15	226125	1530	1196	−590	−3036	−1420	964	561	796
27.27	110123	464	259	119	1244	−2349	39	86	139
20.95	83897	178	559	162	−121	−377	663	−189	−875
18.69	242200	647	703	2693	−1315	−587	−2054	−298	211
17.55	12903	−114	18	47	−4	−32	95	−68	57
16.87	17836	129	74	−86	11	34	−74	−128	39
15.53	39992	−379	572	−83	9	−13	−140	57	−22
Superimposed spatial component		2455	3381	2261	−3211	−4744	−506	20	344

Note: The first row relates to the dominant component, whereas the remaining rows identify the spatial components.

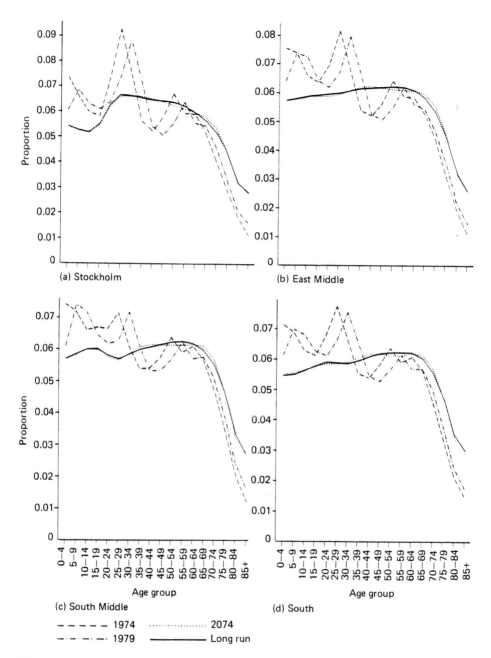

Figure 11.6(a)–(d) The initial, projected, and long-run regional age profiles of the quasi-factorizable multiregional model using 1974 Swedish female population data.

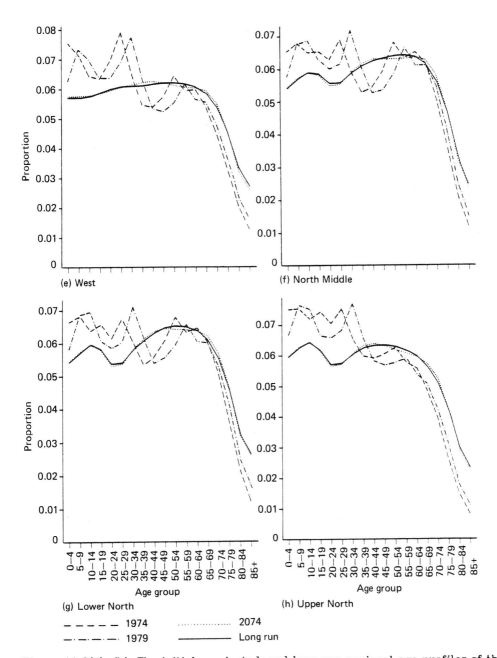

Figure 11.6(e)–(h) The initial, projected, and long-run regional age profiles of the quasi-factorizable multiregional model using 1974 Swedish female population data.

Table 11.7 Half-lives, periods, and regional information about the 0–4 age group of the major cyclical components of the quasi-factorizable multiregional model using 1974 Swedish female population data.

Half-life (t_i)	Period (τ_i)	Stockholm	East Middle	South Middle	South	West	North Middle	Lower North	Upper North
Initial regional upper bounds $(2\delta_i \gamma_{iaj})$									
28.18	32.70	2673	2306	1164	2103	3076	1388	643	887
15.58	32.90	694	289	145	710	391	229	138	198
14.50	32.91	163	83	51	485	854	12	26	45
12.47	33.23	97	213	65	50	145	247	74	345
11.56	33.23	151	142	561	276	119	434	62	44
11.12	33.32	785	126	332	64	224	604	346	312
10.84	33.38	458	199	277	40	112	213	475	160
10.23	33.22	441	718	117	11	14	185	55	26
Initial regional phase angles $(\omega_i + \varphi_{iaj})$									
28.18	32.70	13.46	16.77	14.77	16.96	16.90	12.68	10.54	11.44
15.58	32.90	-131.32	-132.35	41.03	47.37	38.43	-138.92	-143.16	-143.28
14.50	32.91	-80.29	-75.12	-94.48	-88.38	95.23	-18.80	-80.64	-84.92
12.47	33.23	-28.36	-2.62	3.12	173.08	168.80	-9.63	172.07	171.81
11.56	33.23	-0.31	9.87	19.62	-164.48	-160.67	-165.31	-172.79	25.46
11.12	33.32	-43.01	144.07	127.02	-63.24	-51.62	129.79	-66.55	124.71
10.84	33.38	-74.59	-54.89	105.24	-78.31	-76.25	104.44	118.88	-58.38
10.23	33.22	-136.91	43.06	-134.16	48.41	-164.20	-130.97	69.92	-119.91
Initial regional loadings $[2\delta_i \gamma_{iaj} \cos(\omega_i + \varphi_{iaj})]$									
28.18	32.70	2564	2208	1125	2012	2943	1354	632	870
15.58	32.90	-260	-194	110	481	306	-173	-110	-159
14.50	32.91	28	21	-4	14	-78	11	4	4
12.47	33.23	85	213	65	-50	-142	243	-73	-341
11.56	33.23	151	140	528	-265	-112	-419	-61	40
11.12	33.32	574	-101	-200	15	139	-387	138	-177
10.84	33.38	122	115	-73	8	27	-53	-229	84
10.23	33.22	-322	525	-82	7	-14	-121	19	-13
Total	–	2941	2925	1469	2222	3069	455	318	307

Note: The top row of each section of the table relates to the dominant cyclical component, whereas the remaining rows identify the other major cyclical components.

East Middle, South, and West regions, and (c) four profiles with a clear shortage of young adults in the South Middle, North Middle, Lower North, and Upper
North regions. Finally, both models indicate that the initial spatial distribution will change very little in the future, with the South and West regions
being the major gainers and the East Middle, Stockholm, and South Middle
regions being the major losers.

11.6 Comparison of the Dynamic Properties of Four Empirical Population Systems

The four population systems to be compared briefly here are: (a) the
1966–1971, eight-region female population system of Canada; (b) the 1970,
eight-region female population system of Great Britain; (c) the 1974, eight-
region population system of the Soviet Union; and (d) the 1974, eight-region
female population system of Sweden.[11] To facilitate comparison, a few indices
are presented in Table 11.8. A more detailed analysis is given by Liaw (1980a).

Reflecting mainly the differences in fertility level, the annual intrinsic
growth rates range from 0.92% for Canadian females to −0.33% for Swedish
females. The British and Soviet systems have the intermediate values of 0.47
and 0.59%, respectively. Because of the influences of population waves and
population momenta, the projected population growth rates in the short run
may be quite different from the intrinsic growth rates. For Canada and the
Soviet Union, where interregional variation in fertility level is relatively large,
it is important to emphasize that the population momentum of a multiregional
population system is affected by the differences between the initial and the
long-run spatial distributions as well as by the differences between the initial
and the long-run age profiles. If the positive (negative) population momentum
is mainly due to the differences in age profile, then it is usually safe to infer
that the average short-run growth rate of the total population say, for a
period of 30 years in which the effect of population waves is averaged out, will
be higher (lower) than the intrinsic growth rate. However, if the positive
(negative) momentum is mainly a result of the differences in interregional
population distribution, then it may be misleading to infer that the average
short-run growth rate will be higher (lower) than the intrinsic growth rate.

---

[11]The regions in the Canadian system are Atlantic (including the four eastern provinces),
Quebec, Ontario, Manitoba, Saskatchewan, Alberta, British Columbia, and the North (including the Yukon and Northwest Territories). The regions in the remaining three systems are
identical to those in Chapter 6 of this book, except for the British system, which has the
North, Yorkshire and Humberside, and North West regions combined into one region. The
Canadian system has 14 age groups (0–4, 5–9,..., 65+), whereas the other systems have 18
age groups (0–4, 5–9,..., 85+). This chapter's Canadian model differs from that of Termote
(1980) in terms of model observation plan (period–cohort versus period) and number of regions. For all three systems, immigration and emigration rates are set to zero.

Table 11.8 Indices characterizing the dynamic properties of multiregional models of four population systems.

Characteristics	Canada (1966–1971)	Great Britain (1970)	Soviet Union 1974)	Sweden (1974)
Intrinsic growth rate (% per year)	0.92	0.47	0.59	−0.33
Average growth rate in the first 30 years (% per year)	1.21	0.37	0.81	0.05
Population momentum (%)	−4.9	−1.5	7.5	17.7
Period of the most durable major cyclical component (years)	26.7	27.3	26.0	33.0
Relative rate of decline (% per year)[a]:				
Most durable major cyclical component	3.6	4.3	3.3	2.1
Least durable major cyclical component	8.1	7.9	9.9	6.2
Most durable spatial component	0.7	1.6	1.3	1.9
Least durable spatial component	3.1	3.8	7.1	4.1
Dissimilarity index with respect to long-run spatial distribution (%):				
At initial time	24.4	5.1	20.2	4.1
100 years later	11.9	0.7	0.7	0.6
Dissimilarity index with respect to long-run age profile (%):				
At initial time	9.4	4.2	8.3	7.9
100 years later	1.0	0.1	0.4	0.5

[a]The relative rate is computed relative to the growth rate of the dominant component.

The population momentum of the multiregional Canadian population system is −4.9%, which is totally different from that of the corresponding uniregional model (25.0%). The large positive momentum of the uniregional model reflects the initial age profile being much younger than the long-run age profile. In contrast, the negative momentum of the multiregional model results from the tendency of a large reduction in the population share of Quebec (from the initial 29.06% to the long-run 9.18%), which has the lowest fertility level of all the regions. Since the spatial redistribution process in Canada, though persistent, is slow, the negative momentum does not imply that the average short-run growth rate will be lower than the intrinsic growth rate. Actually, the projected average growth rate in the first 30 years is 1.21% per year, which is higher than the intrinsic growth rate of 0.92%. The effect of the negative momentum does not appear until the "middle run" (i.e., more than 50 years into the future).

The population momentum of the 1970 British system is also negative (−1.5%). This negative momentum is the result of the fertility level in 1970 being higher than the average level of the previous five decades (Rees 1979b).

In other words, the long-run age profiles are somewhat younger than the corresponding initial age profiles in most regions. This difference in age profiles results in the negative momentum, which implies that the average short-run growth rate will be lower than the intrinsic growth rate. The average annual rate of the first 30 years is projected to be 0.37%, compared with the intrinsic growth rate of 0.47%.

Positive population momenta are found in the Soviet Union (7.5%) and Sweden (17.7%). These are the result of the initial age profiles being younger than the long-run age profiles and imply that the average short-run growth rates will be higher than the corresponding intrinsic growth rates. The projected average annual growth rates in the first 30 years are 0.81% for the Soviet Union and 0.05% for Sweden, compared with the intrinsic growth rates of 0.59 and −0.33%, respectively.

The dominant major cyclical component indicates that the projected population waves in Canada, Great Britain, and the Soviet Union are similar in periodicity (about 26 or 27 years) and in relative rate of decline (about 3 or 4% per year). In contrast, the waves of the Swedish system have a higher periodicity (33 years) and a lower relative rate of decline (2%). The contrast suggests that Sweden is more "advanced" than the other three countries in the pattern of reproduction — an older mean age and a smaller dispersion. Within each system, all regional population waves are nearly synchronical, reflecting that major fertility changes in each system in recent decades have been truly nationwide.

In the Canadian and British systems, all spatial components have smaller rates of decline than do all cyclical components, suggesting the tendency of a two-stage convergence process: a fast convergence in age profiles followed by a slow convergence in regional shares. In the Soviet and Swedish systems, a few spatial components tend to decline faster than the dominant cyclical component. Of particular interest is the least durable spatial component of the Soviet system; it declines at the relative rate of 7.1% per year and depicts clearly the rapidity of urbanization that is expected to continue in the Soviet Union (Liaw 1981).

The dissimilarity index with respect to the long-run distribution in Table 11.8 shows that in Great Britain and in Sweden the initial population distribution is quite consistent with the observed demographic processes, whereas in Canada and in the Soviet Union major changes in population distribution are expected. In Canada, the major loser is Quebec and the major gainers are the two western provinces of British Columbia and Alberta (Liaw 1980a). In the Soviet Union, the rural region will experience a large relative loss and all urban regions will have significant gains. However, the relative shares *among* the seven urban regions in the Soviet system in 1974 are quite similar to those in the long-run distribution; the dissimilarity between the initial and the long-run distributions is only 4.7%. Thus, if we ignore urbanization, the three

European nations appear to be more stable than Canada in terms of spatial population distribution.

The dissimilarity indices with respect to the long-run age profiles in Table 11.8 suggest that in all four systems the projected regional age profiles converge rapidly to their long-run patterns. Depending on the age selectivity of migration, the long-run regional age profile may be smooth or "irregular". Figure 11.7 shows, for example, that a large deficit of young adults in the rural parts of the Soviet Union is likely to continue, because the initial and the long-run age profiles are similar in shape.

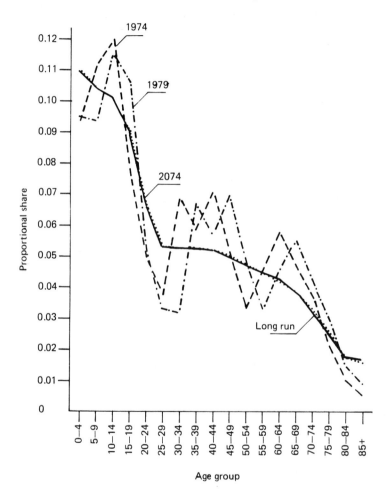

Figure 11.7 The initial, projected, and long-run age profiles of the rural population of the Soviet Union.

11.7 Conclusion

In fitting the multiregional model to several real-world age-by-region population systems, we were amazed to find some common features in the analytic solutions of the empirically constructed models. Among these features are:

(a)   the clustering of eigenvalues around those of the corresponding uniregional models;
(b)   the nearly zero-sum nature of what Liaw (1978b, 1980a) called the spatial components that reveal the characteristics of geographical redistribution;
(c)   the existence of a nearly synchronical cyclical component and many nearly opposite cyclical components;
(d)   the marked irregularities in some stable regional age profiles;
(e)   the behavioral similarity at the national level between a multiregional model and the corresponding uniregional model.

To the extent that the factorizable and quasi-factorizable multiregional models possess some basic properties of an actual multiregional model, the analysis and synthesis carried out in this chapter suggest that the above-mentioned features should indeed be expected. It is worth noting that for most industrialized countries the actual multiregional model must be nearly quasi-factorizable, because the fertility and mortality schedules differ only slightly among regions.

To regional scientists who do not see the relevance of classical renewal theory in explaining such regional phenomena as the contrast in age profiles between economically prosperous and depressed regions, our extension of the theory may prove to be of some value. For example, according to the extended theory, an irregular regional age profile may persist long into the future if the irregularity is the result of the age selectivity in the migration process.

Through the analytic solution we have learned, among other things, that the redistribution potential is weak in Great Britain and Sweden, but strong in Canada and the Soviet Union; that the redistribution in the Soviet Union, which involves not much more than urbanization, will proceed rapidly; and that the redistribution in Canada, which implies a significant relative decline in population of the French-speaking province of Quebec and a marked increase in the two resource-rich provinces of British Columbia and Alberta, will proceed slowly and persistently.

CHAPTER TWELVE

Conclusion

Andrei Rogers

Regional populations increase because of births and inmigration and decrease through deaths and outmigration. If more people leave an area than enter it, the result is negative net migration; the opposite situation gives rise to positive net migration. The point of the multiregional perspective is that there is no such person as a "net migrant". An outmigrant from one region becomes an inmigrant to another, creating a link between two regional populations.

The idea is simple, and it is not new. Its immediate consequence for demographic analysis is the need to focus on multiple interacting populations, on flows rather than on net changes in stocks, and on rates that relate the incidence of such flows to the different populations "exposed to the risk" of experiencing them. Conventional demographic practice follows: from rates to probabilities and from probabilities to standard life table measures, such as life expectancies, or to well established procedures for projecting future populations, such as the cohort-survival model.

The perspective of multiregional demography united the efforts of some 40 scientists, representing over half-a-dozen disciplines and more than 20 countries, and it focused their attention on contemporary migration and settlement patterns in the 17 nations of the IIASA study. The project lasted seven years and produced a large number of publications. What was accomplished and what was learned?

Most of what was accomplished and learned in the course of the Migration and Settlement Study was methodological and descriptive in character. Because the principal aim was to disseminate and expand a methodological tool this is not surprising. The dissemination led to the accumulation of a large data bank, assembled by those adopting the new tool, and this in turn led to a comparative analysis of the data. New problems and ideas arising out of the implementation of the tool in different national settings led to the development of new theoretical findings and methods, most of which contribute to three principal themes: spatial population dynamics, migration measurement and analysis, and multistate demography.

12.1 Spatial Population Dynamics

The evolution of a multiregional population is a consequence of regional patterns of fertility and mortality and of the interregional structure of migration flows. The Migration and Settlement Study contributed to an increased understanding of how such components of change interact to bring about the spatial population distributions that are currently observed in industrialized and industrializing nations.

The populations of most IIASA nations are expected to cease growing within the next two decades and a few are already experiencing negative or zero growth. Consequently, an early concern of the Migration and Settlement Study was a formal analysis of the spatial demographic consequences of national population stabilization. By extending the mathematical apparatus developed by demographers for projecting the evolution of national populations to zero growth, it was demonstrated that the demographic redistributional effects of stabilization depend in a very direct way on the spatial pattern of total births that is occasioned by fertility reduction (Rogers and Willekens 1976, 1978). Introducing the notion of *spatial* reproductive values, the study showed that the "spatial momentum" of zero population growth, the ratio by which the ultimate stationary regional population exceeds the current one, is a function not only of the geography of fertility decline but also of the structure of interregional migration flows.

A rising concern with the social consequences of population processes and a consequent growing interest in population policy led the Migration and Settlement Study to explore the applicability of formal models of demoeconomic policy (Willekens and Rogers 1977, Propoi and Willekens 1978, Willekens 1979). In such models policy objectives and policy instruments are defined explicitly and for different times. Formally, the dynamic policy problem becomes one of choosing time paths for certain *control* variables, from a given set of feasible time paths, so as to optimize a particular objective or to achieve particular targets. When presented in this form the dynamic policy problem becomes a dynamic optimization problem, and a convenient analytical framework for the study of quantitative dynamic demoeconomic policy is then offered by the theory of optimal control. The principal contribution of the research carried out on this topic by the Migration and Settlement Study was the connection of several fundamental themes in two related but largely independent bodies of literature: the mathematical literature in systems engineering that deals with the control of complex systems describable by sets of differential or difference equations and the more substantive literature in the formal theory of economic growth and policy. The logical structures of the two perspectives are similar, and it was shown that their formalisms can be fruitfully transferred to the field of population policy.

Implicit in every multiregional regime of fertility, mortality, and migration is a stable spatial distribution and an intrinsic annual rate of growth. Changes in any single component, such as a particular path of fertility reduction, lead to changed stable relationships. But how do these relationships evolve over time, and how do the individual components affect this evolution? This question also was illuminated by the work of the Migration and Settlement Study (Willekens 1977a, Liaw 1980a, 1981, and Chapter 11 of this book).

Starting with the analytic solution of a multiregional population projection that is generated by a constant multiregional regime of growth, it was shown that such a projection tends toward a fixed asymptotic distribution in two stages: first, a quick disappearance of cyclical behavior and a relatively rapid convergence to stable age compositions in each region; and second, a gradual convergence toward a stable interregional allocation of the national population. Population "waves" are transmitted through regional age groups by the cyclical components of the system's analytic solution, whereas spatial redistribution is controlled by its spatial components.

That convergence to stable regional age compositions generally precedes that of stable regional shares is also suggested by the Migration and Settlement Study's examination of methods of "shrinking" large-scale population projection models by means of aggregation or decomposition (Rogers 1976b). At the core of the shrinking strategies proposed is Simon and Ando's (1961) seminal idea that it might be useful to model different parts of a large system at different levels of detail, treating its evolution as a composite growth process that evolves in distinct temporal phases. They neatly convey the essence of their argument with an illustration that describes the convergence of temperature changes in an office building with many rooms, each of which is partitioned into several offices. Disturbances over time will produce a temperature equilibrium *within* each room rather rapidly, whereas a temperature equilibrium *among* rooms will be reached only slowly.

An important contribution of the Migration and Settlement Study to the understanding of spatial population dynamics is its development of place-of-birth-specific multiregional life tables and population projections (Rogers and Philipov 1980, Ledent 1981, Philipov and Rogers 1981). Although the numerical illustrations for these formulations were made only with data on a single country, the US, the results obtained suggest a general conclusion. The introduction of population heterogeneity by means of a disaggregation of transition probabilities by region of birth significantly alters the values assumed by traditional demographic measures such as region-specific life expectancies and population shares. Because the migration rates of return migrants, for example, are several times higher than the average, according them higher transition probabilities in life table and projection calculations may produce a dramatic impact on the results.

Virtually all of the population projections generated by the Migration and Settlement Study assumed a constant multiregional regime of growth. But the model and the computer programs used in the study can be readily applied to create "scenarios" of future population trajectories that reflect specified changes in growth regimes. IIASA's analysis of the urbanization transition in prospect for today's industrializing Third World nations provides an illustration (Rogers 1978, Rogers and Williamson 1982).

In order to assess some of the important demographic consequences of rapid urbanization, a generalization and expansion of Coale's (1969) now classic analysis of the ways in which alternative demographic trends might affect the economic development of less developed countries was carried out. Coale's scenario of the evolution of a national population was disaggregated by the introduction of urban and rural sectors and rural-to-urban migration flows. Alternative urbanization trajectories were generated, and the various population characteristics studied by Coale were examined. The introduction of migration as a component of change and the concomitant disaggregation of a national population into urban and rural sectors brought into sharp focus urban—rural differentials in dependency burdens, labor force growth rates, and relative population sizes. The sectorally disaggregated demographic projections also indicated how the forces of demographic transition may contribute to reduced urban growth rates in the later stages of the urbanization transition, for example, through the braking forces of lower urban fertility rates.

12.2 Migration Patterns: Measurement and Analysis

Internal migration and national population redistribution are universal phenomena experienced by all nations. But are their patterns, antecedents, and consequences similar worldwide? The answer to this question is bound to remain inconclusive so long as the principal variable, migration, is inadequately measured. Complex behavioral explanations, derived from sophisticated socioeconomic and psychological theories, are unlikely to yield reliable conclusions in the absence of more refined measures of the variable at the core of the analysis.

Migration studies have in the past exhibited a curious ambivalence with regard to the measurement of geographical mobility, an ambivalence that is particularly striking because of the contrast that it poses with respect to the corresponding history of mortality and fertility studies. Thus the Migration and Settlement Study devoted considerable attention to the problem of estimating and measuring migration, generating a number of results that have

enhanced our understanding of appropriate quantitative evaluations of migration rates, probabilities, and age profiles. To do this, the study quite naturally
turned to the corresponding literature in mortality and fertility for guidance,
demonstrating that migration measurement can usefully apply concepts borrowed from that literature, modifying them where necessary to take into
account aspects that are peculiar to spatial mobility.

The analyses of the Migration and Settlement Study, like those of many
other demographic investigations with a comparative component, were sharply
constrained by the availability of data. The lack of adequate migration data in
a few IIASA nations in particular led the study to investigate a class of estimation methods for inferring patterns of interregional flows from aggregate data
(Willekens 1980, Willekens *et al.* 1981, Willekens 1982). Drawing on the related
literature in the analysis of various kinds of interaction matrices and contingency tables, a general estimation procedure was formulated, which unified
much of the previous work on the subject. The underlying strategy of this procedure (as in most such estimation efforts) is a search for those values of missing elements that preserve, in some sense, the structure of the entire data
set.

A related topic in the estimation of migration flows from inadequate or
inaccurate data is the use of hypothetical "model" age profiles to develop
improved approximations of age-specific migration rates. Although model
schedules have been used to summarize and codify observed regularities in
mortality and fertility regimes, they have not been applied in studies of
interregional migration. Thus the Migration and Settlement Study first formulated a mathematical expression that captured the fundamental regularities
exhibited by the age profiles of migration contained in the data bank produced by its national case studies, and then developed a system of hypothetical model schedules for use in multiregional population analyses carried out in
countries that lack adequate migration data (Rogers *et al.* 1978, Rogers and
Castro 1981c, and Chapter 5 of this book).

Having established that migration schedules exhibit a common profile in
most countries, the Migration and Settlement Study then sought to identify
the factors contributing to this regularity. Again drawing on the related
literature in mortality and fertility, the study examined the contributions
made to aggregate age profiles by different causes of migration and by different family dependency relationships (Rogers and Castro 1981b, Castro and
Rogers 1983a, b).

The different cause-specific age patterns were interpreted within the
framework of a life cycle in which individuals pass through different life
stages, such as entries into the educational system, marriage, and the labor
force, and exits such as divorce, retirement, and post-retirement moves to join

relatives or to enter nursing homes. The different family dependency relationships were introduced in recognition that migration often is undertaken by families rather than by individuals and that therefore the age composition of migrants tells us something about family patterns.

The Migration and Settlement Study's concern with migration data, rates, and schedules was complemented by a parallel concern regarding the appropriate computational procedures for translating migration rates into probabilities. Since demographers normally estimate probabilities from observed rates by computing a life table, considerable attention was accorded to alternative multiregional life table construction methods (Rogers and Ledent 1976, 1977, Ledent 1980c, 1982a, b, and Chapters 9 and 10 of this book). Inasmuch as all life table functions originate from a set of age-specific transition probabilities, the study's research particularly illuminated the ways in which counts of *moves* call for different estimation procedures than do counts of the corresponding *movers* at different points in time. Migration data obtained from population registers therefore require a different transition probability estimator than do migrant data collected in national censuses.

In the field of economics a division is generally made between the areas of *mathematical economics* and *econometrics*. The former deals principally with abstract mathematical descriptions of economic dynamics and economic growth; the latter treats statistically estimated relationships between basic economic variables. Analogous distinctions are made to distinguish mathematical psychology from psychometrics, mathematical biology from biometrics, and mathematical sociology from sociometrics. In a similar vein, mathematical demography may be distinguished from demometrics, the development and elaboration of which formed an important component of the Migration and Settlement Study (Rogers 1978, Ledent 1978c, 1982b).

Much of the work in demometrics focused on the establishment of empirically based quantitative relationships between interregional migration flows and regional socioeconomic variables (Miron 1978, Rempel 1981, Liaw and Bartels 1982, Bartels and Liaw 1983). Of particular interest in this regard was the development of an improved method of calibrating the Alonso (1973, 1978a, b) model of movement (Ledent 1980d, 1981). The central feature of the Alonso model is the idea that place-to-place flows not only are determined by the socioeconomic "push" and "pull" attributes of a particular origin and destination, but also are affected by the corresponding attributes of all other potential origins and destinations. The problem of how to estimate simultaneously these "systemic" variables was resolved by viewing the Alonso model as a particular class of spatial interaction model (Wilson 1971), for which various calibration techniques have been proposed. An illustrative application to Canadian data related interprovincial migration patterns to explanatory variables such as population size, unemployment rates, and weekly wage rates (Ledent 1980d).

12.3 Multistate Demography

Demography is concerned with the description, analysis, and projection of human populations disaggregated by age, sex, location, and a number of states of existence (Thompson 1953). Demography also has been characterized as the quantitative study of fundamental demographic processes, such as mortality, fertility, migration, and marriage (Bogue 1968). These processes may be viewed as transitions that persons experience during the course of their life cycle. Individuals are born, age, enroll in school, enter the labor force, marry, reproduce, migrate from one region to another, retire, and ultimately die. These transitions contribute to changes in various population stocks through simple accounting identities. For example, the number of married people at the end of each year is equal to the number at the beginning of the year plus new marriages and arrivals of married migrants minus divorces, deaths, widowings, and the departure of part of the married population.

The Migration and Settlement Study's work in formal multiregional mathematical demography has contributed to a generalization of classical demographic techniques that unifies many of the existing purely demographic methods for dealing with transitions between multiple states of existence. For example, it is now clear that multiple-decrement mortality tables, tables of working life, nuptiality tables, tables of educational life, and multiregional life tables are all members of a general class of increment–decrement life tables called *multistate life tables*. It is also now recognized that projections of populations classified by multiple states of existence can be carried out using a common methodology of *multistate projection*, in which the core model of population dynamics is a multidimensional generalization of either the continuous-age–time model of Lotka or the discrete-age–time Leslie model (Keyfitz 1979, Rogers 1980, Land and Rogers 1982).

The arithmetic for tracking people as they move into and out of the labor force or from the single to the married state is the same as that for handling their moves from one region of residence to another. All three cases present sets of transitions, and the formal demographic problem is the determination of what happens when these transitions occur over successive periods of time and age.

Consider, for example, the conventional table of working life and its estimates of expected remaining working lifetime for individuals at each of several ages. Because of their focus on changes in stocks rather than on flows, such tables generally reflect three restrictive assumptions: first, entry into the labor force occurs only before the peak age of active life; second, retirement occurs only after the peak age, and re-entry into the labor force is not possible; and finally, active and inactive individuals in the labor force ages are exposed to identical mortality regimes. All three assumptions may be dropped in calculating a multistate life table, and the table's survivorship proportions can be entered into a multistate projection model in order to obtain estimates of future labor force totals (Willekens 1980).

Scholars associated with the Migration and Settlement Study also applied multistate life table techniques to examine changes in marital status patterns (Willekens *et al.* 1982, Rogers and Williams 1985). By permitting re-entry into previously vacated marital states (e.g., remarriage), such multistate life tables are able to incorporate the influences of current marital statuses on future ones. By incorporating a regional dimension, they also permit an association between migration and changes in marital status. And together with the standard multistate projection model, they provide the demographer with a convenient apparatus for generating multiregional—multistatus population projections.

Conventional formulas for carrying out actuarial calculations connected with disability insurance, withdrawals from a life insurance plan, pensions, and annuities may be found in standard texts such as Jordan (1975). *Ad hoc* approximations, some of them awkward, are introduced for each. The use of multistate life table techniques can simplify many such multiple-contingency calculations (Keyfitz and Rogers 1982). For example, suppose that a person is now aged x and in the jth state, and that an annuity is payable only while he or she is alive and in the ith state. If money carries no interest, the answer to this annuity problem is simply the expected future lifetime in state i for a person initially in state j. If money carries interest the calculation needs to be modified by introducing a simple discounting factor.

12.4 Closing Remarks: Dissemination, Application, and New Directions

An indicator of the usefulness of a new idea is the degree to which it becomes disseminated and applied. Assessed in such terms, the models and computer programs of the Migration and Settlement Study can be said to have attained some measure of success. Expositional articles dealing with applications of multiregional/multistate demography and using IIASA's computer programs continue to appear in different languages in various international scholarly journals (Kedelski 1981, Paradysz 1981, Philipov 1981b, Espenshade and Braun 1982, Kawashima *et al.* 1982, Partida-Bush 1982, Kuroda and Nanjo 1983, Nair 1983). IIASA's methodological work constituted a major focus of a state-of-the-art conference on multistate demography supported by the US National Science Foundation (Land and Rogers 1982). Government agencies, such as the Quebec Bureau of Statistics (1981) and the US Bureau of Labor Statistics (1982) have adopted this tool, and the new *International Encyclopedia of Population* refers to it as a fundamental new departure in life table application (Ross 1982).

In a relatively short time, the fundamental ideas of multiregional/multistate demography have become widespread and are now receiving attention from scholars in a number of countries. Thus it is likely that the active period of methodological development of the past decade will continue its evolution. Two directions explored by the Migration and Settlement Study in its later stages seem to offer particular promise: event-history analysis and demoeconomics.

Event-history analysis is an analytical approach, developed largely within sociology, for analyzing changes in the distributions of populations across statuses such as married, divorced, employed, and unemployed. Couched in the perspective of causal analysis, the approach emphasizes the effects of population heterogeneity on short-run multistate transitions and combines behavioral hypotheses about the effects of heterogeneity on rates with stochastic process models (Hannan 1982, Tuma and Hannan, 1984). It focuses on the impacts of observed and unobserved heterogeneity, the effects of duration in a state on rates of exit from that state, the reasonableness of assumptions postulating homogeneity over time, and the influence of previous experiences on current and prospective patterns of behavior. Until very recently, however, event-history analysis had accorded little attention to age variation in rates and to long-run projections.

The development of multistate life tables and projection models has brought the demographic tradition much closer to the sociological one, and a marriage between the two perspectives seems possible and desirable. An important consequence of such a merger could be the development of a micro and a macro branch of formal demography. Microdemography would be devoted to the formal causal analysis of the behavior of decision-making units such as the individual or the family; macrodemography would examine the behavior of aggregates, for example, the relationships between various population groups defined with respect to age, sex, and location and various measures of economic performance and well-being.

A noted Harvard University professor used to tell his students that the difference between economics and sociology is simple:

> Economics is all about how people make choices. Sociology is all about why they don't have any choices to make. (Duesenberry 1960, p.233)

Demography, with its roots in sociology and the actuarial sciences, relies principally on *decomposition* as a research method, and accounts for macrodemographic events by considering the shifting weights between groups that exhibit different behaviors. The economist's research perspective, on the other hand, is usually directed at explaining the *choice behavior* of individuals, families, and establishments, and macro events are explained by accounting for changing behavior within groups, regions, and firms.

If economic factors play an important role in determining mortality, fertility, marriage, and migration patterns, then spatial population dynamics are clearly shaped by those same factors. It follows that migration and settlement patterns cannot be analyzed without giving explicit attention to the interaction between the various principal demographic and economic (*demoeconomic*) variables driving national and regional population growth and development.

A number of regional and multiregional macrodemoeconomic models developed at IIASA sought to establish quantitative statements regarding major demographic and economic variables that help to explain the past behavior of such variables or that forecast their future evolution (Ledent 1978c, 1982b, Ledent and Gordon 1980, Gordon and Ledent 1980, Kelley and Williamson 1980, Karlström 1982, Shishido 1982, Rogers and Williams 1985). Focusing on the major components of demoeconomic change and emphasizing the operations of local labor markets, such models provide a connection between migration, labor force dynamics, and spatial development. Together with the causal microdemoeconomic models of the event-history school, they presage the evolution of a more theoretical yet quantitative demographic analysis – one that recognizes the fundamental importance of a theory that is based on a successful combination of socioeconomic and psychological concepts, behavioral causal analysis, mathematics, and statistical inference. The role of multiregional/multistate mathematical demography in such a "new" demography is likely to be modest but vital.

Glossary of Parameters and Variables

An attempt was made to use a single set of parameters and variables throughout the book. In Chapters 5 and 11, however, it was more appropriate not to deviate too much from the notations that have become convention in the specialized literature. The glossary therefore consists of three parts. The parameters and variables that are used throughout the book are summarized first. Next, we list separately the parameters and variables that are special to Chapters 5 and 11.

Parameters

b	state of not yet born
d	state of death
h	width of age interval
i (or k)	region of residence; region of origin
j (or k)	region of destination
t	exact time
u	length of time interval
x (or y)	exact age
N	number of regions
T	time interval $(t, t + u)$
X (or Y)	age interval $(x, x + h)$
α	lowest age of childbearing
β	highest age of childbearing
ω	highest age
Ω	highest age group

Variables

1	column vector of ones (summation vector)
1'	row vector of ones (summation vector)
a^{id}	mean duration to death in region i
a_x^{ij}	mean duration to transfer from region i to region j: exact time spent in i by a person of exact age x at the beginning of the interval, before moving to j during the interval
b_t^i	crude birth rate in region i at time t
b_X^{ij}	average number of babies born in region i during the interval $(t, t + u)$ and alive in region j at the end of that interval, per x- to $(x + h)$-year-old resident (mother) at the beginning of that interval (element of matrix $\mathbf{b}_X$)

c_{xt}^j age composition of the population at time t in region j

d_t^j crude death rate in region j at time t

${}_y^k e_x^i$ number of years an x-year-old person, who was a resident of region k at age y, may expect to live in i in the remainder of his/her lifetime (element of matrix ${}_y\mathbf{e}_x$). If $y = 0$, the variable gives the life expectancy by place of birth. If $y = x$, the variable gives the life expectancy by place of residence at age x

i_t^j crude inmigration rate into region j at time t

l_x^i number of people of exact age x in region i. The number of people is expressed in terms of a unit birth cohort

${}_y^k l_x^i$ probability that a person who is in region k at age y will be in i at exact age x (element of matrix ${}_y\mathbf{l}_x$) (probability that a resident of k, aged y, survives in i at age x)

${}^k l_{xz}^{ij}$ probability that a person who was in region k at exact age y is alive and a resident of i at age x, and will still be alive at age z and residing at that time in j; or the number of persons of region k and of age y who will be in i at age x and in j at age z, the number being expressed in terms of a unit birth cohort

m_X^{ij} annual rate of migrating from region i to region j of persons aged x to $x + h$ (element of matrix $\mathbf{m}_X$)

o_t^j crude outmigration rate of region j at time t

p_x^{ij} probability that an x-year-old resident of region i will be in region j at age $x + h$ (element of matrix $\mathbf{p}_x$)

q_x^i probabiity that an x-year-old resident of region i dies before reaching the age of $x + h$

r growth rate of the stable population

r_t^j rate of growth of region j at time t

s_X^{ij} the proportion of x- to $(x + h)$-year-old residents of region i at time t who are alive and $x + h$ to $x + 2h$ years old in region j at time $t + u$ ($t + u$ is also indicated by $t + 1$, in which case the time is measured in unit intervals of u years each) (element of matrix $\mathbf{s}_X$)

$\bar{x}_\mu$ mean age of the schedule of intensities μ_x

ASFR   age-specific fertility rate

CBR   crude birth rate

G   multiregional growth matrix

GDR   gross death rate

GFR   gross fertility rate

GMR^{ij} gross migraproduction rate: the sum, over all ages, of the age-specific rates of migrating from i to j

GRR   gross reproduction rate: number of daughters a woman may expect to have during her lifetime in the absence of mortality

I   identity matrix

$K^{bi,sj}$ number of persons born in region i during the interval $(t, t + u)$ and alive in region j at the end of the interval ($= k_0^{ij}$)

$K^{ei,sj}$	number of people alive in region i at the beginning of the interval (time t) and surviving in region j at the end of the interval (time $t + u$) $(= K^{ij})$
$K^i_{x\,t}$	observed number of people of **exact** age x in region i at time t
$K^i_{X\,t}$	observed number of people aged x to $x + h$, in region i at time t
$K^{i\,j}_X$	number of x- to $(x + h)$-year-old residents of region i who are in region j, h years later (transitions or migrants – prospective observation)
K^{ij}_X	number of x- to $(x + h)$-year-old residents of region j who were in region i, h years earlier (transitions or migrants – retrospective observation)
K_s	vector of stable population by age and region of residence
K_{Xs}	vector of stable population, x- to $(x + h)$-years old, by region of residence
$_k^y L^i_X$	(i) number of years lived in region i between ages x and $x + h$ by a person who is a resident of k at earlier age y. (ii) Number of survivors in region i, aged x to $x + h$, of those residing in region k at earlier age y. The number is expressed for a unit cohort (element of matrix $\mathbf{L_x}$). If $y = 0$, L refers to birth cohorts
^{i}MNR^j	net migraproduction rate of i-born persons out of region j: the average number of migrations out of j that an i-born person may expect to make during his/her lifetime
NRR	net reproduction rate: number of daughters a woman may expect during her lifetime in the presence of mortality
O^{bi}_X	number of children born in region i during the interval $(t, t + u)$ to mothers of age x to $x + h$
$O^{i\,d}_X$	number of x- to $(x + h)$-year-old residents of region i who die during the interval $(t, t + u)$
O^{ij}_X	number of migrations from region i to region j by x- to $(x + h)$-year-old persons during the interval $(t, t + u)$
$O^{i\,o}_X$	number of x- to $(x + h)$-year-old outmigrants out of region i during the interval $(t, t + u)$
$O^{\rho i}_X$	number of x- to $(x + h)$-year-old inmigrants into region i during the interval $(t, t + u)$
Q	vector of stable equivalent number of births by region
R^k	relative radix: proportion of children that are born in region k in the stationary population
SHA^j_t	share of region j in the total population at time t
$_k^y T^i_x$	average number of years lived in region i beyond age x by a person who is a resident of k at age y (element of matrix $_y\mathbf{T_x}$)
TFR	total fertility rate
Y	total stable equivalent population
$\underline{Y}$	vector of stable equivalent population by age and region
$\bar{Y}$	regional distribution of the stable equivalent population

$i\,{}_{\vartheta}{}^{j}$	migration level with respect to region j of individuals born in i ($= {}_{0}^{t}e_{\cdot}^{j} / {}_{0}^{t}e_{\cdot}$)
λ	dominant eigenvalue of the multiregional growth matrix $\mathbf{G}$
μ_x^b	intensity of childbearing at age x
μ_x^{bi}	intensity of childbearing in region i at age x (other term: instantaneous rate of fertility)
μ_x^{id}	intensity of dying in region i at age x (other terms used in the demographic literature are: force of mortality; instantaneous death rate)
μ_x^{ij}	intensity of moving from region i to region j at age x (i.e., in the interval from x to $x + dx$)
ξ	right eigenvector associated with λ of $\mathbf{G}$

Parameters and Variables Related to Model Migration Schedules (Chapter 5)

Parameters

x	age
y_0	age at which an appreciable number of females first leave home to establish their own household
ω	highest age of the migration schedule

Variables

a_1	level of pre-labor force component
a_2	level of labor force component
a_3	level of post-labor force component
c	constant
$f_1(x)$	single-exponential density function describing $N(x)$
$f_2(x)$	double-exponential density function describing $N(x)$
$f_{1c}(x)$	proportion of the population of dependents that is of age x
$f_{2c}(x)$	proportion of the population of heads of households that is of age x
$g(y)$	probability density function
m_x	migration rate at age x
m_X	migration rate in age group $(x, x + h)$
O	crude outmigration rate ($= O / K$)
O_1	migration rate (propensity) of dependents
O_2	migration rate (propensity) of heads of households
$p_1(x)$	probability that a dependent of age x migrates in the interval $(x, x + h)$
$p_2(x)$	probability that a head of household of age x migrates in the interval $(x, x + h)$

x_h	location on age axis of high peak of model migration schedule
x_l	location on age axis of low point of model migration schedule
$\bar{x}_m$	mean age of model migration schedule
x_r	location on age axis of retirement peak
A	parental shift
B	jump
$C(x)$	proportion of total population aged x at mid-year
D_0	migration dependency ratio $(= \varphi_1 / \varphi_2)$
$G(x)$	distribution function $[\int_{y_0}^{x} g(y)dy]$: proportion of female population who are heads of household by age x
GMR	gross migraproduction rate
K	total population $[= K(\cdot)]$
$K(x)$	population of age x
$N(x)$	proportion of migrants aged x at the time of migration
O	total number of outmigrants $[= O(\cdot)]$
$O(x)$	number of outmigrants of age x
Z	labor force shift
α_1	descent parameter of pre-labor force component
α_2	descent parameter of labor force component
α_3	descent parameter of post-labor force component
β_{12}	α_1 / α_2
δ_{1c}	a_1 / c
δ_{12}	a_1 / a_2
δ_{32}	a_3 / a_2
λ_2	ascent parameter of labor force component
λ_3	ascent parameter of post-labor force component
μ_2	position on the age axis of the labor force component
μ_3	position on the age axis of the post-labor force curve
σ_2	λ_2 / α_2
σ_3	λ_3 / α_3
φ_c	relative share of the constant term in $N(x)$
φ_1	relative share of child component in $N(x)$
φ_2	relative share of adult component in $N(x)$
$\Gamma(\alpha_2 / \lambda_2)$	gamma function value of α_2 / λ_2

Parameters and Variables Related to Spatial Population Dynamics (Chapter 11)

Parameters

a	rank order of the age group
f	last age of last reproductive age group
t	time (time is measured in units of u years; hence u years after time t is the period $t + 1$)

w	number of age groups
N	number of regions

Variables

$\overset{\wedge}{\cdot}$	variable associated with the uniregional age-specific matrix $\hat{G}$
$\overset{\wedge}{\cdot}$	variable associated with the pure migration matrix $\hat{G}$
c_i	coefficient of the ith term in the analytic solution of the multiregional growth model
$g(\lambda)$	characteristic equation of the growth matrix G
k	total population size at $t = 0$
${}^i m_a$	infant age-specific interregional migration matrix
m_a	noninfant age-specific interregional migration matrix
t_i	half-life [number of years to reduce by half the upper bound of the cyclical component determined by the ith (complex) eigenvalue]
G	growth matrix of multiregional demographic growth model
$\hat{G}$	growth matrix of uniregional demographic growth model
$\hat{G}$	pure migration matrix: $N \times N$ column-stochastic matrix, describing the level and pattern of age-independent migration, under absence of regional differentials in fertility and mortality
p_i'	left (row) eigenvector of the growth matrix G, associated with the ith eigenvalue*
Q_i	right column eigenvector of the growth matrix G associated with the ith eigenvalue λ_i*
R	residual vector
γ_{iaj}	auxiliary variable
δ_i	auxiliary variable
λ_i	ith eigenvalue of the growth matrix G
σ_i	magnitude of a complex eigenvalue [$= (\sigma_i^2 + \beta_i^2)^{1/2}$]
τ_i	period (in years) of the cyclical component with frequency Θ_i
φ_{iaj}	auxiliary variable
ω_i	auxiliary variable
Θ_i	amplitude of a complex eigenvalue [$= \tan^{-1}(\beta_i / \alpha_i)$]; also the frequency (in degrees of h years; $h = 5$ in this chapter)

*Several of the eigenvalues are complex numbers. They occur in conjugate pairs and are denoted as $\alpha_i \pm i\beta_i$, with α_i the real part and β_i the imaginary part; i is the square root of -1. The eigenvectors associated with complex eigenvalues are also complex: right eigenvector $X_i + iY_i$; left eigenvector, $U_i + iV_i$

About the Authors

LUIS J. CASTRO (Mexico), a member of the Population Division of the United Nations in New York, spent four and a half years at IIASA during 1977–1982 working on the Migration and Settlement Study. He received a degree in civil engineering from the National Autonomous University of Mexico (UNAM) in 1970 and a Masters degree in urban systems engineering and policy planning from Northwestern University in 1975.

YOUNG J. KIM (Korea) is currently an associate professor at the Department of Population Dynamics, School of Hygiene and Public Health, Johns Hopkins University. She received her PhD in biostatistics in 1972 after obtaining a Master's degree in physics. Professor Kim came to IIASA in 1980 to further develop her interests in mathematical demography, particularly the analysis of multiregional zero growth populations with changing rates.

PIOTR KORCELLI (Poland) is currently a professor at the Institute of Geography and Spatial Organization of the Polish Academy of Sciences, where he heads the Department of Urban and Population Studies. He received his PhD in economic geography from the Polish Academy of Sciences in 1968 and a Habilitation Doctorate in 1973. During his stay at IIASA he worked on problems of human settlement systems development.

JACQUES LEDENT (France) received his degree in engineering from the Ecole Nationale des Ponts et Chaussees in 1969 and his PhD in urban systems engineering and policy planning from Northwestern University in 1982. After five years at IIASA, he moved to Canada where he is currently a professor at the National Institute for Scientific Research (INRS), University of Quebec.

KAO-LEE LIAW (Canada) joined IIASA in 1980 to carry out research on multiregional mathematical demography. He is currently an associate professor at the Department of Geography, McMaster University, Hamilton, Ontario, Canada. He studied at National Taiwan University and Kansas State University, and received his PhD in geography from Clark University in 1974.

PHILIP H. REES (England) is a reader in population geography at the University of Leeds. He did his undergraduate work at the University of Cambridge and his graduate work at the University of Chicago, obtaining a doctorate in 1973. His recent work has focused on the application of population accounting methods to multiregional life table construction and to regional population projection. He has visited IIASA a number of times during the past few years to pursue these interests further and to continue his collaboration with its team of demographers.

ANDREI ROGERS (United States) led the program of demographic and human settlement research at IIASA from 1976 to 1983. Professor Rogers received his Bachelor's degree in architecture in 1960 from the University of California,

Berkeley, and his PhD in urban and regional planning in 1964 from the University of North Carolina, Chapel Hill. Since then he has been a professor of city and regional planning at the University of California, Berkeley, and of civil engineering at Northwestern University. Currently he is professor of geography and Director of the Population Program at the University of Colorado, Boulder.

SVETLANA SOBOLEVA (Soviet Union) came to IIASA in 1979 on a one-year sabbatical from the Institute of Economics and Industrial Engineering, Siberian Branch of the USSR Academy of Sciences, Novosibirsk, where she received her PhD in 1973. Dr. Soboleva's scientific interests include problems of modeling migration, the influence of socioeconomic factors on demographic processes, and methodological problems of modeling.

MARC G. TERMOTE (Canada) came to IIASA in 1979 to work on the migration and settlement study. He was awarded a PhD in law from the University of Louvain, Belgium, in 1960 and a PhD in economics, also from the University of Louvain, in 1969. Between 1969 and 1973 he was a professor in the Department of Demography and the Economics Institute at the University of Louvain. Marc Termote is now a professor at the National Institute for Scientific Research (INRS), University of Quebec.

FRANS J. WILLEKENS (Belgium) came to IIASA in 1975 from Northwestern University for a three-year stay to work on migration and settlement systems research. Dr. Willekens studied agricultural engineering, economics, and sociology at the University of Leuvain, Belgium, and received his Master's degree there in 1970. He began his PhD studies in urban systems engineering and policy planning at Northwestern University in 1973 and completed his dissertation while at IIASA. Since 1980 he has been Deputy Director of the Netherlands Interuniversity Demographic Institute (NIDI).

References

Alonso, W. (1973) *National Interregional Demographic Accounts: A Prototype.* Monograph 17. Berkeley, California: University of California, Institute of Urban and Regional Development.

Alonso, W. (1978a) The Current Halt in the Metropolitan Phenomenon. In C.L. Leven (ed.), *The Mature Metropolis*, pp.23–42. Lexington, Massachusetts: D.C. Heath.

Alonso, W. (1978b) A Theory of Movements. In N. Hansen (ed.), *International Perspectives on Structure, Change, and Public Policy*, pp. 197–211. Cambridge, Massachusetts: Ballinger.

Andersson, A. and I. Holmberg (1980) *Migration and Settlement 3: Sweden.* Research Report RR-80-5. Laxenburg, Austria: International Institute for Applied Systems Analysis.

Bartels, C., and K.L. Liaw (1983) The Dynamics of Spatial Labor Mobility in the Netherlands. *Environment and Planning A* 15:329–342.

Beale, C.L. (1977) The Recent Shift of United States Population to Non-metropolitan Areas, 1970–1975. *International Regional Science Review* 2(2):113–122.

Beaujot, R.P. (1978) Canada's Population: Growth and Dualism. *Population Bulletin* 33(2). Washington, D.C.: Population Reference Bureau.

Berry, B.J.L. (1973) *Growth Centers in the American Urban System*, vols. 1 and 2. Cambridge, Massachusetts: Ballinger.

Berry, B.J.L., and Q. Gillard (1977) *The Changing Shape of Metropolitan America: Commuting Patterns, Urban Fields, and Decentralization Processes 1960–1970.* Cambridge, Massachusetts: Ballinger.

Bies, K., and K. Tekse (1980) *Migration and Settlement 7: Hungary.* Research Report RR-80-34. Laxenburg, Austria: International Institute for Applied Systems Analysis.

Bishop, Y.M., S.E. Fienberg, and P.W. Holland (1975) *Discrete Multivariate Analysis: Theory and Practice.* Cambridge, Massachusetts: Massachusetts Institute of Technology Press.

Bogue, D. (1968) *Principles of Demography.* New York: John Wiley.

Borchert, J.G. (1980) The Dutch Settlement System. In *The National Settlement Systems: Topical and National Reports*, pp. 283–335 International Geographical Union, Commission on National Settlement Systems, Warsaw: Institute of Geography and Spatial Organization, Polish Academy of Sciences.

Boudeville, J. (1978) Les Régions de villes en Europe (The City Regions of Europe). In J.M. Paelinck (ed.), *La Structure Urbaine en Europe Occidentale: Faites, Théories, Modèles* (The Urban Structure of Western Europe: Facts, Theories, Models), pp. 54–84. Farnborough, Hampshire, England: Saxon House.

Bourgeois-Pichat, J. (1981) Recent Demographic Change in Western Europe: An Assessment. *Population and Development Review* 7:19–42.

Bourne, L.S. (1975) *Urban Systems: Strategies for Regulation. A Comparison of Policies in Britain, Sweden, Australia and Canada.* Oxford: Clarendon Press.

Bourne, L.S. (1982) Recent Trends in Urban Growth and Population Redistribution in Canada. In T. Kawashima and P. Korcelli (eds.), *Human Settlement Systems:*

Spatial Patterns and Trends, pp. 139–158. Collaborative Proceedings CP-82-S1. Laxenburg, Austria: International Institute for Applied Systems Analysis, IIASA Collaborative Proceedings Series.

Bourne, L.S., P. Korcelli, and O. Waerneryd (1980) Changing Spatial Configurations in National Settlement Systems. In *The National Settlement Systems: Topical and National Reports*, pp. 51–81. International Geographical Union, Commission on National Settlement Systems. Warsaw: Institute of Geography and Spatial Organization, Polish Academy of Sciences.

Brass, W. (1971) On the Scale of Mortality. In W. Brass (ed.), *Biological Aspects of Demography*, pp. 69–110. London: Taylor and Francis.

Brass, W. (1977) Notes on Empirical Mortality Models. In *Population Bulletin of the United Nations*, No. 9:38–42.

Brass, W. (1980) The Relational Gompertz Model of Fertility by Age of Woman. In *Regional Workshop on Techniques of Analysis of World Fertility Survey Data*. London: WFS Occasional Papers 22.

Brown, K.M., and J.E. Dennis (1972) Derivative Free Analogues of the Levenberg–Marquardt and Gauss Algorithms for Non-Linear Least Squares Approximations. *Numerische Mathematik* 18:289–297.

Brown, A.A., and E. Neuburger (1977) *International Migration: A Comparative Perspective*. New York and London: Academic Press.

Campisi, D., A. La Bella, and G. Rabino (1982) *Migration and Settlement:17. Italy*. Research Report RR-82-23. Laxenburg, Austria: International Institute for Applied Systems Analysis.

Caselli, G., and V. Egidi (1981) *Nouvelles Tendances de la Mortalité en Europe* (New Mortality Trends in Europe). Etudes Démographiques No. 5. Strasbourg, France: Council of Europe.

Castro, L.J., and A. Rogers (1983a) Patterns of Family Migration: Two Methodological Approaches. *Environment and Planning A* 15:237–254.

Castro, L.J., and A. Rogers (1983b) What the Age Composition of Migrants Can Tell Us. *Population Bulletin of the United Nations* 15:63–79.

Central Statistical Office (1973) *Itogi Vsesojuznoj Perepisi Naselenija 1970 Goda*. Tt. 1,2. *Chislennost' Naselenija SSSR, Sojuznyk i Avtonomnykh Respublik, Krajev i Oblasteiji*. (Results of the Soviet Union's Population Census of 1970, vols. 1 and 2. The Size of the Population of the USSR, Union and Autonomous Republics, Territories and Regions). Moscow: Statistika.

Central Statistical Office (1974) *Itogi Vsesojuznoj Perepisi Naselenija 1970 Goda*. T.7 (Results of the Soviet Union's Population Census of 1970, vol.7). Moscow: Statistika.

Central Statistical Office (1975) *Naselenije SSSR (Chislennost', Sostav i Dvizhenije Naselenija) 1973. Statisticheskij Sbornik*. [The Population of the USSR (Population Size, Structure and Migration) 1973. Statistical Yearbook]. Moscow: Statistika.

Central Statistical Office (1976) *Narodnoje Khoziajstvo SSR u 1975*. (National Economy of the USSR in 1975). Moscow: Statistika.

Coale, A.J. (1969) Population and Economic Development. In P.M. Hauser (ed.), *The Population Dilemma*, 2nd edn., pp. 59–84. Englewood Cliffs, New Jersey: Prentice-Hall.

Coale, A.J. (1972) *The Growth and Structure of Human Populations: A Mathematical Investigation*. Princeton, New Jersey: Princeton University Press.

Coale, A.J., and P. Demeny (1966) *Regional Model Life Tables and Stable Populations*. Princeton, New Jersey: Princeton University Press.

Coale, A.J., and D.R. McNeil (1972) The Distribution by Age of the Frequency of First Marriage in a Female Cohort. *Journal of the American Statistical Association* 67:743–749.

Coale, A.J., and T.J. Trussell (1974) Model Fertility Schedules: Variations in the Age Structure of Childbearing in Human Populations. *Population Index* 40(2):185–258.

Compton, P.A. (1971) *Some Aspects of the Internal Migration of Population in Hungary Since 1957*. Budapest: Central Statistical Office, Demographic Research Institute.

Cordey-Hayes, R.D. (1975) Migration and the Dynamics of Multiregional Population Systems. *Environment and Planning A* 7:793–814.

Courgeau, D. (1973a) Migrants et Migrations (Migrants and Migrations). *Population* 28(1):95–129.

Courgeau, D. (1973b) Migrations et Découpages du Territoire (Migrations and Spatial Divisions). *Population* 28(3):511–537.

DaVanzo, J. (1980) *Repeat Migration in the United States: Who Moves Back and Who Moves On?* Working Paper WP-80-158. Laxenburg, Austria: International Institute for Applied Systems Analysis.

DaVanzo, J., and P. Morrison (1978) *Dynamics of Return Migration: Descriptive Findings from a Longitudinal Study*. Report P-5913. Santa Monica, California: The Rand Corporation.

Drewe, P. (1980) *Migration and Settlement: 5. The Netherlands*. Research Report RR-80-13. Laxenburg, Austria: International Institute for Applied Systems Analysis.

Drewett, R., Goddard, J.B., and N. Spence (1975) *British Cities: Urban Population and Employment Trends, 1951–71*. Research Report 10. London: Department of the Environment.

Duesenberry, J.S. (1960) Comment. In *Demographic and Economic Change in Developed Countries: A Conference. National Bureau of Economic Research*, pp. 231–240. Princeton, New Jersey: Princeton University Press.

Dziewoński, K. (1980) Systems of Main Urban Centers (Functioning Within the National Settlement Systems). In *The National Settlement Systems: Topical and National Reports*, pp. 103–120. International Geographical Union, Commission on National Settlement Systems. Warsaw: Institute of Geography and Spatial Organization, Polish Academy of Sciences.

Dziewoński, K., and P. Korcelli (1981) *Migration and Settlement 11: Poland*. Research Report RR-81-20. Laxenburg, Austria: International Institute for Applied Systems Analysis.

East Anglian Economic Planning Council (1978) *The Future Population of East Anglia*. Norwich: Centre for East Anglian Studies.

Economic Commission for Europe (1975) *Post-war Demographic Trends in Europe and the Outlook Until the Year 2000*. New York: United Nations.

Economic Commission for Europe (1979) *United Nations: Labour Supply and Migration in Europe: Demographic Dimensions 1950–1975 and Prospects*. Geneva and New York: United Nations.

Espenshade, T., and R. Braun (1982) Life Course Analysis and Multistate Demography: An Application to Marriage, Divorce, and Remarriage. *Journal of Marriage and the Family* 44:1025–1036.

Feeney, G.M. (1970) Stable Age by Region Distribution. *Demography* 7: 341–348.

Feichtinger, G. (1979) *Demographische Analyse und Populationsdynamische Modelle. Grundzüge der Bevölkerungsmathematik.* Berlin (West): Springer-Verlag.

Feller, W. (1941) On the Integral Equation of Renewal Theory. *Annals of Mathematical Statistics* 12:243–266.

Fisher, R.A. (1930) The Fundamental Theorem of Natural Selection. In *The General Theory of Natural Selection*, pp. 25–30. New York: Dover.

Friedmann, J. (1977) *Territory and Function.* Paper presented at 17th European Congress of Regional Science Association, Cracow.

Gantmacher, F.R. (1964) *The Theory of Matrices* (translated by K.A. Hirsch). New York: Chelsea Publishing Company.

General Register Office (1957) The Registrar General's Statistical Review for England and Wales for the Year 1956. Part II. Tables, Population. London: Her Majesty's Stationery Office.

Glickman, N.J. (1977a) *Growth and Change in the Japanese Urban System: The Experience of the 1970's.* Research Memorandum RM-77-39. Laxenburg, Austria: International Institute for Applied Systems Analysis.

Glickman, N.J. (1977b) *The Japanese Urban System During a Period of Rapid Economic Development.* Research Memorandum RM-77-46. Laxenburg, Austria: International Institute for Applied Systems Analysis.

Goldstein, S. (1976) Facets of Redistribution: Research Challenges and Opportunities. *Demography* 13:423–434.

Gordon, P. (1978) *Deconcentration Without a "Clean Break".* Research Memorandum RM-78-39. Laxenburg, Austria: International Institute for Applied Systems Analysis.

Gordon, P., and J. Ledent (1980) Modeling the Dynamics of a System of Metropolitan Areas: A Demoeconomic Approach. *Environment and Planning A* 12: 125–133.

Grigg, D. (1967) Regions, Models, and Classes. In R.J. Chorley and P. Haggett (eds.), *Models in Geography*, pp. 461–509. London: Methuen.

Grigorev, N. (1978) *Human Settlement Systems: Analysis and Tendencies of Development.* Paper presented at Conference on Analysis of Human Settlement Systems, International Institute for Applied Systems Analysis, Laxenburg, Austria, 18–20 October.

Haggett, P., A. Cliff, and A. Frey (1977) *Locational Methods.* London: Edward Arnold.

Hall, P., and D. Hay (1980) *Growth Centres in the European Urban System.* London: Heinemann Educational.

Hall, P., and D. Metcalf (1978) The Declining Metropolis: Patterns, Problems and Policies in Britain and Mainland Europe. In C.L. Leven (ed.), *The Mature Metropolis*, pp. 65–90. Lexington, Massachusetts: D.C. Heath.

Hall, P., H. Gracey, R. Drewett, and R. Thomas (1973) *The Containment of Urban England*, vols.1 and 2. London: Allen and Unwin.

Hampl,M., J. Jezek, and K. Kühnl (1978) *Socio-Geographic Regionalization of the Czech Socialist Republic.* Paper presented at Conference on Analysis of Human Settlement Systems, International Institute for Applied Systems Analysis, Laxenburg, Austria, 18–20 October.

Hannan, M.T. (1982) *Multistate Demography and Event History Analysis.* Working Paper WP-82-50. Laxenburg, Austria: International Institute for Applied Systems Analysis.

Heligman, J., and J.H. Pollard (1980) The Age Pattern of Mortality. *Journal of the Institute of Actuaries* 107:49–80.

Henry, L. (1972) *Démographie – Analyse et Modèles*. Paris: Sociéte Encyclopédique Universelle. (*Population Analysis and Models*, Edward Arnold, London, 1976).

Hoem, J.M., and M.S. Fong (1976) *A Markov Chain Model of Working Life Tables*. Working Paper WP-2. Copenhagen: University of Copenhagen, Laboratory of Actuarial Mathematics.

Hoem, J.M., and U. Funck-Jensen (1982) Multistate Life Table Methodology: A Probabilist Critique. In K.C. Land and A. Rogers (eds.), *Multidimensional Mathematical Demography*, pp. 155–264. New York: Academic Press.

Hoem, J.M., D. Madsen, J.L. Nielsen, E.M. Ohlsen, H.O. Hansen, and B. Rennerman (1981) Experiments in Modelling Recent Danish Fertility Curves. *Demography* (18):231–244.

Höhn, C. (1981) Les Différences Internationales de Mortalité Infantile: Illusion ou Réalité? (International Differences in Infant Mortality: Illusion or Reality?). *Population* 36(4–5):791–816.

Illingworth, D. (1976) *Testing Some New Concepts and Estimation Methods in Population Accounting and Related Fields*. Ph.D. Dissertation. Leeds: University of Leeds, School of Geography.

Jordan, C.W. (1975) *Life Contingencies*, 2nd edn. Chicago: Society of Actuaries.

Just, P., and L. Liaw (1983) *An Improved Method of Computing Multistate Survivorship Proportions for the Terminal Age Groups*. Working Paper WP-83-65. Laxenburg, Austria: International Institute for Applied Systems Analysis.

Kalinjuk, I.V. (1975) *Vozrastnaja Struktura Naselenija SSSR* (Age Structure of the Population of the USSR). Moscow: Statistika.

Karlström, U. (1982) The Role of Emigration and Migration in Swedish Industrialization. *International Regional Science Review* 7:153–174.

Kawashima, T. (1982) Recent Urban Trends in Japan: Analysis of Functional Urban Regions. In T. Kawashima and P. Korcelli (eds.), *Human Settlement Systems: Spatial Patterns and Trends*, pp. 21–40. Laxenburg, Austria: International Institute for Applied Systems Analysis.

Kawashima, T., and P. Korcelli (eds.) (1982) *Human Settlement Systems: Spatial Patterns and Trends*. Collaborative Proceedings CP-82-S1. Laxenburg, Austria: International Institute for Applied Systems Analysis.

Kawashima, T., T. Ohshika, S. Ohhira, and F. Kimura (1982) Long-Range Population Projections for Japan by Region and Age: Application of IIASA Model. *Gakushuin Economic Papers* 18:3–70 (in Japanese).

Kedelski, M. (1981) Multi-Flow Life Tables of Poland's Population with a Breakdown into Urban and Rural Areas. *Studia Demograficzne* 64:45–63 (in Polish).

Kelley, A.C., and J.G. Williamson (1980) *Modeling Urbanization and Economic Growth*. Research Report RR-80-22. Laxenburg, Austria: International Institute for Applied Systems Analysis.

Kennett, S. (1977) *Migration Trends and Their Contribution to Population Change in the Urban System*. Working Report No. 50. London: London School of Economics and Political Science, Department of Geography.

Kennett, S. (1980) Migration Within and Between the Metropolitan Economic Labour Areas of Britain, 1966–1971. In J.N. Hobcraft and P.H. Rees (eds.), *Regional Demographic Development*. London: Croom Helm.

Keyfitz, N. (1968) *An Introduction to the Mathematics of Population*. Reading, Massachusetts: Addison-Wesley.

Keyfitz, N. (1969) Age Distribution and the Stable Equivalent. *Demography* 6:261–269.

Keyfitz, N. (1971) On the Momentum of Population Growth. *Demography* 7:71–80.

Keyfitz, N. (1972) Population Waves. In T.N.E. Greville (ed.), *Population Dynamics*, pp. 1–38. New York: Academic Press.

Keyfitz, N. (1979) Multidimensionality in Population Analysis. In K. Schuessler (ed.), *Sociological Methodology 1980*, pp. 191–218. San Francisco: Jossey-Bass.

Keyfitz, N. (1980) *Do Cities Grow by Natural Increase or by Migration?*. Research Report RR-80-24. Laxenburg, Austria: International Institute for Applied Systems Analysis.

Keyfitz, N., and D. Philipov (1981) Migration and Natural Increase in the Growth of Cities. *Geographical Analysis* 13(4):287–299.

Keyfitz, N., and A. Rogers (1982) Simplified Multiple Contingency Calculations. *The Journal of Risk and Insurance* 49:59–72.

Khorev, B.J., and V.M. Moiseyenko (1976) *Sdvigi v Razmeschenii Naselenija SSSR* (Changes in the Distribution of the USSR Population). Moscow: Statistika.

Kirk, D. (1960) Some Reflections on American Demography in the Nineteen Sixties. *Population Index* 26:305–310.

Kirk, D. (1983) PAA Meetings Over the Years. *PAA Affairs* (Quarterly Newsletter of the Population Association of America), Spring, pp.3–4.

Kitsul, P., and D. Philipov (1981) The One-Year/Five-Year Migration Problem. In A. Rogers (ed.), *Advances in Multiregional Demography*, pp. 1–33. Research Report RR-81-6. Laxenburg, Austria: International Institute for Applied Systems Analysis.

van der Knaap, G.A., and W.F. Sleegers (1981) *Population Dynamics and Urban Change in the Netherlands*. Paper prepared for Conference on Urbanization and Development, International Institute for Applied Systems Analysis, Laxenburg, Austria, June.

Koch, R., and H.P. Gatzweiler (1980) *Migration and Settlement: 9. Federal Republic of Germany*. Research Report RR-80-37. Laxenburg, Austria: International Institute for Applied Systems Analysis.

Korcelli, P. (1977) *An Approach to the Analysis of Functional Urban Regions: A Case Study of Poland*. Research Memorandum RM-77-52. Laxenburg, Austria: International Institute for Applied Systems Analysis.

Korcelli, P. (1980) *Urban Change: An Overview of Research and Planning Issues*. WP-80-30. Laxenburg, Austria: International Institute for Applied Systems Analysis.

Krishnamoorthy, S. (1979) Classical Approach to Increment–Decrement Life Tables: An Application to the Study of Marital Status of United States Females, 1970. *Mathematical Biosciences* 44(1–2):139–154.

Krönert, R. (1982) The Settlement System and Functional Urban Regions in the German Democratic Republic. Part II: The Hierarchy of Functional Urban Regions. In T. Kawashima and P. Korcelli (eds.), *Human Settlement Systems: Spatial Patterns and Trends*, pp. 73–88. Collaborative Proceedings CP-82-S1. Laxenburg, Austria: International Institute for Applied Systems Analysis.

Kühnl, K. (1978) Selected Aspects of Migration Motivation in the Czech Socialist Republic. *Acta Universitatis Carolinae, Geographica* 13(1):3–11.

Kühnl, K. (1982) *Migration and Settlement: 14. Czechoslovakia*. Research Report RR-82-32. Laxenburg, Austria: International Institute for Applied Systems Analysis.

Kurman, M.V. (1976) *Demograficheskije Processy v SSSR v Poslevojennyi Period* (Demographic Processes in the USSR over the Postwar Period). Moscow: Statistika.

Kuroda, T., and Z. Nanjo (1983) Rogers' Model on Multiregional Population Analysis and Its Application to Japanese Data. *NUPRI Research Paper Series* No. 9. Tokyo: Population Research Institute, Nihon University.

Lackó, L., G. Enyedi, and G. Koszegfalvi (1978) *Functional Urban Regions in Hungary*. Collaborative Paper CP-78-4. Laxenburg, Austria: International Institute for Applied Systems Analysis.

Land, K.C., and A. Rogers (eds.) (1982) *Multidimensional Mathematical Demography*. New York: Academic Press.

Land, K.C., and R. Schoen (1982) Statistical Methods for Markov-Generated Increment–Decrement Life Tables with Polynomial Gross Flow Functions. In K.C. Land and A. Rogers (eds.), *Multidimensional Mathematical Demography*, pp. 265–346. New York: Academic Press.

Latuch, M. (1970) *Migracje Wewnetrzne w Polsce na tle Industrializacji, 1950–60* (Internal Migrations and Industrialization in Poland, 1950–60). Warsaw: Panstwowe Wydawnictwo Ekonomiczne.

Ledent, J. (1978a) *Some Methodological and Empirical Considerations in the Construction of Increment-Decrement Life Tables*. Research Memorandum RM-78-25. Laxenburg, Austria: International Institute for Applied Systems Analysis.

Ledent, J. (1978b) *Temporal and Spatial Aspects in the Conception, Estimation and Use of Migration Rates*. Paper presented at Conference on Migration and Settlement, International Institute for Applied Systems Analysis, Laxenburg, Austria, September.

Ledent, J. (1978c) Regional Multiplier Analysis: A Demometric Approach. *Environment and Planning A* 10:537–560.

Ledent, J. (1980a) *Comparative Dynamics of Three Demographic Models of Urbanization*. Research Report RR-80-1. Laxenburg, Austria: International Institute for Applied Systems Analysis.

Ledent, J. (1980b) *An Improved Methodology for Constructing Increment–Decrement Life Tables from the Transition Perspectives*. Working Paper WP-80-104. Laxenburg, Austria: International Institute for Applied Systems Analysis.

Ledent, J. (1980c) Multistate Life Tables: Movement Versus Transition Perspectives. *Environment and Planning A* 12:533–562.

Ledent, J. (1980d) Calibrating Alonso's General Theory of Movement: The Case of Interprovincial Migration Flows in Canada. *Sistemi Urbani* 2/3:327–358.

Ledent, J. (1981) Constructing Multiregional Life Tables Using Place-of-Birth-Specific Migration Data. In A. Rogers (ed.), *Advances in Multiregional Mathematical Demography*, pp. 35–49. Research Report RR-81-6. Laxenburg, Austria: International Institute for Applied Systems Analysis.

Ledent, J. (1982a) Transition Probability Estimation in Increment–Decrement Life Tables: Using Mobility Data from a Census or a Survey. In K.C. Land and A. Rogers (eds.), *Multidimensional Mathematical Demography*, pp. 347–384. New York: Academic Press.

Ledent, J. (1982b) Long-Range Regional Population Forecasting: Specification of a Minimal Demoeconomic Model, with a Test for Tucson, Arizona. *Papers of the Regional Science Association* 49:37–67.

Ledent, J. with D. Courgeau (1982) *Migration and Settlement: 15. France*. Research Report RR-82-28. Laxenburg, Austria: International Institute for Applied

Systems Analysis.

Ledent, J., and P. Gordon (1980) A Demoeconomic Model of Interregional Growth Rate Differences. *Geographical Analysis* 12(1): 56–67.

Ledent, J., and P. Just (1985) *The Construction of Multiregional Life Tables: Using Migration Versus Migrant Data with an Application to Sweden*. Laxenburg, Austria: International Institute for Applied Systems Analysis.

Ledent, J. and P.H. Rees (1980) *Choices in the Construction of Multi-regional Life Tables*. Working Paper 289. Leeds: University of Leeds, School of Geography (also Working Paper WP-80-173. Laxenburg, Austria: International Institute for Applied Systems Analysis).

Leslie, P.H. (1945) On the Use of Matrices in Certain Population Mathematics. *Biometrica* 33:183–212.

Leven, C.L. (1981) *Regional Shifts and Metropolitan Reversal in the United States*. Paper prepared for Conference on Urbanization and Development. International Institute for Applied Systems Analysis, Laxenburg, Austria, June.

Levenberg, K. (1944) A Method for the Solution of Certain Non-Linear Problems in Least Squares. *Quarterly Journal of Applied Mathematics* 2:164–168.

Ley, D., and J. Mercer (1980) Locational Conflict and the Politics of Consumption. *Economic Geography* 56:89–109.

Liaw, K.L. (1978a) *Derivation and Characterization of the Analytic Solution of the Generalized Rogers Model of Interregional Demographic Growth*. Unpublished Paper. Hamilton, Ontario: McMaster University, Department of Geography.

Liaw, K.L. (1978b) Dynamic Properties of the 1966-1971 Canadian Population System. *Environment and Planning A* 10: 389–398.

Liaw, K.L. (1978c) Sensitivity Analysis of Discrete-Time, Age-Disaggregated Interregional Population Systems. *Journal of Regional Science* 18: 263–281.

Liaw, K.L. (1979a) *Analysis and Projections of the Canadian Interregional Population System*. Research Report to the Social Science and Humanities Research Council of Canada. Hamilton, Ontario: McMaster University, Department of Geography.

Liaw, K.L. (1979b) Implications of Eliminating Foreign Migration upon the Dynamic Properties of the Canadian Interregional Population System. *Modelling and Simulation*, vol.10, part 4. Proceedings of the 10th Annual Pittsburgh Conference, University of Pittsburgh, Pittsburgh, Pennsylvania.

Liaw, K.L. (1980a) Multistate Dynamics: The Convergence of an Age-by-Region Population System. *Environment and Planning A* 12:589–613.

Liaw, K.L. (1980b) The Robustness of the Analytic Solution of a Time-Homogeneous Spatial Population System: A Canadian Case Study. Social Economic Systems. *Modelling and Simulation*, vol.11, part 4, pp.1253–1258. Proceedings of 11th Annual Pittsburgh Conference, University of Pittsburgh, Pittsburgh, Pennsylvania.

Liaw, K.L. (1981) *Multiregional Population Projection: An Analytic Approach*. Working Paper WP-81-81. Laxenburg, Austria: International Institute for Applied Systems Analysis.

Liaw, K.L., and C. Bartels (1982) Estimation and Interpretation of a Nonlinear Migration Model. *Geographical Analysis* 14:229–245.

Long, J.F. (1981) *Using Migration Measures Having Different Time Intervals*. Population Division Working Paper. Washington, D.C.: US Bureau of the Census.

Long, L.H. (1973) New Estimates of Migration Expectancy in the United States. *Journal of the American Statistical Association* 68:37–43.

Long, L.H., and C.G. Boertlein (1976) *The Geographical Mobility of Americans: An International Comparison.* Current Population Reports, Special Studies, Series P-23, No. 64. Washington, D.C.: US Bureau of the Census.

Long, L.H., and W. Frey (1982) *Migration and Settlement: 16. United States.* Research Report RR-82-15. Laxenburg, Austria: International Institute for Applied Systems Analysis.

Long, L.H., and K.A. Hansen (1975) Trends in Return Migration to the South. *Demography* 12(4):601—614.

Long, L.H., and K.A. Hansen (1979) *Reasons for Interstate Migration: Jobs, Retirement, Climate, and Other Influences.* Current Population Reports, Special Studies, Series P-23, No. 81. Washington, D.C.: US Bureau of the Census.

Lotka, A.J. (1907) Relation Between Birth Rates and Death Rates. *Science* N.S. 26:21—22. Reprinted in N. Keyfitz and D. Smith (eds.), *Mathematical Demography*. New York: Springer-Verlag.

Lotka, A.J., with F.R. Sharpe (1911) A Problem in Age-Distribution. *Philosophical Magazine* 21(6):435—438.

Marquardt, D.W. (1963) An Algorithm for Least-Squares Estimation of Nonlinear Parameters. *SIAM Journal of Numerical Analysis* 11:431—441.

McNeil, D.R. (1977) *Interactive Data Analysis.* New York: John Wiley.

McNeil, D.R., T.J. Trussell, and J.C. Turner (1977) Spline Interpolation of Demographic Data. *Demography* 14:245—252.

Miron, J. (1978) Job-Search Perspectives on Migration Behaviour. *Environment and Planning A* 10:519—535.

Mohs, G. (1980) *Migration and Settlement: 4. German Democratic Republic.* Research Report RR-80-6. Laxenburg, Austria: International Institute for Applied Systems Analysis.

Morrison, P.M. (1970) *Implications of Migration Histories for Model Design.* Report P-4342. Santa Monica, California: The Rand Corporation.

Murphy, E.M., and D.N. Nagnur (1972) A Gompertz Fit That Fits: Applications to Canadian Fertility Patterns. *Demography* 9:35—50.

Nair, P.S. (1983) *India's Population: A Multiregional Demographic Analysis.* Working Paper 35. Voorburg: Netherlands Interuniversity Demographic Institute.

Nanjo, Z. (1981) *The Projection Method of Future Regional Population in JapanUsing Migration Data Derived from the Basic Resident Registers.* Paper distributed at Conference on Urbanization and Development, 1—4 June 1981, International Institute for Applied Systems Analysis, Laxenburg, Austria.

Nanjo, Z., T. Kawashima, and T. Kuroda (1982) *Migration and Settlement: 13. Japan.* Research Report RR-82-5. Laxenburg, Austria: International Institute for Applied Systems Analysis.

Office of Population Censuses and Surveys (1974a) *Census 1971, Great Britain, Migration Tables.* London: Her Majesty's Stationery Office.

Office of Population Censuses and Surveys (1974b) *Census 1971, Great Britain, Age, Marital Condition and General Tables.* London: Her Majesty's Stationery Office.

Office of Population Censuses and Surveys (1980a) *Population Trends 21.* London: Her Majesty's Stationery Office.

Office of Population Censuses and Surveys (1980b) *Local Authority Population Estimates Methodology.* Occasional Paper 18. London: Her Majesty's Stationery Office, Population Statistics Division.

Office of Population Censuses and Surveys (1982) *Population Trends 30*. London: Her Majesty's Stationery Office.

Ogilvy, A. (1980a) *Interregional Migration Since 1971: An Appraisal of Data from the National Health Service Central Register and Labour Force Survey*. Occasional Paper 16, Office of Population Censuses and Surveys. London: Her Majesty's Stationery Office, Population Statistics Division.

Ogilvy, A. (1980b) Migration — The Influence of Economic Change. *Futures* 11(5):383–394.

Pankrat'eva, N. (1977) *Naselenije i Socialisticheskoje Vosproizvodstvo* (Population Reproduction Under Socialism). Moscow: Statistika.

Paradysz, J. (1981) Multistate Demographic Analysis. *Studia Demograficzne* 63:75–88 (in Polish).

Partida-Bush, V. (1982) Application of the Multiregional Demographic Model to the Case of Mexico. *Demografia y Economia* 51:449–481 (in Spanish).

Philipov, D. (1981a) *Migration and Settlement: 12. Bulgaria*. Research Report RR-81-21. Laxenburg, Austria: International Institute for Applied Systems Analysis.

Philipov, D. (1981b) Multiregional Demographic Models. *Statistika* 4:36–49 (in Bulgarian).

Philipov, D., and A. Rogers (1981) Multistate Population Projections. In A. Rogers (ed.), *Advances in Multiregional Demography*, pp. 51–82. Research Report RR-81-6. Laxenburg, Austria: International Institute for Applied Systems Analysis.

Polish Central Bureau of Statistics (1973) *Rocznik Demograficzny 1973* (Demographic Yearbook 1973) Warsaw: Polish Central Bureau of Statistics.

van Poppel, F. (1980) *Regional Mortality Differences in Western Europe: A Review of the Situation in the Seventies*. Voorburg: Netherlands Interuniversity Demographic Institute.

Population Reference Bureau (1981, 1982) *World Population Data Sheet*. Washington, D.C.: Population Reference Bureau, Inc.

Pred, A. (1975) On the Spatial Structure of Organizations and the Complexity of Metropolitan Interdependence. *Papers of the Regional Science Association* 35:115–142.

Pressat, R. (1969) *L'Analyse Démographique* (Demographic Analysis). Paris: Presses Universitaires de France.

Preston, S. (1976) *Mortality Patterns in National Populations*. New York: Academic Press.

Preston, S., N. Keyfitz, and R. Schoen (1972) *Causes of Death. Life Tables for National Populations*. New York: Seminar Press.

Propoi, A., and F. Willekens (1978) A Dynamic Linear Programming Approach to National Settlement System Planning. *Environment and Planning A* 10:561–576.

Quebec Bureau of Statistics (1981) *Perspectives Démographiques pour le Québec et ses Régions Administratives, 1976–2001: Analyse des Principaux Résultats (Version Préliminaire)* [Demographic Perspectives for Québec and Its Administrative Regions, 1976–2001: Analysis of the Principal Results (Preliminary Version)]. Quebec: Bureau of Statistics.

Rees, P.H. (1977a) The Measurement of Migration from Census Data and Other Sources. *Environment and Planning A* 9:247–272.

Rees, P.H. (1977b) *The Future Population of East Anglia and Its Constituent Counties (Cambridge, Norfolk and Suffolk)*. Report prepared for East Anglia

Economic Planning Council by University of Leeds Industrial Services Ltd., under Department of the Environment Contract No. DGR/461/23.

Rees, P.H. (1978) Increment–Decrement Life Tables: Some Further Comments from an Accounting Point of View. *Environment and Planning A* 10:705–726.

Rees, P.H. (1979a) *Migration and Settlement in the United Kingdom*. Unpublished Paper. Leeds: University of Leeds, School of Geography.

Rees, P.H. (1979b) *Migration and Settlement: 1. United Kingdom*. Research Report RR-79-3. Laxenburg, Austria: International Institute for Applied Systems Analysis.

Rees, P.H. (1979c) Multiregional Population Analysis: The Accounting Approach. *Sistemi Urbani* 3:3–32.

Rees, P.H. (1980) Multistate Demographic Accounts: Measurement and Estimation Procedures. *Environment and Planning A* 12:499–531.

Rees, P.H. (1981) *Accounts-Based Models for Multiregional Population Analysis: Methods, Program, and Users' Manual*. Working Paper 295. Leeds: University of Leeds, School of Geography.

Rees, P.H. (1984) *Choices in the Construction of Regional Population Projections*. Working Paper 378, School of Geography, University of Leeds, UK. To appear in R.I. Woods and P.H. Rees (eds.), *Developments in Spatial Demography*. London: Allen and Unwin.

Rees, P.H., and J.C.H. Stillwell (1982) *An Integrated Model of Migration Flows and Population Change for a System of UK Metropolitan and Non-Metropolitan Regions: A Framework*. Working Paper 332. Leeds: University of Leeds, School of Geography.

Rees, P.H., and J.C.H. Stillwell (1984) A Framework for Modelling Population Change and Migration in the UK. In A.J. Boyce (ed.), *Migration and Mobility: Biosocial Aspects of Human Movement*. London: Taylor and Francis.

Rees, P.H., and F. Willekens (1981) *Data Bases and Accounting Frameworks for IIASA's Comparative Migration and Settlement Study*. Collaborative Paper CP-81-39. Laxenburg, Austria: International Institute for Applied Systems Analysis.

Rees, P.H., and A.G. Wilson (1975) Accounts and Models for Spatial Demographic Analysis 3: Rates and Life Tables. *Environment and Planning A* 7:199–231.

Rees, P.H., and A.G. Wilson (1977) *Spatial Population Analysis*. London: Edward Arnold.

Rempel, H. (1981) *Rural–Urban Labor Migration and Urban Umemployment in Kenya*. Research Report RR-81-24. Laxenburg, Austria: International Institute for Applied Systems Analysis.

Rikkinen, K. (1979) *Migration and Settlement: 2. Finland*. Research Report RR-79-9. Laxenburg, Austria: International Institute for Applied Systems Analysis.

Rodriguez, G., and J. Trussell (1980) *Maximum Likelihood Estimation of the Parameters of Coale's Model Nuptiality Schedule from Survey Data*. World Fertility Survey, Technical Bulletin 7, Tech.1261. Voorburg, Netherlands: International Statistical Institute.

Rogers, A. (1966) The Multiregional Matrix Growth Operator and the Stable Interregional Age Structure. *Demography* 3:537–544.

Rogers, A. (1968) *Matrix Analysis of Interregional Population Growth and Distribution*. Berkeley, California: University of California Press.

Rogers, A. (1973a) The Multiregional Life Table. *Journal of Mathematical Sociology* 3:127–137.

Rogers, A. (1973b) The Mathematics of Multiregional Demographic Growth. *Environment and Planning* 5:3–29.

Rogers, A. (1975a) *Introduction to Multiregional Mathematical Demography*. New York: John Wiley.

Rogers, A. (1975b) *Spatial Migration Expectancies*. RM-75-77. Laxenburg, Austria: International Institute for Applied Systems Analysis.

Rogers, A. (1976a) *The Comparative Migration and Settlement Study: A Summary of Workshop Proceedings and Conclusions*. Research Memorandum RM-76-1. Laxenburg, Austria: International Institute for Applied Systems Analysis.

Rogers, A. (1976b) Shrinking Large-Scale Population Projection Models. *Environment and Planning A* 8:515–541.

Rogers, A. (1976c) *Two Methodological Notes on Spatial Population Dynamics in the Soviet Union*. Research Memorandum RM-76-48. Laxenburg, Austria: International Institute for Applied Systems Analysis. (Published in revised form in 1978 as Model Migration Schedules: An Application Using Data for the Soviet Union. *Canadian Studies in Population* 5:85–98.)

Rogers, A. (1977) *Migration, Urbanization, Resources, and Development*. Research Report RR-77-14. Laxenburg, Austria: International Institute for Applied Systems Analysis.

Rogers, A. (1978) Demometrics of Migration of Settlement. In P.W.J. Batey (ed.), *Theory and Method in Urban and Regional Analysis*, pp. 1–30. London: Pion.

Rogers, A. (1980) Introduction to Multistate Mathematical Demography. *Environment and Planning A* 12:489–498.

Rogers, A. (1982a) Sources of Urban Population Growth and Urbanization, 1950–2000: A Demographic Accounting. *Economic Development and Cultural Change* 30:483–506.

Rogers, A. (1982b) *Parametrized Multistate Population Dynamics*. Working Paper WP-82-125. Laxenburg, Austria: International Institute for Applied Systems Analysis.

Rogers, A. (ed.) (1982c) Urbanization and Development. *International Regional Science Review* 7(2):99–247.

Rogers, A., and L.J. Castro (1981a) *Model Schedules in Multistate Demographic Analysis: The Case of Migration*. Working Paper WP-81-22. Laxenburg, Austria: International Institute for Applied Systems Analysis.

Rogers, A., and L.J. Castro (1981b) Age Patterns of Migration: Cause-Specific Profiles. In A. Rogers (ed.), *Advances in Multiregional Demography*, pp. 125–159. Research Report RR-81-6. Laxenburg, Austria: International Institute for Applied Systems Analysis.

Rogers, A., and L.J. Castro (1981c) *Model Migration Schedules*. Research Report RR-81-30. Laxenburg, Austria: International Institute for Applied Systems Analysis.

Rogers, A., and J. Ledent (1976) Increment–Decrement Life Tables: A Comment. *Demography* 13(2):287–290.

Rogers, A., and J. Ledent (1977) Rejoinder. *Demography* 14:593.

Rogers, A., and D. Philipov (1980) Multiregional Methods for Subnational Population Projections. *Sistemi Urbani* 2/3:151–170.

Rogers, A., and F. Willekens (1976) Spatial Population Dynamics. *Papers of the Regional Science Association*. 36:3–34.

Rogers, A., and F. Willekens (1978) The Spatial Reproductive Value and the Spatial Momentum of Zero Population Growth. *Environment and Planning A* 10:503–518.

Rogers, A., and P. Williams (1985) Multistate Demoeconomic Modeling and Projection. In A.M. Isserman (ed.), *Population Change and the Economy*, pp. 177–202. Boston: Kluwer-Nijhoff.

Rogers, A., and J.G. Williamson (1982) Migration, Urbanization, and Third World Development: An Overview. *Economic Development and Cultural Change* 30:463–482.

Rogers, A., R. Raquillet, and L.J. Castro (1978) Model Migration Schedules and Their Applications. *Environment and Planning A* 10:475–502.

Ross, J.A. (1982) Life Tables. In J.A. Ross (ed.), *International Encyclopedia of Population*, pp. 400–425. New York: Free Press.

Ryder, N.B. (1964) The Process of Demographic Translation. *Demography* 1:74–82.

Ryder, N.B. (1978) *Methods in Measuring the Family Life Cycle.* Proceedings of International Population Conference, International Union for the Scientific Study of Population.

Rykiel, Z., and A. Zurkowa (1981) Inter-Urban Migration in Poland: National and Urban Systems. In K. Dziewoński and P. Korcelli (eds.), *Studies on Migrations and Settlement Systems of Poland*, pp. 138–188. Wroclaw: Zaklad Narodowy Im. Ossolińskich (in Polish with English summary).

Samuelson, P.A. (1976) Resolving a Historical Confusion in Population Analysis. *Human Biology* 48:559–580.

Sauberer, M. (1981) *Migration and Settlement: 10. Austria.* Research Report RR-81-16. Laxenburg, Austria: International Institute for Applied Systems Analysis.

Schoen, R. (1975) Constructing Increment–Decrement Life Tables. *Demography* 12(2):313–324.

Schoen, R. (1979) Calculating Increment–Decrement Life Tables by Estimating Mean Duration of Transfer from Observed Rates. *Mathematical Biosciences* 47:255–259.

Schoen, R., and K.C. Land (1979) A General Algorithm for Estimating a Markov-Generated Increment–Decrement Life Table with Applications to Marital Status Patterns. *Journal of the American Statistical Association* 74:761–776.

Schoen, R., and V.E. Nelson (1974) Marriage, Divorce and Mortality: A Life Table Analysis. *Demography* 11:267–290.

Sherrill, K. (1977) *Functional Urban Regions and Central Place Regions in the Federal Republic of Germany and Switzerland.* Research Memorandum RM-77-17. Laxenburg, Austria: International Institute for Applied Systems Analysis.

Shishido, H. (1982) Economic Growth and Urbanization: A Study of Japan. *International Regional Science Review* 7:175–191.

Simmons, J.W. (1977) *Migration and the Canadian Urban System: Part I. Spatial Patterns.* Research Report 85. Toronto: University of Toronto, Center for Urban and Community Studies.

Simmons, J.W. (1979) *Migration and the Canadian Urban System: Part III. Comparing 1966–1971 and 1971–1976.* Research Report 112. Toronto: University of Toronto, Center for Urban and Community Studies.

Simon, H.A., and A. Ando (1961) Aggregation of Variables in Dynamic Systems. *Econometrica* 29:111–138.

Soboleva, S. (1980) *Migration and Settlement: 8. Soviet Union.* Research Report RR-80-36. Laxenburg, Austria: International Institute for Applied Systems Analysis.

Stillwell, J.C.H. (1984) *Analysis of Internal Migration in the UK Based on Transition and Movement Data.* Working Paper 367, School of Geography, University of Leeds, UK. To appear in R.I. Woods and P.H. Rees (eds.) *Developments in Spatial Demography.* London: Allen and Unwin.

Stone, R. (1971) *Demographic Accounting and Model-Building.* Paris: Organization for Economic Cooperation and Development.

Swedish Central Bureau of Statistics (1974) *Internal Migration in Sweden 1968–1973,* No. 9. Stockholm: Swedish Central Bureau of Statistics.

Tabah, L.. (1968) Matrix Representation of Changes in the Active Population. *Population* 23:437–470.

Termote, M. (1980) *Migration and Settlement 6: Canada.* Research Report RR-80-29. Laxenburg, Austria: International Institute for Applied Systems Analysis.

Termote, M. (1983) *Changes in Canada's Multiregional Population Dynamics: From the 1960s to the 1970s.* Collaborative Paper CP-83-31. Laxenburg, Austria: International Institute for Applied Systems Analysis.

Theil, H. (1971) *Principles of Econometrics.* New York: John Wiley.

Thompson, W.S. (1953) *Population Problems.* New York: McGraw-Hill.

Tukey, J.W. (1977) *Exploratory Data Analysis.* Reading, Massachusetts: Addison-Wesley.

Tuma, N., and M.T. Hannan (1984) *Social Dynamics: Models and Methods.* New York: Academic Press.

United Nations (1970) *Manual on Methods of Measuring Internal Migration.* New York: United Nations.

United Nations (1979) *United Nations Demographic Yearbook: Special Issue: Historical Supplement.* New York: United Nations.

United Nations (1981) *World Population Prospects as Assessed in 1980.* Population Studies No.78. New York: United Nations, Department of International Economic and Social Affairs.

United Nations (1982) *Levels and Trends of Mortality Since 1950.* New York: United Nations.

US Bureau of the Census (1980) *International Population Dynamics 1950–1979. Demographic Estimates for Countries with a Population of 5 Million or More.* Washington, D.C.: US Government Printing Office.

US Bureau of Labor Statistics (1982) *Tables of Working Life.* Bulletin 2135. Washington, D.C.: US Department of Labor.

Vining, D.R., Jr. (1975) The Spatial Distribution of Human Populations and its Characteristic Evolution over Time: Some Recent Evidence from Japan. *Papers of the Regional Science Association* 35:157–178.

Vining, D.R., Jr., and T. Kontuly (1978) Population Dispersal from Major Metropolitan Regions: An International Comparison. *International Regional Science Review* 3(1):49–73.

Vining, D.R., Jr., and A. Strauss (1977) A Demonstration that the Current Deconcentration of Population in the United States is a Clean Break with the Past. *Environment and Planning A* 9:751–758.

Wilkins, R. (1980) L'Inégalité Sociale Face à la Mortalité à Montréal, 1975–1977 (Social Inequality with Respect to Mortality in Montreal, 1975–1977). *Cahiers Québécois de Démographie* 9(2):159–184.

Willekens, F. (1977a) Sensitivity Analysis in Multiregional Demographic Models. *Environment and Planning A* 9:653–674.

Willekens, F. (1977b) *The Recovery of Detailed Migration Patterns from Aggregate Data: An Entropy Maximizing Approach.* Research Report RR-77-58.

Laxenburg, Austria: International Institute for Applied Systems Analysis.

Willekens, F. (1978) *The Comparative Migration and Settlement Study*. Background Paper for Conference on Migration and Settlement, International Institute for Applied Systems Analysis, Laxenburg, Austria.

Willekens, F. (1979) Optimal Migration Policies: An Analytical Approach: Part I. *Regional Science and Urban Economics* 9:345–367.

Willekens, F. (1980) Multistate Analysis: Tables of Working Life. *Environment and Planning A* 12:563–588.

Willekens, F. (1982) Multidimensional Population Analysis with Incomplete Data. In K.C. Land and A. Rogers (eds.), *Multidimensional Mathematical Demography*, pp. 43–112. New York: Academic Press.

Willekens, F. (1983) *Het Demografische Vooruitberekeningsmodel. Beschryving en Toepassing* (The Demographic Projection Model. Description and Application). Report to the Physical Planning Agency. Voorburg, Netherlands: Interuniversity Demographic Institute.

Willekens, F., and A. Rogers (1977) *Normative Modeling in Demo-Economics*. Research Report RR-77-23. Laxenburg, Austria: International Institute for Applied Systems Analysis.

Willekens, F., and A. Rogers (1978) *Spatial Population Analysis: Methods and Programs*. Research Report RR-78-18. Laxenburg, Austria: International Institute for Applied Systems Analysis.

Willekens, F., A. Pór, and R. Raquillet (1981) Entropy, Multiproportional, and Quadratic Techniques for Inferring Patterns of Migration from Aggregate Data. In A. Rogers (ed.), *Advances in Multiregional Demography*, pp. 83–124. Research Report RR-81-6. Laxenburg, Austria: International Institute for Applied Systems Analysis.

Willekens, F., I. Shah, J.M. Shah, and P. Ramachandran (1982) Multi-State Analysis of Marital Status Life Tables: Theory and Application. *Population Studies* 36:129–144.

Wilson, A.G. (1971) A Family for Spatial Interaction Models and Associated Developments. *Environment and Planning* 3:1–32.

World Bank (1980) *World Development Report, 1980*. Washington, D.C.: World Bank.

Wunsch, G.J., and M.G. Termote (1978) *Introduction to Demographic Analysis: Principles and Methods*. New York: Plenum.

Zaba, B. (1979) The Four-Parameter Logit Life-Table System. *Population Studies* 33(1):79–100.

Zelinsky, W. (1971) The Hypothesis of the Mobility Transition. *Geographical Review* (61):219–249.

AUTHOR INDEX

SUBJECT INDEX

THE INTERNATIONAL INSTITUTE FOR APPLIED SYSTEMS ANALYSIS

is a nongovernmental research institution, bringing together scientists from around the world to work on problems of common concern. Situated in Laxenburg, Austria, IIASA was founded in October 1972 by the academies of science and equivalent organizations of twelve countries. Its founders gave IIASA a unique position outside national, disciplinary, and institutional boundaries so that it might take the broadest possible view in pursuing its objectives:

To promote international cooperation in solving problems arising from social, economic, technological, and environmental change
To create a network of institutions in the national member organization countries and elsewhere for joint scientific research
To develop and formalize systems analysis and the sciences contributing to it, and promote the use of analytical techniques needed to evaluate and address complex problems
To inform policy advisors and decision makers about the potential application of the Institute's work to such problems

The Institute now has national member organizations in the following countries:

Austria
The Austrian Academy of Sciences

Bulgaria
The National Committee for Applied
Systems Analysis and Management

Canada
The Canadian Committee for IIASA

Czechoslovakia
The Committee for IIASA of the
Czechoslovak Socialist Republic

Finland
The Finnish Committee for IIASA

France
The French Association for the
Development of Systems Analysis

German Democratic Republic
The Academy of Sciences of the German
Democratic Republic

Federal Republic of Germany
Association for the Advancement
of IIASA

Hungary
The Hungarian Committee for Applied
Systems Analysis

Italy
The National Research Council

Japan
The Japan Committee for IIASA

Netherlands
The Foundation IIASA–Netherlands

Poland
The Polish Academy of Sciences

Sweden
The Swedish Council for Planning and
Coordination of Research

Union of Soviet Socialist Republics
The Academy of Sciences of the Union
of Soviet Socialist Republics

United States of America
The American Academy of Arts and
Sciences

MIGRATION AND SETTLEMENT

A Multiregional Comparative Study